Ross Mistry
with Hilary Cotter

Microsoft®
SQL Server
2008

Management and Administration

SAMS | 800 East 96th Street, Indianapolis, Indiana 46240 USA

Microsoft® SQL Server 2008 Management and Administration

Copyright © 2009 by Sams Publishing

ISBN-13: 978-0-672-33044-5
ISBN-10: 0-672-33044-X

Library of Congress Cataloging-in-Publication Data

Mistry, Ross.
  Microsoft SQL server 2008 management and administration / Ross Mistry.
  – 1st ed.
    p. cm.
  ISBN 978-0-672-33044-5
  1. SQL server. 2. Database management. I. Title.
  QA76.9.D3M57886 2008
  005.4'476–dc22
                                        2008048922

Printed in the United States of America

Seventh Printing April 2012

Trademarks

Warning and Disclaimer

Bulk Sales

Sams Publishing offers excellent discounts on this book when ordered in quantity for bulk purchases or special sales. For more information, please contact

> **U.S. Corporate and Government Sales**
> **1-800-382-3419**
> **corpsales@pearsontechgroup.com**

For sales outside of the U.S., please contact

> **International Sales**
> **international@pearson.com**

Editor-in-Chief
Karen Gettman

Executive Editor
Neil Rowe

Development Editor
Mark Renfrow

Managing Editor
Patrick Kanouse

Project Editor
Mandie Frank

Copy Editor
Margaret Berson

Indexer
Ken Johnson

Proofreader
Matt Purcell

Technical Editor
Todd Robinson,
MCITP

Publishing Coordinator
Cindy Teeters

Designer
Gary Adair

Compositor
TnT Design, Inc.

Contributing Writers
Hilary Cotter,
MVP;
Shirmattie
Seenarine;
John Welch,
MVP;
Marco Shaw,
MVP;
Maciej Pilecki,
MVP

Contents at a Glance

Table of Contents

About the Author

Ross Mistry, MVP, MCTS, MCDBA, MCSE Ross Mistry is a seasoned professional in the Silicon Valley and a technology advocate with more than a decade of experience in the computer industry. As a principal consultant and partner with Convergent Computing (CCO), Ross designs and implements SQL Server, Active Directory, and Exchange solutions for Fortune 500 organizations with a global presence. Some of the organizations in which Ross Mistry has taken on the role of lead global Microsoft architect include: Network Appliance, Ross Stores Dress for Less, CIBC, Gilead Sciences, Solectron, The Sharper Image, 2Wire, Infinera, and Wells Fargo's small business Ecommerce site.

Ross had the opportunity to work with SQL Server 2008 two years prior to the product release. When he is not focused on his SQL Server specialties—high availability, migrations, and security—his attention turns to SQL Server development and Business Intelligence.

Ross is an author, co-author, and technical editor of more than 10 books. Many of the books have been bestsellers. Recently, he co-authored *Windows Server 2008 Unleashed* and *SQL Server 2005 Management and Administration*. He was a contributing writer on *Hyper-V Unleashed*, *Exchange Server 2007 Unleashed*, and *SharePoint Server 2007 Unleashed*. Ross also took on the role of technical editor for *SQL Server 2005 Unleashed* and *SQL Server 2005: Changing the Paradigm*.

In addition to being an author and consultant, Ross is a public speaker who conducts seminars on Microsoft topics around the world. He frequently speaks at local SQL Server user groups and international conferences. Most recently, he spoke at the SQL Server PASS Community Summit in North America, SQL Server Europe PASS, SQL Server Connections, and the Microsoft campuses in San Francisco and the Silicon Valley.

As a SQL Server Microsoft Most Valuable Professional (MVP), Ross is heavily involved with the SQL Server community and assists by responding to questions in newsgroups, writing articles for magazines, and blogging for networkworld. com and to IT managers on Microsoft's TechNet Community Hub site. His blog site is http://www.networkworld.com/community/mistry.

Dedication

I dedicate this book to my immediate family and the Almighty for providing me with the strength, guidance, and fortitude for completing another unthinkable task. And to the next chapter in the game of life: The New Beginning—01/01/2009.

Ross Mistry, MVP, MCTS, MCDBA, MCSE

Acknowledgments

I would like to acknowledge my wife and children for their patience while I was working on my third title. I know it has been challenging not having a husband and father around on evenings, weekends, and special holidays. Your unwavering support and inspiration is what keeps me motivated and on the right track.

A huge thank you goes out to Hilary Cotter for his contribution on the book and for sharing his knowledge and contacts with me. For this, I am much obliged and look forward to future engagements.

I would also like to acknowledge my other contributing writers: Shirmattie Seenarine, John Welch, Marco Shaw, and Maciej Pilecki. Thanks for putting together great content on short notice. Special thanks to Shirmattie Seenarine for picking up the slack when other writers disengaged from the book. Your assistance ensured we met our deadlines.

To the Sams Publishing team, especially Neil Rowe, Mandie Frank, Mark Renfrow, and Margaret Berson, this was yet another great opportunity and experience for me. Thank you, Burzin Patel, Senior SQL Server Program Manager at Microsoft, for providing insight and responding to my queries in such a timely manner. Also, I can't forget Todd Robinson who was such a meticulous technical editor.

Thanks go out to the various co-authors of my previous books, *SQL Server 2005 Management and Administration* and *Windows Server 2008 Unleashed,* whose knowledge and content are leveraged in this SQL Server 2008 book, including Rand Morimoto, Chris Amaris, Alec Minty, and Omar Droubi.

Lastly, to my best friend Lijon Geeverghese. When I look back, it is hard to believe how far we have come from the days of Pitfield. Stay strong and keep on trading; eventually we will beat the stock market!

Thanks to all—Ross Mistry

We Want to Hear from You!

As the reader of this book, *you* are our most important critic and commentator. We value your opinion and want to know what we're doing right, what we could do better, what areas you'd like to see us publish in, and any other words of wisdom you're willing to pass our way.

You can email or write me directly to let me know what you did or didn't like about this book—as well as what we can do to make our books stronger.

Please note that I cannot help you with technical problems related to the topic of this book, and that due to the high volume of mail I receive, I might not be able to reply to every message.

When you write, please be sure to include this book's title and author as well as your name and phone or email address. I will carefully review your comments and share them with the author and editors who worked on the book.

E-mail: opensource@samspublishing.com

Mail: Neil Rowe
            Executive Editor
            Sams Publishing
            800 East 96th Street
            Indianapolis, IN 46240 USA

Reader Services

Visit our website and register this book at www.informit.com/title/9780672330445 for convenient access to any updates, downloads, or errata that might be available for this book.

INTRODUCTION

SQL Server 2008 is Microsoft's latest data platform providing data management and analytical solutions for the enterprise. The platform is trusted, ensures business continuity, and is more predictable and more scalable than ever before. Although similar to SQL Server 2005, SQL Server 2008 offers a tremendous number of new features and functionality for database administrators, developers, and business intelligence architects.

This book is designed to be the ultimate guide for database administrators as it provides detailed guidance in the areas of planning, installation, management, administration, security, high availability, monitoring, and performance tuning of a SQL Server environment. Moreover, this book includes industry best practices, tips, and step-by-step instructions based on real-world examples.

Some of the classic and new SQL Server 2008 topics covered in the book include: installation, upgrade and migration strategies, Policy Based Administration, Resource Governor, encryption, failover clustering, database mirroring, authorization, hardening, consolidation and virtualization, maintenance plans, monitoring, performance tuning, troubleshooting, log shipping, PowerShell scripting, replication, creating packages and transferring data, indexes, full-text catalogs, and backing up and restoring databases.

The book is also based on Microsoft's latest award-winning server operating system—Windows Server 2008. As a result, not only will readers gain knowledge about SQL Server 2008, but they will also have the opportunity to understand the advantages of running SQL Server 2008 on Windows Server 2008.

What Is in This Book?

This book is organized into five parts, with each part made up of several chapters focusing on core SQL Server 2008 elements. The parts and chapters of the book are detailed in this section.

Part I: Installing, Administering, and Managing the Database Engine

The first part of the book begins by providing an overview of SQL Server 2008, including planning and installing the new platform. After you get SQL Server 2008 installed, the majority of your time will be spent managing and administering the new SQL Server infrastructure. Therefore, the remainder of Part I consists of chapters dedicated to SQL Server 2008 administration and management tasks.

Chapter 1: Installing or Upgrading to the SQL Server 2008 Database Engine

With the recent release of SQL Server 2008, organizations are eager to migrate to the new and improved database platform. However, many organizations feel challenged when trying to establish the best strategies for moving forward. This chapter focuses on the various SQL Server 2008 migration strategies that are available. It answers the question once and for all whether or not organizations should upgrade from a previous version or perform a new SQL Server 2008 installation from scratch and then conduct a migration.

Other topics highlighted in this chapter include: supported migration methodologies, hardware requirements, using the SQL Server 2008 Upgrade Advisor, supported legacy versions of SQL Server, and best practices, tips, and common pitfalls to look out for to achieve a successful migration. Moreover, this chapter describes the benefits associated with running SQL Server on Windows Server 2008, and it also includes upgrade strategies for moving to the latest server operating system.

Chapter 2: Administering the SQL Server 2008 Database Engine

After SQL Server 2008 is installed, it is necessary to configure and administer the server. This chapter focuses on administering the core features and components associated with the Database Engine. Topics include administering the SQL Server properties pages, Database properties pages, Database Engine folders, and the SQL Server Agent. Managing server and database configuration settings—such as memory, processor performance, auditing, compression, database files, and autogrowth—is also covered in depth.

Chapter 3: Creating Packages and Transferring Data with Integration Services

A common database administrator task is transferring data or databases between source and target environments. This chapter focuses on importing, exporting, and transforming data and databases via SQL Server Management Studio and Integration Services. The chapter also covers how packages are created, saved, and executed as well as the management of the Integration Services component.

Chapter 4: Managing and Optimizing SQL Server 2008 Indexes

Similar to an index found in a book, an index in SQL Server is utilized for fast retrieval of data from tables. This chapter explains index concepts, ways to design the appropriate index strategy to maximize performance, creating indexes with SQL Server Management Studio, and how to create indexes with Transact-SQL. The chapter also introduces new SQL Server 2008 index topics, such as creating spatial and filtered indexes, and shares best practices on implementing, managing, and optimizing indexes.

Chapter 5: Administering SQL Server 2008 Full-Text Search

With the data explosion and the ever-increasing amount of data being stored in its native format, full-text search is playing an increasingly important role in databases today. This chapter discusses the new features in SQL Server full-text search and provides step-by-step instructions on how to implement full-text search on your tables, and best practices for full-text search.

Chapter 6: SQL Server 2008 Maintenance Practices

For SQL Server to perform at optimal levels, a DBA should conduct routine maintenance on each database. This chapter focuses on best practices associated with maintaining databases within the SQL Server Database Engine.

The discussion includes creating maintenance plans to check database integrity, shrink databases, reorganize indexes, and update statistics. Additionally, this chapter provides recommendations on daily, weekly, monthly, and quarterly maintenance practices to be conducted on SQL Servers.

Chapter 7: Backing Up and Restoring the SQL Server 2008 Database Engine

Backing and restoring databases is one of the most critical duties of a DBA. It is important that the DBA understand the concepts associated with SQL Server backups, therefore, in the event of a disaster they can restore the database to the point of failure. This chapter covers the new backup compression feature, the importance of backups, creating a backup and recovery plan, storage architecture, transaction log files, recovery model, the various types of backups, backing up with SSMS, automating backups with a maintenance plan, backing up full-text catalogs, creating database snapshots, and of course, best practices.

Part II: SQL Server 2008 Security Practices

Part II of SQL Server 2008 Management and Administration is dedicated to SQL Server security. The first two chapters cover hardening techniques for both SQL Server 2008 and Windows Server 2008 and also discuss administering security and authorization. The next two chapters describe the new features, Policy Based Management, and encryption.

Chapter 8: Hardening a SQL Server Implementation

SQL Server is regularly targeted by hackers because it is a repository of sensitive data for organizations. If an organization's system is breached, hackers can gain access to confidential information including, but not limited to, credit card numbers, social security numbers, and marketing information. As such, it is imperative that database administrators secure both the SQL Server implementation and the data residing in it. This chapter provides an overview of how to harden a SQL Server implementation based on industry best practices so that vulnerabilities and security breaches are minimized.

Some of the security and hardening topics that the chapter delves into include: choosing the appropriate authentication mechanism, hardening the SA account, enforcing strong passwords, leveraging the configuration tools to lock down a SQL Server, configuring the Windows Server 2008 advanced firewall for secure access, selecting the correct service account, and applying security templates with Active Directory.

Chapter 9: Administering SQL Server Security and Authorization

After the SQL Server installation is hardened, the next step involves administering security and granting authorization to the SQL Server environment. Chapter 9 is all about security administration topics: creating logons, granting access and authorization, understanding SQL Server roles, administering password policies, endpoint authentication, SQL Server and database principals, role-based security, and user and schema separation.

Chapter 10: Administering Policy Based Management

Enforcing best practices and standardization on large SQL Server installations was extremely difficult in previous versions of SQL Server. To ensure standardization, SQL Server 2008 introduces Policy Based Management, which allows a DBA to define policies that can be applied to one or more SQL Server instances, databases, and objects. Policy Based Management works on SQL Server 2000 and all its successors.

New concepts, components, terminology, and reporting with Policy Based Management as well as best practices are discussed in Chapter 10. The reader's attention is then turned to real-world step-by-step examples of how to implement Policy Based Management in their environment.

Chapter 11: Encrypting SQL Server Data and Communications

Organizations and DBAs are facing excessive pressure from regulatory agencies to ensure that mission-critical data stored within SQL Server is encrypted. Not only is it important to ensure that data stored within SQL Server is encrypted, but it is equally important to ensure that data in transit is encrypted, database encryption can be implemented without making changes to an application, data can be encrypted at the cell level, and finally, SQL Server volumes can also be encrypted.

Chapter 11 shares many strategies, tips, and best practices on how to leverage the encryption-based technologies included in SQL Server 2008 and Windows Server 2008 for end-to-end data protection. Among these strategies are: leveraging transparent data encryption, integrating security with a

Hardware Security Module (HSM), using certificates to encrypt data in transit, and encrypting SQL Server volumes with BitLocker.

Part III: SQL Server 2008 High-Availability Alternatives

DBAs typically feel compelled to choose just the right technologies to achieve high availability when designing a SQL Server infrastructure. Some of the challenges they face are illustrated in their questions: Should I use failover clustering, database mirroring, log shipping, or replication? Which alternative provides the best protection? How does Windows Server 2008 impact my decision? This part of the book will alleviate pressure and concerns by providing DBAs with best practices and tips on how to design and choose the right SQL Server 2008 high-availability alternative to meet their organization's needs.

In this part, the chapters aim to teach DBAs how to select the appropriate HA technology when designing and implementing SQL Server 2008.

Technologies include failover clustering, log shipping, peer-to-peer replication, and database mirroring, based on Windows Server 2008.

Chapter 12: Implementing and Managing Failover Clustering

The main focus of Chapter 12 is on how to design, configure, and manage a single-instance or multiple-instance high-availability failover cluster with SQL Server 2008.

The chapter is also based on Windows Server 2008. As a result, it includes the new features and prerequisites associated with implementing failover clustering with SQL Server 2008 on Windows Server 2008. Step-by-step procedures for both the Windows Server 2008 failover cluster and SQL Server 2008 failover cluster are also provided.

Chapter 13: Implementing and Managing Database Mirroring

Chapter 13 deals with configuring and managing database mirroring so that organizations can enhance the availability of their SQL Server databases, increase business continuity, and maintain a hot standby of their database in another geographic location. The chapter includes detailed step-by-step instructions for configurations of all three database mirroring modes: high availability, high protection, and high performance.

This chapter also includes best practices from the field, case studies, and discussions of how to integrate database mirroring with other high-availability alternatives such as failover clustering and how to recover from a failed server.

Chapter 14: Implementing and Managing Log Shipping

The focus of Chapter 14 is on configuring and managing log shipping. This chapter supplies step-by-step instructions on how to configure and maintain one or more warm standby databases, typically referred to as *secondary databases*. Like the other high-availability chapters in this part, this chapter includes real-world examples and industry best practices.

Chapter 15: Implementing and Managing SQL Server Replication
SQL Server Replication is another way of distributing data from a source SQL Server to either one or more target SQL Servers. This chapter focuses on replication components and provides a prelude to the different types of replication scenarios that a database administrator can manage, such as snapshot, merge, and transactional replication. Step-by-step replication configurations, including the peer-to-peer replication scenario, a new form of high availability, are also presented.

Part IV: Monitoring and Troubleshooting SQL Server 2008
Part IV of this book covers monitoring, troubleshooting, and performance-tuning techniques to ensure that SQL Server 2008 is optimized and performing at the highest possible levels.

Chapter 16: Managing Workloads and Consumption with Resource Governor
Unfortunately, with the previous releases of SQL Server, there was no way to effectively mitigate performance issues associated with SQL Server workloads. Thankfully, with SQL Server 2008, Microsoft introduced Resource Governor, which provides persistent performance to end users and applications by giving Database Administrators the potential to define resource limits and priorities on different SQL Server workloads. This chapter focuses on introducing, implementing, and configuring Resource Governor from a database administrator perspective.

Chapter 17: Monitoring SQL Server 2008 with Native Tools
SQL Server 2008 includes a tremendous number of native tools that should be leveraged in order to monitor a SQL Server database and infrastructure. This chapter first teaches a DBA how to use native tools to gain quick insight into a SQL Server system. It then focuses on how to leverage the new SQL Server audit functionality to monitor events and SQL Server activity and how to configure database mail. The final technologies described in this chapter are Performance Studio, and Performance and Reliability Monitoring, which are new monitoring technologies introduced with SQL Server 2008 and Windows Server 2008.

Chapter 18: Proactively Monitoring SQL Server 2008 with System Center Operations Manager 2007
Database Administrators and IT managers are under constant pressure to ensure that their SQL Server systems are operating at optimal levels. This can be very

challenging when managing a large SQL Server infrastructure. It is recommended for DBAs to leverage Operations Manager 2007 to proactively monitor and provide a comprehensive view of the health of a SQL Server infrastructure. The discussion in this chapter focuses on the Operations Manager components, installing the SQL Server management pack, and on how to use the operations console to effectively monitor a SQL Server infrastructure. By gaining the upper hand in monitoring and managing a SQL Server infrastructure, Database Administrators can achieve the agility necessary to be successful and focus on other tasks.

Chapter 19: Performance Tuning and Troubleshooting SQL Server 2008

After SQL Server 2008 is placed in operation and is being monitored, it is important to take action on the findings. It is often difficult to anticipate real-world loads during the development phase of application deployment; thus, it is critical to adjust the parameters of the SQL Server 2008 platform to optimize the performance after it is deployed. Frequently, DBAs need to troubleshoot the performance of SQL Server 2008 to address problems that are uncovered by monitoring.

This chapter focuses on how to tune, optimize, and troubleshoot the performance of the SQL Server 2008 system. Specific tools and components include Windows Server 2008 System Monitor, performance thresholds, SQL Server Profiler, Database Engine Tuning Advisor, Query Analysis, and Extended Events.

Part V: SQL Server 2008 Bonus Content

The final part of the book offers bonus content, including leveraging PowerShell to administer SQL Server and implementing Hyper-V to virtualize a SQL Server infrastructure.

Chapter 20: Administering SQL Server 2008 with PowerShell

SQL Server 2008 introduces support for Windows PowerShell. PowerShell is a new command-line shell and scripting language for automating server administration. Microsoft is beginning to integrate this new scripting language into all of their server products. This chapter discusses how to install PowerShell, provides an overview of the language and how it is integrated into SQL 2008, and then dives into how PowerShell can be leveraged to undertake common SQL Server tasks.

Chapter 21: Consolidating and Virtualizing SQL Server 2008 with Hyper-V

Tremendous efforts are being made in the IT industry and the world to sustain the environment. Going green by consolidating and virtualizing servers is a great way to simplify management, minimize data center costs, reduce power consumption, and make the world a better place for future generations. By consolidating SQL Server instances and leveraging Windows Server 2008 Hyper-V for consolidating and virtualizing SQL Server databases and instances, organizations can reduce the number of SQL Server systems within the infrastructure. This chapter focuses on how to plan and implement Hyper-V and create virtualized guest sessions so that SQL Server systems can be consolidated and virtualized. In addition, SQL Server virtualization considerations are also discussed.

Sample Databases

To facilitate running the steps introduced throughout the book, all of the examples are based on either the AdventureWorks2008 or Customer database. Both of these database samples can be downloaded directly from Microsoft's SQL Server sample website at http://www.codeplex.com/SqlServerSamples. The website and downloads also include the step-by-step instructions on how to install the sample databases on SQL Server 2008.

The exact link to the OLTP Adventureworks2008 sample can be found at http://www.codeplex.com/MSFTDBProdSamples/Release/ProjectReleases.asp x?ReleaseId=18407. Be sure to choose the correct MSI file based on the 2008 schema and the processor type of your system.

The Customer database can be downloaded from the sample Integration Services Product Samples website at http://www.codeplex.com/MSFTISProdSamples. The package sample name is "Execute SQL Statements in a Loop Sample Package" and the customer data which needs to be imported into a newly created Customer database is located in Customer.txt file.

In addition, the book is based on SQL Server 2008 Enterprise Edition running on Windows Server 2008 Enterprise Edition. The following elements were used for the scenarios of the book.

Element	Description
Domain	Companyabc.com
Domain Controller	TOR-DC01.companyabc.com
Main Site	Toronto, Ontario
SQL Server Name	TOR-SQL01\Instance01 TOR-SQL01\Instance02
Secondary Site	San Francisco, California
SQL Server Name	SFC-SQL01\Instance01 SFC-SQL02\Instance02
Disaster Recovery Site	New York, New York NYC-SQL01\Instance01 NYC-SQL02\Instance02

PART I

Installing, Administering, and Managing the Database Engine

IN THIS PART

CHAPTER 1

Installing or Upgrading to the SQL Server 2008 Database Engine

SQL Server 2008 Database Engine Services, formerly referred to as "The Database Engine," is the nucleus of SQL Server 2008. Its features are nothing short of impressive. Many organizations today run complex data applications that command the use of a feature like SQL Server's Database Engine that can process, store, and secure data. From a transactional perspective, it is used to store, process, and secure data for the most demanding data-consuming applications within your enterprise. Moreover, the Database Engine offers many other benefits and advantages for organizations. It controls authorization to SQL Server objects, provides high-availability functionality, and includes subfeatures such as Replication and Full-Text Search.

This chapter describes the step-by-step process for installing a clean version of SQL Server 2008 Database Engine and/or upgrading an existing SQL Server Database Engine implementation to SQL Server 2008. In addition, this chapter covers how to leverage the planning tools to ensure a successful installation, upgrade, or transition.

Even though the SQL Server 2008 installation process is very intuitive and has been simplified, a DBA must make several key decisions to ensure that the completed installation or upgrade will meet the needs of the organization. For example, is it beneficial to upgrade an existing SQL Server implementation to SQL Server 2008, or is it preferred to conduct a clean install from scratch? What are the ramifications of these alternatives? Will you lose your existing SQL Server settings, databases, and configurations?

This chapter covers these prerequisite planning tasks to address the questions and concerns of DBAs.

In addition, this chapter also covers the hardware and software prerequisites, supported SQL Server 2008 upgrade paths, supported Windows operating systems for running SQL Server 2008, and benefits of running SQL Server 2008 on the highly anticipated Windows Server 2008 family of operating systems.

What's New for Installation with SQL Server 2008?

SQL Server continues to deliver a robust experience when installing or upgrading to SQL Server 2008. Moreover, SQL Server 2008 introduces significant enhancements to make the installation or upgrade process even more simple and seamless compared to its predecessors. The new installation features for SQL Server 2008 consist of the following:

- A new SQL Server 2008 Installation Center landing page, which includes a tremendous number of options for planning, installing, and maintaining a SQL Server implementation. The Installation Center is also a one-stop shop for planning and reviewing SQL Server documentation before getting started.

- A new planning tool known as the System Configuration Checker, which checks for conditions that could impede a SQL Server installation prior to the actual installation.

- Another great planning tool is the newly refined Install Upgrade Advisor. The Install Upgrade Advisor tool allows a DBA to fully analyze existing SQL Server 2005 and SQL Server 2000 installations for issues that may surface when upgrading to SQL Server 2008. By fixing these issues before conducting the upgrade, an organization will have a smoother experience when transitioning to SQL Server 2008.

- New maintenance tasks have been introduced in the installation process, which allow DBAs to either repair a corrupt SQL Server 2008 installation or conduct a Feature Upgrade. The Feature Upgrade tool is a wizard that allows organizations to upgrade or change their existing edition of SQL Server 2008 after the initial installation or upgrade is complete.

- A discovery report that will provide a detailed report of all SQL Server 2000, 2005, and 2008 components, features, and settings associated with an installation.

- The potential to automate SQL Server installations by using an existing configuration file.

- An Advanced Cluster Preparation tool, which streamlines and prepares a SQL Server 2008 failover cluster installation—which is typically deemed a very difficult task in the industry.

- A tool that will allow for a smooth transition of packages by automatically upgrading them from SQL Server 2005 to the SQL Server 2008 Integration Services format.

Deprecated SQL Server 2008 Database Engine Elements

Not only is it essential to understand the new features and functionality associated with the Database Engine, but it is equally important to understand older elements that have been deprecated in SQL Server 2008. Let's examine the list of deprecated elements that are no longer supported or associated with the Database Engine.

- The DUMP statement associated with backups has been deprecated and replaced with BACKUP.

- The LOAD statement associated with restores has been replaced with RESTORE.

- BACKUP LOG WITH NO_LOG and BACKUP LOG WITH TRUNCATE_ONLY are no longer available as the transaction log is automatically truncated with the database using the Simple recovery model.

- The sp_addalias procedure has been removed.

- SQL Server 60, 65, and 70 compatibility levels are no longer supported. Databases must at least maintain a compatibility level of 80.

- The sp_addgroup, sp_dropgroup, and sp_helpgroup stored procedures have been replaced with roles.

- Sample databases such as Northwind, Pubs, and AdventureWorks are no longer included as optional installation features with the installation program. If you want to use the sample databases, they are offered as out-of-band downloads from Microsoft's samples website.

- The Surface Area Configuration (SAC) tool has been replaced with Policy Based Management.

- Remote servers have been replaced with Linked servers.

> **Note**
>
> The preceding bullets itemize the main features deprecated with the Database Engine. However, for a full list of each item, review the topic "Deprecated Database Engine Features and Discontinued Database Engine Functionality in SQL Server 2008" in SQL Server Books Online (BOL).

Preplanning and Preparing a SQL Server 2008 Server Database Engine Installation

Before you begin the actual installation of SQL Server 2008 Database Engine, you must make several decisions concerning preliminary tasks. How well you plan these steps will determine how successful your installation is—as many of these decisions cannot be changed after the installation is complete.

Verifying Minimum Hardware Requirements

Whether you are installing SQL Server 2008 in a lab or production environment, you need to ensure that the hardware chosen meets the minimum system requirements. In most situations, the minimum hardware requirements presented will not suffice; therefore, Table 1.1 provides not only the minimum requirements, but also the recommended and optimal system requirements for the hardware components.

> **Note**
>
> This book is tailored toward the Standard and Enterprise Editions. As such, the minimum hardware and software requirements documented in Table 1.1 and Table 1.2 of this chapter only cover "core editions" of SQL Server 2008, also known as Standard and Enterprise Editions. To review the hardware and software requirements for the "specialized editions," refer to the section on "Hardware and Software Requirements for Installing SQL Server 2008" in SQL Server 2008 Books Online (BOL).

Table 1.1   **SQL Server 2008 Processor and Memory System Requirements**

SQL Server 2008 Enterprise Edition (64-bit) IA64

Component	Minimum Requirements	Recommended Requirements
Processor	Itanium	1.0GHz or higher: Itanium
Memory	512MB	2.048GB or above

SQL Server 2008 Enterprise Edition (64-bit) x64

Component	Minimum Requirements	Recommended Requirements
Processor	1.4GHz: AMD Opteron, AMD Athlon, Intel Xeon EM64T, and Intel Pentium IV EM64T	2GHz or higher: AMD Opteron, AMD Athlon, Intel Xeon EM64T, and Intel Pentium IV EM64T
Memory	512MB	2.048GB or above

SQL Server 2008 Standard Edition (64-bit) x64

Component	Minimum Requirements	Recommended Requirements
Processor	1.4GHz: AMD Opteron, AMD Athlon, Intel Xeon EM64T, and Intel Pentium IV EM64T	2GHz or higher: AMD Opteron, AMD Athlon, Intel Xeon EM64T, and Intel Pentium IV EM64T
Memory	512MB	2.048GB or above

SQL Server 2008 Enterprise Edition (32-bit) x64

Component	Minimum Requirements	Recommended Requirements
Processor	1.0GHz: Pentium III	2GHz or higher: Pentium III
Memory	512MB	2.048GB or above

SQL Server 2008 Standard Edition (32-bit)

Component	Minimum Requirements	Recommended Requirements
Processor	1.0GHz: Pentium III	2GHz or higher: Pentium III
Memory	512MB	2.048GB or above

The minimum disk space requirements differ depending on which SQL Server 2008 feature will be installed. Table 1.2 depicts these minimum disk space specifications itemized by feature.

Table 1.2 **SQL Server 2008 Minimum Disk Requirements**

SQL Server 2008 Feature	Minimum Disk Space Required in MB
Database Engine and data files, Replication, and Full-Text Search	280
Analysis Services and data files	90
Reporting Services and Report Manager	120
Integration Services	120
Client Components	850
SQL Server Books Online (BOL) and SQL Server Compact Books Online	240

Note

When designing and selecting the system specifications for a SQL Server implementation, even the optimal system requirements recommendations from Microsoft might not suffice. It is a best practice to assess the server specifications of the planned server role while taking the load during the time of deployment and future growth into consideration. For example, a SQL Server 2008 system running 50 instances of the Database Engine will require much more than the recommended specification of 2GB of RAM to run adequately. In addition, SQL Server 2008 running on a Windows 2008 server that is providing business intelligence solutions for 10,000 users might require 32GB of RAM. Therefore, size the system accordingly and test the load before going live into production.

Examining SQL Server 2008 Software Prerequisites

Before installing SQL Server 2008, it is also important to get acquainted with the software prerequisites, as many of these prerequisites outline best practices. As such, you should take the time to review the prerequisites before implementation to ensure installation or upgrade success. The SQL Server 2008 software prerequisites include

- .NET Framework 3.5
- Windows Installer 4.5 or later
- Microsoft Data Access Components (MDAC) 2.8 SP1 or later
- Internet Explorer 6 SP1 or later
- Latest version of PowerShell
- Latest Windows Server hot fixes are recommended
- If SQL Server 2008 will be virtualized, then Hyper-V is required and supported.

Note

For more information and consolidating and virtualizing SQL Server 2008 on Windows Server 2008 Hyper-V, refer to Chapter 21, "Consolidating and Virtualizating with Hyper-V."

The SQL Server installation wizard will first verify if these software prerequisites are already installed. If they are not, don't panic—the SQL Server 2008 installation wizard is very intuitive and will most likely prompt, and then install all of these software prerequisites automatically. Therefore, you won't have to spend hours conducting Google searches, trying to nail down the appropriate downloads, including versions.

Choosing the Appropriate SQL Server Edition

SQL Server 2008 comes in a variety of editions that are tailored to suit the needs and requirements of different organizations and applications. The SQL Server 2008 Editions include the Enterprise, Standard, Workgroup, Express, Compact, and Developer Editions, as described in the following sections.

SQL Server 2008 Enterprise Edition

The SQL Server 2008 Enterprise Edition is the complete feature set of the product and is designed to support the needs of the largest enterprises. It includes all the features for scalability, performance, high availability, enterprise security, data warehousing, business intelligence, and enterprise manageability. The Enterprise Edition is fully 64-bit capable, is optimized to run on 64-bit platforms and can support all the processors and memory found in the operating system.

Some other new features only found in the Enterprise edition include Partitioned Table Parallelism, enhanced database mirroring features, Resource Governor, Backup Compression, online operations, Hot Add CPU, Performance Data Collector, Extensible Key Management, Failover Clustering, Transparent Data Encryption, and Change Data Capture.

SQL Server 2008 Standard Edition

The SQL Server 2008 Standard Edition includes the core set of functionality needed to support data warehouses, electronic commerce applications, and line-of-business applications. It is designed to support the needs of small to medium organizations. The Standard Edition is fully 64-bit capable and can support a maximum of four processors. It is worth mentioning that two nodes of failover clustering is also supported within the Standard Edition.

SQL Server 2008 Workgroup Edition

The SQL Server 2008 Workgroup Edition is designed for small organizations and includes the core database features needed for applications.

SQL Server 2008 Express Edition

The SQL Server 2008 Express Edition is the free edition that is designed to support small or targeted applications with a core set of secure database requirements. This edition replaces the Microsoft SQL Server Desktop Engine (MSDE) platform available in SQL Server 2000 and augments the Express Edition in SQL Server 2005.

SQL Server 2008 Compact Edition

The SQL Server 2008 Compact Edition is the free edition that runs on mobile devices as well as desktops. This provides a single lightweight database platform for client applications. This edition replaces the SQL Server Mobile product and augments the SQL Server 2005 Compact Edition.

SQL Server 2008 Developer Edition

The SQL Server 2008 Developer Edition provides all the same features and functionality as the Enterprise Edition but is licensed only for development purposes.

The following link includes the full list of features supported based on the Editions of SQL Server 2008.

http://msdn.microsoft.com/en-us/library/cc645993.aspx

Choosing the Appropriate Windows Operating System Version and Edition to Support the SQL Server Installation

SQL Server 2008 can run on a number of Windows operating systems. SQL Server 2008 can run on top of Windows Server 2008, Windows Server 2003 SP2, Windows VISTA, and Windows XP. When referring to Windows Server 2008, either the Windows Server 2008 edition with or without Hyper-V can be utilized. Please note that SQL Server 2008 does not support running Windows 2000 or Windows NT 4.0.

Benefits of Running SQL Server 2008 on Windows Server 2008

Hands down, the Windows Server 2008 family of operating systems is the best choice for running SQL Server 2008. By combining the two products, the highest level of security, scalability, reliability, high availability and compliance can be achieved. Some of the major benefits of running SQL Server 2008 on Windows Server 2008 include the following:

- **Authentication**—The Windows Server 2008 authentication mechanism provides the highest level of security for authorization when running Active Directory Domain Services. SQL Server can leverage the following: Active Directory role-based security for authorization and administration, two-factor authentication with SmartCard-based certificates and biometric devices, and integration with certificate services. Finally, Kerberos is now supported for all SQL Server protocols.

- **Encryption**—By combining the encryption technologies included in both SQL Server 2008 and Windows Server 2008, it is finally possible to achieve encryption from an end-to-end perspective.

- **Minimized Footprint**—Both Windows Server 2008 and SQL Server 2008 provide a modularized installation process that is very granular. Therefore, you only install what you need. This strategy minimizes the attack surface, which in turn, mitigates breaches and compromises.

- **Compliance**—New features and functionality such as integrating Audit and Audit Specifications directly with the Windows Server 2008 event and security logs allows for stronger auditing functionality, which is a requirement of many major regulatory compliances.

- **Dynamic Hardware Partitioning**—Allows for both CPU and RAM to be added to the SQL Server system on the fly, without causing a server outage.

- **High Availability Clustering**—Windows Server 2008 supports up to 16 nodes within a SQL Server 2008 failover cluster. In addition, the requirement of having all nodes within the same subnet has been alleviated. Consequently, with the new quorum model and no subnet restriction, it is easier to achieve geographically dispersed clusters.

- **Policy Based Management**—By leveraging the Windows Server 2008 group policy and the configuration management strategies, policies can be created to manage SQL Server databases settings and configurations.

- **PowerShell**—The latest scripting technology geared toward effectively managing Windows Server and Microsoft applications has extended to SQL Server 2008. DBAs can use the powerful command-line scripting technologies to automate administrator tasks for both Windows Server 2008 and SQL Server 2008.

- **Performance Management**—Windows Server 2008 introduces Windows Reliability and a newly refined performance monitor tool for troubleshooting and monitoring SQL Server system performance. In addition, the Windows performance framework has been augmented through the introduction of SQL Server 2008 Performance Data Collector. As a result, collecting, analyzing, and troubleshooting SQL Server data in a centralized solution for end-to-end monitoring can be achieved.

- **Consolidation and Virtualization**—Hyper-V has been introduced with Windows Server 2008. Hyper-V is Microsoft's virtualization technology. By using Hyper-V in conjunction with SQL Server 2008, you can consolidate SQL Servers into a virtualized environment, reduce SQL Server hardware, and reduce total cost of ownership within the infrastructure.

Understanding the Windows Server 2008 Family of Operating Systems

In the Windows 2008 family of operating systems, there are four main editions, and SQL Server 2008 can run on any of them. These editions include Windows Server 2008 Standard, Windows Server 2008 Enterprise Edition, Windows Server 2008 Datacenter Edition, and Windows Web Server 2008.

Organizations and DBAs must understand their workload needs and requirements when selecting the appropriate Windows Server 2008 operating system edition to utilize. In addition, the Windows Server edition selected must also coincide with requirements pertaining to the edition of SQL Server 2008 selected. For example, the Windows Server 2008 Enterprise Edition might be selected if there is a need to sustain an eight-node SQL Server failover cluster; the Standard Edition may be selected in order to save on licensing costs; or Windows Server 2008 Enterprise Edition with Hyper-V may be selected if there is a need to virtualize the SQL Server environment.

Each edition supports both the 32-bit and 64-bit processor architectures and the Standard, Enterprise, and Datacenter editions ship with or without Hyper-V. Hyper-V is the latest Microsoft virtualization technology based on Windows Server 2008.

Finally, when running SQL Server 2008 on Windows Server 2008, the maximum amount of RAM supported by the operating system on 32-bit systems is 4GB when running the Standard Edition and 64GB when running the Enterprise and Datacenter Editions. For a 64-bit system, the numbers increase as the Standard Edition can support 32GB and the Enterprise and Datacenter Editions can support up to 2TB of RAM. Hence it is strongly recommended to be using the x64 versions of the operating system whenever possible as it allows for greater flexibility and upgradability.

Caution

When installing Windows Server 2008, it is possible to select a Server Core installation. Windows Server 2008 Server Core is a stripped-down minimal installation that provides a low-maintenance environment through limited functionality. The present version of Server Core is not intended to be an application platform. Since there are SQL Server dependencies that are not part of the Server Core, SQL Server 2008 *cannot* run on a Windows Server Core installation.

For an overview of the editions and a complete list of Windows 2008 features and functionality, refer to the Microsoft Windows Server 2008 home page at the following link:

http://www.microsoft.com/windowsserver2008/en/us/default.aspx.

New Installation, Upgrade, or Transition?

Organizations that have conducted a SQL Server implementation in the past may need to perform a new SQL Server 2008 installation, a side-by-side installation or upgrade their existing SQL Server system, which is commonly referred to as an *in-place* upgrade. Finally, organizations may choose to transition to SQL Server 2008 by first installing a new installation and then migrating SQL Server databases and objects from the legacy environment. There are benefits to each of these options. The next two sections detail the benefits.

Should You Perform a New SQL Server 2008 Installation?

The primary benefit of a new installation is that, by installing the operating system from scratch, you are starting with a known good server and a brand new SQL Server 2008 implementation. You can avoid migrating problems that might have existed on your previous server—whether due to corrupt software, incorrect configuration settings, or improperly installed applications. Moreover, a new installation provides an opportunity for housecleaning as legacy SQL Server items are not carried over.

For example, it is common for an old SQL Server system to have many outdated databases, packages, user accounts, and stored procedures that have not been touched in over 10 years. Keep in mind, however, that you will also lose all configuration settings from your previous installation. In addition, all SQL Server elements, such as databases, user accounts, packages, and so on, will need to be migrated/transitioned. Moreover, required applications on the legacy server will need to be reinstalled after the installation of the new operating system and the SQL Server 2008 implementation are complete. Make sure you document your server configuration information and back up any data that you want to keep.

When running SQL Server 2008, there may be situations where installing a new installation from scratch is the only option. For example, it is not possible to upgrade a legacy SQL Server Failover Cluster from SQL Server 2005 running on Windows Server 2003 to SQL Server 2008 Failover Clustering running on Windows Server 2008.

Note

When performing a new installation of SQL Server 2008, it is possible to install a new SQL Server 2008 instance on an existing system with SQL Server 2005. Therefore, a side-by-side installation is supported and a migration of existing data from SQL Server 2005 to SQL Server 2008 can be achieved all within the same server.

Should You Upgrade an Existing SQL Server System to SQL Server 2008?

Upgrading, on the other hand, replaces your current SQL Server binaries but keeps existing databases, components, features, packages, users, settings, groups, rights, and permissions intact. In this scenario, you don't have to reinstall applications or restore data. Before choosing this option, keep in mind that you should test your applications and databases for compatibility before migration. Just because they worked on previous versions of SQL Server does not mean they will work on SQL Server 2008.

As always, before performing any type of server maintenance such as a SQL Server or Windows Server 2008 in-place upgrade, you should perform a complete backup of the SQL Server environment, any applications residing on the server, and data that you want to preserve. Do not forget to include the System State when backing up the SQL Server system. It is required when performing a restore if you want to maintain the existing Windows settings.

Table 1.3 lists the upgrade paths for SQL Server 2008.

Table 1.3   **SQL Server 2008 Upgrade Paths**

Previous SQL Server System	Upgrade to SQL Server 2008
SQL Server 2008	SQL Server version upgrades supported
SQL Server 2005	Yes, fully supported to like edition
SQL Server 2000	Yes, fully supported to like edition
SQL Server 7.0	Not supported
SQL Server 6.5	Not supported

> **Note**
>
> In-place upgrades can only be accomplished when using the same edition. For example, an upgrade from SQL Server 2005 Standard to SQL Server 2008 Enterprise cannot be achieved. Nevertheless, there is a way around this situation. It is possible to upgrade from SQL Server 2005 Standard to SQL Server 2008 Standard and then conduct an edition upgrade to SQL Server 2008 Enterprise.

Should You Upgrade the Operating System to Windows Server 2008?

On another note, when upgrading an existing system to SQL Server 2008, there may be situations when an organization would also want to upgrade the underlying operating system to Windows Server 2008. To upgrade to Windows 2008, you must be running a server-level operating system. You cannot upgrade Workstation or Home Editions of operating systems such as Windows XP or Windows Vista to Windows 2008. To upgrade your existing SQL Server's operating system, you must be running Windows Server 2003. An upgrade from Windows NT 4.0 and Windows 2000 Server is not permitted. Table 1.4 lists the available upgrade paths to Windows 2008.

Table 1.4 Windows Server 2008 Upgrade Paths

Previous Operating System	Upgrade to Windows Server 2008
Microsoft Windows Server 2003 R2 Standard, Enterprise, or Datacenter Edition	Yes, fully supported to like edition
Microsoft Windows Server 2003 operating systems with Service Pack 1 (SP1) Standard, Enterprise, or Datacenter Edition	Yes, fully supported to like edition
Microsoft Windows Server 2003 operating systems with Service Pack 2 (SP2) Standard, Enterprise, or Datacenter Edition	Yes, fully supported to like edition
Windows NT 4.0	Not supported
Windows 2000 Server	Not supported
Windows XP	Not supported
Windows Vista	Not supported

Note

For Windows Server 2008, in-place upgrades can only be performed to the same editions of Windows Server 2008. For example, an upgrade from Windows Server 2003 Standard to Windows Server 2008 Enterprise cannot be achieved.

Gathering Additional Information Necessary to Proceed

During the installation of SQL Server 2008, you will have to tell the setup wizard how you want your server configured. The wizard will take the information you provide and configure the server settings to meet your specifications.

Taking the time to gather the information described in the following sections before starting your installation or upgrade will likely make your SQL Server 2008 installation go faster, smoother, and easier.

New SQL Server 2008 Installation or In-place Upgrade

The first and most major decision when moving toward SQL Server 2008 is debating whether to implement a brand new SQL Server installation from scratch or to conduct an in-place upgrade. If you don't already have SQL Server in your existing infrastructure, it is a "no-brainer," and a new installation is warranted. However, if a legacy version of SQL Server resides in the infrastructure, the organization must decide between an in-place upgrade or a new installation. If a new installation is chosen, it is necessary to transition existing SQL Server data from the legacy system to the newly established SQL Server 2008 system. As mentioned earlier, each alternative has benefits and disadvantages.

New SQL Server 2008 Stand-alone Installation or Failover Cluster

Another major decision needs to be made in the planning phases: Should SQL Server 2008 be installed in a stand-alone system or should Failover Clustering be utilized? Failover Clustering provides high availability for a SQL Server instance and should be leveraged if an organization needs maximum availability, protection against server hardware failure, seamless failover that does not require DBA intervention, and finally, automatic client redirects. A stand-alone installation is also sufficient, as it is cheaper, easier to administer, and does not require specific failover clustering hardware.

Note

To install SQL Server 2008 Failover Cluster, review Chapter 12, "Implementing and Managing Failover Clustering."

Single-Instance or Multiple-Instance Installation

For years now, discussions on the topic of single-instance versus multiple-installation have both engulfed and engaged the SQL Server community. Should you install a single-instance SQL Server installation and place all databases on one instance, or scale up and create a multiple-instance SQL Server installation and spread databases across each of these instances? This question continues to echo through every organization. Here are some best practices to assist in making such an arduous decision.

One of the main drawbacks of placing all databases on a single-instance installation involves the tempdb database. The tempdb database is a shared resource between all databases contained within the same SQL Server instance. Performance degradation may occur as the tempdb database is the single point of contention for all temporary database workloads. In multiple-instance installations, a tempdb database is created for each instance, mini-mizing contention and performance degradation.

Many DBAs implement multiple instances for other reasons, including regu-latory compliance, administrator autonomy, different global security policies, global server settings, and compatibility requirements.

> **Note**
>
> Only one instance within the installation can maintain the default instance name. Therefore, if a default instance already exists, SQL Server 2008 must be installed as a named instance.

Side-by-Side Installations with Previous Versions of SQL Server

Organizations also have the option to install a brand new installation of SQL Server 2008 on a server that is already running a legacy instances of SQL Server 2005. Based on this methodology, more than one version of SQL Server will reside on the system.

Typically, the preference is to either conduct an in-place upgrade or install SQL Server 2008 on new hardware to minimize hardware contention and performance degradation. However, side-by-side installations are sometimes warranted. Let's look at the situations that support this installation. SQL Server 2008 will coexist with SQL Server 2005 and SQL Server 2000. Unfortunately, SQL Server 7.0 is not supported, but hopefully the majority of the organizations out there have already transitioned out of SQL Server 7.0 because it is no longer supported by Microsoft.

Determine Which SQL Server 2008 Features to Install

Give serious thought to the SQL Server 2008 features before installing them. The modular setup of SQL Server 2008 is made up of many independent features, previously referred to as components, allowing for complete customization by organizations. This typically results in minimal surface area and more granularity compared with older editions of SQL Server. This improved modular installation process is said to be "slim and efficient" like other new Microsoft products such as Windows Server 2008 and Exchange Server 2007.

The following bullets depict the modular installation including shared features that can be selected during the installation of SQL Server 2008:

- **Database Engine Services**—This is the core service for storing, processing, and securing data. It is designed to provide a scalable, fast, and high-availability platform for access and the other components. Two subfeatures within the Database Engine are

  - **SQL Server Replication**—Replication allows DBAs to copy databases to different locations and keep the copies synchronized. This can be used for data distribution, synchronization, fault tolerance, disaster recovery, load balancing, or testing. The Replication component manages database replication and interacts primarily with the Database Engine features.

  - **Full-Text Search**—The Full-Text Search engine populates and manages the full-text catalogs. The Full-Text engine also makes full-text searches easier by maintaining indexes, a thesaurus, noise words, and linguistic analysis of the full-text indexes.

- **Analysis Services**—The SQL Server 2008 Analysis Services (SSAS) feature provides online analytical processing (OLAP) and data mining. OLAP is a modification of the original database concept of online transaction processing (OLTP). OLAP is designed to provide immediate answers to analytical and ad hoc queries from a multidimensional cube known as an OLAP cube. Data mining is the process of searching large volumes of data for patterns and trends. SSAS allows SQL Server 2008 to provide both these capabilities and is the core feature of business intelligence.

- **Reporting Services**—The Microsoft SQL Server 2008 Reporting Services (SSRS) feature allows for the presentation and delivery of data in a variety of ways. The reports can include tables, matrices, and free-form data. The source data for the reports can be provided by the Database Engine component, the Analysis Services component, or any Microsoft .NET data provider such as ODBC or OLE DB to access data sources such as Oracle or file-based data.

- **Shared Features**—Features designated as "Shared Features" include

  - **Business Intelligence Development Studio**—The Business Intelligence Development Studio is essentially Microsoft Visual Studio 2008 with some additional SQL Server 2008 business intelligence project types. It is an applications development environment that allows developers to build applications that include Analysis Services, Integration Services, and Reporting Services.

  - **Client Tools Connectivity**—This feature includes the installation of communication components between clients and servers.

- **Integration Services**—The SQL Server 2008 Integration Services (SSIS) feature integrates data from different sources. This integration includes importing, exporting, and transforming data from disparate sources. The data can be copied, merged, restructured, and cleaned as part of the integration processing, which makes the integration services a powerful tool in the development of data warehouses. It is imperative to mention that the Integration Services component fills an important gap in the extract.

- **Client Tools Backward Compatibility**—This feature was heavily requested by the SQL Server community. When Client Tools Backward Compatibility is installed, a DBA can manage legacy SQL Server systems.

- **Client Tools SDK**—This feature includes the Software Development Kit containing resources for developers.

- **SQL Server Books Online**—SQL Server Books Online (BOL) is Microsoft's documentation for SQL Server 2008.

- **Management Tools Complete**—When installed, SQL Server 2008 will possess all the management tools, including but not limited to Management Studio, support for Reporting Services, Analysis Services, Integration Services, SQL Server Profiler, and Database Tuning Advisor.

- **Management Tools Basic**—This refers to the scaled-down version of the management toolset. It only includes management studio support for the Database Engine, SQL Server Express, SQL Server Command-Line Utility, and PowerShell.

- **SQL Client Connectivity SDK**—This feature includes the Software Development Kit containing connectivity resources for developers.

- **Microsoft Sync Framework**—This is a comprehensive synchronization platform enabling collaboration and offline of applications, services and devices with support for any data type, any data store, any transfer protocol, and network topology.

When installing the SQL Server 2008 Database Engine, the additional optional subfeatures to install include

- Replication
- Full-Text Search

- Integration Services
- Connectivity components
- Programming models
- Management tools
- Management Studio
- SQL Server Books Online

Installing a Clean Version of SQL Server 2008

The following sections depict the step-by-step instructions for installing a clean version of the SQL Server 2008 Database Engine feature including supplementary subfeatures such as SQL Server Replication, Full-Text Search, Integration Services, and Shared Components.

1. Log in to the server with administrative privileges and insert the SQL Server 2008 media. Autorun should launch the SQL Server 2008 Installation Center landing page; otherwise, click Setup.exe

Note

If SQL Server's setup software prerequisites have not been met, the installation wizard will prompt, and then install the prerequisites. After the prerequisites have been installed, the SQL Server installation process will resume. SQL Server 2008 software prerequisites may include hotfixes, .NET Framework 3.5 and the latest Windows Installer, version 4.5. In addition, system restarts may be required after SQL Server's setup software prerequisites are installed. If so, rerun setup after the reboot to continue with the SQL Server installation.

2. On the SQL Server Installation Center landing page, first select the Installation page, and then click the New SQL Server Stand-alone Installation or Add Features to an Existing Installation link, as displayed in Figure 1.1.

3. On the Setup Support Rules page, review the outcome of the System Configuration Checker. Ensure that all tests associated with the operation passed without any failures, warnings, or skipped elements. Alternatively, you can review a standard or comprehensive report by selecting the Show Details button or View Detailed Report. To continue with the installation, click OK, as illustrated in Figure 1.2.

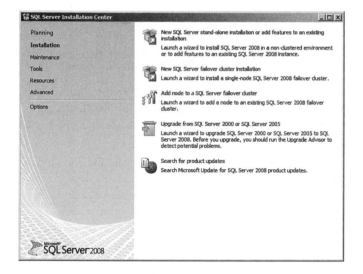

FIGURE 1.1
Performing a new SQL Server stand-alone installation.

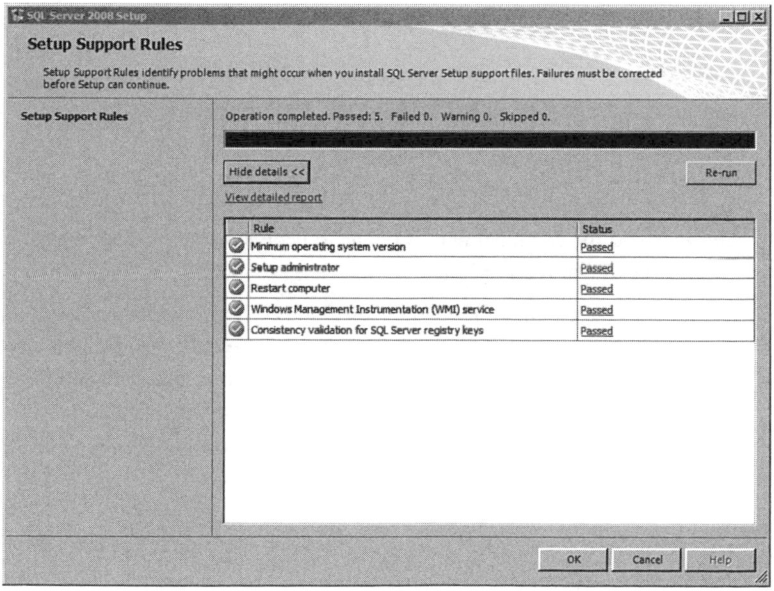

FIGURE 1.2
Reviewing potential problems identified with the Setup Support Rules.

4. On the Product Key page, enter the SQL Server Product Key and click Next.

5. On the License Agreement page, Accept the Licensing Terms, and then click Next.

6. On the Setup Support Files page, the wizard will prompt whether or not additional setup support files are required for the installation. If additional files are required, review the status of the files required, and then click Install.

7. The Setup Support Rules page will be displayed again and will identify any outstanding items that may hinder the installation process associated with the SQL Server installation. Review and correct failures and warnings before commencing the installation. If failures are not displayed, click Next to start the installation. Once any outstanding installation are complete, review the details, and then click Next.

Note

Some of the items that will be tested for in step 7 are: Fusion Template Library, Unsupported SQL Server products, whether the server is a Domain Controller, the version of Windows PowerShell, and Windows Firewall Settings.

---

8. On the Feature Selection page, select the desired features to be installed and provide the path for the Shared Feature Directory. For this example, the Database Engine Services, SQL Server Replication, Full-Text Search, and appropriate Shared Features such as Integration Services and the Management Tools have been selected. Click Next to proceed as illustrated in Figure 1.3.

9. On the Instance Configuration page, specify the Name and Instance ID for the SQL Server installation. The options include either the Default Instance name, which is MSSQLServer, or a Named Instance. In addition, click the ellipsis button in the Instance Root Directory area and specify the path for the installation. Click Next as displayed in Figure 1.4.

Note

Each instance name provided must be unique and there can only be one default instance per SQL Server system.

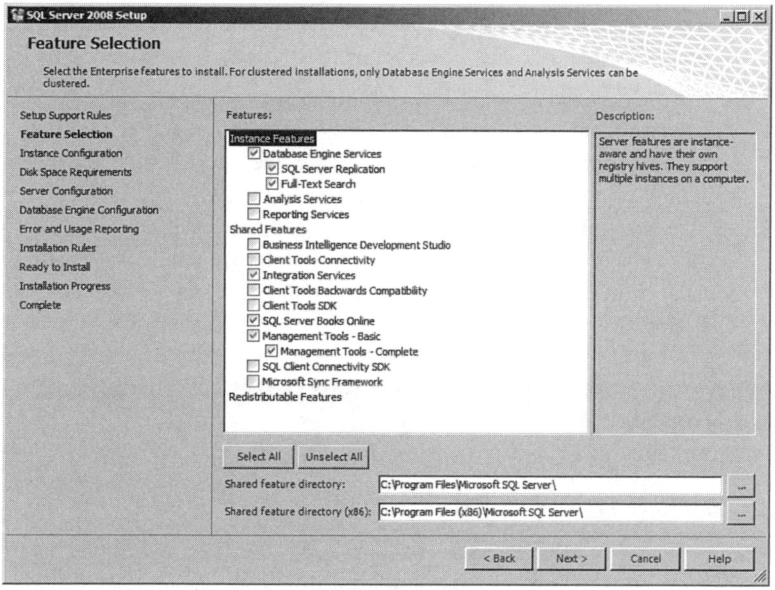

FIGURE 1.3
Specifying the SQL Server features to be installed.

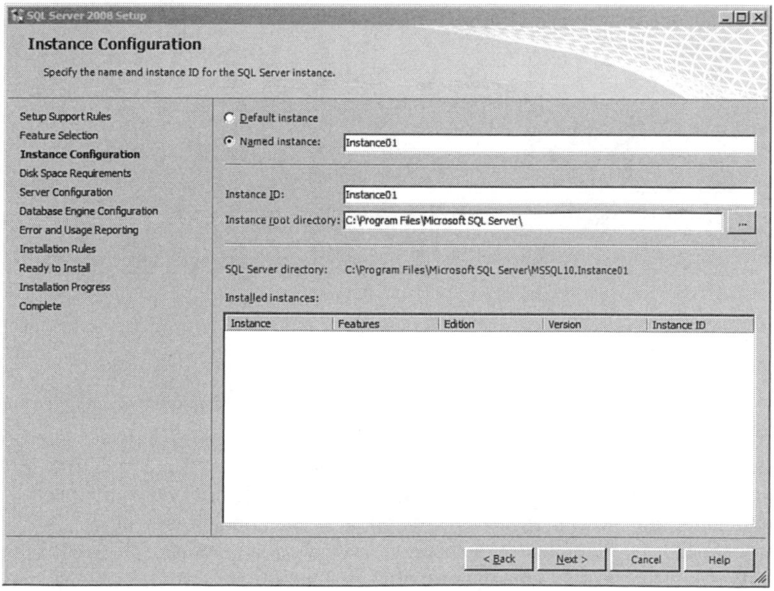

FIGURE 1.4
Configuring the SQL Server instance.

10. The next page is the Disk Space Requirements. Review the disk space summary for the SQL Server components and features selected to be installed, and then click Next.

11. The Server Configuration page includes configuration settings for both Service Accounts and Collation. On the Service Accounts tab, enter a valid low-privilege service account name and password for each service account. Next, specify the Startup Type for each service account listed, as illustrated in Figure 1.5. Options include Automatic, Manual or Disabled. Before proceeding to the next step, click the Collation tab,

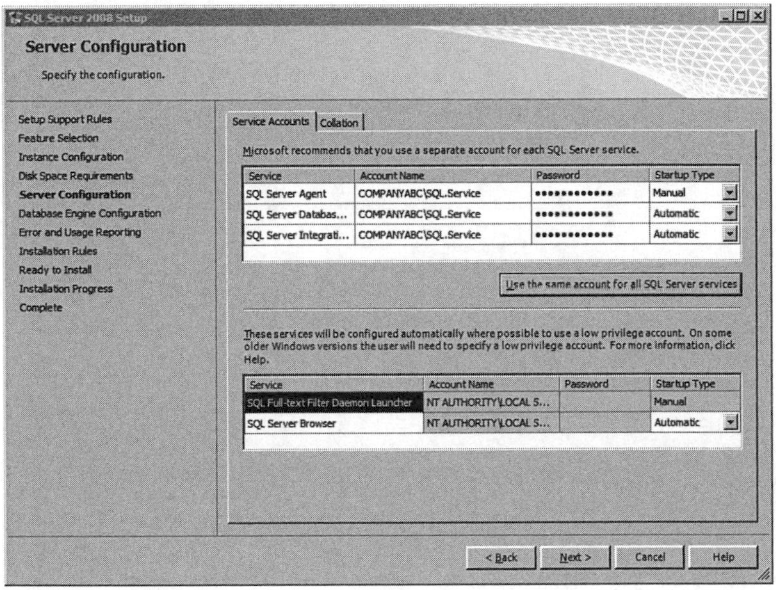

FIGURE 1.5
Specifying the SQL Server service accounts.

Note

From a hardening perspective, Microsoft recommends entering a separate service account for each SQL Server component and feature being installed. In addition, the account specified should follow the principle of least privilege. For more information on selecting the desired service account, and hardening a SQL Server implementation, see Chapter 8, "Hardening a SQL Server Implementation."

12. On the Collation tab, enter the desired collation option for the Database Engine. It is possible to change default collation settings used by the Database Engine and Analysis Services for language and sorting by selecting Customize. Click Next to continue.

13. The Database Engine Configuration page consists of three tabs. The tabs include Account Provisioning, Data Directories, and FILESTREAM. On the first tab, in the Account Provisioning section, specify the Authentication Mode, which consists of either Windows Authentication Mode or Mixed Mode (SQL Server authentication and Windows authentication). If mixed mode is selected, enter and confirm the password for the Built-in SQL Server administrator account. The next step is to provision a SQL Server Administrator by either selecting the option Add Current User or clicking Add and specifying a SQL Server administrator account.

Note

New to SQL Server 2008 is the opportunity to rename the SA account during installation. Renaming the SA account increases security as the account name is well known in the industry.

---

14. The second tab, Data Directories, located still within the Database Engine Configuration page, is used for specifying the location of the default directories associated with the installation of this SQL Server instance. The directories include Data Root Directory, System Database Directory, User Database Directory, User Database Log Directory, TempDB Directory, TempDB Log Directory, and Backup Directory. Either maintain the default directories or specify a new directory for performance and availability.

Tip

Because I/O to log files is sequential and I/O to database files is random, for increased performance, it is a best practice to place log files on a separate disk from database files. In addition, placing the tempdb on its own disk also bolsters performance.

---

15. The final tab on the Database Engine Configuration page is FILESTREAM. Here, decide whether you want to enable FILESTREAM. If FILESTREAM is enabled, additional parameters must be entered such as Enable FILESTREAM for File I/O Streaming Access, Windows Share Name, and whether to allow remote clients to have streaming access to FILESTREAM data. Click Next to proceed.

16. On the Error and Usage Reporting page, help Microsoft improve SQL Server features and services by sending error reports and feature usage to Microsoft. Specify the level of participation, and then click Next.

17. The final check will take place to ensure that the installation process will not be blocked. On the Installation Rules page, review for any outstanding errors or warnings and then click Next to continue.

18. Before commencing the SQL Server 2008 Installation, review the features to be installed on the Ready to Install page, and then click Install.

19. When the installation process starts, you can monitor its progress accordingly. When the installation setup completes, review the success status based on each SQL Server feature and then click Next.

20. On the Complete page, review the location of the SQL Server summary upgrade log file and additional items, which can be found in the supplemental information section. Click Close to finalize the installation.

21. To conduct post-installation tasks, review the upcoming section "Finalizing the SQL Server 2008 Installation or Upgrade" in this chapter.

Upgrading the Database Engine to SQL Server 2008

When upgrading an existing SQL Server system to SQL Server 2008, all SQL Server databases, configuration settings, security settings, and programs are retained from the previous installation. However, there are still several important prerequisite tasks that you perform before the upgrade, as discussed in the following sections.

Tip

It is not possible to change the installation path when upgrading a system to SQL Server 2008. In addition, there must be enough free space on the system and SQL Server partition to support the upgrade; otherwise, the upgrade will come to a halt.

Creating a SQL Server Feature Discovery Report

One of the first tasks a DBA should conduct when upgrading an existing SQL Server system to SQL Server 2008 is to create a discovery report. A SQL Server discovery report, ultimately, is an inventory of the SQL Server components and features installed on an existing SQL Server installation. SQL Server 2008 comes with a new tool called the SQL Server Feature Discovery Report, which will generate a list of features and products. This report can automatically be generated for SQL Server 2008, SQL Server 2005, and SQL Server 2000, by selecting Installed SQL Server Features Discovery Report, on the Tools page, located on the SQL Server Installation Center landing page.

Backing Up the Server

Whenever you are making a major change on a server, something could go wrong. A complete backup of the SQL Server environment, including the SQL Server system databases and Windows Server System State, can make the difference between confidently telling the boss you had a setback so you conducted a rollback, or quivering while you try to find a way to tell your boss a complete disaster has taken place.

Verifying System Compatibility

The first action when upgrading an existing SQL Server system to SQL Server 2008 is running the System Configuration Checker. Launch the System Configuration Checker by first selecting Planning and then System Configuration Checker via the SQL Server 2008 Installation Center landing page.

The System Configuration Checker is an informative tool that conducts a scan on the existing system and indicates problems that might occur when the SQL Server support files are installed. After the scan is completed, a detailed report is presented that indicates the operations that passed, failed, skipped, or presented warnings. View the detailed report, correct any issues, and rerun the scan to ensure absolute success. Then move on to the next prerequisite task, which is running the SQL Server 2008 Upgrade Advisor.

Running the SQL Server Upgrade Advisor

Make it a prerequisite task to test the existing SQL Server system that you plan on upgrading for compatibility issues. Accomplish this by running the SQL Server Upgrade Advisor. The SQL Server Upgrade Advisor is an intuitive tool included with the SQL Server 2008 installation media.

When invoked, the wizard will first analyze previously installed SQL Server components and then produce a detailed report indicating possible upgrade anomalies. In addition, the report provides links to information on how to resolve the issues identified—how convenient!

Caution

Before conducting an in-place upgrade, it is imperative to acknowledge and fix all anomalies. If anomalies go unresolved, the upgrade is sure to fail, resulting in a production outage.

It is important to mention that the Upgrade Advisor can be installed on a remote system and still analyze the following SQL Server components: the Database Engine, Analysis Services, Reporting Services, Integration Services, and Data Transformation Services. Notification Services is not included as this component has been deprecated in SQL Server 2008.

Note

The exhaustive analysis performed by the wizard is unable to examine stored procedures if they are encrypted. Moreover, it is necessary to input a password if DTS or Integration Services packages are password protected.

Installing the SQL Server Upgrade Advisor

1. Launch the SQL Server Installation Center.

2. Select the Planning link and then click Install Upgrade Advisor.

3. Click Next on the SQL Server 2008 Upgrade Advisor Setup Welcome screen.

4. Accept the License Agreement, and then click Next.

5. On the Registration Information screen, enter your name and company name, and then click Next.

6. Provide the installation path on the Feature Selection page. Click Next to continue.

7. Click Install to initiate the installation, and then click Finish to finalize.

Performing a Compatibility Test with SQL Server Upgrade Advisor

When running the SQL Server 2008 Upgrade Advisor, the high-level steps include identifying SQL Server components to analyze, providing credentials for authentication, providing additional parameters, executing analysis, and finally, reviewing the results. Conduct the following steps on the SQL Server system you plan on upgrading in order to perform a compatibility test using the SQL Server 2008 Upgrade Advisor:

1. Click Start, All Programs, SQL Server 2008, SQL Server 2008 Upgrade Advisor.

2. On the Welcome to SQL Server 2008 Upgrade Advisor page, select the link Launch Upgrade Advisor Analysis Wizard, and then click Next.

3. On the SQL Server Components page, provide the name of the SQL Server and then specify the components that will be analyzed. Click Next as displayed in Figure 1.6.

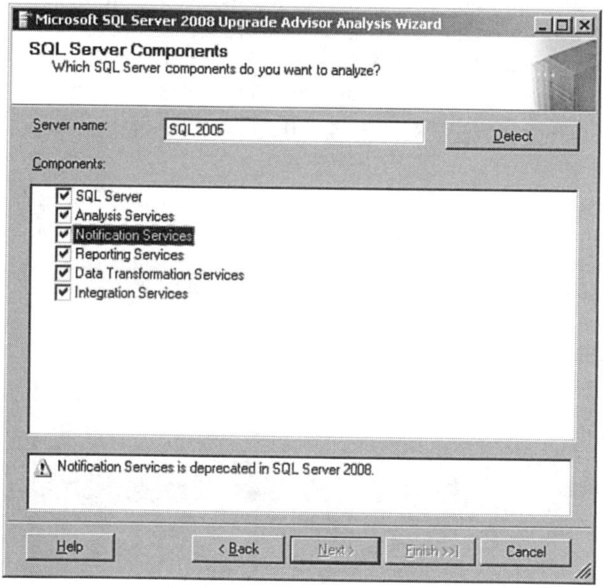

FIGURE 1.6
Specifying the SQL Server Components to analyze.

4. Provide the authentication mechanism for the SQL Server instance and then click Next.

5. On the SQL Server Parameters page, indicate what additional elements should be analyzed. Options include databases, trace files, and SQL Server batch files. Click Next to continue.

6. The Reporting Services Parameters page is an optional step. If a reporting services scan was selected, enter the name of the Reporting Services instance and then choose the authentication mechanism that will be used. Click Next.

7. The Analysis Services Parameters page is an another optional step. If an Analysis Services scan was selected, enter the name of the Analysis Services instance. Next, choose the authentication mechanism that will be used. Click Next.

8. The next optional screen focuses on DTS parameters for DTS packages. Select either the Analyze DTS Packages on Server option or the Analyze DTS Package Files option. If the second option is selected, specify the path to the DTS packages. Click Next to continue.

9. On the final page, SSIS Parameters, indicate whether you want to analyze SSIS packages on the server or files. If the second option is selected, specify the path to the SSIS packages. In addition, if the packages are password protected, enter a password. Click Next to continue.

10. Confirm the Upgrade Advisor Settings and then click Run to commence the analysis.

11. The Upgrade Advisor Progress page provides progress messages for each component being analyzed. The status message includes any of the words error, failure, or success. View the status messages in the details pane or alternatively, launch the report. Click Close as indicated in Figure 1.7.

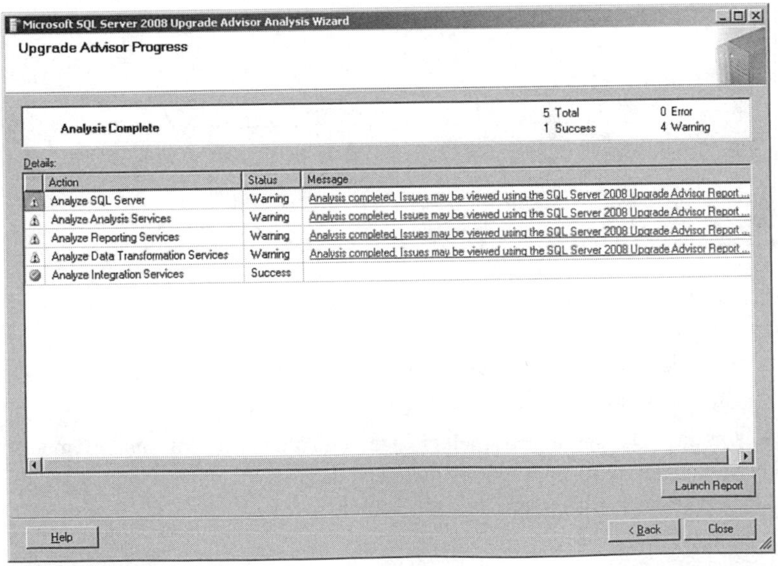

FIGURE 1.7
Reviewing the Upgrade Advisor Analysis Complete Report.

> **Note**
>
> The analysis output is written to a file; therefore, the report can be viewed from the Upgrade Advisor Progress page or at a later date. To review the report at another time, launch the Upgrade Advisor Report Viewer from the Upgrade Advisor start page.

The report can be viewed by server and then by instance or component. Moreover, the report can be filtered by All Issues, All Upgrade Issues, Pre-Upgrade Issues, All Migration issues, Resolved Issues, or Unresolved Issues. The output report also indicates when issues should be addressed. For instance, the report may indicate the issue should be addressed before the upgrade or after the upgrade. It is beneficial to review each message to ensure there are no issues when upgrading the existing SQL Server system to SQL Server 2008. When drilling through each message, it is possible to expand upon an issue and gain additional information on how to resolve the anomaly by clicking the link titled Tell Me More About This Issue and How to Fix It.

Additional Considerations Before Upgrading the Database Engine to SQL Server 2008

The following additional considerations apply before upgrading the Database Engine to SQL Server 2008:

- Even though this book does not focus on Analysis Services, if you are upgrading a 64-bit edition of SQL Server, it is imperative to upgrade Analysis Service first and then the Database Engine.

- Run the appropriate DBCC commands to ensure that both the system and user databases are in good health. A maintenance plan can be generated to complete these tasks.

- Make certain that all databases, specifically the system databases, are configured to autogrow. The system databases includes master, model, msdb, and tempdb.

- Ensure that you have administrative access to all user and system databases and that each database has logon information in the master system database.

- Configure the Max Worker Threads setting to a value of 0.

- Disable all startup stored procedures as the upgrade process may restart the server.

- If Replication is enabled, stop replication during the upgrade process.

- Conduct a rolling upgrade if Database Mirroring is used. First upgrade the mirrored instance, failover services, and then upgrade the principal instance (which is now the mirror). It is also recommended to remove the witness and change the operation mode to high safety during the upgrade.

- In SQL Server 2000, Log Shipping was established with a Database Maintenance Plan. Because the installation in SQL Server 2005 and SQL Server 2008 no longer uses a maintenance plan to implement Log Shipping, it is not possible to upgrade a SQL Server 2000 system running log shipping to SQL Server 2008.

Performing the SQL Server 2008 Upgrade

At this point, you have accomplished quite a few tasks. Let's review: your data is backed up, you have read the release notes, you ran the SQL Server System Configuration Checker and the SQL Server Upgrade Advisor, and you addressed the issues or warnings identified. It is now time to upgrade to SQL Server 2008.

1. Log in to the server and insert the SQL Server 2008 media. Autorun should launch the SQL Server 2008 Installation Center landing page; otherwise, click Setup.exe.

2. On the SQL Server Installation Center landing page, first select the Installation link, and then Upgrade from SQL Server 2000 or SQL Server 2005.

3. On the Setup Support Rules page, review the outcome of the System Configuration Checker. Ensure that all tests associated with the operation passed without any failures, warnings, or skipped elements. Alternatively, you can review a standard or comprehensive report by selecting the Show Details button or View Detailed Report. Click OK to continue with the installation.

4. On the Setup Support Files page, the wizard will prompt whether or not additional setup support files are required for the installation. If additional files are required, review the status of the files required and click Install.

5. The Setup Support Rules page will be displayed again and will identify any outstanding items that may hinder the installation process associated with the SQL Server cluster. Review and correct failures and warnings before commencing the installation. If failures are not displayed, click Next to start the installation.

6. On the Product Key page, enter the SQL Server Product Key and click Next.

7. On the License Agreement page, accept the Licensing Terms, and then click Next.

8. On the Select Instance page, use the drop-down menu and specify a SQL Server instance to upgrade. Click Next as displayed in Figure 1.8.

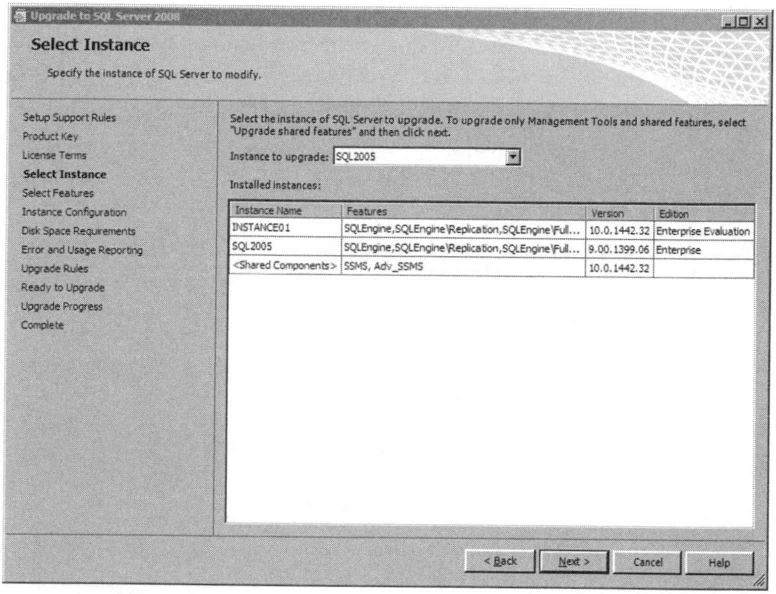

FIGURE 1.8
Specify the SQL Server instance to upgrade.

> **Note**
>
> The Installed Instances section displays all the instances installed on the system. In addition, to upgrade only SQL Server Management Tools, choose the option Upgrade Shared Features Only in the Instance to Upgrade drop-down list.

9. Review the features to be upgraded in the Select Features page, and then Click Next.

> **Note**
>
> It is not possible to modify the SQL Server features being released during an upgrade.

10. Review the name and InstanceID for the SQL Server instance being upgraded and click Next.

11. The next page is the Disk Space Requirements. Review the disk space summary for the SQL Server components and features selected to be upgraded, and then click Next.

12. On the Full-Text Upgrade page, specify an option of how the existing Full-Text catalogs will be processed after the upgrade. Click Next as displayed in Figure 1.9.

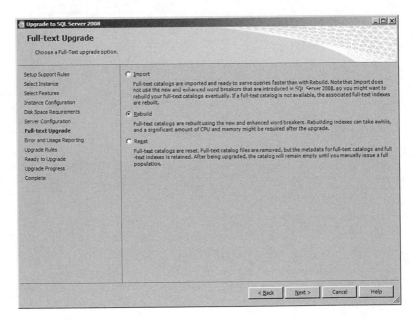

FIGURE 1.9
Specifying the Full-Text Upgrade option.

- **Import**—Full-Text catalogs are imported "as is" and are ready to serve queries. This process is much faster than rebuilding the Full-Text catalogs; however, the import does not leverage the new Full-Text features and functionality associated with SQL Server 2008.

- **Rebuild**—When this option is selected, the Full-Text catalogs are rebuilt using the new and enhanced word breakers associated with SQL Server 2008. This process is typically slower, and a significant amount of processor and memory will be required to tackle this operation.

- **Reset**—The final option is Reset. The Full-Text catalogs will be removed; therefore, after the upgrade is complete, the catalogs will remain empty until they are manually processed with a full population.

13. On the Error and Usage Reporting page, help Microsoft improve SQL Server features and services by sending error reports and feature usage to Microsoft. Specify the level of participation, and then click Next.

14. The final check will take place to ensure that the upgrade process will not be blocked. On the Upgrade Installation Rules page, review for any outstanding errors or warnings and then click Next to continue.

15. Before commencing the SQL Server 2008 upgrade, review the features to be upgraded on the Ready to Upgrade page, and then click Install.

16. When the upgrade process starts, you can monitor its progress accordingly. When the upgrade setup completes, review the success status based on each SQL Server feature. Click Next as illustrated in Figure 1.10.

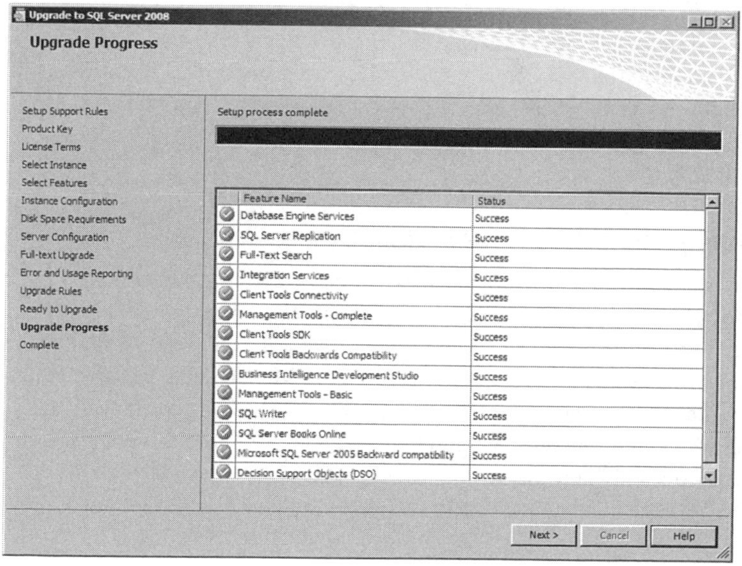

FIGURE 1.10
Reviewing the results of the SQL Server 2008 upgrade.

17. On the Complete page, review the location of the SQL Server summary upgrade log file and items in the Supplemental Information section. Click Close to finalize the upgrade.

18. To conduct post-installation tasks, review the upcoming section "Finalizing the SQL Server 2008 Installation or Upgrade."

Finalizing the SQL Server 2008 Installation or Upgrade

Once the installation or upgrade of SQL Server 2008 is complete, it is beneficial to review the following tasks in order to finalize the installation.

Reviewing SQL Server 2008 Logs

When the installation or upgrade is complete, it is best practice to review the setup log file, review the Windows application log, and review SQL Server logs for any issues or warnings. As noted earlier, the location to the SQL Server 2008 installation setup file can be found on the Complete page during the final stages of the installation or upgrade.

Downloading and Installing Updates

Even though the Windows Server 2008 system may be configured to automatically obtain server updates, it is still a best practice to check for missing SQL Server 2008 and Windows Server 2008 service packs and critical fixes. These outstanding service packs and critical fixes can be installed with Microsoft Update or a software distribution tool such as System Center 2007 Configuration Manager.

Hardening the SQL Server Installation

Another important step to finalize the SQL Server 2008 installation or upgrade is hardening the SQL Server implementation. There are a number of tasks that should be completed in order to harden the SQL Server installation. Some of these tasked include using Policy Based Management to reduce the surface attack area, enabling a Windows Server 2008 advanced firewall, and leveraging the SQL Server Configuration Manager Tool to disable unnecessary protocols and features.

> **Note**
>
> The SQL Server Surface Area Configuration Tool has been deprecated in SQL Server 2008. Therefore, Policy Base Management and `sp_configure` should be utilized instead, in order to harden and configure the surface area of a SQL Server installation.

Items to Consider After an Upgrade

This section describes additional items to take into consideration after an upgrade to SQL Server 2008 is complete.

Running SQL Server Management Studio for the First Time

After the upgrade is complete and you launch SQL Server Management Studio for the first time, you will be prompted to import customized user settings from SQL Server 2005 Management Studio. Click Yes or No and be aware that some SQL Server 2008 default settings might be changed after you import your customized settings.

Choosing the Database Compatibility Level After the Upgrade

When SQL Server systems are upgraded to SQL Server 2008, it is beneficial to understand how compatibility level settings affect databases. The compatibility levels include

- SQL Server 2008—Version 100
- SQL Server 2005—Version 90
- SQL Server 2000—Version 80

If you select one of these options, the database behaviors are to be compatible with that specified version of SQL Server. This setting only affects a specific database and not all databases associated with a SQL Server instance.

> **Note**
>
> After the upgrade, SQL Server automatically sets the compatibility level to the earlier version of SQL Server.

The settings can be changed by right-clicking a database and specifying the compatibility level on the Database Options page or by using the ALTER DATABASE command. The following Transact-SQL sample illustrates how to change the compatibility level.

```
Alter Database <database name>
Set Compatibility_Level =<80 | 90 | 100>
```

From a best-practice perspective, it is recommended to change the database to single-user mode before changing the database compatibility settings. This prevents inconsistent results if active queries are executed.

Additional Post-Upgrade Tasks

- Update Statistics on all users and system databases.

- Execute DBCC_UPDATEUSAGE on all databases to ensure that all databases have the correct row and page counts.

- With SQL Server 2008, queries on partitioned tables and indexes are processed differently. Therefore, it is recommended to remove the USE PLAN hint from the query.

Managing SQL Server 2008 Installations

The following sections explain how to manage SQL Server 2008 installations.

Employing Additional SQL Server 2008 Instances

As mentioned earlier, many organizations decide on scaling up their SQL Server infrastructure by creating consolidated SQL Server systems with multiple-instance installations. To achieve the goal of installing additional instances on an existing system, a DBA must relaunch the SQL Server 2008 installation utility, and then select the option New SQL Server Stand-alone Installation or Add Features to an Existing Installation.

When the new SQL Server installation wizard begins, follow the steps in the earlier section "Installing a Clean Version of SQL Server 2008"; however, on the Installation Type page, select the option Perform a New Installation of SQL Server 2008, as displayed in Figure 1.11. Then on the Feature Selection page, select the desired features to be installed for the new instance. Finally, on the Instance Configuration page, provide the instance with a unique name and proceed with the installation.

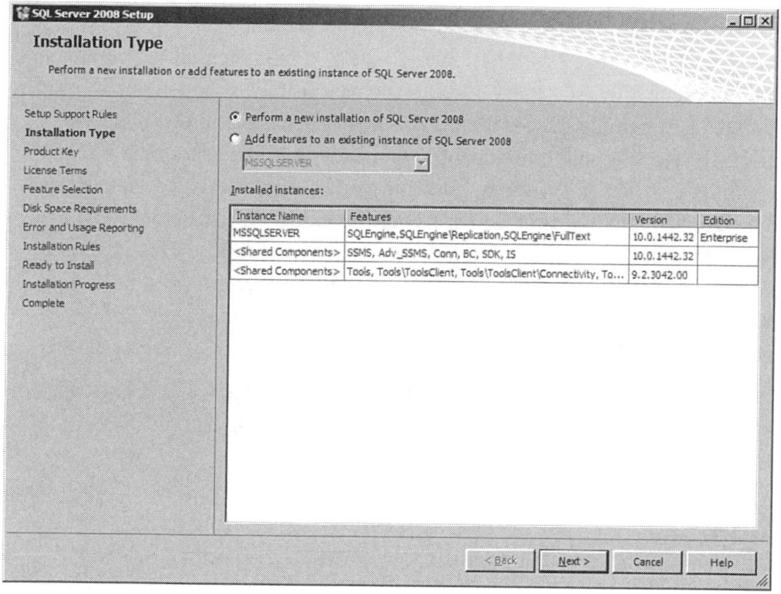

FIGURE 1.11
Adding additional SQL Server instances to an existing installation.

Adding Features to an Existing SQL Server 2008 Installation

The process for adding and removing SQL Server features to an existing Installation is similar to the steps involved when adding additional SQL Server instances. The DBA must select New SQL Server Stand-alone Installation or Add Features to an Existing Installation from the SQL Server 2008 Installation Center's Installation page. However, on the Installation Type screen, the option Add Features to an Existing Instance of SQL Server 2008 must be selected. Then on the Feature Selection page, select the features to be added and continue through the wizard.

Note

It is not possible to add features when upgrading to SQL Server 2008; therefore, this strategy should be used for adding additional features after the SQL Server upgrade is complete.

Changing SQL Server 2008 Editions

Another feature included with SQL Server 2008 is the potential to conduct an Edition upgrade after SQL Server 2008 has been installed. For example, if an organization is running the Standard Edition and decides that they want to leverage the features and functionality associated with the Enterprise Edition, they simply conduct an edition upgrade instead of formatting and reinstalling from scratch. Another advantageous scenario includes moving from SQL Server 2005 Standard to SQL Server 2008 Enterprise Edition. This objective would be achieved by first upgrading the SQL Server system from SQL Server 2005 Standard to SQL Server 2008 Standard, and then running the Edition Upgrade to upgrade the installation Enterprise Edition of SQL Server 2008.

To conduct an Edition Upgrade on SQL Server 2008, the Edition Upgrade must be selected from the Maintenance page on the SQL Server 2008 Installation Center landing screen.

Summary

The SQL Server 2008 installation process and deployment tools bear similarities to those found in previous versions of SQL Server. However, feature and performance enhancements associated with the new SQL Server 2008 Installation Center tool have improved the installation experience—whether you are installing a single SQL Server implementation from scratch or upgrading an existing system to SQL Server 2008.

Best Practices

The following are best practices from this chapter:

- Verify that your hardware, devices, and drivers are supported by SQL Server 2008.

- Stick to using the recommended or optimal hardware and software requirements when installing or upgrading to SQL Server 2008.

- Leverage the planning tools and documentation associated with the SQL Server Installation Center when installing or upgrading to SQL Server 2008.

- Run the System Configuration Checker tool as a prerequisite task when either installing or upgrading to SQL Server 2008.

- Install and run the Upgrade Advisor to identify any upgrade anomalies when upgrading a system to SQL Server 2008.

- When performing an upgrade, make sure you document your SQL Server system and database configuration information and perform a backup of any SQL Server data and objects that you want to keep.

- Leverage Windows Server 2008 as the operating system when running SQL Server 2008.

- Finalize a SQL Server implementation by hardening the system based on the best practices listed in Chapter 8.

- Because the SAC tool has been deprecated, utilize Policy Based Management to configure the surface area of one or many SQL Server systems.

- The Windows Server 2008 Advanced Firewall is enabled by default; therefore, review Chapter 8 to understand how to configure the firewall for SQL Server access.

- Review Books Online if you need to upgrade other SQL Server 2008 features above and beyond the Database Engine.

- Data, log, and tempdb directories should be on separate physical disks or Logical Unit Numbers (LUNs) for performance whenever possible.

CHAPTER 2

Administering the SQL Server 2008 Database Engine

Although SQL Server 2008 is composed of numerous components, one component is often considered the foundation of the product. The Database Engine is the core service for storing, processing, and securing data for the most challenging data systems. Note that the Database Engine is also known as Database Engine Services in SQL Server 2008, Likewise, it provides the foundation and fundamentals for the majority of the core database administration tasks. As a result of its important role in SQL Server 2008, it is no wonder that the Database Engine is designed to provide a scalable, fast, secure, and highly available platform for data access and other components.

This chapter focuses on administering the Database Engine component, also referred to as a feature in SQL Server 2008. Administration tasks include managing SQL Server properties, database properties, folders within SQL Server Management Studio, and the SQL Server Agent based on SQL Server 2008. In addition, Database Engine management tasks are also covered.

Even though the chapter introduces and explains all the management areas within the Database Engine, you are directed to other chapters for additional information. This is a result of the Database Engine feature being so large and intricately connected to other features.

What's New for DBAs When Administering the Database Engine on SQL Server 2008

SQL Server 2008 introduces a tremendous number of new features, in addition to new functionality, that DBAs need to be aware of.

The following are some of the important Database Engine enhancements:

- Built-in on-disk storage compression at several different areas. DBAs can compress database files, transaction logs, backups, and also database table elements at the row level and the page level.

- A new storage methodology for storing unstructured data. SQL Server FILESTREAM allows large binary data to be stored in the filesystem yet remains an integral part of the database with transactional consistency.

- Improved performance on retrieving vector-based data by creating indexes on spatial data types.

- A new data-tracking feature, Change Data Capture and Merge, allows DBAs to track and capture changes made to databases with minimal performance impact.

- A new database management approach to standardizing, evaluating, and enforcing SQL Server configurations with Policy Based Management. This dramatically improves DBA productivity because simplified management can be easily achieved. In addition, the policies can scale to hundreds or thousands of servers within the enterprise.

- A DBA can leverage standard administrative reports included with the Database Engine to increase the ability to view the health of a SQL Server system.

- Performance Studio can be leveraged to troubleshoot, tune, and monitor SQL Server 2008 instances.

- New encryption technologies such as Transparent Data Encryption (TDE) can be leveraged to encrypt sensitive data natively without making any application changes.

- New auditing mechanisms have been introduced; therefore, accountability and compliance can be achieved for a database.

- A DBA can add processors to the SQL Server system on the fly. This minimizes server outages; however, the hardware must support Hot CPU Add functionality.

- Resource Governor is a new management node found in SQL Server Management Studio. Resource Governor will give DBAs the potential to manage SQL Server workload and system resource consumption.

- SQL Server 2008 enhances table and index partitioning by introducing an intuitive Create Partition Wizard tool.

- SQL Server 2008 and PowerShell are integrated; therefore, DBAs can use Microsoft's extensible command-line shell to perform administrative SQL Server tasks by execution of cmdlets.

- The Database Engine Query Editor now supports IntelliSense. IntelliSense is an autocomplete function that speeds up programming and ensures accuracy.

Administering SQL Server 2008 Server Properties

The SQL Server Properties dialog box is the main place where you, as database administrator (DBA), configure server settings specifically tailored toward a SQL Server 2008 Database Engine installation.

You can invoke the Server Properties dialog box for the Database Engine by following these steps:

1. Choose Start, All Programs, Microsoft SQL Server 2008, SQL Server Management Studio.
2. Connect to the Database Engine in Object Explorer.
3. Right-click SQL Server and then select Properties.

The Server Properties dialog box includes eight pages of Database Engine settings that you can view, manage, and configure. The eight Server Properties pages are similar to what was found in SQL Server 2005 and include

- General
- Memory
- Processors
- Security
- Connections
- Database Settings
- Advanced
- Permissions

Note

Each SQL Server Properties setting can be easily scripted by clicking the Script button. The Script button is available on each Server Properties page. The Script output options available include Script Action to New Query Window, Script Action to a File, Script Action to Clipboard, and Script Action to a Job.

> **Note**
>
> In addition, it is possible to obtain a listing of all the SQL Server configuration settings associated with a Database Engine installation by executing the following query, in Query Editor.
>
> ```
> SELECT * FROM sys.configurations
> ORDER BY name ;
> GO
> ```

The following sections provide examples and explanations for each page in the SQL Server Properties dialog box.

Administering the General Page

The first Server Properties page, General, includes mostly information pertaining to the SQL Server 2008 installation, as illustrated in Figure 2.1. Here, you can view the following items: SQL Server name; product version such as Standard, Enterprise, or 64-bit; Windows platform, such as Windows 2008 or Windows 2003; SQL Server version number; language settings; total memory in the server; number of processors; Root Directory; Server Collation; and whether the installation is clustered.

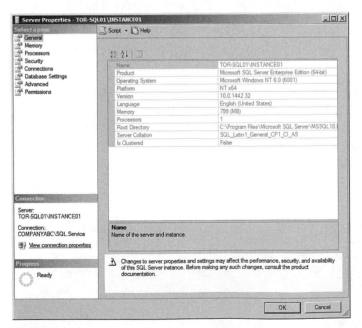

FIGURE 2.1
Administering the Server Properties General page.

Administering the Memory Page

Memory is the second page within the Server Properties dialog box. As shown in Figure 2.2, this page is broken into two sections: Server Memory Options and Other Memory Options. Each section has additional items to configure to manage memory; they are described in the following sections.

Administering the Server Memory Options

The Server Memory options are as follows:

- **Use AWE to Allocate Memory**—If this setting is selected, the SQL Server installation leverages Address Windowing Extensions (AWE) memory. Typically, this setting is no longer needed when running 64-bit systems as they can natively handle more than 4GB of RAM out of the box. Therefore, the setting is only tailored toward 32-bit systems.

- **Minimum Server Memory and Maximum Server Memory**—The next items within Memory Options are for inputting the minimum and maximum amount of memory allocated to a SQL Server instance. The memory settings inputted are calculated in megabytes.

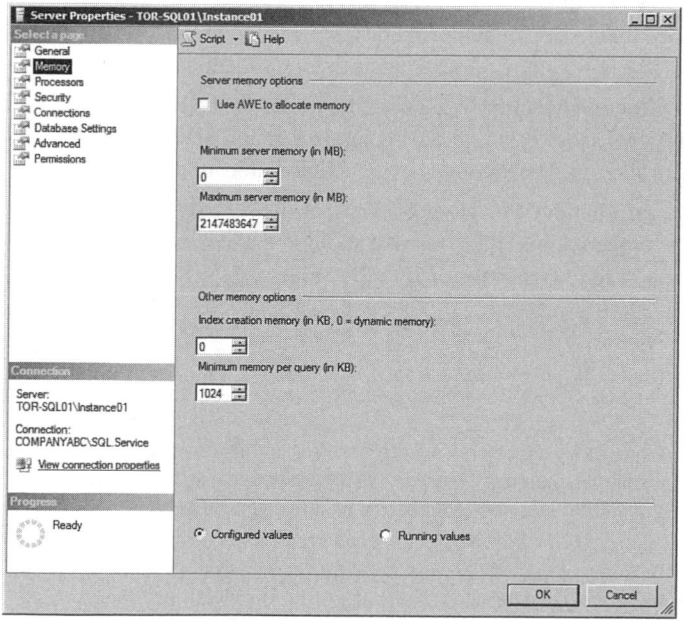

FIGURE 2.2
Administering the Server Properties Memory page.

The following Transact-SQL (TSQL) code can be used to configure Server Memory Options:

```
sp_configure 'awe enabled', 1
RECONFIGURE
GO
sp_configure 'min server memory', ,<MIN AMOUNT IN MB>
RECONFIGURE
GO
sp_configure 'max server memory', <MAX AMOUNT IN MB>
RECONFIGURE
GO
```

> **Note**
>
> The information enclosed in angle brackets < > needs to be replaced with a value specific to this example. This applies to this Transact-SQL example and subsequent ones to follow in this chapter and book.

Other Memory Options

The second section, Other Memory Options, has two additional memory settings tailored toward index creation and minimum memory per query:

- **Index Creation Memory**—This setting allocates the amount of memory that should be used during index creation operations. The default value is 0, which represents dynamic allocation by SQL Server.

- **Minimum Memory Per Query**—This setting specifies the minimum amount of memory in kilobytes that should be allocated to a query. The default setting is configured to the value of 1024KB.

> **Note**
>
> It is best to let SQL Server dynamically manage both the memory associated with index creation and the memory for queries. However, you can specify values for index creation if you're creating many indexes in parallel. You should tweak the minimum memory setting per query if many queries are occurring over multiple connections in a busy environment.

Use the following TSQL statements to configure Other Memory Options:

```
sp_configure 'index create memory, <NUMBER IN KB>
RECONFIGURE
GO
```

```
sp_configure 'min memory per query, <NUMBER IN KB>
RECONFIGURE
GO
```

Administering the Processors Page

The Processors page, shown in Figure 2.3, should be used to administer or manage any processor-related options for the SQL Server 2008 Database Engine. Options include threads, processor performance, affinity, and parallel or symmetric processing.

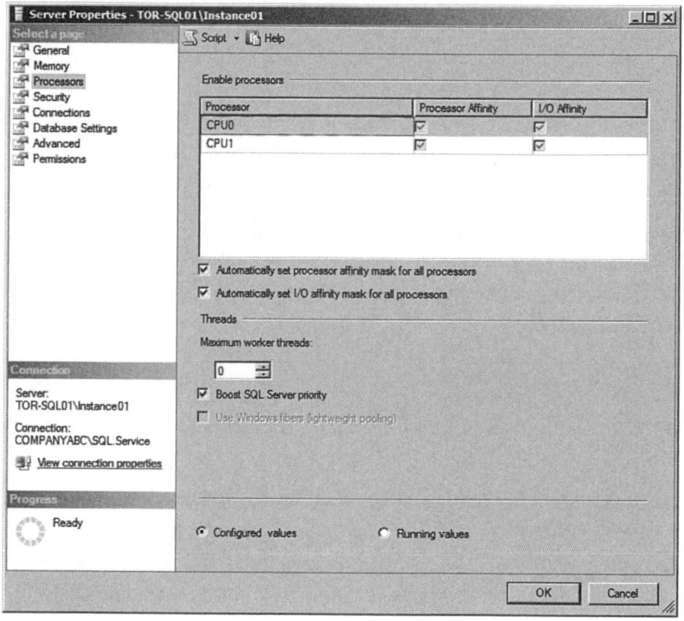

FIGURE 2.3
Administering the Server Properties Processor page.

Enabling Processors

Similar to a database administrator, the operating system is constantly multi-tasking. Therefore, the operating system moves threads between different processors to maximize processing efficiency. You should use the Processors page to administer or manage any processor-related options such as parallel or symmetric processing. The processor options include:

- **Enable Processors**—The two processor options in this section include Processor Affinity and I/O Affinity. Processor Affinity allows SQL Server to manage the processors; therefore, processors are assigned to specific threads during execution. Similar to Processor Affinity, the I/O Affinity setting informs SQL Server about which processors can manage I/O disk operations.

Tip

SQL Server 2008 does a great job of dynamically managing and optimizing processor and I/O affinity settings. If you need to manage these settings manually, you should reserve some processors for threading and others for I/O operations. A processor should not be configured to do both.

- **Automatically Set Processor Affinity Mask for All Processors**—If this option is enabled, SQL Server dynamically manages the Processor Affinity Mask and overwrites the existing Affinity Mask settings.
- **Automatically Set I/O Affinity Mask for All Processors**—Same thing as the preceding option: If this option is enabled, SQL Server dynamically manages the I/O Affinity Mask and overwrites the existing Affinity Mask settings.

Threads

The following Threads items can be individually managed to assist processor performance:

- **Maximum Worker Threads**—The Maximum Worker Threads setting governs the optimization of SQL Server performance by controlling thread pooling. Typically, this setting is adjusted for a server hosting many client connections. By default, this value is set to 0. The 0 value represents dynamic configuration because SQL Server determines the number of worker threads to utilize. If this setting will be statically managed, a higher value is recommended for a busy server with a high number of connections. Subsequently, a lower number is recommended for a server that is not being heavily utilized and has a small number of user connections. The values to be entered range from 10 to 32,767.

Tip

Microsoft recommends maintaining the Maximum Worker Threads setting at 0 in order to negate thread starvation. Thread starvation occurs when incoming client requests are not served in a timely manner due to a small value for this setting. Subsequently, a large value can waste address space as each active thread consumes 512KB.

- **Boost SQL Server Priority**—Preferably, SQL Server should be the only application running on the server; therefore, it is recommended to enable this check box. This setting tags the SQL Server threads with a higher priority value of 13 instead of the default 7 for better perform-ance. If other applications are running on the server, performance of those applications could degrade if this option is enabled because those threads have a lower priority. If enabled, it is also possible that resources from essential operating system and network functions may be drained.

- **Use Windows Fibers (Lightweight Pooling)**—This setting offers a means of decreasing the system overhead associated with extreme context switching seen in symmetric multiprocessing environments. Enabling this option provides better throughput by executing the context switching inline.

Note

Enabling fibers is tricky because it has its advantages and disadvantages for performance. This is derived from how many processors are running on the server. Typically, performance gains occur if the system is running a lot of CPUs, such as more than 16, whereas performance may decrease if there are only 1 or 2 processors. To ensure the new settings are optimized, it is a best practice to monitor performance counters, after changes are made. In addition, this setting is only available when using Windows Server 2003 Enterprise Edition.

These TSQL statements should be used to set processor settings:

```
sp_configure 'affinity mask', <VALUE>;
RECONFIGURE;
GO


sp_configure 'affinity I/O mask', :<VALUE>;
RECONFIGURE;
GO
```

```
sp_configure 'lightweight pooling', <0 or 1>;
RECONFIGURE;
GO

sp_configure 'max worker threads', :<INTEGER VALUE>;
RECONFIGURE;
GO

sp_configure 'priority boost', <0 or 1>;
RECONFIGURE;
GO
```

Administering the Security Page

The Security page, shown in Figure 2.4, maintains server-wide security
configuration settings. These SQL Server settings include Server
Authentication, Login Auditing, Server Proxy Account, and Options.

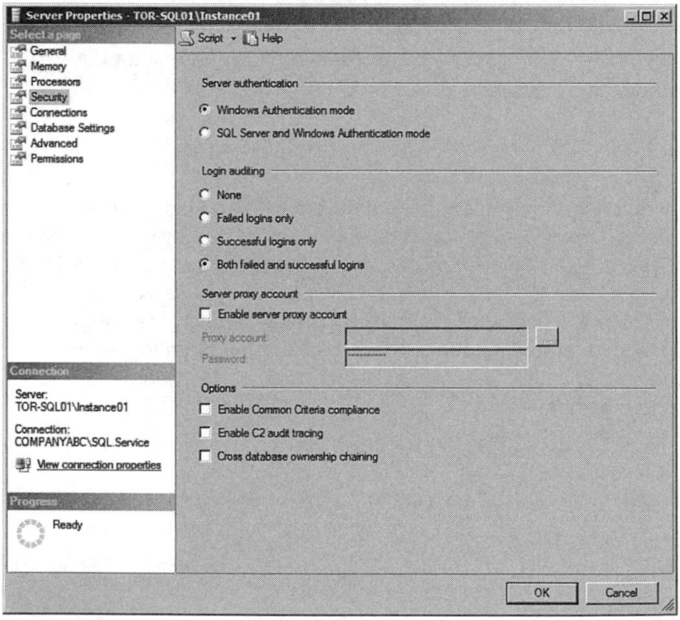

FIGURE 2.4
Administering the Server Properties Security page.

Server Authentication

The first section in the Security page focuses on server authentication. At present, SQL Server 2008 continues to support two modes for validating connections and authenticating access to database resources: Windows Authentication Mode and SQL Server and Windows Authentication Mode. Both of these authentication methods provide access to SQL Server and its resources. SQL Server and Windows Authentication Mode is regularly referred to as *mixed mode authentication*,

---

Note

During installation, the default authentication mode is Windows Authentication. The authentication mode can be changed after the installation.

The Windows Authentication Mode setting is the default Authentication setting and is the recommended authentication mode. It leverages Active Directory user accounts or groups when granting access to SQL Server. In this mode, you are given the opportunity to grant domain or local server users access to the database server without creating and managing a separate SQL Server account. It's worth mentioning that when Windows Authentication Mode is active, user accounts are subject to enterprise-wide policies enforced by the Active Directory domain, such as complex passwords, password history, account lockouts, minimum password length, maximum password length, and the Kerberos protocol. These enhanced and well-defined policies are always a plus to have in place.

The second authentication option is SQL Server and Windows Authentication (Mixed) Mode. This setting, uses either Active Directory user accounts or SQL Server accounts when validating access to SQL Server. Starting with SQL Server 2005, Microsoft introduced a means to enforce password and lockout policies for SQL Server login accounts when using SQL Server Authentication.

Note

Review the authentication sections in Chapter 8, "Hardening a SQL Server 2008 Implementation," for more information on authentication modes and which mode should be used as a best practice.

Login Auditing

Login Auditing is the focal point on the second section on the Security page. You can choose from one of the four Login Auditing options available: None, Failed Logins Only, Successful Logins Only, and Both Failed and Successful Logins.

Tip

When you're configuring auditing, it is a best practice to configure auditing to capture both failed and successful logins. Therefore, in the case of a system breach or an audit, you have all the logins captured in an audit file. The drawback to this option is that the log file will grow quickly and will require adequate disk space. If this is not possible, only failed logins should be captured as the bare minimum.

Server Proxy Account

You can enable a server proxy account in the Server Proxy section of the Security page. The proxy account permits the security context to execute operating system commands by the impersonation of logins, server roles, and database roles. If you're using a proxy account, you should configure the account with the least number of privileges to perform the task. This bolsters security and reduces the amount of damage if the account is compromised.

Additional Security Options

Additional security options available in the Options section of the Security page are as follows:

- **Enable Common Criteria Compliance**—When this setting is enabled, it manages database security. Specifically, it manages features such as Residual Information Protection (RIP), controls access to login statistics, and enforces restrictions where, for example, the column titled GRANT cannot override the table titled DENY.

- **Enable C2 Audit Tracing**—When this setting is enabled, SQL Server allows the largest number of the success and failure objects to be audited. The drawback to capturing for audit data is that it can degrade performance and take up disk space. The files are stored in the Data directory associated with the instance of the SQL Server installation.

- **Cross-Database Ownership Chaining**—Enabling this setting allows cross-database ownership chaining at a global level for all databases. Cross-database ownership chaining governs whether the database can be accessed by external resources. As a result, this setting should be enabled only when the situation is closely managed because several serious security holes would be opened.

Administering the Connections Page

The Connections page, as shown in Figure 2.5, is the place where you examine and configure any SQL Server settings relevant to connections. The

Connections page is broken up into two sections: Connections and Remote Server Connections.

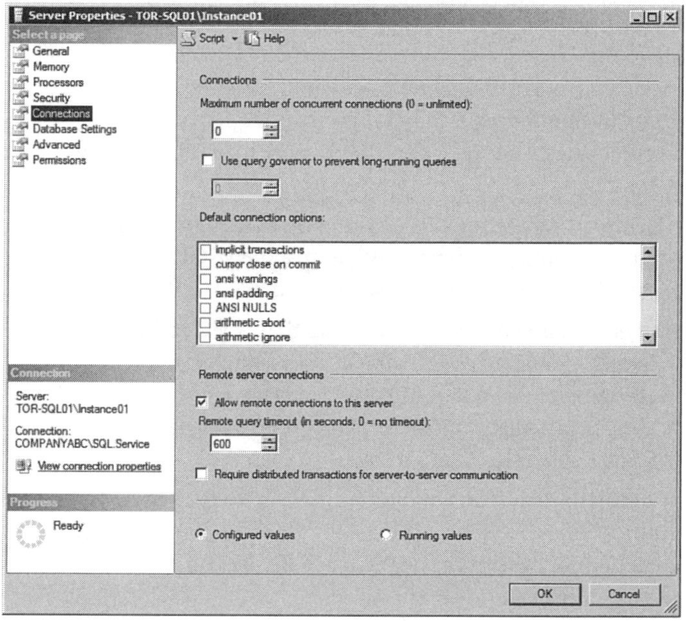

FIGURE 2.5
Administering the Server Properties Connections page.

Connections

The Connections section includes the following settings:

- **Maximum Number of Concurrent Connections**—The first setting determines the maximum number of concurrent connections allowed to the SQL Server Database Engine. The default value is 0, which represents an unlimited number of connections. The value used when configuring this setting is really dictated by the SQL Server hardware such as the processor, RAM, and disk speed.

- **Use Query Governor to Prevent Long-Running Queries**—This setting creates a stipulation based on an upper-limit criteria specified for the time period in which a query can run.

- **Default Connection Options**—For the final setting, you can choose from approximately 16 advanced connection options that can be either enabled or disabled, as shown in Figure 2.5.

Note

For more information on each of the default Connection Option settings, refer to SQL Server 2008 Books Online. Search for the topic "Server Properties Connections Page."

Remote Server Connections

The second section located on the Connections page focuses on Remote Server settings:

- **Allow Remote Connections to This Server**—If enabled, the first option allows remote connections to the specified SQL Server. With SQL Server 2008, this option is enabled by default.

- **Remote Query Timeout**—The second setting is available only if Allow Remote Connections is enabled. This setting governs how long it will take for a remote query to terminate. The default value is 600, however, the values that can be configured range from 0 to 2,147,483,647. Zero represents infinite.

- **Require Distributed Transactions for Server-to-Server Communication**—The final setting controls the behavior and protects the transactions between systems by using the Microsoft Distributed Transaction Coordinator (MS DTC).

Note

When using Windows Server 2008, MS DTC is now referred to as DTC.

Administering the Database Settings Page

The Database Settings page, shown in Figure 2.6, contains configuration settings that each database within the SQL Server instance will inherit. The choices available on this page are broken out by Fill Factor, Backup and Restore, Recovery, and Database Default Locations.

Default Index Fill Factor

The Default Index Fill Factor setting specifies how full SQL Server should configure each page when a new index is created. The default setting is 0, and the ranges are between 0 and 100. The 0 value represents a table with room for growth, whereas a value of 100 represents no space for subsequent insertions without requiring page splits. A table with all reads typically has a higher fill factor, and a table that is meant for heavy inserts typically has a low fill factor. The value 50 is ideal when a table has plenty of reads and writes. This setting is global to all tables within the Database Engine.

For more information on fill factors, refer to Chapter 4, "Managing and Optimizing SQL Server 2008 Indexes" and Chapter 6, "SQL Server 2008 Maintenance Practices."

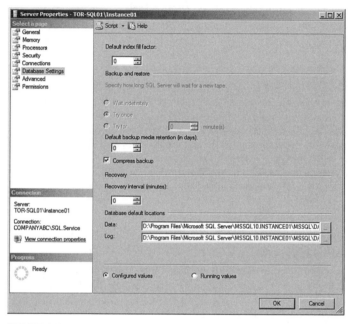

FIGURE 2.6
Administering the Server Properties Database Settings page.

Backup and Restore

The Backup and Restore section of the Database Settings page includes the following settings:

- **Specify How Long SQL Server Will Wait for a New Tape**—The first setting governs the time interval SQL Server will wait for a new tape during a database backup process. The options available are Wait Indefinitely, Try Once, or Try for a specific number of minutes.

- **Default Backup Media Retention (In Days)**—This setting is a system-wide configuration that affects all database backups, including the translation logs. You enter values for this setting in days, and it dictates the time to maintain and/or retain each backup medium.

- **Compress Backup**—Backup compression is one of the most promising and highly anticipated features of SQL Server 2008 for the DBA. If the Compress Backup system-wide setting is enabled, all new backups associated with the SQL Server instance will be compressed. Keep in mind there is a tradeoff when compressing backups. Space associated with the backup on disk is significantly reduced; however, processor usage increases during the backup compression process. For more information on compressed backups, refer to Chapter 7, "Backing Up and Restoring the SQL Server 2008 Database Engine."

Note

It is possible to leverage Resource Governor in order to manage the amount of workload associated with the processor when conducting compressed backups. This will ensure that the server does not suffer from excessive processor resource consumption, which eventually leads to performance degradation of the server. For more information on Resource Governor, refer to Chapter 16, "Managing Workloads and Consumption with Resource Governor."

Recovery

The Recovery section of the Database Settings page consists of one setting:

- **Recovery Interval (Minutes)**—Only one Recovery setting is available. This setting influences the amount of time, in minutes, SQL Server will take to recover a database. Recovering a database takes place every time SQL Server is started. Uncommitted transactions are either committed or rolled back.

Database Default Locations

Options available in the Database Default Locations section are as follows:

- **Data and Log**—The two folder paths for Data and Log placement specify the default location for all database data and log files. Click the ellipsis button on the right side to change the default folder location.

Administering the Advanced Page

The Advanced Page, shown in Figure 2.7, contains the SQL Server general settings that can be configured.

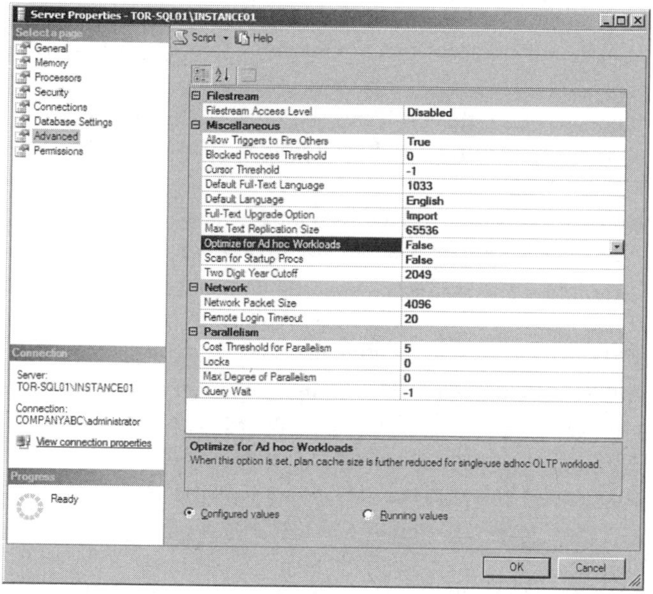

FIGURE 2.7
Administering the Server Properties Advanced Settings page.

Filestream

FILESTREAM is a new storage methodology introduced with SQL Server 2008. There is only one item that can be configured via the Advanced page.

■ **Filestream Access Level**—This setting displays how the SQL Server instance will support FILESTREAM. FILESTREAM is a new feature associated with SQL Server 2008, and it allows for the storage of unstructured data. The global server options associated with FILESTREAM configuration include:

    ■ **Disabled**—The Disabled setting does not allow Binary Large Object (BLOB) data to be stored in the file system.

    ■ **Transact-SQL Access Enabled**—FILESTREAM data is accessed only by Transact-SQL and not by the file system.

    ■ **Full Access Enabled**—FILESTREAM data is accessed by both Transact-SQL and the file system.

Miscellaneous Settings

Options available in the Miscellaneous section of the Advanced page are as follows:

- **Allow Triggers to Fire Others**—If this setting is configured to True, triggers can execute other triggers. In addition, the nesting level can be up to 32 levels. The values are either True or False.

- **Blocked Process Threshold**—The threshold at which blocked process reports are generated. Settings include 0 to 86,400.

- **Cursor Threshold**—This setting dictates the number of rows in the cursor that will be returned for a result set. A value of 0 represents that cursor keysets are generated asynchronously.

- **Default Full-Text Language**—This setting specifies the language to be used for full-text columns. The default language is based on the language specified during the SQL Server instance installation.

- **Default Language**—This setting is also inherited based on the language used during the installation of SQL. The setting controls the default language behavior for new logins.

- **Full-Text Upgrade Option**—Controls the behavior of how full-text indexes are migrated when upgrading a database. The options include; Import, Rebuild or Reset.

- **Max Text Replication Size**—This global setting dictates the maximum size of text and image data that can be inserted into columns. The measurement is in bytes.

- **Optimize for Ad Hoc Workloads**—This setting is set to False by default. If set to True, this setting will improve the efficiency of the plan cache for ad hoc workloads.

- **Scan for Startup Procs**—The configuration values are either True or False. If the setting is configured to True, SQL Server allows stored procedures that are configured to run at startup to fire.

- **Two Digit Year Cutoff**—This setting indicates the uppermost year that can be specified as a two-digit year. Additional years must be entered as a four-digit number.

Network Settings

Options available in the Network section of the Advanced page are as follows:

- **Network Packet Size**—This setting dictates the size of packets being transmitted over the network. The default size is 4096 bytes and is sufficient for most SQL Server network operations.

- **Remote Login Timeout**—This setting determines the amount of time SQL Server will wait before timing out a remote login. The default time is 30 seconds, and a value of 0 represents an infinite wait before timing out. The default setting is 20.

Parallelism Settings

Options available in the Parallelism section of the Advanced page are as follows:

- **Cost Threshold for Parallelism**—This setting specifies the threshold above which SQL Server creates and runs parallel plans for queries. The cost refers to an estimated elapsed time in seconds required to run the serial plan on a specific hardware configuration. Set this option only on symmetric multiprocessors. For more information, search for "cost threshold for parallelism option" in SQL Server Books Online.

- **Locks**—The default for this setting is 0, which indicates that SQL Server is dynamically managing locking. Otherwise, you can enter a numeric value that sets the utmost number of locks to occur.

- **Max Degree of Parallelism**—This setting limits the number of processors (up to a maximum of 64) that can be used in a parallel plan execution. The default value of 0 uses all available processors, whereas a value of 1 suppresses parallel plan generation altogether. A number greater than 1 prevents the maximum number of processors from being used by a single-query execution. If a value greater than the number of available processors is specified, however, the actual number of available processors is used. For more information, search for "max degree of parallelism option" in SQL Server Books Online.

- **Query Wait**—This setting indicates the time in seconds a query will wait for resources before timing out.

Administering the Permissions Page

The Permissions Page, as shown in Figure 2.8, includes all the authorization logins and permissions for the SQL Server instance. You can create and manage logins and/or roles within the first section. The second portion of this page displays the Explicit and Effective permissions based on the login or role.

For more information on permissions and authorization to the SQL Server 2008 Database Engine, refer to Chapter 9, "Administering SQL Server Security and Authorization."

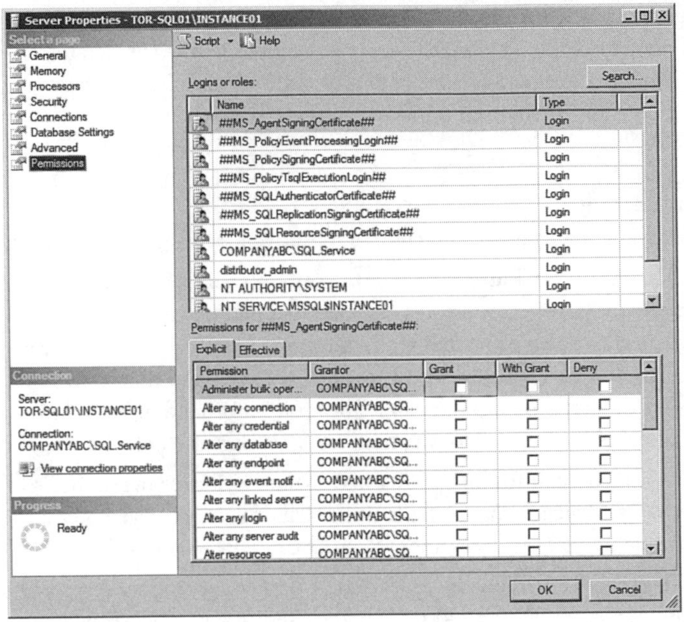

FIGURE 2.8
Administering the Server Properties Permissions page.

Administering the SQL Server Database Engine Folders

After you configure the SQL Server properties, you must manage the SQL Server Database Engine folders and understand how the settings should be configured. The SQL Server folders contain an abundant number of configuration settings that need to be managed on an ongoing basis. The main SQL Server Database Engine top-level folders, as shown in Figure 2.9, are as follows:

- Databases
- Security
- Server Objects
- Replication
- Management

Each folder can be expanded, which leads to more subfolders and thus more management of settings. The following sections discuss the folders within the SQL Server tree, starting with the Databases folder.

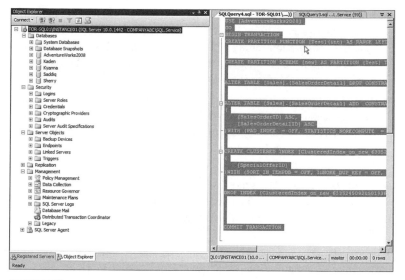

FIGURE 2.9
Viewing the Database Engine folders.

Administering the Databases Folder

The Databases folder is the main location for administering system and user databases. Management tasks that can be conducted by right-clicking the Database folder consist of creating new databases, attaching databases, restoring databases, and creating custom reports.

The Databases folder contains subfolders as a repository for items such as system databases, database snapshots, and user databases. When a Database folder is expanded, each database has a predefined subfolder structure that includes configuration settings for that specific database. The database structure is as follows: Database Diagrams, Tables, Views, Synonyms, Programmability, Service Broker, Storage, and Security.

Let's start by examining the top-level folders and then the subfolders in subsequent sections.

Administering the System Databases Subfolder

The System Databases subfolder is the first folder within the Database tree. It consists of all the system databases that make up SQL Server 2008. The system databases consist of

- **Master Database**—The master database is an important system database in SQL Server 2008. It houses all system-level data, including system configuration settings, login information, disk space, stored procedures, linked servers, and the existence of other databases, along with other crucial information.

- **Model Database**—The model database serves as a template for creating new databases in SQL Server 2008. The data residing in the model database is commonly applied to a new database with the Create Database command. In addition, the tempdb database is re-created with the help of the model database every time SQL Server 2008 is started.

- **Msdb Database**—Used mostly by the SQL Server Agent, the msdb database stores alerts, scheduled jobs, and operators. In addition, it stores historical information on backups and restores, SQL Mail, and Service Broker.

- **Tempdb**—The tempdb database holds temporary information, including tables, stored procedures, objects, and intermediate result sets. Each time SQL Server is started, the tempdb database starts with a clean copy.

TIP

It is a best practice to conduct regular backups on the system databases. In addition, if you want to increase performance and response times, it is recommended to place the tempdb data and transaction log files on different volumes from the operating system drive. Finally, if you don't need to restore the system databases to a point in failure, you can set all recovery models for the system databases to Simple.

Administering the Database Snapshots Subfolder

The second top-level folder under Databases is Database Snapshots. A *snapshot* allows you to create a point-in-time read-only static view of a database. Typical scenarios for which organizations use snapshots consist of running reporting queries, reverting databases to state when the snapshot was created in the event of an error, and safeguarding data by creating a snapshot before large bulk inserts occur. All database snapshots are created via TSQL syntax and not the Management Studio.

For more information on creating and restoring a database snapshot, view the database snapshot sections in Chapter 7.

Administering a User Databases Subfolder

The rest of the subfolders under the top-level Database folder are all the user databases. The user database is a repository for all aspects of a database, including administration, management, and programming. Each user database running within the Database Engine shows up as a separate subfolder. From within the User Database folder, you can conduct the following tasks: backup, restore, take offline, manage database storage, manage properties, manage database authorization, encryption, shrink, and configure log shipping or database mirroring. In addition, from within this folder, programmers can create the database schema, including tables, views, constraints, and stored procedures.

Note

Database development tasks such as creating a new database, views, or stored procedures are beyond the scope of this book, as this book focuses only on administration and management tasks affiliated with the Database Engine.

Administering the Security Folder

The second top-level folder in the SQL Server instance tree, Security, is a repository for all the Database Engine securable items meant for managing authorization. The sublevel Security Folders consist of

- **Logins**—This subfolder is used for creating and managing access to the SQL Server Database Engine. A login can be created based on a Windows or SQL Server account. In addition, it is possible to configure password policies, server role and user mapping access, and permission settings.

- **Server Roles**—SQL Server 2008 leverages the role-based model for granting authorization to the SQL Server 2008 Database Engine. Predefined SQL Server Roles already exist when SQL Server is deployed. These predefined roles should be leveraged when granting access to SQL Server and databases.

- **Credentials**—Credentials are used when there is a need to provide SQL Server authentication users an identity outside SQL Server. The principal rationale is for creating credentials to execute code in assemblies and for providing SQL Server access to a domain resource.

- **Cryptographic Providers**—The Cryptographic Providers subfolder is used for managing encryption keys associated with encrypting elements within SQL Server 2008. For more information on Cryptographic Providers and SQL Server 2008 encryption, reference Chapter 11, "Encrypting SQL Server Data and Communications."

- **Audits and Server Audit Specifications**—SQL Server 2008 introduces enhanced auditing mechanisms, which make it possible to create customized audits of events residing in the database engine. These subfolders are used for creating, managing, storing, and viewing audits in SQL Server 2008. For more information on creating and managing audits including server audit specifications, refer to Chapter 17, "Monitoring SQL Server 2008 with Native Tools."

Administering the Server Objects Folder

The third top-level folder located in Object Explorer is called Server Objects. Here, you create backup devices, endpoints, linked servers, and triggers.

Backup Devices

Backup devices are a component of the backup and restore process when working with user databases. Unlike the earlier versions of SQL Server, backup devices are not needed; however, they provide a great way to manage all the backup data and transaction log files for a database under one file and location.

To create a backup device, follow these steps:

1. Choose Start, All Programs, Microsoft SQL Server 2008, SQL Server Management Studio.

2. In Object Explorer, connect to the Database Engine, expand the desired server, and then expand the Server Objects folder.

3. Right-click the Backup Devices folder and select New Backup Device.

4. In the Backup Device dialog box, specify a Device Name and enter the destination file path, as shown in Figure 2.10. Click OK to complete this task.

This TSQL syntax can also be used to create the backup device:

```
USE [master]
GO
EXEC master.dbo.sp_addumpdevice  @devtype = N'disk',
@logicalname = N'Rustom''s Backup Device',
@physicalname = N'C:\Rustom''s Backup Device.bak'
GO
```

For more information on using backup devices and step-by-step instructions on backing up and restoring the Database Engine, refer to Chapter 7.

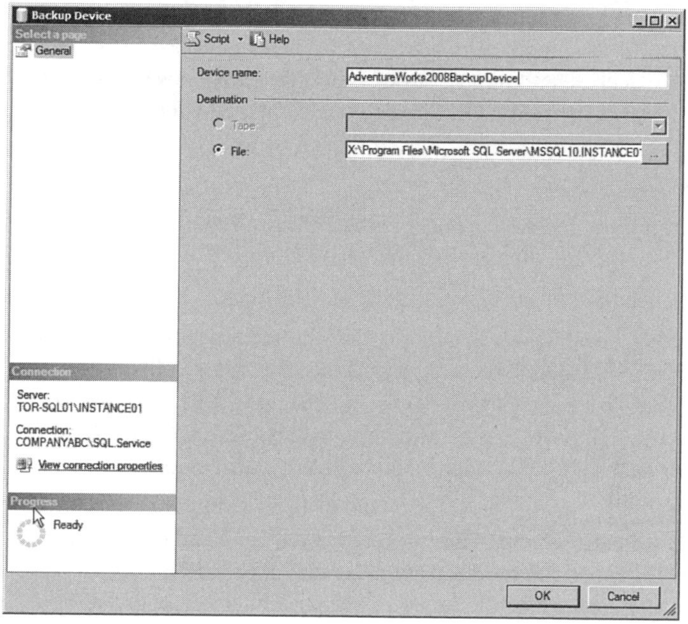

FIGURE 2.10
Creating a backup device with SQL Server Management Studio.

Endpoints

To connect to a SQL Server instance, applications must use a specific port that SQL Server has been configured to listen on. In the past, the authentication process and handshake agreement were challenged by the security industry as not being robust or secure. Therefore, SQL Server uses a concept called *endpoints* to strengthen the communication security process.

The Endpoint folder residing under the Server Objects folder is a repository for all the endpoints created within a SQL Server instance. The endpoints are broken out by system endpoints, database mirroring, service broker, Simple Object Access Protocol (SOAP), and TSQL.

The endpoint creation and specified security options for Database Mirroring endpoints are covered in Chapter 13.

Linked Servers

As the enterprise scales, more and more SQL Server 2008 servers are introduced into an organization's infrastructure. As this occurs, you are challenged to provide a means to allow distributed transactions and queries between different SQL Server instances. Linked servers provide a way for organizations to overcome these hurdles by providing the means of distributed transactions, remote queries, and remote stored procedure calls between separate SQL Server instances or non–SQL Server sources such as Microsoft Access.

Follow these steps to create a linked server with SQL Server Management Studio (SSMS):

1. In Object Explorer, first connect to the Database Engine, expand the desired server, and then expand the Server Objects Folder.

2. Right-click the Linked Servers folder and select New Linked Server.

3. The New Linked Server dialog box contains three pages of configuration settings: General, Security, and Server Options. On the General Page, specify a linked server name, and select the type of server to connect to. For example, the remote server could be a SQL Server or another data source. For this example, select SQL Server.

4. The next page focuses on security and includes configuration settings for the security context mapping between the local and remote SQL Server instances. On the Security page, first click Add and enter the local login user account to be used. Second, either impersonate the local account, which will pass the username and password to the remote server, or enter a remote user and password.

5. Still within the Security page, enter an option for a security context pertaining to the external login that is not defined in the previous list. The following options are available:

   - **Not Be Made**—Indicates that a login will not be created for user accounts that are not already listed.

   - **Be Made Without a User's Security Context**—Indicates that a connection will be made without using a user's security context for connections.

   - **Be Made Using the Login's Current Security Context**—Indicates that a connection will be made by using the current security context of the user which is logged on.

   - **Be Made Using This Security Context**—Indicates that a connection will be made by providing the login and password security context.

6. On the Server Options page, you can configure additional connection settings. Make any desired server option changes and click OK.

> **Note**
>
> Impersonating the Windows local credentials is the most secure authentication mechanism, provided that the remote server supports Windows authentication.

Triggers

The final folder in the Server Objects tree is Triggers. It is a repository for all the triggers configured within the SQL Server instance. Again, creating triggers is a development task, so it is not covered in this book.

Administering the Replication Folder

Replication is a means of distributing data among SQL Server instances. In addition, peer-to-peer replication can also be used as a form of high availability and for offloading reporting queries from a production server to a second instance of SQL Server. When administering and managing replication, you conduct all the replication tasks from within this Replication folder. Tasks include configuring the distributor, creating publications, creating local subscriptions, and launching the Replication Monitor for troubleshooting and monitoring.

Administering, managing, and monitoring replication can be reviewed in Chapter 15, "Implementing and Managing SQL Server Replication."

Administering the Management Folder

The Management folder contains a plethora of old and new elements used to administer SQL Server management tasks. The majority of the topics in the upcoming bullets are covered in dedicated chapters, as the topics and content are very large. The subfolders found in the Management folder consist of the following:

- **Policy Management**—A new feature in SQL Server 2008, Policy Management allows DBAs to create policies in order to control and manage the behavior and settings associated with one or more SQL Server instances. Policy Based Management ensures that a system conforms to usage and security practices of an organization and its industry by constantly monitoring the surface area of a SQL Server system, database, and/or objects. To effectively establish and monitor policies for a SQL Server environment, review Chapter 10, "Administering Policy Based Management."

- **Data Collection**—Data Collection is the second element in the Management folder. It is the main place for DBAs to manage all aspects associated with the new SQL Server 2008 feature, Performance Studio. Performance Studio is an integrated framework that allows database administrators the opportunity for end-to-end collection of data from one or more SQL Server systems into a centralized data warehouse. The collected data can be used to analyze, troubleshoot, and store SQL Server diagnostic information. To further understand how to administer Performance Studio, data collections, and the central repository and management reports, review Chapter 17.

■ **Resource Governor**—The paramount new feature included with the release of SQL Server 2008. Resource Governor can be used in a variety of ways to monitor resource consumption and manage the workloads of a SQL Server system. By leveraging Resource Governor and defining the number of resources a workload can use, it is possible to establish a SQL Server environment that allows many workloads to run on a server, without the fear of one specific workload cannibalizing the system. For more information on managing Resource Governor, refer to Chapter 16.

■ **Maintenance Plans**—The Maintenance Plan subfolder includes an arsenal of tools tailored toward automatically sustaining a SQL Server implementation. DBAs can conduct routine maintenance on one or more databases by creating a maintenance plan either manually or by using a wizard. Some of these routine database tasks involve rebuilding indexes, checking database integrity, updating index statistics, and performing internal consistency checks and backups. For more information on conducting routine maintenance, review Chapter 6.

■ **SQL Server Logs**—The SQL Server Logs subfolder is typically the first line of defense when analyzing issues associated with a SQL Server instance. From within this subfolder, it is possible to configure logs, view SQL Server logs, and view Windows Logs. By right-clicking the SQL Server Log folder, you have the option to limit the number of error logs before they are recycled. The default value is 6; however, a value from 6 to 99 can be selected. The logs are displayed in a hierarchical fashion with the Current log listed first.

■ **Database Mail**—The Database Mail folder should be leveraged to configure SQL Server email messages using the SMTP protocol. Management tasks include configuring mail system parameters, creating mail accounts, administering profiles, and mail security. For more information on managing Database Mail, see Chapter 17.

■ **Distributed Transaction Coordinator**—There isn't much to manage; however, the Distributed Transaction Coordinator (DTC) provides status on the DTC service from within SSMS. Although status is presented, such as running or stopped, the DTC service must be managed with the Services snap-in included with Windows Server 2008.

■ **Legacy**—The Legacy subfolder includes a means of managing legacy SQL Server 2008 elements that are still supported and not yet decommissioned. Typically, these elements are pre–SQL Server 2005 and include Database Maintenance Plans, Data Transformation Services, and SQL Mail.

Note

Notification Services, which was previously found in the Management folder, has been deprecated.

Administering Database Properties

The Database Properties dialog box is the place where you manage the configuration options and values of a user or system database. You can execute additional tasks from within these pages, such as database mirroring and transaction log shipping. The configuration pages in the Database Properties dialog box include

■ General

■ Files

■ Filegroups

■ Options

■ Change Tracking

■ Permissions

■ Extended Properties

■ Mirroring

■ Transaction Log Shipping

The upcoming sections describe each page and setting in its entirety. To invoke the Database Properties dialog box, perform the following steps:

1. Choose Start, All Programs, Microsoft SQL Server 2008, SQL Server Management Studio.

2. In Object Explorer, first connect to the Database Engine, expand the desired server, and then expand the Databases folder.

3. Select a desired database such as AdventureWorks2008, right-click, and select Properties. The Database Properties dialog box, including all the pages, is displayed in the left pane.

Administering the Database Properties General Page

General, the first page in the Database Properties dialog box, displays information exclusive to backups, database settings, and collation settings. Specific information displayed includes

- Last Database Backup
- Last Database Log Backup
- Database Name
- State of the Database Status
- Database Owner
- Date Database Was Created
- Size of the Database
- Space Available
- Number of Users Currently Connected to the Database
- Collation Settings

You should use this page for obtaining information about a database, as displayed in Figure 2.11.

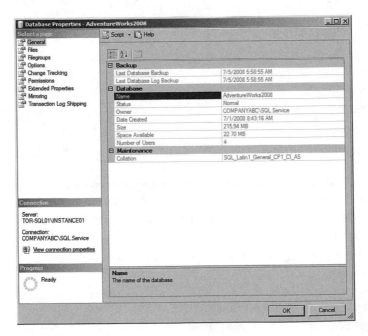

FIGURE 2.11
Viewing the General page in the Database Properties dialog box.

Administering the Database Properties Files Page

The second Database Properties page is called Files. Here you can change the owner of the database, enable full-text indexing, and manage the database files, as shown in Figure 2.12.

Managing Database Files

The Files page is used to configure settings pertaining to database files and transaction logs. You will spend time working in the Files page when initially rolling out a database and conducting capacity planning. Following are the settings you'll see:

- **Data and Log File Types**—A SQL Server 2008 database is composed of two types of files: data and log. Each database has at least one data file and one log file. When you're scaling a database, it is possible to create more than one data and one log file. If multiple data files exist, the first data file in the database has the extension *.mdf and subsequent data files maintain the extension *.ndf. In addition, all log files use the extension *.ldf.

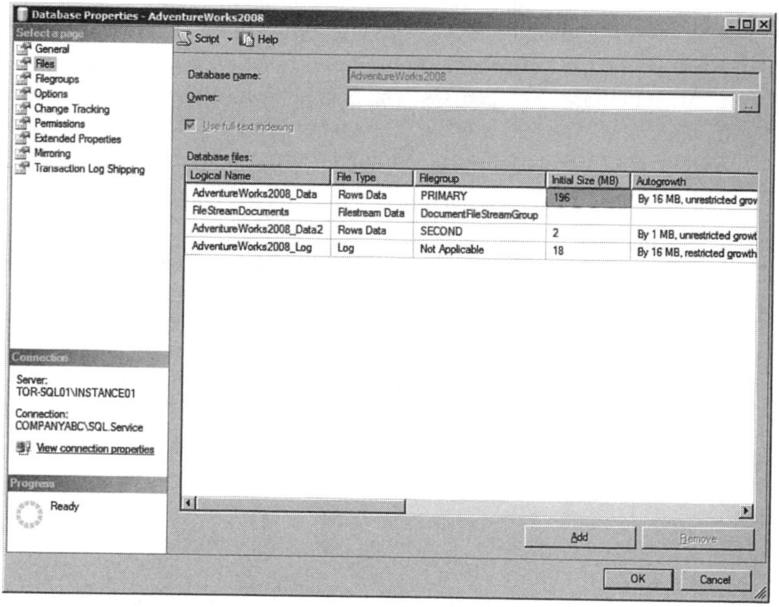

FIGURE 2.12
Configuring the database files settings from within the Files page.

Tip

To reduce disk contention, many database experts recommend creating multiple data files. The database catalog and system tables should be stored in the primary data file, and all other data, objects, and indexes should be stored in secondary files. In addition, the data files should be spread across multiple disk systems or Logical Unit Number (LUN) to increase I/O performance.

- **Filegroups**—When you're working with multiple data files, it is possible to create filegroups. A filegroup allows you to logically group database objects and files together. The default filegroup, known as the Primary Filegroup, maintains all the system tables and data files not assigned to other filegroups. Subsequent filegroups need to be created and named explicitly.

- **Initial Size in MB**—This setting indicates the preliminary size of a database or transaction log file. You can increase the size of a file by modifying this value to a higher number in megabytes.

- **Autogrowth**—This feature enables you to manage the file growth of both the data and transaction log files. When you click the ellipsis button, a Change Autogrowth dialog box appears. The configurable settings include whether to enable autogrowth, and if autogrowth is selected, whether autogrowth should occur based on a percentage or in a specified number of megabytes. The final setting is whether to choose a maximum file size for each file. The two options available are Restricted File Growth (MB) or Unrestricted File Growth.

Tip

When you're allocating space for the first time to both data files and transaction log files, it is a best practice to conduct capacity planning, estimate the amount of space required for the operation, and allocate a specific amount of disk space from the beginning. It is not a recommended practice to rely on the autogrowth feature because constantly growing and shrinking the files typically leads to excessive fragmentation, including performance degradation.

Note

Database Files and RAID Sets—Database files should reside only on RAID sets to provide fault tolerance and availability, while at the same time increasing performance. If cost is not an issue, data files and transaction logs should be placed on RAID 1+0 volumes. RAID 1+0 provides the best availability and performance because it combines mirroring with striping. However, if this is not a possibility due to budget, data files should be placed on RAID 5 and transaction logs on RAID 1.

Increasing Initial Size of a Database File

Perform the following steps to increase the data file for the AdventureWorks2008 database using SSMS:

1. In Object Explorer, right-click the AdventureWorks2008 database and select Properties.

2. Select the Files Page in the Database Properties dialog box.

3. Enter the new numerical value for the desired file size in the Initial Size (MB) column for a data or log file and click OK.

Creating Additional Filegroups for a Database

Perform the following steps to create a new filegroup and files using the AdventureWorks2008 database with both SSMS and TSQL:

1. In Object Explorer, right-click the AdventureWorks2008 database and select Properties.

2. Select the Filegroups page in the Database Properties dialog box.

3. Click the Add button to create a new filegroup.

4. When a new row appears, enter the name of new the filegroup and enable the option Default.

Alternatively, you can use the following TSQL script to create the new file-group for the AdventureWorks2008 database:

```
USE [master]
GO
ALTER DATABASE [AdventureWorks2008] ADD FILEGROUP [SecondFile-
Group]
GO
```

Creating New Data Files for a Database and Placing Them in Different Filegroups

Now that you've created a new filegroup, you can create two additional data files for the AdventureWorks2008 database and place them in the newly created filegroup:

1. In Object Explorer, right-click the AdventureWorks2008 database and select Properties.

2. Select the Files page in the Database Properties dialog box.

3. Click the Add button to create new data files.

4. In the Database Files section, enter the following information in the appropriate columns:

Columns	Value
Logical Name	AdventureWorks2008_Data2
File Type	Data
FileGroup	SecondFileGroup
Size	10 MB
Path	C:\
File Name	AdventureWorks2008_Data2.ndf

5. Click OK.

Note

For simplicity, the file page for the new database file is located in the root of the C: drive for this example. In production environments, however, you should place additional database files on separate volumes to maximize performance.

It is possible to conduct the same steps by executing the following TSQL syntax to create a new data file:

```
USE [master]
GO
ALTER DATABASE [AdventureWorks2008]
ADD FILE (NAME = N'AdventureWorks2008_Data2',
FILENAME = N'C:\AdventureWorks2008_Data2.ndf',
SIZE = 10240KB , FILEGROWTH = 1024KB )
TO FILEGROUP [SecondFileGroup]
GO
```

Configuring Autogrowth on a Database File

Next, to configure autogrowth on the database file, follow these steps:

1. From within the File page on the Database Properties dialog box, click the ellipsis button located in the Autogrowth column on a desired database file to configure it.

2. In the Change Autogrowth dialog box, configure the File Growth and Maximum File Size settings and click OK.

3. Click OK in the Database Properties dialog box to complete the task.

You can use the following TSQL syntax to modify the Autogrowth settings for a database file based on a growth rate at 50% and a maximum file size of 1000MB:

```
USE [master]
GO
ALTER DATABASE [AdventureWorks2008]
MODIFY FILE ( NAME = N'AdventureWorks2008_Data',
MAXSIZE = 1024000KB , FILEGROWTH = 50%)
GO
```

Managing FILESTREAM Data

Until SQL Server 2008, organizations have been creatively inventing their own mechanisms to store unstructured data. Now SQL Server 2008 introduces a new file type that can assist organizations by allowing them to store unstructured data such as bitmap images, music files, text files, videos, and audio files in a single data type, which is more secure and manageable.

From an internal perspective, FILESTREAM creates a bridge between the Database Engine and the NTFS filesystem included with Windows Server. It stores varbinary(max) binary large object (BLOB) data as files on the filesystem, and Transact-SQL can be leveraged to interact with the filesystem by supporting inserts, updates, queries, search, and backup of FILESTREAM data. FILESTREAM will be covered in upcoming sections of this chapter.

Administering the Database Properties Filegroups Page

As stated previously, filegroups are a great way to organize data objects, address performance issues, and minimize backup times. The Filegroup page is best used for viewing existing filegroups, creating new ones, marking filegroups as read-only, and configuring which filegroup will be the default.

To improve performance, you can create subsequent filegroups and place database files, transaction log files, Filestream data and indexes onto them. In addition, if there isn't enough physical storage available on a volume, you can create a new filegroup and physically place all files on a different volume or LUN if Storage Area Network (SAN) is being used.

Finally, if a database has static data, it is possible to move this data to a specified filegroup and mark this filegroup as read-only. This minimizes backup times; because the data does not change, SQL Server marks this filegroup and skips it.

Note

Alternatively, you can create a new filegroup directly in the Files page by adding a new data file and selecting New Filegroup from the Filegroup drop-down list.

Administering the Database Properties Options Page

The Options page, shown in Figure 2.13, includes configuration settings on Collation, Recovery Model, and other options such as Automatic, Cursor, and Miscellaneous. The following sections explain these settings.

Collation

The Collation setting located on the Database Properties Options page specifies the policies for how strings of character data are sorted and compared, for a specific database, based on the industry standards of particular languages and locales. Unlike SQL Server collation, the database collation setting can be changed by selecting the appropriate setting from the Collation drop-down box.

Recovery Model

The second setting within the Options page is Recovery Model. This is an important setting because it dictates how much data can be retained, which ultimately affects the outcome of a restore.

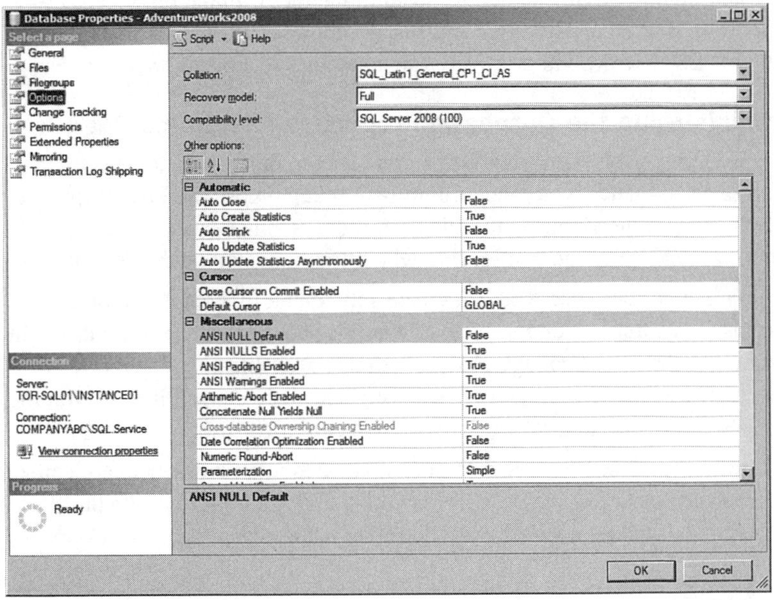

FIGURE 2.13

Viewing and configuring the Database Properties Options page settings.

Understanding and Effectively Using Recovery Models

Each recovery model handles recovery differently. Specifically, each model differs in how it manages logging, which results in whether an organization's database can be recovered to the point of failure. The three recovery models associated with a database in the Database Engine are as follows:

- **Full**—This recovery model captures and logs all transactions, making it possible to restore a database to a determined point in time or up to the minute. Based on this model, you must conduct maintenance on the transaction log to prevent logs from growing too large and disks becoming full. When you perform backups, space is made available again and can be used until the next planned backup. Organizations may notice that maintaining a transaction log slightly degrades SQL Server performance because all transactions to the database are logged. Organizations that insist on preserving critical data often overlook this issue because they realize that this model offers them the highest level of recovery capabilities.

- **Simple**—This model provides organizations with the least number of options for recovering data. The Simple recovery model truncates the transaction log after each backup. This means a database can be recovered only up to the last successful full or differential database backup. This recovery model also provides the least amount of administration because transaction log backups are not permitted. In addition, data entered into the database after a successful full or differential database backup is unrecoverable. Organizations that store data they do not consider mission-critical may choose to use this model.

- **Bulk-Logged**—This recovery model maintains a transaction log and is similar to the Full recovery model. The main difference is that transaction logging is minimal during bulk operations to maximize database performance and reduce the log size when large amounts of data are inserted into the database. Bulk import operations such as BCP, BULK INSERT, SELECT INTO, CREATE INDEX, ALTER INDEX REBUILD, and DROP INDEX are minimally logged.

Since the Bulk-Logged recovery model provides only minimal logging of bulk operations, you cannot restore the database to the point of failure if a disaster occurs during a bulk-logged operation. In most situations, an organization will have to restore the database, including the latest transaction log, and rerun the Bulk-Logged operation.

This model is typically used if organizations need to run large bulk operations that degrade system performance and do not require point-in-time recovery.

> **Note**
>
> When a new database is created, it inherits the recovery settings based on the Model database. The default recovery model is set to Full.

Next, you need to determine which model best suits your organization's needs. The following section is designed to help you choose the appropriate model.

Selecting the Appropriate Recovery Model

It is important to select the appropriate recovery model because doing so affects an organization's ability to recover, manage, and maintain data.

For enterprise production systems, the Full recovery model is the best model for preventing critical data loss and restoring data to a specific point in time. As long as the transaction log is available, it is possible to even get up-to-the-minute recovery and point-in-time restore if the end of the transaction log is backed up and restored. The trade-off for the Full recovery model is its impact on other operations.

Organizations leverage the Simple recovery model if the data backed up is not critical, data is static or does not change often, or if loss is not a concern for the organization. In this situation, the organization loses all transactions since the last full or last differential backup. This model is typical for test environments or production databases that are not mission-critical.

Finally, organizations that typically select the Bulk-Logged recovery model have critical data, but logging large amounts of data degrades system performance, or these bulk operations are conducted after hours and do not interfere with normal transaction processing. In addition, there isn't a need for point-in-time or up-to-the-minute restores.

> **Note**
>
> It is possible to switch the recovery model of a production database and switch it back. This would not break the continuity of the log; however, there could be negative ramifications to the restore process. For example, a production database can use the Full recovery model and, immediately before a large data load, the recovery model can be changed to Bulk-Logged to minimize logging and increase performance. The only caveat is that the organization must understand that it lost the potential for point-in-time and up-to-the-minute restores during the switch.

Switching the Database Recovery Model with SQL Server Management Studio

To set the recovery model on a SQL Server 2008 database using SSMS, perform the following steps:

1. In Object Explorer, first connect to the Database Engine, expand the desired server, and then expand the database folder.

2. Select the desired SQL Server database, right-click on the database, and select Properties.

3. In the Database Properties dialog box, select the Options page.

4. In Recovery Model, select either Full, Bulk-Logged, or Simple from the drop-down list and click OK.

Switching the Database Recovery Model with Transact-SQL

It is possible not only to change the recovery model of a database with SQL Server Management Studio, but also to make changes to the database recovery model using Transact-SQL commands such as ALTER DATABASE. You can use the following TSQL syntax to change the recovery model for the AdventureWorks2008 Database from Simple to Full:

```
--Switching the Database Recovery model
Use Master
ALTER DATABASE AdventureWorks2008 SET RECOVERY FULL
GO
```

Compatibility Level

The Compatibility Level setting located on the Database Properties Options page is meant for interoperability and backward compatibility of previous versions of SQL Server. The options available are SQL Server 2008 (100), SQL Server 2005 (90), and SQL Server 2000 (80).

Note

Unlike SQL Server 2005, SQL Server 2008 does not support SQL Server 7.0 (70) compatibility mode.

Other Options (Automatic)

Also available on the Database Properties Options page are these options:

- **Auto Close**—When the last user exits the database, the database is shut down cleanly and resources are freed. The values to be entered are either True or False.

- **Auto Create Statistics**—This setting specifies whether the database will automatically update statistics to optimize a database. The default setting is True, and this value is recommended.

- **Auto Shrink**—Similar to the shrink task in a maintenance plan or Integration Services, if this setting is set to True, SQL Server removes unused space from the database on a periodic basis. For production databases, this setting is not recommended.

- **Auto Update Statistics**—Similar to the Auto Create Statistics settings, this setting automatically updates any out-of-date statistics for the database. The default setting is True, and this value is recommended.

- **Auto Update Statistics Asynchronously**—If the statistics are out of date, this setting dictates whether a query should be updated first before being fired.

Other Options (Cursor)

The following options are also available on the Database Properties Options page:

- **Close Cursor on Commit Enabled**—This setting dictates whether cursors should be closed after a transaction is committed. If the value is True, cursors are closed when the transaction is committed, and if the value is False, cursors remain open. The default value is False.

- **Default Cursor**—The values available include Global and Local. The Global setting indicates that the cursor name is global to the connection based on the `Declare` statement. In the `Declare Cursor` statement, the Local setting specifies that the cursor name is Local to the stored procedure, trigger, or batch.

Other Options (Miscellaneous)

The following options are also available on the Database Properties Options page:

- **ANSI NULL Default**—The value to be entered is either True or False. When set to False, the setting controls the behavior to supersede the default nullability of new columns.

- **ANSI NULLS Enabled**—This setting controls the behavior of the comparison operators when used with null values. The comparison operators consist of Equals (=) and Not Equal To (<>).

- **ANSI Padding Enabled**—This setting controls whether padding should be enabled or disabled. Padding dictates how the column stores values shorter than the defined size of the column.

- **ANSI Warnings Enabled**—If this option is set to True, a warning message is displayed if null values appear in aggregate functions.

- **Arithmetic Abort Enabled**—If this option is set to True, an error is returned, and the transaction is rolled back if an overflow or divide-by-zero error occurs. If the value False is used, an error is displayed; however, the transaction is not rolled back.

- **Concatenate Null Yields Null**—This setting specifies how null values are concatenated. True indicates that string + NULL returns NULL. When this setting is False, the result is string.

- **Cross-Database Ownership Chaining Enabled**—Settings include either True or False. True represents that the database allows cross-database ownership chaining, whereas False indicates that this option is disabled.

- **Date Correlation Optimization Enabled**—If this option is set to True, SQL Server maintains correlation optimization statistics on the date columns of tables that are joined by a foreign key.

- **Numeric Round-Abort**—This setting indicates how the database will handle rounding errors.

- **Parameterization**—This setting controls whether queries are parameterized. The two options available are Simple and Forced. When you use Simple, queries are parameterized based on the default behavior of the database, whereas when you use Forced, all queries are parameterized.

- **Quoted Identifiers Enabled**—This setting determines whether SQL Server keywords can be used as identifiers when enclosed in quotation marks.

- **Recursive Triggers Enabled**—When this setting is enabled by setting the value to True, SQL Server allows recursive triggers to be fired.

- **Trustworthy**—This setting allows SQL Server to grant access to the database by the impersonation context. A value of True enables this setting.

- **VarDecimal Storage Format Enabled**—When this option is set to True, the database is enabled for the VarDecimal storage format. When using SQL Server 2008, True is the default setting. In addition, it is not possible to disable this feature if tables within the database are using the VarDecimal storage format.

Other Options (Recovery)

Also available on the Database Properties Options page is page verification:

- **Page Verify**—This option controls how SQL Server will handle incomplete transactions based on disk I/O errors. The available options include Checksum, Torn Page Detection, and None.

Other Options (Service Broker)

The Service Broker section includes the following settings:

- **Broker Enabled**—This is a database-level setting indicating whether or not Service Broker is enabled or disabled.

- **Honor Broker Priority**—The second setting controls the Honor Broker Priority behavior. The options available are True and False.

- **Service Broker Identifier**—The third setting displays the identifier associated with the Service Broker.

Other Options (State)

The following options are available on the Database Properties Options page:

- **Database Read Only**—Setting the database value to True makes the database read-only.

  The default syntax for managing the read-only state of a database is

  ```
  ALTER DATABASE database_name
  <db_update_option> ::=
    { READ_ONLY ¦ READ_WRITE }
  ```

- **Database State**—This field cannot be edited; it informs you of the state of the database. Possible states include Online, Offline, Restoring, Recovering, Recovery Pending, Suspect, and Emergency.

  To change the state of a database with TSQL, use the default syntax:

  ```
  ALTER DATABASE database_name
  <db_state_option> ::=
  { ONLINE ¦ OFFLINE ¦ EMERGENCY }
  ```

- **Encryption Enabled**—This field indicates whether or not encryption is enabled for a specific database. The options include True and False.

- **Restrict Access**—This setting manages which users can connect to the database. Possible values include Multiple, Single, and Restricted. The Multiple setting is the default state, which allows all users and applications to connect to the database. Single-user mode is meant for only one user to access the database. This is typically used for emergency administration. The final setting, Restricted, allows only members of the db_owner, dbcreator, or sysadmin accounts to access the database.

The TSQL code for setting the Restrict Access value is as follows:

```
ALTER DATABASE database_name
<db_user_access_option> ::=
    { SINGLE_USER ¦ RESTRICTED_USER ¦ MULTI_USER }
```

Administering the Change Tracking Page

The Change Tracking page is another new feature associated with SQL Server 2008. This page is used to administer change tracking settings for a particular database. Four configurable change tracking settings are provided:

- **Enable or Disable Change Tracking** by configuring the first setting to either True or False.

- **Retention Period** indicates the number of days to maintain change tracking information. The default value is set to 2.

- **Retention Period Units** is the third setting. When selecting options associated with this setting, a DBA can choose from Days, Hours, and Minutes. Typically, organizations choose days, unless there is an unexpected breach and tracking is required for a smaller increment of time.

- **Auto Cleanup** is the final setting. The default setting is True, which indicates that it is enabled. When this setting is enabled, change tracking information will automatically be removed after the retention period entered has expired.

The basic Transact-SQL syntax to enable Change Tracking for a specific database is as follows:

```
Use [Master]
Go
Alter Database [Desired Database] Set CHANGE_TRACKING = ON
GO
```

Administering the Database Properties Permissions Page

The Database Properties Permissions page is used to administer database authorization and role-based access and to control permissions on the database. Chapter 9 covers these topics in their entirety.

Administering the Database Properties Extended Permissions Page

The Database Properties Extended Permissions page is used for managing extended properties on database objects, such as descriptive text, input masks, and formatting rules. The extended properties can be applied to schema, schema view, or column view.

Administering the Database Properties Mirroring Page

Database mirroring is a SQL Server high-availability alternative for increasing availability of a desired database. Database mirroring transmits transaction log records directly from one SQL Server instance to another SQL Server instance. In addition, if the primary SQL Server instance becomes unavailable, the services and clients automatically fail over to the mirrored server. Automatic failover is contingent on the settings and versions used.

The Database Properties Mirroring page is the primary tool for configuring, managing, and monitoring database mirroring for a database. The Mirroring page includes configuration settings for security; mirroring operating mode; and the principal, mirror, and witness server network addresses. For more information on configuring database mirroring, review Chapter 13.

Administering the Database Properties Transaction Log Shipping Page

The final Database Properties page is Transaction Log Shipping. Transaction log shipping is one of four SQL Server 2008 high-availability options. Similar to database mirroring, in log shipping, transactions are sent from a primary server to the standby secondary server on an incremental basis. However, unlike with database mirroring, automatic failover is not a supported feature.

The configuration settings located on the Transaction Log Shipping page in the Database Properties dialog box are the primary place for you to configure, manage, and monitor transaction log shipping.

For more information on administering transaction log shipping, including step-by-step installation instructions, review Chapter 14, "Implementing and Managing Log Shipping."

SQL Server Database Engine Management Tasks

The following sections cover additional tasks associated with managing the SQL Server Database Engine.

Changing SQL Server Configuration Settings

Presently, most of the configuration settings can be changed from within
SQL Server Management Studio. These settings can also be changed using
the SP_CONFIGURE TSQL command. The syntax to change configuration
settings is

```
SP_CONFIGURE ['configuration name'], [configuration
setting&value]
GO
RECONFIGURE WITH OVERRIDE
GO
```

The *configuration name* represents the name of the setting to be changed,
and the *configuration setting value* is the new value to be changed.
Before you can change settings, however, you must use the SP_CONFIGURE
command. You must enable advanced settings by first executing the following
script:

```
SP_CONFIGURE 'show advanced options', 1
GO
RECONFIGURE
GO
```

For a full list of configuration options, see SQL Server 2008 Books Online.

Managing Database Engine Informational Reports

To succeed in today's competitive IT industry, you must be armed with information pertaining to SQL Server 2008. SQL Server 2008 continues to deliver
a tremendous number of canned reports that can be opened directly from
within SQL Server Management Studio. These reports provide information
that allows you to maximize efficiency when conducting administration and
management duties.

You can open these canned reports by right-clicking a SQL Server instance in
Management Studio and selecting Reports and then Standard Reports. The
standard server reports include the following:

- Server Dashboard
- Configuration Changes History
- Schema Changes History
- Scheduler Health
- Memory Consumption
- Activity - All Blocking Transactions

- Activity - All Cursors
- Activity - Top Cursors
- Activity - All Sessions
- Activity - Top Sessions
- Activity - Dormant Sessions
- Activity - Top Connections
- Top Transactions by Age
- Top Transactions by Blocked Transactions Count
- Top Transactions by Locks Count
- Performance - Batch Execution Statistics
- Performance - Object Execution Statistics
- Performance - Top Queries by Average CPU Time
- Performance - Top Queries by Average IO
- Performance - Top Queries by Total CPU Time
- Performance - Top Queries by Total IO
- Server Broker Statistics
- Transaction Log Shipping Status

The standard report titled Server Dashboard, displayed in Figure 2.14, is a great overall report that provides an overview of a SQL Server instance, including activity and configuration settings. However, if a standard report does not suffice, a DBA can also create a custom report.

You can also open canned reports for a specific database by right-clicking a database in Management Studio and selecting Reports and then Standard Reports. The standard database reports include the following:

- Disk Usage
- Disk Usage by Top Tables
- Disk Usage by Tables
- Disk Usage by Partition
- Backup and Restore Events
- All Transactions
- All Blocking Transactions
- Top Transactions by Age
- Top Transactions by Blocked Transaction Count
- Top Transactions by Locks Count

- Resource Locking Statistics by Object
- Object Execution Statistics
- Database Consistency History
- Index Usage Statistics
- Index Physical Statistics
- Schema Changes History
- User Statistics

Detaching and Attaching Databases

Another common task you must conduct is attaching and detaching databases.

Detaching a Database

When a database is detached, it is completely removed from a SQL Server instance; however, the files are still left intact and reside on the filesystem for later use. Before a database can be detached, all user connections must be terminated; otherwise, this process fails. The detach tool includes the options to automatically drop connections, update statistics, and keep full text catalogs.

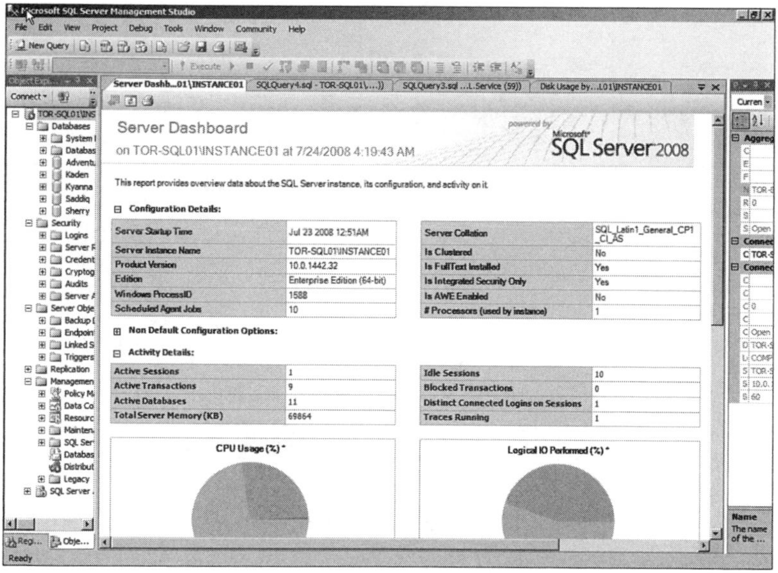

FIGURE 2.14
Viewing the standard Server Dashboard SQL Server canned report.

To drop the sample AdventureWorks2008 database, follow these steps:

1. In Object Explorer, first connect to the Database Engine, expand the desired server, and then expand the Database folder.

2. Select the AdventureWorks2008 database, right-click on the database, select Tasks, and then select Detach.

3. In the Detach Database dialog box, enable the following options, as displayed in Figure 2.15: Drop Connections, Update Statistics, and Keep Full Text Catalogs. Click OK.

Attaching a Database

Here's a common usage scenario for attaching databases: Say you need to move the database from a source to a target SQL Server. When a database is attached, the state of the database is exactly the same as when it was detached.

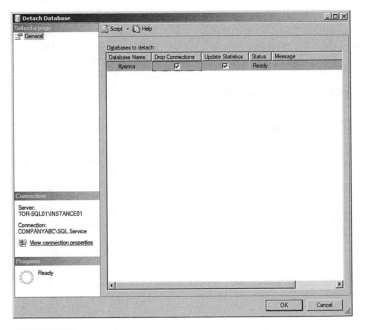

FIGURE 2.15
Specifying detach settings in the Detach Database dialog box.

The following steps illustrate how to attach a database with SQL Server Management Studio:

1. In Object Explorer, first connect to the Database Engine, expand the desired server, and then select the Database folder.

2. Right-click the Database folder and select Attach.

3. In the Attach Databases dialog box, click the Add button to add the database to be attached.

4. In the Locate the Database Files dialog box, specify the path to the *.mdf file and click OK.

5. Optionally, change the name or owner of the database.

6. Click OK to attach the database.

Alternatively, you can use the following TSQL syntax to attach the AdventureWorks2008 database:

```
USE [master]
GO
CREATE DATABASE [AdventureWorks2008] ON
( FILENAME = N'D:\AdventureWorks2008_Data.mdf' ),
( FILENAME = N'D:\AdventureWorks2008_Log.ldf' )
 FOR ATTACH
GO
if exists (select name from master.sys.databases
sd where name = N'AdventureWorks2008' and
SUSER_SNAME(sd.owner_sid) = SUSER_SNAME() )
EXEC [AdventureWorks2008].dbo.sp_changedbowner @loginame=
N'COMPANYABC\SQL.Service', @map=false
GO
```

Scripting Database Objects

SQL Server 2008 has two levels of scripting functionality that assist you in automatically transforming a SQL Server task or action into a TSQL script. The scripting functionality is a great way to automate redundant administration responsibilities or settings. Moreover, you don't have to be a TSQL scripting expert to create solid scripts.

You can generate a script from within a majority of the SQL Server dialog boxes or pages. For example, if you make changes to the SQL Server Processor Properties page, such as enabling the options Boost SQL Server Priority or User Windows Fibers, you can click the Script button at the top of the screen to convert these changes to a script. In addition, this script can be fired on other SQL Servers to make the configuration automatically consistent across similar SQL Servers.

When you click the Script button, the options available are Script Action to New Query Window, Script Action to File, Script Action to Clipboard, and Script Action to Job.

Another alternative to creating scripts is right-clicking a specific folder within Object Explorer and selecting Script As or right-clicking a database, selecting Tasks, and then selecting Generate Script to invoke the Script Wizard. Some of these tasks include scripting database schemas, jobs, tables, stored procedures, and just about any object within SQL Server Management Studio. Additional scripting statements include Create, Alter, Drop, Select, Insert, and Delete.

Managing SQL Server with PowerShell

PowerShell is now integrated and supported in SQL Server 2008. PowerShell is a command-line shell and scripting language that bolsters administrators' management experiences as they achieve greater control and productivity by leveraging a new standardized admin-focused scripting language, which includes more than 130 standard cmdlets, and consistent syntax and utilities. PowerShell is a prerequisite for installing SQL Server 2008 and for the first time, it is included with the Windows Server 2008 operating system as an optional feature that can be installed. For an overview of PowerShell with SQL Server 2008 including the provider, cmdlets, and most common DBA tasks with PowerShell, review to Chapter 20, "Administering SQL Server 2008 with PowerShell."

Backing Up and Restoring the Database

Creating a backup and recovery strategy is probably the most important task you have on your plate. When you're creating backups, it is imperative that you understand the recovery models associated with each database such as Full, Simple, and Bulk-Logged and understand the impact of each model on the transaction log and the recovery process. In addition, it is a best practice to back up the user databases, but to restore a full SQL Server environment, the system database should be included in the backup strategy.

For more information on recovery models and backing up and restoring the Database Engine, see Chapter 7.

Transferring SQL Server Data

There are many different ways to transfer data or databases from within SQL Server Management Studio. There are tasks associated with importing and exporting data and copying and/or moving a full database with the Copy Database Wizard. To use the transferring tasks, right-click a database, select Tasks, and then select Import Data, Export Data, or Copy Database.

Each of these ways to move data is discussed in its entirety in Chapter 3.

Taking a SQL Server Database Offline

As a database administrator, you may sometimes need to take a database offline. When the database is offline, users, applications, and administrators do not have access to the database until it has been brought back online.

Perform the following steps to take a database offline and then bring it back online:

1. Right-click on a desired database such as AdventureWorks2008, select Tasks, and then select Take Offline.

2. In the Task Database Offline screen, verify that the status represents that the database has been successfully taken offline and then select Close.

Within Object Explorer, a red arrow pointing downward is displayed on the Database folder, indicating that the database is offline. To bring the database back online, repeat the preceding steps but select Online instead.

In addition, you can use the following TSQL syntax to change the state of a database from Online, Offline, or Emergency:

```
ALTER DATABASE database_name
<db_state_option> ::=
    { ONLINE ¦ OFFLINE ¦ EMERGENCY }
```

> **Note**
>
> When the database option is configured to an Emergency state, the database is considered to be in single-user mode; the database is marked as read-only. This mode is meant for addressing crisis situations.

Shrinking a Database

The Shrink Database task reduces the physical database and log files to a specific size. This operation removes excess space in the database based on a percentage value. In addition, you can enter thresholds in megabytes, indicating the amount of shrinkage that needs to take place when the database reaches a certain size and the amount of free space that must remain after the excess space is removed. Free space can be retained in the database or released back to the operating system.

The following TSQL syntax shrinks the AdventureWorks2008 database, returns freed space to the operating system, and allows for 15% of free space to remain after the shrink:

```
USE [AdventureWorks2008]
GO
DBCC SHRINKDATABASE(N'AdventureWorks2008', 15, TRUNCATEONLY)
GO
```

> **Tip**
>
> It is best practice not to select the option to shrink the database. First, when shrinking the database, SQL Server moves pages toward the beginning of the file, allowing the end of the files to be shrunk. This process can increase the transaction log size because all moves are logged. Second, if the database is heavily used and there are many inserts, the database files will have to grow again. SQL 2005 and above addresses slow autogrowth with instant file initialization; therefore, the growth process is not as slow as it was in the past. However, sometimes autogrow does not catch up with the space requirements, causing performance degradation. Finally, constant shrinking and growing of the database leads to excessive fragmentation. If you need to shrink the database size, you should do it manually when the server is not being heavily utilized.

Alternatively, you can shrink a database by right-clicking a database and selecting Tasks, Shrink, and Database or File.

Data Compression in SQL Server 2008

With data explosion occurring in the industry and enterprise, more and more data is being stored within SQL Server. However, the databases are no longer averaging 100GB in size as they were 10 years ago. Now databases are becoming larger than ever, ranging in sizes from 10 to 50 TB on average. In addition, many times it is only a select few tables within the database that are growing to these record-breaking sizes. In order to combat this, even though storage is getting cheaper, Microsoft has introduced data compression and a Data Compression Wizard or new Transact-SQL statements; therefore, a DBA can compress tables and indexes to conserve storage space. One of the main design goals of compression with SQL Server 2008 was the potential to shrink data warehouse fact tables. Fact tables are typically the largest tables within a data warehouse as it contains majority of the data associated with a database.

> **Note**
>
> Compression is available only in the Enterprise Edition of SQL Server 2008. Moreover, the sp_estimate_data_compression_savings stored procedure can be used to calculate the storage savings associated with a compressed object.

Using the Data Compression Wizard to Compress Space

The Data Compression Wizard can be used to analyze and compress space associated with a whole table that is stored in a heap or clustered index structure. In addition, it can also support compression tables using nonclustered index and index views. Finally, if the table is partitioned, a DBA can compress portions of the tables and various partitions do not have to maintain the same compressed settings.

The Data Compression wizard can be invoked by right-clicking any table or index and selecting Storage and then Manage Compression. The first step is to select the compression type based on a partition number, or you can choose to use the same compression for all partitions. The compression options include row compression, page compression or none, indicating no compression. The next step is to click the Calculate button to review the disk cost savings. The cost savings will be displayed in the Requested Compressed Space column based on a partition number. This is displayed in Figure 2.16. The final step includes selecting an output option. It is possible to create a script, run immediately, or schedule the task to commence at a later time.

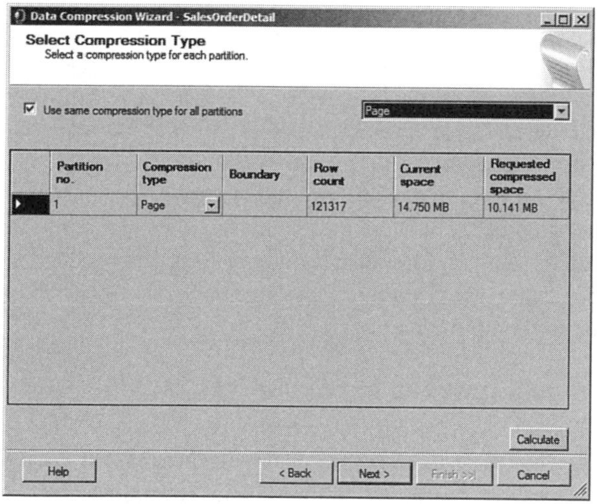

FIGURE 2.16
Specifying the Compression Type with the Data Compression Wizard.

Data Compression with Transact SQL

For those of you who do not like using a wizard interface, the following examples outline the default syntax for compressing data with Transact-SQL.

Creating a Table with Row Compression Enabled

```
CREATE TABLE <Table Name>
(<Column 1. int, <Column 2> nvarchar(50) )
WITH (DATA_COMPRESSION = ROW);
GO
```

Creating a Table with Page Compression Enabled

```
CREATE TABLE <Table Name>
(<Column 1. int, <Column 2> nvarchar(50) )
WITH (DATA_COMPRESSION = PAGE);
GO
```

The following Transact-SQL syntax illustrates compressing the Sales Order Detail table in the AdventureWorks2008 database by the page compression setting.

```
USE [AdventureWorks2008]
ALTER TABLE [Sales].[SalesOrderDetail]
REBUILD PARTITION = ALL
WITH
(DATA_COMPRESSION = PAGE
)
```

As mentioned earlier, compression is only included in the Enterprise Edition of SQL Server 2008. Compression technologies dramatically cut I/O requests and storage; however, the storage gained is typically at the sacrifice of processor performance. Therefore, test scenarios in a prototype lab to ensure that performance degradation of the system does not occur when using this new feature. Finally, use the new performance counters Page Compression Attempts /sec and Page Compressed/Sec found in the SQL Server Access Methods Object to monitor compression.

Partitioning Tables and Indexes in SQL Server 2008

Another common phenomena over the past few years is table and index partitioning in order to make large tables and indexes more manageable. By partitioning tables and indexes across multiple filegroups, data retrieval and management is much quicker as only subsets of the data are used; however, the integrity of the total data collection remains is intact. After partitioning, data is stored horizontally across multiple filegroups, so groups of data are mapped to individual partitions. Typical scenarios for partitioning include large tables that become unmanageable, tables that are suffering performance degradation, maintenance costs that exceed maintenance periods, and moving historical data from the table to another partition.

The next section provides an overview of using the Create Partition Wizard, which is a new feature in SQL Server 2008.

Leveraging the Create Partition Wizard to Create Table and Index Partitions

The Create Partition Wizard can be used to divide data in large tables across multiple filegroups in order to increase performance. The Create Partition wizard can be invoked by right-clicking any table or index, selecting Storage and then selecting Create Partition. The first step is to identify which columns to partition by reviewing all of the columns available in the Available Partitioning Columns section located on the Select a Partitioning Column dialog box, as displayed in Figure 2.17. This screen also includes additional options such as:

- **Collocate to an Available Partitioned Table**—Displays related data to join with the column being partitioned.

- **Storage Align Non Unique Indexes and Unique Indexes with an Indexed Partition Column**—Aligns all indexes of the table being partitioned with the same partition scheme.

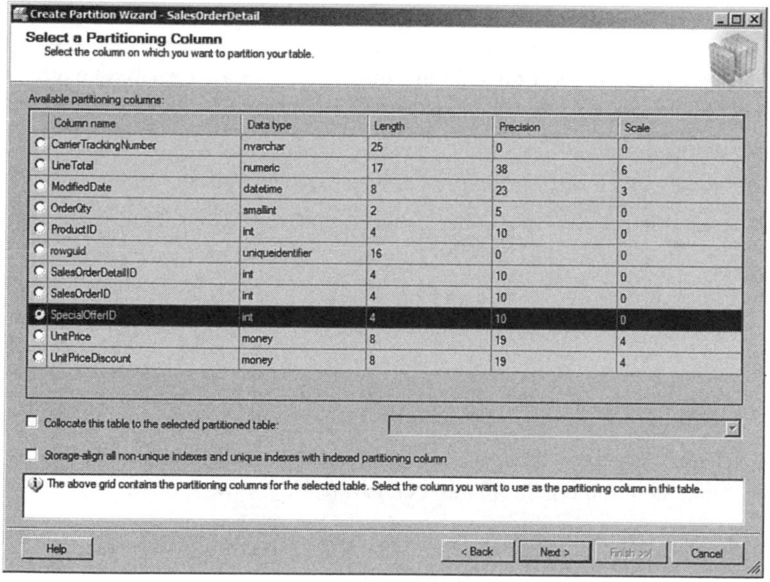

FIGURE 2.17
Specifying Data Compression Type Settings.

The next screen is called Select a Partition Function. This page is used for specifying the partition function where the data will be partitioned. The options available include using an existing partition or creating a new partitioning. The subsequent page is called New Partition Scheme. Here a DBA will conduct a mapping of the rows selected of tables being partitioned to a desired filegroup. Either a new partition scheme should be used or a new one needs to be created. The final screen is used for doing the actual mapping. On the Map Partitions page, specify the partitions to be used for each partition and then enter a range for the values of the partitions. The ranges and settings on the grid include:

- **Filegroup**—Enter the desired Filegroup for the partition
- **Left and Right Boundary**—Used for entering range values up to a specified value. Left boundary is based on `Value <= Boundary` and Right boundary is based on `Value < Boundary`.

Note

By opening the Set Boundary Values dialog box, a DBA can set boundary values based on dates (for example, partition everything in a column after a specific date). The data types are based on dates.

- **RowCount**—Read-only columns that display required space and are only determined when the Estimate Storage button is clicked.
- **Required Space**—Read-only columns that display required space and are only determined when the Estimate Storage button is clicked.
- **Available Space**—Read-only columns that display available space and are only determined when the Estimate Storage button is clicked.
- **Estimate Storage**—When selected, this option determines the rowcount, required, and available space.

Designing table and index partitions is a DBA task that typically requires a joint effort with the database development team. The DBA must have a strong understanding of the database, tables, and columns to make the correct choices for partitioning. For more information on partitioning, review Books Online.

Enabling FILESTREAM Data for a SQL Server Instance

The first step for managing FILESTREAM data is to enable it on the instance of SQL Server. The following steps indicate how to enable FILESTREAM data.

1. Choose, Start, All Programs, Microsoft SQL Server 2008, Configuration Tools, and then select SQL Server Configuration Manager.

2. In SQL Server Configuration Manager, highlight SQL Server Services and then double-click the SQL Server Instance for which you want to enable FILESTREAM. The SQL Server Instance is located in the right pane.

3. In the SQL Server Properties dialog box, select the FileStream tab.

4. Enable the desired FILESTREAM settings and then click OK. The options include: Enable FILESTREAM for Transact-SQL Access, Enable FILESTREAM for File I/O Streaming Access, and Allow Remote Clients to have Streaming Access to FILESTREAM Data.

5. The final step is to fire the following Transact-SQL code in Query Editor.

```
Exec sp_configure_filestream_access_level,2
RECONFIGURE
```

Renaming a Database

The following steps illustrate how to change the name of a database by using SQL Server Management Studio:

1. In Object Explorer, right-click the name of the database and select Rename.

2. Type the new name for the database and press Enter.

Administering the SQL Server Agent

The SQL Server Agent is a Microsoft Windows Service that executes scheduled tasks configured as SQL Server jobs. Ultimately, in SQL Server 2008, any task can be transformed into a job; therefore, the task can be scheduled to reduce the amount of time wasted on manual database administration. The SQL Server Agent can be managed from within SQL Server Management Studio.

Note

The SQL Server Agent service must be running to execute jobs and tasks. This is the first level of investigation when you're troubleshooting why agent jobs are not firing.

Administering the SQL Server Agent Properties

Before utilizing the SQL Server Agent, you should first verify and configure the Agent properties to ensure that everything is copacetic. The SQL Server Agent Properties dialog box is invoked by right-clicking the SQL Server Agent in SSMS and selecting Properties. The SQL Server Agent Properties dialog box has six pages of configuration settings, described in the following sections.

The General Page

The SQL Server Agent page maintains configurable settings such as Auto Restart SQL Server If It Stops Unexpectedly and Auto Restart SQL Server Agent If It Stops Unexpectedly.

From a best-practice perspective, both the restart settings should be enabled on mission-critical databases. This prevents downtime in the event of a server outage because the service will restart if failure is inevitable.

You can change the error log path if preferred and configure a send receipt via the Net send command. In addition, you can include execution trace messages to provide meticulous information on SQL Server Agent operations.

The Advanced Page

The Advanced page controls the behavior of SQL Server Event Forwarding and Idle CPU conditions. It is possible to forward unhandled events, all events, or events based on predefined severity levels selected in the drop-down list to a different server. The target server must be specified in the server drop-down list. The differences between unhandled and handled events are that unhandled events forward only events that no alert responds to, whereas handled events forward both the event and the alert. The final section is tailored toward SQL Server Agent and CPU settings. These settings define the conditions when jobs will run based on values such as Average CPU Usage Falls Below in Percentage and And Remains Below This Level for In Seconds.

> **Note**
>
> In enterprise production environments, a SQL Server instance should have enough processing power that these CPU condition settings are not required.

The Alert System Page

The Alert System page includes all the SQL Server settings for sending messages from agent alerts. The mail session settings are based on the prerequisite task of configuring SQL Server Database Mail. These topics are discussed in Chapter 17.

The Job System Page

The Job System page controls the SQL Server Agent shutdown settings. You can enter a numeric value based on a time increment that governs how long a job can run before automatically being shut down. It is also possible to specify a non-administrator Job Step Proxy Account to control the security context of the agent; however, this option is available only when you're managing earlier SQL Server Agent versions.

The Connections Page

The Connections Page should be used to configure a SQL Server alias for the SQL Server Agent. An alias is required only if a connection to the Database Engine will be made without using the default network transport or an alternate named pipe.

The History Page

You should use the final page, History, for configuring the limit size of a job history log setting. The options include setting maximum job history log size in rows and maximum job history rows per job.

Administering SQL Server Agent Jobs

The first subfolder located under the SQL Server Agent is the Job folder. Here, you create new jobs, manage schedules, manage job categories, and view the history of a job.

Follow these steps to create a new job:

1. In Object Explorer, first connect to the Database Engine, expand the desired server, and then expand the SQL Server Agent folder.
2. Right-click the Jobs folder and select New Job.
3. On the General page in the New Job dialog box, enter a name, owner, category, and description for the new job.
4. Ensure that the Enabled check box is set to True.
5. Click New on the Steps page. When the New Job Steps page is invoked, type a name for the step and enter the type of job this will be. The options range from Transact-SQL, which is the most common, to other items such as stored procedures, Integrations Services packages, and replication. For this example, select TSQL Type and enter the following TSQL syntax in the command window:

```
BACKUP DATABASE [AdventureWorks2008] TO  DISK =
N'C:\Program Files\Microsoft SQL Server
```

```
\MSSQL.1\MSSQL\Backup\AdventureWorks2008.bak'
WITH NOFORMAT, NOINIT,
NAME = N'AdventureWorks2008-Full Database Backup',
SKIP, NOREWIND, NOUNLOAD,  STATS = 10
GO
```

6. From within the General page, parse the command to verify that the syntax is operational and click the Advanced page.

7. The Advanced page includes a set of superior configuration settings. For example, you can specify actions on successful completion of this job, retry attempts including intervals, and what to do if the job fails. This page also includes Output File, Log to Table, History, and the potential to run the job under a different security context. Click OK to continue.

8. Within the New Job dialog box, you can use the Schedules page to view and organize schedules for the job. Here, you can create a new schedule or select one from an existing schedule.

9. Click OK to finalize the creation of the job.

Enabling or Disabling a SQL Server Agent Job

Each SQL Server Agent job can be either enabled or disabled by right-clicking the job and selecting either Enable or Disable.

Viewing SQL Server Agent Job History

From a management perspective, you need to understand whether a SQL Server Agent job was fired properly, completed successfully, or just outright failed. The Job History tool, which is a subcomponent of the Log File Viewer, provides thorough diagnostics and status of job history. Perform the following steps to review job history for a SQL Server Agent job from within SQL Server Management Studio:

1. In Object Explorer, first expand the SQL Server Agent and then the Jobs folder.

2. Right-click a desired job and select View Job History.

3. In the Log File Viewer, review the log file summary for any job from within the center pane.

4. Choose from additional options such as loading saved logs, exporting logs, creating a filter, parsing through logs with the search feature, and deleting logs.

Administering SQL Server Alerts and Operators

The SQL Server Alerts and Operators folders are used for monitoring the SQL Server infrastructure by creating alerts and then sending out notifications to operators. For more information on creating alerts and operators, review Chapter 17.

Administering SQL Server Proxies

The Proxies Folder found within the SQL Server Agent enables you to view or modify the properties of the SQL Server Agent Proxy account. You enter a proxy name and credentials and select the subsystem the proxy account has access to.

Administering SQL Server Error Logs

The final folder in the SQL Server is Error Logs. You can configure the Error Logs folder by right-clicking the folder and selecting Configure. The configuration options include modifying the error log file location, reducing the amount of disk space utilized by enabling the option Write OEM Error Log, and changing the Agent Log Level settings. These settings include enabling Error, Warnings, and/or Information.

Perform the following steps to view SQL Server Agent Error Logs:

1. In Object Explorer, first expand the SQL Server Agent and then the Error Logs folder.

2. When all the error logs are listed under the Error Logs folder, double-click any of the error logs to view them.

Summary

The Database Engine is the core component within SQL Server; it provides a key service for storing, processing, and securing data. SQL Server 2008 introduces many new features that improve your success at administering and managing this core component. In addition, reading this chapter will help you to fully understand how to manage and administer a SQL Server instance server properties, configuration settings, Database Engine folders, database properties, and SQL Server Agent.

Best Practices

The following list is a summary of some of the best practices from the chapter:

- Leverage the scripting utility within SQL Server Management Studio to transform administration tasks into Transact-SQL syntax.

- Unless there is a specific need to do otherwise, it is a best practice to allow SQL Server to dynamically manage the minimum and maximum amount of memory allocated to SQL Server. However, if multiple applications are running on SQL Server, it is recommended to specify minimum and maximum values for SQL Server memory. Then the application cannot starve SQL Server by depriving it of memory.

- The preferred authentication mode is Windows Authentication over SQL Server Authentication because it provides a more robust authorization mechanism.

- Use Change Tracking to ensure accountability and compliance on databases and database objects.

- Leverage the compression technologies to reduce storage utilization.

- Configuring SQL auditing is recommended to capture both failed and successful logins.

- Do not set the database to automatically shrink on a regular basis because this leads to performance degradation and excessive fragmentation over time.

- The first Database Engine administration task after a successful SQL installation should involve tuning and configuring the server properties.

- Configure the recovery model for each database accordingly and implement a backup and restore strategy. This should also include the system databases.

- Database files, transaction log files, and operating system files should be located on separate volumes for performance and availability.

- When multiple database files and transaction log files exist, organize them through the use of filegroups.

- Create basic reports in Management Studio to better understand the SQL Server environment.

- Automate administration tasks by using SQL Server 2008 Agent jobs.

- Review the other break-out chapters in the book for more information on items such as hardening a SQL Server infrastructure, encryption, Policy Based Management, Resource Governor, backups, and maintenance plans.

CHAPTER 3

Creating Packages and Transferring Data with Integration Services

SQL Server 2008 Integration Services (SSIS) provides data movement and transformation capabilities for SQL Server. Just as in SQL Server 2005, SSIS replaces SQL Server 2000 Data Transformation Services (DTS). SSIS provides for the following data services:

- Extraction
- Transformation
- Loading

This triumvirate of data services is frequently referred to as ETL. The process encapsulates the extraction of data from a source, the transformation of the data to suit the requirements of the application, and finally the loading of the data into a destination. The transformations can include normalizing, sanitizing, merging, aggregating, and copying the data. The sources and destinations for the data can be SQL databases, third-party ODBC data, flat files, or any number of other data locations.

SSIS delivers high-performance ETL services with a rich set of tools for designing, testing, executing, and monitoring these integrations. SSIS consists of packages that define the logic for the extraction, transformation, and loading steps, and an engine that performs the steps defined in the package. There is a service that allows administration and monitoring of the packages on the server, and a development environment for creating and debugging the package definitions.

> **Note**
>
> The DTS backward compatibility components are still available in SQL Server 2008. However, since DTS was a deprecated feature in SQL Server 2005, it is unlikely that it will continue to be supported in the next version of SQL Server, making migration of DTS packages to SSIS something to strongly consider for this release of SQL Server.

What's New in Integration Services for SQL Server 2008

SSIS has a number of new features and enhancements in SQL Server 2008. The following list describes the principal changes:

- The Lookup Transform has had numerous improvements. A Cache Transform has been added that allows data to be stored in local files so that it can be reused across multiple Lookup Transforms. The cache can now be populated from any data source that SSIS supports, rather than being limited to OLE DB sources. The Lookup Transform now supports a Not Matched output, in addition to the Matched and Error Outputs.

- A debug dump file can be created when SSIS packages are executed. The file contains detailed information about the package state and execution progress. This allows additional troubleshooting to be performed in the event of package errors.

- Performance of the data flow has been improved through enhancements to the threading model. It now makes better use of multiple-processor computers.

- There are now both ADO.NET Sources and ADO.NET Destination components that make use of ADO.NET data providers.

- There is a new Data Profiling Task that allows you to evaluate the quality of data in SQL Server databases. It allows profiling of individual columns for distribution of values, percentage of nulls, and column statistics. It also allows relationships between columns to be analyzed for candidate keys and dependencies between columns.

- SSIS now uses the Visual Studio Tools for Applications (VSTA) environment for working with script tasks and components. This enables either Visual Basic.NET or C# to be used as the scripting language, and allows managed assemblies and web references to be added to the script code.

- The data types DT_DBTIMESTAMP2, DT_DBTIMESTAMPOFFSET, and DT_DBTIME2 have been added. These data types support additional precision in fractional seconds and time zone offsets.

- The Import and Export Wizard now supports the ability to review and accept any data type conversions that the wizard will perform.

- There are two new features of the relational engine that have particular relevance to SSIS: change data capture and the MERGE statement. Both of these features can be leveraged from SSIS to make a package faster and more efficient.

Note

If you have installed a new SQL Server 2008 system from scratch, the packages, tools, and wizards included in this chapter provide ways to migrate data and databases from older versions of SQL Server.

Options for Creating Packages

There are several options for creating SSIS packages and transferring data in SQL Server 2008. Some of the options do not require in-depth knowledge of SSIS, and are appropriate for simple importing and exporting of data. Other options require a more detailed understanding, but offer more flexibility and capability for transforming and manipulating data.

Import and Export Wizard

The Import and Export Wizard is useful for quickly importing or exporting data from SQL Server when there is little need for manipulation of the data. Behind the scenes, the wizard produces an SSIS package. The package can be run once and discarded, or it can be saved to a file or in the MSDB database for later use. The wizard will handle basic data type conversions, but will not address more complex cleansing of data, such as reformatting telephone numbers. The wizard can be launched from SQL Server Management Studio by right-clicking a database, and selecting Tasks, Import Data, or Tasks, Export Data.

The packages produced by the Import and Export Wizard can provide a useful starting point for developing new packages. The wizard will create the basic structure of the package. The package can then be opened and edited in Business Intelligence Development Studio (BIDS). This can make it easier to add additional transformations to the package. An example of the Import and Export Wizard will be covered in the "Creating a Package" section later in this chapter.

Copy Database Wizard

The Copy Database Wizard is used to copy databases from an instance of
SQL Server 2000 or later to SQL Server 2008. The wizard produces an SSIS
package, like the Import and Export Wizard. Unlike the packages produced
by the Import and Export Wizard, the package created is useful only for
copying databases. It can be edited in Business Intelligence Development
Studio. The package will be stored in the MSDB database, and located in the
<*SERVERNAME*>\DTS Packages\Copy Database Wizard Packages folder,
which you can browse to using the Integration Services Object Explorer in
SQL Server Management Studio. This wizard will be covered in the "Using
the Copy Database Wizard" section later in the chapter.

Business Intelligence Development Studio

Business Intelligence Development Studio (BIDS) offers the most flexibility
in creating SSIS packages. It offers complete access to all of the tasks, transformations, and connectivity options available in SSIS. It can be used to
create new packages or edit existing packages. This flexibility also requires
more understanding of how SSIS works. The next section will cover the
features and options available in SSIS in more detail.

A package can be created directly in BIDS by using the Import and Export
Wizard to add the package to the project, and then editing it using the full set of
design tools available. New for 2008, the Integration Services Connection
Project template will present a wizard for configuring your source and destination connections, and create a basic package as a starting point for moving data.

Packages

Packages allow you to control not only the transfer of data in and out of the
SQL Server 2008 server (commonly referred to as extraction, transformation,
and loading, or ETL for short), but also to automate a variety of maintenance
and administrative functions. This can all be done through a graphical development environment that provides debugging and troubleshooting support.

The types of tasks you are likely to want to automate include the following:

- Importing and exporting data from SQL Server
- Maintaining databases, rebuilding indexes, and other administrative
  tasks
- Running commands and coordinating multiple steps of a process

The package model gives you access to intensive script-like control and
power, but in an easy-to-use and modular interface. Similar capabilities exist

in scripting, batch files, or programming languages such as Visual Basic. However, Integration Services packages bring those capabilities to a model that is built around the database architecture and a data integration toolset. It has predefined tasks that are database oriented and geared toward a database administrator (DBA).

Throughout this chapter, the optional SQL Server 2008 sample files will be used. This allows you to do the procedures shown in the chapter with the same data and follow the steps exactly.

Note

The SQL Server 2008 Integration Services provide a complex and rich set of development tools for integrating and processing information. These tools allow sophisticated programmatic solutions to be developed to meet complex business needs.

However, the administration and maintenance requirements of DBAs are usually more straightforward and simple, and require less development effort. The SQL Server 2008 Integration Services tools also simplify the process of developing administration and maintenance solutions. This chapter focuses on the needs of the DBAs rather than those of a developer.

Packages consist of control flows and control flow tasks, data flows and data flow components, connections, and various supporting structures such as event handlers, variables, and logging. Although each package is self-contained, packages are organized into projects for ease of development and distribution.

Understanding how these various pieces fit together is the key to being able to use packages to automate administrative and maintenance tasks.

Projects and Solutions

Packages are organized into projects and solutions. Projects are containers for packages. Each project can contain multiple packages. In addition to the packages, a project contains the definitions for data sources and data source views that are used by the packages.

A *solution* is a container for organizing projects that are related or that compose a business solution. When a project is created, the Business Intelligence Development Studio automatically creates a solution for the project if one does not already exist.

DBAs rarely use solutions or projects, because most packages used by DBAs are stand-alone packages. However, a package must be part of a project in order to debug it in Business Intelligence Development Studio.

Control Flow

The control flow is the organizing element of the package. Control flows contain a series of tasks that determine what the package will do, including data flows to orchestrate data movement. Each package has one primary control flow. There can be additional control flows associated with event handlers, as discussed in the "Event Handlers" section in this chapter. Each control flow can contain nested control flows in the form of containers. Containers allow package developers to organize tasks and set up repeating tasks, such as conditional loops. Containers can contain tasks and other containers, allowing for sophisticated nested logic and processing.

The available types of containers are listed in Table 3.1.

Table 3.1   **Container Types**

Container	Description
For Each Loop and For Loop	Repeats the tasks contained in the container until the end of the collection or test condition is reached.
Sequence	Used to sequence and isolate tasks into smaller control flows.

> **Note**
>
> SSIS also uses an internal container called the TaskHost that can contain a single task. Every task is automatically hosted in this container. This is transparent when developing packages, but it can be helpful to remember that every task is essentially a container that only holds one task.

Tasks

Tasks are the individual units of work in a package. You can use tasks to do such things as execute a SQL statement, import data, copy a database, send mail, or initiate a data flow. Each task has a set of properties associated with it that control its behavior at runtime. There are a multitude of different tasks that provide a rich set of tools to automate work. Table 3.2 shows several of the commonly used control flow tasks. There is a complete list of control flow tasks in the Books Online topic "Integration Services Tasks."

Table 3.2   **Control Flow Tasks**

Task	Description
Data Flow Task	Runs data flows to extract data, apply column-level transformations, and load data
File System Task	Performs common operations on files and directories
Execute Package Task	Allows one package to execute another
Execute SQL Task	Executes a SQL statement against a relation database
Data Profiling Task	Task that profiles the data in SQL Server databases for statistical information, correlation of data, and patterns in the data
Transfer Database Task and Transfer SQL Server Objects Tasks	These tasks move SQL Server databases or objects in those databases from one instance to another.

Data Flow

The data flow determines how data is moved, which is the main goal of any data integration process. This is the nuts and bolts of the extraction, transformation, and loading of the data. Data flows are also referred to as *pipelines* because data flows from one location to another within them. Individual units of work in a data flow are known as *components*. Data flow components are organized into sources, transformations, and destinations. These control where data comes from, how it is changed, and where it goes, respectively. Depending on the function of the component, it may have several inputs and outputs. Components can be connected together by joining the output from one component to the input on another component. This connection is a *data flow path*, and it shows how data will move through the pipeline.

A variety of sources and destination are available in the data flow components. Most sources have an equivalent destination. For example, there is an ADO.NET source and an ADO.NET destination. The XML Source, however, does not have an equivalent destination, and there are several destinations (such as the Data Reader destination) that do not have equivalent sources. The common sources and destinations are listed in Table 3.3. The complete list can be found in the Books Online topics "Integration Services Sources" and "Integration Services Destinations."

Table 3.3   **Common Source and Destination Components**

Source or Destination	Description
ADO.NET Source	Consumes data from a .NET Framework data provider
Excel Source	Extracts data from an Excel file
Flat File Source	Extracts data from a flat file
OLE DB Source	Consumes data from an OLE DB provider
ADO.NET Destination	Loads data using a .NET Framework data provider
Excel Destination	Writes data to an Excel Workbook
Flat File Destination	Writes data to a flat file
OLE DB Destination	Loads data using an OLE DB provider

The possible transformations are where the data flow really shows its versatility. There are transformations that operate on individual rows and on sets of rows. There are transformations that can join rows, split rows, or even do lookups into another table for references. This gives you a multitude of options for what to do with the data that is being moved between a source and a destination.

The transformations can also be executed sequentially to allow more than one transformation to be done on the data, and different flow paths can be taken dependent on the data as well, allowing decisions to be made for each row of data.

Row transformations are the most commonly used data-flow transformation elements. They can transform column values or create new columns. Typical uses are to change the data type of a column, manipulate text (such as splitting a name field into first and last names), or create a copy of a column for future manipulation.

The rowset transformations output a new set of rows based on the input rows. Typical uses include sorting a rowset through the Sort transform or averaging columns in a rowset using the Aggregate transform.

There is a set of transformations that allow data to be split, joined, or used as a lookup reference. Frequently, rowsets must be split into separate groups. For example, a table of customers may need to be cleaned by removing those below a certain age. The conditional split would be used to separate the data on the basis of that condition.

There are also transformations that allow data to move in and out of the data flow. For example, the import and export transformations allow data to be brought into and out of the data flow via files. The audit transformation allows data from the running environment to be brought into the data flow, for example, by allowing the login name of the user to be put into a column.

Table 3.4 lists the commonly used data flow components. The complete list can be found in the Books Online topic "Integration Services Transformations."

Table 3.4   **Data Flow Transformation Components**

Transformation	Description
Data Conversion Transformation	The transformation that converts the data type of a column to a different data type
Derived Column Transformation	The transformation that populates columns with the results of expressions
Script Component	The transformation that uses .NET script to extract, transform, or load data
OLE DB Command Transformation	The transformation that runs SQL commands for each row in a data flow
Aggregate Transformation	The transformation that performs aggregations such as AVERAGE, SUM, and COUNT
Sort Transformation	The transformation that sorts data
Conditional Split Transformation	The transformation that routes data rows to different outputs
Union All Transformation	The transformation that merges multiple data sets
Lookup Transformation	The transformation that looks up values in a reference table using an exact match
Row Count Transformation	The transformation that counts rows as they move through it and stores the final count in a variable

Connections

Connections allow the package to connect to a variety of sources, destinations, and services. Connections include databases, flat files, Excel spreadsheets, FTP services, and others. Table 3.5 contains a list of the commonly used connection types. A complete list is in Books Online under the topic "Connection Managers."

Table 3.5   **Connection Types**

Connection Managers	Description
ADO.NET Connection Manager	For connecting to relational data sources by using ADO.NET
Excel Connection Manager	For connecting to Excel workbooks
Flat File Connection Manager	For accessing data in a single flat file
ODBC Connection Manager	For connecting to data sources by using ODBC
OLE DB Connection Manager	For connecting to data sources by using OLE DB

Connections are instantiated through connection managers, which are logical representations of the connections. The connection managers contain all the properties needed for the connection. A single connection manager can be reused throughout a package, such as a connection to a database, or a connection to an SMTP mail server. In addition, there can be more than one connection manager of the same type, such as when connections to multiple flat files are needed.

Event Handlers

Event handlers trigger when the package or tasks raise events. These events are raised when significant conditions occur, including errors (OnError), warnings (OnWarning), information messages (OnInformation), or when the package or task completes (OnPostExecute). The complete list of events can be found in Books Online under the topic "Integration Services Event Handlers."

Event handlers launch control flows, which can include all the same tasks as the package control flow. In effect, the event handlers are containers with control and data flows that execute only when their trigger condition is encountered.

Variables

Variables are used to store values that the package can use at runtime. For example, a variable can be used to store the count of rows processed by a Row Count Transformation in the data flow. Or it can be used to store the value for a parameterized SQL statement to be run from an Execute SQL Task. Variables can be defined at the package level, or they can be scoped to a container or individual task.

There are a number of system variables that provide additional information about the package execution. These include ContainerStartTime, which indicates the start time of the package or task, and ExecutionInstanceGUID, which provides a unique identifier each time the package is executed. A complete list of system variables can be found in Books Online under the topic "System Variables."

Log Providers and Logging

When packages execute, detailed information is generated about the execution of the package. This information is very useful for troubleshooting and auditing the package. By default, this information is displayed in the console but not stored anywhere. This information can be captured in logs for later review and analysis.

SSIS can log to a number of different destinations, including text files, SQL Server, or the Windows Event Log, through the use of log providers. Custom log providers can be created as well. Log providers abstract the actual mechanics of writing log information to a specific destination away from the package.

> **Note**
>
> Under SQL Server 2005, when logging to SQL Server, the log table name was sysdtslog90. The new name under 2008 is sysssislog. It is also now marked as a system table, so it will now be displayed under *<Database>*\ Tables\System Tables in SQL Server Management Studio.

The package can log to more than one provider at a time—for example, to both the Windows Event Log and to the SQL Server. The same events will be logged to both providers.

Developing Packages

As stated earlier, packages are the core of the Integration Services. Packages are developed in the Business Intelligence Development Studio, which is a sophisticated development environment with extensive development and debugging features. The specific tool used for Integration Services is the SSIS Designer, which is the graphical tool to develop and maintain the SSIS packages. The SSIS Designer allows you to

- Build control and data flows
- Configure event handlers
- Execute and debug packages
- Graphically follow the package execution

This section will cover using the SSIS Designer in creating a package, reviewing the package, and finally running the package.

Creating a Project

To start this sample, a project needs to be created to contain the packages. This project can contain multiple packages that are related for ease of maintenance and organization. A solution will be created automatically for any new project.

To create a project, follow these steps:

1. Launch SQL Server Business Intelligence Development Studio.
2. Select File, New, Project.
3. Select the Integration Services Project template.
4. Change the name—in this case, Customer Project.
5. Select a location to store the project, such as `c:\projects\`.
6. Leave the Solution Name as is—in this case, Customer Project. A directory will be created for the new solution. Click OK to create the project.

The project will be opened with a default package name, `Package.dtsx`.

Creating a Package

A simple package will now be created. This package will import the
Customers.txt sample file (available in the Integration Services samples
from CodePlex at http://www.codeplex.com/MSFTISProdSamples/Release/
ProjectReleases.aspx?ReleaseId=16043), which contains customer records
for more than 2,000 customers. The data contains name, birth date, yearly
income, occupation, and other key data.

To create the import package, follow these steps:

1. If necessary, launch the SQL Server Business Intelligence
   Development Studio.

2. Open the Customer Project created in the previous section.

3. Click Project, SSIS Import and Export Wizard. Click Next on the first
   page of the wizard.

4. In the Data Source drop-down list, select Flat File Source.

5. In the File Name field, click Browse to browse for the file to import.

6. Navigate to C:\Program Files\Microsoft SQL
   Server\100\Samples\Integration Services\Package
   Samples\ExecuteSQLStatementsInLoop Sample\Data Files\.

7. Select the Customers.txt file and click Open.

8. Check the box Column Names in the first data row and click Next.

9. Review the columns and data the wizard will import and click Next.

10. Select SQL Server Native Client 10.0 in the Data Source drop down
    list. In the Server Name field, select TOR-SQL01\INSTANCE01.
    Select AdventureWorks2008 in the Database field and click Next.

11. Ensure that the Destination table name is [dbo].[Customers]. Click
    Preview to review the columns and data. Click Close to close the
    preview window, and click Next.

12. Review the summary. Note the location where the package will be
    saved and that the package will not be run immediately.

13. Click Finish to build and save the package. A new package name,
    Package1.dtsx, will be created.

14. Click Close to exit the wizard, and select File, Save All to save the
    project.

The project now has a package that will import the Customers.txt source
file into a Customers table in the AdventureWorks2008 database.

Walkthrough of a Package

To better familiarize you with the SSIS Designer package development user interface in Business Intelligence Development Studio, this section will explore the interface using the newly created customer import package.

The Solution Explorer shows the view of the Customer project with the packages, as can be seen in Figure 3.1. This view is located in the SSIS Designer in the upper-right pane. The package that was created in the previous section can be seen.

Selecting the Package1.dtsx package will show the properties of the package in the Properties window in the lower-right pane. This is true of the interface in general; selecting an object will show its properties.

The name of the package can be changed here to something more appropriate, such as Import Customers. To do this:

1. Select the Package1.dtsx package in the Solution Explorer.

2. In the Properties pane, change the filename to CustomerImport.dtsx.

3. The interface asks whether the package object name should be changed as well. Click Yes to accept the change.

4. Select File, Save All to save the changes.

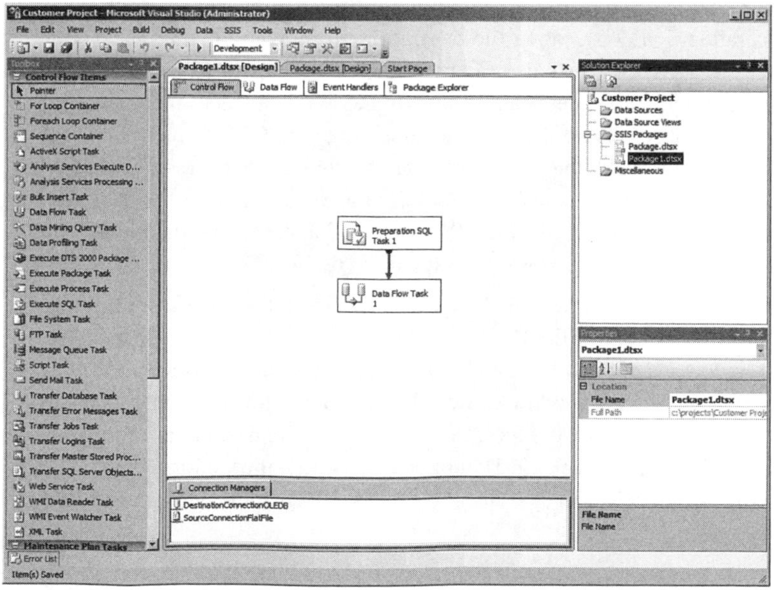

FIGURE 3.1
The Customer Import project.

The SSIS Packages folder in the Solution Explorer will show the updated name. The default package `Package.dtsx` can be deleted in the Solution Explorer window as well by right-clicking the package and selecting Delete. After the changes, only one package, named `CustomerImport.dtsx`, should be visible in the Solution Explorer.

The Error List window is located below the Connection Managers window and shows any errors, warnings, or messages that the package generates. This window is active and will show messages as soon as they are detected by the interface during the design of the package. The Error List may be hidden or minimized, and can be displayed by selecting View, Error List from the menu.

Walkthrough of the Control Flow

In the Control Flow window, the control steps of the CustomerImport package can be seen. These steps are instances of control flow tasks. There are only two tasks in this particular package, the Preparation SQL Task 1 and the Data Flow Task 1. Clicking the Preparation SQL Task 1 will change the focus of the Properties pane and show the properties of the task. These properties can be difficult to interpret until you are familiar with the tasks.

An alternate method of reviewing the configuration of a task is to use the edit function. This can be accessed by selecting the task in the designer pane and right-clicking to select Edit. Doing this for the CustomerImport package Preparation SQL Task shows the configuration shown in Figure 3.2. The figure shows that the task is an Execute SQL Task type, and the SQLStatement parameters can be seen in the SQLStatement field, although the statement scrolls off the window. Selecting the SQLStatement field will display an ellipsis button ("...") that you can click to view the SQL statement in a larger window. This task will execute the SQL statement to create the Customers table in the AdventureWorks2008 database in preparation for the import. Click Cancel to close the Execute SQL Task Editor.

The Task Editor window will change depending on the specific task being edited. The left side of the BIDS interface contains the Toolbox window. If the window is not visible, it can be displayed by selecting View, Toolbox from the menu. This window shows all the control flow tasks that are available. These range from the Execute SQL Task to Send Mail Task to maintenance tasks such as Back Up Database Task. When the Control Flow designer window is open, the Toolbox window will show only control flow tasks.

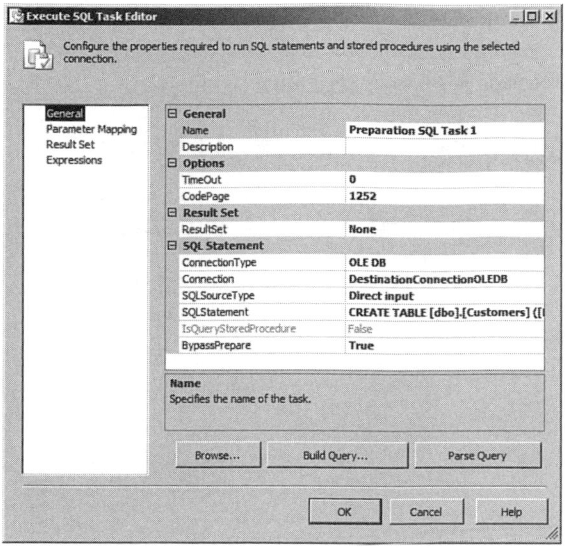

FIGURE 3.2
The Task Editor window.

The tasks in the control flow are connected by arrows. These arrows are precedence constraints, and they control the flow of execution between tasks. Preparation SQL Task 1 has a green arrow that connects to Data Flow Task 1. This indicates that Preparation SQL Task 1 must complete before Data Flow Task 1 can begin executing. The fact that the arrow is green indicates that it is a Success precedence constraint, meaning that Preparation SQL Task 1 must complete successfully before Data Flow Task 1 can begin. A red arrow would indicate that the preceding task must fail, and a blue arrow would indicate that as long as the preceding task completes (regardless of success or failure), the subsequent task can begin.

Walkthrough of the Data Flow

The Data Flow Task shown in the Control Flow designer window is expanded in the Data Flow designer window, which can be accessed by editing the Data Flow Task or by clicking the Data Flow tab in the designer window. The steps in the data flow are called components, which helps differentiate them from control flow tasks. The Data Flow designer window for the CustomerImport package shows two items, the Source - Customers_txt component, and the Destination - Customers component.

These two items are shown in Figure 3.3. The overall architecture of the data flow is to take data from a source, transform it in some manner if needed, and finally put the transformed data into a destination.

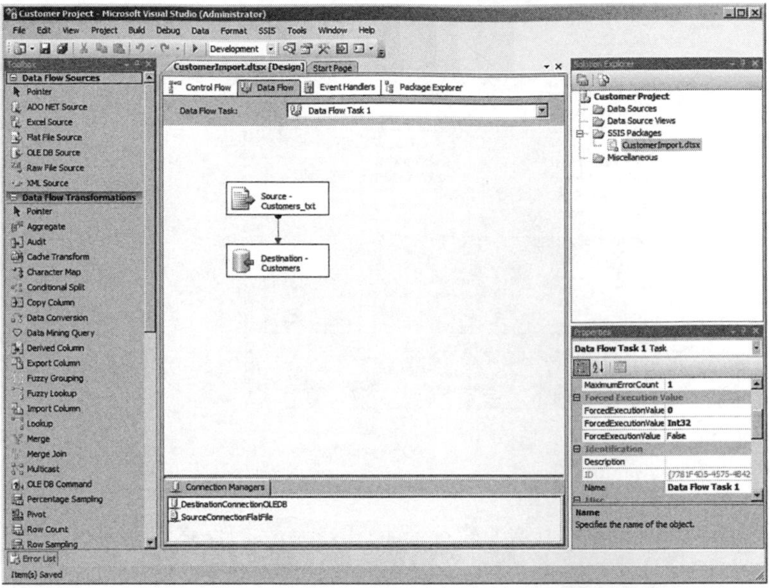

FIGURE 3.3
The Data Flow designer window.

Right-clicking the Source - Customers_txt item and selecting Edit shows the configuration of the source. The item in this case is a Flat File Source, as indicated by the title of the window. Clicking the Connection Managers option shows the name of the connection manager, which will be examined in "Walkthrough of the Connection Managers," later in this section. Clicking the Preview button shows a preview of the first 200 rows that will be imported from the source. Selecting the Columns option on the left shows the columns that are available from the source (the external columns) and also how the columns are mapped into the output. Columns can easily be renamed in this area. As an example of this, change EmailAddress to SMTP in the Output Column. Finally, selecting the Error Output option on the left allows you to indicate what to do, on a column-by-column basis, in response to errors. In the case of either errors in or truncation of the column data, the choices are to either fail the component (the default behavior), ignore the failure, or to redirect the row. Clicking OK saves the changes to the item.

Right-clicking the Destination - Customers item and selecting Edit shows the configuration properties of the OLE DB Destination. Selecting the Connection Managers option shows the destination connection. The OLE DB Connection Manager setting specifies the destination connection manager, which will be discussed in the next section, "Walkthrough of the Connection Managers." The Data access mode shows how the data will be inserted into the destination, and the table or view within the database can be selected as well. Various other options exist on this screen, as well, such as whether to lock the table when inserting.

Selecting the Mappings option on the left results in an error, because the Customers table does not exist in the AdventureWorks2008 database. Click OK to clear the error and then click the New button next to the Name of the table or the view field. This will create a SQL script to create the table. The name of the table will default to the name of the data flow component (Destination - Customers), so change the name in the script to dbo.Customers. Then click OK to create the table.

Select the Mappings options in the OLE DB Destination Editor again to show the mappings of the columns. The mappings can be adjusted here if needed. Scroll to the bottom of the list of columns, and locate the row that has the destination column set to SMTP, and the input column set to <ignore>. Select SMTP as the input column.

Finally, the Error Output option on the left shows what will be happen if errors occur during the insertion of the data. Unlike the Flat File Source, the OLE DB Destination does not allow column-specific error handling. Either the entire row is inserted, or the entire row fails.

Much like the control flow, the Data Flow designer window has associated Toolbox items that can be accessed via the vertical tab on the left pane. The Toolbox is organized by sources, transformations, and destinations.

The components in a data flow are connected with data flow paths, which are represented by arrows, just like with the control flow tasks. However, in the data flow, the arrows indicate the flow of data from one component to another, rather than the flow of execution. Data flow paths show the connection of one component's output to another component's input. Green arrows indicate the successful data output from a component, and red arrows indicate an output that contains data with errors. Different components offer different numbers of inputs and outputs, depending on their purpose. For example, Source components do not have inputs, as they are the starting point for data entering the data flow. Destination components may have no outputs, or they may have only an error output, because they are endpoints for data in a data flow.

Walkthrough of the Connection Managers

The Connection Managers window, located below the designer window, shows the source and destination connections. Right-click the SourceConnectionFlatFile connection manager and select Edit to see the properties of the source. In the General options, the filename and the format of the file are specified. Selecting the Columns option to the left will display the columns of the source, with the first 100 rows for verification. In the Advanced options window, you can adjust the details for each column, including the data type, the name of the column, and the length. You can click the Suggest Types button to scan the data and adjust the data type. Finally, use the Preview option window to preview the first 200 rows to ensure that the data is being read properly.

Editing the DestinationConnectionOLEDB connection shows the configuration setting of the destination. In this case, under the Connection options, the provider is shown as Native OLE DB\SQL Native Client 10.0. The server name is specified, as well as the form of authentication to use and the database to connect to. A Test Connection button lets you verify whether the connection is configured successfully. The All options window allows you to set the configuration at a very detailed level, such as encryption or timeout settings.

Interestingly, the specific table within the database is not specified in the destination connection manager. The connection is to the database rather than the table. The table into which the data will be inserted is specified at the item level in the data flow.

Running a Package

One of the nice features of the Business Intelligence Development Studio interface is the capability to run the package in the UI. This allows you to test and debug packages in a controlled environment before unleashing them on production.

The Control Flow and Data Flow windows of the package show the graphical view of the tasks in the package. In the graphical view of the flows, the status of the box is reflected in the color of the box:

- Green—Task Successful
- Yellow—Task in Progress
- Red—Task Failed

The Progress tab of the package shows the detailed progress, including useful information such as phase start and end, the percentage complete, and key diagnostic information. Within this window, it is easy to copy any message to paste it into a search or documentation. This information will be available even after ending debugging of the package, on the Execution Results tab.

> **Caution**
>
> The shortcut for running the debugger is the F5 key. This key conflicts with the standard Refresh key, which is also F5. This means if you attempt to refresh the screen using the standard shortcut key, the package may unexpectedly execute.
>
> Be careful when refreshing in the Business Intelligence Development Studio.

The package in the designer runs in debugging mode. To start debugging the package, follow these steps:

1. Launch the Business Intelligence Development Studio.
2. Open the Customer Project created earlier.
3. Click the CustomerImport.dtsx in the Solution Explorer.
4. Select Debug, Start Debugging to run the package.
5. The CustomerImport package control flow Preparation SQL Task 1 will change to yellow and then to red, indicating a problem in the execution of the package.
6. Review the messages in the Output window in the lower-right corner. In particular, note the message "There is already an object named 'Customers' in the database."
7. Select the Data Flow tab and note that the data flow items have not executed, as they are still white (rather than yellow, green, or red).
8. From the menu, select Debug, Stop Debugging to halt the execution.

The problem is that the Customers table was already created earlier. This table could be manually deleted, but maybe it should be dropped as part of the package execution on a normal basis. To do this, the control flow of the CustomerImport package will be adjusted to drop the Customers table. To add this task to the control flow, follow these steps:

1. With the CustomerImport package Control Flow tab selected, click the Toolbox tab.
2. Select the Execute SQL Task control flow item and drag it to the Control Flow window. Position the task above the Preparation SQL Task 1.

> **Note**
>
> Two errors will come up immediately in the Error List, which are validation errors. One indicates that no connection manager is specified, and the other indicates that validation errors exist.
>
> These errors are normal and will be resolved as the task is configured.

3. Edit the newly created task by right-clicking it and selecting Edit.

4. In the Name field, enter **Drop Customers Table SQL Task**. Enter this same text into the Description field.

5. In the Connection drop–down list, select the DestinationConnectionOLEDB connection manager.

6. In the SQLStatement field, click the button to expand the field and enter the text: `drop table[dbo].[Customers]`

7. Click OK to close the SQLStatement window. Click OK again to close the Task Editor.

8. On the Drop Customers Table SQL Task, there is a green arrow. Click the arrow and drag it to the top of the Preparation SQL Task. Click to attach the arrow.

9. Save the project.

The control flow for the package should now have the Drop Customers SQL Task connected to the Preparation SQL Task 1, and the Preparation SQL Task 1 should be connected to the Data Flow Task 1 by green arrows. There should be no errors in the Error List.

Now the CustomerImport package can be run again using the menu command Debug, Start Debugging. The control flow steps will change from white to yellow as they execute, then from yellow to green as they complete successfully. The Data Flow Task 1 will fail during this execution. The status of the data flow can be seen by selecting the Data Flow tab in the designer. The Destination - Customers destination component will be red, indicating that the error occurred there. Selecting the Progress tab will display the detailed execution results of the package. The problem can be identified by scrolling through these results. There are three error messages, designated by the red exclamation points. The errors indicate that the column that was renamed from EmailAddress to SMTP is not found on the destination table. To correct this, the Preparation SQL Task 1 needs to be updated.

1. Select Debug, Stop Debugging to stop the package execution.

2. Select the Control Flow tab, then right-click the Preparation SQL Task 1 and choose Edit.

3. In the SQLStatement field, click the button to expand the field and change the line reading "`[EmailAddress] varchar(50),`" to "`[SMTP] varchar(50),`".

4. Click OK, and then OK again to exit the Task Editor.

Run the package again by selecting Debug, Start Debugging from the menu. The package should execute successfully, with all control flow task and data flow components turning green.

The tabs can be changed during package debugging. The Control Flow tab is useful to observe where the package is in its execution, and the Data Flow tab can be used to observe the data movement in a data flow. The color coordination helps identify where the package is in its execution, which is very useful in large or complex packages.

Another useful tab is the Progress tab in the design window. The Progress tab shows the detailed progress of each task in the control and each component in the data flows. It includes start and stop times, as well as detailed activities and percentages of completion. In the case of the Drop Customers Table SQL Task that was added to the package, the actual SQL query can be seen. As illustrated earlier, this information can be very useful for debugging packages.

Successful execution of the package can also be verified by reviewing the Output window, which gives a more concise view of the package status than the Progress window. If the Output window is not visible, it can be displayed by selecting View, Output from the menu. The window should show a series of messages (the first and last three messages are shown) similar to the following:

```
SSIS package "CustomerImport.dtsx" starting.
....
Information: 0x4004300B at Data Flow Task 1,SSIS.Pipeline:
"component "Destination - Customers" (94)" wrote 2058 rows.
Information: 0x40043009 at Data Flow Task 1,SSIS.Pipeline:
Cleanup phase is beginning.
SSIS package "CustomerImport.dtsx" finished: Success.
```

The last line indicates that the package completed successfully. The third message from the bottom indicates that 2,058 rows were written to the destination, in this case the Customers table in the AdventureWorks2008 database.

After the execution has been verified, select Debug, Stop Debugging to return to design mode. Even after exiting the debugging mode, the previous package execution results can be reviewed in the Execution Results tab of the design window.

Caution

Even though the package executed in the SSIS Designer in debugging mode, the changes to the data were real. The data was read from the customers.txt file, the Customers table in the AdventureWorks2008 database was deleted, and a new table was created with the data from customers.txt. Any data in the original Customers table is lost.

When developing packages and projects, it is important to use a development database server to ensure there is no impact to production data.

Now that the package has been run, the next step is to save it where it can be used in production. It is rare to execute packages in Business Intelligence Development Studio for production use. See "Deploying the Package" later in this chapter for ways to import and export, store, and execute packages that are created in the designer.

Enhancing Packages

This section will discuss various ways that SSIS packages can be modified to include additional functionality. This will include performing additional transformations on the data, logging messages from the package, and enabling packages to run on multiple servers without modification to the package files.

Transforming Data

In the CustomerImport package, the data was transferred without any transformation. This section will examine how the data can be transformed while being transferred.

Suppose there is a request to import the Customer data into the AdventureWorks2008 database, but the data owner wants the customers partitioned into two separate tables. One table (HighIncomeCustomers) will contain the customers with a yearly income of $100,000 or more, and the other table (ModerateIncomeCustomers) will contain customers with less than a yearly income of $100,000.

The CustomerImport package will need to be modified to support this. This requires a conditional split, which is essentially a case statement based on the yearly income.

The first step is to adjust the control flow. In the Control Flow designer of the CustomerImport package, do the following:

1. Copy and paste the Drop Customers Table SQL Task.

2. Next, edit the Drop Customers Table SQL Task, changing the Name and Description to `Drop HighIncomeCustomers Table SQL Task`.

3. Edit the SQLStatement to change the `[dbo].[Customers]` to `[dbo].[HighIncomeCustomers]`.

4. Edit the second Drop Customers Table SQL Task (named Drop Customers Table SQL Task 1), changing the Name and Description to `Drop ModerateIncomeCustomers Table SQL Task`.

5. Edit the SQLStatement to change the `[dbo].[Customers]` to `[dbo].[ModerateIncomeCustomers]`.

6. Copy and paste the Preparation SQL Task 1.

7. Edit the first Preparation SQL Task 1, changing the Name and Description to `HighIncomeCustomers Preparation SQL Task`.

8. Edit the SQLStatement to change the [dbo].[Customers] to `[dbo].[HighIncomeCustomers]`.

9. Edit the second Preparation SQL Task 1 (named Preparation SQL Task 1 1), changing the Name and Description to `ModerateIncomeCustomers Preparation SQL Task`.

10. Edit the SQLStatement to change the `[dbo].[Customers]` to `[dbo].[ModerateIncomeCustomers]`.

11. Remove the existing arrows between the tasks by highlighting them and pressing Delete.

12. Drag the tasks into order with the drop tasks first, the preparation tasks next, and finally the Data Flow Task.

13. Select each task starting at the top and then drag the green arrow on the task to make them sequential.

14. Save the package as `CustomerImport2.dtsx`, by selecting File, Save CustomerImport.dtsx As. When prompted to rename the object, choose Yes.

The control flow should now look like the control flow shown in Figure 3.4. The boxes in the figure have been adjusted to improve the readability.

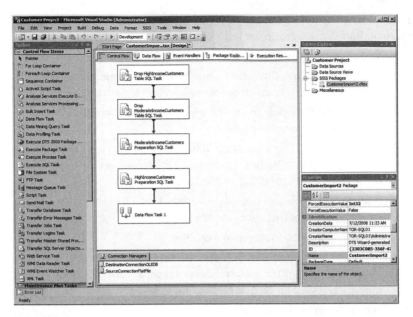

FIGURE 3.4
The CustomerImport2 package control flow.

The next adjustment to the package is to change the data flow. This is where the actual work of splitting the customers tasks place.

In the Data Flow designer of the CustomerImport2 package, do the following to set up the conditional split:

1. Drag the Conditional Split item from the Toolbox.

2. Rename the Conditional Split to Conditional Split on Yearly Income. This can be done from the Properties window by setting the Name property, or by selecting the Conditional Split and pressing F2.

3. Remove the existing arrow between the Source Customers_txt source and the destination by highlighting it and pressing Delete.

4. Select the Source Customers_txt source and then click the green arrow. Drag the arrow to the Conditional Split component.

5. Edit the Conditional Split item.

6. Expand the Type Casts folder on the right and drag the (DT_I4) type cast to the first Condition Field. The Output Name will automatically be labeled Case 1.

7. Expand the Columns folder and drag the Yearly Income column to the end of the condition for Case 1.

8. Expand the Operators folder and drag the Greater Than or Equal To (>=) operator to the end of the condition for Case 1.

9. Enter **100000** after the >= operator. Click the Output Name column, and the Condition should be black, indicating that it parsed correctly and that the data types match. The condition should be (DT_I4)[YearlyIncome]>=100000.

10. Copy the entire condition for Case 1, and paste it into the Condition field immediately below the first one. The Output Name will be labeled Case 2.

11. Change the operator from Greater Than or Equal To (>=) to Less Than (<). The condition should be (DT_I4)[YearlyIncome]<100000. The condition should be black, indicating that it parsed correctly.

12. Change the Output Name Case 1 to High Income and the Case 2 to Moderate Income. Click OK to save the changes.

The Conditional Split item is now ready to split the customers between high income and moderate income. The next step is to set up the destinations and link them to the conditional split to complete the flow.

To set up the destinations, follow these steps:

1. Copy and paste the Destination - Customers item to create a second one.

2. Rename the first Destination - Customers to Destination - High Income Customers.

3. Select the Conditional Split component, and drag the green line to Destination - High Income Customers. Select High Income from the Output Selection dialog, and click OK.

4. Edit the Destination - High Income Customers destination, and click the New button next to the name of the table or view the drop–down list.

5. On the first line, change the text [Destination - High Income Customers] to [HighIncomeCustomers] and click OK, then click OK again to save the item.

6. Rename the second Destination - Customers 1 to Destination - Moderate Income Customers.

7. Select the Conditional Split component, and drag the green line to Destination - Moderate Income Customers. Select Moderate Income from the Output Selection dialog, and click OK.

8. Edit the Destination - Moderate Income Customers and click the New button next to the Name of the table or view the drop–down list.

9. On the first line, change the text [Destination - Moderate Income Customers] to [ModerateIncomeCustomers] and click OK, then click OK again to save the item.

10. Drag the tasks into order with the Source - Customers_txt item first, followed by the Conditional Split next, and finally, the two Destinations next to each other on the same line.

11. Save the package.

The data flow should now look like the flow in Figure 3.5. Again, the boxes have been adjusted to improve the readability of the flow.

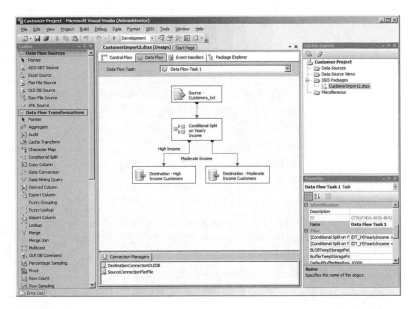

FIGURE 3.5
The CustomerImport2 package data flow.

The CustomerImport2 package is now ready to execute. Clicking Debug, Start Debugging executes the package. The package executes and shows the following messages in the Output window.

```
SSIS package "CustomerImport2.dtsx" starting.
....
Information: 0x4004300B at Data Flow Task 1,SSIS.Pipeline:
"component "Destination - High Income Customers" (94)" wrote 210
rows.
```

```
Information: 0x4004300B at Data Flow Task 1,SSIS.Pipeline:
"component "Destination - Moderate Income Customers" (252)" wrote
1848 rows.
Information: 0x40043009 at Data Flow Task 1,SSIS.Pipeline:
Cleanup phase is beginning.
SSIS package "CustomerImport2.dtsx" finished: Success.
```

The results of the execution can also be viewed graphically in the Data Flow design window when you are debugging the package in the Business Intelligence Development Studio. This view, shown in Figure 3.6, is a color-coded representation of the data flow, as discussed before. In this instance, the graphic also shows the count of rows output at each step. In the figure, the number of rows from the source is 2,058. At the output of the conditional split, 210 rows went to the high income table and 1,848 rows went to the moderate income table. This information matches the results in the Output window.

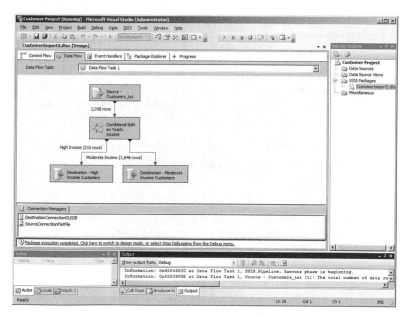

FIGURE 3.6
Graphical view of the data flow execution.

This example illustrates how easy it is to transform and manipulate the data during the data flow. A multitude of different data flow transformations exist, which are discussed in the "Data Flow" section near the beginning of the chapter.

Adding Logging

During the execution of the package, it might be important to log what is happening inside the package. Logging can be enabled for an entire package or for a single container or task, since a task is considered to be a container by SSIS.

To add logging to the CustomerImport2 package, follow these steps:

1. From the menu, select SSIS, Logging.

2. Enable logging by checking the top-level package item in the Containers window, in this case the CustomerImport2.

3. Select the Provider type for the log. In this case, use the SSIS log provider for Text files.

4. Click Add. A row will be added to the list of logs. Ensure that the check box under the Name column on the new row is checked.

5. In the window, click Configuration and use the drop-down list to select New Connection.

6. In the File Connection Manager Editor, from the Usage Type drop-down list, select Create File.

7. Enter the filename into the File field, in this case c:\data\CustomerImport2.txt. If c:\data does not exist, it will need to be created before the package is executed. Then click OK.

8. Click the Details tab to select the events to log.

9. Select the check box next to the Events column to select all the events.

10. Click OK to save the logging configuration.

11. Save the package.

To test the logging, debug the package. After the package has executed, review the log file CustomerImport2.txt. It should contain complete details of the package execution. Logging all events does incur some overhead, however, so in real world implementations, a subset of events should be used. The most important events for troubleshooting are the OnError, OnWarning, OnPreExecute, and OnPostExecute events. In many scenarios, these provide enough information to identify the source of a problem.

Using Expressions

Expressions are a very powerful feature of SSIS that allows packages to adjust their properties at runtime. They are a key element in developing flexible packages that do not require manual intervention each time they are run.

For an example of using expressions, consider the logging that was added to the CustomerImport2 package. If the package is executed again, the log entries for the new execution will be appended to the existing file. In a production environment, where the package may be executed nightly or multiple times a day, this can result in very large and difficult-to-read log files. However, expressions can be used to start a new log file each day that the package is run. To modify the CustomerImport2 package to use an expression, follow these steps:

1. Select the `CustomerImport2.txt` connection manager in the Connection Managers window. Press F4 to ensure that the Properties window is open.

2. Locate the Expressions item in the list of properties. Select it, and click the ellipsis button (...) to open the Property Expressions Editor.

3. Under Property, select ConnectionString. The ConnectionString property holds the filename for File connection managers.

4. Click the ellipsis button next to the Expressions column.

5. In the Expression Builder dialog, type the following into the Expression field:

```
"C:\\data\\CustomerImport2_" + ((DT_WSTR,5)YEAR(GETDATE()))
+ "-" + ((DT_WSTR,5)MONTH(GETDATE())) + "-" +
((DT_WSTR,5)DAY(GETDATE())) + ".txt".
```

The backslashes need to be doubled, as they are escape characters in the SSIS expression language.

6. Click the Evaluate Expression button to see the results of the expression. It should appear similar to `c:\data\CustomerImport2_2008-7-31.txt`, but with the current date.

7. Click OK to close the Expression Builder, and OK again to close the Property Expressions Editor.

If the package is executed again, a new log file will be created in the data directory, with the current date appended to the filename. This is a simple example of using expressions to make a package more dynamic. Because they can be applied to task properties, selected data flow component properties, and variables, they offer a great deal of power in developing the package.

Sending Email

It can be useful to have the package notify someone when it completes. For example, it might be desirable to send an email message when the CustomerImport2 package completes.

Follow these steps:

1. Select the Control Flow tab in the designer window of the CustomerImport2 package.

2. Drag the Send Mail Task from the Toolbox to the Control Flow designer window.

3. Select the Data Flow Task.

4. Select the green arrow and drag it to the Send Mail Task.

5. Edit the Send Mail Task and select the Mail options.

6. From the SmtpConnection drop-down list, select New Connection.

7. In the SMTP Server field, enter the fully qualified domain name (FQDN) of the SMTP server, such as smtphost.companyabc.com. Then click OK.

8. In the From field, enter the From email address.

9. In the To field, enter the destination email address.

10. In the Subject field, enter a subject, such as `CustomerImport2 Completed`.

11. In the MessageSource field, enter a message body.

12. Click OK to save the settings and then save the package.

The modified CustomerImport2 should have the Data Flow Task 1 task connected to the Send Mail Task by a green arrow. The package will send an email after the Data Flow Task completes. Notice in the Connection Manager window that there is a new SMTP Connection Manager.

The feature could be used to send an email when the control flow starts, ends, or even in intermediate stages as required.

Adding Error Handling

In spite of the best-laid plans, errors will occur during the execution of packages. However, errors in the package can be handled through the use of events.

To notify someone if the CustomerImport2 package experiences an error, execute the following steps:

1. Open the CustomerImport2 package created previously.

2. Select the Event Handler tab.

3. The CustomerImport2 executable (the package) and the `OnError` event handler are selected by default. The drop–down list shows other event handler types.

4. Click the link in the middle of the pane, which reads "Click here to create an 'OnError' event handler for executable 'CustomerImport2'."

5. Drag the Send Mail Task from the Toolbox to the Event Handler window.

6. Edit the Send Mail Task and select the Mail options.

7. From the SmtpConnection drop-down list, select the SMTP Connection Manager. This is the same one created previously, which will be reused for this task.

8. In the From field, enter the From email address.

9. In the To field, enter the destination email address.

10. In the Subject field, enter a subject, such as `CustomerImport2 Error`.

11. In the MessageSource, enter a message body.

12. Click OK to save the settings, then save the package.

To introduce an error to test the error handling, rename the source file `Customers.txt` in the directory `C:\Program Files\Microsoft SQL Server\100\Samples\Integration Services\Package Samples\ExecuteSQLStatementsInLoop Sample\Data Files\` to `Customers.tst`. This will cause an error when the package attempts to import the data.

After renaming the source data file, running the package will cause an error and the `OnError` event handler will trigger and execute the Send Mail Task. Interestingly, the task color will show the execution status as with any other task. If no errors exist, the event handler tasks remain white. If an error occurs, the event handler tasks will change color to reflect the execution (yellow) and their completion (green).

Restore the original filename for the source data file Customers.txt to run the package. The package should now generate the successful completion email message and not the error email message.

Although this example is a single simple task, more complex control and data flows can be created to handle error events in a more sophisticated fashion. All the tasks that are available in the Control Flow designer are also available in the event handler, including the ability to add data flows to the event handler.

Adding Configurations

Many of the configuration settings in packages are static, meaning they don't need to change between environments. But the servers to which the package will be deployed may have different configurations and settings, which can cause the package to fail. A different package could be created with different settings for each server, but this would become a maintenance headache. Package configurations are a feature in SSIS that help make packages portable, meaning that they can be moved between environments without having to modify the package itself. Package configurations allow you to store some settings for the package outside of the package itself, creating a package with dynamic settings that make it adaptable to the local conditions.

Package configurations can come from the following sources:

- Environment variables
- Registry entries
- SQL Server
- Parent package variables
- XML configuration file

An example of a static setting is the CustomerImport2 package using the SQL Server 2008 instance TOR-SQL01\INSTANCE01. Perhaps this is the development instance of the database. After the package has developed to a sufficient point, it needs to be moved to a QA environment for additional testing. This QA environment is in a second instance of SQL Server 2008, TOR-SQL01\INSTANCE02. To address this problem, the server name can be stored in an XML configuration file. This allows the package to be deployed to different servers easily by updating the configuration file, without having to customize the package for each environment.

The steps needed to accomplish this are as follows:

1. Launch the SSIS Designer and open the Customer project.
2. Open the CustomerImport2 package.
3. Select SSIS, Package Configurations.
4. Check the Enable Package Configurations check box.
5. Click the Add button. Click Next.
6. From the Configuration Type drop-down list, select the XML Configuration file type.
7. Enter `c:\projects\Customer Project\Customer Project\CustomerImport2.dtsconfig` into the Configuration filename field. Then click Next.

> **Note**
>
> SSIS does not have full support for relative paths. Instead, the full path to the configuration file should be entered here. The path to the configuration file can be modified when the package is deployed or executed.

8. In the Objects window, locate and expand the DestinationConnectionOLEDB connection manager in the Connection Managers folder. Expand the Properties folder that appears under it.

9. Select the ConnectionString property.

10. Click Next.

11. Enter **Destination Connection Configuration** for the Configuration name. The result should look like the screen in Figure 3.7.

12. Click Finish.

13. Click Close to close the Package Configurations Organizer.

14. Save the project.

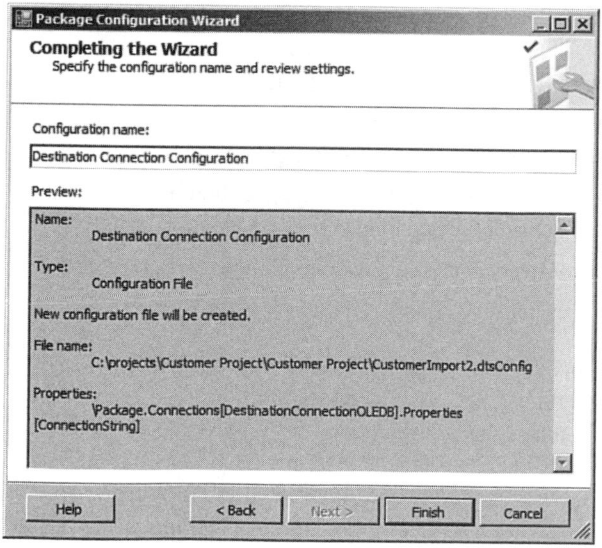

FIGURE 3.7
Package configurations.

The package configuration will now dynamically replace the destination database connection string with the contents of the XML configuration file at runtime.

Before deploying the package, it is important to test that the configuration works in the SSIS Designer. Configurations are loaded in the design environment, as well as at runtime. To test it, follow these steps:

1. Open the configuration file (`c:\projects\Customer Project\` `Customer Project\CustomerImport2.dtsconfig`) in a text editor, such as Notepad, or in Business Intelligence Development Studio.

TIP

The XML syntax for the configuration can be a little confusing, but BIDS makes it much easier to understand. Not only does it have syntax highlighting, but it includes an autoformatting feature that makes the XML much more readable. To use it, just open the XML document, click inside it, and press Crtl+K, then Ctrl+D.

---

2. Locate the `<ConfiguredValue>` and `</ConfiguredValue>` tags within the XML. The connection string is contained between these two tags.

3. Update the text in the connection string that reads `Data Source=TOR-SQL01\INSTANCE01;` to `Data Source=TOR-SQL01\INSTANCE02;`.

4. Save the configuration file. Now close and reopen the CustomerImport2 package in the SSIS Designer.

5. Select the DestinationConnectionOLEDB connection manager, and edit it. The Server Name field should show `TOR-SQL01\INSTANCE02`.

6. Now open the configuration file again, and change the server instance back to the original value.

The fact that BIDS applies the configurations at design time makes it easy to verify that they are working correctly. The package's destination server can now be modified by altering the configuration file. When executing the package outside of the BIDS environment, a command-line switch can be applied that allows the package to use a different configuration file at runtime. This will be discussed further in the section "Running Packages."

> **TIP**
>
> A common problem encountered with configurations is related to passwords. For security reasons, SSIS will not save passwords in any type of configuration. For example, if a configuration is created for a connection string, and the connection string uses a password instead of Windows Authentication, the password will be removed from the connection string that is stored in the configuration.
>
> The workaround for this is to open the configuration directly, using the appropriate tool for the configuration type (Notepad for XML, SQL Server Management Studio for SQL Server, and so on) and add the password into the connection string directly. Be aware that the configuration should be stored securely if it will contain passwords.

Adding Maintenance Tasks

Packages are not just for ETL (extraction, transformation, and loading). Packages are very useful in the maintenance of SQL Server 2008. You can execute maintenance tasks such as backing up a database, rebuilding indexes, or shrinking a database. These tasks can be executed in a series and include conditional elements to control the execution.

> **Note**
>
> Many of the maintenance tasks can be executed in a Maintenance Plan in SQL Server Management Studio. This provides a rich wizard-driven interface to create and modify maintenance plans to back up, reindex, shrink, and perform all the other maintenance tasks. These are the same SSIS maintenance tasks available in the BIDS environment.
>
> SQL Server Management Studio is the preferred method of running maintenance in SQL Server 2008. However, when specific maintenance tasks need to be executed in line with control flows in a package or in response to errors in a package, BIDS can be used to add the appropriate tasks to the package.

Deploying and Running Integration Services Packages

After a package is designed and tested, the package will need to be deployed to an instance of SQL Server Integration Services. You can run the packages from the SSIS Designer, but they will not perform as quickly and can't be scheduled from that interface. Running packages on the server will be discussed in the "Running Packages" section later in this chapter.

Two factors are involved in deploying packages. The first is choosing a storage location for the packages. The second is how to deploy the packages to the chosen storage location.

Storing Packages

Packages can be stored in the SQL Server MSDB database, SSIS package storage, or the file system.

- **MSDB**—Packages stored in the MSDB database are stored in the sysssispackages table. Folders can be created in MSDB to help organize the packages.

> **Note**
>
> In SQL Server 2005, SSIS packages were stored in the sysdtspackages90 table.

- **Package Store**—Packages stored in the Package Store database are stored by default in the %Program Files%\Microsoft SQL Server\100\DTS\Packages\ directory. Folders can be created in the Package Store to help organize the packages.

- **File System**—Packages stored in the file system can be located on any accessible drive and path. File system storage is not managed by the SSIS service. The administrator simply copies .dtsx files to the designated folder.

Both MSDB storage and the Package Store can be managed from SQL Server Management Studio by connecting the Integration Services instance. Folders can be used to organize the packages in both, and packages can be imported and exported from both locations through SQL Server Management Studio. The export features allow administrators to save packages to other SSIS instances, or to a file with a .dtsx extension. The exported file can be edited in BIDS. The Import feature can be used to import .dtsx files or packages from another SSIS instance to the local instance.

> **Note**
>
> Unfortunately, packages cannot be dragged and dropped within the folder structure of the SSIS storage. You must use the export and import feature to move the packages around.
>
> However, you can drag and drop files within the native Windows file system. When you do, the changes are reflected in the SSIS file system folder.

Deploying Packages

Packages can be deployed in three ways:

- Manually
- Using a Package Manifest
- Using DTUTIL.exe

Each method has its advantages and disadvantages. Manual deployment requires little preparation, but does not scale well if deploying to many servers. Packaged deployments are very customizable and can adapt to different server configurations, but require effort to create the deployment packages.

Manual Deployment

Manual deployment is straightforward and consists of importing the package into the SSIS, either to the File System storage or the SQL Server storage (MSDB).

To import a package in SQL Server Management Studio, follow these steps:

1. Open SQL Server Management Studio.

2. Select Integration Services from the Server Type drop-down list and click Connect.

3. Expand the Stored Packages folder and right-click the File System folder. Select Import Package.

4. Select the location of the package, in this case File System. Enter the path and filename for the package. Alternatively, click the button next to the Package path field to browse for a package. Browse to the locations of the CustomerImport2 package, which is in C:\Projects\Customer Projects\Customer Project\, and select the CustomerImport2.dtsx file. Click Open.

5. Click in the Package Name field. The package name CustomerImport2 will be filled in automatically, but can be changed if needed. Click OK to import the package.

The package will be displayed in the File System folder and can now be run or scheduled from there.

TIP

An alternative to going through the import process described in the preceding steps is to simply copy the .dtsx file to the file system directory, by default %Program Files%\Microsoft SQL Server\100\DTS\Packages. This can be useful if you want to deploy an entire folder of packages at once. However, this method can't be used if you want to store the packages in MSDB.

Building a Package Deployment Utility

Deploying the package requires that a deployment utility be built. This utility is the executable that will install the package on a target server.

To build the deployment utility, execute the following steps:

1. Right-click on the Customer Project in the Solution Explorer window and select Properties.

2. Select the Deployment Utility option page.

3. Change the CreateDeploymentUtility value to True.

4. Note the DeploymentOutputPath option. This is the location where the utility will be built underneath the project directory structure. Click OK to save the settings.

5. Select Build, Build Customer Project. This will create the files needed to deploy the package to another server.

The build will have created three files: `Customer Project.SSISDeploymentManifest`, `CustomerImport2.dtsx`, and `CustomerImport2.dtsConfig`. These will be located in the project directory, specifically `C:\Projects\Customer Project\Customer Project\bin\Deployment\`.

Note

The deployment build is for the entire project, so all the packages in the project will be deployed to the destination server. This allows a set of packages that deliver a solution to be bound and installed together as a unit.

The next step is to install the package on the destination server.

1. Copy the files in `C:\Projects\Customer Project\Customer Project\bin\Deployment\` to the destination server, in this case TOR-SQL02.

2. On the destination server, in this case TOR-SQL02, double-click the `Customer Project.SSISDeploymentManifest` file. This launches the Package Installation Wizard. Click Next on the first page.

3. Leave the default File System deployment and click Next.

4. Ensure that the folder is `C:\Program Files\Microsoft SQL Server\100\DTS\Packages\Customer Project`, and click Next.

5. Click Next to install the package.

6. The package configuration file can be updated on this page. Expand the Properties item and update the text under the Value column from `Data Source=TOR-SQL01\INSTANCE01` in the connection string to `Data Source=TOR-SQL02`. Then click next.

7. Click Finish to close the Summary window.

The package installation can be verified by launching the SQL Server Management Studio. The Customer Project and the CustomerImport2 package should be visible in Stored Packages, File System. The package can now be run or scheduled as described in "Running Packages," later in this chapter.

Using DTUTIL

DTUTIL is a command-line utility that can be used to deploy packages, among other things. It has the ability to apply a password to the package when it is deployed, regenerate package identifiers (used to uniquely identify a package for logging purposes), and to digitally sign packages. Unlike the package manifest, it can be run without requiring user interaction, making it ideal for large-scale, automated deployments.

Securing SSIS Packages

SQL Server Integration Services supports a number of security features. These security features protect the packages from unauthorized execution, modification, sensitive information, and even protect the entire contents of the packages. This section describes the database roles and the protection levels for packages.

Note

In addition to the security that SSIS provides to packages, you must also be concerned with other areas of security with regard to packages. Packages frequently use data files, configuration files, and log files. These files are not protected by the security mechanisms within SSIS.

To ensure that confidential information is not exposed, you must protect the locations of these files as well. Typically, you do this at the operating system level through Access Control List (ACL) controls and the Encrypting File System (EFS).

SSIS has three database roles for controlling access to packages. They roughly fall into the categories of administrator, user, and operator. If more granularity is needed in the rights assignment, you can create user-defined roles.

The fixed database level roles and their rights are listed in Table 3.6.

Table 3.6   **Fixed Security Roles**

Role	Description
db_ssisadmin or sysadmin	This role gives users all the available SSIS rights. This includes enumerating, viewing, executing, importing, exporting, and deleting any package.
db_ssisltduser	This role gives users the ability to enumerate all packages. However, the user is limited to viewing, executing, importing, exporting, and deleting only the user's own packages.
db_ssisoperator	This role gives users the ability to enumerate, view, execute, and export any package.
Windows Administrators	Windows Administrators can view all currently executing packages, and stop the execution of any package.

Protection levels are set on packages when they are created in the Business Intelligence Development Studio or the wizards. These protection levels prevent the unauthorized execution or modification of packages. Protection levels can be updated on packages when they are imported into the SSIS package store.

The protection levels refer to sensitive information in what they protect. These are typically passwords in connection managers, but can include any task property or variable that is marked as sensitive.

The options for protection levels are listed in the following sections.

Do Not Save Sensitive (DontSaveSensitive)

The DontSaveSensitive option suppresses sensitive information in the package when it is saved. This protection level does not encrypt; instead, it prevents properties that are marked sensitive from being saved with the package and therefore makes the sensitive data unavailable when the package is closed and reopened. This protection level is often combined with Package Configurations to store the secure information.

Caution

Configurations must have secure information manually entered, as SSIS will not save sensitive data to a configuration. After sensitive information has been added, the configuration needs to be protected, as the SSIS security mechanisms do not apply to configuration files.

Encrypt All / Sensitive with Password (`EncryptAllWithPassword` / `EncryptSensitiveWithPassword`)

The `EncryptAllWithPassword` or `EncryptSensitiveWithPassword` option encrypts the package by using a password the user supplies when the package is created or exported. To open the package in SSIS Designer or run the package by using the DTEXEC command-prompt utility, the user must provide the package password. Using the `EncryptAll*` option encrypts the entire package, and the `EncryptSensitive*` option will encrypt just the items designated as sensitive.

Encrypt All / Sensitive with User Key (`EncryptAllWithUserKey` / `EncryptSensitiveWithUserKey`)

The `EncryptSensitiveWithUserKey` option is the default setting for packages. The `EncryptAllWithUserKey` or `EncryptSensitiveWithUserKey` option encrypts the package by using a key based on the user profile. Only the user who created or exported the package can decrypt the information in the package, preventing other users from using the package with the sensitive information included. Using the `EncryptAll*` option encrypts the entire package, and the `EncryptSensitive*` option will encrypt just the items designated as sensitive. This Protection Level option can create challenges in real-world scenarios, as only a single user can use or modify the package.

Rely on Server Storage for Encryption (`ServerStorage`)

The `ServerStorage` option protects the whole package using SQL Server database roles. This option is supported only when a package is saved to the SQL Server MSDB database. It is not supported when a package is saved to the file system from Business Intelligence Development Studio.

Running Packages

You can trigger the packages from within the SQL Server Management Studio and monitor their execution progress in detail.

Using Management Studio to Run Packages

To run a package (using the CustomerImport2 package) within SSIS, do the following:

1. Open SQL Server Management Studio.
2. Select Integration Services from the Server Type drop-down list and click Connect.
3. Expand the Stored Packages folder, then the File System folder.

4. Right-click the CustomerImport package imported earlier and select Run Package. The Execute Package Utility runs.

5. In the General options page, you will see the package source, the server, the authentication, and the package name.

6. Click the Reporting options page to see the reporting options available.

7. Click the Set Values options page to see the options available. Using this page, properties on the package can be overridden at runtime. This is a useful feature for changing values that may need to be unique for each execution of the package.

8. Click the Command Line options page to see the command-line version of the execution. This capability is useful to automate the package execution in the future.

Note

You can add parameters to the command line by selecting the Edit the Command Line Manually option.

---

9. Click Execute to run the package.

10. The Package Execution Progress window opens, displaying the package progress and information. This is the same information displayed on the Progress tab in Business Intelligence Development Studio. The message should indicate that 210 rows were written to the HighIncomeCustomers table, and 1,848 rows were written to the ModerateIncomeCustomers table.

11. Click Close to close the Progress window.

12. Click Close to close the Execute Package utility.

Note

The Execute Package Utility can be opened without using SQL Server Management Studio. Simply run DTEXECUI at a command prompt and it will open.

Caution

The Execute Package Utility is useful for setting up a package to execute. However, packages that report a large amount of information will run progressively slower when run from the Execute Package Utility. For this reason, it is better to execute large or long-running packages from DTEXEC (the command-line version of the Execute Package Utility) or from SQL Server Agent.

Also, running a package from SQL Server Management Studio through the Execute Package Utility or DTEXEC uses the local machine's resources to execute the package. If SQL Server Management Studio is connected to a remote server, the package is executed using the resources of the local machine, not the remote server. To ensure that the server resources are used, run the package from SQL Server Agent.

Using DTEXEC to Run Packages

DTEXEC is a command-line utility for executing packages. It supports all the options of the Execute Package Utility, but does not use a GUI. This makes it ideal for automating package executions. It can be used from a CmdExec step in a SQL Agent job, or from any tool capable of calling a command-line utility. The complete list of command-line switches for DTEXEC is available in Books Online.

Scheduling Packages

Packages can be scheduled to run automatically using the SQL Server Agent. The package needs to be accessible to the SQL Server Agent to be scheduled.

In this example, the CustomerImport2 package needs to be run every day at 6 a.m. to update the Customer table. To schedule a package for execution, follow these steps:

1. Open SQL Server Management Studio.

2. Connect to the Database Engine of the SQL Server.

3. Right-click on SQL Server Agent and select New, Job.

4. In the General options page, enter the name of the job, in this example `Daily Customer Update`.

5. Select the Steps option page and click New to create a new step.

6. Enter the Step name, in the example `Update Customer`.

7. In the Type drop-down list, select SQL Server Integration Services Package.

8. In the Package Source drop-down list, select the SSIS Package Store.

9. In the Server drop-down list, select TOR-SQL01 as the server name.

10. Click the Package selection button to the right of the Package field.

11. Browse the Select an SSIS Package window to find the CustomerImport2 package imported earlier. Then click OK.

12. Click OK to save the step.

13. Select the Schedules option page and click New to create a new job schedule.

14. In the Name field, enter **Daily at 6 AM**. In the Occurs drop-down list, select Daily. Change the Occurs Once at field to **6:00:00** AM.

15. Click OK to save the schedule, and click OK again to save the job.

The job will now run the SSIS package at 6 a.m. every day. The job is saved in the database and can be reviewed in the Jobs folder within the SQL Server Agent. You can test it by right-clicking on the job and selecting Start Job.

Jobs can run a series of packages in a sequence of steps and even with conditional branches that depend on the output of the preceding packages. This allows packages to be chained together to complete a larger task.

By default, packages will be run under the permissions of the SQL Agent account. If the packages need additional privileges, a proxy account can be used for the SQL Server Agent job, see the topic 'Creating SQL Server Agent Proxies' in Books Online.

Transferring Data with Integration Services

The Data Flow Task is the primary means of transferring data with SSIS. However, there are additional options for specific needs that DBAs face on a regular basis. Among the items available are the ability to copy databases and to perform bulk inserts of data.

Using the Copy Database Wizard

SSIS includes a Transfer Database Task that can be included in packages. This is useful if other tasks need to be performed in conjunction with the database transfer, as the SSIS package can be used to coordinate them. In addition to the Transfer Database Task, a database can be copied using the SQL Server Management Studio Copy Database Wizard. This process is useful if the database will only need to be copied once, or if the transfer of the database is all that needs to be accomplished. Follow these steps to copy the AdventureWorks database from TOR-SQL01\INSTANCE01 to TOR-SQL01\INSTANCE02 using the Copy Database Wizard:

1. Launch SQL Server Management Studio.

2. Connect to the source database server, in this case TOR-SQL01\INSTANCE01. Expand the Databases folder.

3. Right-click the AdventureWorks (not AdventureWorks2008) database and select Tasks, Copy Database. Click Next at the first page of the wizard.

4. Select the Source server, which should be the TOR-SQL01\INSTANCE01 server, and click Next.

5. Select the Destination server, which should be the TOR-SQL01\INSTANCE02 server, and click Next.

6. The default Transfer Method is to use the detach and attach method, which will bring the source database offline. Because this would be disruptive, select Use the SQL Management Object Method. This will keep the source database online. Click Next to continue.

7. Verify that the AdventureWorks database is selected, and click Next.

8. Change the option to drop the destination database if it already exists, which is the Drop Any Database option. This forces an overwrite of the database on the destination server. Click Next.

9. Don't select any additional objects to transfer. Ensure that Logins are not selected to transfer. Click Next.

10. Click Next to leave the package defaults. Then click Next to run immediately.

11. Review the choices and click Finish to execute the transfer.

Note

Depending on the security context that the SQL Agent account is run under, a proxy account may need to be specified that has access to both the source and destination databases.

This method is easy to use for a one-time copy of a database. Note that the wizard actually creates a package in the MSDB storage of the destination server, which can be seen by connecting to the SSIS on the destination server. This package can be run more than once, if there is a need to copy the database on a regular basis.

Using the Bulk Insert Task

The Bulk Insert Task can be used to import text files into SQL Server tables. The Bulk Insert Task is very efficient at loading large amounts of data, but can't perform any data conversion or transformations. The text file to be imported must be delimited, and can use a format file to define the rows and columns. To use it, follow these steps:

1. Launch the SSIS Designer and open the Customer project.

2. Create a new package by selecting Project, New SSIS Package.

3. Rename the package to `BulkInsertCustomer.dtsx` by right-clicking the package in the Solution Explorer, and selecting Rename. When prompted, select Yes to rename the package object.

4. Drag the Bulk Insert Task from the Toolbox to the Control Flow designer. Edit the task by right-clicking and selecting Edit.

5. Select the Connection option. Click the Connection drop-down list and select New Connection. In the Configure OLE DB Connection Manager dialog box, click New to create a new connection. Specify the Server name as TOR-SQL01\INSTANCE01 and the database as AdventureWorks2008. Click OK, and then click OK again to return to the Bulk Insert Task Editor.

6. In the Destination Table field, select the [AdventureWorks2008].[dbo].[Customers] table that was created in earlier samples.

7. Ensure that the ColumnDelimiter field is set to Tab.

8. Click the File drop-down list, and select New Connection. Set the Usage Type to Existing File, and browse to the `C:\Program Files\Microsoft SQL Server\100\Samples\Integration Services\Package Samples\ExecuteSQLStatementsInLoop Sample\Data  Files\Customers.txt` file. Click Open, and then OK to return to the Bulk Insert Task Editor.

9. Select the Options option to the left, and set the FirstRow field to 2, to skip the first row containing the column headers.

10. To see the package run, select Debug, Start Debugging. The package should run and the Bulk Insert Task should turn green.

Caution

The Bulk Insert Task will append the rows to what already exists in the table. To delete the existing rows first, add an Execute SQL Task to truncate the table first.

> **Note**
>
> There is also the Bulk Copy utility (bcp.exe), whichcan be used to manually import or export data from a table. The bcp utility bulk copies data from or to a data file from an existing table in a database.
>
> The Bulk Copy utility is less convenient than the wizards because it requires that the table be created in advance, and the command options are relatively obscure. However, it can be useful for getting information from older versions of SQL Server.

Summary

Packages and the Business Intelligence Development Studio provide a rich environment for creating packages for automating and controlling the movement of data. Packages are very useful, not only to import or export data but also to automate maintenance activities. The SSIS Designer is a graphical development interface that makes it easy for even the beginning DBA to create, test, and deploy packages.

Best Practices

Some important best practices from the chapter include the following:

- Debug and monitor progress of the package in the Business Intelligence Development Studio.
- Don't use the F5 shortcut key to try to refresh the screen, because it executes the current package instead.
- Use logging to track the package execution.
- Use the OnError event to handle and report errors in packages.
- Use manual package deployments for few packages and few servers.
- Use packaged deployments or DTUTIL for larger numbers of servers and packages.
- Use package configurations to dynamically adjust the settings of packages for multiple environments.
- Use expressions to make packages more dynamic.
- Use maintenance plans to set up maintenance for databases, rather than packages.
- Use package tasks to include specific maintenance tasks within packages.
- Use the Copy Database Wizard for one-time database transfers.

CHAPTER 4

Managing and Optimizing SQL Server 2008 Indexes

SQL Server 2008 uses indexes to structure and optimize access to data found within the tables of a database. Index design, maintenance, and optimization are key factors that contribute to how well a database performs. Although the lack of indexes or the use of poorly designed indexes, along with inadequate maintenance, can lead to performance degradation, well-designed and maintained indexes can significantly improve the overall performance of a database by reducing the cost associated with locating data.

When you are performing management and administrative tasks on indexes, it is important to understand the different options and powerful tools that help DBAs to make indexing management and optimization decisions.

What's New for Indexes with SQL Server 2008

- Filtered indexes have been introduced as a way of optimizing nonclustered indexes on a subset of data.

- The number of indexes that can be created per table has increased. Tables can now contain a total of 1,000 indexes per table, 1 clustered index, and up to 249 nonclustered indexes.

- A maximum of 249 XML indexes can be created.

- *Spatial data* is a new feature introduced in SQL Server 2008 for storing coordinate information pertaining to physical locations and geometric objects. SQL Server 2008 allows indexes to be created on spatial data stored within a table.

The Importance of Indexes

A well-planned indexing strategy allows fast and efficient access to the underlying data. Indexes can be created on tables or views and ideally allow SQL Server to locate and manage data more efficiently. When efficiency is improved, the amount of time each operation takes is reduced, along with the cost associated with performing the operation.

Index design is typically performed during development of the database application. The reason is that the ability to create effective indexes is based on understanding how application queries are coded and how the data is stored in the database. However, indexes also require management after the database application is deployed and as usage patterns emerge or change.

Managing and optimizing indexes as an ongoing process allows potential performance improvements without requiring changes to the underlying schema. As data is queried, the SQL Server Query Optimizer automatically determines the best method to access the data based on the type of operation and the available indexes.

How Indexes Work

The data within a SQL Server 2008 database is stored within tables. The data within a table is grouped together into allocation units based on the column data type. The data within each allocation unit is physically stored in 8KB pages.

Note

For efficiency, groups of eight pages are physically managed together. This 64KB group of pages is referred to as an *extent*.

Pages within a table store the actual data rows along with the different structures to facilitate locating the data. When the rows of data associated with a table are not logically sorted, the table is referred to as a *heap* structure.

When an index is created, the data in the heap can be rearranged and becomes part of the index, as in the case of a clustered index. An index can also be created as a separate structure that simply points to the location of the data in the heap or clustered index, as in the case of a nonclustered index. A new type of index is also available in SQL Server 2008; this new index can be created on spatial data columns in the table to improve the efficiency of spatial queries. In addition, filtered indexes can be generated to improve queries that select from a well-defined subset of data.

The different types of indexes have advantages and disadvantages along with different characteristics that need to be considered as part of the ongoing indexing maintenance strategy.

> **Note**
>
> By default, an index with a single partition is comparable to the organizational structure of tables and indexes in previous versions of SQL Server as it is stored within a single filegroup. If multiple partitions are leveraged, the index will span the partitions horizontally and can ultimately be placed in multiple filegroups for increased performance.

Heap Structures

Ultimately, a *heap* is a table without a clustered index where data is not stored in any particular order. A heap structure is often the least efficient method of querying data rows in a table because all rows in the table are scanned each time the data is queried, making it a laborious process. For example, when a specific row of data is needed or when a range of data is needed, all pages in the table are scanned to ensure the correct result is returned. A simile may help further explain heap structures. Searching for data on the heap structure would be like looking up a word in a dictionary that wasn't presented in alphabetical order or looking for a particular topic in a book that didn't contain an index. In any dictionary or book, an individual can look up the words "SQL Server" by scanning the words under the letter S—simple. On the other hand, if all words in a dictionary were stored based on a heap structure, the words would not be stored in a logical order, forcing people to search the dictionary page by page—ouch!

There are a few situations when the heap structure may be an efficient structure when dealing with small tables, infrequently accessed tables, or when large amounts of data are frequently written to or deleted from the table. The index maintenance cost can often outweigh any potential performance improvement on these types of tables. It is often recommended to avoid creating indexes on tables that fall into these categories.

Clustered Indexes

Clustered indexes are tables that have been sorted based on one or more table columns. Only one clustered index can be created for a table, and it is commonly placed on *key* columns or columns used frequently, such as the ones referenced by the WHERE clause. When a clustered index is created, the table is sorted into a *b-tree* structure, allowing SQL Server to quickly locate the correct data. Figure 4.1 shows an example of a clustered index based on b-tree storage structure.

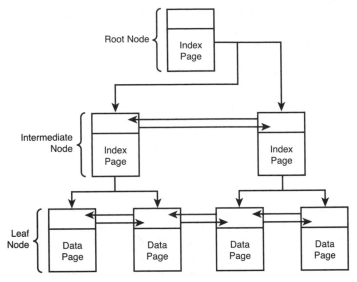

FIGURE 4.1
Clustered index b-tree structure.

The top of the index contains the root node, the starting position for the index. The intermediate level contains the index key data; the index data can point to other intermediate pages or the data in the leaf level. The leaf level nodes located at the bottom of the b-tree contain the actual table data. When the data in the table is queried, the Database Engine can quickly navigate the b-tree structure and locate specific data without having to scan each page.

Nonclustered Indexes

Nonclustered indexes are implemented as a separate b-tree structure that does not affect the pages in the underlying table. Unlike a clustered index, more than one nonclustered index can be placed on columns within a table. Figure 4.2 shows an example of a nonclustered index b-tree.

The top of the index contains the root node, the starting position for the index. However, unlike clustered indexes, a nonclustered index does not contain any data pages and does not modify the data in the source table. The index pages on the leaf node contain a *row locator* that references the data in the associated table.

If the underlying table is also clustered, as in a clustered index, leaf node pages in the nonclustered index point to the corresponding clustered index key. If the underlying table does not have a clustered index, the leaf node pages in the nonclustered index point to the corresponding row in the heap.

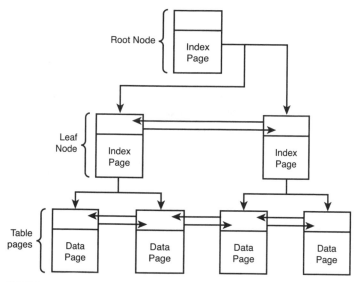

FIGURE 4.2
Nonclustered index b-tree structure.

Indexed Views

When a view is queried, the resulting data is materialized at runtime. Depending on the amount of data returned, a high cost can be associated with the materialization process. To reduce the cost of using complex views, you can create an index on a column in the view.

Note

The Query Optimizer may select a view index automatically, even if the view is not explicitly named in the FROM clause.

The data that would normally be materialized during runtime is stored are stored in the database based on the same format as the table. When the underlying data is changed, the related indexed views are automatically maintained just as clustered and nonclustered indexes are maintained.

Filtered Indexes

Add *filtered index* to the list of new features introduced with SQL Server 2008. This new feature can be described as an optimized nonclustered index that essentially behaves like a normal index with one exception: It only covers a well-defined subset of data found in a column. It might help to think of a filtered index as a regular index with a WHERE clause that identifies and indexes specific pieces of data in a column. Some advantages of using filtered indexes over traditional nonclustered indexes include smaller indexes, which in turn improves performance and reduce storage costs. In addition, filtered indexes reduce maintenance costs because a filter index only needs to update the subset of data when changes take place. It is a best practice to include a small number of keys or included columns in a filtered index definition, and to incorporate only the columns that are necessary for the query optimizer to choose the filtered index for the query execution plan. The query optimizer can choose a filtered index for the query regardless of whether it does or does not cover the query. However, the query optimizer is more likely to choose a filtered index if it covers the query.

Spatial Indexes

As mentioned earlier, one can create an index on spatial objects residing in a column associated with the spatial data types. The new spatial data types include the geography data type for storing geodetic data and the geometry data type to store planar data. As more and more businesses seek applications and devices that deliver location intelligence, storing spatial data directly in SQL Server relational tables will eventually become a very popular and regularly requested task. As such, database administrators should become familiar with creating indexes for spatial data as there will be a need to enhance queries associated with this new data type.

XML Indexes

XML indexes can be created on XML table columns and should be considered when working with XML data types. The XML columns in a table are stored as binary large objects (BLOBs). Normally, when XML columns are queried, the data is shredded during runtime and placed into a relational table. The cost associated with this operation can be very high, depending on the size of the XML column. An XML index shreds the data when the index is created, eliminating the cost of this operation during runtime.

A single primary index and three different types of secondary indexes can exist on each XML column in a table for a total of 249 different XML indexes. Unlike traditional indexes, XML indexes cannot be created on views.

General Index Characteristics

Whereas pages in a heap are not linked or related to each other, index pages are linked; this link type is typically referred to as a *doubly linked list*. This means one link points to the previous page, and one points to the next page.

The doubly linked list effectively allows the Database Engine to quickly locate specific data or the starting and ending points of the range by moving through the index structure.

Both clustered and nonclustered indexes are stored as a b-tree structure. The b-tree structure logically sorts pages with the intention of reducing the amount of time needed to search for data. For example, when you're querying a heap, the entire table must be scanned because the data is not sorted. However, when you're querying a b-tree, the logical and physical organization of data allows the correct rows to be located quickly.

When creating an index, you must select one or more key columns. The index key can be any column with the exception of the varchar(max), nvarchar(max), varbinary(max), ntext, text, image, and XML data types. The combined length of the selected key column cannot exceed 900 bytes.

The effectiveness of an index is based on the key columns, so choosing the correct key columns is an important part of the clustered index design.

How Column Constraints Affect Indexes

Constraints can be defined on columns to ensure data integrity. For example, a constraint can be configured on a column that contains phone numbers to make sure that only valid phone numbers are entered in the correct format with the correct number of digits.

When the primary key constraint is applied to a column, a unique clustered index is automatically created. If a clustered index already exists for the table, a nonclustered index is created.

How Computed Columns Affect Indexes

A computed column uses an expression to generate its value. Unless the computed column is marked as PERSISTED, the value of the computed column is not stored in the table like other columns; it is calculated when the data is queried.

Indexes can be created that include these columns. However, because of the complexity associated with computed columns, specific prerequisites must be met. Following are the prerequisites for indexes on computed columns:

- **Determinism**—The computed column expression must be deterministic. For example, the computed column expression can't use the SUM, AVG, or GETDATE functions because the result may change. On the other hand, the DATEADD and DATEDIFF functions are considered deterministic as they will always produce the same result based on the dates being calculated.

- **Precision**—The computed column expression must use precise data types. For example, the computed column expression can't normally use the float or real data types because the returned value may change slightly between queries. However, the float and real data types can be used if the column is also marked as PERSISTED because the imprecise data is calculated and stored in the table.

- **Data Type**—The computed column expression cannot evaluate to the text, ntext, or image data types. However, these columns can be included as nonkey columns in a nonclustered index.

- **Ownership**—The table and all functions referenced by the computed column must have the same owner.

- **Set Options**—The ANSI_NULLS option must be ON when using the CREATE TABLE and ALTER TABLE statements. When you're using the INSERT, UPDATE, and DELETE statements, the NUMERIC_ROUNDABORT option must be set to OFF, and the ANSI_NULLS, ANSI_PADDING, ANSI_WARNINGS, ARITHABORT, CONCAT_NULL_YIELDS_NULL, and QUOTED_IDENTIFIER options must be set to ON.

Clustered Index Characteristics

When a clustered index is created, the data in the table is actually sorted into the leaf nodes of a b-tree, essentially making the data in the table part of the index. Each table can contain only one clustered index because the data can be physically sorted only one time.

Nonclustered Index Characteristics

When a nonclustered index is created, the data in the table is not modified. Instead, the leaf nodes of the b-tree contain a pointer to the original data. This pointer can either reference a row of data in a heap or a clustered index key, depending on the structure of the underlying table. For example, if the underlying table has a clustered and nonclustered index defined, the leaf nodes of the nonclustered index point to the key location in the clustered index. Conversely, if the underlying table is a heap, because it does not have a clustered index defined, the nonclustered index simply points to rows in the heap to locate the queried data.

Nonclustered Index Include Columns

Just as with clustered indexes, the combined length of the selected key columns cannot exceed 900 bytes. However, nonclustered indexes are able to "include" columns in the index that are not counted as part of the key. This feature is important because it allows indexes designed to cover all columns used by queries while maintaining a key length below the 900-byte limit.

Also like clustered indexes, the index key can be any column with the exception of the `ntext`, `text`, `image`, `varchar(max)`, `nvarchar(max)`, `varbinary(max)`, and `XML` data types. However, the `varchar(max)`, `nvarchar(max)`, `varbinary(max)`, and `XML` data types can be selected as included columns.

XML Index Characteristics

An XML index should be used when dealing with XML column types. The first index on the XML column must be the primary index. The primary XML index shreds the XML data, allowing faster access to the data because the shredding operation does not need to be performed at runtime.

After a primary XML index is created, up to three secondary XML indexes can be created. Each secondary index is a different type and serves a different purpose. The different secondary indexes can be based on the path, value, or properties of the XML data.

Traditional indexes can be stored in different filegroups separate from the associated table. However, XML indexes are always stored in the same filegroup as the underlying table.

Filtered Index Characteristics

A filtered index may be useful when dealing with subsets of data. The storage format of a filtered index is not unlike the typical nonclustered indexes that are stored within the b-tree hierarchy. With a filtered index, however, only a subset of the data is indexed. When implementing filtered indexes, it is very important to understand the data stored within the table including the desired column to be indexed, so that the appropriate `WHERE` clauses can be selected correctly.

A common scenario for implementing a filtered index usually includes queries that contain many null values within a column. Take, for example, a column such as column X with 10,000 rows of data, but only 700 rows contain data within column X. Therefore, a filtered index can be applied for the non-null data rows within the column, which equates to 700 rows of data. As a result of using a filtered index, the index is slimmer and more efficient from a cost perspective. Another scenario would include creating a filtered index on a data column and only including days after a specific date value, such as May 7, 2008, in the subset of data.

Spatial Index Characteristics

Using the new `geography` and `geometry` data types, organizations can store and manipulate both geodetic and planar spatial data directly in the relational database. It will be necessary for DBAs to leverage spatial indexes to provide fast execution of queries involving spatial data. Fortunately, DBAs can make informed decisions when identifying the most suitable spatial index as the Query Optimizer has been enhanced to include spatial data. When making these decisions, it is still beneficial to understand the internals and characteristics of how spatial data is stored in the database.

Similar to clustered and nonclustered indexes, spatial indexes use the same b-tree method for storing the indexed data. However, SQL Server breaks down the spatial data into a grid hierarchy, therefore, the data can be stored based on two-dimensional spatial data in linear order. The index construction process consists of breaking down the space into a grid hierarchy based on four levels. Level 1 is the top level.

In a multilevel grid hierarchy, each level of the index subdivides the grid sector that is defined in the level above it. For example, each successive level further breaks down the level above it, so each upper-level cell contains a complete grid at the next level. On a given level, all the grids have the same number of cells along both axes (for example, 4×4 or 8×8), and the cells are all one size.

In addition, because spatial data and indexes are stored directly in the SQL Server Database Engine, the SQL Server Query Optimizer can make cost-based decisions on which spatial indexes to use for a given query. This process is similar to any other index within SQL Server 2008.

Index Design and Strategy

Data in a SQL Server 2008 database can be accessed and managed through a variety of methods depending on how the database application was developed. This can make the index design process relatively complicated because the correct indexes must be created for the correct scenario. The following sections provide guidance and strategy for the index design process.

Using Clustered Indexes

You should select the smallest number of key columns within the 900-byte limit. The selected key column or columns should provide uniqueness that allows the data to be searched quickly.

It is recommended to avoid making clustered indexes on columns with few unique values because the Query Optimizer often skips the index and resorts to a table scan. This means the index is not used, yet the index still needs to be maintained by the Database Engine, causing unnecessary overhead. Following are some general guidelines and best practices for creating clustered indexes:

- A clustered index is often used when large amounts of data or a range of data is queried, such as the data spanning a single month from a table that contains data for an entire year.

- Queries that use the ORDER BY or GROUP BY clauses generally benefit from a clustered query because the data is already sorted and doesn't need to be re-sorted.

- A clustered index is effective when the data is accessed sequentially, the data is searched frequently, or the data would have to be sorted.

The data in the table is sorted as the clustered index is built. From this point, the index is automatically maintained. One downside of a clustered index is the potential cost of index maintenance. Specific operations such as frequent inserts into the middle of the table or many delete operations cause the entire table to shift because the order of the data is automatically maintained. These types of operations also cause nonclustered queries to be updated because the nonclustered index relies on the location of index data within the clustered index.

Using Nonclustered Indexes

Nonclustered indexes cover costly queries with the smallest number of key and included columns. Each nonclustered index introduces additional cost associated with maintaining the index; for this reason, it is important to select the key and include columns carefully. Following are some general guidelines and best practices for creating nonclustered indexes:

- A nonclustered index is often used when smaller data sets or exact matches are returned because the data page can be located quickly, and additional nonkey columns can be included to avoid exceeding the 900-byte key length limit.

- Nonclustered indexes should also be used to cover additional query scenarios the clustered index does not cover. As many as 249 nonclustered indexes can be created per table.

When the underlying table has a clustered index defined, all nonclustered indexes on that table depend on the clustered index. If the clustered index is disabled, the nonclustered indexes are also automatically disabled.

Using Unique Indexes and the Uniqueifier Column

When creating new indexes or altering existing indexes, you can enable the unique option to force unique values across the key column rows. If the unique option is not selected, the SQL Server Database Engine appends a 4-byte uniqueifier column to the index key. This column is used to ensure uniqueness when nonunique data is included in the key. This column is maintained internally and cannot be changed.

Calculating Disk Space Requirements

When index creation and maintenance operations are performed, enough temporary space must exist in the filegroup the index will be created in; otherwise, the operation will fail.

When the index operation is performed, the sorting is done either in the same filegroup as the table or the filegroup where the index is located. However, the sort operation can also be done in the tempdb to potentially improve performance at the expense of temporary disk space. For additional information on how to use the tempdb with indexes, see the section "Sorting Indexes in the tempdb" later in this chapter.

The sum of space needed for both the old and new structure is the starting point to determine the approximate amount of free space needed to perform the index operation. For example, if a heap has 64,000 rows and each row is 1000 bytes, approximately 61MB of free space is required for the source data. This can be calculated with the following formula:

Current Number of Rows * Average Row Length in bytes = Source structure size

or

64000 * 1000 bytes = 61.0351562 megabytes

The size estimate should be rounded up for the calculation. In this case, the 61MB heap size is rounded to 70MB. To create a clustered index on this heap, you need a total of 70MB free space. When the new index has been created, the space used by the old structure is reclaimed.

When a new index is created or an existing index is rebuilt, a fill factor can be defined. The target structure requires additional space if the fill factor setting is configured.

> **Note**
>
> The fill factor index option allocates additional space in each index page to anticipate growth. This reduces the chance of page splits and fragmentation as data is changed but reduces the performance of the index as the index becomes larger.

For example, if an 80 percent fill factor is specified, the 70MB heap requires approximately 88MB free space because 20 percent additional space is allocated for each page. You can use the following calculation to determine additional space needed due to the fill factor:

Source structure size / Fill Factor Percentage

Or

70 MB / 80% = 87.5 megabytes

Existing nonclustered indexes also have to be worked into the formula. When a new clustered index is created, existing nonclustered indexes must be rebuilt because the leaf nodes must now use the clustered key instead of the heap row indicator to find data.

For example, if an existing nonclustered index has 64,000 rows and each row is 100 bytes, approximately 8MB is used for the existing nonclustered index. The following formula can be used to calculate the size of the existing nonclustered index:

Rows in Index * Average Row Length in bytes / Current Fill Factor Percentage

or

(64000 * 100 bytes) / (80%) = 7.62939453 megabytes

The expected size of the nonclustered key can be estimated by adding the new clustered key size to the existing row length and then subtracting the existing 8-byte row indicator. For example, if the new clustered key size is 36 bytes, the expected space needed for the rebuilt nonclustered index is about 10MB. You can then use the following calculation to estimate the size of the new nonclustered index:

Rows in Index * (Average Row Length in bytes − 8 + Clustered Key Size in bytes) / Fill Factor Percentage

or

(64000 * ((100 bytes) − (8 bytes) + (36 bytes))) / (80%) = 9.765625 megabytes

The total source structure would then be 78MB (70MB heap + 8MB nonclustered index) and the total destination structure would be 98MB (88MB cluster + 10MB nonclustered index). A total of 98MB free space is required to complete the index operation with 78MB space reclaimed after the operation has completed.

If the option to sort the index in the tempdb is enabled, the tempdb must have enough space to hold the equivalent of the source table. In this example, the source table is about 70MB. The sort in tempdb option is ignored if the sort operation can be performed in memory.

Administering Indexes

The administration of SQL Server 2008 indexes can be performed through the SQL Server Management Studio interface or through Transact-SQL (TSQL) code. When you are performing administration of SQL Server indexes, it is important to understand the different options available in the different versions of SQL Server.

The code examples provided in the following sections can be executed through the Query Editor window in SQL Server Management Studio.

Transact-SQL Index Syntaxes

Transact-SQL code can be used to manage indexes on tables in a SQL Server database. The CREATE INDEX statement can be used to create new indexes, the modification of existing indexes can be performed through the ALTER INDEX statement, and the removal of indexes can be performed through the DROP INDEX statement. Examples that use each of these index-related TSQL statements are provided throughout this chapter.

Creating Relational Indexes with Transact-SQL

The following code shows the complete syntax of the CREATE INDEX TSQL statement. You can use the CREATE INDEX statement to create a relational index on a table or view, or an XML index on an XML column.

```
CREATE [ UNIQUE ] [ CLUSTERED ¦ NONCLUSTERED ] INDEX index_name
    ON <object> ( column [ ASC ¦ DESC ] [ ,...n ] )
    [ INCLUDE ( column_name [ ,...n ] ) ]
    [ WHERE <filter_predicate> ]
    [ WITH ( <relational_index_option> [ ,...n ] ) ]
    [ ON { partition_scheme_name ( column_name )
        ¦ filegroup_name
        ¦ default
        }
    ]
    [ FILESTREAM_ON { filestream_filegroup_name
 ¦ partition_scheme_name ¦ "NULL" } ]
  [ ; ]
<object> ::=
{
    [ database_name. [ schema_name ] . ¦ schema_name. ]
        table_or_view_name
}
<relational_index_option> ::=
```

```
{
    PAD_INDEX = { ON ¦ OFF }
  ¦ FILLFACTOR = fillfactor
  ¦ SORT_IN_TEMPDB = { ON ¦ OFF }
  ¦ IGNORE_DUP_KEY = { ON ¦ OFF }
  ¦ STATISTICS_NORECOMPUTE = { ON ¦ OFF }
  ¦ DROP_EXISTING = { ON ¦ OFF }
  ¦ ONLINE = { ON ¦ OFF }
  ¦ ALLOW_ROW_LOCKS = { ON ¦ OFF }
  ¦ ALLOW_PAGE_LOCKS = { ON ¦ OFF }
  ¦ MAXDOP = max_degree_of_parallelism
  ¦ DATA_COMPRESSION = { NONE ¦ ROW ¦ PAGE}
      [ ON PARTITIONS (
➥{ <partition_number_expression> ¦ <range> }
      [ , ...n ] ) ]
}
<filter_predicate> ::=
    <conjunct> [ AND <conjunct> ]
<conjunct> ::=
    <disjunct> ¦ <comparison>
<disjunct> ::=
        column_name IN (constant ,…)
<comparison> ::=
        column_name <comparison_op> constant
<comparison_op> ::=
    { IS ¦ IS NOT ¦ = ¦ <> ¦ != ¦ > ¦ >= ¦ !> ¦ < ¦ <= ¦ !< }
<range> ::=
<partition_number_expression> TO <partition_number_expression>
```

The following code shows the CREATE INDEX options used in previous
versions of SQL Server. Backward compatibility is provided to allow easier
transition to SQL Server 2008 from previous versions of SQL Server. You
should not use these options when developing new code.

```
CREATE [ UNIQUE ] [ CLUSTERED ¦ NONCLUSTERED ] INDEX index_name
    ON <object> ( column_name [ ASC ¦ DESC ] [ ,...n ] )
    [ WITH <backward_compatible_index_option> [ ,...n ] ]
    [ ON { filegroup_name ¦ "default" } ]
<object> ::=
{
    [ database_name. [ owner_name ] . ¦ owner_name. ]
        table_or_view_name
```

```
}
<backward_compatible_index_option> ::=
{
    PAD_INDEX
  ¦ FILLFACTOR = fillfactor
  ¦ SORT_IN_TEMPDB
  ¦ IGNORE_DUP_KEY
  ¦ STATISTICS_NORECOMPUTE
  ¦ DROP_EXISTING
}
```

Modifying Relational Indexes with Transact-SQL

The following example shows the complete syntax of the ALTER INDEX
TSQL statement. You can use this code to rebuild indexes, disable indexes,
reorganize indexes, or modify or set options on existing relational indexes.

```
ALTER INDEX { index_name ¦ ALL }
    ON <object>
    { REBUILD
        [ [PARTITION = ALL]
                    [ WITH ( <rebuild_index_option>
                        [ ,...n ] ) ]
          ¦ [ PARTITION = partition_number
              [ WITH ( <single_partition_rebuild_index_option>
                      [ ,...n ] )
              ]
          ]
        ]
    ¦ DISABLE
    ¦ REORGANIZE
        [ PARTITION = partition_number ]
        [ WITH ( LOB_COMPACTION = { ON ¦ OFF } ) ]
  ¦ SET ( <set_index_option> [ ,...n ] )
    }
[ ; ]
<object> ::=
{
    [ database_name. [ schema_name ] . ¦ schema_name. ]
        table_or_view_name
}
<rebuild_index_option > ::=
{
```

```
    PAD_INDEX = { ON ¦ OFF }
  ¦ FILLFACTOR = fillfactor
  ¦ SORT_IN_TEMPDB = { ON ¦ OFF }
  ¦ IGNORE_DUP_KEY = { ON ¦ OFF }
  ¦ STATISTICS_NORECOMPUTE = { ON ¦ OFF }
  ¦ ONLINE = { ON ¦ OFF }
  ¦ ALLOW_ROW_LOCKS = { ON ¦ OFF }
  ¦ ALLOW_PAGE_LOCKS = { ON ¦ OFF }
  ¦ MAXDOP = max_degree_of_parallelism
  ¦ DATA_COMPRESSION = { NONE ¦ ROW ¦ PAGE }
      [ ON PARTITIONS (
➡{ <partition_number_expression> ¦ <range> }
      [ , ...n ] ) ]
}
<range> ::=
<partition_number_expression> TO <partition_number_expression>
}
<single_partition_rebuild_index_option> ::=
{
    SORT_IN_TEMPDB = { ON ¦ OFF }
  ¦ MAXDOP = max_degree_of_parallelism
  ¦ DATA_COMPRESSION = { NONE ¦ ROW ¦ PAGE } }
}
<set_index_option>::=
{
    ALLOW_ROW_LOCKS = { ON ¦ OFF }
  ¦ ALLOW_PAGE_LOCKS = { ON ¦ OFF }
  ¦ IGNORE_DUP_KEY = { ON ¦ OFF }
  ¦ STATISTICS_NORECOMPUTE = { ON ¦ OFF }
}
```

Deleting Indexes with Transact-SQL

The following example shows the complete syntax of the DROP INDEX TSQL
statement. You can use this code to remove a relational or XML index.

```
DROP INDEX
{ <drop_relational_or_xml_or_spatial_index> [ ,...n ]
¦ <drop_backward_compatible_index> [ ,...n ]
}
<drop_relational_or_xml_or_spatial_index> ::=
      index_name ON <object>
    [ WITH ( <drop_clustered_index_option> [ ,...n ] ) ]
```

```
<drop_backward_compatible_index> ::=
    [ owner_name. ] table_or_view_name.index_name
<object> ::=
{
    [ database_name. [ schema_name ] . ¦ schema_name. ]
        table_or_view_name
}
<drop_clustered_index_option> ::=
{
    MAXDOP = max_degree_of_parallelism
    ¦ ONLINE = { ON ¦ OFF }
  ¦ MOVE TO { partition_scheme_name ( column_name )
              ¦ filegroup_name
              ¦ "default"
              }
  [ FILESTREAM_ON { partition_scheme_name
              ¦ filestream_filegroup_name
              ¦ "default" } ]
}
```

Creating Spatial Indexes with Transact-SQL

The following code shows the complete syntax of the CREATE SPATIAL
INDEX TSQL statement. You can use the CREATE SPATIAL INDEX statement
to create a spatial index on a spatial column.

```
Create Spatial Index
CREATE SPATIAL INDEX index_name
  ON <object> ( spatial_column_name )
    {
        [ USING <geometry_grid_tessellation> ]
          WITH ( <bounding_box>
                   [ [,] <tesselation_parameters> [ ,...n ] ]
                   [ [,] <spatial_index_option> [ ,...n ] ] )
      ¦ [ USING <geography_grid_tessellation> ]
          [ WITH ( [ <tesselation_parameters> [ ,...n ] ]
                   [ [,] <spatial_index_option> [ ,...n ] ] ) ]
    }
  [ ON { filegroup_name ¦ "default" } ]
;
<object> ::=
    [ database_name. [ schema_name ] . ¦ schema_name. ]
                table_name
```

```
<geometry_grid_tessellation> ::=
{ GEOMETRY_GRID }

<bounding_box> ::=
BOUNDING_BOX = ( {
        xmin, ymin, xmax, ymax
    ¦ <named_bb_coordinate>, <named_bb_coordinate>,
<named_bb_coordinate>, <named_bb_coordinate>
  } )
<named_bb_coordinate> ::= { XMIN = xmin ¦ YMIN = ymin
 ¦ XMAX = xmax ¦ YMAX=ymax }
<tesselation_parameters> ::=
{
    GRIDS = ( { <grid_density> [ ,...n ] ¦ <density>, <density>,
<density>, <density> } )
  ¦ CELLS_PER_OBJECT = n
}
<grid_density> ::=
{
     LEVEL_1 = <density>
   ¦ LEVEL_2 = <density>
   ¦ LEVEL_3 = <density>
   ¦ LEVEL_4 = <density>
}
<density> ::= { LOW ¦ MEDIUM ¦ HIGH }
<geography_grid_tessellation> ::=
{ GEOGRAPHY_GRID }

<spatial_index_option> ::=
{
    PAD_INDEX = { ON ¦ OFF }
  ¦ FILLFACTOR = fillfactor
  ¦ SORT_IN_TEMPDB = { ON ¦ OFF }
  ¦ IGNORE_DUP_KEY = OFF
  ¦ STATISTICS_NORECOMPUTE = { ON ¦ OFF }
  ¦ DROP_EXISTING = { ON ¦ OFF }
  ¦ ONLINE = OFF
  ¦ ALLOW_ROW_LOCKS = { ON ¦ OFF }
  ¦ ALLOW_PAGE_LOCKS = { ON ¦ OFF }
  ¦ MAXDOP = max_degree_of_parallelism
}
```

Creating Filtered Indexes with Transact-SQL

The following code shows examples of the CREATE FILTERED INDEX TSQL statement. You can use the CREATE FILTERED INDEX statement to create a filtered index on a subset of data residing in a column. The first example displays a filtered index based on a subset of products subcategories in the product table in the AdventureWorks2008 database.

```
CREATE NONCLUSTERED INDEX AK_ProductSubCategory
ON Production.Product(ProductSubCategoryID)
WHERE (ProductSubcategoryID = 17)
```

The next example illustrates creating a filtered index on ComponentID and Start date columns in the Production.BillOfMaterials table in the AdventureWorks2008 database. The filtered criteria is based on the EndDate columns, which are not null.

```
CREATE NONCLUSTERED INDEX FIBillOfMaterialsWithEndDate
ON Production.BillOfMaterials (ComponentID, StartDate)
WHERE EndDate IS NOT NULL
```

Creating Indexes with SQL Server Management Studio

When working with indexes, not only is it possible to create indexes with Transact-SQL, but indexes can also be created via SQL Server Management Studio. Use the following steps to create either a clustered, nonclustered, XML or spatial index with SQL Server Management Studio.

1. Launch SQL Server Management Studio and connect to a Database Engine instance.

2. Expand the SQL Server instance, the Database folder, and then select the database that contains the table on which the index will be generated.

3. Expand the desired table, right-click the Indexes folder, and then select new Index.

4. In the Index Name text box, enter a name for the new index.

5. Specify the type of index to use in the Index Type drop-down list. The options include Clustered, NonClustered Primary XML, and spatial.

6. To specify the index columns to be added, click Add.

7. Specify the column to be indexed in the Select Columns From dialog box, and then click OK.

8. On the New Index screen, either click OK to finalize the creation of the index or proceed to the next steps to enter advanced configuration settings for the index being created.

Options Page

Some additional options are available when creating indexes with SQL Server Management Studio. The Options page includes the following configurable settings, as displayed in Figure 4.3:

- **Drop Existing Index**—This option is only available if the index already exists. If you select this option, the pre-existing index will be dropped and re-created.

- **Rebuild Index**—Used to re-create a pre-existing index on a table.

- **Ignore Duplicate Values**—This option will specify whether a duplicate key value can be inserted into the indexed column.

- **Automatically Recompute Statistics**—Enabled by default, this option will automatically update index statistics when the index is being generated.

- **Use Row Locks When Accessing the Index**—This setting performs row-level locking, which is also enabled by default. If this setting is cleared, index maintenance will be conducted faster; however, additional blocks on users may occur.

- **Use Page Lock When Accessing the Index**—SQL Server uses page-level, row-level, or table-level locking. When this option is enabled, page locking is implemented.

- **Store Immediate Sort Results in tempdb**—This setting is not enabled by default, and if it is enabled, the intermediate sort results associated with building the index are conducted in tempdb.

- **Set Fill Factor**—This setting controls how full the leaf level of each index should be during generation.

- **Allow Online Processing of DML Statements While Creating the Index**—If this option is enabled, the setting permits concurrent users access to the underlying clustered or nonclustered index data during the index operation.

- **Set Maximum Degree of Parallelism**—Limits the number of processors that can be utilized when carrying out the index task. The default setting is 0, which represents the usage of all processors.

- **Use Index**—The final setting on the Options page is Use Index. This setting, when selected, allows SQL Server to use the index.

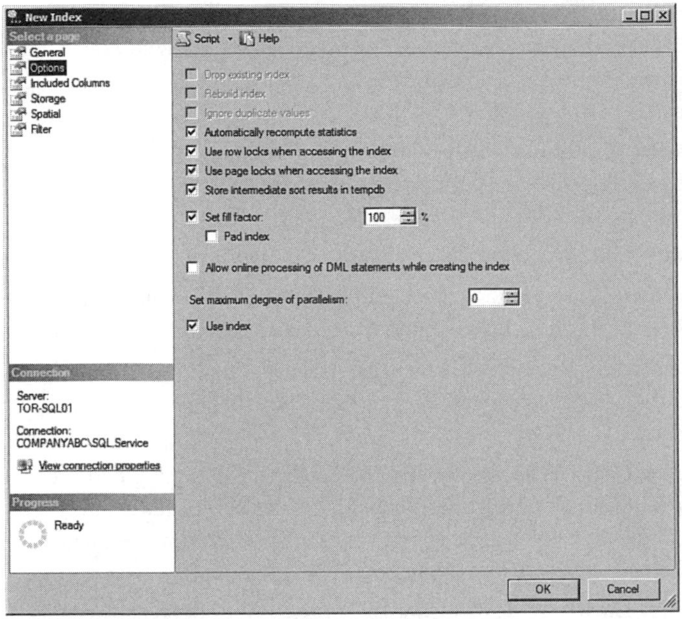

FIGURE 4.3
The Advanced New Index Settings on the Options page.

Included Columns Page

The next page in the New Index dialog box is known as Included Columns. In addition to the index key, extra nonkey columns can be added to the index by selecting the Add button. This invokes a new Select Columns dialog box where the DBA can specify the additional nonkey columns to add to the index. The advantages associated with creating Included Columns are; the 900 byte size limit for the indexes does not apply as the columns defined in the include statement, called non-key columns, are not counted in the number of columns by the Database Engine, also the index maintenance overhead associated with the actual composite index columns are reduced.

Storage Page

The Storage page, as illustrated in Figure 4.4, includes settings for the placement of the indexes and whether or not compression will be leveraged. Indexes can be placed on additional or specified filegroups in order to maximize performance. In addition, new settings include placement for FILESTREAM data and which logical partition should be used. If compression is enabled, compression type settings can be enabled on the row or page.

Finally, it is possible to enable the Allow Online Processing of DML
Statement setting to allow access to the underlying clustered and nonclustered index during the creation process.

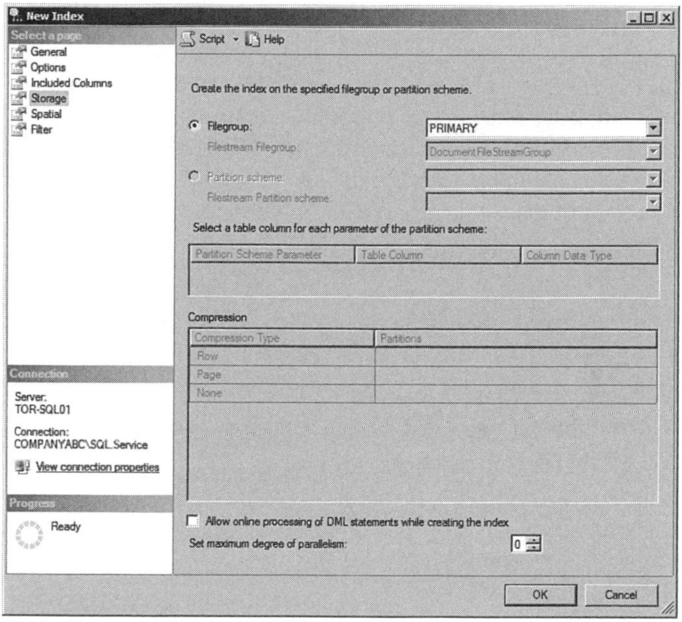

FIGURE 4.4
The Advanced New Index Settings on the Storage page.

Spatial Page

First of all, options associated with the Spatial page are only available if an
spatial index is being created. If a spatial index will be created, the values
associated with the spatial properties must be entered in the following spatial
page. The options on this page include

- **Bounding box**—The perimeter of the top-level grid of the geometric
  plane. The grid includes the X and Y minimum and maximum coordi-
  nates associated with the bounding box.

- **General**—The General section includes the Geometry and Geography
  grid of the tessellation scheme of the associated index.

- **Grids**—The Final Grid section displays the density of the grid at each
  level of the tessellation scheme. Settings include Low, Medium and High.

Filter Page

The final page in the Index Creation dialog box is the Filter page. Here a DBA can create filter expressions for a new or existing index.

Creating Clustered Indexes

The following procedure demonstrates the creation of a clustered index and shows the effect of creating a clustered index on a table. To begin the demonstration, run the following code within SQL Server Management Studio. This code creates a table called AllItems in the AdventureWorks2008 database. If an existing table called AllItems already exists, it is dropped. When the table is created, three rows of three columns of data are inserted.

Follow these steps to create the AllItems table in the AdventureWorks2008 database:

1. Launch SQL Server Management Studio and connect to the Database Engine.

2. Select the New Query button from the toolbar. Type the following code in the Query Editor window and then click the Execute button.

```
IF  EXISTS (SELECT * FROM sys.objects
WHERE object_id = OBJECT_ID(N'[dbo].[Allitems]')
 AND type in (N'U'))
USE AdventureWorks2008
DROP TABLE [dbo].[Allitems]
GO
USE [AdventureWorks2008]
GO
CREATE TABLE [dbo].[Allitems](
    [ID] [int] NOT NULL,
    [Item] [int] NOT NULL,
    [Value] [int] NOT NULL
) ON [PRIMARY]
GO
INSERT INTO AllItems VALUES (4, 23, 66)
INSERT INTO AllItems VALUES (2, 27, 28)
INSERT INTO AllItems VALUES (3, 28, 93)
SELECT * FROM AllItems
```

When the code is executed, the results pane located below the Query Editor window displays the following data:

```
ID    Item    Value
4     23      66
2     27      28
3     28      93
```

When a clustered index is added to the table, the data is sorted into the clustered index b-tree. Follow these steps to add a clustered index to the AllItems table:

1. In SQL Server Management Studio, expand the AdventureWorks2008 database and then Tables.

2. Expand the dbo.AllItems table, which should be located near the top of the list. If the AllItems table is not displayed, click F5 to refresh the table list.

3. Right-click the Indexes folder located beneath the AllItems table and select New Index from the menu. The New Index Properties dialog box opens.

4. In the Index Name field, type **IX_ID**. In the Index Type field, select Clustered from the drop-down menu. Click the Add button, select the ID column, and then click OK. Click OK to create the index.

5. Select the New Query button from the toolbar. Type the following code in the Query Editor window and then click the Execute button.

```
SELECT * FROM AllItems
```

When the code is executed, the results pane located below the Query Editor window displays the following data:

ID	Item	Value
2	27	28
3	28	93
4	23	66

The results show that the data has been sorted based on the ID column in the table. The data has been sorted into a b-tree structure. The index nodes contain the ID, and the leaf nodes contain the Item and Value columns.

You can easily create a clustered index through the CREATE INDEX statement. The following code looks for an existing index called IX_ID, and if the index is found, it is dropped with the DROP INDEX statement. A new clustered index using the ID column as the index key is then created.

```
USE AdventureWorks2008
IF EXISTS (SELECT name FROM sys.indexes WHERE name = 'IX_ID')
  DROP INDEX [IX_ID] ON [dbo].[AllItems]
USE [AdventureWorks2008]
GO
CREATE CLUSTERED INDEX [IX_ID] ON [dbo].[AllItems]
(
    [ID] ASC
) ON [PRIMARY]
GO
```

Creating Nonclustered Indexes

The following procedure can be used to create a non-clustered index which includes the Item column as a nonkey column:

1. In SQL Server Management Studio, expand the AdventureWorks2008 database and then Tables.

2. Expand the dbo.AllItems table, right-click the Indexes folder located beneath the AllItems table, and select New Index from the menu. The New Index Properties dialog box opens.

3. In the Index Name field, type `NX_ID_Item`. In the Index Type field, select Nonclustered from the drop-down menu. Click the Add button, select the ID column, and then click OK.

4. Select the Included Columns page. Click the Add button, select the Item column, and then click OK. Click OK to create the index.

When you create a clustered index and include the Item column as a nonkey column, SQL Server can locate all the data required to support queries that include only the ID and Item columns. This can reduce the cost of executing queries that include these columns because all the data necessary to satisfy the query can be found in the index.

Disabling and Deleting Indexes

When a clustered index is disabled, the underlying data in the table is inaccessible. In addition, nonclustered indexes on the table are also disabled because nonclustered indexes rely on the clustered index key data to locate data in the table.

Follow these steps to disable the clustered index on the Person.Address table located in the AdventureWorks2008 database:

1. From within SQL Server Management Studio, expand a SQL Server instance, Databases, AdventureWorks2008, and then Tables. Expand the Person.Address table.

2. Expand the Indexes folder located beneath the Person.Address table. Right-click the PK_Address_AddressID index and select Disable.

3. When the Disable Index window opens, verify that the correct index is listed and then click OK.

4. The Disable Index information dialog box is displayed as a reminder that disabling the index prevents access to the underlying table. Click Yes.

When the clustered index has been disabled, data in the table cannot be accessed. The following code demonstrates using the ALTER INDEX statement to disable the index:

```
USE [AdventureWorks2008]
GO
ALTER INDEX [PK_Address_AddressID] ON [Person].[Address] DISABLE
GO
```

Use the following code to query the table. The results pane should state: "The query processor is unable to produce a plan because the index 'PK_Address_AddressID' on table or view 'Address' is disabled." This shows that the table is inaccessible when the index is disabled.

```
USE [AdventureWorks2008]
SELECT *
FROM [Person].[Address]
GO
```

Disabling nonclustered indexes and indexed views does not prevent access to the underlying data. Disabling this type of index simply prevents the Query Optimizer from potentially selecting the index as part of the execution plan.

With nonclustered and view indexes, the b-tree structure is physically deleted when the index is disabled; only the index metadata is kept. You can use the same procedure used to disable a clustered index to disable a nonclustered index.

If all indexes on a table will be deleted, remove the clustered index last. If the clustered index is removed before nonclustered indexes, the nonclustered indexes have to be maintained when the clustered index is removed.

Enabling and Rebuilding Indexes

When an index is disabled, you can enable it by either rebuilding the index or re-creating the index. When a clustered index is disabled, nonclustered indexes for the table are automatically disabled, too. When the clustered index is rebuilt or re-created, the nonclustered indexes are not automatically enabled unless the option to rebuild all indexes is used.

Follow these steps to enable the clustered index on the Person.Address table located in the AdventureWorks2008 database:

1. From within SQL Server Management Studio, expand a SQL Server instance, Databases, AdventureWorks2008, and then Tables. Expand the Person.Address table.

2. Expand the Indexes folder located beneath the Person.Address table. Right-click the PK_Address_AddressID index and select Rebuild.

3. When the Rebuild Index window opens, verify that the correct index is listed and then click OK.

When the clustered index has been rebuilt, the data can once again be queried. However, the nonclustered indexes cannot be selected by the Query Optimizer because they need to be enabled individually. You can use the same procedure to enable each nonclustered index.

Alternatively, you can use the following code to rebuild all indexes on the table, effectively enabling each index as the rebuild is complete:

```
USE [AdventureWorks2008]
GO
ALTER INDEX ALL ON [Person].[Address] REBUILD
GO
```

Implementing Index Maintenance and Maintenance Plans

A SQL Server 2008 maintenance plan allows different maintenance tasks to be performed automatically based on a customizable schedule. These tasks help reduce the administrative effort needed to keep the database healthy because the tasks are scheduled and executed automatically.

You can access maintenance plans through the SQL Server Management Studio by navigating to the Management\Maintenance Plans folder in the Object Explorer pane. You can create a new maintenance plan by right-clicking the Maintenance Plans folder and selecting New Maintenance Plan. You also can access the Maintenance Plan Wizard by right-clicking the Maintenance Plans folder and selecting Maintenance Plan Wizard.

Use the following code to enable the Agent XPs component:

```
sp_configure 'show advanced options', 1;
GO
RECONFIGURE;
GO
sp_configure 'Agent XPs', 1;
GO
RECONFIGURE
GO
```

When a maintenance plan is created either manually or through the Maintenance Plan Wizard, several tasks are available to maintain indexes.

Following are the index-related maintenance plan options:

- **Check Database Integrity**—This task performs consistency checks on one or more databases. When you're configuring this task, an option is available to include the indexes in the integrity verification process.

- **Rebuild Index**—This task can be used to rebuild a specific index or all indexes in a database. This task can specify the fill factor and can sort the index results in tempdb to improve efficiency. This task can also use the online indexing option available in the SQL Server 2005 Enterprise and Developer Editions.

- **Reorganize Index**—This task can be used to reorganize a specific index or all indexes in a database. This task can also compact large objects during the reorganize process.

For additional information on how to administer SQL Server 2008 maintenance plans, see Chapter 6, "SQL Server 2008 Maintenance Practices."

SQL Server 2008 also provides the ability to back up indexes. For more information, see Chapter 7, "Backing Up and Restoring the Database Engine."

Configuring Indexes for Maximum Performance

When you are administering indexes, several options are available and should be considered to improve the overall performance of the indexes and index management operations.

Configuring Index Statistics

When an index is created, the option to recompute statistics is enabled by default. The Query Optimizer uses these statistics to determine the best method of accessing the data. Inaccurate statistics may cause the Query Optimizer to select a less than optimal execution plan.

The Database Engine periodically updates the statistics by testing them for accuracy. If necessary, the maintenance of statistics can be disabled. You can use the ALTER INDEX statement to disable collection of statistics. The following code demonstrates using the ALTER INDEX statement to disable statistics on the PK_Address_AddressID index on the Person.Address table:

```
USE [AdventureWorks2008]
GO
ALTER INDEX PK_Address_AddressID ON [Person].[Address]
SET(STATISTICS_NORECOMPUTE=ON);
GO
```

During the creation of an index through the SQL Server Management Studio, you can disable the collection of index statistics by deselecting the Automatically Recomputed Statistics option on the Option page.

Examining Fragmentation Considerations

When a row is added to a full index page, a page split occurs, and about half the rows are moved to a new page. This is a costly operation because additional I/O operations are necessary to move the data. Additional I/O operations are then needed each time the data is accessed because the data is no longer continuous. When an index is created or altered, the fill factor option can be used to address fragmentation issues. This option can reduce the amount of fragmentation as the index grows by preallocating free space in the index data pages.

Follow these steps to determine the amount of fragmentation for an index:

1. From within SQL Server Management Studio, expand a SQL Server instance, Databases, AdventureWorks2008, and then Tables. Expand the Person.Address table.

2. Expand the Indexes folder located beneath the Person.Address table. Right-click the PK_Address_AddressID index and select Properties.

3. When the Index Properties dialog box opens, select the Fragmentation page to view the total fragmentation percentage for the index.

The DBCC SHOWCONTIG command can also be used to determine index fragmentation. The following code shows how to use DBCC to show the fragmentation of all indexes in the Person.Address table:

```
DBCC SHOWCONTIG ('Person.Address')
WITH ALL_INDEXES, FAST;
GO
```

The results are as follows:

```
DBCC SHOWCONTIG scanning 'Address' table...
Table: 'Address' (85575343); index ID: 1, database ID: 5
TABLE level scan performed.
- Pages Scanned................................: 340
- Extent Switches.............................: 43
- Scan Density [Best Count:Actual Count].......: 97.73% [43:44]
- Logical Scan Fragmentation ..................: 0.29%
DBCC SHOWCONTIG scanning 'Address' table...
Table: 'Address' (85575343); index ID: 2, database ID: 5
LEAF level scan performed.
```

```
- Pages Scanned...............................: 56
- Extent Switches.............................: 6
- Scan Density [Best Count:Actual Count].......: 100.00% [7:7]
- Logical Scan Fragmentation .................: 0.00%
DBCC SHOWCONTIG scanning 'Address' table...
Table: 'Address' (85575343); index ID: 3, database ID: 5
LEAF level scan performed.
- Pages Scanned...............................: 211
- Extent Switches.............................: 26
- Scan Density [Best Count:Actual Count].......: 100.00% [27:27]
- Logical Scan Fragmentation .................: 0.00%
DBCC SHOWCONTIG scanning 'Address' table...
Table: 'Address' (85575343); index ID: 4, database ID: 5
LEAF level scan performed.
- Pages Scanned...............................: 27
- Extent Switches.............................: 4
- Scan Density [Best Count:Actual Count].......: 80.00% [4:5]
- Logical Scan Fragmentation .................: 7.41%
DBCC execution completed. If DBCC printed error messages, contact
your system administrator.
```

The DBCC command will be deprecated in future versions of SQL Server. It is recommended to use the management function sys.dm_db_index_physical_ stats to replace the DBCC SHOWCONTIG command when checking index fragmentation. The upcoming example illustrates the management function alternative for checking fragmentation.

You also can use the following code to show the fragmentation. When this code is executed, the percentage of fragmentation for all indexes in the Person.Address table is returned.

```
USE AdventureWorks2008;
GO
SELECT
  a.index_id,
  b.name,
  a.avg_fragmentation_in_percent
FROM sys.dm_db_index_physical_stats (DB_ID(),
 OBJECT_ID(N'Person.Address'), NULL, NULL, NULL) AS a
  JOIN sys.indexes AS b
    ON a.object_id = b.object_id
      AND a.index_id = b.index_id;
GO
```

The result is

```
1    PK_Address_AddressID     0
2    AK_Address_rowguid      0
3    IX_Address_AddressLine1_AddressLine2_City_StateProvinceID_
➥PostalCode     0
4    IX_Address_StateProvinceID    7.40740740740741
```

Implementing Fill Factor Administration

The fill factor can be configured so that each page in the leaf level allocates extra space for new rows. By default, the fill factor is set to 0, allowing only one additional row to be added to the page before a split operation is necessary. If the pages in the leaf level are expected to grow, you can use the Fill Factor setting to allocate extra space in each page. For example, set the Fill Factor setting to 80 percent to leave 20 percent room in each page for growth. The fill factor can be configured only when an index is created or rebuilt.

> **Note**
>
> Increasing the amount of free space in each page results in a larger index. A larger index increases the I/O cost when accessing the data and degrades performance.

You can use the ALTER INDEX statement to set an 80 percent fill factor on the PK_Address_AddressID index located on the Person.Address table in the AdventureWorks2008 database:

```
USE [AdventureWorks2008]
GO
ALTER INDEX PK_Address_AddressID ON [Person].[Address]
REBUILD WITH(FILLFACTOR=80);
GO
```

The fill factor can also be configured through the SQL Server Management Studio. For example, to set the fill factor, create a new index by right-clicking the Indexes folder located beneath the Person.Address table and select New Index. In the New Index window, select the Options page and set the fill factor to the desired level.

Figure 4.5 shows the Set Fill Factor option set to 80 percent, allowing 20 percent free space within the leaf node of the index. The Pad Index option can also be configured to provide the intermediate level with additional free space.

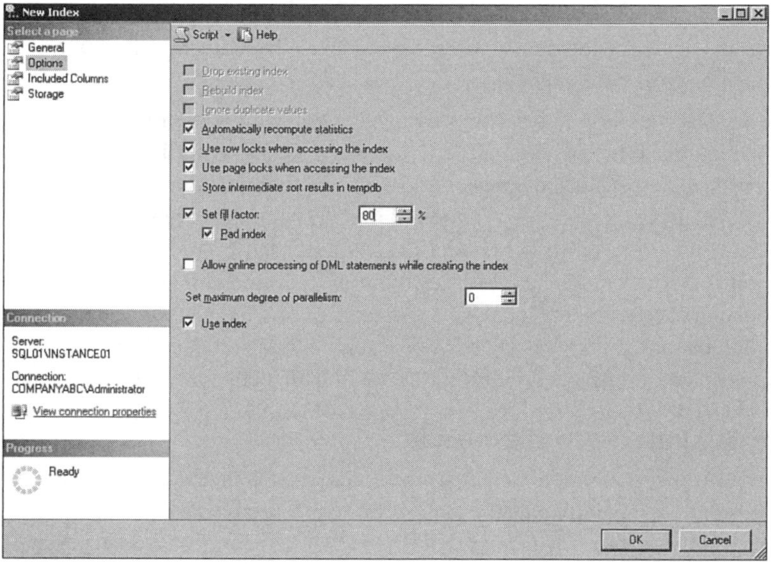

FIGURE 4.5
Fill factor options.

> **Note**
>
> The free space allocated by the fill factor setting is not maintained; the space is allocated once. When the additional space is filled, a split operation occurs. To reallocate the space again, you must rebuild the index.

To view the fill factor value of one or more indexes, use the sys.indexes catalog view. You can use the following code to determine the fill factor on the PK_Address_AddressID index. The fill factor number is located in the fill_factor column.

```
USE AdventureWorks2008
SELECT fill_factor FROM sys.indexes
WHERE name = 'PK_Address_AddressID'
```

Determining When to Rebuild or Reorganize an Index

When a split operation occurs, the data pages can become fragmented, and fragmentation can lead to performance-related issues. Two different options exist for dealing with fragmentation: The first is to reorganize the index, and the second is to rebuild the index.

When the level of fragmentation is greater than 5 percent but less than 30 percent, the reorganize option is recommended. When an index has 30 percent or greater fragmentation, a rebuild is recommended.

The reorganize process physically reorganizes the leaf nodes of the index, allowing more efficient access. The reorganize process is much lighter on the server and doesn't block queries or updates, essentially minimizing the impact on people using the database. The rebuild process actually drops the existing index and re-creates it with the specified settings, such as fill factor. This option is more thorough but also uses more server resources, and if the Online option is not selected, the index is unavailable during the rebuild process. The sys.dm_db_index_physical_stats DMV is a great way for identifying size and fragmentation for data and indexes associated with a table or view.

Sorting Indexes in the tempdb

Normally, when an index is created, the sorting of the index data is done within the same filegroup as the table or the filegroup where the index is stored. However, when you are rebuilding existing indexes or creating new indexes, you can sort the data in the tempdb.

If the tempdb is physically located on a different set of disks, performance improvement can be achieved because the reading of data from one set of disks can be separated from the writing of data to the tempdb.

Note

To increase processing effectiveness, one tempdb file should be created per CPU.

You can use the ALTER INDEX statement to rebuild all indexes located on the Person.Address table in the AdventureWorks2008 database, using the tempdb to sort the data:

```
USE AdventureWorks2008;
GO
ALTER INDEX ALL ON Person.Address
REBUILD WITH (SORT_IN_TEMPDB = ON);
```

Using the Database Engine Tuning Advisor

The Database Engine Tuning Advisor is an effective tool to analyze and report the indexing potential. This tool allows the selection of a single table, single database, or multiple databases for analysis. This is one of the key tools that you should use when attempting to determine the appropriate indexes and the effect of indexes.

This tool works by placing a load on the selected objects. The results of this load are evaluated, and a recommendation is provided, along with a potential improvement percentage. The recommended changes can then be implemented directly from within the tool.

This demonstration creates a sample workload file and then runs it against the Production.Product table in the AdventureWorks2008 database. Before you start, the existing clustered indexes on the table are dropped using the DROP INDEX statement. To drop the nonclustered indexes on the Production.Product table, run the following code:

```
USE [AdventureWorks2008]
GO
DROP INDEX [AK_Product_Name] ON [Production].[Product],
[AK_Product_ProductNumber]ON [Production].[Product],
[AK_Product_rowguid] ON [Production].[Product]
GO
```

After the nonclustered indexes have been deleted, the table can be more effectively analyzed for possible indexes. The next step is to create a workload file; this is SQL code that will be used in the analysis process of the table. Follow these steps to create the workload file:

1. Choose Start, All Programs, Microsoft SQL Server 2008, SQL Server Management Studio.

2. Type the name of a SQL Server instance in the Server Name field, select Windows Authentication from the Authentication drop-down menu, and then click the Connect button.

3. Select the New Query button from the toolbar. Then type the following code in the Query Editor window:

```
USE [AdventureWorks2008]
SELECT [Name],
  [ProductNumber],
  [StandardCost],
  [ListPrice]
FROM Production.Product
WHERE [ListPrice] - [StandardCost] > 50
```

4. Select File, Save SQLQuery1.sql As. Then type **Workload.sql** in the File Name field and select a path to save the file.

After the workload file has been created, follow these steps to analyze a table for indexing purposes:

1. Choose Start, All Programs, Microsoft SQL Server 2008, Performance Tools, Database Engine Tuning Advisor.

2. Type the name of a SQL Server instance in the Server Name field, select Windows Authentication from the Authentication drop-down menu, and then click the Connect button.

3. On the General tab, select the File option and then browse for the Workload.SQL file created in the previous steps. Select AdventureWorks2008 from the Database for Workload Analysis drop-down menu.

4. Click the down arrow next to the AdventureWorks2008 database and select the Product table from the list, as shown in Figure 4.6.

5. Select the Tuning Options tab and review the available options. Options include the ability to analyze different types of indexes and partitioning strategies. Click the Advanced button to specify space and online processing restrictions. The default options are acceptable for this demonstration.

6. The default options evaluate the table for nonclustered index potential and disable partitioning recommendations. Click the Start Analysis button.

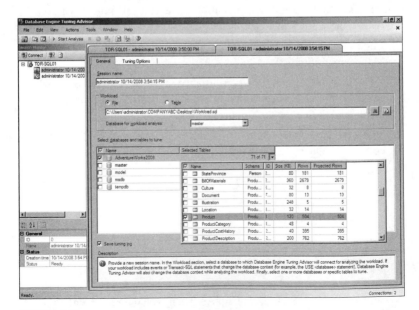

FIGURE 4.6
AdventureWorks2008 Index Tuning table selection.

The analysis of the table is performed. The results, shown in Figure 4.7, show a nonclustered index with ListPrice and StandardCost as key columns, and ProductNumber as an included nonkey column that would improve performance by 46 percent.

From within the Recommendation tab of the Database Engine Tuning Advisor, click the blue text in the Definition column to see the code necessary to create the recommended indexes. To apply all the recommendations, choose Actions, Apply Recommendation from the menu. The Apply Recommendations dialog box is displayed, allowing you to apply the recommendations immediately or schedule them for later.

This demonstration used a simple workload file to place a load on the database. This is often not appropriate or practical for large complex databases. As an alternative, you can use the information captured from the SQL Server profiler utility to place a more real-world load on the database.

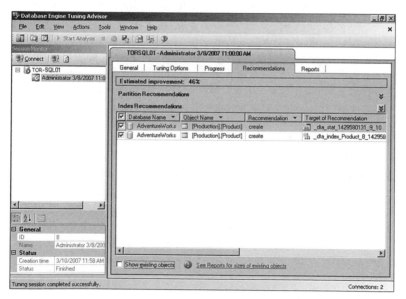

FIGURE 4.7
Database tuning recommendations.

Examining Additional Indexing Options

When you're creating new indexes or altering existing indexes, additional options are available. These options are listed on the General and Options pages found in the Index Properties dialog box. Follow these steps to access

the Properties dialog box for the PK_Address_AddressID index on the
Person.Address table in the AdventureWorks2008 database:

1. From within SQL Server Management Studio, expand a SQL Server
   instance, Databases, AdventureWorks2008, and then Tables. Expand
   the Person.Address table.

2. Expand the Indexes folder located beneath the Person.Address table.
   Right-click the PK_Address_AddressID index and select Properties.

The Index Properties dialog box opens. The General page contains the
Unique option, and the Options page contains the other options available:

- **Unique**—When creating new indexes or altering existing indexes, you
  can enable the Unique option to force unique values across the key
  columns. When defined, this option forces uniqueness across all columns.
  For example, if a unique index is created and multiple columns are
  selected as index key columns, each column can have duplicate values as
  long as the entire row is unique.

- **Ignore Duplicate Values**—When the Unique option is selected on the
  General page, Ignore Duplicate Values on the Options page is available.
  This option changes how SQL Server reacts when a duplicate key is
  inserted into a unique column. When this option is disabled, the entire
  transaction fails; when this option is enabled, only the duplicate insert
  part of the transaction fails.

- **Automatically Recompute Statistics**—This option allows SQL Server
  to track statistics on indexes. This is important because the Query
  Optimizer uses statistics to calculate the best execution plan.

- **Use Row and Page Locks**—This option allows the SQL Server granular
  control when altering and building indexes. A table lock is often necessary
  when the index is created or altered; however, this option allows single
  rows or individual pages to be locked, effectively reducing the possibility
  of blocking users. The result is that the index operation will take longer.

Enterprise Indexing Features

The Enterprise Edition of SQL Server 2008 offers additional features not
available in the Standard Edition. Note that these features are also available in
the Developer Edition of SQL Server 2008.

Partitioning Indexes

The table that holds data and the index pages, along with stand-alone index
structures, can be partitioned. This physically divides the data into partitions

that can reside in different filegroups across different physical disks. This feature allows large tables and indexes to be physically managed as smaller sets of data while maintaining one logical table.

When you create an index through the SQL Server Management Studio or through TSQL statements, you can set the partition scheme of the index. However, the partition scheme must already exist before the index can be configured to use the partition scheme.

If you create the index on a table that is already partitioned, the index automatically uses the same partition scheme as the parent table. Because of this, it is often easier to create the partition scheme for the underlying table first before creating the index. In this scenario, the table and index are "aligned" because they are using the same partition scheme.

However, if the index is stored away from the table in a different filegroup, the index partition scheme is not inherited from the underlying table and must be specified if necessary. In this scenario, the table and index can be "unaligned."

Online Indexing

When an index is created or rebuilt, the operation can be performed online. This allows the underlying table to be accessed during the operation. Use the following command to rebuild each of the indexes on the HumanResources.Shift table while keeping the data online:

```
USE [AdventureWorks2008]
GO
ALTER INDEX ALL ON HumanResources.Shift
REBUILD WITH(ONLINE = ON);
GO
```

You also can access the online indexing option through the SQL Server Management Studio as follows:

1. From within SQL Server Management Studio, expand a SQL Server instance, Databases, AdventureWorks2008, and then Tables. Expand the Production.Product table.

2. Right-click the Indexes folder located beneath this table and select new Index.

3. In the Name field, type **IX_SellStartDate_SellEndDate**, and in the Index Type field, select Nonclustered from the drop-down menu. Click the Add button and choose the SellStartDate and SellEndDate columns. Then click the OK button.

4. Click the Options page. Enable the option Allow Online Processing of DML Statements While Creating the Index option. Then click OK.

The index is then created online because the Allow Online Processing of DML Statements While Creating the Index option was selected.

Parallel Indexing

When an index is created, altered, or dropped, the number of processors used can be limited. Use the following command to rebuild each of the indexes on the Person.Address table in the AdventureWorks2008 database, specifying that the maximum number of processors to use is four:

```
USE [AdventureWorks2008]
GO
ALTER INDEX ALL ON [Person].[Address]
REBUILD WITH(MAXDOP=4);
GO
```

By default, the MAXDOP is set to 0, allowing the Database Engine to configure the number of processors based on how busy the server is. When the MAXDOP option is used, additional memory is used on the server.

Summary

Index design needs to be tested because different indexes are used for different situations. Creating indexes on the correct key columns and including appropriate nonkey data can significantly improve the efficiency of database operations. Creating the wrong types of indexes, too many indexes, or even setting the wrong indexing options can increase the overhead of the index along with the associated maintenance cost, resulting in decreased database performance. For this reason, it is important to understand the characteristics of each type of index along with the limitations and advantages of each.

In addition, it is also important to understand how to use the different SQL Server 2008 tools available to assist with the index design and maintenance process.

Best Practices

The following best practices were demonstrated and discussed in this chapter:

- Managing and optimizing indexes is an ongoing process because performance can suffer both with the lack of indexes and poorly implemented and managed indexes.

- Create clustered indexes on columns that are frequently used and are lean data types. For example, the clustered index could be an identity column. However, it is not uncommon to create the clustered index on a column used in WHERE, ORDER BY, and GROUP BY clauses and in joins.

- Nonclustered indexes are dependent on the clustered index. Be careful when disabling a clustered index because the nonclustered indexes are also automatically disabled.

- A table can have only one clustered index. Take care to ensure that the key length of the clustered index doesn't exceed 900 bytes.

- Use nonclustered indexes to cover frequent or costly queries that are not covered by the clustered index. As many as 999 nonclustered indexes can be created on a table.

- Take care to ensure the key length of the nonclustered index doesn't exceed 900 bytes. Add columns as nonkey include columns to place additional data into the index.

- In order to alleviate performance degradation caused by fragmentation, maintain indexes by either updating or rebuilding indexes.

- If the tempdb is stored in a different filegroup or on a different set of physical disks, use the option to sort the index in the tempdb for a performance improvement.

- Leverage the Enterprise Edition's online indexing feature to eliminate downtime when removing fragmentation from indexes.

- When deleting all indexes on a table, remember to remove the clustered index last. If the clustered index is removed first, any nonclustered indexes are unnecessarily maintained as part of the removal process.

- Spatial indexes should be created to increase the response time of spatial queries.

- Leverage Filtered indexes to improve performance and reduce maintenance costs on columns that have nulls.

CHAPTER 5

Administering SQL Server 2008 Full-Text Search

SQL Server full-text search is an optional component of SQL Server 2008. It first shipped as part of beta 3 of SQL Server 7. With each release of SQL Server, full-text search becomes significantly faster and more powerful. Full-text search in SQL Server 2008 is orders of magnitude faster than it was in the previous versions.

SQL Server full-text search allows you to rapidly search for words and tokens (like MSFT, XXX, FBI, and so on) in binary, char, nchar, varchar, nvarchar, XML, image, sysname, text, and varbinary columns. It creates an index very similar to the index that you will find at the back of this book. For example, if you wanted to find rows containing the word "test" in the full-text indexed column notes in the Authors table, you would issue the following query:

```
Select * From Authors where contains(notes,'test')
```

Although you could use the LIKE predicate for such a search, full-text searches have the following advantages over using the LIKE predicate:

- In general, they are orders of magnitude faster than using a LIKE predicate.

- They can search binary content.

- They can use language features.

However, searches using the LIKE predicate can

- Search for patterns in the middle of a word, for example:

```
select * From tableName where column  like '%una%'
```

- Search for sequences. For example, 'abc[a,b][0-9]%' will search on content beginning with abc, then either the letter a or b, then a number, and then anything else.

- Can be faster than a full-text search if you have a nonclustered index on the column, or if you are only searching on word beginnings.

SQL full-text search is typically used to allow users to conduct searches against content (for example, a jewelry store might want to allow users to search their online store catalogs), or to satisfy relational searches.

The purpose of this chapter is to explain the features of SQL full-text search and how to implement and administer them in SQL Server 2008.

New Features of SQL 2008 Full-Text Search

The following is a list of the new features in SQL Server 2008 full-text search.

- Full-text catalogs are now stored inside the database.

- SQL Server Query Optimizer now can use highly optimized execution plans against the full-text indexes stored in the catalogs.

- Noise lists (also known as stop word lists, or noise files) are now stored in the database. Microsoft now refers to there as Full-Text stoplists or more simply as stoplists. You can create any number of noise word lists, and each full-text index table or indexed view can have its own specific noise word list.

- A Dynamic Management View (DMV) is provided to troubleshoot querying.

- Two DMVs are provided to troubleshoot indexing.

- Full-text language support has been increased.

- Full-text catalogs in log-shipped or mirrored databases do not need to be repopulated when you fail over. In previous versions of SQL Server, if you log-shipped or mirrored a database that was full-text indexed, you would have to repopulate the full-text indexes when you failed over to the secondary or mirror. In SQL Server 2008 this is no longer necessary—on failover the full-text indexes are immediately accessible and queryable.

- Full-text search now works with the FILESTREAM property of varbinary(max) columns.

- A new external engine does the content extraction and indexing, called FDHost (Filter Daemon Host) also known as SQL Full-Text Host.

- Full-text search has increased language support and now supports 48 languages, up from the 23 supported in SQL Server 2005.

- Full-text search provides the ability to define a filegroup where the full-text catalogs can be stored.

- DBCC CHECKDB validates SQL full-text structures, but does not validate their contents.

- A considerable number of performance improvements have been added.

Of all the features described in the preceding list, the one that is going to have the most significant impact on developers is the performance improvements while querying. Tests on large tables reveal a significant increase in querying, especially when performing mixed queries. A mixed query is a query which combines relational and full-text predicates.

Architecture

SQL Server Full-Text Search has two essential functions, indexing and searching. The indexing process creates the full-text index that the searching function searches to determine which rows contain columns containing the word, token, or phrase you are searching for.

Indexing

The indexing engine (hosted by a process called FDHost and launched by a service called MSSQLFTLauncher) connects to your database (using a component called a *protocol handler*) and reads the tables. It extracts the textual data from the columns you are full-text indexing, using components called *word breakers*. The filters (also known as iFilters) are able to read the varchar/char, XML, and binary documents, extract the text, and then send the text to the word breakers. The filters are specific for the type of documents that are stored in the columns you are full-text indexing. By default this will be char (character) or text data. If you are storing data in columns using the char, varchar, nchar, nvarchar, or the text data types, the text filter will be used.

If you are storing XML documents in columns of the XML data type, an XML filter will be used, which has special logic that can be used to interpret and index the contents of XML documents.

Binary data requires different handling. *Binary data* is data stored in a format that is only understood by the application that reads and writes documents in that format. Typically, a text editor cannot read binary data. If you store binary data in SQL Server, for SQL full-text search to be able to full-text index it, it must be able to extract the textual data from it. To be able to index and search full-text data, you need to do the following:

1. Store it in its native format in the image or varbinary(max) columns.

2. Install the appropriate Filter or IFilter for the document type and for the bit version of your OS (32 bit or 64 bit). Filters extract the textual information and sometimes properties from the documents. You can see a list of the document types that SQL Server 2008 has filters for by querying:

```
select document_type from sys.fulltext_document_types
```

Table 5.1 documents the file extension with the document type.

For example, SQL Server 2008 contains filters for all Office documents, HTML files, and TIFF files (it can do OCR on faxes stored in the TIFF format), but it does not contain the filter for Adobe's Portable Document Format (PDF). You will need to search the Adobe web site to obtain this filter, download it, and install it on your system.

3. Add a char or varchar column to the tables you are full-text indexing that will contain the extension the binary data would have if it were stored in the file system. This column is referred to as the *document type column*.

4. Construct your full-text index referencing this document type column. Please refer to the sections "Creating a Full-Text Index Using the Wizard" and "Creating a Full-Text Index Using TSQL" later in this chapter for more information on how to do this.

For example, execute this query in the AdventureWorks 2008 database and you will get the following:

```
use AdventureWorks2008
GO
select FileExtension, BinaryData=
substring(Document,0,20)
from Production.Document
where document is not null
FileExtension
.doc        0xD0CF11E0A1B11AE1000000000000000000000000
.doc        0xD0CF11E0A1B11AE1000000000000000000000000
.doc        0xD0CF11E0A1B11AE1000000000000000000000000
.doc        0xD0CF11E0A1B11AE1000000000000000000000000
.doc        0xD0CF11E0A1B11AE1000000000000000000000000
.doc        0xD0CF11E0A1B11AE1000000000000000000000000
.doc        0xD0CF11E0A1B11AE1000000000000000000000000
.doc        0xD0CF11E0A1B11AE1000000000000000000000000
.doc        0xD0CF11E0A1B11AE1000000000000000000000000
(9 row(s) affected)
```

Table 5.1   **File Extensions of Documents Indexable by SQL FTS**

.a	Ada and Pascal code files
.ans	Word text layout files
.asc	ASCII text
.ascx	Web User Control*
.asm	Assembler source file*
.asp	Active Server Pages source file *
.aspx	Active Server Pages .NET source file*
.asx	Advanced Stream redirector file
.bas	Basic source file
.bat	Batch file
.c	C source file
.cc	C++ source file
.cls	Class source file
.cmd	Batch file
.cpp	C++ source file
.cs	Visual C# source file
.csa	Comma-separated file
.css	Cascading Style Sheets source file
.csv	Comma-separated variables list
.cxx	Borland C++ source file
.dbs	Word Printer Description file
.def	Visual C++ definition file
.dic	Microsoft Office custom dictionary
.doc	Microsoft Office Word document
.docm	Microsoft Office Word Open XML Format Document with Macros Enabled
.docx	Microsoft Office Word Open XML Format Document
.dos	Text file/DOS specification info
.dot	Word document template
.dsp	Developer Studio project
.dsw	Visual Studio workspace
.ext	SQL Extended Properties script file
.faq	Frequently Asked Questions document
.fky	Visual FoxPro macro

Table 5.1   **continued**

.h	C Header source file
.hhc	Microsoft HTML Help Contents
.hpp	HTML Help Project
.hta	HTML Program file
.htm	HTML source file
.html	HTML source file
.htt	Microsoft Hypertext Template
.htw	HTML file
.htx	Enhanced HTML template
.hxx	C++ header source file
.i	HTML file
.ibq	IsoBuster CD/DVD image file
.idl	Interface Definition Language source file
.idq	Internet Data Query source file
.inc	Include file
.inf	Install information file
.ini	Configuration file
.inl	Visual C++ inline function file
.inx	ACL for Windows index
.jav	Java source file
.java	Java source file
.jnt	Windows XP Tablet PC Edition Journal
.js	JavaScript source file
.jsl	Visual J# source file
.kci	SQL Key Constraint and Index script file
.lgn	Windows application log
.log	Generic ASCII log file
.lst	PowerPoint view file
.m3u	MP3 Playlist file
.mak	Make file (compiler instruction file)
.map	Visual Studio .NET Linker Map
.mdb	Access database
.mht	MHTML document—archived web page
.mhtml	MHTML document—archived web page

.mk	Make file (compiler instructions file)
.msg	Exchange Mail message
.obd	Office Binder document
.obt	Office Binder template
.odc	Office Data Connection
.odh	Visual Studio Interface Definition Language file
.odl	Visual C++ Type Library source (Interface Definition Language file)
.one	OneNote note file
.pl	Perl source file
.pot	PowerPoint template
.pps	PowerPoint Show
.ppt	PowerPoint document
.pptm	PowerPoint document
.pptx	PowerPoint document
.rc	C++ resource compiler script file
.rc2	Visual Studio noneditable resources
.rct	Visual Studio Resource template
.reg	Registry data file
.rgs	InstallShield script for Windows Registry
.rtf	Rich Text Format file
.rul	InstallShield rules file
.s	Assembler source code
.scc	Visual SourceSafe Control file
.shtm	HTML file containing server-side Directives
.shtml	HTML file containing server-side Directives
.snippet	Common source file format for Visual Studio products
.sol	Flash MX SharedObject
.sor	Access Snapshot file
.srf	Visual Studio Server Response file
.stm	HTML document
.tab	SQL Table script file
.tdl	Visual Studio Template Description Language file
.tif	Image file
.tiff	Image file—default for MS Fax
.tlh	Visual Studio—Typelib Generated C/C++ header file

Table 5.1 **continued**

.tli	Visual Studio—Typelib Generated C/C++ inline file
.txt	ASCII text file
.udf	SQL Function source file
.udt	SQL User Defined Type source file
.url	Internet Location file
.user	Visual Studio Project User Options
.usr	Visual Studio Project User Options
.vbs	VBScript source file
.vcproj	Visual Studio project file
.vdx	Visio document
.viw	SQL View script file
.vsd	Visio document
.vspscc	Visual Studio Source Control Project Metadata file
.vss	Visio document
.vsscc	Visual Studio Source Control Solution Root metadata file
.vssscc	Visual Studio Source Control Solution metadata file
.vst	Visio template
.vsx	XML for Visio Stencil file
.vtx	XML for Visio Template file
.wri	WordPad document
.wtx	ASCII text file
.xlb	Excel worksheet
.xlc	Excel chart
.xls	Excel document
.xlsb	Excel binary workbook
.xlsm	Excel macro-enabled workbook
.xlsx	Excel 2007 document
.xlt	Excel template
.xml	Extensible Markup Language document
.xps	XML Paper Specification
.xsd	methodXML Schema
.xslt	XSL Transform file
.zip	Compressed document

In the Production.Document table, there are nine Word documents stored in binary format in the Document column. For SQL full-text search to be able to properly index these documents, it has to know that they are Word documents, and it uses the FileExtension column to do this. If you do not give a type column or the extension you give is not recognized, the default text filter will be used.

The filters are specific for the document type; that is, the Word filters understand the file format for Word documents and the XML filters understand the file format of the XML documents, and they will emit text data from the binary documents stored in the columns you are full-text indexing. If you need to index documents for which the file type does not appear in the results of sys.full_text_document_types, you will need to install that filter on the server running SQL Server 2008, and then allow SQL Server 2008 to use them. To allow SQL Server to use these third-party filters, you will need to issue the following two commands:

```
sp_FullText_Service 'load_os_resources',1
sp_FullText_Service 'verify_signature',0
```

The first command will load all the filters installed on the OS, and the second will disable the need to verify certificates of the third-party filters. This is important if you are using an unsigned filter like Adobe's PDF filter. If you fail to do this, your filter may not load, and all filters will take longer to load as the third-party filters certificates are checked.

You can write your own filters to extend what is shipped by default in SQL Server 2008 full-text search. Refer to the following document for more information on how to do this:

```
http://msdn2.microsoft.com/en-us/library/ms916793.aspx
```

During the indexing process, the filters will read the content you want to full-text index from the base tables and then send the stream of text data to another set of components called *word breakers*. The word breakers are language specific. They will apply language rules to the text stream emitted by the filters, and they break the text stream into words or tokens that are ready for indexing. The US and UK (or International English) word breakers don't do a lot during the indexing process as the language rules applied during indexing are very simple. However, for German they will break a compound word down into its constituent words, so the word Wanderlust is broken down into Wanderlust, Wandern, and Lust—and all three words are stored in the index as such (only they are lowercased—all words are stored as Unicode and lower-cased in the index). For Far Eastern languages, the word breakers have to inter-pret the entire word and pull it apart character by character looking for constituent characters and subcharacters—each character is stored in the index.

By default the word breaker that will be used by FTHost is the language speci-fied in the `sp_configure` (unless you specify that you want the contents of the columns you are full-text indexing to be indexed in a different language).

The following T-SQL command will show you your default full-text language

```
sp_configure 'default-full-text language'
```

Results:

```
name                            minimum maximum         config_value run_value
----------------------------    ------- -------         ------------ ---------
default full-text language 0           2147483647  1033         1033
```

Here we see that we are using the Locale ID (LCID) of 1033, which corre-sponds to US English.

Please refer to the sections "Configuring Full-Text Indexes Using the Wizard" and "Configuring Full-Text Indexes Using TSQL." Note that some documents have language-specific tags in them, which will launch different word breakers than the ones you specify on your server, or in your full-text index creation statement. For example, Word and XML documents have language tags embed-ded in them; if your Word documents are in German, but you specify in your full-text index creation statement that they are to be indexed in French, your Word document will be indexed in German, not French.

There is a lot of discussion about the differences between the UK and US word breakers. Basically they are identical except for how they handle words like *realize* (US spelling) and *realise* (UK spelling). These differences show up during query time (when you are searching, not during indexing time). So if you are searching on *realize* using a FreeText search, you will get rows returned where your full-text indexed cloumns contain the words *realize*, *real-izing*, and *realized*, but not to the UK spelling of these words: *realise*, *realising*, and *realised*.

The word breaker will also break acronyms and tokens like C# in different ways. FBI will be indexed as FBI and F.B.I.; fbi will only be indexed as fbi. C# will be indexed as C with a placeholder indicating that a nonindexable character occurred after the C. Searching on C# will return rows where your full-text columns contain C#, C+, C++, C!, and so on. But c# will be indexed as c (if c is not in your noise word list).

When the word breaker has completed its task, it sends the list of words to be indexed to the indexer (also known as the *index writer*). Stop words are removed from the list of words to be indexed. *Stop words* are words that occur too frequently to be helpful in searching. For example, if you were to search on the word *the* or *internet* on a search engine, so many results would be returned that you would likely be unable to find what you are looking for. You need more specific search terms to narrow or refine your search. Stop words are considered to occur too frequently to be useful in searches and as such no one will search on them. Stop words are also called *noise words*; lists of stop words are called *stoplists*, stop word lists, or noise word lists.

In SQL Server 2008 full-text search, noise words are stored in system tables. Before a word or token is indexed in the full-text indexes by the indexer, it is checked to see if this word is in the stop word list. If it is a positional character, it is stored in the full-text index, noting that a stop word occurred at that position. Noise word lists were important in search engines a decade ago when disk costs were expensive. Now they are used to prevent terms from being indexed; for example, a Microsoft search engineer told me that a customer would add the word *sex* to his noise word list so that any searches including this term would be unable to find any documents containing the word *sex*. The search engine that powers the Microsoft public web sites adds words that occur infrequently (and the word Microsoft) to its stop word lists. The stop word lists that ship with SQL Server 2008 contain letters, numbers, personal pronouns (*I, me, mine, yours*), articles (*a, at, the, of, to*), and so on. Whenever you make a change to a stop word list, you must repopulate your full-text indexes for accurate results.

Here are the steps to maintain your stop word lists:

1. In SQL Server Management Studio, connect to a SQL Server instance.

2. Expand the database that contains the tables you want to full-text index.

3. Expand the Storage Folder.

4. Right-click on Full-Text Stop Lists.

5. Select New Full-Text Stoplist.

6. Give a name to your stoplist and assign an owner.

7. If you are adding stop words that you do not want to be indexed, the best approach is to create an empty stoplist. If you want to modify an existing stop list, select Create from the System Stoplist.

8. After your stop list is created, locate it in the Full Text Stoplists folder and select Properties. In the dialog you can add stop words or delete stop words for each language.

9. After you have made your changes, you will need to rebuild your full-text catalogs. Expand the Full Text Catalogs folder, right-click on each of your catalogs, and select Rebuild.

10. Click OK in the dialog that asks "Do you want to drop the full-text catalog and rebuild it?"

11. Click Close to exit this dialog.

The indexer builds an inverted file index, which is basically two tables, one a table of words, and the other table showing which words occur in which rows and columns, and what position they occur in. For example, consider the phrase "Peas porridge hot, peas porridge cold, peas porridge in the pot nine days old." The word table is illustrated in Table 5.2.

Table 5.2   **Hypothetical Table of Words for an Inverted File Index**

WordPK	Word
1	peas
2	porridge
3	Hot
4	Cold
5	In
6	The
7	Pot
8	Nine
9	Days
10	old

The hypothetical word position table is illustrated in Table 5.3.

Table 5.3 **Hypothetical Word Position Table**

WordPositionPK	WordPK	Position
1	1	1
2	2	2
3	3	3
4	1	4
5	2	5
6	4	6
7	1	7
8	2	8
9	5	9
10	6	10
11	7	11
12	8	12
13	9	13
14	10	14

To illustrate how this works, the first word (Peas) is stored in the word table with a value of 1, the second (porridge) is stored in the word table with a value of 2, the third word (hot) is stored in the word table with a value of 3, and the fourth word (Peas) is already in the word table with a value of 1, so it is not added again. This process is continued until all the words present in the phrase are stored in the word table. Then in the word position table, the first word (Peas) is stored with a pk of 1, and the word pk value of 1 (from the word table), and it is the first word in the phrase, so its word position is 1. The second word (porridge) is stored with a pk of 2, and its word pk has a value of 2 (from the word table) and its word position is 3. The third word (hot) is stored with a pk of 3, and its word pk has a value of 3 (from the word table) and a word position of 3. The fourth word (peas again) is stored with pk of 4, its word pk is 1, and it is the fourth word in the phrase, so its word position is 4. This continues for the entire phrase.

At any one time there may be multiple inverted file indexes for a full-text indexed table. At periodic intervals while indexing is occurring, the multiple inverted file indexes are combined into a single inverted file index through a process called a *master merge*. You can force a master merge by doing a catalog reorganize in either of two ways:

- By using the TSQL statement

  ```
  ALTER FULLTEXT CATALOG
  AW2008FullTextCatalog  REORGANIZE
  ```

  where your catalog is named `AW2008FullTextCatalog`
- By using optimization (an option available to you in the Catalog Properties dialog box).

Searching

Unlike the indexer, the search components are completely within the SQL Server query engine. When you issue your search queries using the SQL `Contains` or `FreeText` predicates (or their analogues `ContainsTable` or `FreeTextTable`), the search is conducted against the inverted file index and sometimes your base tables. Depending on the language you search in and the type of search you do, the word breakers may expand your search beyond the original search terms. For example, if you do a `FreeText` search on the word *exercise*, the search will actually be done on the following words: *exercise, exercised, exercises,* and *exercising*; and this search will return rows that contain any of the variants of the word exercise in the columns you are full-text indexing. If you are searching on a term like "University of California," the search will be conducted on "University [any word] California" as *of* is a noise word. So you will get rows returned where the full-text columns contain the word *University* before a noise word and then the word *California* occurs; for example *University of California, University to California, University at California,* and even *University Southern California* where *Southern* is not a noise word. Key to understanding why *University Southern California* is returned is that the Full-Text Search engine will return rows containing *University*, then any single word or token, and then *California*. *University of Southern California* would not be returned as there are two words between *University* and *California*. Also, at query time the query engine can do thesaurus expansions. For example, with your thesaurus file enabled, a `FreeText` query on IE would return rows where the full-text indexed columns contained IE, IE5, or Internet Explorer.

Now that we understand the architecture of full-text search, let's discuss how to create our full-text catalogs.

Implementing SQL Server 2008 Full-Text Catalogs

Full-text catalogs are essentially provided for backward compatibility with previous versions of SQL Server. In previous versions of SQL Server they would contain the full-text indexes of the tables and views you were full-text indexing. Each table you are full-text indexing can have a single full-text index on it. You can place this full-text index in only one catalog. A catalog can contain multiple full-text indexes.

The only reason you might want to have different full-text catalogs is different levels of accent sensitivity.

There are basically two steps to implementing a full-text solution. Before you create a full-text index, you must create a full-text catalog. In the wizard, full-text catalog creation can be done alongside the full-text index creation, but under the covers the catalog is always created first.

We'll first discuss creation of the full-text catalog using the wizard, and then by using the TSQL commands.

Creating a Full-Text Catalog Using the Wizard

There are two entry points to creating a full-text catalog:

- Using SQL Server Management Studio
- Using TSQL

Using SQL Server Management Studio

1. In SQL Server Management Studio, connect to a SQL Server instance.

2. Expand the Database folder that contains the tables you want to full-text index.

3. Expand the Storage folder, and right-click on the Full-Text catalog folder.

4. Select and click the New Full-Text Catalog menu item, which will display the New Full-Text Catalog dialog box as illustrated in Figure 5.1.

5. After you have set the options for your catalog, click on OK to close the dialog box.

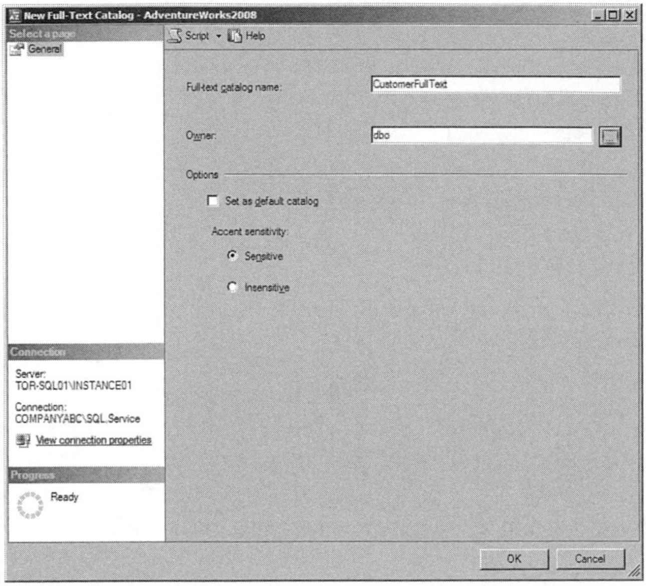

FIGURE 5.1
New Full-Text Catalog dialog.

There are several options here:

- Full-Text Catalog Name—This is the name of your full-text catalog.
  The name should be descriptive of the function of the catalog. The
  name will be used when creating full-text indexes (unless you create a
  default catalog).

- Owner—This is the owner of the full-text catalog. The owner "owns"
  the catalog: Anyone in the dbo_role in the database or sys_admin role
  on the server will be able to manage the full-text catalog, but the owner
  "owns" the full-text catalog, and the owner is the only one who will be
  able to drop it.

- Set as Default Catalog—If you select this option, you will not need to
  specify which catalog you want to use for your full-text indexes. By
  default all full-text indexes will be created in this catalog.

- Accent Sensitivity—This option controls how accents are handled in
  the full-text indexing process. If you specify that your catalog is accent
  insensitive, all words indexed have their accents removed, so if you
  search on an accented version of the word, you will get hits to all
  possible variants of that accented word, so a search on *café* will give

hits to *café, cafe, cafè, café, cafê,* and *cafë*! If you specified that you wanted your catalog to be accent sensitive, the words would be indexed with their accents, so a search on *café* would only return rows with full-text columns containing the word *café.*

Creating a Full-Text Catalog Using TSQL

The TSQL commands used to create a catalog are highly symmetrical with the SQL Full-text Search Wizard options. The TSQL syntax used to create the full-text catalog is

```
CREATE FULLTEXT CATALOG CatalogName
ON FILEGROUP FileGroupName
WITH ACCENT_SENSITIVITY=OFF
AS DEFAULT
AUTHORIZATION dbo
```

These options map to the options in the Full-Text Catalog dialog box, with the exception of the IN PATH option. This is a legacy parameter that provides backward compatibility with SQL 2005, where it specified the file system directory where the full-text catalog would be created. Values specified for this parameter in SQL Server 2008 have no effect.

The only required parameter is the catalog name parameter. There can only be one default catalog per database, and by default accent sensitivity is on.

Creating a Full-Text Index Using the Full-Text Wizard

The full-text indexes are what the SQL Server references to determine which rows match your search phrase. There are three ways to create a full-text index on your table or indexed view:

- Using TSQL commands
- Using the Full-Text Index Wizard, accessible by right-clicking on your table in SQL Server Management Studio
- Using the Full-Text Catalog Properties dialog by selecting tables in the Tables/Views tab

We will defer how to create full-text indexes on your tables or indexed views using TSQL commands until the next section. We'll discuss how to use the Full-Text Index Wizard before we talk about using the Catalog Properties dialog.

To launch the Full-Text Index Wizard:

1. In SQL Server Management Studio, connect to a SQL Server instance.

2. Expand the database that contains the tables or indexed views you want to full-text index in SQL Server Management Studio.

3. Locate the table (you can only full-text index one table at a time) and right-click on it.

4. Click the Full-Text Index menu option, and then select Define Full-Text Index as illustrated in Figure 5.2.

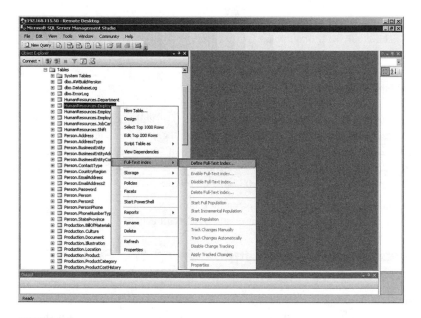

FIGURE 5.2
Launching the Full-Text Index Wizard.

We will defer the discussion of the other menu options until we have completed the Full-Text Index Wizard. Clicking on Define Full-Text Index will launch the Full-Text Index Wizard, which is illustrated in Figure 5.3.

5. Click on Next to advance the wizard to the Select an Index dialog as illustrated in Figure 5.4.

FIGURE 5.3
The Full-Text Indexing Wizard splash screen.

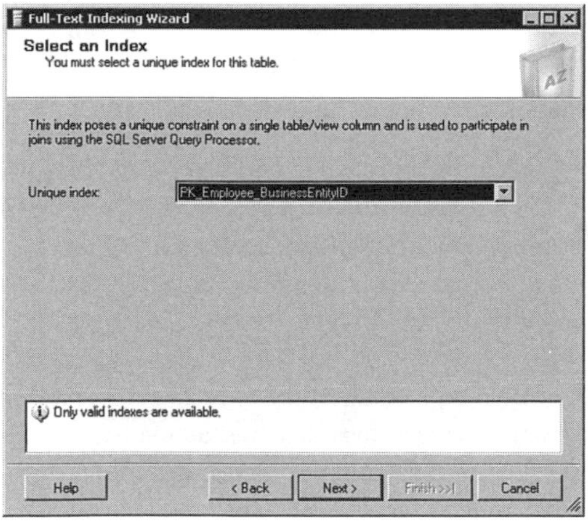

FIGURE 5.4
Select an Index dialog box.

In Figure 5.4, note that the Unique Index drop-down box displays a list of all the unique indexes that are available to use as basis for full-text indexing. Full-text indexing uses a key index to be able to identify the row it is indexing and the row returned in response to full-text searches. The key index values must be unique; otherwise, full-text indexing will be unable to determine which row it has already indexed and which rows it has yet to index.

If your table does not have any unique indexes on it, this dialog will display a message in the lower half stating that a unique column must be defined on this table/view. You will also notice that if your table does not have a unique index/primary key on it that SQL full-text indexing can use, the Unique Index drop-down list box will not be enabled.

There are three other criteria for an index to be used as a basis for a full-text index table:

    a. It must be a single-column index.

    b. The column must be nondeterministic; that is, it cannot be a computed column.

    c. It must be non-null.

4. After you have made your key index selection, click Next. This will launch the Select Table Columns dialog box, illustrated in Figure 5.5.

The Select Tables Columns dialog box is where you

- Choose which columns you want to full-text index.

- Choose which language you want your content stored in each column to be indexed in.

- Specify which column will be used to indicate to the full-text indexing engine what type of data is stored in varbinary(max) or image data type columns.

This table illustrates all the data type columns that you can full-text index: binary, char, image, nchar, ntext, nvarchar, sysname, text, varbinary, varchar, and XML data type columns. Select the columns you want to full-text index and then select the language in which you want your content to be full-text indexed, by clicking on the text box under the Language for Word Breaker column. As we discussed in the "Architecture" section, the word breaker is a COM component that applies language rules to the text stream emitted by the filters.

The Language for Word Breaker drop-down list box displays all the language options.

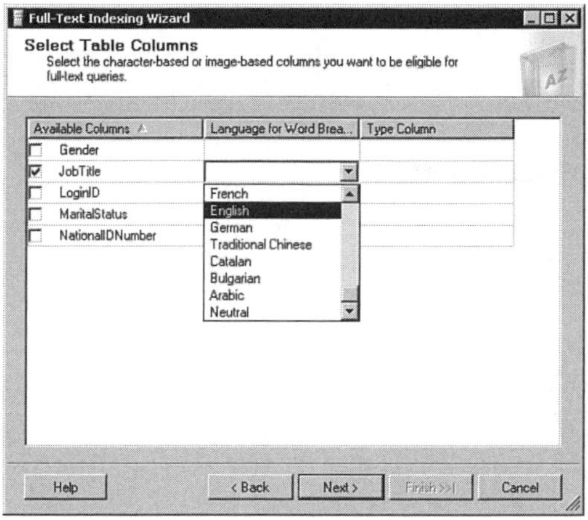

FIGURE 5.5
Select Table Columns dialog box.

See Table 5.4 for a list of all supported full-text indexing languages. If you do not select a language, the default full-text language setting for your server will be the language used. You can set this or determine the setting by using the following command:

```
sp_configure  'show advanced options', 1
RECONFIGURE WITH OVERRIDE
Sp_configure 'default full-text language'
```

This will display the following results:

```
default full-text language 0 2147483647 1033 1033
```

What is important to note here is the run_value 1033. This is the LCID (LoCale IDentifier), which corresponds to an entry in sys.fulltext_Languages, as the following query demonstrates:

```
select lcid, name From sys.fulltext_languages
where lcid=1033
```

6. After you have selected the language to be used to index your column's content, you may want to select a document type column that will tell the indexer what type of content is in your varbinary and image data type columns. This drop-down option will only be enabled for the varbinary and image data type columns.

7. When you have completed step 6, you can select Next or Finish. If you select Next, the Select Change Tracking dialog box (illustrated in Figure 5.6) will be displayed.

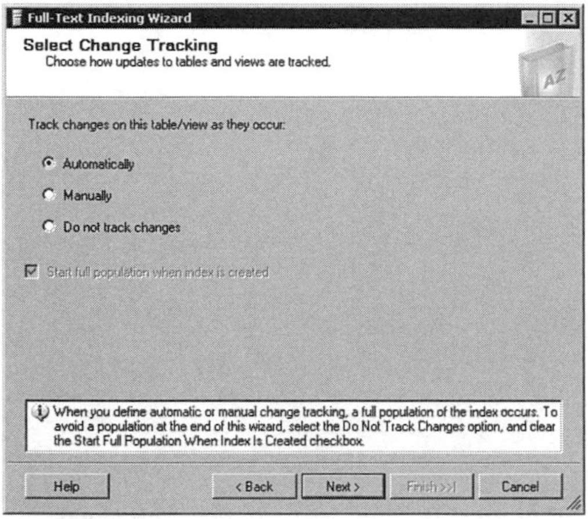

FIGURE 5.6
Select Change Tracking dialog box.

There are four options to index your content.

- Change Tracking—Apply Changes in Background
- Change Tracking—Apply Changes Manually
- Full Population
- Incremental Population

We will cover population types in the next section, "Population Types."

8. After you have selected your population method, click the Next button in the Select Change Tracking dialog box. This will launch the Select Catalog, Index FileGroup, and Stoplist dialog box illustrated in Figure 5.7.

We have already discussed the options in catalog creation in the section "Creating a Full-Text Catalog Using the Wizard." The only new option that appears here is the Select Full-Text Stoplist drop-down. By default you will be using the system stop list. If you click the drop-down box, you have the option to select other stop word lists that you have created for this database, or the <off> option. The <off> option will essentially give you an empty stop word list—in other words, full-text indexing will index all words or tokens.

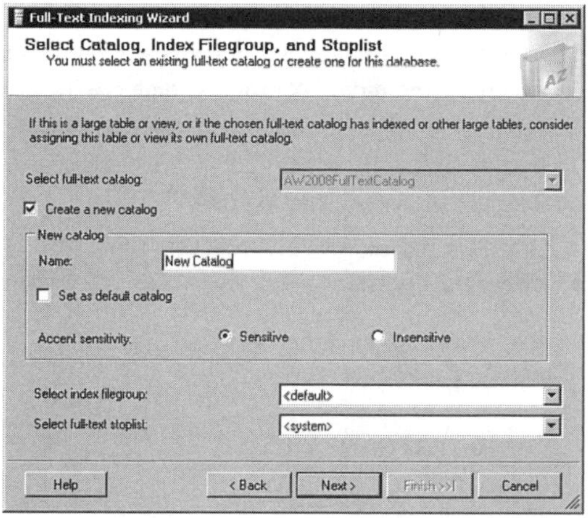

FIGURE 5.7
Select Catalog, Index Filegroup, and Stoplist dialog box.

9. After you have configured your catalog, select Next. The Define
   Population Schedules dialog box will allow you to define schedules for
   full or incrementation populations, as illustrated in Figure 5.8.

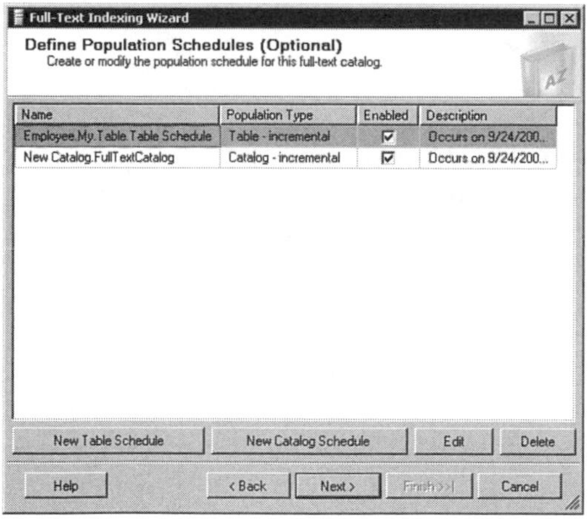

FIGURE 5.8
Define Population Schedules dialog box filled in for an incremental table and catalog
population.

10. Clicking Next will present the Full-Text Indexing Wizard Description,
    which is a summary of what the full-text indexing wizard will create. You

can expand any of the nodes for more information on how the Full-Text Indexing wizard will create your full-text index and/or catalog. Click Back to make changes, or Finish to create the index. A progress dialog will display the status of each creation step. Figure 5.9 illustrates the dialog displayed when the progress is complete. If you do get an error there will be a hyperlink you can click to get more information on the error.

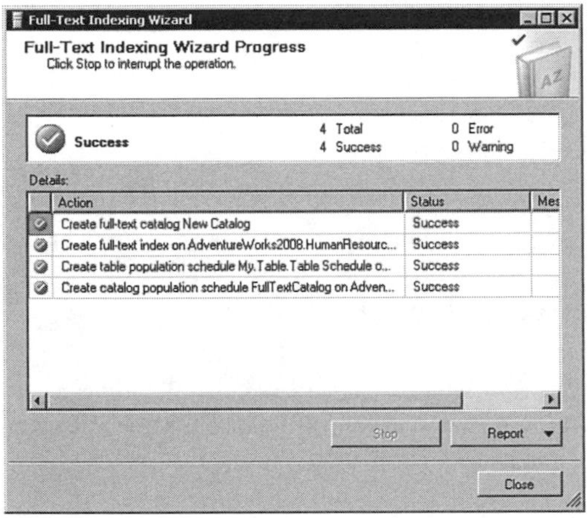

FIGURE 5.9
Full-Text Indexing progress report.

Table 5.4   **Languages Supported in Full-Text Indexing**

Chinese (Macau SAR)	Chinese (Singapore)	Serbian (Cyrillic)	Spanish
Chinese (Hong Kong SAR, PRC)	Serbian (Latin)	Portuguese	British English
Simplified Chinese	Marathi	Malayalam	Kannada
Telugu	Tamil	Gujarati	Punjabi
Bengali (India)	Malay - Malaysia	Hindi	Vietnamese
Lithuanian	Latvian	Slovenian	Ukrainian
Indonesian	Urdu	Thai	Swedish
Slovak	Croatian	Russian	Romanian
Brazilian	Norwegian (Bokmål)	Dutch	Korean
Japanese	Italian	Icelandic	Hebrew
French	English	German	Traditional Chinese
Catalan	Bulgarian	Arabic	Neutral

You can also create a full-text index on a table from the Catalog folder. To do this, use the following steps:

1. In SQL Server Management Studio, connect to a SQL Server instance.

2. Expand the database that contains the tables you want to full-text index.

3. Right-click on your catalog, select Properties, and click on the Tables/Views tab as illustrated in Figure 5.10.

4. To add a table or view, you will need to click on the arrow tab to move tables in and out of the list box titled Tables/View Objects Assigned to the Catalog.

After a table/view is assigned to the catalog, you will note that you have an option to include columns to be full-text indexed in the Eligible Columns text box at the bottom of the dialog as well as selecting Language for Word Breaker and Data Type Column (if you are indexing image or varbinary data type columns). You also have the option to select how you want this table to be populated—change tracking with update in background, change tracking with update index manually, or no population type (the Do Not Track Changes option). If you select the option to not track changes, you will be responsible for controlling the population yourself.

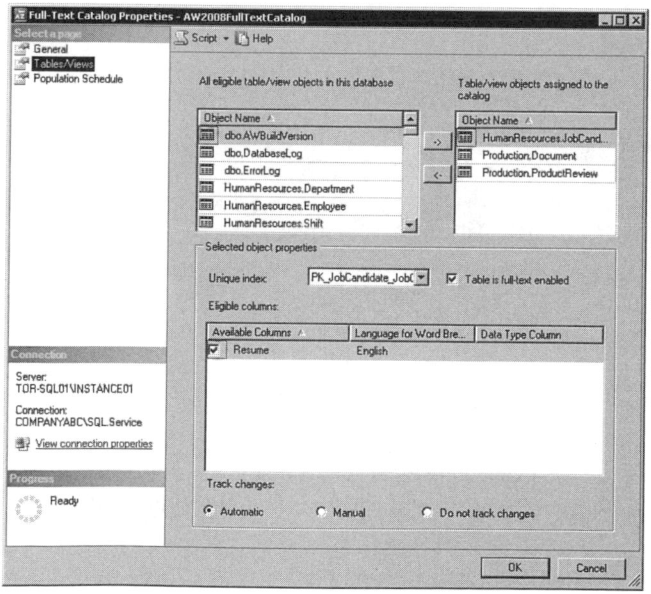

FIGURE 5.10
Creating a full-text index on a table using the Tables/Views tab of the Catalog properties dialog box.

Population Types

SQL full-text search builds indexes by gathering the data to be indexed from the base tables. This process is called *population* and there are four types of populations.

Change Tracking—Track Changes Automatically

The Automatic option is the Track Changes Automatically. Figure 5.11 illustrates where you can find this menu option in the full-text index menu options when you right click on a table. This option is also visible in the catalog properties dialog, illustrated in the lower half of Figure 5.10.

Change tracking is the process by which the full-text indexing process keeps track of changes that have occurred in the tables you are full-text indexing. By default when a change occurs in one of the columns in a row you are full-text indexing, change tracking will queue a list of the rows and their columns that changes. The indexing host then processes this change in near-real time.

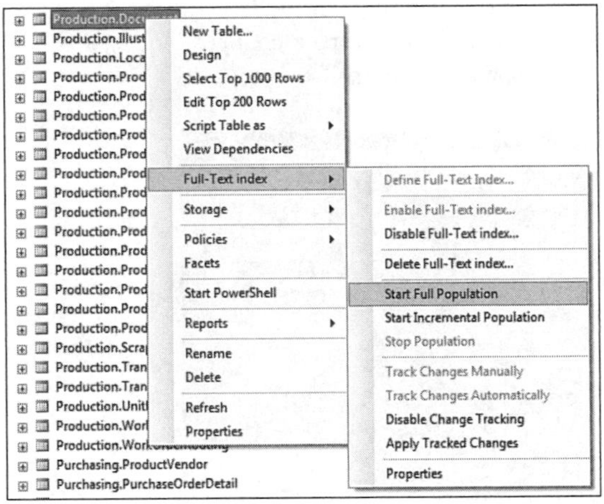

FIGURE 5.11
Selecting the change tracking options.

What is important to note about change tracking is that if you update a column that you are not full-text indexing, that row will not be full-text indexed again.

Change Tracking—Track Changes Manually

In extreme load cases there may be some locking associated with change tracking, so you have the option of postponing the indexing process until a later point in time. This is the Manually option (visible in the lower half of Figure 5.10), also known as Track Changes, Manually (visible in Figure 5.11). If you right-click on a table that you have already full-text indexed and select the Full-Text Index option, you will notice the Track Changes Manually option, which corresponds to the Manually option. If data is modified in a full-text column on your full-text index table, a list of the keys corresponding to these rows will be stored in a change tracking queue until you manually apply the changes to the indexing process—you do this by a scheduleor by right-clicking on your table and selecting full-text indexing and then the Apply Tracked Changes option. For example, you can schedule all of your full-text changes to be indexed at night or another quiet period, or you could have them scheduled to be "manually" applied every 5 minutes. You also have the option of manually applying them yourself. Keep in mind that if you choose this option you will not get real-time indexing; in other words, searches done on your full-text index will only be up to date to the last time you applied the changes.

Full-Population
As we discussed earlier, change tracking tracks changes to the full-text indexed columns and indexes the rows that have changed. This process occurs in near-real time. *Full-population* is a process that extracts each row and full-text indexes the columns you are full-text indexing. There is no change tracking involved; every row is reindexed, whether it has been changed or not. Full-populations are best used when the bulk of your data changes at one time, and consequently you have no real-time requirements. For example, if a jewelry chain wants to allow their customers to search a table with item descriptions, and the items that they have for sale only change quarterly, a full-population will work best. Change tracking introduces too much overhead.

You may find that if your data changes daily at some point in time, change tracking will work better than a full-population, but it all depends on how much data you have and how frequently you want it updated. A rough rule of thumb is that if 80% or more of your data changes at any one time, you should use full-text indexing. If less than 80% changes and you want real-time index updates, use change tracking with apply changes in background. If you experience locking between DML processes and the full-text indexing process, use Change Tracking with Apply Changes Manually. In some cases, you may find that incremental populations work best when less than 80% of your data changes at one time and you do not require near-real-time index-ing. We will cover this in the next topic.

To select Full-Population, select the Do Not Track Changes option, and ensure that the Start Full-Population When Index Is Created option is selected.

Incremental Population

An *incremental population* is best used when a significant portion of your data changes at one time and at infrequent intervals. With an incremental population, a timestamp column is required on the table you are full-text indexing. The incremental population process records the highest timestamp value each time it runs. It compares the timestamp value from the previous run and then returns a list of rows that have higher timestamp values than the last run. This way it gets a list of all the rows that have changed since the last run. Key to understanding how an incremental population are three facts:

1. If the time stamp column does not exist, a full-population is run.

2. All rows that have a higher timestamp value than the last time recorded stamp value are reindexed, even if the data in the columns you are full-text indexing has not changed. If a change is made to an ancillary column, the row will still be full-text indexed again.

3. The timestamp column only returns a list of inserted or updated rows. The incremental population process still has to retrieve key values from the entire table to determine which rows have been deleted and remove the corresponding entries from the full-text index.

Depending on how many rows have been deleted or updated, a full-population may be faster than an incremental population. You will need to do benchmarking tests to see which population method will work best for you.

Creating a Full-Text Index Using TSQL

Creating full-text indexes on your tables is syntactically similar to the way you create indexes on your tables.

In its simplest form the TSQL creation statement would look like this:

```
CREATE FULLTEXT INDEX on [HumanResources].[Department]
(Name LANGUAGE 1033)
KEY INDEX PK_Department_DepartmentID  ON (AW2008FullTextCatalog,
FILEGROUP [PRIMARY])
```

Where Name is the column you are full-text indexing, 1033 is the language you are indexing in (this is American English), PK_Department_DepartmentID is the primary key of the table [HumanResources].[Department] that you are full-text indexing, AW2008FullTextCatalog is the name of the catalog, and Primary is the name of the file group.

The arguments of the full-text index creation statement are as follows:

- **TableName**—This is the name of the table or index view that you want to full-text index.

- **ColumnName**—This is the name of the column or columns you want to full-text index. If you are indexing multiple columns, you would separate them with commas. Here is an example:

```
CREATE FULLTEXT INDEX on [HumanResources].[Department]
(Name LANGUAGE 1033, GroupName LANGUAGE 1036)
KEY INDEX PK_Department_DepartmentID  ON
(AW2008FullTextCatalog,
FILEGROUP [PRIMARY])
```

  Here we are full-text indexing two columns, Name, and GroupName. We are indexing Name using American English (I033) and GroupName using French (1036). The Language argument is completely optional.

- **Type Column**— The Type Column argument is to be used when you are full-text indexing image or varbinary columns. It contains the name of a column that tells the indexer what the type of content is in the image or varbinary column for that row; for example, for one row it might contain the value doc, and for another the value pdf. Here is an example of using the Type Column option that is used in the table [Production].[Document]:

```
--if you entered the above full-text index creation command
--you will need to drop the existing full-text index
--use this command to do it
--DROP FULLTEXT INDEX on [Production].[Document]
CREATE FULLTEXT INDEX ON [Production].[Document](
[Document] TYPE COLUMN [FileExtension] LANGUAGE [English])
KEY INDEX [PK_Document_DocumentNode]ON
([AW2008FullTextCatalog], FILEGROUP [PRIMARY])
WITH (CHANGE_TRACKING = AUTO, STOPLIST = SYSTEM)
GO
```

  Note that as this full-text index is already in place, you will need to drop it before you run the preceding command. Use this command to drop it:

```
Use AdventureWords2008
GO
DROP FULLTEXT INDEX on [Production].[Document]
```

The warning applies to inserts or updates made to your image or varbinary columns using WRITETEXT or UPDATETEXT operations that are not logged. If you use these operations to update the tables you are full-text indexing, these changes will not be indexed.

- Language—This option is used to apply different language word breakers to your full-text indexed columns. It is optional and if you do not use this option, the default full-text language setting will determine which language word breaker will be used. To determine the LCID to be used, consult sys.fulltextlanguages. In addition, note that if you are indexing language-aware documents (like Word and XML documents), the language settings in these documents will override whatever language you have specified your columns to be indexed in.

- Key Index—Key Index is the unique index that you are using as a key for full-text indexing operations. Please refer to the Type Column discussion for a sample of its usage.

- Full-Text Catalog Name—This is the name of your full-text catalog. If you have a default full-text catalog set up for the database that contains your tables that you are full-text indexing, you will not need to specify a catalog. Please refer to the Type Column discussion for a sample of its usage.

- FileGroup—This parameter is for backward compatibility only.

- Change_Tracking—This parameter determines how your full-text index is populated. By default, Change Tracking with Update Index in Background will be done. You can also select Change Tracking with Update Index Manually, or that no population should occur after full-text index creation.

Here are some examples of these features. The following three statements are all equivalent. The = is optional, and Change Tracking with Update Index in Background is the default.

```
CREATE FULLTEXT INDEX ON [Production].[Document](
[Document] TYPE COLUMN [FileExtension] LANGUAGE [English])
KEY INDEX [PK_Document_DocumentNode]ON ([AW2008FullText
Catalog],
FILEGROUP [PRIMARY])
WITH CHANGE_TRACKING=AUTO
CREATE FULLTEXT INDEX ON [Production].[Document](
[Document] TYPE COLUMN [FileExtension] LANGUAGE [English])
```

```
KEY INDEX [PK_Document_DocumentNode]ON ([AW2008FullText
Catalog],
FILEGROUP [PRIMARY])
WITH CHANGE_TRACKING AUTO
CREATE FULLTEXT INDEX ON [Production].[Document](
[Document] TYPE COLUMN [FileExtension] LANGUAGE [English])
KEY INDEX [PK_Document_DocumentNode]ON ([AW2008FullText
Catalog],
FILEGROUP [PRIMARY])
```

For manual change tracking the following command would be used:

```
CREATE FULLTEXT INDEX ON [Production].[Document](
[Document] TYPE COLUMN [FileExtension] LANGUAGE [English])
KEY INDEX [PK_Document_DocumentNode]ON ([AW2008FullText
Catalog],
FILEGROUP [PRIMARY])
WITH CHANGE_TRACKING MANUAL
```

For no populations you would use the following command

```
CREATE FULLTEXT INDEX ON [Production].[Document](
[Document] TYPE COLUMN [FileExtension] LANGUAGE [English])
KEY INDEX [PK_Document_DocumentNode]ON ([AW2008FullText
Catalog],
FILEGROUP [PRIMARY])
```

Users may see this warning... Warning: Request to start a full-text index population on table or indexed view 'Production.Document' is ignored because a population is currently active for this table or indexed view.

```
WITH CHANGE_TRACKING=OFF,NO POPULATION
```

If you wanted to do a full population after the fact, you would use the `ALTER FULLTEXT INDEX` command as in the following example:

```
ALTER FULLTEXT INDEX ON [Production].[Document]
START FULL POPULATION
```

If you were using Change Tracking with Update Index Manually and you wanted all tracked changes updated in the index, you would use the following command:

```
ALTER FULLTEXT INDEX ON [Production].[Document]
START UPDATE POPULATION
To drop a full-text catalog use the following command:
DROP FULLTEXT INDEX ON MyTable
```

Maintaining Full-Text Indexes

When you have completed creating a full-text index using the wizard, you may need to control the index population on the table or catalog level.

To do this, right-click on your table and select Full-Text Indexing. This option is illustrated in Figure 5.12.

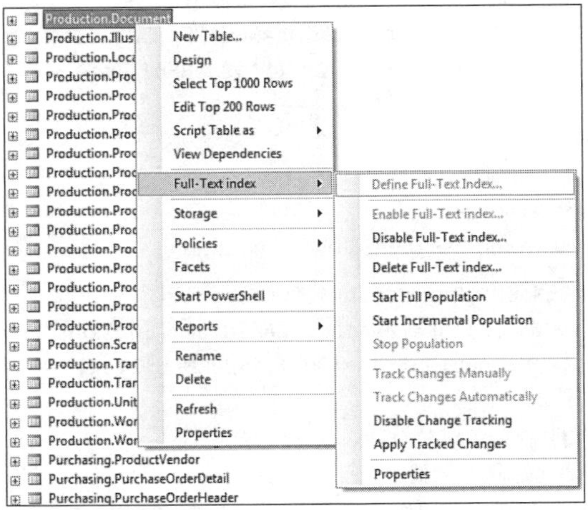

FIGURE 5.12
Options to control the full-text index.

You will notice the following options:

- Define Full-Text Index (disabled in Figure 5.12)—Use this option to create a full-text index on your table.

- Enable Full-Text Index (disabled in Figure 5.12)—Use this option to enable a disabled full-text index.

- Disable Full-Text index—Used to disable a full-text index. The index will be searchable, but will not index any new rows or changes until it is enabled. After an index is enabled, you will need to run a full or incremental population. If change tracking is enabled, SQL Server will automatically start a full or incremental population. Incremental populations will be done if there is a timestamp column on the table and a full population has already been run. Otherwise SQL Server will automatically do the full-population.

- Delete Full-Text Index—Used to delete a full-text index. You will no longer be able to search this index after it is deleted.

- Start Full-Population—Will start a full-population. Use this if you are manually controlling your populations or have made a change to the full-text index, or the stop word list.

- Start Incremental Population—Will start an incremental population if there is a timestamp column on the table you are full-text indexing.

- Stop Population (disabled in Figure 5.12)—Use this option if you need to stop a population for performance reasons, or if you need to do maintenance on your full-text index, for example, to change a stop word list.

- Disable Change Tracking—This option will disable change tracking permanently. To keep your full-text index up to date, you will need to enable this option again (using the Track Changes Manually or Track Changes Automatically option, or by running a full or incremental population).

- Apply Tracked Changes—Use this option if you have enabled Track Changes Manually. You will need to select Apply Tracked Changes to feed the latest changes that have occurred on your full-text indexed table to the indexing process.

- Start PowerShell—This option provides a window into PowerShell to create and run PowerShell scripts.

- Properties—This option launches the Full-Text Index Properties dialog box where you can configure properties on your full-text index.

The options Define Full-Text Index, Enable Full-Text Index, Stop Population, Track Changes Manually, and Track Changes Automatically are not enabled in this dialog as they are mutually exclusive with an already created full-text index on a table that has change tracking enabled.

Creating Stop Lists

Stop lists are used when you want to hide words in searches or to prevent words from being indexed that would otherwise bloat your full-text index and might cause performance problems. Stop lists (also known as noise word lists or stop word lists) are a legacy component from decades ago when disk prices were very expensive. Back then, using stop lists could save considerable disk space. However, with disk prices being relatively cheap, the use of stop lists is no longer as critical as it once was. You can create your own stop word list using the following instructions:

1. In SQL Server Management Studio, connect to your SQL Server.

2. Expand your database in SQL Server Management Studio, and then right-click on the Full-Text Stop Lists node.

3. Select New Full-Text StopList.

You have an option of creating your own stop list, basing it on a system stop list, creating an empty one, or creating one based on another stop list in a different database. Each catalog can have its own stop list, which is a frequently demanded feature, as some search consumers want to be able to prevent some words from being indexed in one table, but want the same words indexed in a different table.

To maintain your stop word lists:

1. In SQL Server Management Studio, connect to a SQL Server instance.

2. Expand the database, the Storage folder, and the Full-Text Stop Lists folder.

3. Right-click on the stop list you need to maintain. Select Properties. Figure 5.13 illustrates this option.

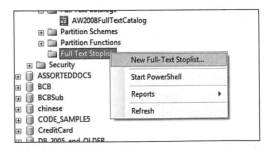

FIGURE 5.13
Maintaining a full-text stop list.

The options are to add a stop word, delete a stop word, delete all stop words, and clear the stop list. After you select which option you want, you can enter a stop word, and then the language to which you want that stop word to be applied.

Keep in mind that the stop lists are applied at query time (while searching) and at index time (while indexing). Changes made to a stop list will be reflected in real time in searches, but will only be applied to newly indexed words. The stop words will still be in the catalog until you rebuild the catalog. It is a best practice to rebuild your catalog as soon as you have made changes to your stop word list. To rebuild your full-text catalog, right-click on the catalog in SQL Server Enterprise Manager and select the Rebuild option.

Thesaurus Option

Frequently searchers will want their search automatically expanded to another term; for example, if you search on *cars* you might want also want results returned for *automobiles,* or if you search on the word *center,* you might want results coming back that include the alternative spelling *centre.* This type of thesaurus capability is called an *expansion.* Alternatively, some search administrators will want a search term replaced by another term altogether. For example, some searchers might search on *Bombay,* a city in India that is now called *Mumbai.* If all of the content in the database used the term *Mumbai,* search administrators will want to replace the search term *Bombay* with *Mumbai.*

SQL Server full-text search has a Thesaurus option, which allows for both expansions and replacements. At the command prompt, navigate to `C:\Program Files\Microsoft SQL Server\MSSQL10.MSSQLSERVER\MSSQL\FTData`. Note that Vista users will have to run the command prompt as an administrator or log on as an administrator to enable this feature. You will notice 48 language-specific XML thesaurus files there. Use the `TSGlobal.xml` thesaurus file if you want to add patterns and replacements that will be applied to all language-specific thesaurus files. Otherwise, edit the thesaurus file for your language. The thesaurus file will look something like this:

```
<XML ID="Microsoft Search Thesaurus">
<!-- Commented out
    <thesaurus xmlns="x-schema:tsSchema.xml">
        <diacritics_sensitive>0</diacritics_sensitive>
        <expansion>
            <sub>Internet Explorer</sub>
```

```
            <sub>IE</sub>
            <sub>IE5</sub>
        </expansion>
        <replacement>
            <pat>NT5</pat>
            <pat>W2K</pat>
            <sub>Windows 2000</sub>
        </replacement>
        <expansion>
            <sub>run</sub>
            <sub>jog</sub>
        </expansion>
    </thesaurus>
-->
</XML>
```

What is important to note here is that before you can start to use the thesaurus
options, you will need to edit your thesaurus file using a text editor (preferably
Notepad as some commercial text editors will not save the thesaurus file
correctly), and edit out the two comment tags. There are three options in the
thesaurus file:

- Diacritics_sensitive—This is analogous to the accent sensitivity
  settings on your catalog. With Diacritics Sensitive set to 0, accents will
  not be respected. So if you have a replacement of *café* with *coffee*, a
  search on *cafe* will be replaced with the search term *coffee*. Setting this
  value to 1 will replace both search terms *café* and *cafe* with *coffee*.

- Replacements—These are search terms you want to have replaced with
  another search term. The pat tag indicates this is a pattern you want
  replaced. The sub tag indicates what the replacement search word or
  phrase is to be. As the sample thesaurus file indicates, you can have
  more than one replacement. To add your own replacement, you must
  start and end the replacement with <replacement> and </replacement>
  respectively. The word or phrase you want to be replaced must be delimited by the pat tags, for example, if you want *sex* replaced by *gender*,
  you would need to wrap *sex* in the pat tags like this:

```
<pat>sex</pat>
```

Then your substitute gender would be wrapped in the sub tags like this:

```
<sub>gender</sub>
```

So your entire replacement section would look like this:

```
<replacement><pat>sex</pat><sub>gender</sub></replacement>
```

- Expansions—These are search terms where you want results returned to the original search word, but also to other words or phrases. The example in the thesaurus file is for *Internet Explorer*. The expansions are *IE* and *IE5*. So if you were searching on *Internet Explorer*, you would get search results to rows containing the terms *Internet Explorer*, rows containing *IE*, and rows containing *IE5*. The same formatting rules apply to the expansion tags as the replacement tags.

To test the thesaurus option, create a small table that contains the pattern and substation terms on different rows and then do FreeText searches. FreeText searches do implicit thesaurus expansion and replacements.

Using Full-Text Search

The focus of this book is on administering SQL Server 2008, and the focus of this chapter is on administering SQL Server 2008 full-text search. Complete coverage of full-text queries is beyond the scope of this book and more appropriate for a book on SQL Server 2008 programming. However, as it is essential for the DBA to test full-text search to ensure that it is working correctly, this section will present the basics on how to search the full-text indexes.

There are two types of searches:

- Contains—A strict word/phrase-based search: exact matches only by default.

- FreeText—A more natural way to search where the search terms are linguistically expanded so that a search is conducted on both singular and plural forms of nouns, articles, and all declensions of a verb. So a search on *apple* would return rows containing *apple* and *apples*, and a search on *mouse* would return rows containing *mouse* and *mice*. This expansion of terms is called *stemming*.

There are two variants of these searches:

- Contains/ContainsTable
- FreeText/FreeTextTable

Typical Contains/FreeText searches can be conducted like this:

```
select *
from [Production].[Document]
where CONTAINS(Document, 'arm')
```

```
select *
from [Production].[Document]
where FREETEXT(Document, 'arm')
```

There are several points to note here:

- You can search on all columns (*), or one or more columns (Col1, Col2). If you search on more than one column, you must delimit them with commas.

- All searches whether they are on a word/token or a phrase must be wrapped in single quotes. If you are searching on phrases using the Contains predicate, you must wrap the phrase in double quotes. If you wrap a phrase in double quotes in a FreeText query, the search will be the functional equivalent of a Contains query; that is, you will get no stemming.

FreeText queries by default are expanded by all expansions in the TSGlobal.xml file and the thesaurus file for your language.

Contains queries can be made more FreeText-like by using the following predicates:

- FormsOf(Inflectional, "my search term")—Where your phrase is stemmed:

  ```
  SELECT Title FROM production.Document
  WHERE CONTAINS (*, 'FormsOf(Inflectional, cycle)')
  ```

- FormsOf(Thesaurus, "my search term")—Where your phrase is expanded according to your thesaurus file and the global thesaurus file (TSGlobal.xml).

- Near—By using NEAR or ~, for example:

  ```
  Select * from [Production].[Document]
  where CONTAINS(Document, '"crank" NEAR "arm"')
  ```

- Boolean operators—You can use AND, OR, and NOT, for example:

  ```
  Select * from [Production].[Document]
  where CONTAINS(Document, '"crank" AND NOT "hand"')
  ```

- Weighted—You can weigh the importance of search terms:

```
Select * from [Production].[Document]
where CONTAINS(Document, 'ISABOUT("crank", arm
WEIGHT(0.9))')
```

- * (a wildcard operator)—Using this predicate will wild-card the search term, so a search on *hel** will return rows containing *hell, Helen, help,* and *Helwig.* Note that if you wild-card one term in a search phrase, all terms in the search phrase will be wild-carded. Here is a example:

```
SELECT Title FROM production.Document
WHERE CONTAINS (*, '"reflect*"')
```

The Contains Table/FreeTextTable clause returns a ranked rowset. Here is an example of its usage:

```
SELECT Title, RANK  FROM production.Document join
CONTAINSTABLE(production.Document, *,'reflector') AS k ON
k.[Key]=production.Document.DocumentNode ORDER BY RANK DESC
```

ContainsTable and FreeText tables are especially valuable as they return a rank that can be used to order so that the most relevant searches are returned first. They also have a top_n_by_rank parameter, which allows you to limit the number of rows returned. Performance might be unacceptable if you were to conduct a complex query that returns several hundred thousand rows. This parameter is especially useful for such searches where you only want 100 rows returned. Here is an example of its usage:

```
SELECT Title, rank FROM production.Document join
CONTAINSTABLE(production.Document, *,'reflector',100) AS k ON
k.[Key]=production.Document.DocumentNode ORDER BY RANK DESC
```

Troubleshooting Full-Text Indexing

The first question you should ask yourself when you have a problem with SQL full-text search is: Is the problem with searching or with indexing? To make this determination Microsoft has included three Dynamic Management Views (DMVs) in SQL Server 2008 to help you answer this question:

- sys.dm_fts_index_keywords
- sys.dm_fts_index_keywords_by_document
- sys.dm_fts_parser

The first two DMVs will display the contents of your full-text index. The first DMV will return the following columns:

- Keyword—Each keyword in varbinary form
- Display _term—The keyword as indexed; all the accents will be removed from the word.
- Column_ID—The column ID in which the word exists
- Document_Count—The number of times the word exists in that column

The second DMV breaks down the keywords by document. Like the first DMV it also contains the Keyword, display_term, and Column_ID columns, but in addition it contains the following two columns:

- Document_ID—The row in which the keyword occurred
- Occurrence_count—The number of times the word occurred in the cell (a cell is also known as a *tuple*; it is a row-column combination, that is, the contents of the third column in the fifth row)

The first DMV is used primarily to determine candidate noise words and hapax legomena (words that occur once in your index and are likely typos) and can be used to diagnose indexing problems. The second DMV is used to determine what was stored in your index for a particular cell.

Here are some examples of their usage:

```
select * From sys.dm_fts_index_keywords(DB_ID(),
Object_iD('Production.Document'))
select * From sys.dm_fts_index_keywords_by_document(DB_ID(),
Object_iD('Production.Document'))
```

These two DMVs are used to determine what occurs at index time. The third DMV is used primarily to determine what happens at search time; in other words, how SQL Server full-text search interprets your search phrase. Here is an example of its usage.

```
select * from sys.dm_fts_parser(@queryString,
@LCID, @StopListID, @AccentSensitive)
```

@QueryString is your search word or phrase, @LCID is the LoCale ID for your language (determinable by querying sys.fulltext_languages), @StopListID is your stoplist file (determinable by querying

sys.fulltext_stoplists), and @AccentSensitive allows you to set accent
sensitivity (0 not sensitive, 1 sensitive to accents). Here is an example of how
this works:

```
select * from sys.dm_fts_parser('café', 1033, 0, 1)
select * from sys.dm_fts_parser('café', 1033, 0, 0)
```

In the second example, you will notice that the display_term is cafe and not
café. These queries return the following columns:

- Keyword—A varbinary representation of your keyword.

- Group_id—The query parser builds a parse tree of the search phrase. If
  you have any Boolean searches, it will assign different Group_IDs to
  each part of the search term. For example, in the search phrase '"Hillary
  Clinton" OR "Barak Obama"' Hillary and Clinton will belong to
  Group_ID 1 and Barak and Obama will belong to Group_ID 2.

- Phrase_id— Some words are indexed in multiple forms, for example
  data-base is indexed as data, base, and database. In this case data and
  base will have the same Phrase_id and database will have another
  phrase_id.

- Occurence_count—This is how frequently the word appears in the
  search string.

- Special_term—Refers to any delimiters that the parser finds in the
  search phrase. Possible values are Exact Match, End of Sentence, End
  of Paragraph, and End of Chapter.

- Display_term—This is how the term would be stored in the index.

- Expansion_type—The type of expansion: whether it is a thesaurus
  expansion (4) , an inflectional expansion (2), or not expanded (0). For
  example, this query will show the stemmed variants of the word run:

```
select * from sys.dm_fts_parser('FORMSOF( INFLECTIONAL,
run)',
1033, 0, 0)
```

- Source_Term—This is the source term as it appears in your query.

When troubleshooting indexing problems, consult the full-text error log,
which can be found in C:\Program Files\Microsoft SQL Server\
MSSQL10.MSSQLSERVER\MSSQL\LOG and will start with the prefix SQLFT
followed by the database ID (padded with leading 0s), the catalog_id (query
sys.fulltext_catalogs for this value), and then an extension of LOG. You

may find many versions of the log each with a numerical extension, such as `SQLFT0001800005.LOG.4`. This is the fourth version of this log. These full-text indexing logs can be read by any text editor.

You may find entries in this log indicating that documents were retried or documents failed indexing along with error messages returned from the filters.

Best Practices

Here are some general best practices for improving SQL Server 2008 full-text search performance:

- Make your key index as narrow as possible—preferably an integer column with a nonclustered index on it. If your key index is your clustered index, place a nonclustered index on it as well and consider making this index a covering index.

- Consider partitioning very large tables into different physical tables (full-text indexing does not take advantage of partitioned tables). By doing so you can issue full-text queries in parallel and union all the results.

- Consider converting any binary data to text before storing it in the database to increase indexing performance and decrease indexing time. Note that OCR documents (TIFFs) are the most resource-intensive documents to full-text index.

- If you are using change tracking, reorganize your indexes periodically to improve performance and decrease fragmentation. Right-click on your catalog, select Properties, and click Optimize Catalog.

- If you are using change tracking, and experience locking while full-text indexing (especially when using the change tracking population types), use trace flag 7464, i.e.

```
DBCC TRACEON (7646, -1)
```

Microsoft has provided the following DMVs to help you monitor the indexing process:

- `Sys.dm_fts_outstanding_batches`—This is a list of what is currently in the queue to be full-text indexed. Watch for entries in the is_retry_batch, retry_hints, retry_hints_description, and doc_failed columns. These indicate problems with locking between user activity and the indexing process as well as the filters malfunctioning or being unable to index the contents of binary object in the row.

- Sys.dm_fts_fdhosts—This provides information on the index's host process. Watch to see if the number of batches increases or remains high. This can indicate memory pressure in the OS, or insufficient resources; for example, when you index Asian-language content, you will see this value remain high as it is a CPU-intensive process.

- Sys.dm_fts_memory_buffers—The indexing process is not only CPU intensive but also can be memory intensive if you are indexing large numbers of large documents.

- Sys.dm_fts_index_population—Use this DMV to check the status of your indexing processes. Under resource pressure (for example, low disk space), the population process may pause. Check the status_description column for more information on your indexing progression.

- Sys.dm_fts_active_catalogs—This DMV reports on the status of your full-text catalogs.

- Sys.dm_fts_memory_pools—This DMV reports on memory use of the full-text indexing process. If the buffer_count is consistently high, you may need to cap the amount of memory SQL Server uses to dedicate some memory to the OS (and consequently the indexing process).

- Sys.dm_fts_population_ranges—This DMV returns information about the specific ranges related to a full-text index population currently in progress.

Summary

SQL Server full-text search is a powerful component in SQL Server; the new features in SQL Server 2008 make it a compelling upgrade for high full-text search consumers. The performance of SQL Server 2008 full-text search is orders of magnitude faster than previous versions.

CHAPTER 6

SQL Server 2008 Maintenance Practices

For SQL Server databases to perform at optimal levels, a database administrator (DBA) should conduct routine maintenance on each database. Some of these routine database tasks involve rebuilding indexes, checking database integrity, updating index statistics, and performing internal consistency checks and backups. These routine database maintenance tasks are often overlooked because they are redundant, tedious, and often time-consuming. Moreover, today's DBAs are overwhelmed with many other tasks throughout the day. In recognition of these issues, SQL Server provides a way to automate or manually create these routine DBA chores with a maintenance plan. After the maintenance tasks are identified and created, routine maintenance should commence daily, weekly, monthly, or quarterly, depending on the task. Ultimately, these tasks will put organizations on the path to having healthier, consistent, and more trustworthy databases.

What's New for Maintenance with SQL Server 2008?

SQL Server 2008 doesn't necessarily introduce any new compelling features and functionality associated with creating maintenance plans; however, the SQL Server Program team continues to deliver rich features that were introduced with the release of Service Pack 2 for SQL Server 2005. The following list describes some of these features:

- With SQL Server 2005, the installation of SQL Server Integration Services (SSIS) was warranted if organizations wanted to run maintenance plans. Integration Services is not required because maintenance plans are now a fully supported feature within the Database Engine.

- The Maintenance Plan designer continues to support multiple subplans within a maintenance plan and the functionality to create independent schedules for each subplan.

- For increased administration, maintenance plans continue to support multiserver environments and logging maintenance plan information to remote servers. Maintenance plans can be configured for all target servers from one central master server.

- With the release of SQL Server 2008, new backup compression options have been added to the Database Backup maintenance plan tasks.

- Separate execution schedules can be created for each subtask within a maintenance plan.

Establishing a SQL Server Maintenance Plan

A maintenance plan performs a comprehensive set of SQL Server jobs that run at scheduled intervals. The maintenance plan conducts scheduled SQL Server maintenance tasks to ensure that relational databases within the database engine are performing optimally, conducting regular backups, and checking for anomalies. The Database Maintenance Plan, a feature included within the SQL Server Database Engine, can be used to automatically create and schedule these daily tasks. A comprehensive maintenance plan includes these primary administrative tasks:

- Running database integrity checks
- Updating database statistics
- Reorganizing database indexes
- Performing database backups
- Cleaning up database historical operational data
- Shrinking a database
- Cleaning up leftover files from the maintenance plan
- Executing SQL Server jobs
- Cleaning up maintenance tasks

Check Database Integrity Task

The Check Database Integrity Task verifies the health and structural integrity of both user and system tables within relational databases selected in the SQL Server Database Engine. When running this task, you have the option to also check the integrity of all index pages. This specific task can be created in the Maintenance Plan Wizard, which will manually create a maintenance task. On the other hand, you can use TSQL to create this task. When you create the Database Integrity Task, the database options available include all system databases, all user databases, or specific databases.

Although the following example shows basic syntax, it supplies the information you need to assess the health and integrity of the database on the AdventureWorks2008 database.

```
USE [AdventureWorks2008]
GO
DBCC CHECKDB(N'AdventureWorks2008') WITH NO_INFOMSGS
```

Shrink Database Task

The Shrink Database Task reduces the physical database and log files to a specific size, similar to the Automatic Shrink Task available in SSMS. When creating a maintenance task, you can shrink all databases, all system databases, all user databases, or specific databases within a single task. This operation removes excess space in the database based on a percentage value you enter in MB. In addition, thresholds must be entered, indicating the amount of shrinkage that needs to take place after the database reaches a certain size and the amount of free space that must remain after the excess space is removed.

Finally, free space can be retained in the database or released back to the operating system. For example, if you believe that the database will grow again after a shrink operation, then it is a best practice to retain freed space in database files. This will condense the database based on contiguous pages, however, the pages are not de-allocated and the database files will not physically shrink. On the other hand, if you anticipate that the files will not regrow after a shrink operation, the second option will physically shrink the files and release the free space back to the operating system.

This TSQL syntax shrinks the AdventureWorks2008 database, returns freed space to the operating system, and allows for 15 percent of free space to remain after the shrink:

```
USE [AdventureWorks2008]
GO
DBCC SHRINKDATABASE(N'AdventureWorks2008', 15, TRUNCATEONLY)
GO
```

> **Tip**
>
> When you create maintenance plans, it is a best practice not to select the option to shrink the database. First, when shrinking the database, SQL Server moves pages toward the beginning of the file, allowing the tail end of the files to be shrunk. This process can increase the transaction log size because all moves are logged. Second, if the database is heavily used and there are many inserts, the database files will have to grow again. Since SQL Server 2005, Microsoft has addressed slow autogrowth with instant data file initialization; therefore, the growth process is not as slow as it was in the past. It should be noted that instant file initialization only occurs on the data file and not the log file. If the log file must grow, it still must "zero" out the new space to ensure consistency, which will cause performance issues. However, at times autogrow does not catch up with the space requirements, causing performance degradation.
>
> Third, constant shrinking and growing of the database leads to excessive fragmentation. Therefore, if you need to shrink the database size, it should be done manually when the server is not being heavily utilized.

Reorganize Index Task

When there is a need to improve index scanning performance, look to the Reorganize Index Task.

This task defragments and compacts clustered and nonclustered indexes on all tables or views, or a particular table or view. The Reorganize Index Task can also be applied to all databases, system databases, user databases, or individually targeted databases. By also selecting an additional option, large object (LOB) data types such as images, text and FILESTREAM data will also be included in the compacting process.

To gain better insight into the operation of this task, use the TSQL syntax that follows to reorganize indexes for the AdventureWorks2008 [Sales].[SalesOrderDetail] table. This example also includes the option to compact large objects:

```
USE [AdventureWorks2008]
GO
ALTER INDEX [AK_SalesOrderDetail_rowguid]
ON [Sales].[SalesOrderDetail]
REORGANIZE WITH ( LOB_COMPACTION = ON )
GO
USE [AdventureWorks2008]
GO
```

```
ALTER INDEX [IX_SalesOrderDetail_ProductID]
ON [Sales].[SalesOrderDetail]
REORGANIZE WITH ( LOB_COMPACTION = ON )
GO
USE [AdventureWorks2008]
GO
ALTER INDEX [PK_SalesOrderDetail_SalesOrderID_SalesOrderDetailID]
ON [Sales].[SalesOrderDetail]
REORGANIZE WITH ( LOB_COMPACTION = ON )
```

Rebuild Index Task

The Rebuild Index Task aims to eliminate fragmentation by reorganizing all the table indexes in the database. This task is particularly good for ensuring that query performance and application response do not degrade. Therefore, when SQL is called on to conduct index scans and seeks, it operates at its full potential. In addition, this task optimizes the distribution of data and free space on the index pages, which allows for growth to take place faster.

The two Rebuild Index Task free space options consist of the following:

- **Reorganize Pages with the Default Amount of Free Space**—Drop the indexes on the tables in the database and re-create them with the fill factor that was specified when the indexes were created.

- **Change Free Space per Page Percentage To**—Drop the indexes on the tables in the database and re-create them with a new, automatically calculated fill factor, thereby reserving the specified amount of free space on the index pages. The higher the percentage, the more free space is reserved on the index pages, and the larger the index grows. Valid values are from 0 through 100.

The Rebuild Index Task advanced options consist of the following:

- **Sort Results in tempdb**—The Sort Results in tempdb option is the first advanced option available in the Rebuild Index Task. This option is comparable to the SORT_IN_TEMPDB option for the index. When this option is enabled, the intermediate results are stored in tempdb during the rebuild of an index.

- **Keep Index Online While Reindexing**—The second advanced option allows users to access the underlying table, clustered index data, and the associated indexes during the index rebuild operation. It is worth mentioning that the online index option requires a significant amount of free space on the hard disk. For example, if the indexes on the table take up 3GB of space, then an additional 3GB of disk space is required for this process as the old indexes get swapped out once the new ones have been created.

Armed with the knowledge of what the Rebuild Index Task can do, use the following information to gain some hands-on experience. Use the Rebuild Index syntax that follows to rebuild indexes for the AdventureWorks2008 [Sales]. [SalesOrderDetail] table. The option to Reorganize pages using the default amount of free space has been selected. This example will also sort results in tempdb and keep the index online while reindexing.

```
USE [AdventureWorks2008]
GO
ALTER INDEX [AK_SalesOrderDetail_rowguid] ON [Sales].[SalesOrder
Detail] REBUILD PARTITION = ALL WITH ( PAD_INDEX  = OFF,
STATISTICS_NORECOMPUTE  = OFF, ALLOW_ROW_LOCKS  = ON,
ALLOW_PAGE_LOCKS  = ON, IGNORE_DUP_KEY  = OFF, ONLINE = ON,
SORT_IN_TEMPDB = ON, DATA_COMPRESSION = NONE )
GO
USE [AdventureWorks2008]
GO
ALTER INDEX [IX_SalesOrderDetail_ProductID] ON [Sales].[Sales
OrderDetail] REBUILD PARTITION = ALL WITH ( PAD_INDEX  = OFF,
STATISTICS_NORECOMPUTE  = OFF, ALLOW_ROW_LOCKS  = ON,
ALLOW_PAGE_LOCKS  = ON, ONLINE = ON, SORT_IN_TEMPDB = ON,
DATA_COMPRESSION = NONE )
GO
USE [AdventureWorks2008]
GO
ALTER INDEX [PK_SalesOrderDetail_SalesOrderID_SalesOrderDetailID]
ON [Sales].[SalesOrderDetail] REBUILD PARTITION = ALL WITH (
PAD_INDEX  = OFF, STATISTICS_NORECOMPUTE  = OFF, ALLOW_ROW_LOCKS
= ON, ALLOW_PAGE_LOCKS  = ON, ONLINE = ON, SORT_IN_TEMPDB = ON,
DATA_COMPRESSION = NONE )
```

Update Statistics Task

The Update Statistics Task ensures the data in the tables and indexes on one or more SQL Server databases are up to date by resampling the distribution statistics of each index on user tables.

Numerous choices are available to customize this task. Each of the options is explained next:

- **Databases**—First select the databases that will be impacted by this task. The choices range from All Databases, System Databases, or User Databases and These Databases.

- **Object**—After the databases are selected, decide in the Objects box whether to display both tables and views or only one of these options.

- **Selection**—Choose the tables or indexes that will be impacted. If the Tables and Views option was selected in the Objects box, this box will be unavailable.

- **Update**—The Update box offers three choices. Select All Existing Statistics if you need to update both columns and indexes. Select Column Statistics if you need to update only column statistics, and select Index Statistics if you need to update only index statistics.

- **Scan Type**—The Scan Type section allows you to update statistics based on a Full Scan or by entering a Sample By value. The Sample By values can be either a percentage or a specific number of rows.

The syntax to update statistics on the AdventureWorks2008 [Sales].[SalesOrderDetail] table with the advanced options to update all existing statistics and conduct a full scan is as follows:

```
use [AdventureWorks2008]
GO
UPDATE STATISTICS [Sales].[SalesOrderDetail]
WITH FULLSCAN
```

History Cleanup Task

The History Cleanup Task offers organizations the perfect opportunity to remove historical data in a few simple steps. You can delete several types of history data using this task. The following two options are associated with this task.

- **Historical Data to Be Deleted**—Use the Maintenance Plan Wizard to purge several types of data, including Backup and Restore history, SQL Server Agent Job history, and Maintenance Plan history.

- **Remove Historical Data Older Than**—Use the wizard also to select the age of the data you want to delete. For example, you can choose to periodically remove older data based on daily, weekly, monthly, and yearly increments.

When the History Cleanup Task is complete, you can save a report to a text file or email the report to an operator by clicking Next. The Select Report

Options page is invoked and you must enable the check box Write a Report to a Text File, and then indicate the storage location of the report by specifying the file and folder location.

The following TSQL example removes historical data older than four weeks for the following items: Backup and Restore history, SQL Server Agent Job history, and Maintenance Plan history.

```
declare @dt datetime
select @dt = dateadd(wk,-4,getdate())
exec msdb.dbo.sp_delete_backuphistory @dt
EXEC msdb.dbo.sp_purge_jobhistory  @oldest_date=@dt
EXECUTE msdb..sp_maintplan_delete_log null,null,@dt
```

Execute SQL Server Agent Job

The Execute SQL Server Agent Job Task allows you to run SQL Server Agent jobs that already exist as well as SSIS packages as part of the maintenance plan. This is done by selecting the job in the Available SQL Server Agent Jobs section in the Define Execute SQL Server Agent Job Task page. Alternatively, TSQL syntax can be used to execute a job by entering the appropriate Job ID of a specific job that already exists.

The syntax to execute a SQL Server Agent job is as follows:

```
EXEC msdb.dbo.sp_start_job @job_
id=N'35eca119-28a6-4a29-994b-0680ce73f1f3'
```

Back Up Database Task

The Back Up Database Task is an excellent way to automate and schedule full, differential, or transaction log backups.

You can choose from an expanded set of options when creating full, differential, or transaction log backups with maintenance plans. With these expanded options, you can choose to back up a database or an individual component, set expiration dates, verify integrity, and even determine whether to use disk or tape. Each of the backup options is described in more detail in the following list:

- **Specify the Database**—A maintenance plan can be generated to perform a variety of backups, including backing up a single database, all databases, system databases, or all user databases.

- **Backup Component**—The Backup Component section offers the option of either backing up the entire database or individual files or filegroups.

- **Backup Set Will Expire**—To stipulate when a backup set will expire and can be overwritten by another backup, you need only to specify the number of days or enter a hard date such as September 5, 1974, for the set to expire.

- **Back Up To**—This option allows the backup to be written to a file or a tape. A tape drive must be present on the system to back up to tape. The other option is having a backup written to a file residing on a network share.

- **Back Up Databases Across One or More Files**—When selecting the backup destination, you can either add or remove one or more disk or tape locations. In addition, you can view the contents of a file and append to the backup file if it already exists.

- **Create a Backup File for Every Database**—Instead of selecting the preceding option, Back Up Databases Across One or More Files, you can let SQL Server automatically create a backup file for every database selected. In addition, you can automatically create a subdirectory for each database selected.

Note

If the Automatically Create a Subdirectory option is selected, the new subdirectory created will inherit permissions from the parent directory. NTFS permissions should be used to secure the root folder to restrict unauthorized access.

- **Verify Backup Integrity**—This option verifies the integrity of the backup when it is completed by firing a TSQL command that determines whether the backup was successful and is accessible.

- **Set Backup Compression**—When using the Enterprise Edition of SQL Server 2008, the options available include: leverage backup compression based on the server default settings, compress the backup regardless of the server-level default, and finally, do not compress backup.

Note

For a more thorough and detailed discussion of full, differential, and transaction log backups, see Chapter 7, "Backing up and Restoring the SQL Server 2008 Database Engine."

You can choose to back up a database in one of three ways when you create a maintenance plan. Using the wizard, you select the Define Back Up Database (Full) Task when it is necessary to capture the full database. Similarly, select Define Back Up Database (Differential) Task if it is important to record only data that has changed since the last full backup, or select the Define Back Up Database (Transaction Log) Task, which will back up only entries that are recorded to logs. The backup file extension for the Full and Differential Task is *.bak, whereas the Transaction Log Task is *.trn. Other than these noted differences, the options for each task are the same. If the Maintenance Plan wizard will not be used, then a DBA must choose the Back Up Database Task and specify the backup type. Backup types include Full, Differential and Transaction Log.

Caution

It is probably abundantly clear by now that maintenance plans are regularly used by DBAs to back up databases, including the transaction logs. A problem may occur during the restore process if you create a transaction log backup with the maintenance plan on a database that has already been configured for log shipping or is already part of another backup set. Ultimately, two sets of transaction log backups are created, one from the maintenance task and the other from the log shipping task or other backup job. Therefore, if a restore is needed, a combination of the transaction log backups is required to conduct the restore; otherwise, it is not possible to restore the database to the point of failure. If transaction log backups already exist based on log shipping, it is a best practice not to create additional transaction log backups with the maintenance plan. This will eliminate confusion and the potential of a botched restore resulting in lost data.

Maintenance Cleanup Task

The Maintenance Cleanup Task is used to delete files such as backups and reports that reside on the database after the maintenance plan is completed. There are many options for deleting data using this task:

- **Delete Files of the Following Type**—You can choose to delete database backup files or maintenance plan text reports.

- **File Location**—You can also choose to delete a specific file using the File Name box.

- **Search Folder and Delete Files Based on an Extension**—You can delete numerous files with the same extension within a specified folder using this option; for example, all files with the extension *.txt. You can also select to delete all first-level subfolders within the folder identified with this option.

■ **File Age**—Files can be deleted by age. You will need to indicate the age of the files to be deleted. For example, you may choose to delete files older than two years. The unit of time also includes hours, days, weeks, and months.

Creating a Maintenance Plan

You can use several methods for creating a maintenance plan. You can use the Database Maintenance Plan Wizard from SQL Server Management Studio (SSMS), or you can manually create a maintenance plan using the tasks associated with the Maintenance Plan Tasks Toolbox. Review the following sections to appreciate how easy and straightforward it is to create a maintenance plan manually and with the wizard.

Creating a Maintenance Plan with the Wizard

Maintaining SQL Server databases is a vital activity for DBAs everywhere. A well-maintained system requires the use of a maintenance plan that automates administrative tasks according to each organization's needs. This section demonstrates using the Maintenance Plan Wizard to create a customized maintenance plan of all system and user databases.

For this example, the steps include the following maintenance tasks: Check Database Integrity, Reorganize Index, Rebuild Index, Update Statistics, and Clean Up History. In a production environment, you should not include both the Reorganize Index and Rebuild Index task in the same plan. These tasks would be considered redundant because one task rebuilds the indexes from scratch and the other reorganizes the indexes. They have only been included for explanation purposes. In production environments it is a best practice to create separate maintenance plans for system and user databases.

Note

How to create database and transaction log backups with the Maintenance Plan Wizard is discussed in Chapter 7 in the section titled "Automating Backups with a Maintenance Plan."

---

1. Choose Start, All Programs, Microsoft SQL Server 2008, SQL Server Management Studio.

2. In Object Explorer, first connect to the Database Engine, expand the desired server, expand the Management folder, and then the Maintenance Plans folder.

3. Right-click Maintenance Plans and choose Maintenance Plan Wizard.

4. In the Welcome to the Database Maintenance Plan Wizard page, read the message and then click Next.

5. In the Select Plan Properties page, enter a name and description for the maintenance plan.

6. Choose either the first option (Separate Schedules for Each Task) or the second option (Single Schedule for the Entire Plan or No Schedule). For this example, a separate schedule will be created for the backup plan. Click Next as shown in Figure 6.1.

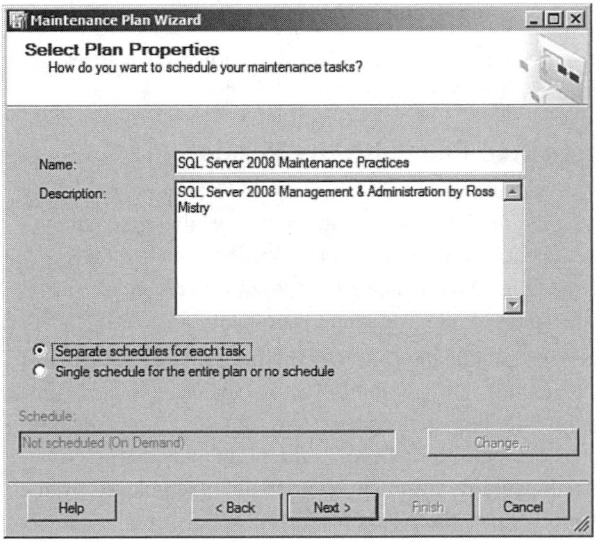

FIGURE 6.1
Scheduling and selecting the Maintenance Plan properties.

Note

Creating separate independent schedules for each subtask within a single maintenance plan is possible when working with SQL Server 2008. This was a new feature introduced with the release of SQL Server 2005 Service Pack 2. A scenario when this can be done includes; a weekly schedule for a full backup and an hourly schedule for a transaction log backup.

---

7. On the Select Maintenance Tasks page, as shown in Figure 6.2, place a check next to the following maintenance tasks: Check Database Integrity, Reorganize Index, Rebuild Index, Update Statistics, and Clean Up History, and then click Next.

8. On the Select Maintenance Task Order page, select the order in which the tasks should be executed and then click Next.

Tip

Many maintenance tasks, including reindexing or updating statistics, alter the database when they run. In recognition of this situation, it is a best practice to make the full database backup maintenance task the first order of operation when prioritizing maintenance tasks. This ensures that the database can be rolled back if the maintenance plan tasks that change the database fail.

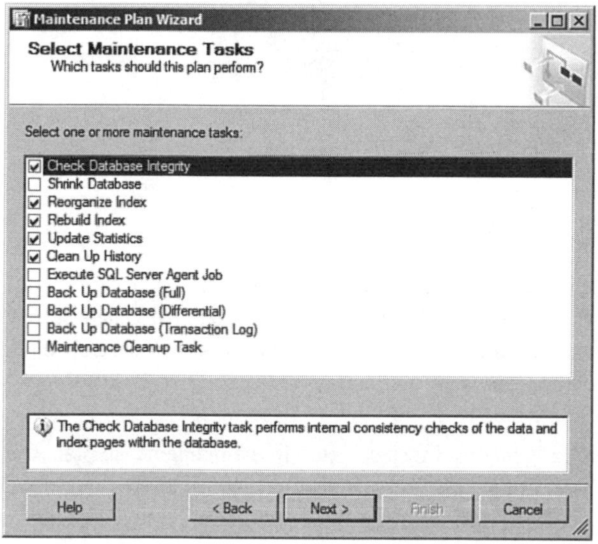

FIGURE 6.2
Selecting database maintenance tasks.

9. The first option in the maintenance plan is checking the database integrity. In the Define Database Check Integrity Task page, select All Databases from the drop-down list. The next item is to accept the defaults. Do this by validating that the Include Indexes Check option is enabled, which will that ensure all index pages and table databases have an integrity check run against them. Proceed to change the schedule by clicking Change, and then set this task so it reoccurs every week starting during nonpeak times, such as Sunday at midnight. Click Next to proceed as in Figure 6.3.

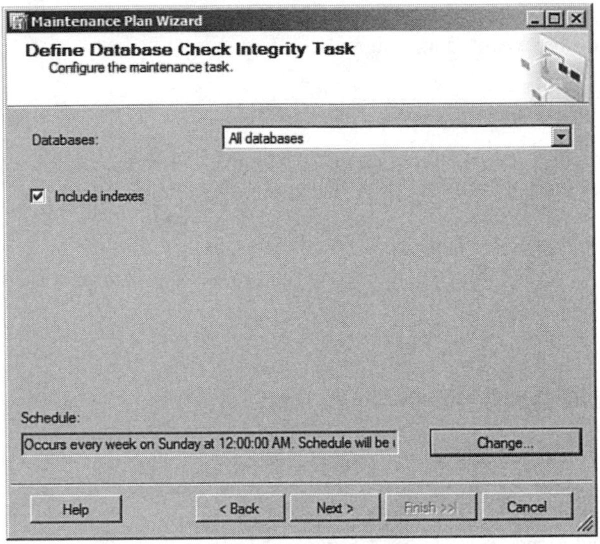

FIGURE 6.3
The Define Database Check Integrity Task page.

10. The second option selected is Reorganize Index. From the drop-down
box on the Define Reorganize Index Task page, select All Databases.
Ensure that the option for Compact Large Objects is enabled. Schedule
this task to occur once a week on Sunday at 1 a.m. Click Next to
proceed as in Figure 6.4.

11. The Rebuild Index is the third task selected in the maintenance plan. On
the Define Rebuild Index Task page, first select All Databases and then
proceed to schedule this task to occur once a week on Sunday at 2 a.m.
Verify in the Free Space Options area that the Reorganize Pages with
the Default Amount of Free Space option is selected. In the Advanced
Options section, enable Sort Results in tempdb and Keep Index Online
While Reindexing, as shown in Figure 6.5. Click Next to proceed.

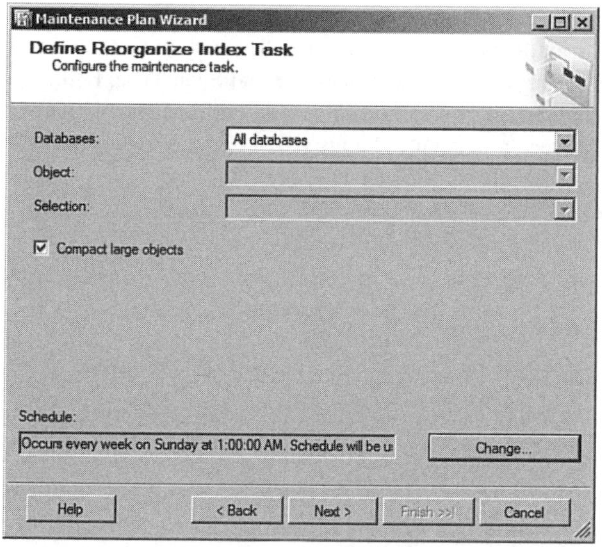

FIGURE 6.4
The Define Reorganize Index Task page.

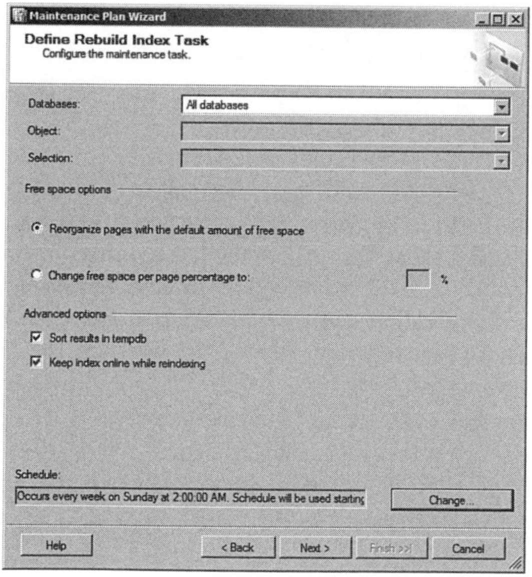

FIGURE 6.5
The Define Rebuild Index Task page.

12. For the fourth task, on the Define Update Statistics Task page, select All Databases from the Databases drop-down list. Ensure that the default Update settings, All Existing Statistics and Scan Type, Full Scan, are selected. Set this task to occur weekly on Sundays at 3 a.m. Click Next to proceed as shown in Figure 6.6.

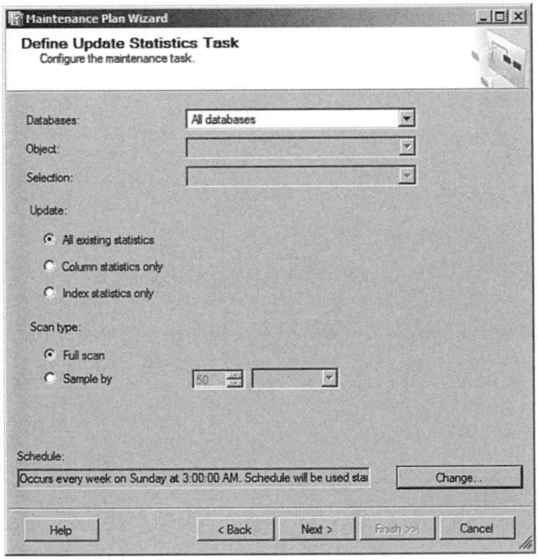

FIGURE 6.6
Specifying options on the Define Update Statistics Task page.

13. In the Define History Cleanup Task page, select the options to delete historical data, such as Backup and Restore History, SQL Server Agent Job History, and Maintenance Plan History. For the Remove Historical Data Older Than option, you can use the default of 4 weeks. This value should be based on the organization's retention requirements, as shown in Figure 6.7. Schedule the task to reoccur on a weekly basis on Sundays at 5 a.m. and then click Next.

14. In the Select Report Options page, set the option to either write a report to a text file and enter a folder location, or to email the report. To email the report, Database Mail must be enabled, configured, and an Agent Operation with a valid email address must already exist. Click Next to continue.

15. The Complete the Wizard page summarizes the options selected in the Maintenance Plan Wizard. It is possible to drill down on a task to view advanced settings. Review the options selected, and click Finish to close the summary page.

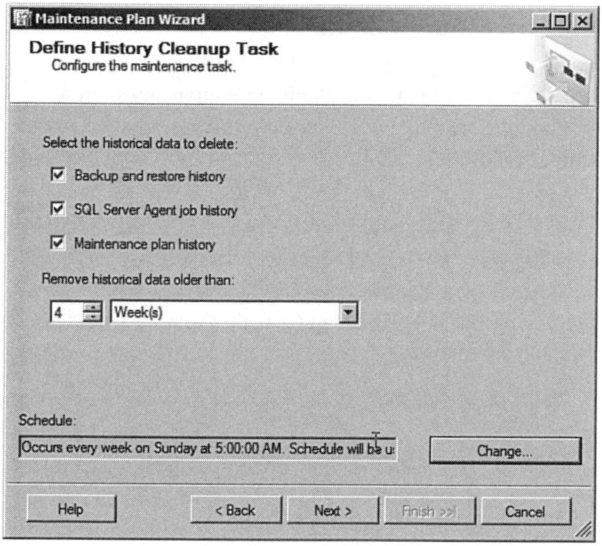

FIGURE 6.7
Specifying options on the Define History Cleanup Task page.

16. On the Maintenance Plan Wizard Progress page, review the creation
status as shown in Figure 6.8, and click Close to end the Maintenance
Plan Wizard.

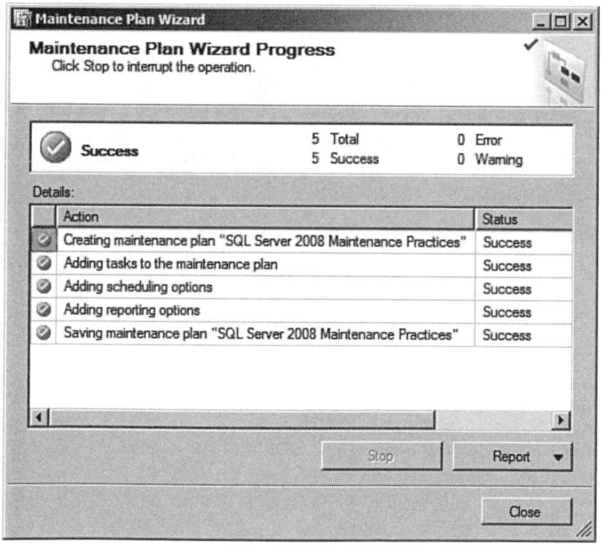

FIGURE 6.8
Viewing the Maintenance Plan Wizard Progress page.

Creating a Maintenance Plan Manually

Maintenance plans can also be created manually with the aid of the Maintenance Plan (Design tab). You can create a much more flexible maintenance plan with an enhanced workflow using the Maintenance Plan Design tab compared to the Maintenance Plan Wizard, because it is equipped with better tools and superior functionality.

Since the release of Service Pack 2 for SQL Server 2005, maintenance plan history can still be logged to a remote server when you're creating a manual plan. This is a great feature when managing many SQL Servers within an infrastructure because all data that is logged can be rolled up to a single server for centralized management.

> **Note**
>
> Creating manual maintenance plans with the Maintenance Plan (Design tab) is very similar to the design surface available when creating packages with SSIS. For more information on creating Integration Service projects, see Chapter 3, "Creating Packages and Transferring Data with Integration Services."

The Maintenance Plan design surface, as shown in Figure 6.9, can be launched by right-clicking the Maintenance Plans folder and selecting New Maintenance Plan.

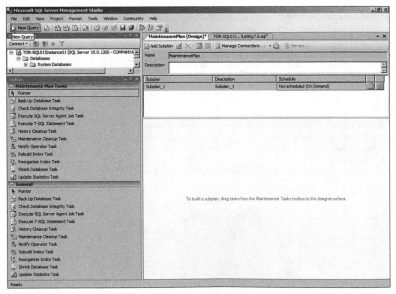

FIGURE 6.9
Viewing the Maintenance Plan design surface and toolbar screen

You will find the Maintenance Tasks toolbox in the left pane of the Maintenance Plan (Design tab). You can drag maintenance tasks from this toolbox to the design surface in the center pane. If more than one task is dragged to the designer, it is possible to create a workflow process between the two objects by establishing relationships between the tasks. The workflow process can consist of precedence links. As such, the second task will only execute based on a constraint, which is defined in the first task such as "on success, failure or completion." For example, you can choose to create a workflow that will first back up the AdventureWorks2008 database and then, on completion, rebuild all the AdventureWorks2008 indexes, as illustrated in Figure 6.10.

The Precedence Constraint link between two objects can control the work-flow if there is a statement to execute the second rebuild index task when the first backup task is successful. In this situation, when a backup task fails, the second task will not fire. As for creating a precedence constraint, you should first highlight both of the maintenance tasks in the designer, right-click, and then choose Add Precedence Constraint. After the Precedence Constraint is created, either double-click the connector arrow or right-click it and select Edit. This will bring up the Precedence Constraint Editor, where you can define the constraint options, as shown in Figure 6.11.

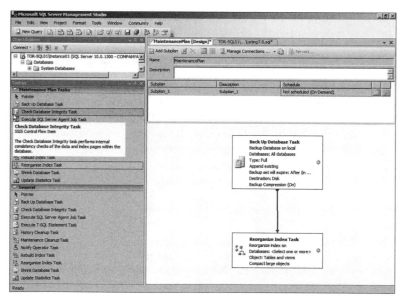

FIGURE 6.10
Implementing a Precedence Constraint between two maintenance plan tasks.

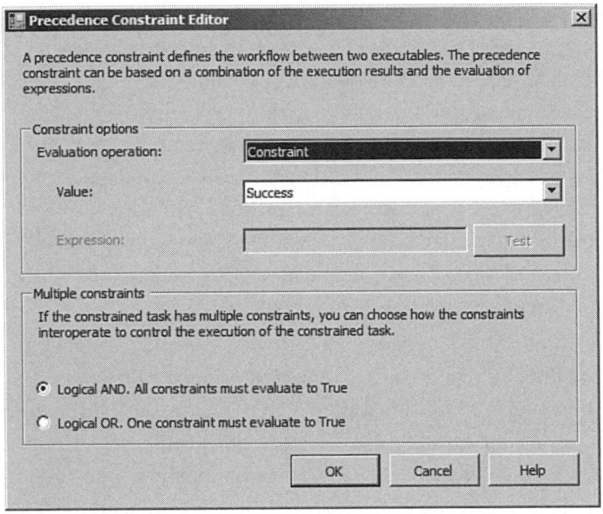

FIGURE 6.11
Setting the Precedence Constraints on the Maintenance Plan Tasks page.

In addition to creating precedence links, you also can execute tasks simultaneously. This is known as *task parallelism* and is commonly used when executing the same type of maintenance tasks on different SQL Servers. For example, you can execute a full backup of the master database on all the SQL Servers from a central master SQL Server starting on Sunday at 9:00 p.m.

The final item worth mentioning is the reporting capabilities. After the maintenance plan is completed, you can create a report. To do this, locate the Reporting and Logging icon in the Maintenance Plan designer. The Reporting and Logging dialog box as shown in Figure 6.12 displays options such as Generate a Text File Report and Send Reports to an Email Recipient. Additional logging functionality exists, such as logging extended information and log maintenance plan history to a remote server.

Tip

When working with maintenance plan tasks, you can use the View TSQL Command button to convert the options selected for the task into TSQL syntax. This is a great feature for DBAs who do not have an extensive background in programming.

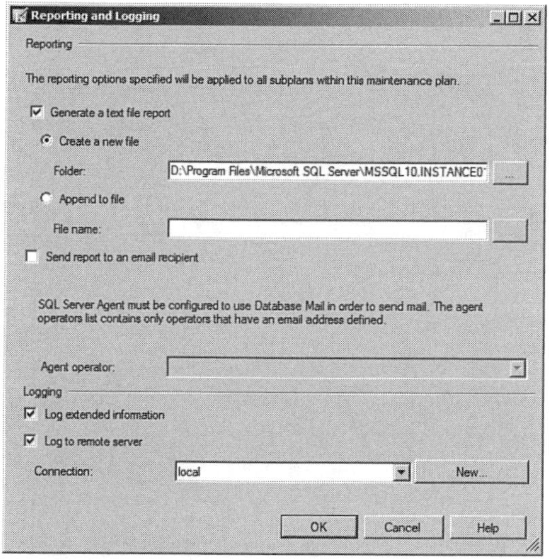

FIGURE 6.12
Configuring Maintenance Plan Reporting and Logging options.

Viewing Maintenance Plans

All maintenance plans can be viewed under the Maintenance Plan folder in SSMS and stored in SQL Server as jobs. They require the SQL Server Agent to be running to launch the job at the scheduled interval. If the SQL Server Agent is stopped, the jobs will not commence. In addition, all jobs can be edited or changed for ongoing support or maintenance.

Follow these steps to view the maintenance plan jobs in SQL Server Management Studio:

1. Choose Start, All Programs, Microsoft SQL Server 2008, SQL Server Management Studio.

2. In Object Explorer, first connect to the Database Engine, expand the desired server, expand SQL Server Agent, and then expand the jobs folder.

3. Click Jobs to see a list of jobs created by the Maintenance Plan Wizard. The jobs are displayed in the Object Explorer Details tab located in the right pane; otherwise, the jobs are displayed under the Jobs folder in Object Explorer. This is shown in Figure 6.13.

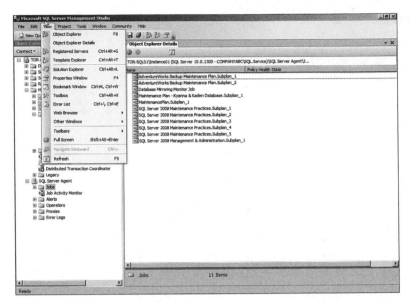

FIGURE 6.13
Viewing Maintenance Plan scheduled jobs.

If the SQL Server Agent is not running, a dialog box may appear, stating that the SQL Server Agent on the target server is not running. The SQL Server Agent must be started for SQL Server jobs to commence. Follow these steps to start the SQL Server Agent:

1. Choose Start, All Programs, Microsoft SQL Server 2008, SQL Server Management Studio.

2. In Object Explorer, first connect to the Database Engine, and then expand the desired server.

3. Right-click SQL Server Agent and then click Start.

Creating Multiserver Maintenance Plans

In the past, DBAs encountered numerous challenges when managing more than one maintenance plan within their pre—SQL Server 2005 Service Pack 2 infrastructure. The task of creating maintenance plans in a multiserver environment was exceedingly tedious because a maintenance plan had to be created on each and every server. Moreover, the task of verifying success, failure, and job history was equally difficult and time-consuming; it had to be conducted on each server because a method to centrally manage these plans did not exist. To clearly illustrate just how difficult life could get for DBAs, it is worth mentioning that a typical global organization may have well over 100 SQL Servers within its infrastructure; therefore, imagine the heartache and lack of operational efficiency that came along with managing maintenance plans.

Today, these nuisances continue to be alleviated. SQL Server 2008 offers support for multiserver maintenance plans. Specifically, you can now create maintenance plans for each of your SQL servers from a single central master server. This provides a significant difference in operational efficiency and administration.

To take full advantage of this new feature in SQL Server 2008, a multiserver environment containing one master server and one or more target servers must be constructed before a multiserver maintenance plan can be created. It should be mentioned that target servers can be used only to view the maintenance plans. As a result, multiserver maintenance plans must be created and maintained on the master server so that you can provide regular maintenance.

> **Note**
>
> To create or manage multiserver maintenance plans, you must be a member of the sysadmin fixed server role on each of the SQL Servers.

Multiserver maintenance plans can be created with either the Maintenance Plan Wizard or by manually using the Maintenance Plan (Design tab).

Establishing Maintenance Schedules for SQL Server

With each new release, SQL Server has become more self-maintaining. However, even with self-maintenance and automated maintenance plans, DBAs must conduct additional maintenance. Some maintenance procedures require daily attention, whereas others may require only yearly checkups. The maintenance processes and procedures that an organization follows depend strictly on the organization's individual environment.

The categories described in the following sections and their corresponding procedures are best practices for organizations of all sizes and with varying IT infrastructures. The following sections will help organizations establish sound maintenance practices to help them ensure the health of their SQL Server Database Engine. The suggested maintenance tasks that follow are based on daily, weekly, monthly, and quarterly schedules.

Daily Routine Maintenance Tasks

Maintenance tasks requiring close and regular attention are commonly checked each day. DBAs who take on these tasks daily ensure system reliability, availability, performance, and security. Some of the daily routine maintenance tasks include the following:

- Check that all required SQL Server services are running.
- Check Daily Backup logs for success, warnings, or failures.
- Check the Windows Event logs for errors.
- Check the SQL Server logs for security concerns such as invalid logins.
- Conduct full or differential backups.
- Conduct Transaction Log backups on databases configured with the Full or Bulk-Logged recovery model.
- Verify that SQL Server jobs did not fail.
- Check that adequate disk space exists for all database files and transaction logs.
- At least monitor processor, memory, or disk counters for bottlenecks.

Weekly Routine Maintenance Tasks

Maintenance procedures that require slightly less attention than daily checking are categorized in a weekly routine. The following list details these weekly tasks:

- Conduct full or differential backups.
- Review Maintenance Plan reports.
- Check database integrity.
- Shrink the database if needed.
- Compact clustered and nonclustered tables and views by reorganizing indexes.
- Reorganize data on the data and index pages by rebuilding indexes.
- Update statistics on all user and system tables.
- Delete historical data created by backups, restores, SQL Server agent, and maintenance plan operations.
- Manually grow database or transaction log files if needed. Adjust automatic growth values if needed.
- Remove files left over from executing maintenance plans.

Monthly or Quarterly Maintenance Tasks

Some maintenance task are managed more infrequently, such as on a monthly or quarterly basis. Do not interpret these tasks as unimportant because they don't require daily maintenance. These tasks also require maintenance to ensure the health of their environment, but on a less regular basis because they are more self-sufficient and self-sustaining. Although the following tasks may appear mundane or simple, they should not be overlooked during maintenance.

- Conduct a restore of the backups in a test environment.
- Archive historical data if needed.
- Analyze collected performance statistics and compare them to baselines.
- Review and update maintenance documentation.
- Review and install SQL Server patches and service packs (if available).
- Test failover if running a cluster, database mirroring, or log shipping.
- Validate that the backup and restore process adheres to the Service Level Agreement defined.
- Update SQL Server build guides.
- Update SQL Server disaster recovery documentation.
- Update maintenance plan checklists.
- Change Administrator passwords.
- Change SQL Server service account passwords.

Summary

The maintenance plan feature alone should be one of the key selling points for SQL Server 2008. The ability to use an uncomplicated wizard to automate administrative tasks that SQL Server will perform against a single database or multiple databases has decreased the amount of manual work DBAs must do and ensures that tasks do not get overlooked. To take advantage of running tasks concurrently, or using precedence constraints to run tasks sequentially, you should create plans manually. This is the best way to develop maintenance plans for those looking for a lot of flexibility on advanced workflow.

SQL Server 2008 continues to allow organizations to extend their use of maintenance plans. The following are just some of the features SQL Server 2008 has brought to the table. SQL Server 2008 offers support for multi-server maintenance plans, SQL Server 2008 does not require SSIS to be installed, and supports the potential for remote logging.

In the end, the most important thing to take away from this chapter is the importance of having a maintenance plan in place early and ensuring that maintenance is scheduled accordingly to preserve the health of each database.

Best Practices

Some important best practices from the chapter include the following:

- DBAs should fully understand all maintenance activities required and implemented within the SQL Server environment.
- Use the Maintenance Plan Wizard to automate and schedule routine maintenance operations.
- When creating maintenance plans with the wizard, leverage the features included in SQL Server 2008 and create independent schedules for subtasks.
- Maintenance tasks should be scripted, automated, and fully documented.
- Maintenance tasks should be conducted during nonpeak times or after hours, such as on weekends and after midnight.
- When you configure the order of the maintenance tasks, backups should be executed first, and then other tasks that change the database.
- Do not include the Shrink Task when creating Maintenance Plans. Manually shrink the database if needed during nonpeak hours.
- Maintenance tasks should be grouped into daily, weekly, and monthly schedules.
- Schedule and conduct routine maintenance tasks on a daily, weekly, and monthly basis.
- For a large enterprise environment running many SQL Servers, take advantage of subplans and the multiserver maintenance plan.

CHAPTER 7

Backing Up and Restoring the SQL Server 2008 Database Engine

One of the most important tasks of a DBA is to ensure that the new SQL Server infrastructure is being correctly backed up. Designing and implementing a proper backup strategy lends assurance that a successful recovery process can be initiated if an organization experiences problems with its databases, systems, servers, or sites.

This chapter covers the areas database administrators and organizations need to consider when conducting SQL Server backups and recoveries of databases associated with SQL Server 2008 Database Engine. Specifically, this chapter highlights how to back up and restore a database by using SQL Server Management Studio, maintenance plans, and Transact-SQL.

What's New for Backup and Recovery with SQL Server 2008?

With the tremendous amounts of data explosion occurring in our digital society, the size of databases used in organizations has increased exponentially over the past few years. As database sizes increase, so does the challenge of managing backups, while the cost of storage and storage management increases as well. Fortunately, Microsoft addresses these concerns by introducing backup compression in SQL Server 2008.

Another new and highly anticipated feature introduced with SQL Server 2008 is backup encryption. When a database is encrypted with Transparent Data Encryption (TDE), all backups associated with the encrypted database are also encrypted. The certificate used to encrypt the database must be present in order to restore the database, or the data restore will fail and the data will be left in a decrypted, unusable state. Therefore, ensure that the certificates associated with TDE and the encrypted databases are stored safely. For more information on Transparent Data Encryption. reference Chapter 11.

Backup Compression

Backup compression allows a DBA to compress database backups associated with the Database Engine, thus reducing the cost linked to backup storage. Backup compression is disabled by default, and must be enabled at the server level in order to leverage this new rich feature. This can be achieved by enabling the Compress Backup option in the Database Settings page associated with the Server properties. Server properties can be accessed by right-clicking a desired SQL Server and selecting properties in SQL Server Management Studio. Alternatively, the following TSQL syntax can be used to enable backup compression at the server level:

```
USE master;
GO
EXEC sp_configure 'backup compression default', '1';
RECONFIGURE WITH OVERRIDE;
```

There may be situations when backup compression at the server level is enabled; however, the compression feature is not required when backing up a specific database. Therefore, a DBA can override the backup compression default server setting when conducting a database backup on a specific database. The backup compression override option is available when creating backups with SQL Server Management Studio, Transact-SQL, Maintenance Plan Wizard, and the SQL Server 2008 Integration Services Back Up Database Task.

Note

Backup compression is a feature included only in the Enterprise and Developer editions of SQL Server 2008. It is straight forward to implement in existing TSQL scripts as you can simply add COMPRESSION or NO COMPRESSION in the WITH options.

Finally, database compression has great results. Obviously, compression results will vary and are indicative of what kind of data is stored in the database. However, compression ratios of 4 to 1 have been achieved. Unfortunately, with any compression technology, there is always a performance trade-off. Backup compression does not increase disk I/O as compressed data is smaller; however, CPU usage typically increases. It is beneficial to test backup compression before using it in production, so that as a DBA, you are fully aware of the performance impact on the SQL Server system and associated SQL workload.

Note

It is recommended to create a policy with Policy Based Management that will govern the amount of CPU that can be consumed when conducting compressed backups. This will ensure that the compressed backup do not place excessive CPU pressure on the system causing performance degradation. For more information on Resource Governor, refer to Chapter 16 "Managing Workloads and Consumption with Resource Governor."

The Importance of Backups

Understanding how to back up the SQL Server 2008 Database Engine remains a big challenge for many organizations today, even for those organizations that make an effort to execute a backup strategy. Unfortunately, in many situations, it takes a disaster for them to realize that their backup strategy is inappropriate, or that specific SQL Server elements such as the transaction log or recovery model were overlooked. This awakening is far too late for those organizations, however, because they may have already experienced a horrific data loss.

Data loss is unacceptable in today's competitive economy. Losing mission-critical data residing in SQL Server can be particularly harmful to an organization's success because that data provides key information that ultimately gives an organization its competitive advantage. Organizations suffering catastrophic data loss are more susceptible to going out of business. Moreover, regulatory requirements such as compliance with the Sarbanes-Oxley Act or PCI place tremendous pressure on organizations to be more trustworthy and accountable for their data, especially financial information.

With organizations beginning to understand the value of their data, more and more organizations are also beginning to recognize that the backup and recovery operations of the SQL Server 2008 Database Engine are some of the most important SQL Server administrative tasks of database administrators. When you understand all the intricate details that make up SQL Server and the backup options available, you can better develop a database backup and restoration strategy that minimizes or eliminates data loss and corruption in your organization.

Say you're working with a full installation of SQL Server, which includes all its components. With the ability to identify all these parts and understand how they are associated, you can understand that your focus should be not only on backing up databases, but also on the other SQL Server components and items installed such as Analysis Services, Reporting Services, Full-Text Catalogs, and Internet Information Services. You should take all of these components into account to successfully back up and restore a SQL Server environment.

Note

To successfully backup and restore a complete SQL Server environment involves backing up not only databases, but all other SQL Server components and items installed. However, this chapter focuses strictly on backup and recovery tasks associated with the SQL Server 2008 Database Engine.

Items to Consider When Creating a Backup and Recovery Plan

The objective of all SQL Server 2008 backups is to restore a database to a known state. The most common need for backups is to recover data from accidental deletions due to human error. Other factors that might call for a recovery of data may include application errors, hardware failure, or the need to recover data to a prior state.

When organizations understand the objective and necessity for backups, they must attend to the business scope of their SQL Server backup and recovery plan. To help identify the scope, an organization needs to ask some of the following questions:

- Has a Service Level Agreement (SLA) already been defined?
- Is the data in each database considered to be mission-critical?
- Is there a clear statement of what should and shouldn't be backed up?
- What is the frequency of the backups?
- What standards are acceptable for offsite storage and retrieval?
- What is the escalation path for failed backups?
- What are the decision criteria for overrun jobs?
- Will the backups be password protected?
- How long will data be retained?
- How much data can the organization afford to lose at any given moment?

- What is the availability of resources governing the backup and restore process?

- What is the financial cost of downtime?

- Are there any regulatory requirements dictating how backups and restores should be conducted and managed?

After some of these questions are answered, the high-level scope of the desired backup starts to take shape. The organization then needs to address the technical aspects of the backup and recovery plan. Some of the technical questions may include the following:

- What SQL Server databases should be included in the backup and recovery plan?

- Should I back up the system databases?

- Which database recovery model should be used?

- How often should the backups occur?

- What type of media should be used?

- Should I leverage the new SQL Server 2008 Backup Compression feature? If so, do I have the Enterprise Edition?

- Which utilities such as Transact-SQL (TSQL), SQL Server Management Studio (SSMS), or third-party tools should be leveraged when creating backups?

Backing Up and Recovering the Database Engine

The Database Engine is the heart of SQL Server. It is responsible for storing data, databases, stored procedures, security, and many more functions such as full-text search, Database Mail, replication, and high availability. Because the Database Engine is one of the most vital components of the SQL Server database as a result of the crucial data it holds, it is essential for organizations to create a backup and recovery plan for the Database Engine.

The Storage Architecture

Executing a successful database backup and restore plan begins with understanding the Database Engine storage architecture. This involves having intimate knowledge of how SQL Server leverages database files, filegroups, transaction logs, and the newly introduced file type, FILESTREAM.

SQL Server 2008 databases have three kinds of file types associated with them: database files, transaction log files, and FILESTREAM files. A SQL

Server database is always made up of at least one data file and one transaction log file and FILESTREAM data is optional. The following sections elaborate on each of these files.

Database Files
The default database files reside within a primary filegroup. A *filegroup* is a logical structure for grouping data files and managing them as a logical unit. The primary filegroup contains the primary data file and any secondary data files not stored in another filegroup. If you want to increase performance and the speed of the backup and recovery, it is recommended that you create additional files or filegroups and split database objects across these several filegroups to establish parallel processing.

The default extension for the database file within the primary filegroup is .mdf. Likewise, filegroups inherit the default extension .ndf. It is possible to create up to 32,766 user-defined filegroups.

Transaction Log Files
Every relational database has a transaction log to record database activity. Transaction logs are responsible for recording every modification made to the database. As such, these logs are a critical component of the database, especially during recovery because the log is counted on to restore the database to a point in time or the point of failure. The default extension for a transaction log is .ldf. As with database files, additional transaction log files can be added to increase performance, backups, and restore times.

FILESTREAM Files
Until SQL Server 2008, organizations have been creatively inventing their own mechanisms to store unstructured data. Now SQL Server 2008 introduces a new data type that can assist organizations by allowing them to store unstructured data such as bitmap images, music files, text files, videos, audio files in a single data type which is more secure and manageable. If FILESTREAM data is being leveraged, the DBAs must also take these files into consideration when backing up the database.

Tip

It is a best practice to place the database, transaction logs and backups on separate disks. This will prevent catastrophic failure in the event that a single disk fails. In addition, this also increases performance and allows a DBA to restore a database to the point of failure.

When you're confident that you understand the database and transaction log files within the Database Engine, you should turn your attention to the various Database Engine recovery models in SQL Server. The level of understanding you have of each of these models significantly affects your database backup and restore strategy.

Using Recovery Models Effectively

Each model handles recovery differently. Specifically, each model differs in how it manages logging, which governs whether an organization's database can be recovered to the point of failure. The three recovery models associated with a database in the Database Engine are Full, Simple, and Bulk-Logged:

- **Full**—This model captures and logs all transactions, making it possible to restore a database to a given point in time or up to the minute. Based on this model, you must conduct maintenance on the transaction log to prevent logs from growing too large and disks from becoming full. When you perform backups, space is made available again and can be used until the next planned backup. Organizations may notice that maintaining a transaction log slightly degrades SQL Server performance because all transactions to the database are logged. Organizations that insist on preserving critical data often overlook this issue because they realize that this model offers them the highest level of recovery capabilities.

- **Simple**—This model provides organizations with the least number of options for recovering data. It truncates the transaction log after each backup. This means a database can be recovered only up to the last successful full or differential database backup. This recovery model also requires the least amount of administration because transaction log backups are not permitted. In addition, data entered into the database after a successful full or differential database backup is unrecoverable. Organizations that store data they do not deem to be mission-critical may choose to use this model.

- **Bulk-Logged**—This model maintains a transaction log and is similar to the Full recovery model. The main difference is that transaction logging is minimal during bulk operations to maximize database performance and reduce the log size when large amounts of data are inserted into the database. Bulk import operations such as BCP, BULK INSERT, SELECT INTO, CREATE INDEX, ALTER INDEX REBUILD, and DROP INDEX are minimally logged.

Because the Bulk-Logged recovery model provides only minimal logging of bulk operations, you cannot restore the database to the point of failure if a disaster occurs during a bulk-logged operation. In most situations, an organization has to restore the database, including the latest transaction log, and rerun the bulk-logged operation.

This model is typically used if organizations need to run large bulk operations that degrade system performance and do not require point-in-time recovery.

Note

When a new database is created, it inherits the recovery settings based on the model database. The default recovery model is set to Full.

Now that you're familiar with the three recovery models, you need to determine which model best suits your organization's needs. The next section is designed to help you choose the appropriate model.

Selecting the Appropriate Recovery Model

Selecting the appropriate recovery model affects an organization's ability to recover, manage, and maintain data.

For enterprise production systems, the Full recovery model is the best model for preventing critical data loss and restoring data to a specific point in time. As long as the transaction log is available, it is even possible to get up-to-the-minute recovery and point-in-time restore if the tail-end of the transaction log is backed up and restored. The trade-off for the Full recovery model is its impact on other operations.

Organizations leverage the Simple recovery model if the data backed up is not critical, data is static and does not change often, or loss is not a concern. In this situation, the organization loses all transactions since the last full or last differential backup. This model is typical for test environments or production databases that are not mission-critical.

Finally, organizations that typically select the Bulk-Logged recovery model have critical data, but do not want to degrade system performance by logging large amounts of data, or they conduct these bulk operations after hours so as not to interfere with normal transaction processing. In addition, such organizations do not need point-in-time or up-to-the-minute restores.

> **Note**
>
> You can switch the recovery model of a production database and switch it back. This does not break the continuity of the log; however, there could be negative ramifications to the restore process. For example, a production database can use the Full recovery model, and immediately before a large data load, the recovery model can be changed to Bulk-Logged to minimize logging and increase performance. The only caveat is that your organization must understand that it lost the potential for point-in-time and up-to-the-minute restores during the switch.

Switching the Database Recovery Model with SSMS

To set the recovery model on a SQL Server 2008 database using SSMS, perform the following steps:

1. Choose Start, All Programs, Microsoft SQL Server 2008, SQL Server Management Studio.

2. In Object Explorer, first connect to the Database Engine, expand the desired server, and then expand the database folder.

3. Select the desired SQL Server database, right-click on the database, and select Properties.

4. In the Database Properties dialog box, select the Options tab.

5. In the Recovery Model field, select either Full, Bulk-Logged, or Simple from the drop-down list, as shown in Figure 7.1, and click OK.

Switching the Database Recovery Model with TSQL

Not only can you change the recovery model of a database with SSMS, but you can also make changes to the database recovery model using TSQL commands such as ALTER DATABASE. You can use the following TSQL script to change the recovery model for the AdventureWorks2008 database from Simple to Full:

```
—Switching the Database Recovery model
Use Master
ALTER DATABASE AdventureWorks2008 SET RECOVERY FULL
GO
```

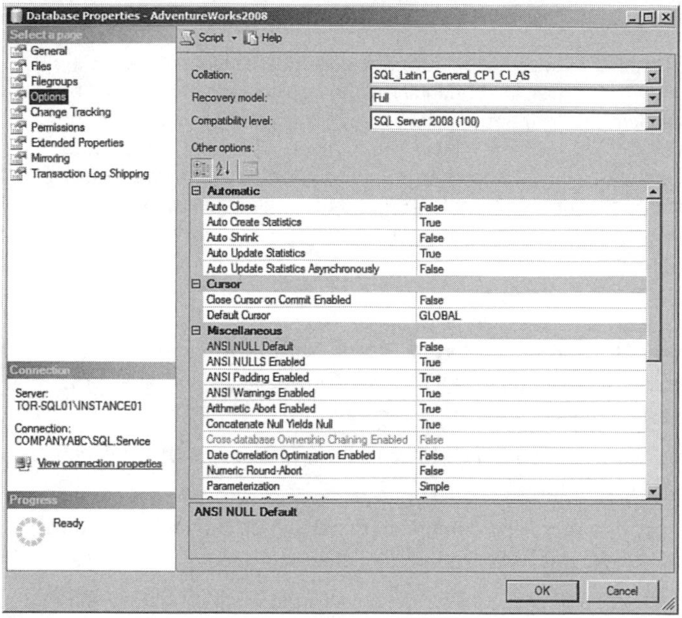

FIGURE 7.1
Selecting a recovery model.

SQL Server Backup Methods

Now that you've selected the appropriate recovery model, you should turn your attention to fully understanding the different backup methods available. This is the third step in successfully creating a backup and recovery solution for the Database Engine. The backup utility included in SQL Server offers several options for backing up databases. The following sections identify the following SQL Server backup methods:

- Full backups
- Differential backups
- Transaction log backups
- File and filegroup backups
- Partial backups
- Differential partial backups
- Copy-only backups
- Mirrored backups

Full Backup

The full backup is also commonly referred to as *full database backup*. Its main function is to back up the entire database as well as transaction logs, filegroups, and files. As a result, a full backup can be used to restore the entire database to its original state when the backup was completed.

Equally important, many people refer to the full database backup as the *baseline* for all other backups. The reason is that the full database backup must be restored before all other backups can be created or restored, such as differential backups, partial backups, and transaction logs.

The following script illustrates how to conduct a full database backup for the AdventureWorks2008 database.

> **Note**
>
> For this example and others in this chapter, the backup set is located on the X: drive on a proprietary backup file called SQLBackup. Please change the syntax in these examples to reflect the backup location and file of your choice based on your environment.

```
—SQL SERVER 2008 MANAGEMENT & ADMINISTRATION BY ROSS MISTRY
—CHAPTER 7 BACKING UP AND RESTORING
➡THE SQL SERVER 2008 DATABASE ENGINE

—FULL BACKUP EXAMPLE
USE AdventureWorks2008
BACKUP DATABASE [AdventureWorks2008]
TO  DISK = N'X:\SQLBackup.bak'
WITH  DESCRIPTION = N'SQL Server 2008 Management &
➡Administration', NOFORMAT, NOINIT,  NAME = N'AdventureWorks2008-
FullDatabaseBackup', SKIP, NOREWIND, NOUNLOAD,
COMPRESSION,  STATS = 10, CHECKSUM, CONTINUE_AFTER_ERROR
GO
declare @backupSetId as int
select @backupSetId = position from msdb..backupset where
database_name=N'AdventureWorks2008'
and backup_set_id=(select max(backup_set_id)
from msdb..backupset where database_name=N'AdventureWorks2008' )
if @backupSetId is null begin raiserror
(N'Verify failed. Backup information for database
➡ ''AdventureWorks2008'' not found.', 16, 1) end
```

```
RESTORE VERIFYONLY FROM  DISK = N'X:\SQLBackup.bak'
WITH  FILE = @backupSetId,  NOUNLOAD,  NOREWIND
GO
```

This example conducts a full database backup on the AdventureWorks2008 database. The additional options consist of Backup Set Will Not Expire, Backing Up to Disk, Append to the Existing Backup Set, Verify Backups When Finished, Perform Checksum Before Writing to Media, Continue on Error and Compress Backup.

Differential Backups

Unlike a full database backup, a differential database backup backs up only data that changed after the last successful full database backup was conducted, resulting in a smaller backup.

The following script illustrates how to conduct a differential database backup for the AdventureWorks2008 database.

```
-SQL SERVER 2008 MANAGEMENT & ADMINISTRATION BY ROSS MISTRY
-CHAPTER 7 RESTORING THE SQL SERVER 2008 DATABASE ENGINE
-DIFFERENTIAL BACKUP EXAMPLE
USE AdventureWorks2008
BACKUP DATABASE [AdventureWorks2008] TO  DISK =
N'X:\SQLBackup.bak' WITH  DIFFERENTIAL , DESCRIPTION = N'SQL
Server 2008 Management & Administration', NOFORMAT, NOINIT,  NAME
= N'AdventureWorks2008-DifferentialDatabaseBackup', SKIP,
NOREWIND, NOUNLOAD, COMPRESSION,  STATS = 10, CHECKSUM,
CONTINUE_AFTER_ERROR
GO
declare @backupSetId as int
select @backupSetId = position from msdb..backupset where
database_name=N'AdventureWorks2008' and backup_set_id=(select
max(backup_set_id) from msdb..backupset where database_name=
N'AdventureWorks2008' )
if @backupSetId is null begin raiserror(N'Verify failed. Backup
information for database ''AdventureWorks2008'' not found.', 16,
1) end
RESTORE VERIFYONLY FROM  DISK = N'X:\SQLBackup.bak' WITH  FILE =
@backupSetId,  NOUNLOAD,  NOREWIND
GO
```

This differential example creates a copy of all the pages in the database modified after the last successful full or differential AdventureWorks2008 database backup. The additional options consist of Backup Set Will Not Expire, Backing Up to Disk, Append to the Existing Backup Set, Verify Backups When Finished, Perform Checksum Before Writing to Media, Continue on Error, and Compress Backup.

Transaction Log Backup

Transaction log backups are useful only for those databases using a Full or Bulk-Logged recovery model. The transaction log backs up all data as of the last full backup or transaction log backup. As with a differential backup, it is worth remembering that a transaction log backup can be executed only after a full backup has been performed.

Additional options for backing up the transaction log include

- **Truncate the Transaction Log**—If log records were never truncated, they would constantly grow, eventually filling up the hard disk and causing SQL Server to crash. This option is the default transaction log behavior and truncates the inactive portion of the log.

- **Back Up the Tail of the Log**—This option is typically used as the first step when restoring SQL Server to a point in failure or point in time. Backing up the tail portion of the log captures the active log that has not been captured by a previous backup before a disaster occurs. This option allows you to recover the database and replay any transactions that have not been committed to the database or included in the backup sets already taken.

The following script illustrates how to create a transaction log backup for the AdventureWorks2008 database.

```
—SQL SERVER 2008 MANAGEMENT & ADMINISTRATION BY ROSS MISTRY
—CHAPTER 7 BACKING UP AND RESTORING
►THE SQL SERVER 2008 DATABASE ENGINE
—TRANSACTION LOG BACKUP EXAMPLE
USE AdventureWorks2008
BACKUP LOG [AdventureWorks2008] TO
DISK = N'X:\SQLBackup.bak'
WITH  DESCRIPTION = N'SQL Server 2008
Management & Administration',
NOFORMAT, NOINIT,
NAME = N'AdventureWorks2008-TransactionLogBackup',
SKIP, NOREWIND, NOUNLOAD, COMPRESSION,
```

```
STATS = 10, CHECKSUM, CONTINUE_AFTER_ERROR
GO

declare @backupSetId as int
select @backupSetId = position
from msdb..backupset
where database_name=N'AdventureWorks2008'
and backup_set_id=(select max(backup_set_id)
from msdb..backupset
where database_name=N'AdventureWorks2008' )
if @backupSetId is null begin raiserror(N'Verify failed.
Backup information for database
➡''AdventureWorks2008'' not found.', 16, 1) end
RESTORE VERIFYONLY FROM
DISK = N'X:\SQLBackup.bak'
WITH  FILE = @backupSetId,
NOUNLOAD,  NOREWIND
GO
```

This example conducts a transaction log database backup on the AdventureWorks2008 database. The additional options consist of Backing Up to Disk, Append to the Existing Backup Set, Verify Backups When Finished, and Perform Checksum Before Writing to Media, Continue on Error, and Compress Backup. The transaction log behavior truncates the transaction log when complete.

The following script illustrates how to create a transaction log (tail-log) backup for the AdventureWorks2008 database.

Note

It is a best practice to use the master database when performing the tail-log transaction log backup with TSQL.

```
—SQL SERVER 2008 MANAGEMENT & ADMINISTRATION BY ROSS MISTRY
—CHAPTER 7 BACKING UP AND RESTORING
➡THE SQL SERVER 2008 DATABASE ENGINE
—TRANSACTION LOG - TAIL LOG BACKUP EXAMPLE
USE Master
BACKUP LOG [AdventureWorks2008]
TO  DISK = N'X:\SQLBackup.bak'
WITH  NO_TRUNCATE ,
```

```
DESCRIPTION = N'SQL Server 2008 Management &
Administration', NOFORMAT, NOINIT,
NAME = N'AdventureWorks2008-TransactionLogBackup',
SKIP, NOREWIND, NOUNLOAD,  NORECOVERY ,
COMPRESSION,  STATS = 10,
CHECKSUM, CONTINUE_AFTER_ERROR
GO
declare @backupSetId as int
select @backupSetId = position
from msdb..backupset
where database_name=N'AdventureWorks2008'
and backup_set_id=(select max(backup_set_id)
from msdb..backupset
where database_name=N'AdventureWorks2008' )
if @backupSetId is null begin raiserror
(N'Verify failed. Backup information for database
 ''AdventureWorks2008'' not found.', 16, 1) end
RESTORE VERIFYONLY FROM  DISK = N'X:\SQLBackup.bak'
WITH  FILE = @backupSetId,  NOUNLOAD,  NOREWIND
GO
```

This example conducts a backup of the tail of the transaction log on the
AdventureWorks2008 database and leaves the database in the restoring state.
The additional options consist of Back Up to Disk, Append to the Existing
Backup Set, Verify Backups When Finished, Perform Checksum Before
Writing to Media, Continue on Error and Compress Backup. The transaction
log behavior truncates the transaction log when complete.

File and Filegroup Backups

Instead of conducting a full backup, organizations can back up individual
files and filegroups. This backup method is often favorable to organizations
that just can't consider backing up or restoring their databases because of
size and the time required for the task. When you use file and filegroup
backups, backing up the transaction log is also necessary because the database must use the Full or Bulk-Logged recovery model.

The basic syntax for creating a file or filegroup backup is as follows:

```
BACKUP DATABASE { database_name ¦ @database_name_var }
 <file_or_filegroup> [ ,...n ]
  TO <backup_device> [ ,...n ]
  [ <MIRROR TO clause> ] [ next-mirror-to ]
  [ WITH { DIFFERENTIAL ¦ <general_WITH_options> [ ,...n ] } ]
[;]
```

Partial Backups

Partial backups were introduced as a new feature in SQL Server 2005. Primary filegroups and read-write filegroups are always backed up when a partial backup is executed. Any filegroups marked as read-only are skipped to save time and space. Partial backups should not be confused with differential backups. Unlike differential backups, partial backups are best used when read-only filegroups exist and you have chosen not to back up this data because it is static. If you choose to back up a read-only filegroup, this choice must be identified in the BACKUP command. It is worth mentioning that a partial backup can only be created with TSQL; this functionality is not included in SSMS.

The basic syntax for creating partial and differential backups is as follows:

```
—Creating a Partial Backup
BACKUP DATABASE { database_name ¦ @database_name_var }
 READ_WRITE_FILEGROUPS [ , <read_only_filegroup> [ ,...n ] ]
  TO <backup_device> [ ,...n ]
  [ <MIRROR TO clause> ] [ next-mirror-to ]
  [ WITH { DIFFERENTIAL ¦ <general_WITH_options> [ ,...n ] } ]
[;]
```

Differential Partial Backups

A differential partial backup has many of the features of a differential backup and a partial backup. Only data that has been modified in the primary filegroups and read-write filegroups and not marked as read-only is backed up since the last partial backup. As with partial backups, this functionality is not included in SSMS and can be created only with TSQL.

Copy-Only Backups

The capability to make copy-only backups was introduced in SQL Server 2005 and continues to exist with SQL Server 2008. This backup type provides an entire independent backup of a database without affecting the sequence of the backup and restore process.

A common scenario for creating a copy-only backup is when you need to refresh a staging database from production. You can simply create a copy-only backup and restore it to the staging environment without affecting the sequence of the conventional backup or restore process. SSMS now supports copy-only backups. It is possible, however, to create copy-only backups on both the database files and logs.

The basic syntax for creating a copy-only backup for a database file is as follows:

```
BACKUP DATABASE database_name TO
 <backup_device> ... WITH COPY_ONLY …
```

The basic syntax for creating a copy-only backup for a transaction log file is
as follows:

```
BACKUP LOG database_name TO <backup_device>
.. WITH COPY_ONLY …
```

> **Note**
>
> In SQL Server 2005, it was only possible to create a copy-only backup with
> Transact-SQL; however, with SQL Server 2008 it can be done with the GUI in
> SSMS.

Mirrored Backups

Mirrored backups, also called *mirrored media sets*, another new feature that
was introduced with SQL Server 2005, but that continues to be delivered in
SQL Server 2008, are a large timesaver. Unlike in the past when you were
given the arduous task of creating additional backup copies in the event of a
media failure, SQL Server 2008 can create a maximum of four mirrors during
a backup operation, which increases reliability and performance. Moreover,
SQL Server 2008 also ensures the reliability of the media through database
and backup checksums. The only shortcoming to mirrored backups is that the
media for each mirror must be the same. For instance, if a backup is committed to tape, all mirrors must also be committed to tape.

A mirrored backup is not necessarily a backup type, per se, but an optional
clause available when you're creating full, differential, or transaction log
backups.

The following TSQL syntax creates a media set called
AdventureWorks2008MediaSet using three tape drives as backup devices:

```
BACKUP DATABASE AdventureWorks2008 TO TAPE = '\\.\tape01', TAPE =
➡'\\.\tape02', TAPE = '\\.\tape03'
WITH
    FORMAT,
    MEDIANAME = 'AdventureWorks2008MediaSet'
```

Typically, the speed of a backup device is a bottleneck that causes backup
performance degradation. To increase the speed of any type of backup, it is a best
practice to use multiple backup devices. When using multiple backup devices,
backups are written in parallel, thus increasing backup times and performance.

> **Note**
>
> For a complete listing of TSQL syntax conventions on backups, including the arguments, options, and explanations, see "Backup Transact-SQL" in the SQL Server 2008 Books Online.

Backing Up and Recovering Examples

The following sections focus on SQL Server 2008 backup and restore strategies for databases within the Database Engine. The examples include backing up all user and system databases to disk with a maintenance plan, compressing backups, backing up the AdventureWorks2008 database using the Full recovery model, and restoring the AdventureWorks2008 database to the point of failure.

Understanding the Need to Back Up the System Databases

If you want to restore a SQL Server 2008 installation, it is imperative not only to back up SQL Server user databases such as AdventureWorks2008, but also the system databases. The main SQL Server 2008 system databases are

- **Master Database**—The master database is an important system database in SQL Server 2008. It houses all system-level data, including system configuration settings, login information, disk space, stored procedures, linked servers, and the existence of other databases, along with other crucial information.

- **Model Database**—The model database serves as a template for creating new databases in SQL Server 2008. The data residing in the model database is commonly applied to a new database with the Create Database command. In addition, the tempdb database is re-created with the help of the model database every time SQL Server 2008 is started.

- **Msdb Database**—Used mostly by SQL Server Agent, the msdb database stores alerts, scheduled jobs, and operators. In addition, it also stores historical information on backups and restores, Mail, and Service Broker.

- **Tempdb**—The tempdb database holds temporary information, including tables, stored procedures, objects, and intermediate result sets. Each time SQL Server is started, the tempdb database starts with a clean copy.

> **Note**
>
> By default, the master, msdb, and tempdb databases use the Simple recovery model, whereas the model database uses the Full recovery model by default.

It is a best practice to include the system database with the existing user database backup strategy. At a minimum, the system databases should be backed up at the time a configuration is added, changed, or removed relative to a database, login, job, or operator.

Conducting a Full Backup Using SSMS

To perform a full SQL database backup on the AdventureWorks2008 database using SSMS, do the following:

1. Choose Start, All Programs, Microsoft SQL Server 2008, SQL Server Management Studio.

2. In Object Explorer, first connect to the Database Engine, expand the desired server, and then expand the database folder.

3. Select the AdventureWorks2008 database.

4. Right-click on the AdventureWorks2008 database, select Tasks, and then select Backup.

5. On the General page in the Back Up Database window, review the name of the database being backed up and validate that the Backup Type option is set to Full.

6. Type the desired name and description for the backup, and in the Backup Component section, choose Database, as shown in Figure 7.2.

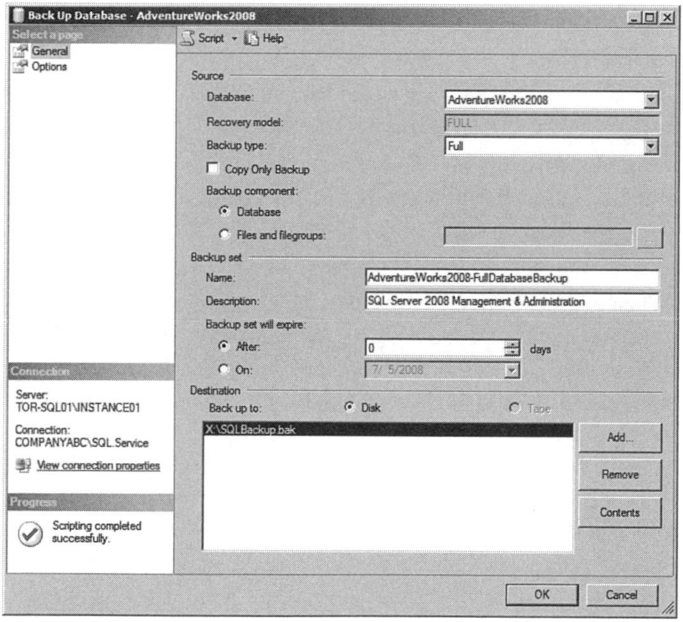

FIGURE 7.2
Viewing the SQL Server Back Up Database page.

The Destination section identifies the disk or tape media that will contain the backup. You can specify multiple destinations in this section by clicking the Add button. For disk media, a maximum of 64 disk devices can be specified. The same limit applies to tape media. If multiple devices are specified, the backup information is spread across those devices. All the devices must be present to restore the database. If no tape devices are attached to the database server, the Tape option is disabled.

7. In the Destination section, choose the Disk option, as shown in Figure 7.2. Accept the default backup location, or remove the existing path and click Add to select a new destination path for the backup.

8. In the Select Backup Destination window, type the path on the hard disk where the database backup will be created, including the backup filename, and then click OK. Alternatively, you can choose a backup device instead of storing the backup on hard disk.

As mentioned earlier, the Copy Only Backup option can now be enabled when conducting a backup with SQL Server Management Studio. The option is found in the Back Up Database window (see Figure 7.2).

9. Initialize the backup or enter advanced backup options by clicking Options in the Select a Page pane.

The Overwrite Media section allows you to specify options relative to the destination media for the backup. The two options available are Back Up to the Existing Media Set and Back Up to A New Media Set, and Erase All Existing Backup Sets.

- When the first option, Back Up to the Existing Media Set, is selected, there are three potential settings to be configured. The first setting, Append to the Existing Backup Set, assumes that any prior backups that were contained on the media set are preserved and the new backup is added to them. The second setting, Overwrite All Existing Backup Sets, replaces any former backups on the existing media set with the current backup. An optional setting exists; Check Media Set Name and Backup Set Expiration, forces SQL Server to verify the media set name and backup set expiration settings before a backup occurs on an existing media set by providing a media set name to be utilized.

- The second option, Back Up to a New Media Set, and Erase All Existing Backup Sets, allows you to create a new media set and erase previous backups sets by inputting a new media set name and description.

Options in the Reliability section can be used to ensure that the backup that has been created can be used reliably in a restore situation. Verifying the Backup When Finished is highly recommended but causes the backup time to be extended during the backup verification. Similarly, the Perform Checksum Before Writing to Media option helps ensure that you have a sound backup but again causes the database backup to run longer. Finally, the backup process will fail if errors are found in the checksum analysis; therefore, indicate whether or not you want the backup process to proceed or stop by enabling the setting Continue on Error.

The options in the Transaction Log section are available for databases that are in the Full or Bulk-Logged recovery model. These options are disabled in the Simple recovery model and are only available if a Transaction Log backup is selected The Truncate the Transaction Log option causes any inactive portion of the transaction log to be removed after the database backup is complete. This is the default option and helps keep the size of your transaction log manageable. The Backup the Tail of the Log option is related to point-in-time restores.

The options in the Tape Drive section are enabled only when you select Tape for the destination media. The Unload the Tape After Backup option rejects the media tape after the backup is complete. This feature can help identify the end of the backup and prevent the tape from being overwritten the next time the backup runs. The Rewind the Tape Before Unloading option is self-explanatory and causes the tape to be released and rewound prior to unloading the tape.

The last set of options is the compression settings to be used during the backup process. The options include: Use the Default Server Settings, Compress Backup, and Do Not Compress Backup.

10. On the Options page, in the Overwrite Media section, maintain the default settings, Back Up to the Existing Media Set, and Append to the Existing Backup Set.

11. In the Reliability section, choose the options Verify Backup When Finished, Perform Checksum Before Writing Media, and Continue on Error.

12. In the Compression section, set the compression for this database backup to Compress Backup, as shown in Figure 7.3. Click OK to execute the backup.

13. Review the success or failure error message and click OK to finalize.

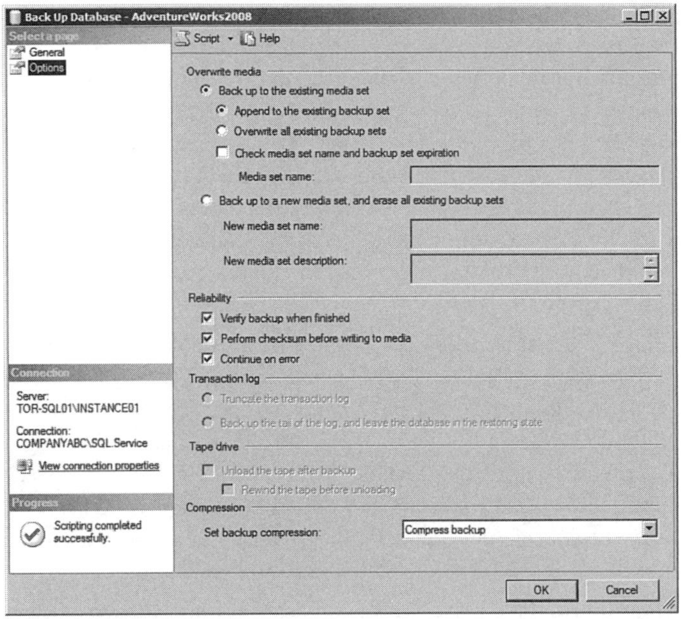

FIGURE 7.3
Setting SQL Server full backup advanced options.

Conducting a Differential Backup Using SSMS

To perform a differential SQL database backup on an individual database using SSMS, do the following:

1. Right-click on the AdventureWorks2008 database, select Tasks, and then select Backup.

2. On the General page in the Back Up Database window, review the name of the database being backed up and validate that the Backup Type option is set to Differential.

3. Type the desired name and description for the backup, and in the Backup Component section, choose Database.

4. In the Destination section, choose the Disk option. Accept the default backup location, or remove the existing path and click Add to select a new destination path for the backup.

5. In the Select Backup Destination window, type the path on the hard disk where the database backup will be created, including the backup filename, and then click OK. For this example, use the same destination path and filename used in the previous full backup steps.

6. On the Options page, in the Overwrite Media section, maintain the default settings, Back Up to the Existing Media Set and Append to the Existing Backup Set.

7. In the Reliability section, choose the options Verify Backup When Finished, Perform Checksum Before Writing to Media, and Continue on Error.

8. Set the desired backup compression settings. Then click OK to execute the backup.

9. Review the success or failure error message and click OK to finalize.

Conducting a Transaction Log Backup Using SSMS

To perform a transaction log SQL database backup on an individual database using SSMS, do the following:

1. Choose Start, All Programs, Microsoft SQL Server 2008, SQL Server Management Studio.

2. In Object Explorer, first connect to the Database Engine, expand the desired server, and then expand the database folder.

3. Select the AdventureWorks2008 database.

4. Right-click on the AdventureWorks2008 database, select Tasks, and then select Backup.

5. On the General page in the Back Up Database window, review the name of the database being backed up and validate that the Backup Type option is set to Transaction Log.

6. Type the desired name and description for the backup, and in the Backup Component section, choose Database.

7. In the Destination section, choose the Disk option. Accept the default backup location, or remove the existing path and click Add to select a new destination path for the backup.

8. In the Select Backup Destination window, type the path on the hard disk where the database backup will be created, including the backup filename, and then click OK. For this example, use the same destination path and filename used in the previous full backup steps.

9. Initialize the backup or enter advanced backup options by clicking on Options in the Select a Page pane.

   The Transaction Log section allows you to specify options relative to how the transaction log should be handled during the backup. The two choices are

- Truncate the Transaction Log
- Back Up the Tail of the Log, and Leave the Database in the Restoring State

After a checkpoint is performed, the inactive portion of the transaction log is marked as reusable. If the default option—Truncate the Transaction Log—is selected, the backup truncates the inactive portion of the transaction log, creating free space. The physical size of the transaction log still remains the same, but the usable space is reduced.

The second option—Back Up the Tail of the Log, and Leave the Database in the Restoring State—is typically used if a disaster occurs and you are restoring the database to a point in failure. Ultimately, this option backs up the active logs that were not already backed up. These active logs can then be used against the recently recovered database to a point in failure or point in time.

10. On the Options page, in the Overwrite Media section, maintain the default settings, Back Up to the Existing Media Set and Append to the Existing Backup Set.

11. In the Reliability section, choose the options Verify Backup When Finished, Perform Checksum Before Writing Media, and Continue on Error.

12. In the Transaction Log section, choose the option Truncate the Transaction Log.

13. In the Compression section, set the compression for this database backup to Compress Backup.

14. Review the settings, as shown in Figure 7.4, and click OK to execute the backup.

15. Review the success or failure error message and click OK to finalize.

Automating Backups with a Maintenance Plan

Instead of backing up a database and transaction logs individually with SSMS or TSQL, you can automate and schedule this process with a single task by creating a maintenance plan. The Database Backup maintenance plan reduces the efforts required to create individual backups on all user and system databases. In addition, it is possible to create subtasks and schedule these items at separate times. Maintenance plans are discussed further in Chapter 6, "SQL Server 2008 Maintenance Practices."

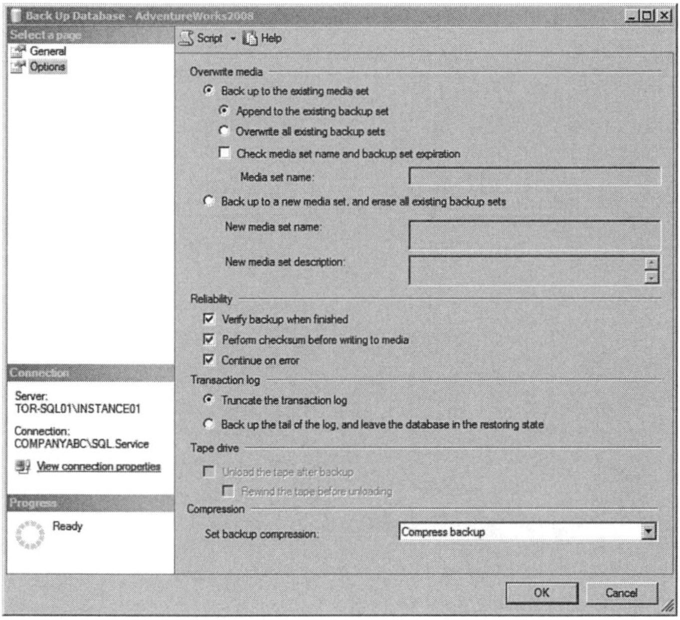

FIGURE 7.4
Setting SQL Server Backup transaction log advanced options.

Follow these steps to start the creation of a customized backup maintenance plan for all user and system databases by using the Maintenance Plan Wizard:

1. Choose Start, All Programs, Microsoft SQL Server 2008, SQL Server Management Studio.

2. In Object Explorer, first connect to the Database Engine, expand the desired server, and then expand the Management folder.

3. Right-click Maintenance Plans and choose Maintenance Plan Wizard.

4. In the Welcome to the Database Maintenance Plan Wizard page, read the message and click Next.

5. On the Select Plan Properties page, enter a name and description for the maintenance plan.

6. Choose either the first option, Separate Schedules for Each Task, or the second option, Single Schedule for the Entire Plan or No Schedule. For this example, create a separate schedule for the backup plan, as shown in Figure 7.5. Then click Next.

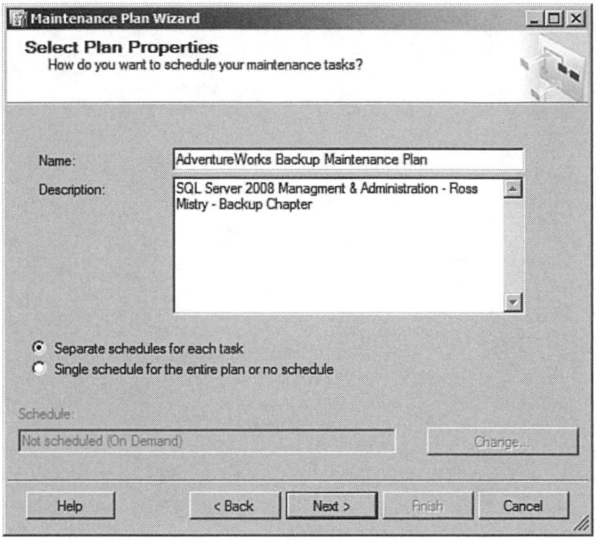

FIGURE 7.5
Selecting the maintenance plan properties.

> **Note**
>
> The ability to create separate independent schedules for each subtask within a single maintenance plan was a new feature released with SQL Server 2005 Service Pack 2.

7. In the Select Maintenance Tasks page, check the Back Up Database (Full) and Back Up Database (Transaction Log) maintenance tasks, as shown in Figure 7.6, and click Next.

8. On the Select Maintenance Task Order page, review the order in which the tasks will be executed and click Next. For this example, the Back Up Database (Full) task should be listed first and then the Back Up Database (Transaction Log) task should follow.

The Define Back Up Database (Full) page includes an expanded set of options when you're creating full backups with the Maintenance Plan Wizard. You can choose a database to be backed up, choose an individual component, set expiration, verify integrity, and decide whether to use disk or tape. The backup options are

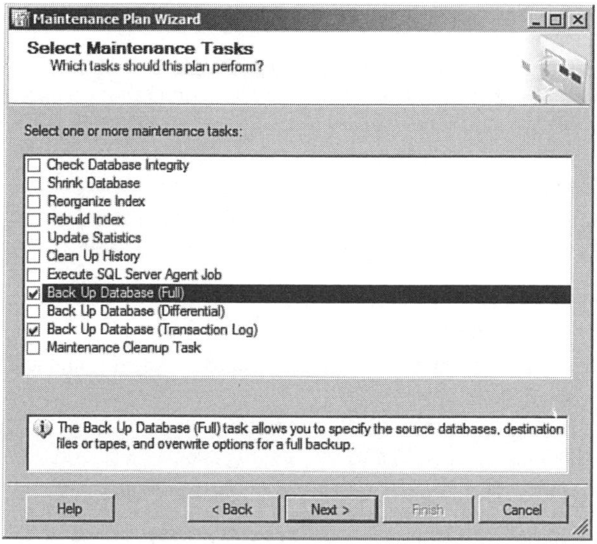

FIGURE 7.6
Selecting maintenance task options.

- **Database(s)**—Specify the database. It is possible to generate a maintenance plan to back up an individual database, all databases, systems databases, or all user databases.

- **Backup Component**—In the Backup Component section, you can select either the entire database or individual files or filegroups.

- **Backup Set Will Expire**—This option allows you to specify when the backup set will expire and can be overwritten by another backup based on a number of days or a specific date.

- **Back Up To**—This option allows the backup to be written to a file or tape. A tape drive must be present on the system, and it is possible to write to a file residing on a network share.

- **Back Up Databases Across One or More Files**—For the backup destination, you can either add or remove one or more disk or tape locations. In addition, you can view the contents of a file and append to the backup file if it already exists.

- **Create a Backup File for Every Database**—Instead of selecting the option Back Up Databases Across One or More Files, you can let SQL Server automatically create a backup file for every database selected. In addition, it is also possible to automatically create a subdirectory for each database selected.

> **Note**
>
> The subdirectory inherits permissions from the parent directory. Therefore, use NTFS permissions to secure this folder and restrict unauthorized access.

- **Verify Backup Integrity**—This option verifies the integrity of the backup when completed by firing a TSQL command that verifies whether the backup was successful and accessible.

- **Set Backup Compression**—This option controls the compression settings associated with a database backup.

- **Schedule**—This option enables you to create a separate schedule for this specific task.

9. In the Define Back Up Database (Full) Task page, choose All Databases from the drop-down list next to Databases and click OK.

10. Check the Backup Set Will Expire option and enter **0** days so that the backup set will not expire.

11. Select the option Create a Backup File for Every Database and then click the ellipsis button to specify a backup folder. In the Locate Folder page, select a folder on the hard disk where the database backup will be created and click OK.

12. Check the option Verify the Backup Integrity.

13. In the Compression section, set the compression for this database backup to Compress Backup.

14. Click Change in the Schedule section. In the Job Schedule Properties page, configure this schedule type to repeat on a weekly basis. Set the frequency for every Sunday starting at 12:00 a.m., as shown in Figure 7.7, and click OK.

15. Review the Define Back Up Database (Full) Task settings, configured as shown in Figure 7.8, and click Next to continue configuring the maintenance plan.

The next page, Define Backup Database (Transaction Log) Task, focuses on backup settings for the transaction logs. The settings and options within this page are similar to the settings and options for creating full database backups explained previously. The only difference with the transaction logs is that databases using the Simple recovery model are excluded and the backup file extension is .trn, not .bak.

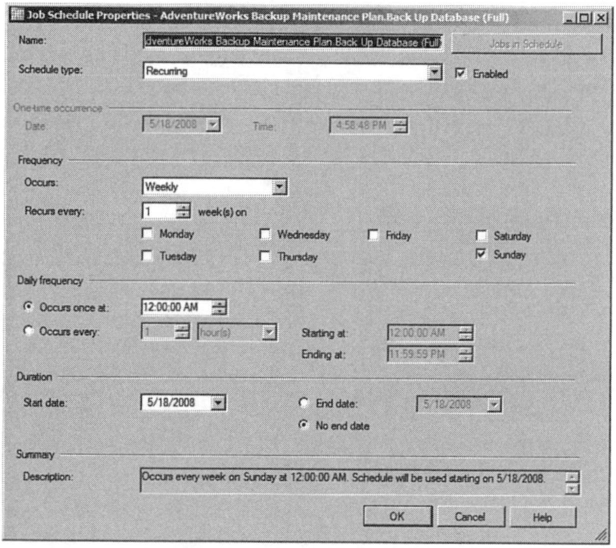

FIGURE 7.7
Setting the job scheduled properties for the maintenance plan.

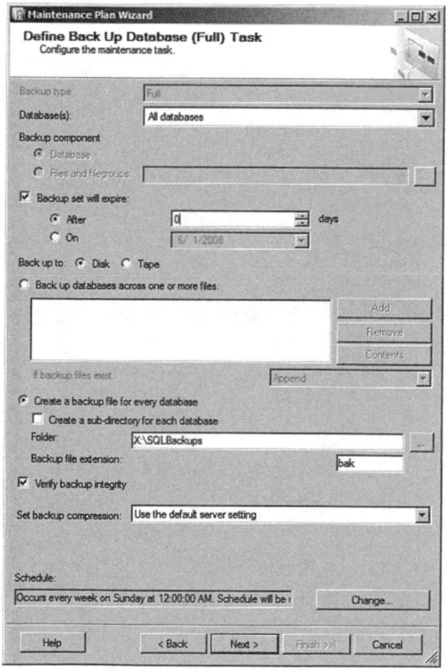

FIGURE 7.8
Selecting the Define Back Up Database (Full) Task settings.

16. Similar to the preceding steps, in the Define Back Up Database
(Transaction Log) Task, select All Databases, Backup Set Will Not Expire,
Create a Backup File for Every Database, and Create a Sub-Directory for
Each Database. In addition, select a backup folder and check the option
Verify Backup Integrity and Compress Backup, as shown in Figure 7.9.

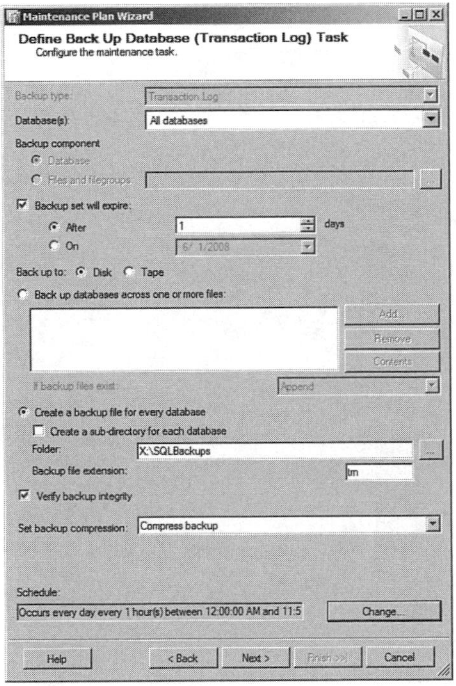

FIGURE 7.9
Selecting the Define Back Up Database (Transaction Log) Task settings.

Note

When you select the option to back up all databases, databases with the simple
recovery model will be excluded as Transaction Log backups do not apply.

---

17. Click Change in the Schedule section. In the Job Schedule Properties
page, configure the frequency of this job to daily and the daily
frequency to every 1 hour, and click OK.

18. Review the Define Back Up Database (Transaction Log) Task settings
and click Next to continue configuring the maintenance plan.

19. On the Select Report Options page, set the option to either write a report to a text file and enter a folder location, or email the report. If you want to email the report, Database Mail must be enabled and configured, and an Agent Operation with a valid email address must already exist. Click Next to continue.

20. The Complete the Wizard page summarizes the options selected in the Maintenance Plan Wizard. It is possible to drill down on a task to view advanced settings. Review the options selected and click Finish to close the summary page.

21. In the Maintenance Plan Wizard Progress page, review the creation status, as shown in Figure 7.10, and click Close to end the Maintenance Plan Wizard.

21. The maintenance plan is then created and should be visible under the Maintenance Plan folder in SSMS. In addition, you can find the maintenance plan jobs in the Jobs folder within the SQL Server Agent.

Note

For these backup examples, SQL Server is being backed up to disk. In production, backups should not be stored on the same disks as the database or transaction logs. For retention and recovery purposes, backups stored to disks should eventually be committed to tape and stored offsite.

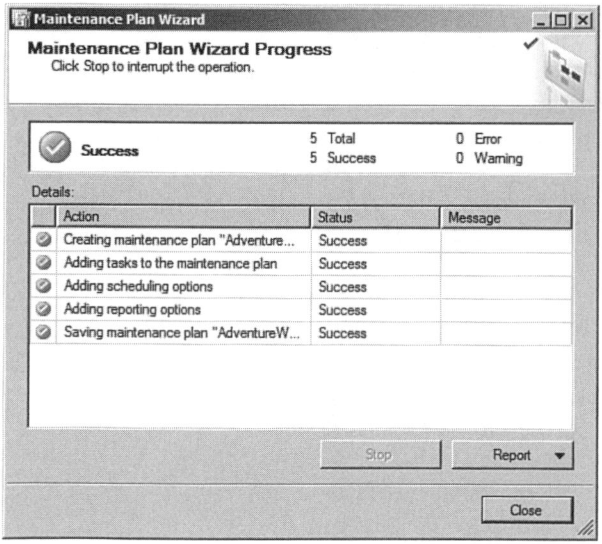

FIGURE 7.10
Viewing the Maintenance Plan Wizard progress.

Conducting a Full Database Recovery Using SSMS

When database corruption or a disaster occurs, you need to restore the database to the point of failure or until a specific date and time. If the database is set to the Full recovery model during the backup, the high-level plan for restoring the database consists of the following sequential tasks: The first step, if possible, is to back up the active transactions (the tail-log), and leave the database in a restoring state. The next step includes restoring the latest full backup and then the most recent differential backups, provided that differential database backups were taken. Finally, subsequent log files should be restored in sequence with the final log being the tail-log.

If the Simple recovery model is used, it is not possible to make transaction log backups; therefore, the restore process consists of restoring the last full backup and most recent differential backup.

Follow these steps to restore the database to the point of failure:

1. Choose Start, All Programs, Microsoft SQL Server 2008, SQL Server Management Studio.

2. In Object Explorer, first connect to the Database Engine, click New Query, and execute the following code to conduct full database, differential, and multiple transaction log backups.

```
— FULL BACKUP ADVENTUREWORKS2008
USE AdventureWorks2008
BACKUP DATABASE [AdventureWorks2008]
TO  DISK = N'X:\AdventureWorks2008.bak'
WITH  DESCRIPTION = N'SQL Server 2008 Management
and Administration',
NOFORMAT,
NOINIT,
NAME = N'AdventureWorks2008-Full Database Backup',
SKIP, NOREWIND, NOUNLOAD,  STATS = 10
GO


—DIFFERENTIAL BACKUP ADVENTUREWORKS2008
USE AdventureWorks2008
BACKUP DATABASE [AdventureWorks2008]
TO  DISK = N'X:\AdventureWorks2008.bak'
WITH  DIFFERENTIAL ,
DESCRIPTION = N'SQL Server 2008 Management
and Administration',
NOFORMAT, NOINIT,
NAME = N'AdventureWorks2008-
```

```
➥Differential Database Backup',
SKIP, NOREWIND, NOUNLOAD,  STATS = 10
GO
– TRANSACTION LOG BACKUP
USE AdventureWorks2008
BACKUP LOG [AdventureWorks2008]
TO  DISK = N'X:\AdventureWorks2008.bak'
WITH  DESCRIPTION = N'SQL Server 2008 Management
and Administration',
NOFORMAT,
NOINIT,
NAME = N'AdventureWorks2008-Transaction Log  Backup',
SKIP, NOREWIND, NOUNLOAD,  STATS = 10
GO
```

3. To restore the database to the point in failure, first close any connections to the database including any outstanding query windows and then execute the following script to perform the tail-log backup to begin disaster recovery. Close the query window before moving on to the next step, which includes restoring full, differential, and transaction log backups taken in step 2 using SSMS.

```
– TAIL LOG TRANACTION LOG BACKUP
BACKUP LOG [AdventureWorks2008]
TO  DISK = N'X:\AdventureWorks2008.bak'
WITH  NO_TRUNCATE ,
DESCRIPTION = N'SQL Server 2008 Management
and Administration',
NOFORMAT,
NOINIT,
NAME = N'AdventureWorks2008-
➥Transaction Tail Log  Backup',
SKIP, NOREWIND, NOUNLOAD,  NORECOVERY ,  STATS = 10
GO
```

4. In Object Explorer, right-click on the AdventureWorks2008 database, select Tasks, Restore, and then select Database. (Notice that the database is in a recovering state and is not operational.)

5. On the General page in the Restore Database window, check all the database, differential, and transaction log backups in the Select the Backup Sets to Restore section, as shown in Figure 7.11. Notice that the tail-log backup is the final backup in the list.

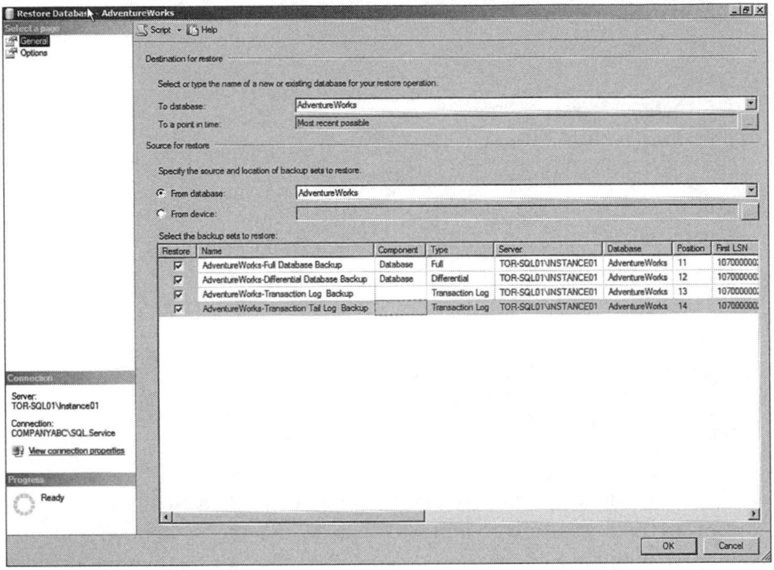

FIGURE 7.11
Selecting general restore options.

6. On the General page in the Restore Database window, select the options Overwrite the Existing Database and Leave the Database Ready to Use by Rolling Back Uncommitted Transactions, as shown in Figure 7.12, and click OK.

7. Review the restore success message and click OK.

Note

If there is a need to restore the database to a specific point in time, it is possible to input a date and time value in the To a Point in Time section on the General page of the Restore page. The restore process will stop rolling back any entries in the transaction log after this specified period.

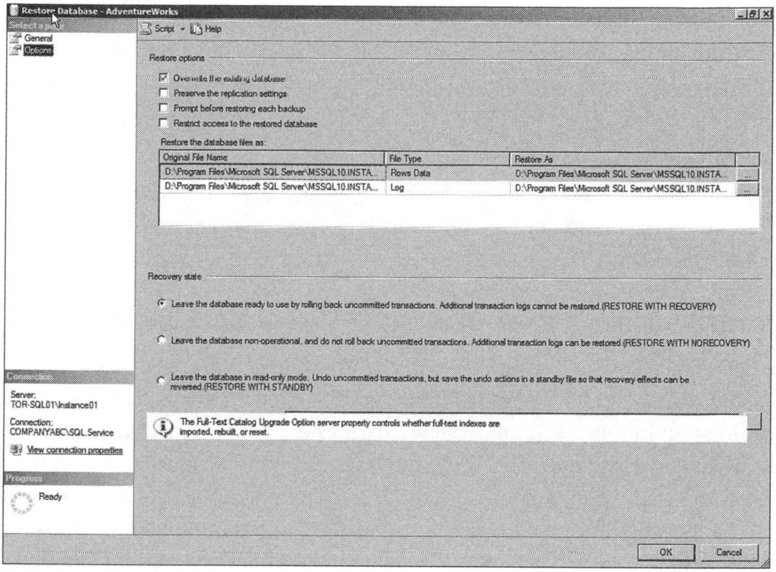

FIGURE 7.12
Selecting additional restore options.

Backing Up and Recovering Full-Text Catalogs

The process of backing up and restoring full-text catalogs is similar to backing up and restoring database files. Unlike in SQL Server 2000, each full-text catalog in SQL Server 2008 is treated as a file and is automatically included in regular full or differential backups. As a result, when backing up the full-text catalog, you should follow the full and differential backup steps described earlier in the chapter.

Backing Up Full-Text Catalogs

In SQL 2005, it was possible to back up and restore your full-text catalog separately from the rest of your database. During a backup, your full text catalog would be stored in a separate file group and then backed up with this file group. When you restored this file group, the catalog would be restored into the file system. This allowed your full-text catalogs to be more portable as they could be stored in - a database backup, or in a separate file group backup.

In SQL 2008, the catalog is essentially a container of properties for a group of full text indexes. It exists in the database completely; it is no longer stored in the file system. When you back up your database, your full-text catalog and indexes are backed up with your database; you can't do more granular backups that only contain the full-text catalog. Nor is there a way to restore only the full-text catalog; database restores contain the database objects as well as any full-text indexes or catalogs that are in that database backup.

Full-text indexing is now aware of both log shipping and database mirroring. In SQL 2005, you could log-ship and mirror a full-text-enabled database, but on recovery you would need to run a full population. This is no longer necessary in SQL 2008.

Understanding and Creating Database Snapshots

Database snapshots were first introduced with SQL Server 2005. The *database snapshot* provides a read-only copy of a SQL Server database at a specific point in time. This static view provides a comprehensive picture of the full database, tables, views, and stored procedures. Organizations can use a database snapshot to protect the state of a database at a specific time, to do offload reporting, or to maintain historical data. For instance, an organization can revert to a snapshot in the event it runs into problems. Keep in mind that this feature is available only with SQL Server 2008 Enterprise Edition.

When using database snapshots, some limitations exist, as follows:

- It is not possible to drop, detach or restore a database if a snapshot already exists. The snapshot must be removed first.

- Snapshots of the system databases such as the model, master or tempdb are not supported.

- Full text indexing is not supported with database snapshots.

Caution

Database snapshots are a convenient feature, but they are not a replacement for maintaining a backup and restore plan. A backup and recovery plan is still necessary because changes made after the snapshot is taken are lost unless an organization also maintains regular and full backups that include the latest transaction log. This ensures that the most recent data is available for recovery. As a result, a snapshot should be viewed only as an extra layer of protection for preserving a database to a specific point in time.

If you want to fully use and manage snapshots, two tools are necessary. You must use TSQL to create and revert to snapshots and SSMS to view snapshots. Both TSQL and SSMS can be used to delete snapshots. The following sections show how to create, view, revert to, and delete database snapshots.

Creating a Database Snapshot with TSQL

In the Query Analyzer, execute the following script to create a database snapshot for the AdventureWorks2008 database:

```
—Creating a database Snapshot with Transact-SQL
Use AdventureWorks2008
CREATE DATABASE AdventureWorks2008_Snapshot_05072007_1200_SS ON
( NAME = AdventureWorks2008_Data, FILENAME =
"X:\AdventureWorks2008_Snapshot_0507200711/16/2004_1200_SS.ss" )
AS SNAPSHOT OF AdventureWorks2008;
GO
```

Viewing a Database Snapshot with SSMS

After creating the database snapshot, you can view it using SSMS. Follow the steps in the preceding section to view the AdventureWorks2008 database snapshot and then follow these steps to view the snapshot:

1. In Object Explorer, first connect to the Database Engine, expand the desired server, expand the Database folder, and then expand the Database Snapshots folder.

2. Select the desired database snapshot to view (for this example, AdventureWorks2008_SS_05_07_2007), as shown in Figure 7.13.

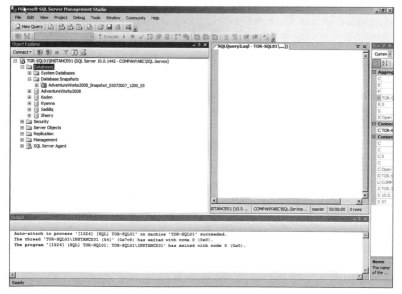

FIGURE 7.13
Viewing database snapshots with SSMS.

Reverting to a Database Snapshot with TSQL

In Query Analyzer, execute the following script to revert the AdventureWorks2008 database with the database snapshot created in the preceding steps:

```
USE Master
RESTORE DATABASE AdventureWorks2008
FROM DATABASE_SNAPSHOT =
➥'AdventureWorks2008_Snapshot_0507200705072007_1200_SS'
GO
```

Dropping a Database Snapshot

You can drop a database snapshot by either right-clicking on the snapshot in SSMS and choosing Delete or by issuing a DROP statement that identifies the name of the snapshot to be dropped.

The following script drops the AdventureWorks2008 snapshot created in the preceding steps:

```
DROP DATABASE 'AdventureWorks2008_Snapshot_05072007_1200_SS'
```

Tip

When naming snapshots, it is a best practice to first include the name of the source database supplemented with the date and time of when the snapshot was taken. For example; <DatabaseName>_snapshot_ <yyyy_mm_dd>_<hhmm>

For more information on database snapshots, see the topic "Database Snapshots" in SQL Server 2008 Books Online.

Summary

Although you, as database administrator, are charged with maintaining the SQL Server database, you can easily get caught up in daily administration and fire-fighting because your workload is often laborious. It is nonetheless imperative for you to develop and implement a strategic SQL Server backup and recovery plan. Currently, the backup maintenance task is likely the easiest tool available to implement the backup strategy for all user and system relational databases. In the event that Analysis Services, Reporting Services, or Internet Information Services is being used, it is important for each component to find its way into your organization's backup and restore plan. Finally, your organization should make it a habit to test and document your backup and recovery plan prior to implementation.

Best Practices

The following are best practices for backing up and restoring SQL
Server 2008:

- Define and document an SLA relevant to the SQL Server 2008 environment.

- Test the backup and recovery plan on a periodic basis and also before production to validate that it is operational and the SLA can be met.

- Select the appropriate recovery model for all systems and user databases. Use the Full recovery model for mission-critical databases that need to be restored to the point of failure in the event of a disaster.

- Isolate database and transaction log files on separate spindles for recovery purposes.

- Save the backups locally on a redundant disk drive separate from the online databases and back up to tape on a regular basis.

- If database or transaction log backups are stored locally on disk, do *not* store them on the same volumes as the database and transaction log files. If a drive or volume failure occurs, both the files and backups could be lost.

- For retention and recovery purposes, the backups stored to disk should be committed to tape.

- Commit to doing frequent backups if the system is an online transaction processing (OLTP) environment. An OLTP database is also known as the databases residing in the SQL Server Database Engine.

- Try to schedule backups when SQL Server is not in the process of being heavily updated.

- Use maintenance plans to streamline, automate, and schedule backups for all system and user databases.

- For large databases, consider introducing additional files or filegroups and include a combination of full, differential, filegroup, and transaction log backups to reduce backup and restore times.

- Speed up the backup process by selecting multiple backup devices.

- Leverage the new Backup Compression feature to minimize the backup footprint on disk. However, first test the impact in a dedicated lab before rolling out into production.

- When restoring the database to the point in failure, remember to first back up the tail-log and then conduct the restore.

PART II

SQL Server 2008 Security Practices

IN THIS PART

CHAPTER 8

Hardening a SQL Server Implementation

SQL Server is regularly targeted by hackers because it is a repository of sensitive data for organizations. If the server is breached, hackers can gain access to confidential information, including credit card numbers, Social Security numbers, or marketing information.

To prevent cybercrime or, at the very least, reduce it, Microsoft has been working very hard since 2002 in bringing the community more secured products with the Microsoft Trustworthy Computing Initiative. Although Microsoft products are being transformed and are more secure by default and design due to Trustworthy Computing, the company is not delusional about where things stand today. Microsoft knows it still has much work to do to bolster security. This is important for all database administrators to understand because it means that you should take additional steps to further harden your SQL Server implementation until you can rely fully on Trustworthy Computing.

This chapter shows how important it is to harden the SQL Server implementation when the SQL Server installation is complete. The chapter explains how to manage a secure SQL Server implementation based on industry best practices so that vulnerabilities and security breaches are minimized. The following security topics are covered to harden a SQL Server implementation: using configuration tools to minimize the attack surface, deciding which authentication method to use, enforcing strong passwords, using SQL Server security logs, choosing the appropriate service account, verifying security with Microsoft Baseline Security Analyzer, and installing Windows and SQL Server Service Packs.

What's New for Hardening a SQL Server 2008 Implementation?

- The Surface Area Configuration Tool (SAC), used for enabling or disabling services and features within SQL

Server 2005, has been deprecated and replaced with Policy Based Management. Policy Based Management enables DBAs to create system policies in order to enforce granular configuration settings for one or more SQL Server systems.

■ In the past, Kerberos was only available when using the TCP/IP protocol. Now, Kerberos authentication has been expanded to include all protocols in the SQL Server stack such as named pipes and shared memory protocols.

■ SQL Server 2008 is tightly integrated with Windows Server 2008 and Active Directory Domain Services. Windows Server 2008 offers the most secure platform, the strongest authentication mechanism, the ability to leverage Active Directory Certificates Services, and multiple-factor authentication with items such as smart cards.

■ It is now possible to rename the SA account during a fresh installation or upgrade of SQL Server 2008. Renaming the SA account is a recommended step when hardening a SQL Server implementation as it minimizes the chances of the account being hacked and misused.

■ The local Windows Group BUILTIN\Administrator is no longer included in the SQL Server sysadmin server role.

■ SQL Server accounts are following the principle of least privilege as they are better protected and now further isolated from the operating system.

> **Note**
>
> Policy Based Management is a hardening technique; however, this book includes a dedicated chapter on this subject. For more information, see Chapter 10, "Administering Policy Based Management."

Windows and SQL Server Authentication

Authentication is commonly identified as a security measure designed to establish the validity of a user or application based on criteria such as an account, password, security token, or certificate. After a user or an application's validity is verified, authorization to access the desired object is granted.

At present, SQL Server 2008 continues to support two modes for validating connections and authenticating access to database resources: "Windows Authentication mode" and "SQL Server and Windows Authentication mode." Both of these authentication methods provide access to SQL Server and its resources.

> **Note**
>
> During installation, the default authentication mode is Windows. The authentication mode can be changed after the installation, however.

Windows Authentication Mode

Windows Authentication mode is the default and recommended authentication mode. It leverages local accounts, Active Directory user accounts, and groups when granting access to SQL Server. In this mode, you, as the database administrator, are given the opportunity to grant domain or local server users access to the database server without creating and managing a separate SQL Server account.

When Windows Authentication mode is used, Active Directory user accounts are subject to enterprise-wide policies enforced by the Active Directory domain such as complex passwords, password history, account lockouts, minimum password length, maximum password length, and the Kerberos protocol. If the server is not partaking in a domain, then the local security policies will govern the account's password and lockout behavior.

SQL Server and Windows Authentication (Mixed) Mode

SQL Server and Windows Authentication mode, which is regularly referred to as *mixed mode authentication*, uses either Active Directory user accounts or SQL Server accounts when validating access to SQL Server. Like SQL Server 2005, SQL Server 2008 continues to support a means to enforce password and lockout policies for SQL Server login accounts when using SQL Server authentication. These SQL Server policies include enforcing password complexity, password expiration, and account lockouts. As a reminder, this functionality, which was introduced with SQL Server 2005, was not available in SQL Server 2000, and this was a major security concern for most organizations and database administrators. Essentially, this security concern played a role in helping define Windows authentication as the recommended practice for managing authentication in the past. Today, SQL Server and Windows Authentication mode (Mixed Mode) may be able to successfully compete with Windows Authentication mode.

Which Mode Should Be Used to Harden Authentication?

When you are aware of the authentication methods, the next step is choosing one to manage SQL Server security. Although SQL Server 2008 now can enforce policies, Windows Authentication mode is still the recommended alternative for controlling access to SQL Server because this mode carries added advantages; Active Directory provides an additional level of protection with the Kerberos protocol. As a result, the authentication mechanism is more mature and robust; therefore, administration can be reduced by leveraging Active Directory groups for role-based access to SQL Server. In addition, it is now possible to utilize Kerberos with all network protocols associated with SQL Server 2008. Network protocols include TCP, Named Pipes, Shared Memory, and Virtual Interface Adapter (VIA).

Nonetheless, this mode is not practical for everything out there. Mixed authentication is still required if there is a need to support legacy applications, application requires it or clients coming in from platforms other than Windows and a need for separation of duties exists.

It is common to find organizations where the SQL Server and Windows teams do not trust one another. Therefore, a clear separation of duties is required because SQL Server accounts are not managed via Active Directory.

Using Windows authentication is a more secure choice. However, if mixed mode authentication is required, you must make sure to leverage complex passwords and the SQL Server 2008 password and lockout policies to further bolster security.

> **Note**
>
> The capability for SQL Server authentication in SQL Server 2008 to manage both password and lockout properties is available only if SQL Server is installed on Windows Server 2003 and above. The policies are enforced by the local security policy associated with the operating system

Configuring SQL Server 2008 Authentication Modes

To select or change the server authentication mode, follow these steps:

1. In SQL Server Management, right-click on a desired SQL Server and then click Properties.

2. On the Security page, as shown in Figure 8.1, select the desired server authentication mode under Server Authentication and then click OK.

3. In the SQL Server Management Studio dialog box, click OK to acknowledge the need to restart SQL Server.

4. In Object Explorer, right-click on a desired server and then click Restart. If the SQL Server Agent is running, it requires a restart also.

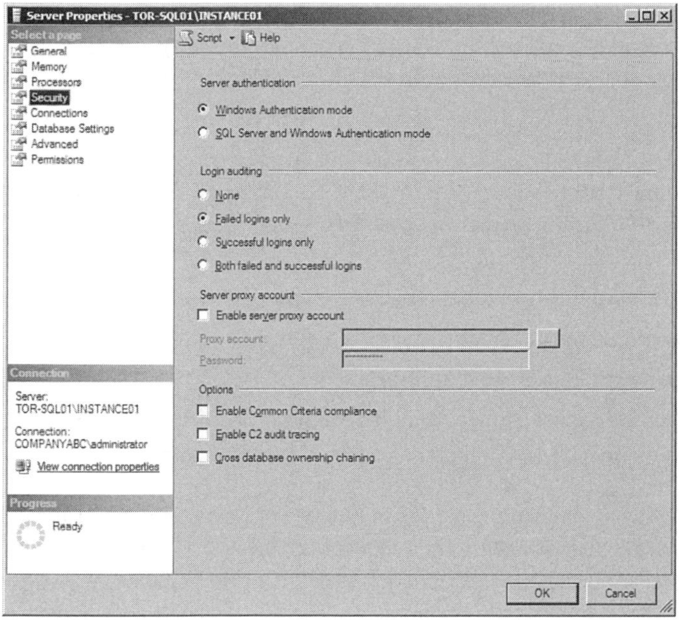

FIGURE 8.1
Configuring SQL Server 2008 authentication modes.

> **Note**
>
> If Windows Authentication mode is selected during installation, the SA login is disabled by default. If the authentication mode is switched to SQL Server mixed mode after the installation, the SA account is still disabled and must be manually enabled. It is a best practice to reset the password when the mode is switched.

Security Ramifications of the SA Account

If SQL Server Authentication mode is used, a strong SA password should also be used. By default, the SA account has full administrative privileges over a SQL Server installation; therefore, in the event this account is compromised, the intruder will have full access to SQL Server and all databases.

In the past, it was common to find production SQL Server installations with a weak or blank SA password, which naturally increased the risk of security vulnerabilities and compromises. Microsoft introduced the idea of checking for blank SA passwords during the installation of Service Pack 4 on SQL Server 2000. Database administrators were further informed of the security vulnerabilities associated with maintaining a blank password; however, they were not forced to enter a password, which again left the account and server in a vulnerable state.

This situation is no longer an issue since SQL Server 2005.

If you use SQL Server authentication, you must enter a strong SA password; otherwise, you cannot continue with the SQL Server installation. A strong password for SQL Server must contain at least six characters and satisfy at least three of the following four criteria:

- The password must contain uppercase letters.

- The password must contain lowercase letters.

- The password must contain numbers.

- The password must contain non-alphanumeric characters such as #, %, or ^.

In addition, a strong password cannot use typical or commonplace words that everyone in the IT field is accustomed to, such as *Password*, *Admin*, *Administrator*, *SA*, or *Sysadmin,* and cannot use either the name of the user logged on to the computer or the computer name. These are all considered weak passwords.

Not allowing a weak or blank password reinforces the fact that Microsoft is serious about its ongoing Trustworthy Computing Initiative. In the past few years, Microsoft has invested significant time and resources in enhancing the security of each of its products, including SQL Server 2008.

Tip

It is a best practice not to use the SA account for day-to-day administration, logging on to the server remotely, or having applications use it to connect to SQL.

Enforcing or Changing a Strong Password

To change or assign a strong SA password, do the following:

1. In Object Explorer, first expand the Security folder and then the Logon folder. Right-click on the SA account and then click Properties.

2. On the General page in the Login Properties dialog box, as shown in Figure 8.2, enter a new complex SA password, confirm it, and then click OK.

3. Restart Microsoft SQL Server Services, including SQL Server Agent.

Disabling and Renaming the SA Account

When attackers want to compromise a SQL Server, they don't want to access the system as common users; they want complete control of the server so that they can gain access to all the data within it. Because most hackers already know the SA account exists, this makes hacking one step easier because this account would grant them complete control of the SQL Server if compromised. Similar to the way you use a Windows Administrator account, it is a best practice to rename and disable the SA account in SQL Server 2008 when running in mixed authentication mode. This technique increases security one step further because most hackers are familiar with the SA account and the rights associated with it.

> **Note**
>
> Don't forget that SQL Server 2008 now provides you with the option to rename the SA account during the installation of SQL Server 2008.

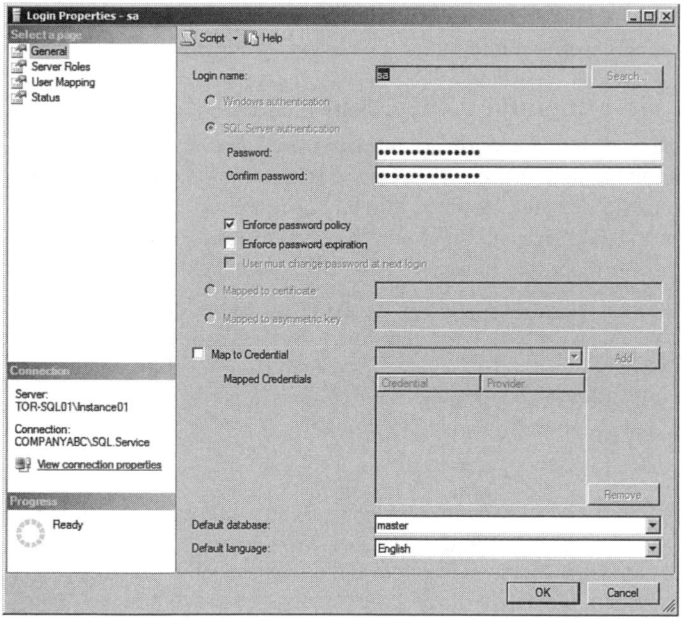

FIGURE 8.2
The SQL Server Login Properties dialog box for the SA account.

The following syntax first disables the SA account and then renames it to something not easily identified. This example uses the name Ross-Mistry:

```
USE MASTER
ALTER LOGIN sa DISABLE;
GO
ALTER LOGIN sa WITH NAME = [Ross-Mistry];
GO
```

> **Tip**
>
> Before renaming or disabling the SA account, make sure another account exists with administrator privileges; otherwise, you will not have access to the SQL Server.

Also, it is a best practice to rename the account to something that is not related to an administrator, SA, or service, or is easily identifiable so that it's not so obvious that this account was previously SA.

Using Configuration Tools to Harden the Installation

After you've installed SQL Server 2008, you should run the SQL Server Configuration Manager to harden the SQL Server implementation.

Reducing the SQL Server 2008 Surface Area

It is beneficial to maintain a slim and efficient installation of SQL Server 2008 by minimizing its footprint. This can be achieved by reducing the SQL Server system's surface area by only installing necessary components and disabling unwanted services and features. These hardening techniques make SQL Server less susceptible to hackers and malicious attacks.

The Surface Area Configuration tool (SAC), which was included in SQL Server 2005, has been replaced with the Policy Based Management framework; therefore, Policy Based Management should be utilized in order to manage the SQL Server surface area.

> **Note**
>
> Because SAC has been deprecated, the connectivity management features need to be configured using the Configuration Manager tool. The Configuration Manager tool is discussed in the next section, whereas Policy Based Management should be utilized when reducing surface area.

Using the SQL Server Configuration Manager Tool to Harden an Installation

The SQL Server Configuration Manager tool is a tool that you can use when hardening a SQL Server implementation. This tool should be used to configure and lock down unwanted services and features associated with a SQL Server implementation. Elements that can be configured include services, network configurations, native client configurations, client protocols, and aliases installed on a server.

To launch this tool, choose Start, All Programs, Microsoft SQL Server 2008, Configuration Tools, SQL Server Configuration Manager. The SQL Server Configuration Manager window is shown in Figure 8.3. The following nodes appear in the tool:

- **SQL Server Services**—This node enables you to start, stop, pause, resume, or configure services. In addition, you should use the tool when changing service account names and passwords.

- **SQL Server Network Configuration**—This node is the place where you can configure, enable, or disable SQL Server network protocols for the SQL Server Services installed on a server. In addition, you can configure encryption and expose or hide a SQL Server database instance.

- **SQL Native Client Configuration**—This node enables you to lock down network protocols or make changes to settings associated with ports for client connections.

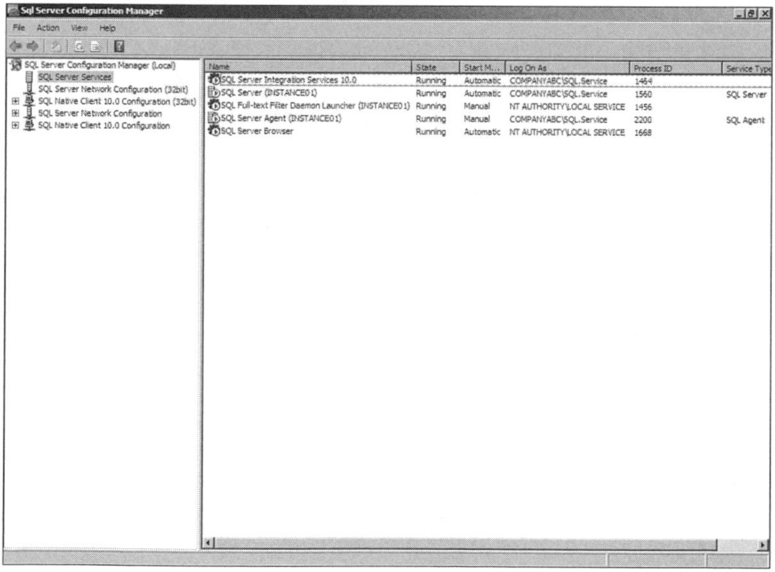

FIGURE 8.3
Managing services and connections, and disabling unnecessary SQL services.

Hardening SQL Server Ports with SQL Configuration Manager

A default installation of SQL Server 2008 uses TCP port 1433 for client requests and communications. These ports are well known in the industry, which makes them a common target for hackers. Therefore, it is a best practice to change the default ports associated with the SQL Server installation to put off hackers from port-scanning the default ports of the SQL Server installation. Unfortunately, SQL Server requires an open port for network communications. Therefore, this procedure prolongs the inevitable, as the used port will eventually be found.

Note

SQL Server 2008 does not automatically listen on port UDP 1434. Similar to SQL Server 2005, the task has been turned over to SQL Server Browser Services, which listens and resolves client connection requests made to the server. It also provides name and port resolution to clients when multiple instances are installed.

Follow these steps to change the default port using SQL Server Manager Configuration tools:

1. Choose Start, All Programs, Microsoft SQL Server 2008, Configuration Tools, SQL Server Configuration Manager.

2. Expand the SQL Server 2008 Network Configuration node and select Protocols for the SQL Server instance to be configured.

3. In the right pane, right-click the protocol name TCP/IP and choose Properties.

4. In the TCP/IP Properties dialog box, select the IP Addresses tab.

5. There is a corresponding entry for every IP address assigned to the server. Clear the values for both the TCP Dynamic Ports and TCP Port for each IP address except for the IP addresses under IPAll.

6. In the IPAll section for each instance, enter a new port that you want SQL Server 2008 to listen on, as shown in Figure 8.4.

7. Click Apply and restart the SQL Server Services.

Note

The TCP Port for the default instance is automatically set to 1433 and the TCP Dynamic Ports setting is blank. The second and subsequent instances by default do not have the TCP Port set and have TCP Dynamic Ports set to 0. Using Dynamic Ports requires the use of the SQL Server Browser Service in order to direct incoming connections to the current port for that instance. This however makes it more difficult to setup firewalls etc as the port can change each restart.

Hiding a SQL Server Instance from Broadcasting Information

It is possible for SQL Server clients to browse the current infrastructure and retrieve a list of running SQL Server instances. The SQL Server Browser service enumerates SQL Server information on the network. When the SQL Server is found, the client obtains the server name and can connect to it if it has the appropriate credentials. This can present a large security threat to organizations because sensitive production data can be compromised. Note, that the SQL Server Browser service is required when running multiple instances on a single server. As indicated earlier, the Browser Service directs incoming connections to specific ports associated to an instance.

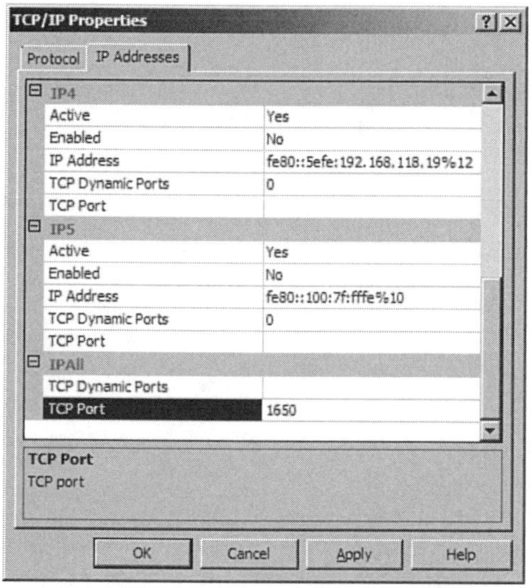

FIGURE 8.4
Changing the default SQL Server ports.

Organizations don't need to worry —there is help for this type of situation. The SQL Server Configuration Manager tool can be used to hide an instance of SQL Server. This is typically a best practice for mission-critical production database servers that host sensitive data because there is no need to broadcast this information. Clients and applications still can connect to SQL Server if needed; however, they need to know the SQL Server name, protocol, and which port the instance is using to connect.

To hide a SQL Server instance with SQL Server Configuration Manager, follow these steps:

1. Choose Start, All Programs, Microsoft SQL Server 2008, Configuration Tools, SQL Server Configuration Manager.

2. Expand the SQL Server 2008 Network Configuration node and select Protocols for the SQL Server instance to be configured.

3. Right-click Protocols for [Server\Instance Name] and then choose Properties.

4. In the Hide Instance box on the Protocols for [Server\Instance Name] Properties page, shown in Figure 8.5, select Yes.

5. Click OK and restart the services for the change to take effect.

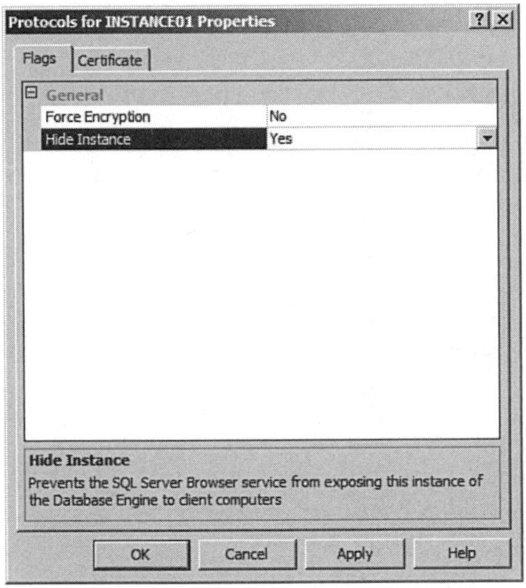

FIGURE 8.5
Hiding a SQL Server instance.

Hardening a Server with the Security Configuration Wizard in Windows Server 2008

The most impressive hardening tool and useful addition to the Windows Server operating system has to be the Security Configuration Wizard (SCW). SCW was first introduced as an add-in with Windows Server 2003 Service Pack 1; however, it is now included out of the box with Windows Server 2008. SCW is an attack-surface reduction tool that allows you to completely lock down a server, except for the particular services that it requires to perform specific duties. The role-based security policies are predefined and assist you by configuring services, network security, auditing, Registry settings, and more. This way, a WINS server responds only to WINS requests, a DNS server has only DNS enabled, and a SQL Server responds only to SQL requests. Windows Server 2008 continues to deliver this type of long-sought-after functionality.

SCW allows you to build custom role-based templates that can be exported to additional servers, thus streamlining the security process when setting up multiple systems. In addition, current security templates can be imported into SCW so that existing intelligence can be maintained. The SCW included with Windows Server 2008 includes new improved features and functionality such as more server role configurations and security settings out of the box, the possibility to disable unneeded services based on the server role, the capability to establish restrictive audit policies, advanced firewall configurations, and the power to transform a SCW policy into a Group Policy object (GPO) and link it to an Organizational Unit (OU) for centralized SQL Server infrastructure management when using Active Directory Domain Services (AD DS).

The advantages to using the SCW service on SQL Server are immediately identifiable. SQL Server, because it houses sensitive data and is often indirectly exposed to the Internet by web service applications, is vulnerable to attack and therefore should have all unnecessary services and ports shut down. A properly configured firewall normally drops this type of activity, and although the preceding section focused on minimizing surface attacks, it is always a good idea to put in an additional layer of security for good measure.

The Security Configuration Wizard can be run to lock down SQL Server based on a SQL Server role-based template, therefore, only the bare necessities required will be operational. This includes SQL access, web and ASP-related web access, and any other access methods required for the server. In addition, network security, port configuration, and Registry settings can be configured. Each SQL Server implementation differs, so it is important to run the wizard on a prototype to determine what settings are right for each individual SQL Server.

Note

For best results, when you're locking down a server with the Security Configuration Wizard, it is a best practice to first harden the SQL Server installation with the configuration tools described in the previous sections and then run this tool.

To launch the Security Configuration Wizard, choose Start, All Programs, Administrative Tools, Security Configuration Wizard. Use the wizard to create a role-based SQL Server security policy that locks down unnecessary services, network security, ports, Registry settings, and audit policies.

Verifying Security Using the Microsoft Baseline Security Analyzer (MBSA)

Like Windows Server 2008, Microsoft SQL Server 2008 also requires the latest service packs and updates to reduce known security vulnerabilities. Microsoft offers an intuitive, free downloadable tool called the Microsoft Baseline Security Analyzer (MBSA). This tool identifies common security vulnerabilities on SQL Servers by identifying incorrect configurations and missing security patches for SQL Server, Windows Server 2008, and Internet Information Services (IIS).

Not only MBSA can scan a single SQL Server, but it can also scan multiple instances of SQL Server. The MBSA SQL Server scan works by detecting and displaying SQL Server vulnerabilities, including the following: members of the sysadmin role, weak or blank SQL Server local accounts and SA passwords, SQL Server Authentication mode, SQL Server on a domain controller, and missing service packs and critical fixes.

> **Note**
>
> Unfortunately, MBSA does not provide all the scanning bells and whistles for SQL Server 2008 administration vulnerabilities yet. Microsoft is currently working on upgrading the tool to support SQL Server 2008. In the meantime, the tool still identifies missing security patches and service packs. In addition, it will find vulnerabilities on existing SQL Server 2005 installations.

Before installing MBSA, you should become acquainted with some specific Microsoft system requirements for the installation. Being familiar with the following list will help you on your way to a successful installation:

- The operating system must be Windows Server 2008, Windows Server 2003, Windows Vista, or Windows XP.
- Internet Explorer must be version 5.01 or higher.
- An XML parser such as the one available with Internet Explorer 5.01 or MSXML version 3.0 SP2 must be available.

Installing MBSA on a Server

Installation of MBSA is predictably straightforward. It can be installed on any workstation or server in the network. To install, complete these steps:

1. Download the latest version of the MBSA from the Microsoft website. The current link is http://www.microsoft.com/mbsa.

2. Double-click the MBSA installation file such as `mbsasetup-en.msi` to launch the installation.

Scanning for Security Vulnerabilities with MBSA

MBSA can scan a single computer or a range of computers, or all computers in a domain based on an IP address, range of IP addresses, or computer name. The security scanner can identify known security vulnerabilities on several Microsoft technologies such as Windows, IIS, or SQL Server.

To scan SQL Server for known SQL or Windows vulnerabilities, weak passwords, and security updates, follow these steps:

1. Choose Start, All Programs, Microsoft Baseline Security Analyzer.

2. Click on Scan a Computer to pick the system to scan. You can scan more than one computer here by entering either a valid IP address range or domain name.

3. In the next window, which is Which Computer Do You Want to Scan?, enter the computer name or IP address of the desired SQL Server. Select all options you want, as shown in Figure 8.6, and click Start Scan.

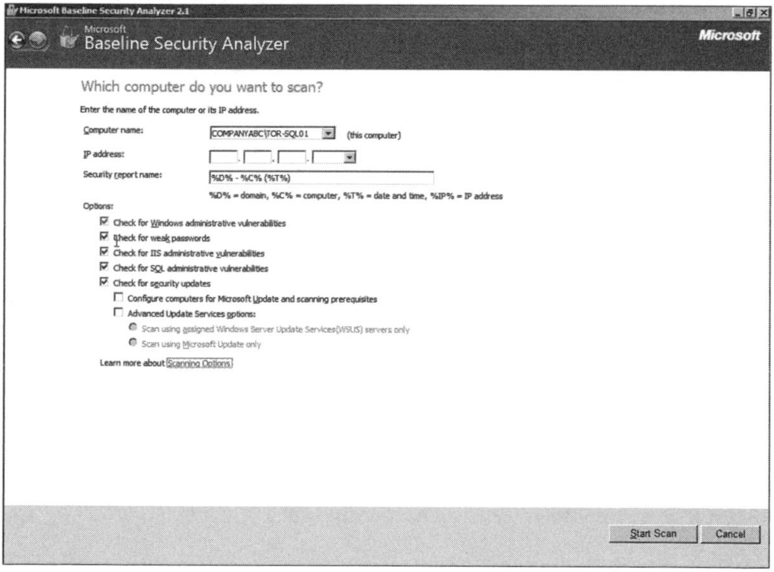

FIGURE 8.6
MBSA computer scan and options screen.

Viewing MBSA Security Reports

A separate security report is generated for the desired SQL Server on completion of the computer scan. This report is generated regardless of whether a local or remote scan is conducted. In addition, scanned reports are stored for future viewing on the same computer where the Microsoft Baseline Security Analyzer is installed.

The information yielded in the MBSA security reports is quite intuitive and addresses each vulnerability detected. For example, if MBSA detects a missing SQL Server service pack, Windows patch, or hot fix, it displays the vulnerability in the Security Update Scan section and provides the location that focuses on the fix.

In the security report example shown in Figure 8.7, note that each section scanned has a score associated with it. An end user or administrator can easily browse each section identifying known security vulnerabilities, verifying what was scanned, checking the results, and analyzing how to correct anomalies that MBSA detected.

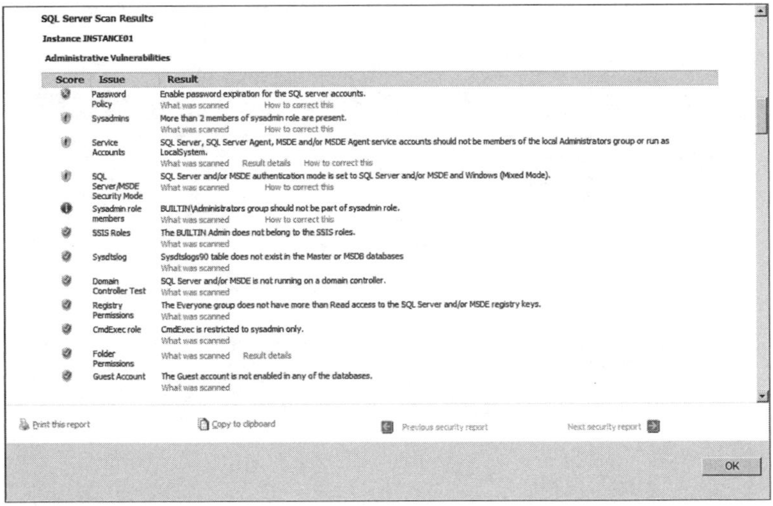

FIGURE 8.7
Viewing a Microsoft Baseline Security Analyzer vulnerability report.

Using the SQL Server 2008 Best Practice Analyzer (BPA) Tool to Harden an Installation

Another tool that is typically a database administrator's best friend is the much-awaited SQL Server 2008 Best Practice Analyzer (BPA) tool. The BPA gathers data from Microsoft Windows and SQL Server configuration settings. The BPA is a database management tool that uses a predefined list of SQL Server 2008 recommendations and best practices to determine whether there are potential issues in the database environment. The BPA also covers security hardening best practices.

Hardening SQL Server Service Accounts

You are prompted to enter a service account during the initial installation of SQL Server. Services can run under domain-based accounts, local service accounts, or built-in accounts such as Local System or Network Service. You can select to use a single service account for all instances and components being installed or to customize the installation by entering a dedicated service account for each instance and component.

The following SQL Server service accounts are available:

- **SQL Server Database Engineer Service**—This account provides core database functionality by facilitating storage, processing, and controlled access of data and rapid transaction processing.

- **SQL Server Agent Service**—This account provides auxiliary functionality by executing jobs, monitoring SQL Server, creating alerts, and automating administrative tasks.

- **SQL Server Integration Services Service**—This account provides management support for SSIS package storage and execution.

- **SQL Server Analysis Services Service**—This account provides business intelligence applications by supplying online analytical processing (OLAP) and data mining functionality.

- **SQL Server Reporting Services**—This account acts as a liaison between Reporting Services and SQL Server by managing, executing, rendering, and delivering reports.

- **SQL Server Full-Text Filter Daemon Launcher**—This account manages full-text indexes on content and properties of structured and semistructured data to allow fast linguistic searches on this data.

- **SQL Server Browser**—This account acts as a liaison with client computers by enumerating SQL Server connection information.

- **SQL Server Active Directory Helper**—This account enables integration between SQL Server and Active Directory.

- **SQL Server VSS Writer**—This account provides the interface to back up and restore SQL Server via the Windows Server Volume Shadow Copy Service (VSS) infrastructure.

There aren't necessarily any hard and fast rules to follow when trying to determine the type of service account to use. The main objective is to understand the limitations and positive offerings of the service account being used. It is equally important to analyze the value of the data residing within SQL Server and the risks and amount of security exposure that would take place if the SQL Server database was compromised. Lastly, when hardening and choosing SQL Server service accounts, you should employ the principle of least privilege and isolation.

The Principle of Least Privilege

It is a best practice to configure a service account based on the principle of least privilege. According to the *principle of least privilege*, SQL Server service accounts should be granted the least number of rights and permissions to conduct a specific task. Based on this recommendation, you should *not* grant a service account unnecessary elevated privileges such as domain administrator, enterprise administrator, or local administrator privileges. This enhances the protection of data and functionality from faults. Also, you should recognize that these highly elevated privileges are really not required. In fact, gone are the days when the SQL Server service accounts required domain administrator or local administrator privileges.

Service Account Isolation

For isolation purposes, a separate account should be created for each SQL Server instance and component being installed. Therefore, if the service account is compromised, only the one instance or component associated with the service account is breached. For example, suppose a bank is running 100 SQL Server instances and each instance maintains financial information. If one service account is used for all these instances, all 100 instances would be compromised in the event of a service account breach. This type of situation could be disastrous for a bank, especially with today's laws and regulatory requirements.

The need to create and manage more than one service account definitely increases administration and can be monotonous; however, it is a best practice to isolate each instance or component. One other notable benefit of isolation is witnessed with the amount of control organizations achieve through it. Organizations can grant specific permissions to one service account without elevating permissions to another service account that does not need elevated permissions.

The Types of Service Accounts Available

The following types of service accounts are available to choose from:

- **Local System Account**—This account grants full administrative rights to users on the local computer, which makes it a highly privileged account. As such, its use should be closely monitored. Note that this account does not grant network access rights.

- **Network Service Account**—This built-in account grants users the same level of access as members of the User group. This account allows services to interrelate with other services on the network infrastructure.

- **Domain User Account**—This account is used if the service will interrelate with other services on the network infrastructure.

- **Local Service Account**—Users of this built-in account have the same level of access that is designated to members of the Users group. This limited access protects against service breaches.

Determining Which Type of Account to Use for SQL Server Services

The question that always surfaces regarding service accounts is, "Which service account should be used with implementing SQL Server 2008?" The answer depends on your intended use of the service account and the relationship it will have to the server and network.

Services that run as the local service account access network resources with no credentials. As a result, this account should not be used if you want the services to interact with other network resources.

If you are looking for a service account that grants limited privileges like the local service account but also runs services that can interrelate with other services on the network infrastructure, you should consider using a network service account. This account uses the credentials of the computer account to gain access to the network. It is not recommended that you use this account for either the SQL Server service or the SQL Server Agent service account.

Consideration should also be given to the domain user account if its services will interact with other services on the network infrastructure. If you also want to perform certain activities including replication, remote procedure calls, or network drive backups, a domain user account is preferred over a network service account because only this account allows server-to-server activity. One point to keep in mind when using a domain account is that it must be authenticated on a domain controller.

The local system account is not recommended for use for the SQL Server service or SQL Server Agent services. The reason is that it is a best practice to configure a service so that it runs effectively with the least number of privileges granted. The local system account is a highly privileged account, which means it should be used very carefully. In addition, it probably has privileges that neither SQL Server Agent services nor SQL Server services actually require.

> **Tip**
>
> Microsoft recommends that you do not use a network service account if an account with lesser privileges is available. The reason is that the network service account is a shared account and can be utilized by other services running on the Windows Server system. Local User or Domain User accounts are preferred, specifically if they are not associated with highly privileged groups such as Domain Administrator.

Changing a SQL Server Service Account with SQL Server Configuration Manager

Typically, server administrators use the Services Snap-in component included with Windows Server 2008 Server Manager or the Administrative tools to make changes to Windows Services. There are serious negative ramifications if SQL Server service accounts are changed using this tool. SQL Server service accounts require special Registry settings, NTFS file system permissions, and Windows user rights to be set, which the Windows tool does not address, thus causing a SQL Server outage. Fortunately, these additional permission requirements can be updated automatically if you use SQL Server native configuration tools such as the SQL Server Configuration Manager or SQL Server Surface Area Configuration. Therefore, it is a best practice to use the native SQL Server configuration tools when making changes to SQL Server service accounts; changes should not be made using the Windows Server 2008 Services tool.

Follow these steps to change the user account, including credentials for a SQL Server service such as the SQL Server Agent, using the SQL Server Configuration Manager:

1. Choose Start, All Programs, Microsoft SQL Server 2008, Configuration Tools, SQL Server Configuration Manager.
2. Select the SQL Server Services node.
3. In the right pane, double-click on the SQL Server Agent Service.
4. In the SQL Server Agent box, enter a new service account name and password.

5. Confirm the password by retyping it, as shown in Figure 8.8, and click Apply.

6. Accept the message to restart the services and click OK.

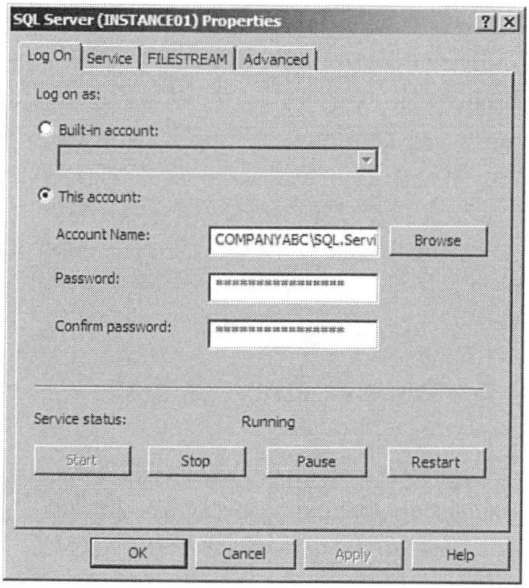

FIGURE 8.8
Changing the service account credentials.

The SQL Server Agent now uses the new service account credentials for authentication. In addition, Registry settings, NTFS permissions, and Windows rights are updated automatically.

Installing Service Packs and Critical Fixes

SQL Server 2008, like all other Microsoft applications and server products, is subject to periodic software updates. Interim updates can be downloaded and installed through the Microsoft/Windows Update option on the system or by visiting the Windows Update website (http://update.microsoft.com), which initiates the installer to check for the latest updates for Windows.

Likewise, major updates are essentially bundled as service packs that roll up patches and updates into a single installation. Installation of the latest service pack brings a server up to date, which means to the point in time when the service pack was issued. It is also worth noting that the future service packs for both SQL Server 2008 will most likely be cumulative. You can install a service pack update in one of three ways:

- **Microsoft/Windows Update**—The service pack can be downloaded and automatically installed as part of the normal update process.
- **Download and Install**—The service pack can be downloaded as a file. This file can then be launched to install the update. This is frequently done when a system is not connected to the Internet or when a scheduled installation is desired as opposed to an immediate installation after downloading from the Internet.
- **Automated Patch Management and Deployment Tools**—Software distribution tools can be used to install service pack updates. Systems Center 2007 Configuration Manager and Windows Software Update Services (WSUS) are examples of two tools you can use to accomplish the task.

Updating and Patching SQL Server and the Operating System

In addition to the patches that are installed as part of a SQL Server 2008 service pack, security updates and patches are constantly being released by Microsoft. It is advantageous to install these updates made available for SQL Server and the operating system. These patches can be manually downloaded and installed, or they can be automatically applied by using Microsoft Update.

It is a best practice to install critical fixes for both SQL Server and the operating system when they are released. In addition, major service packs and security rollups should be installed in a timely manner. All patches should be tested in a prototype lab before being installed in production, and it is recommended that you conduct a full backup of the system prior to the installation of the patches.

Understanding How SQL Server Security Logs Play a Part in Security

In the previous sections, you learned ways of minimizing security vulnerabilities on SQL Server. Now that SQL Server is hardened, it is beneficial to enable auditing. SQL Server security auditing monitors and tracks activity to log files that can be viewed through Windows application logs or SQL Server Management Studio. SQL Server offers the following four security levels with regards to security auditing:

- **None**—Disables auditing so no events are logged
- **Successful Logins Only**—Audits all successful login attempts
- **Failed Logins Only**—Audits all failed login attempts
- **Both Failed and Successful Logins**—Audits all login attempts

At the very least, security auditing should be set to Failed Logins Only. As a result, failed logins can be saved, viewed, and acted on when necessary. Unless a change is made, security auditing is set, by default, to Failed Logins Only. On the other hand, it is a best practice to configure security auditing to capture Both Failed and Successful Logins. All logins are captured in this situation and can be analyzed when advanced forensics are required.

Configuring SQL Server Security Logs for Auditing

To configure security login auditing for both failed and successful logins, follow these steps:

1. In SQL Server Management Studio, right-click on a desired SQL Server and then click Properties.

2. On the Security page, as shown in Figure 8.9, under Login Auditing, select the desired auditing criteria option button, such as Both Failed and Successful Logins, and then click OK.

3. Restart the SQL Server Database Engine and SQL Server Agent to make the auditing changes effective.

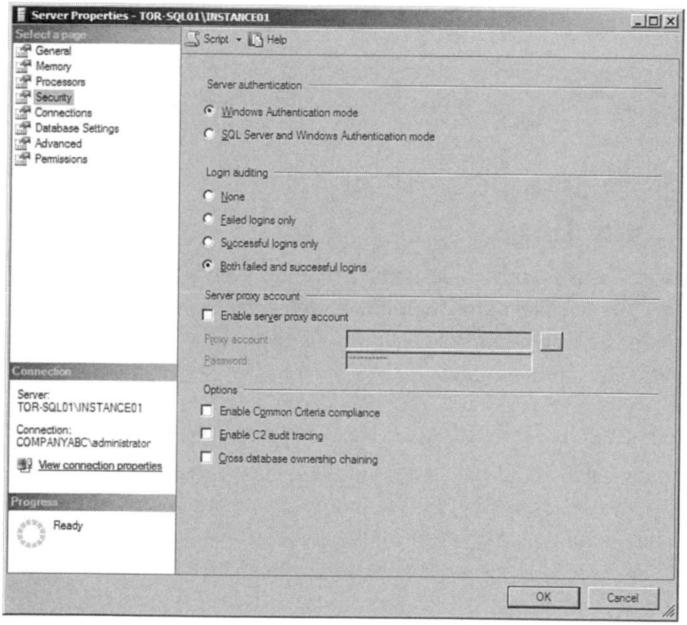

FIGURE 8.9
Configuring security auditing to both failed and successful logins.

Enhanced Auditing Functionality included with SQL Server 2008

SQL Server systems are strong candidates to fall subject to the rules and regulations governed by regulatory requirements. SQL Server is typically a repository for organizations' and customers' data that tends to be both mission-critical and sensitive if it falls into the wrong hands.

One of the latest compliance rules some organizations are subject to includes the ability to successfully log events in a central repository and produce reports of all activity being captured. Microsoft understands the push toward better logging and auditing capabilities and has introduced new features and functionality in SQL Server 2008 that facilitate stronger auditing for compliance reasons.

By introducing two new objects, Audit object and Audit Specification object, organizations can now log every SQL Server action to the Windows Application Log, Windows Security Log, or to a file. In addition, when using Windows Server 2008 or System Center 2007 Operations Manager, it is possible to create a central repository for all events collected across many SQL Server systems within the enterprise.

> **Note**
>
> For more information on "how-to" topics associated with enhanced auditing, review Chapter 17, "Monitoring SQL Server 2008 with Native Tools."

Additional SQL Server Hardening Recommendations

The following sections focus on additional hardening techniques to further lock down SQL Server. The items include removing the BUILTIN\Administrators Windows group, using a firewall to filter out unwanted traffic, and hardening IIS.

Removing the BUILTIN\Administrators Windows Group

In the past, many database administrators in the industry were concerned about the BUILTIN\Administrators Windows group having sysadmin privileges by default over a SQL Server instance. Some people believe that this situation was one of the biggest out-of-the-box security flaws for SQL Server. The reason is that all local Windows administrators, including domain administrators, are given full control over SQL Server because they are part of the BUILTIN\Administrators Windows group. This led to a best practice to remove the BUILTIN\Administrators group to address this situation. Doing this hardens the SQL Server installation.

Microsoft realized that this was a major security flaw, and with SQL Server 2008 BETA versions the local Windows Group BUILTIN\Administrator is no longer included in the SQL Server sysadmin server role. When the official RTM version released, Microsoft removed the group outright. Therefore, it is up to you to decide whether there is still a need to add this group, if desired.

Removing the BUILTIN\Administrators Windows Group with Transact-SQL

If the group existed from previous versions of SQL Server or using BETA code, the following Transact-SQL (TSQL) syntax removes the BUILTIN\Administrators Windows Group from a SQL Server instance. If you decide to run this syntax, you should execute it on each SQL Server instance installed in the organization:

```
Use Master
IF EXISTS (SELECT * FROM sys.server_principals
WHERE name = N'BUILTIN\Administrators')
DROP LOGIN [BUILTIN\Administrators]
GO
```

Using a Firewall to Filter Out Unwanted Traffic

Now that the default SQL Server ports have been changed according to the instructions in the previous section, the next step is to enable a firewall that will filter out unwanted traffic and allow connections only to the SQL Server designated from within the organization's infrastructure. The Windows firewall included with Windows Server 2008 should be sufficient. However, if more advanced firewall features are sought, a full-fledged hardware-based firewall or software-based firewall should be used, such as Internet Security and Acceleration (ISA) Server 2006.

Note

A common problem in the past was that some organizations had their SQL Server reside within the demilitarized zone (DMZ) or configured with a public IP address. This made their SQL Server public-facing and, therefore, accessible from the outside world. As a rule of thumb, when you're implementing SQL Server from within an infrastructure, it should never be Internet-facing, within the DMZ, or publicly accessible.

The following table summarizes the default ports utilized by common SQL Server components.

SQL Server Default Instance	1433
SQL Server Named Instance	Dynamic Port
Admin Connection	1434
Browser Service	1434
Default Instance running over HTTP Endpoint	80
Default Instance running over HTTPS Endpoint	443
Service Broker	4022
Analysis Services	2383
Reporting Services Web Services	80
Reporting Services Web Services HTTPS	443
Integration Services	135

Using the Integrated Windows Server 2008 Firewall with Advanced Security

Windows Server 2008 includes a vastly improved integrated firewall that is turned on by default in all installations of the product. The firewall, administered from a Microsoft Management Console (MMC) snap-in shown in Figure 8.10 gives unprecedented control and security to a server. It can be accessed by choosing Start, All Programs, Administrative Tools, Windows Firewall with Advanced Security.

The firewall is fully integrated with the Server Manager utility and the Server Roles Wizard. Both the Server Manager utility and the Server Roles Wizard are new management tools included with Windows Server 2008. For example, if an DBA runs the Server Roles Wizard and chooses to make the server a file server or a domain controller, only then are those ports and protocols that are required for file server or domain controller access opened on the server. Unfortunately, this is not the case with SQL Server, and firewall rules must be created and configured manually.

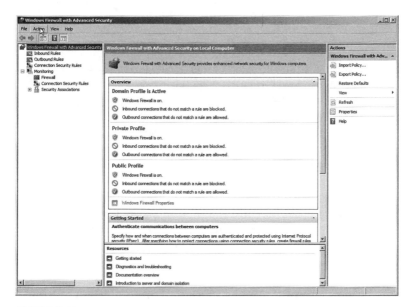

FIGURE 8.10
Using the integrated Windows Firewall with Advanced Security.

> **Note**
>
> It is instinctive for most DBAs or Windows administrators to disable soft-
> ware firewalls on servers, as they have caused problems with functionality in
> the past. This is not recommended in Windows Server 2008, however, as
> the product is tightly integrated with its firewall, and the firewall provides for
> a much greater degree of security than previous versions of Windows Server
> provided.

Creating Rules for SQL Server 2008 on the Windows Server 2008 Firewall

In certain cases, when a third-party application is not integrated with Server
Manager, or when needing to open specific individual ports, it may become
necessary to create firewall rules for individual services to run properly. This is
the case when working with SQL Server 2008. Both inbound rules addressing
traffic to the server, and outbound rules, addressing how the server can communicate out, can be created. Rules can be created based on the following factors:

■ **Program**—A rule can be created that allows a specific program executable access. For example, you can specify that the `C:\Program Files\Custom Program\myprogram.exe` file has full outbound access when running. The Windows Firewall program will then allow any type of connections made by that program full access. This can be useful in scenarios when a specific application server uses multiple varied ports, but the overall security that the firewall provides is still desired.

■ **Port**—Entering a traditional UDP or TCP port into the Add Rules Wizard is supported. This covers traditional scenarios such as "We need to open port 1433 on the SQL Server system."

■ **Predefined**—Windows Server also has built-in, predefined rules, such as those that allow AD DS, DFS, BITS, HTTP, and many more. The advantage to using a predefined rule is that Microsoft has done all the legwork in advance, and it becomes much easier to allow a specific service.

■ **Custom**—The creation of custom rule types not covered in the other categories is also supported.

When configuring the Windows firewall, you can either create an exception for SQL Server based on the instance's port number or by adding the path to the SQL Server program. The default instance of SQL Server uses port 1433; however, ports are assigned dynamically when running more than one instance. Therefore, it is a best practice to utilize the path of the program.

Follow these steps to create a SQL Server exception on the Windows firewall by adding the path of the SQL Server program:

1. Open the Windows Firewall MMC Console (Start, All Programs, Administrative Tools, Windows Firewall with Advanced Security).

Note

A message box will be displayed if the Windows Firewall/Internet Connection Sharing (ICS) service is not running. Click Yes to activate the service and the firewall. In addition, another warning will appear indicating that your computer is not protected and you must turn on Windows Firewall if the firewall setting is configured to Off.

---

2. Click on the Inbound Rules node in the node pane.

3. In the Action Pane, click the link labeled New Rule.

4. In the Rule Type dialog box, shown in Figure 8.11, select to create a rule based on Add Program and click Next to continue.

5. Select the SQL Server instance from the program list. If the program is not available in the list, click Browse to search for it and provide the path for the appropriate SQL Server instance, for example, `D:\Program Files\Microsoft SQL Server\MSSQL10.Instance01\MSSQL\Binn\ sqlservr.exe`, as illustrated in Figure 8.12. Then click Open.

Note

Microsoft SQL Server provides an instance ID for every SQL Server instance installed on a server. Typically, the ID is incremented by 1 when more than one instance is installed on a server. Use the SQL Server Configuration Manager tool to obtain the instance ID and installation path of a SQL Server instance. To find it, double-click the server name, and the Advanced tab displays the instance ID and installation path to the SQL Server instance.

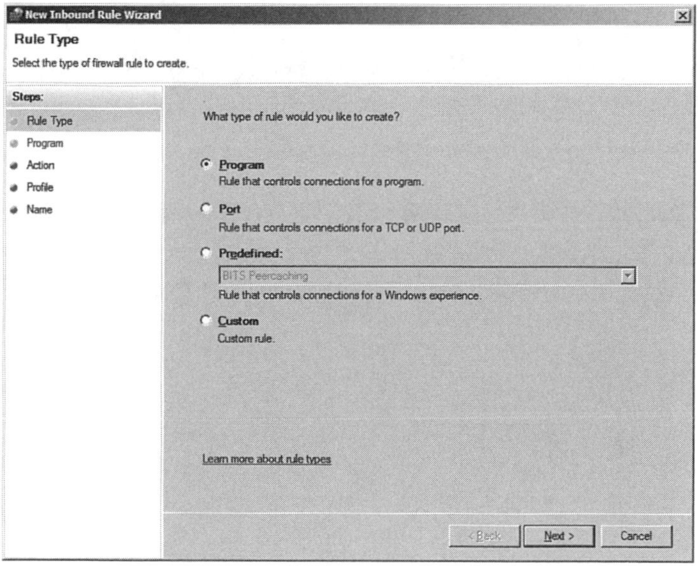

FIGURE 8.11
Setting Windows firewall options.

6. In the next window, on the Action tab, specify the action that should be taken when a connection matches the condition of the rule. The options are Allow the Connection, Allow the Connection If It Is Secure, and Block the Connection. Select Allow the Connection as displayed in Figure 8.13 and then click Next.

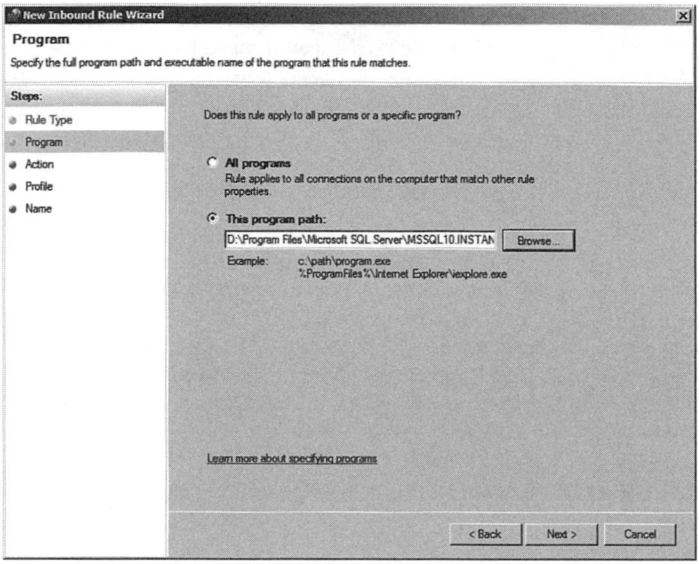

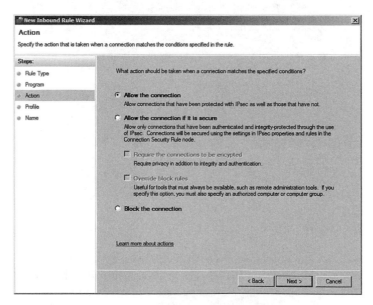

FIGURE 8.12
Setting the Windows firewall exception screen.

FIGURE 8.13
Specifying the connection action.

7. On the Profile page, shown in Figure 8.14, specify the desired profile box. This allows a DBA to specify that a rule only applies when connected to specific networks. Click Next to continue.

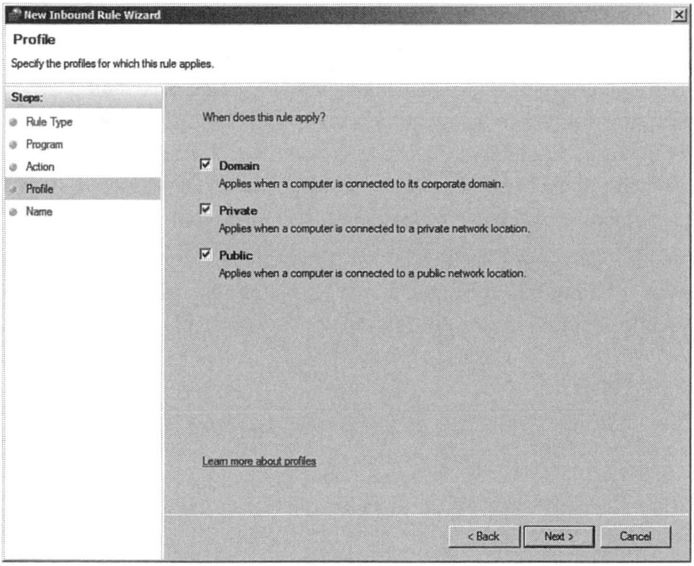

FIGURE 8.14
Specifying the profiles to which the rule applies.

8. Enter a descriptive name for the rule and click Finish.

9. Repeat these steps for every SQL Server instance or SQL component that requires an exception, such as Analysis Services, Integration Services, and so on.

10. Test the connection to the SQL Server from a desired client to validate both that the firewall is enabled and the appropriate exceptions were created.

Note

Create an exception for the SQL Server Browser service if there is a need to broadcast SQL Server information to clients over the network. Otherwise, SQL Server clients must know the names and ports of the clients when connecting.

Using the Integrated Windows Firewall is no longer just a good idea—it's a vital part of the security of the product. The addition of the ability to define rules based on factors such as scope, profile, IPSec status, and the like further positions the Server OS as one with high levels of integrated security.

Summary

One of the best features of SQL Server 2008 is that it's secure by default; however, when the SQL Server installation is complete, it is imperative that you harden the SQL Server implementation. You should understand all hardening techniques available so that you can determine which hardening strategies work best for your organization. Not every hardening technique works for everyone.

Additional security strategies such as encrypting SQL Server data and communications, Policy Based Management, and administering SQL Server authorization and security are covered in the upcoming chapters.

Best Practices

Following is a summary of best practices for hardening a SQL Server environment:

- When the SQL Server installation is complete, harden the SQL Server environment.

- Install the most recent critical fixes and service packs for both Windows and SQL Server.

- When you're selecting authentication modes, Windows Authentication is a more secure choice; however, if mixed mode authentication is required, leverage complex passwords and SQL Server 2008 password and lockout policies to further bolster security.

- Do *not* use the SA account for day-to-day administration, logging on to the server remotely, or having applications use it to connect to SQL. It is best if the SA account is disabled and renamed.

- Create a role-based security policy with the Security Configuration Wizard tool.

- After SQL Server 2008 is installed, run the SQL Server Configuration Manager tool to disable unnecessary features and services and create policies with Policy Based Management.

- Install only required components when installing SQL Server.

- After the server has been hardened, periodically asses the server's security using the MBSA and SQL Server BPA.

- For production SQL Servers running mission-critical databases, either hide the instance or disable the SQL Server Browser service.

- Change the default ports associated with the SQL Server installation to put off hackers from port-scanning the server.

- Enable a firewall to filter unnecessary and unknown traffic.

- At the very least, set security auditing to failed login attempts; otherwise, both failed and successful logins should be captured and monitored.

- If upgrading previous versions of SQL Server, remove the BUILTIN/Administrators group from the SQL Server Logins.

CHAPTER 9

Administering SQL Server Security and Authorization

By maintaining a strategy that is secure by design, secure by default, and secure in deployment, SQL Server 2008 allows for a much more effective method of design, implementation, and administration of security across resources and services provided by the SQL environment. Security permissions can be defined on a wide range of objects, from network endpoints that facilitate client communication, to execute permissions on a stored procedure, even down to the column level within a table. Complex security implementations can be efficiently controlled with granular role-based authorization and database schemas.

Administering SQL security is a key database administrator task that normally begins immediately following the hardening of the system. Understanding the different components related to security is essential to effective SQL security administration. This chapter discusses and demonstrates common administrative security tasks, incorporating best practices and new features introduced with SQL Server 2008.

What's New for Security and Authorization with SQL Server 2008?

- In previous versions of SQL Server, the local Windows Group BUILTIN\Administrators automatically had elevated privileges and full control of a SQL Server system as it was automatically placed in the sysadmin role. With SQL Server 2008, the BUILTIN\Administrators group was stripped from the installation, and the group must be added explicitly, if needed.

■ SQL Server 2008 still creates and leverages Windows local groups, but they are no longer granted rights in SQL Server. These groups are strictly used to provide operating-system rights to a SQL Server via Access Control List (ACL). Only accounts provisioned during the installation process are granted rights within SQL Server 2008.

SQL Server Security

SQL Server 2008 continues to support two modes for validating connections and authenticating access to database resources: *Windows Authentication mode* and *SQL Server authentication mode*. Both modes provide the ability for users to authenticate to SQL Server and access database resources.

> **Note**
>
> It is important to understand that security can be most effectively managed when the environment has been prepared and hardened. See Chapter 8, "Hardening a SQL Server Implementation," for additional information.

When you're administering SQL Server security, it is important to follow the *principle of least privilege*. This basically means that only the permissions necessary to accomplish the task should be granted to the different user and service accounts. The principle of least privilege ensures that only the required resources are exposed to the client, while other resources are inaccessible and locked down. This improves the environment in multiple ways, including lowering the probability of accidental or intentional damage, increasing system scalability, and simplifying administration and deployment.

SQL Server 2008 facilitates flexible and scalable management of object permissions by allowing database users to be added to roles. Database roles serve a purpose similar to that of groups in the Windows operating system— they allow you to group accounts with common permission requirements and grant those permissions to a role instead of individual users. Figure 9.1 depicts at a high level how database objects are accessed by clients.

In Figure 9.1 the client communicates to SQL Server through an endpoint. The client provides credentials used for authentication either by explicitly entering them in SQL authentication mode or with pass-through Windows-based authentication. Server logins can be assigned permissions —to server-level securable objects including the SQL Server, endpoints, and other logins.

> **Note**
>
> A SQL Server login cannot be given permissions for database securable objects directly.
>
> A login must be mapped to a database user; the database user then can be given permissions on database-scoped securable objects either directly or through database roles and schemas.

To grant permissions on database securable objects, you map the server login to a database user. Permissions for database objects can be granted directly to the database user; however, it is a best practice to add the database user to a database role or roles and then grant the appropriate permissions to those roles. Review the section on Role-Based Access best practices on granting access to SQL Server.

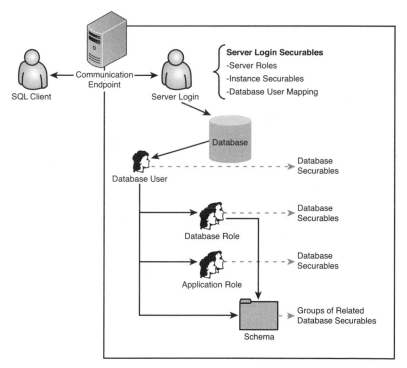

FIGURE 9.1
Overview of SQL Server security.

Endpoints and Communication

To communicate and access resources provided by a SQL Server, you must establish a connection to a server endpoint. In most cases, Tabular Data Stream (TDS) () endpoints are used for communication with SQL Server. TDS packets sent by the client to the endpoint are encapsulated with a standard network protocol by way of the SQL Server Network Interface (SNI) protocol layer. The SNI layer used for TDS encapsulation is common to both the SQL Server and SQL client.

Endpoints for several common network protocols supported by SQL Server are created by default. In addition, an endpoint is created by default for the Dedicated Administrator Connection (DAC); this endpoint can be used only by members of the sysadmin fixed server role to establish an administrative connection to the server. Following are the default endpoints and protocols:

- Dedicated Administrator Connection (TCP)
- TSQL Local Machine (Shared Memory)
- TSQL Named Pipes (Named Pipes)
- TSQL Default TCP (TCP)
- TSQL Default VIA (VIA)

Default system endpoints cannot be dropped or disabled. However, they can be stopped and started, and the permissions for the endpoints can be altered as necessary. For each SQL Server instance, only a single named pipe and shared memory endpoint are supported. User-defined endpoints can have multiple instances per SQL Server instance; the protocol for user-defined endpoints is always HTTP or TCP.

The default system endpoints are all configured for the TSQL payload type. This means they communicate with the endpoint using Transact-SQL. When a user defines an endpoint, the payload type can be configured as TSQL, SOAP, Service Broker, or Database Mirroring. For example, a database that is using database mirroring communicates with its partners through endpoints configured with the Database Mirroring payload type.

> **Note**
>
> The Dedicated Administrator Connection (DAC) allows you to connect to a server when the Database Engine does not respond to regular connections. By default, the DAC endpoint cannot be accessed remotely and is available only from the local computer. To allow remote access to DAC, you can enable the `remote admin connections` option through the `sp_configure` system stored procedure.

With the exception of HTTP, the protocols for each of the default endpoints are listed and can be configured in the SQL Server Configuration Manager. In addition, all endpoints are listed in Object Explorer in SQL Server Management Studio, under Server Objects > Endpoints.

When a protocol is disabled, the endpoint that implements the protocol cannot be used, although the endpoint may still be in the started state. In SQL Server 2008 Enterprise, Standard, and Workgroup Editions, only TCP/IP is enabled by default. In the Developer and Evaluation Editions, TCP/IP is disabled by default.

You can use the sys.endpoints catalog view to see the status of all endpoints on the server. The following query returns all the endpoints configured on the server:

```
USE MASTER
SELECT * FROM sys.endpoints
```

The sys.http_endpoints, sys.soap_endpoints, and sys.endpoint_webmethods catalog views can be used to get additional information about specific types of endpoints.

The sys.server_permissions catalog view can be used to see the permissions on server-level securable objects, including endpoints. You can use the sys.server_principals catalog view to retrieve the name of the server principal listed in the grantee_principal_id column.

For example, the following query returns the grantee permissions and grantee name for all endpoints on a server. Note that endpoints have a value of 105 in the class column:

```
USE MASTER
SELECT
  p.class_desc,
  p.major_id,
  p.minor_id,
  p.grantee_principal_id,
  sp.name as grantee_name,
  p.permission_name,
  p.state_desc
FROM sys.server_permissions p
  INNER JOIN sys.server_principals sp
    ON p.grantee_principal_id = sp.principal_id
WHERE class = 105
```

The result set of the query shows that the principal public has been granted CONNECT permission on each of the endpoints by default. This essentially allows all logins to connect to any of the default endpoints, if the underlying protocol has also been enabled.

> **Note**
>
> It is a best practice to enable only communication protocols that are neces-
> sary and to allow only specific CONNECT permissions on endpoints.

You can administer existing protocols and endpoints through the SQL Server
Configuration Manager Policy Based Management, the database mirroring
wizard and by using data definition language (DDL). However, you can
create new endpoints only through the CREATE ENDPOINT DDL.

Server Logins and Database Users

Server logins and database users are both principals—logins are principals on
the server level, and database users are principals on the database level. SQL
Server permissions on securable objects can be granted to principals at the
appropriate level. Logins can be granted permissions on server-level securable
objects and database users can be granted permissions on database-level securable objects, but logins cannot be granted permission to database-level objects
and database users cannot be granted permissions to server-level objects.

Table 9.1 shows all the SQL Server principals.

Table 9.1   **SQL Server Principals**

Type	Description
Server	SQL Server login
Server	SQL Server login from Windows login
Server	SQL Server login from certificate
Server	SQL Server login from asymmetric key
Database	Database user
Database	Database role
Database	Database user mapped to Windows user
Database	Database user mapped to Windows group
Database	Database user mapped to certificate
Database	Database user with no login

> **Note**
>
> Principals are also securable objects; for example, users can be granted
> control permissions on other users, database roles, and so on.

Clients authenticate to the server using a login. The authentication used for the login can be either Windows-based or SQL-based. Windows authentication logins are recommended over SQL authentication logins because Windows logins can leverage Active Directory security, native authentication encryption, and pass-through (transparent) authentication.

When you're using Windows Authentication mode, the account can be either a local or domain-based user account, or an account that is a member of a group (local or domain) that has been added as a login to SQL Server. When you're using SQL authentication, the account information, including hashed password, is stored in the master database of your SQL Server instance.

Both SQL- and Windows-based logins provide access to server instance objects but not to database objects. The following securable objects can have permissions assigned to server logins:

- Servers
- Endpoints
- Logins

SQL logins can be mapped to database users. Database users are then granted permissions on securable objects in the database. Following are database-level securable objects:

- Databases
- Stored procedures
- Tables
- Views
- Inline functions
- Scalar functions
- Table-valued functions
- Aggregate functions
- Application roles
- Assemblies
- Asymmetric keys
- Certificates
- Database roles
- Full-text catalogs
- Schemas
- Symmetric keys
- Synonyms
- Users
- User-defined data types
- XML schema collections

Both SQL logins and users are considered securable objects and can have permissions assigned in the same fashion as any other object in the database.

Role-Based Access

Although database users can be granted permissions on objects directly, this is generally considered a bad practice when dealing with complex security scenarios. It is much more effective to create roles for each type of user, assign the correct permissions to the role, and make individual user accounts members of that role. Role-based access reduces the cost of ongoing security administration because users can be added and removed from roles without having to re-create complex permissions for each user.

Role-based access can be established at both the SQL Server level and in Active Directory. It is common to establish role-based access for all network services through Active Directory with the added benefit of organization-wide control of data services.

Using Active Directory for role-based access follows the standard of placing user accounts into domain global *role groups* and the role groups into domain local *access groups*. The access groups are then added to the SQL instance as logins and mapped to database users. The database users can then be added to the correct database role and/or security schemas. As a result, users added to role groups in Active Directory automatically obtain the correct permissions. Security management for the environment is transferred from SQL Server into Active Directory, where it can be controlled centrally.

Note

Active Directory can be leveraged to establish access and role-based security groups for accessing SQL Server resources. However, a limitation exists using this security model because a default schema cannot be assigned to a database user that maps to a server login that in turn maps to a Windows group. The reason for this limitation is quite obvious: because a single user can be a member of multiple Windows groups and each of those groups can be granted access to SQL Server, this could lead to irresolvable ambiguities when such groups have different default schemas.

This is typically not an issue as long as the security design accounts for this limitation. Role-based access through Active Directory is still highly recommended and effective.

Several server-level roles exist in each SQL Server instance. Server roles are used to grant administrative permissions on the server and are not used to grant permission to normal user accounts. Table 9.2 lists each server-level role and the permissions associated with each role.

Table 9.2   **Server-Level Roles**

Server Role	Default Permissions
bulkadmin	Granted: ADMINISTER BULK OPERATIONS
dbcreator	Granted: CREATE DATABASE
diskadmin	Granted: ALTER RESOURCES

Server Role	Default Permissions
processadmin	Granted: ALTER ANY CONNECTION, ALTER SERVER STATE
securityadmin	Granted: ALTER ANY LOGIN
serveradmin	Granted: ALTER ANY ENDPOINT, ALTER RESOURCES, ALTER SERVER STATE, ALTER SETTINGS, SHUTDOWN, VIEW SERVER STATE
setupadmin	Granted: ALTER ANY LINKED SERVER
sysadmin	Granted with GRANT option: CONTROL SERVER
public	Granted: VIEW ANY DATABASE

> **Note**
>
> All logins belong to the public server role by default. The public role is granted VIEW ANY DATABASE by default.

Several fixed database-level roles exist in each SQL Server database. Those predefined roles are used to grant a predefined set of permissions to database users and, with the exception of the public role, they are not used to assign permissions to individual objects. Table 9.3 lists each fixed database-level role and the permissions associated with each role.

Table 9.3   **Fixed Database-Level Roles**

Database Role	Default Permissions
db_accessadmin	Granted: ALTER ANY USER, CREATE SCHEMA
db_backupoperator	Granted: BACKUP DATABASE, BACKUP LOG, CHECKPOINT
db_datareader	Granted: SELECT
db_datawriter	Granted: DELETE, INSERT, UPDATE
db_ddladmin	Granted: ALTER ANY ASSEMBLY, ALTER ANY ASYMMETRIC KEY, ALTER ANY CERTIFICATE, ALTER ANY CONTRACT, ALTER ANY DATABASE DDL TRIGGER, ALTER ANY DATABASE EVENT NOTIFICATION, ALTER ANY DATASPACE, ALTER ANY FULLTEXT CATALOG, ALTER ANY MESSAGE TYPE, ALTER ANY REMOTE SERVICE BINDING, ALTER ANY ROUTE, ALTER ANY SCHEMA, ALTER ANY SERVICE, ALTER ANY SYMMETRIC KEY, CHECKPOINT, CREATE AGGREGATE, CREATE DEFAULT, CREATE FUNCTION, CREATE PROCEDURE, CREATE QUEUE, CREATE RULE, CREATE SYNONYM, CREATE TABLE, CREATE TYPE, CREATE VIEW, CREATE XML SCHEMA COLLECTION, REFERENCES

Table 9.3   **continued**

Database Role	Default Permissions
db_denydatareader	Denied: SELECT
db_denydatawriter	Denied: DELETE, INSERT, UPDATE
db_owner	Granted with GRANT option: CONTROL
db_securityadmin	Granted: ALTER ANY APPLICATION ROLE, ALTER ANY ROLE, CREATE SCHEMA, VIEW DEFINITION
public	Granted: SELECT on system views

> **Note**
>
> All database users belong to the public database role by default. It is a best practice to avoid using the public database role when assigning permissions.

Database Schema

The database schemas were first introduced in SQL Server 2005 and provide several improvements when compared to previous versions of SQL Server. The schema is a key part of establishing flexible database security administration.

When objects are accessed in SQL Server 2005 or 2008, they are referenced by a four-part identifier, where parts have the following meaning:

[DatabaseServer].[DatabaseName].[DatabaseSchema].[DatabaseObject]

For example, the following query can be used to access the Employee table created as part of the HumanResources schema in the AdventureWorks2008 database. The AdventureWorks2008 database is hosted on INSTANCE01 on the server TOR-SQL01.

```
SELECT *
FROM [TOR-SQL01\INSTANCE01].[AdventureWorks2008].
➥[HumanResources].[Employee]
```

The *database schema* is a namespace used to reference objects in the database. The schema provides a way to manage security on groups of objects as a unit. As new database objects are defined, they must be associated with a schema and automatically inherit the permissions granted on the schema.

The principal defined as the schema owner effectively owns all objects in the schema. When the owner of a schema is changed, all objects in the schema are owned by the new principal, with the exception of objects for which a different owner was explicitly defined.

This is a significant improvement over SQL Server 2000 because the schema takes the place of the user account that owned the database objects, allowing much easier transfer of object ownership. When the ownership of the object changes, there is no need to change your queries, as the fully qualified name of the object is not changed.

Password Policies

Domain policies and local security policies provide the password and account lockout configuration that affects users' ability to authenticate and access SQL Server resources.

When Windows Authentication mode is used, these settings govern all users according to the defined password policy.

When SQL Server authentication is used, a SQL login can be configured to be subject to the password and lockout policies of the underlying local security or domain group policy. This functionality is supported only with the Windows Server 2003 or later operating systems, such as Windows Server 2008.

> **Note**
>
> If SQL authentication is used, it is highly recommended to enable these options to enforce the local security policies in order to increase the level of security for SQL logins.

The following password policies can be used to help secure Windows and SQL Server authentication:

- **Enforce Password History**—This security setting determines the number of unique new passwords that have to be associated with a user account before an old password can be reused.

- **Maximum Password Age**—This security setting determines the period of time (in days) that a password can be used before the system requires the user to change it.

- **Minimum Password Age**—This security setting determines the period of time (in days) that a password must be used before the user can change it.

- **Minimum Password Length**—This security setting determines the least number of characters that a password for a user account may contain.

- **Password Must Meet Complexity Requirements**—This security setting determines whether passwords must meet complexity requirements.

Complex passwords cannot contain the user's login name, must be at least six characters in length, and must contain characters from three of the four available character categories. Character categories include uppercase, lowercase, base 10 digits, and non-alphabetic characters.

- **Store Passwords Using Reversible Encryption**—This security setting determines whether the operating system stores passwords using reversible encryption. This setting affects only Windows authentication and has no effect on SQL Server logons.

Note

In Windows Server 2003, there can be only a single password policy for each Active Directory domain. Password policy settings for the domain must be defined in the root node for the domain.

This limitation was lifted in Windows Server 2008, as password policies can now be defined on a per-group and per-user basis.

These security policies can be accessed through the Windows Settings\Security Settings\Account Policies\Password Policies node in the Default Domain Policy. Figure 9.2 shows the default Active Directory password policies.

The following account lockout policies can be used to help secure Windows and SQL Server authentication:

- **Account Lockout Threshold**—This security setting determines the number of minutes a locked-out account remains locked out before automatically becoming unlocked. The available range is from 0 minutes through 99,999 minutes. If you set the account lockout duration to 0, the account is locked out until an administrator explicitly unlocks it.

- **Account Lockout Duration**—This security setting determines the number of failed logon attempts that causes a user account to be locked out. A locked-out account cannot be used until it is reset by an administrator or until the lockout duration for the account has expired. You can set a value between 0 and 999 failed logon attempts. If you set the value to 0, the account is never locked out.

- **Reset Lockout Counter After**—This security setting determines the number of minutes that must elapse after a failed logon attempt before the failed logon attempt counter is reset to 0 bad logon attempts. The available range is 1 minute to 99,999 minutes.

These security policies can be accessed through the Windows Settings\Security Settings\Account Policies\Account Lockout Policy node in the Default Domain Policy. Figure 9.3 shows the default Active Directory account lockout policies.

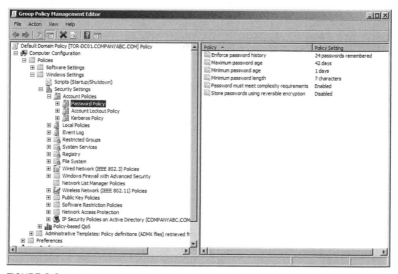

FIGURE 9.2
Windows password policies.

When these policies are configured, the resulting domain-level group policy or the local security policy helps secure the environment by preventing low-security passwords.

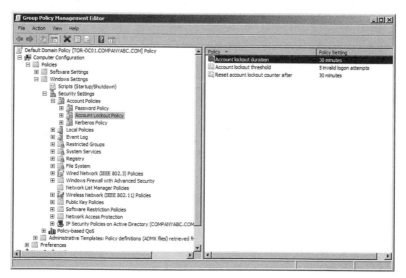

FIGURE 9.3
Windows account lockout policies.

Logon Triggers

Logon triggers were first introduced in SQL Server 2005 Service Pack 2 and this functionality is also included in SQL Server 2008. Logon triggers allow you to handle logon events on the server and enforce your own authentication policies based on logic implemented in the trigger. This enables you to create flexible logon policies, based on multiple criteria.

The following code listing gives an example of a trigger that disallows login attempts from user Bob between 6 p.m. and 6 a.m.

```
CREATE TRIGGER trg_after_hours_logins
ON ALL SERVER
FOR LOGON
AS
BEGIN
IF SUSER_SNAME()= 'Bob' AND
    ((SELECT DATEPART(hh, GETDATE())) >= 18
    OR (SELECT DATEPART(hh, GETDATE())) < 6)
    ROLLBACK;
END;
```

Security Management DDL

The data definition language (DDL) statements used to administer SQL Server 2008 security is provided in the following sections as a reference. The Transact-SQL (TSQL) statements shown here are demonstrated in the section "Administering SQL Server Security" later in this chapter.

Managing Logins with DDL

The CREATE LOGIN statement can be used to define new SQL Server logins. The SQL Server login can be a Windows user account, a Windows security group, or a SQL Server account. The CREATE LOGIN statement replaces the sp_addlogin system stored procedure used in previous versions of SQL Server.

```
CREATE LOGIN login_name { WITH <option_list1> ¦ FROM <sources> }

<sources> ::=
    WINDOWS [ WITH <windows_options> [ ,... ] ]
    ¦ CERTIFICATE certname
    ¦ ASYMMETRIC KEY asym_key_name

<option_list1> ::=
    PASSWORD = 'password' [ HASHED ] [ MUST_CHANGE ]
    [ , <option_list2> [ ,... ] ]
```

```
<option_list2> ::=
    SID = sid
    ¦ DEFAULT_DATABASE = database
    ¦ DEFAULT_LANGUAGE = language
    ¦ CHECK_EXPIRATION = { ON ¦ OFF}
    ¦ CHECK_POLICY = { ON ¦ OFF}
    ¦ CREDENTIAL = credential_name

<windows_options> ::=
    DEFAULT_DATABASE = database
    ¦ DEFAULT_LANGUAGE = language
```

The ALTER LOGIN statement can be used to modify existing SQL Server logins. For example, if the password policy of a SQL user causes the account to become locked out, the security administrator can use the ALTER LOGIN statement to unlock the account.

```
ALTER LOGIN login_name
    {
    <status_option>
    ¦ WITH <set_option> [ ,... ]
    }

<status_option> ::=
        ENABLE ¦ DISABLE

<set_option> ::=
    PASSWORD = 'password' [HASHED]
    [
      OLD_PASSWORD = 'oldpassword'
      ¦ <password_option> [ <password_option> ]
    ]
    ¦ DEFAULT_DATABASE = database
    ¦ DEFAULT_LANGUAGE = language
    ¦ NAME = login_name
    ¦ CHECK_POLICY = { ON ¦ OFF }
    ¦ CHECK_EXPIRATION = { ON ¦ OFF }
    ¦ CREDENTIAL = credential_name
    ¦ NO CREDENTIAL

<password_option> ::=
    MUST_CHANGE ¦ UNLOCK
```

The DROP LOGIN statement can be used to remove logins from the server:

```
DROP LOGIN login_name
```

The preceding DDL statements replace their older counterparts in the form of system stored procedures. The following stored procedures are still available; however, these stored procedures are considered deprecated and should not be used:

- sp_addlogin
- sp_grantlogin
- sp_denylogin
- sp_revokelogin

Managing Users with DDL

The CREATE USER statement can be used to define a new database user. After the SQL Server login is created, the login can be mapped to a database as a user; from this point, permissions for the database can be assigned.

```
CREATE USER user_name
    [ { { FOR ¦ FROM }
      {
        LOGIN login_name
        ¦ CERTIFICATE cert_name
        ¦ ASYMMETRIC KEY asym_key_name
      }
      ¦ WITHOUT LOGIN
    ]
    [ WITH DEFAULT_SCHEMA = schema_name ]
```

The ALTER USER statement can be used to modify existing database users. For example, if you need to update the default schema for a user, you can use this statement.

```
ALTER USER user_name
    WITH <set_item> [ ,...n ]

<set_item> ::=
    NAME = new_user_name
    ¦ DEFAULT_SCHEMA = schema_name
```

> **Note**
>
> It is possible to create a database user without mapping it to a login. This allows you to create such a login, grant necessary permissions, and map it to a login at a later stage. Such logins can also be used inside the database to provide impersonated security context while executing code modules, such as stored procedures or functions.

The DROP USER statement can be used to remove a database user from a database. Removing a database user does not remove an associated login and, conversely, when the login is removed, the mapped database user account is not automatically removed; this step must be done manually to complete the removal.

```
DROP USER user_name
```

Managing Roles with DDL

The CREATE ROLE and ALTER ROLE statements can be used to define and modify database roles. Users should be assigned to database roles instead of being assigned to objects directly to get the appropriate permissions.

```
CREATE ROLE role_name [ AUTHORIZATION owner_name ]
ALTER ROLE role_name WITH NAME = new_name
```

The sp_addrolemember statement can be used to add principals to database roles. If a login is specified, a database user is automatically created for the login and added to the role.

```
sp_addrolemember [ @rolename = ] 'role',
    [ @membername = ] 'security_account'
```

The sp_droprolemember statement can be used to remove database users from database roles:

```
sp_droprolemember [ @rolename = ] 'role' ,
          [ @membername = ] 'security_account'
```

The sp_addsrvrolemember statement can be used to add logins to fixed server roles. Note that role membership for login sa and public server role cannot be changed.

```
sp_addsrvrolemember [ @loginame= ] 'login'
    , [ @rolename = ] 'role'
```

The `sp_dropsrvrolemember` statement can be used to remove logins from fixed server roles.

```
sp_dropsrvrolemember [ @loginame = ] 'login' ,
  [ @rolename = ] 'role'
```

Managing Schemas with DDL

The CREATE SCHEMA statement can be used to define a new database schema. Database roles and users can be granted permissions on a schema level. The schema is used to group database objects together, so permissions don't need to be assigned to individual objects.

```
CREATE SCHEMA schema_name_clause [ <schema_element> [ ...n ] ]

<schema_name_clause> ::=
    {
        schema_name
    ¦ AUTHORIZATION owner_name
    ¦ schema_name AUTHORIZATION owner_name
    }

<schema_element> ::=
    {
        table_definition ¦ view_definition ¦ grant_statement ¦
        revoke_statement ¦ deny_statement
    }
```

The ALTER SCHEMA statement can be used to transfer ownership to another database user or role. This statement cannot be used to add or remove securable items from the schema. To add or remove securable objects from the schema, you use the ALTER SCHEMA statement:

```
ALTER SCHEMA schema_name TRANSFER securable_name
```

Managing Permissions with DDL

The statements shown in this section can be used to grant, deny, or revoke permissions on objects to principals. Only the basic syntax is shown; you can find additional object-specific syntax in SQL Server 2008 Books Online.

Note

Normally, deny permissions take precedence over grant permissions. However, for backward compatibility, column-level permissions take precedence over object permissions.

The GRANT statement gives principals such as database roles, users, and logins permissions to securable objects such as databases and tables. The WITH GRANT option essentially allows the grantee principal to give other principals the same permissions on the object.

```
GRANT { ALL [ PRIVILEGES ] }
      ¦ permission [ ( column [ ,...n ] ) ] [ ,...n ]
      [ ON [ class :: ] securable ] TO principal [ ,...n ]
      [ WITH GRANT OPTION ] [ AS principal ]
```

The DENY statement prevents principals from accessing objects and inheriting permissions through membership in database roles:

```
DENY { ALL [ PRIVILEGES ] }
     ¦ permission [ ( column [ ,...n ] ) ] [ ,...n ]
     [ ON [ class :: ] securable ] TO principal [ ,...n ]
     [ CASCADE] [ AS principal ]
```

The REVOKE statement removes any existing permissions, either granted or denied:

```
REVOKE [ GRANT OPTION FOR ]
     {
       [ ALL [ PRIVILEGES ] ]
       ¦
               permission [ ( column [ ,...n ] ) ] [ ,...n ]
     }
     [ ON [ class :: ] securable ]
     { TO ¦ FROM } principal [ ,...n ]
     [ CASCADE] [ AS principal ]
```

Administering SQL Server Security

The following sections provide detailed instructions for administering SQL Server permissions and authorizing access to SQL Server resources. The demonstrations are shown using logins configured for either SQL Server or Windows Authentication mode because both can be added to roles and are given permissions the same way.

Note

Using Windows authentication is considered a more secure choice and is recommended over SQL logins because Windows authentication protocols such as NT LAN Manager (NTLM) and Kerberos can be leveraged.

Using Windows authentication provides several advantages over SQL Server authentication, including enterprise-wide control of access accounts governed by domain security policies. In addition, Windows authentication can leverage Active Directory authentication protocols such as NTLM and Kerberos when SQL Server is located in an Active Directory domain.

If SQL authentication is used, it is recommended that you leverage password and lockout policies in addition to login encryption to further bolster security.

The section "Password Policies" earlier in this chapter contains additional information on how to configure password policies.

Server Login Administration

The SQL login is the basic method of authenticating to the SQL Server. When Windows accounts are used, either NTLM or Kerberos authentication is used to authenticate the user. Kerberos will be the first preference, and then it will fall back to NTLM if Kerberos is not available. The user's credentials are sent in an encrypted form, making it difficult to discover them as they travel across the network.

Enabling Mixed Mode Authentication

SQL Server can be configured for Windows Authentication mode only or SQL Server and Windows Authentication mode. For simplicity, some of the demonstrations use SQL authentication and require the server to support both authentication modes.

Follow these steps to enable both Windows Authentication mode and SQL Server and Windows Authentication mode:

1. Launch SQL Server Management Studio, and then connect to a SQL Server Instance.

2. In Object Explorer, right-click on a desired SQL Server and then click Properties.

3. On the Security page, under Server Authentication, select SQL Server and Windows Authentication mode, and then click OK.

4. In the SQL Server Management Studio dialog box, click OK to acknowledge the need to restart SQL Server.

5. In Object Explorer, right-click on a desired server and then click Restart. If the SQL Server Agent is running, it also requires a restart.

> **Note**
>
> If Windows Authentication mode is selected during installation, the sa login is disabled by default. If the authentication mode is switched to SQL Server mixed mode after the installation, the sa account is still disabled and must be manually enabled. It is a best practice to reset the password when the mode is switched.

Creating SQL Authentication Logins

The Logins node holds all the Windows and SQL logins for the server. From this node, the different server logins can be managed. The following procedure can be used to create a new SQL login within SQL Server Management Studio:

1. Launch SQL Server Management Studio, and then connect to a SQL Server Instance.

2. In Object Explorer, expand Security and select the Logins node

3. Right-click the Logins node and select New Login. The Login—New window opens.

The following relevant login options are located on the General configuration page:

- **Login Name**—When Windows authentication is used, this is the name of the existing Windows user or Windows security group. When SQL authentication is used, this is the name selected for the login.

- **Windows Authentication**—This option allows the selection of a Windows user account or security group for the logon. The Windows user account or security group can reside in Active Directory or the local server.

- **SQL Server Authentication**—This option allows the creation of an account where the account information including the account password is stored in the SQL database.

The following additional options are available on the General tab when you use SQL Server authentication:

- **Enforce Password Policy**—This option configures the SQL Server to enforce domain or local server password policies. If SQL Server authentication is used, this option is highly recommended to help improve security.

- **Enforce Password Expiration**—This option configures the SQL Server to enforce domain or local server password expiration policies. This option should be enabled if the database application provides a way for the user to change the password.

■ **User Must Change Password**—When this option is enabled, the user must change the password during the first authentication. This option should be enabled if the database application provides a way for the user to change the password.

Follow these steps to create the SQL Server login and complete the configuration page:

1. Enter **Test.User1** in the Login Name field.

2. Select SQL Server authentication.

3. Enter the password.

4. Confirm the password.

5. Select Enforce Password Policy.

6. Select Enforce Password Expiration.

7. Select User Must Change Password at Next Login.

8. Leave Master as the Default database.

9. Leave <default> as the Default language.

10. Figure 9.4 shows how the Logon Properties window should look. Click OK to complete the page and create the login.

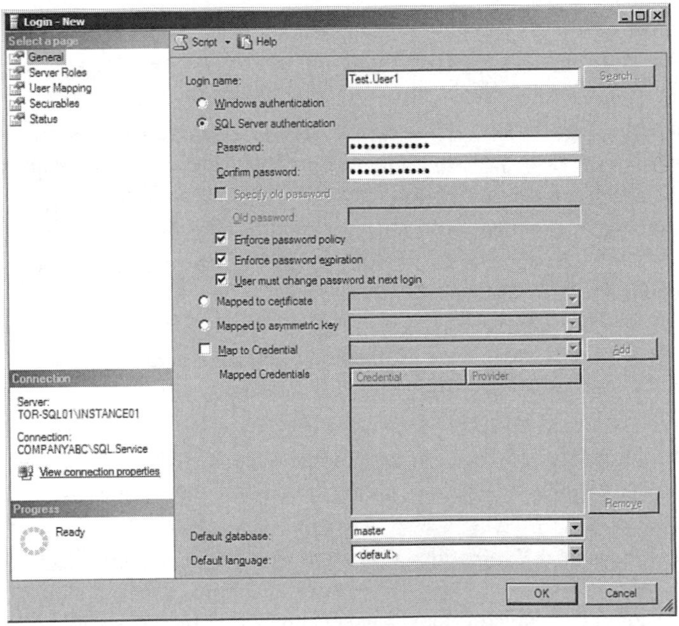

FIGURE 9.4
New SQL authentication logon properties.

The SQL login Test.User1 is created but currently has only a limited set of permissions. By default, all users are members of the public fixed server role.

You can use the following TSQL code to accomplish the same task. This code creates a user called Test.User2 with `Password!!` set as the default password for the account:

```
USE [master]
GO
CREATE LOGIN [Test.User2] WITH
    PASSWORD=N'Password!!'
    MUST_CHANGE,
    DEFAULT_DATABASE=[master],
    CHECK_EXPIRATION=ON,
    CHECK_POLICY=ON
GO
```

After the account is created, the next step is to verify the account can authenticate to the server. Configuring permissions for the login is described later in this chapter. To continue, do the following:

1. Launch a new instance of SQL Server Management Studio.

2. Select Database Engine from the Server Type drop-down; then enter the server and instance name.

3. Select SQL Server Authentication from the Authentication drop-down list.

4. Enter **Test.User1** in the Login field and enter the password assigned to the logon. Then click the Connect button.

5. A change password prompt is displayed because the User Must Change Password policy was enabled when the login was defined.

6. Enter and confirm the new password; then click OK.

7. A connection to the database engine is made. If the Object Explorer pane is not visible, press the F8 key.

8. From within the Object Explorer pane, expand Databases and select the AdventureWorks2008 database.

9. An error message is displayed, notifying the login that the database is inaccessible.

Although the account cannot access any of the databases, the authentication should be successful.

Creating Windows Authentication Logins

Creating a Windows login is similar to creating a SQL Server login. Another one of the many advantages to using Windows authentication includes the ability to add domain security groups as the login instead of just the user account.

> **Note**
>
> One of the drawbacks to using Windows security groups for logins is that you cannot assign a default schema.

Before you add a Windows account or security group as a SQL Server login, it must exist in Active Directory or on the local computer. Follow these steps to create a Windows user account in Active Directory:

1. On the SQL Server system, select Start, Run.

2. Type **DSA.MSC** and then click OK.

3. Create a domain user account called **Test.Domain1**.

After creating the Active Directory user account, you can add the account as a login. Follow these steps:

1. In Object Explorer, expand the Security node.

2. Right-click the Logins node and select New Login.

3. Click the Search button.

4. Click Locations and select Entire Directory, and then click OK.

5. Type **Test.Domain1** in the Object field.

6. Click the Check Name button to confirm the account name.

7. Click OK to return to the Login Properties window.

8. Select Master as the Default database.

9. Select <default> as the Default language.

10. Figure 9.5 shows how the Logon Properties window should look. Click OK to complete the page and create the login.

The user account is listed in the Logins folder. Perform the following steps to verify that the account can authenticate to the server. The SQL Server Management Studio can be executed as a different user account through the Run As command.

1. Add Choose, Start, All Programs, Microsoft SQL Server 2008. Then right-click on SQL Server Management Studio and select Run As.

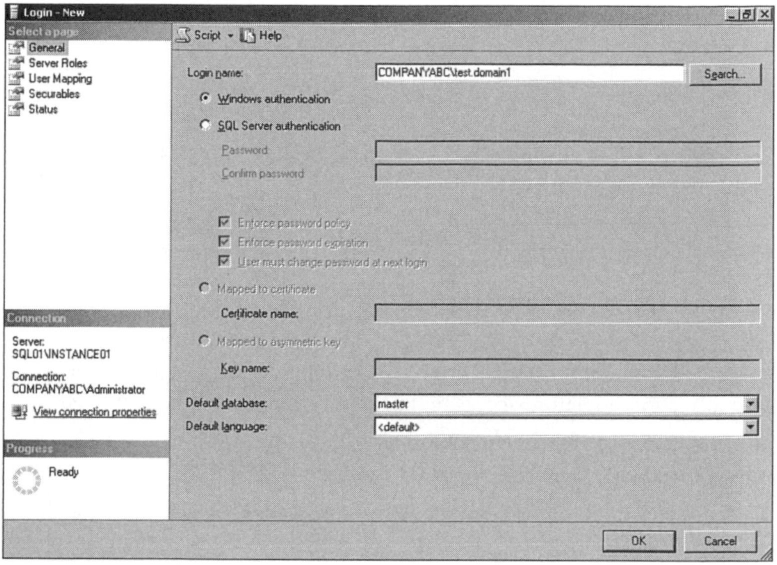

FIGURE 9.5
New Windows authentication logon properties.

2. In the Run As window, enter **COMPANYABC\Test.Domain1** in the User Name field.

3. Enter the associated account password and click OK. The SQL Server Management Studio opens under the Test.Domain1 account.

4. Select Database Engine from the Server Type drop-down list; then enter the server and instance name.

5. Select Windows Authentication from the Authentication drop-down list and then click the Connect button.

6. A connection to the database engine is made. If the Object Explorer pane is not visible, press the F8 key.

7. From within the Object Explorer pane, expand Databases and select the AdventureWorks2008 database.

8. An error message is displayed, notifying the login that the database is inaccessible.

The authentication should be successful because the default database was set to Master and the login is a member of the public server role. The public role has limited access to the master database. If you set the default database to something else, such as AdventureWorks2008, the authentication would fail because the public role does not have access to this database by default.

You can use the following TSQL code to add the Test.Domain1 user as a SQL login:

```
USE [master]
GO
CREATE LOGIN [COMPANYABC\Test.Domain1] FROM WINDOWS WITH
DEFAULT_DATABASE=[master]
GO
```

Database User Administration

After adding a login to the server, you can create a database user. The database user is essentially mapped back to the original login; this means the login is normally required before access to database resources can be authorized.

Follow these steps to manage database users. This procedure adds the login Test.User1 to the AdventureWorks2008 database in a SQL Server instance.

1. In Object Explorer, expand the AdventureWorks2008, Security, and select Users.

2. Right-click Users and select New User.

3. Click the ellipsis button next to the Login Name field.

4. On the Select Login page, click Browse.

5. Select Test.User1 and then click OK.

6. Click OK to return to the Database User page.

7. Enter **Test.User1** in the User Name field.

8. Click the ellipsis button next to the Default Schema field.

9. On the Select Schema window, click Browse.

10. Select Human Resources and then click OK.

11. Click OK to return to the Database User properties window.

12. The Database User properties window should look similar to Figure 9.6. Click OK to create the database user.

A user called Test.User1 is added to the database. You can use the following TSQL code to add a login and an associated database user:

```
USE [AdventureWorks2008]
CREATE LOGIN [Test.User2]
  WITH PASSWORD=N'Password!'
  MUST_CHANGE,
  DEFAULT_DATABASE=[master],
  CHECK_EXPIRATION=ON, CHECK_POLICY=ON
```

```
GO
CREATE USER [Test.User2]
  FOR LOGIN [Test.User2]
  WITH DEFAULT_SCHEMA=[HumanResources]
GO
```

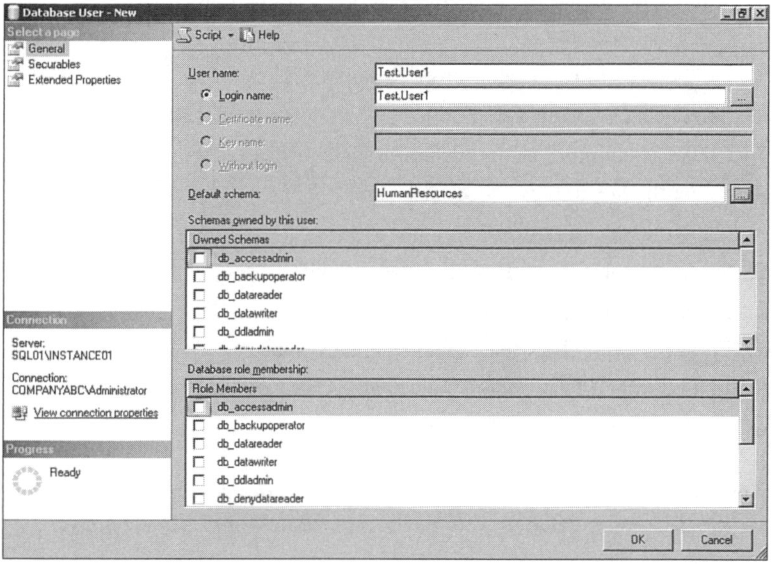

FIGURE 9.6
New database user properties.

Now that you've added the login to the database, you can assign the correct permissions. Although permissions to objects can be assigned directly to users, it is recommended to create roles and database schemas to control access to database objects.

Windows-based logins can be mapped to database users using the exact same method. Database mapping for logins can also be configured on the Mapping Options page of the Login Properties window.

Database Role Administration

For efficient and effective management of data, users should be added to database roles. Each database role can be assigned permissions on a different object found in SQL Server.

The following procedure creates a new database role called Human Resources Reporting, the Test.User1 database user is added to this new role, and the role is given SELECT permissions to the HumanResources schema. Just follow these steps:

1. In Object Explorer, expand AdventureWorks2008, Security, Roles, and select Database Roles.
2. Right-click Database Roles and select New Database Role.
3. Type **Human Resources Reporting** in the Name field.
4. Click the Add button.
5. On the Select Database User or Role page, click Browse.
6. Select Test.User1 and click OK.
7. Click OK to return to the Database Role properties window.
8. Select the Securables properties page.
9. Click the Search button.
10. Select All Objects of Type and then click OK.
11. Select Schemas and click OK.
12. From the Securables list, select HumanResources.
13. In the Explicit Permissions list, enable Grant on the Select permission.
14. Click OK to complete the new role.

You can use the following TSQL code to create and configure the Human Resources Reporting database role in the AdventureWorks2008 database:

```
USE [AdventureWorks2008]
GO
CREATE ROLE [Human Resources Reporting]
GO
USE [AdventureWorks2008]
GO
EXEC sp_addrolemember N'Human Resources Reporting',
 N'Test.User1'
GO
use [AdventureWorks2008]
GO
GRANT SELECT ON SCHEMA::[HumanResources]
TO [Human Resources Reporting]
GO
```

The code example first creates the database role and then adds the user Test.User1 to the role. Finally, the role is given permissions to the schema object named HumanResources.

The `sys.database_role_members` and `sys.database_principals` catalog views can be used to display database roles.

Security Schema Administration

The security schema for a database essentially provides a container for a group of objects in the database. Besides the default schemas found in all databases, the AdventureWorks2008 database has several different schemas defined, including HumanResources, Person, Production, Purchasing, and Sales.

Follow these steps to establish a new schema called Test Schema for the AdventureWorks2008 database:

1. In Object Explorer, expand AdventureWorks2008, Security, and select Schemas.

2. Expand the Schemas node. Each of the default schemas for the AdventureWorks2008 database is listed.

3. Right-click the Schemas node and select New Schema. The new Schema Properties window opens.

4. In the Schema Name field, type **Test Schema**.

5. Click the Search button.

6. Click the Browse button.

7. Select Test.User1 and click OK.

8. Click OK to return to the Schema properties page.

On the Permissions page of the schema, you can define the permissions for each database user and role. These permissions can also be defined on the Database User or Role Property pages.

The permissions configured on the schema are applied to each object created in the schema for each principal given rights on the schema. This is very important when managing security because new objects can now inherit the correct permissions automatically.

Managing Application Roles

An application role is another type of principal that can be created in a SQL Server database. Like the database role, the application role is given permissions to database objects, can be added to other roles, and granted permissions through schemas. However, unlike the database role, the application role does not contain database users. The application role is designed to allow applications to obtain permissions on database objects.

When a user runs a database application, the application executes a specific stored procedure designed to activate the application role. The database application must be configured to provide the correct password for the role. If the authentication is successful, the user's security context changes completely to that of the application role. The only way to revert to the original context is through disconnecting and connecting again. The following syntax is used to define a new application role:

```
CREATE APPLICATION ROLE application_role_name
    WITH PASSWORD = 'password' [ , DEFAULT_SCHEMA = schema_name ]
```

You can also configure application roles through the SQL Server Management studio by selecting the Application Roles node in the Security\Roles node of a database.

The sp_setapprole stored procedure must be executed by the application to activate the application role. Here's the syntax of the stored procedure:

```
sp_setapprole [ @rolename = ] 'role',
      [ @password = ] { encrypt N'password' }
    ¦
    ¦
      'password' [ , [ @encrypt = ] { 'none' ¦ 'odbc' } ]
      [ , [ @fCreateCookie = ] true ¦ false ]
    [ , [ @cookie = ] @cookie OUTPUT ]
```

The sp_unsetapprole stored procedure must be executed by the application to change the user's context back to the original settings. Following is the syntax of this stored procedure. Note that the cookie option must be used in the sp_setapprole for this stored procedure to work.

```
sp_unsetapprole @cookie
```

As an alternative to application roles, database users can be created without explicit logins. Applications can then be configured to execute database code under the security context of this database user instead of the application role.

Server Endpoint Administration

Server endpoints allow communication with the SQL Server through one or more of the supported protocols. All endpoints for a SQL Server instance can be viewed through the SQL Server Management Studio. Follow these steps to view endpoints on a SQL Server instance:

1. In Object Explorer, expand Server Objects, Endpoints, Systems Endpoints, TSQL.
2. The default TSQL endpoints are listed.

If database mirroring or SOAP web services user-defined endpoints have been created, they are listed under the corresponding nodes within the Endpoints node.

The SQL Server Management Studio offers limited management of endpoints, allowing only the administration of permissions for endpoints and providing the ability to drop user-defined endpoints.

Note

System default endpoints cannot be dropped. However, you can start and stop these endpoints and change the permission on system default endpoints.

Endpoint security is important because it controls the different aspects of the endpoint, such as who can connect and who can administer an endpoint for a specific instance or application.

Follow these steps to change the permissions on the default system TSQL Local Machine endpoint:

1. In Object Explorer, expand Security and select the Logins node.

2. Double-click the Test.User1 login created previously in the section "Creating SQL Authentication Logins."

3. Select the Securables page; then click the Add button.

4. Select All Objects of the Type; then click OK.

5. Enable Endpoints and then click OK.

6. Select TSQL Local Machine from the Securables list.

7. Select the Deny column for the Connect permission.

8. Figure 9.7 shows how the Securables option page should look for the login. Click OK to change the permissions.

Open another instance of the SQL Server Management Studio from the test server TOR-SQL01 and attempt to authenticate as Test.User1. Because of the deny permission created, an attempt to authenticate as Test.User1 should fail even though the login is active.

Note

Endpoint permissions are associated with the actual name of the endpoint. This can be a problem when an endpoint is configured for dynamic ports because the name changes when the port changes. As a result, the security associated with the endpoint is lost.

As a best practice, avoid using endpoints with dynamic ports, specifically when endpoint permissions are used.

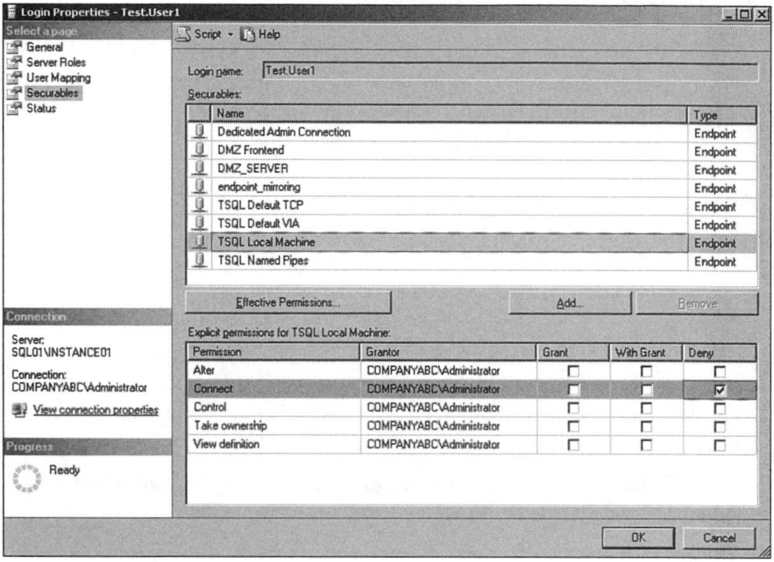

FIGURE 9.7
Login endpoint permissions.

You can create a new endpoint only through TSQL statements. The CREATE, ALTER, and DROP ENDPOINT statements have many options; for additional information, see SQL Server 2008 Books Online.

The following code shows how to create a TCP endpoint called DMZ Frontend that listens on port 48620:

```
CREATE ENDPOINT [DMZ Frontend]
AS TCP (LISTENER_PORT=48620) FOR TSQL()
GO
```

The following warning message is displayed when the endpoint is created:

```
Creation of a TSQL endpoint will result in the revocation of any
'Public' connect permissions on the 'TSQL Default TCP' endpoint.
If 'Public' access is desired on this endpoint, reapply this
permission using 'GRANT CONNECT ON ENDPOINT::[TSQL Default TCP]
to [public]'.
```

If necessary, you must add the public role to the default endpoint by running the command identified in the warning message.

You can use the following TSQL statement to allow the user Test.User1 to connect to the newly created endpoint:

```
USE MASTER
GRANT CONNECT ON ENDPOINT::[DMZ Frontend] to [Test.User1]
GO
```

Summary

Administering SQL Server security is a key task bestowed upon database administrators. Understanding and leveraging the different security features associated with the SQL Server 2008 Database Engine and the different SQL Server 2008 components is essential to ensuring the integrity of the environment.

A properly implemented and well-maintained security model helps reduce the likelihood of sensitive data exposure, while increasing the overall scalability and reliability of the environment.

Best Practices

The following best practices can be taken from this chapter:

- To manage security most effectively, prepare and harden the environment. See Chapter 8 for additional information.

- When administering SQL Server security, follow the principle of least privilege. This basically means giving only the necessary permissions to the different user and service accounts needed to accomplish the task.

- Enable only communication protocols that are necessary and allow only specific CONNECT permissions on endpoints.

- Leverage Active Directory, specifically running Windows Server 2008 to establish access and role-based security groups for accessing SQL Server resources.

- When you are using Active Directory for role-based access, you cannot assign a default schema to the user accounts. Ensure that the security model accounts for this limitation.

- All database users belong to the public database role by default. Avoid using the public database role when assigning permissions unless absolutely necessary.

- The schema provides a way to manage security on groups of objects with a granular level of control. Use the schema to group related objects together—that is, objects that can have the same permissions given to the same principals.

- If possible, always use Windows Authentication mode to leverage Windows Server 2008 authentication protocols, such as Kerberos, along with domain-level password policies.

- If you use SQL authentication, enable the options to enforce the local security policies and implement encrypted authentication.

- Create database users without logins in SQL Server 2008. This approach can be used as an alternative to application roles in the database.

- Endpoint permissions are associated with the actual name of the endpoint. This can be a problem when an endpoint is configured for dynamic ports because the name changes when the port changes. As a result, the security associated with the endpoint is lost. Avoid using endpoints with dynamic ports, specifically when endpoint permissions are used.

CHAPTER 10

Administering Policy Based Management

Policy Based Management, formerly known as Declarative Management Framework in the Community Technology Previews (CTPs), is one of the most sought-after new management features in SQL Server 2008. Policy Based Management gives an organization the potential to create policies to manage one or more SQL Server instances, databases, or objects within the enterprise. In addition, policies can be evaluated against target systems to ensure that the standard configuration settings are not out of compliance. Policy Based Management was developed in response to the following industry trends:

- Increasing amounts of data being stored
- Data center consolidation and virtualization
- Growing product capabilities
- Proliferation of SQL Server systems within the enterprise
- Need for a way to manage SQL Server settings from a holistic perspective
- Regulatory compliance demanding secure and standardized settings

Introduction to Policy Based Management

Policy Based Management is a new feature in SQL Server 2008. Essentially DBAs are being required to do more, frequently with less. There has been a data explosion over the past several years. In a 2006 study IDC (International Data Corporation— http://www.idc.com) reported that 5 exabytes of digital media (5 billion gigabytes) were stored in 2003, and in 2006 this had ballooned to 161 exabytes. Not only is more data being stored, but users are accessing more data than before.

Business Intelligence delivering actionable insights is becoming more critical in the enterprise, and these insights require large data volumes for trending and forecasting. Data warehouses are becoming more critical in every enterprise.

Frequently this data explosion means a proliferation of SQL Servers, and distributed data is now often consolidated from distributed servers to data centers.

SQL Servers are increasingly being consolidated in data centers. Rising power and cooling costs, the increasing per-square-foot cost of data centers, and physical space shortages are forcing IT management to move to SQL Server consolidation and even virtualization. Complexities of the SQL Server product set are forcing DBAs to focus on efficient, scalable management and standardization. Due to the large numbers of SQL Servers involved, management by automation becomes critical as well to lessen the administrative burden. Monitoring also becomes more important to provide proactive support.

A well-managed SQL Server enterprise that follows best practices offers the following advantages:

- **Standardization**—Every SQL Server will have a common disk layout and settings. As a result, DBAs moving from one SQL Server to another will not be surprised by different disk layouts or unusual settings that could account for a performance problem.

- **Best practices**—Microsoft internal studies have shown that 80 percent of the support calls to their Customer Service and Support (CSS) could have been avoided if the customer had been following best practices. Best practices not only offer performance advantages but also lead to fewer failure events caused by poorly configured SQL Servers, and security breaches due to SQL Servers that have not been hardened (security holes not locked down).

- **Ease of deployment**—A well-managed data center will have automated procedures for building SQL Servers (that is, unattended installations using the template.ini file) that require less time to build and minimal administrative interaction, resulting in fewer mistakes in a build and a reduction in administrative tasks.

- **Regulatory compliance**—By maintaining controlled and standardized settings, organizations can easily adhere to the demanding requirements of regulations such as Sarbanes-Oxley, HIPPA, and PCI.

The intent of Policy Based Management is to provide a management framework that allows DBAs to automate management in their enterprise according to their own set of predefined standards. By implementing Policy Based Management within a SQL Server infrastructure, organizations will reap the following benefits: Total cost of ownership associated with managing SQL Server systems will be reduced, configuration changes to the SQL Server system can be monitored, unwanted system configuration changes can be prevented, and policies will ensure compliance.

The stated goals of Policy Based Management fall into three categories:

- **Management by intent**—Allows DBAs to enforce standards and best practices from the start rather in response to a performance problem or failure event

- **Intelligent monitoring**—Allows DBAs to detect changes that have been made to their SQL Server environments that deviate from the desired configuration

- **Virtualized management**—Provides a scalable framework that allows for establishment management across the enterprise

Microsoft SQL Server 2008 also ships with several policies that are not imported into a default installation of SQL Server 2008. These can be found in `C:\Program Files\Microsoft SQL Server\100\Tools\Policies\DatabaseEngine\1033`. Note that there are also policies for Reporting Services and Analysis Services, which can be found in the `ReportingServices` and `AnalysisServices` subdirectories of the `Policies` directory. Also note that Policy Based Management can also be used to manage SQL 2005 and 2000 servers.

> **Note**
>
> Microsoft has a blog focusing on Policy Based Management (http://blogs. msdn.com/sqlpbm/) where they will be publishing scripts that can be used to enforce Microsoft best practices for SQL Server.

Policy Based Management Concepts

Before we start learning about enforcing Policy Based Management, there are a few key concepts DBAs must understand. These concepts include

- Facets
- Conditions
- Policies
- Categories
- Targets
- Execution mode
- Central Management Servers

Facets

A *facet* is a logical grouping of predefined SQL Server 2008 configuration settings. When a facet is coupled with a condition, a policy is formed and can be applied to one or more SQL Server instances and systems. Common facets include: Surface Area Configuration, Server Audit, Database File, and Databases. Table 10.1 illustrates the complete list of predefined facets that can be selected. Facets are included with SQL Server 2008 and cannot be modified.

The complete list of facets can be viewed in SQL Server 2008 Management Studio by expanding the Management folder, the Policy Based Management node, and then the Facets folder. Alternatively, to view facets applied to a specific database, right-click the database and select Facets.

Note

Currently, there is a sum of 38 facets with the potential of 1,330 properties to be configured. Going forward, Microsoft will undoubtedly create more facets, which will be included with upcoming service packs.

Table 10.1   **Facets for Policy Based Management**

Facet Name	Check on Change: Prevent	Check on Change: Log	Check on Scan
Application Role	X	X	X
Asymmetric Key	X	X	X
Audit			X
Backup Device			X
Broker Priority			X
Broker Service			X
Certificate			X
Credential			X
Cryptographic Provider			X
Data File			X
Database			X
Database Audit Specification			X
Database DDL Trigger			X
Database Maintenance			X
Database Option		X	X
Database Performance			X
Database Role	X	X	X
Database Security			X
Default			X

Facet Name	Check on Change: Prevent	Check on Change: Log	Check on Scan
Endpoint	X	X	X
File Group			X
Full Text Catalog			X
Full Text Index			X
Full Text Stop List			X
Index			X
Linked Server			X
Log File			X
Login			X
Login Options	X	X	X
Message Type			X
Multipart Name	X	X	X
Name			X
Partition Function			X
Partition Scheme			X
Plan Guide			X
Remote Service Binding			X
Resource Governor			X
Resource Pool	X	X	X
Rule			X
Schema	X	X	X
Server			X
Server Audit			X
Server Audit Specification			X
Server Configuration		X	X
Server DDL Trigger			X
Server Information			X
Server Performance			X
Server Security			X
Server Settings			X
Server Setup			X
Service Contract			X
Service Queue			X

Table 10.1   **continued**

Facet Name	Check on Change: Prevent	Check on Change: Log	Check on Scan
Service Route			X
Statistic			X
Stored Procedure	X	X	X
Surface Area		X	X
Surface Area for AS			
Surface Area for RS			
Symmetric Key			X
Synonym			X
Table			X
Table Options	X	X	X
Trigger			X
User			X
User Defined Aggregate			X
User Defined Data Type			X
User Defined Function	X	X	X
User Defined Table Type			X
User Defined Type			X
User Options	X	X	X
View			X
View Options	X	X	X
Workload Group	X	X	X
Xml Schema Collection			X

Conditions

A *condition* is a Boolean expression that dictates an outcome or desired state of a specific management condition, also known as a facet. Condition settings are based on properties, comparative operators, and values such as String, equal, not equal, LIKE, NOT LIKE, IN, or NOT IN. For example, a check condition could verify that data and log files reside on separate drives, that the state of the database recovery model is set to Full Recovery, that database file sizes are not larger than a predefined value, and that database mail is disabled.

Policies

A *policy* is a standard for a single setting of an object. It ultimately acts as a verification mechanism of one or more conditions of the required state of SQL Server targets. Typical scenarios for creating policies include: imposing Surface Area Configuration settings, enforcing naming conventions on database objects, enforcing database and transaction log placement, and controlling recovery models. As mentioned earlier, a tremendous number of policies can be created against SQL Server 2008 systems. Surface Area Configurations are a very common policy, especially since the SQL Server 2005 Surface Area Configuration tool has been deprecated in SQL Server 2008.

> **Note**
>
> A policy can only contain one condition and can be either enabled or disabled.

Categories

Microsoft recognized that although you may want to implement a set of rigid standards for your internal SQL Server development or deployments, your enterprise may have to host third-party software that does not follow your standards. Although your internally developed user databases will subscribe to your own policies, the third-party user applications will subscribe to their own categories. To provide flexibility you can select which policies you want a table, database, or server to subscribe to and group them into groups called *categories*, and then have a database subscribe to a category and unsubscribe from a group of other policies.

Targets

A *target* is one or more SQL Server instances, databases, or database objects that you want to apply your categories or policies to. Targets can only be SQL Server 2008, 2005, or 2000 systems. Due to the changes with the Database Engine in 2008, Policy Based Management does not support full functionality with SQL Server 2005 or earlier systems. If necessary, it is still possible to create system configuration policies with the Security Configuration Wizard, which is included with Windows Server 2008.

> **Note**
>
> The use of the Security Configuration Wizard is covered in Chapter 8, "Hardening a SQL Server Implementation."

Execution Modes

When implementing policies, there are three types of execution modes. The On Change mode has two variations:

- **On demand**—The On Demand policy ensures that a target or targets are in compliance. This task is invoked manually by right-clicking on the policy in the Management folder, Policy Management folder, Policy folder, and selecting Evaluate. The policy will not be enforced, and will only be verified against all targets that have been subscribed to that policy. You can evaluate a policy also by right clicking on the database and selecting Policies and Evaluate.

- **On schedule**—Policies can be evaluated on a schedule. For example, a policy can be scheduled to check all SQL Server 2008 systems once a day. If any anomalies arise, these out-of-compliance policies will be logged to a file. This file should be reviewed on a periodic basis. In addition, whenever a policy fails, the complete tree in SQL Server Management Studio would display a red downward pointing arrow next to the policy as illustrated in Figure 10.1.

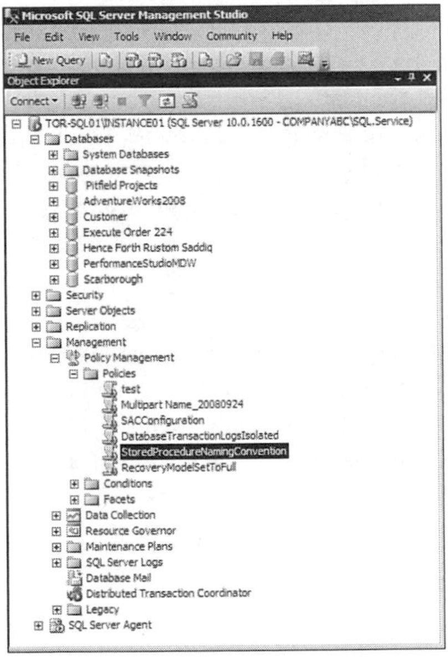

FIGURE 10.1
SQL Server management tree illustrating failed policies for table name.

- **On Change Prevent**—The On Change Prevent execution mode prevents changes to server, server object, database, or database objects which would make them out of compliance. For example, if you select a policy that restricts table names that to begin with the prefix `tbl`, and you attempt to create a table called MyTable, you will get the following error message, and your table will not be created.

```
Policy 'table name' has been violated by
'/Server/(local)/Database/iFTS/Table/dbo.mytable'.
This transaction will be rolled back.
Policy description: ''
Additional help: '' : ''.
Msg 3609, Level 16, State 1, Procedure sp_syspolicy_
dispatch_event, Line 50
The transaction ended in the trigger.
The batch has been aborted.
```

- On Change Log Only—If you select On Change Log Only, a policy condition that is evaluated as failed will be logged in the SQL Server Error log. The change does not prevent out-of-compliance changes.

Central Management Servers

In large enterprises, organizations will most likely have more than one SQL Server system they want to effectively manage from a Policy Based Management perspective. Therefore, if DBAs want to implement policies to multiple servers, they have two options. The first option includes exporting the policy and then importing it into different SQL Server systems. After the policy is imported, it must be configured to be evaluated on demand, on schedule, or on change.

The second option includes creating one or more Central Management Servers. Central Management Servers are a new philosophy with SQL Server 2008. Basically, by registering one or more SQL Servers with a Central Management Server, a DBA can deploy multi-server policies and administration from a central system.

For example, you could create two Central Management Servers, one called OLAP and another called OLTP, and then register servers into each Central Management Server, import the different policies into each Central Management Server, and then evaluate the polices on each different Central Management Server. So, on your OLTP Central Management Server, the servers OLTP1, OLTP2, OLTP3, which are registered in the OLTP Central Management Server, would have the OLTP policies evaluated on them.

Creating a Central Management Server

Follow these procedures to register a Central Management Server.

1. In SQL Server Management Studio, click Registered Servers from the View menu.

2. In Registered Servers, expand the Database Engine, right-click Central Management Servers, and then select Register Central Management Server.

3. In the New Server Registration dialog box, specify the name of the desired Central Management Server.

4. If needed, specify additional connection properties on the Connection Properties tab or click Save.

Registering SQL Server Instances in a Central Management Server

The next step registers SQL Server instances to be associated with a Central Management Server. The following procedures outline these tasks:

1. Right click on the Central Management Server you wish to associate your SQL Server instance with.

2. Select New Server Registration.

3. In the New Server Registration dialog box, specify the name of the desired Central Management Server.

4. Repeat step 4 for all SQL Server instances that you want to register with this Central Management Server.

Figure 10.2 illustrates a Central Management Server with one Server Group and two SQL Server instances registered.

Importing and Evaluating Polices to the Central Management Server

After the Central Management Server has been established, the Server Group has been created, and the desired SQL Server instances registered, it is time to import and evaluate policies. Importing policies for multiple instances can be done by right-clicking the Central Management Server or Server Group and selecting Import Policies. After the policies have been imported, the next step is to evaluate the policies by right-clicking the Central Management Server or Server Group and selecting Evaluate. The output will indicate the status of policies associated with all the SQL Server instances associated with the Central Management Server or Server Group.

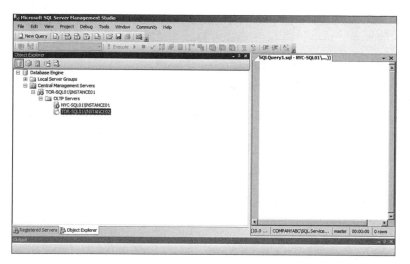

FIGURE 10.2
Central Management Server.

> **Note**
>
> Importing, exporting, and evaluating policies are covered later throughout the chapter.

Implementing Policy Based Management

Now that you understand the basic purpose and concepts behind Policy Based Management, let's look at how to administer Policy Based Management, then how to apply it to a server, and then a group of servers.

There are essentially five steps to implementing and administering Policy Based Management:

- Creating a condition based on a facet
- Creating a policy based on that condition
- Creating a category
- Creating a Central Management Server
- Subscribing to a category
- Exporting or importing a policy

Let's look at each of these in turn. The upcoming sections explain each step in its entirety.

Creating a Condition Based on a Facet

When creating conditions, the general principle includes three elements: selecting a property, an operator, and then a value. Follow the steps to create a condition based on a facet. This example will enforce a naming standard on a table.

1. To create a condition, connect to a SQL Server 2008 instance on which you want to create a policy.

2. Launch SQL Server Management Studio. In Object Explorer, expand the Management folder, expand the Policy Management Folder, and then expand the Facets folder.

3. Within the Facets folder, browse to the desired facet on which you want to create the policy.

4. To invoke the Create New Condition window, right-click the facet, such as Table, and select New Condition.

5. In the Create New Condition dialog box, type a name for the condition and ensure that the facet selected is correct.

6. In the Expression section, perform the following tasks:

    a. Select the property on which you want to create your condition. For this example, the Name property will be used.

    b. In the Operator drop-down box, select the NOT LIKE operator

    c. In the value text box enter `'tbl%'`.

6. Repeat step 6 for any additional expressions. For this example the following expressions were entered, as displayed in Figure 10.3.

AndOr	Field	Operator	Value
	@Name	NOT LIKE	'tbl%'
AND	Len(@Name)	<=	50
AND	@Name	NOT LIIKE	'%s'

> **Note**
>
> You can create conditions that query Windows Management Instrumentation (WMI) (using the ExecuteWSQL function) or SQL Server (using the (ExecuteSQL function). For example you can do this to check on available disk space, or number of processors on the server. WMI allows you to issue SQL like queries against Management Objects which can return information on the physical machine hosting SQL Server; configuration and performance information which is not accessible from within SQL Server itself.

7. Click OK to finalize the creation of the condition. You may have to click on the Field text box again for the OK button to be enabled.

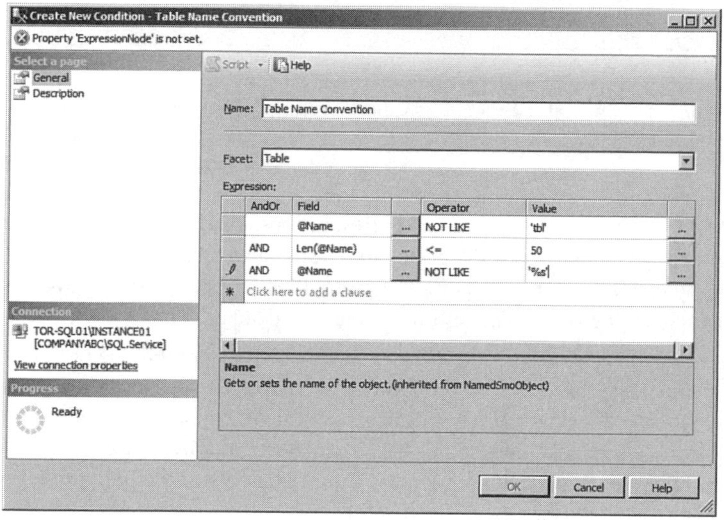

FIGURE 10.3
Creating a condition based on a facet.

Creating a Policy

After the condition or conditions have been created, it is necessary to create the policy. The *policy* is a standard that can be enforced on one or more SQL Server instances, systems, server objects, databases, or database objects. This procedure includes the step-by-step instructions for creating a policy with SQL Server Management Studio.

1. In Object Explorer, expand the Management folder, expand the Policy Management Folder, and then click on Policies.

2. Right-click on the Policies folder and select New Policy.

3. On the General tab in the Create New Policy dialog box, enter a name for the new policy, such as **Stored Proc Naming**.

4. In the Check Condition drop-down box, select a condition, such as the one created in the previous example, or select New to generate a new condition from scratch.

5. The Against Targets section indicates which objects the policy should be evaluated against. For example, you could create a new condition that applies to a specific database, all databases, a specific table, all tables, or to databases created after a specific date. In the Action Targets section, indicate which targets this condition should apply to.

6. Specify the Evaluation Mode by selecting one of the options in the drop-down menu. The options include On Demand, On Schedule, On Change Log Only, and On Change Prevent.

Note

If On Schedule is selected, specify a schedule from the predefined list or enter a new schedule.

---

7. The final drop-down box is Server Restrictions. You can restrict which servers you do not want the policy to be evaluated against or enforced on by creating a server condition. Create a server restriction or leave the default setting None. The policy settings are displayed in Figure 10.4.

8. Before you close the Create New Policy dialog, ensure that the policy is Enabled, and then click on the Description page. The description page allows you to categorize your policy, but it also allows you to display a custom text message when a policy is violated and a hyperlink where the DBA/developer can go for more information about the policy.

9. Click OK to finalize the creation of the new policy.

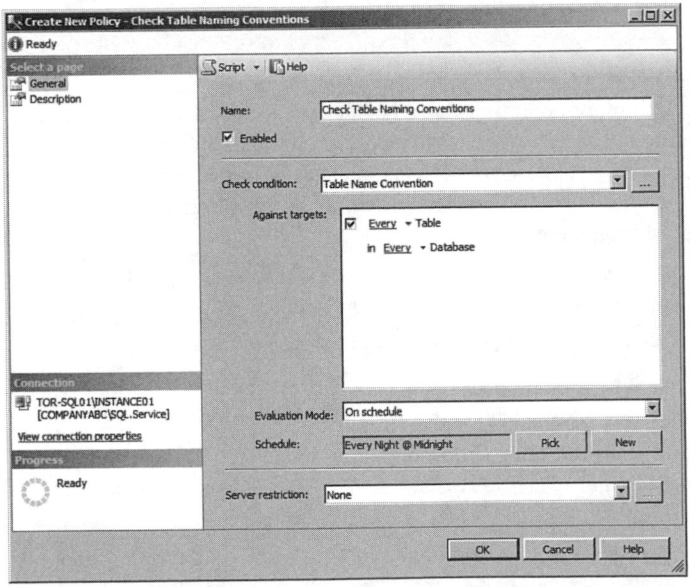

FIGURE 10.4
The Create New Policy dialog box.

An Alternative to Creating Policies

As you can imagine, for complex policies you may need to create many conditions. In some cases it may be easier to create a table, database, or server that is configured to conform to the policy you want to create, and then right-click on the specific object, select Facets, and then click the New Policy from Facets button.

This will export a policy and a single condition to which the existing object will conform. Figure 10.5 illustrates the dialog that prompts you for a name for your policy and dialog as well as where you want to store the policy. You can store it in the file system and then import it to a Central Management Server or other servers where you want the policy to be evaluated, or you can import it directly to a server. Note that this policy will contain conditions specific to the object you use as a template; for example, if you use the AdventureWorks database, the policy will test for the condition where the database name is equal to AdventureWorks. For this to be useful, you will likely need to edit the conditions to ensure that they are generic and will evaluate exceptions correctly.

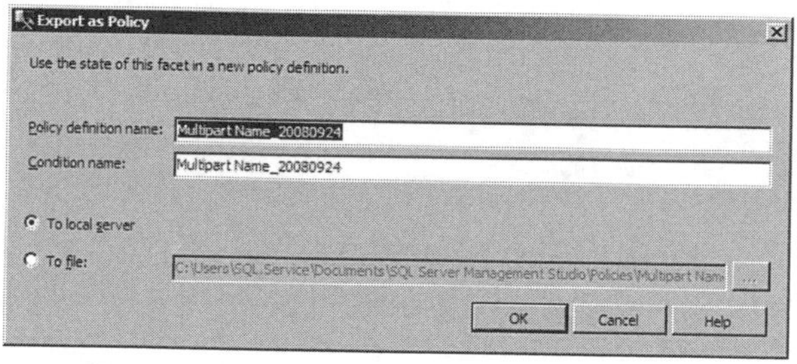

FIGURE 10.5
Exporting a policy based on an existing object.

Creating a Category

After you have created a policy, it should be categorized. Categorization allows you to group policies into administrative or logical units, and then allow database objects to subscribe to specific categories. It is worth mentioning that server objects can't subscribe to policies.

To create a category, click on the Description page in the Create New Policy Dialog box. Policies can be placed in the default category, or a specific category, or you can create a new category. Specifying a category is illustrated in Figure 10.6.

You can also create categories by right clicking on Policy Management and selecting Manage Categories.

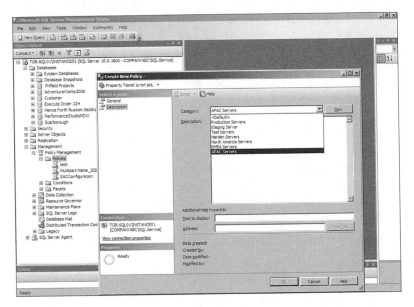

FIGURE 10.6
The Category Selection dialog.

If you choose to create a new category, click on the New button. This will present a dialog that allows you to name the category. By default this policy will be parked in the new category.

You can also select which category you want policies to belong to by selecting a specific category in the drop-down box. After you have categorized your policies, you can select which categories you want your database to subscribe to. Right-click on the Policy Management folder and select Manage Categories. The Manage Policy Categories dialog box (illustrated in Figure 10.7) will appear. Check the categories to which you want all databases on your server to subscribe, and deselect the ones that you do not want your server database to be subscribed to by default.

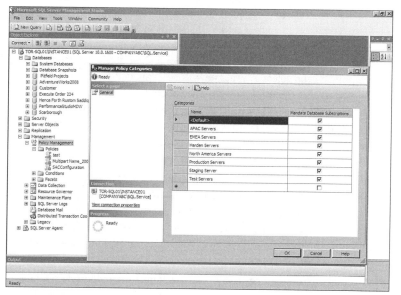

FIGURE 10.7
The Manage Policy Categories dialog box.

Other than the default category, DBAs can select which category (and policies belonging to that category) they want their databases to subscribe to. For
example, if you have third-party software that does not follow your naming
standards, you should ensure that the policies that enforce your naming standards are not in the default category. Then selectively have each of your user
databases on your server subscribe to these database.

Evaluating Policies

After you have created an organization's policies and categories, you will
want to evaluate them to determine which of your servers and databases are
out of compliance. There are three management points that can be leveraged
in order to evaluate policies.

- For the first alternative, right-click on a server, server object, database,
  or database object in SQL Server Management Studio 2008, and select
  Policies and then Evaluate.

- For the second alternative, expand the Management Folder, expand
  Policy Management, right-click on Policies, and select Evaluate. It is
  also possible to select an individual policy, in the Policy folder, right-
  click on it, and select Evaluate.

■ Finally, the preferred way to evaluate all of your servers, or a group of your servers, is to connect to a SQL Server in SQL Server Management Studio 2008 and select View Registered Servers, and then select a Central Management Server If you select a Central Management Server, the policies you select to evaluate will be evaluated on all SQL Servers defined on that Central Management Server, for example, all member servers in all Server Groups. If you select a Server Group, all member servers in that Server Group will be evaluated. To evaluate the policies, you will need to right-click on the Central Management Server, or Server Group, or even Member Server and select Evaluate Policies.

When you right click on the Central Management Server or Server Group, and select Evaluate Polices you will be presented with a dialog which prompts you for a Source, with a Choose Source prompt. For select source enter the server name into which you have imported your policies, or browse to a file share. Then highlight all the policies you want to import and click on the close button to close the dialog.

After the policies are imported, you can select the individual policies you want to run and click Evaluate. The policies will be evaluated on the member servers and the results will be displayed in the Evaluation Results pane, as illustrated in Figure 10.8.

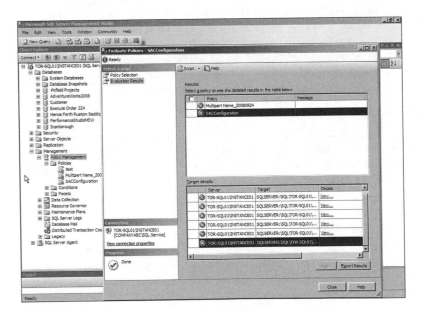

FIGURE 10.8
The Evaluation Results pane.

The Evaluation Results pane will display servers where a policy has failed. You will notice that in the target details there is a View hyperlink, which will allow you to browse to get more details on why the individual target server failed compliance to the policy you evaluated.

Importing and Exporting Policies

There may be situations when a DBA wants to export one or many policies with their conditions from one or many SQL Server systems and import them to another SQL Server instance or system. Fortunately, this can be easily done with an export and import wizard as the policies fully integrate with XML files.

Follow these steps to export a policy with SQL Server Management Studio:

1. In Object Explorer, expand the Management folder, expand the Policy Management Folder, and then click on Policies.

2. Right-click a desired policy to export and then click Export Policy.

3. In the Export Policy dialog box, specify a name and path for the policy and click Save.

Importing a policy from an XML file is just as simple. Follow these steps to import a policy with SQL Server Management Studio:

1. In Object Explorer, expand the Management folder, expand the Policy Management Folder, and then select Policies.

2. Right-click on the Policy Folder and click Import.

3. The import screen has three options to be aware of:

   a. First, provide the path to the file to import.

   b. Second, enable the option to Replace Duplicate Items When Imported.

   c. Finally, in the Policy State drop-down box, specify the state of the policy being imported. The options include Preserve Policy State on Import, Enable All Policies on Import, and Disable All Policies on Import.

Sample Templates and Real-World Examples

The following sections illustrate the sample policy templates included with SQL Server 2008 and real world examples for using Policy Based Management.

Sample Policy Templates

SQL Server 2008 includes a plethora of predefined sample policies, which can be leveraged by importing them into a SQL Server 2008 system. The policies available for import are located in the default installation drive at `C:\Program Files\Microsoft SQL Server\100\Tools\Policies`. As mentioned earlier, import the desired policies by right-clicking the Policies node and selecting Import. The sample templates are categorized by SQL Server feature such as Database Engine, Reporting Services, and Analysis Services.

Recovery Models

Recovery models determine how SQL Server uses the transaction log. On OLTP systems, the most appropriate recovery model is generally the Full Recovery model. For OLAP systems the most appropriate recovery model is generally the simple recovery model. For most development environments the most appropriate recovery model is also the simple recovery model.

For mission critical databases, or databases where point in time recovery is important, having a transaction logged backed up every five minutes may be required. Policy Based Management can be used to determine if the appropriate recovery model is in place for each user database for each server type. Central Management Servers could be created for each server type and a policy can be created to ensure that the appropriate recovery model is in place.

Surface Area Configuration

SQL Server 2005 shipped with the SQL Server Surface Area Configuration tool (SAC). This tool allowed you to enable or disable various components and services on individual SQL 2005 Servers. This feature was deprecated in SQL Server 2008, as the Microsoft team felt that the better way to handle these configuration tasks was through Policy Based Management.

If you want to implement the Surface Area Configuration feature in SQL Server 2008 to configure components and services, import the following policies:

- `Surface Area Configuration for Database Engine 2005 and 2000 Features.xml`
- `Surface Area Configuration for Database Engine 2008 Features.xml`
- `Surface Area Configuration for Service Broker Endpoints.xml`
- `Surface Area Configuration for SOAP Endpoints.xml`

SQL Server Health Checks

One of the SQL Server Support Engineers has blogged on how to do server health checks using PBM. You can access his blog using this URL. http://blogs.msdn.com/bartd/archive/2008/09/11/defining-complex-server-health-policies-in-sql-2008.aspx

The main part of the SQL Server health check revolves around ensuring the disk response times are less than 100 ms. The Policy uses ExecuteSQL to query the DMV sys.dm_io_virtual_file_stats to ensure that the disk response time is within this limit. You can extend this policy to query other DMVs for other health checks, for example the use of excessive parallelism or checking to ensure that cumulative wait stats have not exceeded predefined boundaries.

Object Naming conventions

Your company may have standards for naming objects. For example, stored procedures must start with the prefix usp, tables must start with the prefix tbl, and functions must start with the prefix ufnc. Policy based management can be used to ensure that all objects are compliant with this policy. This policy can be implemented on change, which will prevent the creation of such noncompliant objects.

Best Practices

You can implement policies which check for best practices. For example, databases can be configured with the auto-close and auto-shrink options. Although these options have their place on production systems, they are not recommended as the auto-close option will cause a time delay while the database is opened by a connection trying to access it. This can lead to timeouts. The auto-shrink option can lead to fragmentation and is in general not recommended. A policy can check for these settings and other settings to ensure that all your databases are following best practices.

Summary

Policy Based Management is a new component in SQL Server 2008 that allows you to manage your SQL 2000, 2005, and 2008 servers by creating policies that can be used to enforce compliance to best practices, or to report on out-of-compliance servers. It provides a highly granular, flexible, and extensible toolset that allows you to manage all aspects of your SQL Server. Properly used, it is a great tool to enforce standardization in your environment and to ease the management burden.

Best Practices

- When deploying Policy Based Management in your environment, be very careful about using On Change Prevent. For example, a policy that prevents stored procedure creation with the sp_ prefix will prevent the enabling of replication on a SQL Server.

- When you create a policy that you want enforced on all user databases, place this policy in the default category and it will be subscribed to all databases. Otherwise, you will need to manually subscribe all databases to the categories that contain the policies you want enforced.

- Make use of multiple Configuration Servers or Server Groups to group your SQL Servers according to logical groupings on which you want to group your policies.

- Importing policies into centralized SQL Server 2008 servers makes it easier to deploy groups of policies against groups of servers using Central Management Servers, for example, to store data warehouse policies on Server A. Use this server as a source when selecting policies to evaluate against your data warehouse servers registered in the Data Warehousing Central Management Server.

- You may find that your environment may contain 3rd party user applications/databases which are not in compliance with the policies you have created for your enterprise. Policy Based Management uses the opt in metaphor were all policies are enforced by default. For servers you do not wish the policy to be enforced on you will need tag the database, perhaps with an extended property or a specially named table which the server exception category or the target will detect and exempt that server or database from the policy.

- Use the ExecuteWSQL task to issue WMI queries to extend conditions and policies beyond the SQL Server environment, for example, to check what other services may be running on a server hosting SQL Server.

CHAPTER 11

Encrypting SQL Server Data and Communications

The data stored in Microsoft SQL Server 2008 can be both valuable and confidential. The information stored in databases in SQL Server could be medical histories, income data, or company trade secrets. This information needs to be protected against unauthorized access. In many cases, government and industry regulations require that this data be stored in an encrypted format.

Many of the controls presented in this book have been *access* controls—that is, controls that determine who has authorization to access what. A determined hacker can circumvent these controls through various means, such as sniffing network traffic, going dumpster diving for backup tapes, or making inference attacks.

A more sophisticated approach to data protection is to use an in-depth defense strategy, where there are multiple layers of defense. If a hacker breaches one layer, other layers underneath provide protection. In addition to the access-based controls, encryption provides another layer of protection.

Ultimately, there isn't just one encryption technology included with SQL Server 2008 or Windows Server 2008 that will provide end-to-end encryption of a SQL Server implementation from a holistic perspective. However, by combining the encryption technologies included with SQL Server 2008 and Windows Server 2008, it is possible to achieve the goal of end-to-end encryption.

This chapter shows how to encrypt data in the database, at the disk level, and over the wire to prevent a hacker from obtaining valuable data.

What's New for Encryption with SQL Server 2008?

SQL Server 2008 introduces new features and functionality when it comes to encrypting SQL Server data. Moreover, when running SQL Server 2008 on Windows Server 2008, organizations can also reap additional benefits. The new encryption elements associated with SQL Server 2008 and Windows Server 2008 consist of

- **Transparent Data Encryption**—Encryption can be enabled on an entire database, which includes data files and log files without the need for application changes.

- **Extensible Key Management**—Using a newly introduced interface driver, encryption key management and storage can be handled by external devices such as a Hardware Security Module (HSM). The HSM performs encryption and decryption of keys, resulting in heightened security of key management and key storage utilized by the encryption infrastructure.

- **BitLocker**—BitLocker can be leveraged to encrypt the volumes associated with the SQL Server system. This can be achieved when running any version of the latest Windows Server 2008 operating system.

Encryption in SQL

The confidentiality of the data stored in your SQL Server system or transmitted between the server and the client application can be compromised. A hacker can eavesdrop on communications between the client and server, as shown in Figure 11.1. The hacker might also obtain a database file or a backup media of the database.

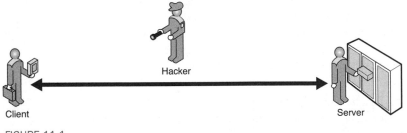

FIGURE 11.1
Unprotected client/server traffic.

To protect against these potential attacks, SQL Server 2008 allows you, as database administrator, to encrypt the data in the database and the network communications. Encryption allows you to protect the confidentiality of data during storage and transmission, as shown in Figure 11.2.

Hacker

Client

Server

FIGURE 11.2
Encrypted client/server traffic.

Encryption does not prevent an attacker from capturing the data. Rather, it prevents the attacker from understanding what that data means. For example, if confidential salary information is stored in a database, it is open to potential discovery by a hacker. If the hacker can capture the value 100000, it is reasonably clear what the salary is. Suppose, instead, the hacker captures this value:

```
0x00057978740EBC4882D182DE0BC8943401000000B0D2747903102AD4696BC980
217970DAD5B4C38314DB45D065079C9B43F922D0A04517C38EC8CA9B5CD19702DE
E0A042
```

This binary string makes it much more difficult to understand what the salary figure is. In this case, it is the encrypted version of the value 100000.

This chapter shows how to encrypt data both while stored in the database and while in transit over the network between the client and server.

In terms of the data stored in the database, there are two main methods to protect it with encryption: either using column encryption (first introduced in SQL Server 2005) or using Transparent Data Encryption (TDE, new in SQL Server 2008). Those two features are independent of each other and quite different in the way they work. We will look into both of them—let's start with column encryption.

Column Encryption

The column encryption feature was first introduced in SQL Server 2005. It is based on a simple principle: You create encryption keys and certificates within the database and use them, through special functions, to encrypt and decrypt your data as it is stored and read from a table column.

Encryption Hierarchy

SQL Server 2008 has an encryption hierarchy to protect the data and the encryption keys. The various levels are

- **Windows level**—The highest level of the hierarchy is the Windows operating system. This level uses Windows Data Protection (DP) API to encrypt and protect the next level.

- **SQL Server level**—This level contains the Service Master Key (SMK), which is protected by the Windows level. The Service Master Key is used to protect the next level.

- **Database level**—This level contains the Database Master Key (DMK) and the remaining keys and certificates. The Database Master Key encrypts and protects the certificates, symmetric keys, and asymmetric keys within the database.

The encryption hierarchy provides a scalable and granular mechanism for protecting the data within the server and databases. It allows for multiple database owners to coexist on the same server without compromising security of other databases.

Service Master Key

The Service Master Key is the root of all encryption within SQL Server 2008. This key is generated during the first time it is needed to encrypt a linked password, credential or database master key.

This key is accessible only by the Windows account used by the SQL Server service.

Database Master Key

The Database Master Key is used to secure the keys and certificates used to encrypt data. This key is manually created for each database.

If you don't want a Database Master Key, you can encrypt the keys and certificates with a password rather than the Database Master Key. This can be a useful alternative to prevent the owner of a database from gaining access to encrypted data in highly secure environments. However, when the key is encrypted with a password instead of the Database Master Key, a weaker algorithm is used.

Keys and Certificates

Asymmetric and symmetric keys are used to encrypt keys, certificates, and data. Each has its own specific uses and pros and cons.

Symmetric keys are relatively straightforward. The keys are used to both encrypt and decrypt. The encryption is relatively fast, so symmetric keys are useful for encrypting large quantities of data. However, symmetric keys need to be shared, and this can make them difficult to use.

Asymmetric keys are composed of a public and private key pair. These pairs of keys are used to both encrypt and decrypt, but with a twist. Each key can decrypt what the other key encrypted, but not its own. Asymmetric encryption is resource intensive, so it is not suitable for encrypting large volumes of data. However, it is uniquely suited for encrypting symmetric keys for the purpose of sharing them.

Certificates are used to vouch for the identity of an entity presenting the public key contained in the certificate. In effect, a *certificate authority (CA)* issues a certificate that presents a public key and an identity that a third party can trust. Certificates can be issued by well-known third-party CAs such as VeriSign, by private CAs on Windows Server 2003 and 2008 servers, or they can be self-signed certificates issued by SQL Server instances.

Third-party certificates are typically expensive, private certificates require additional configuration, and self-signed certificates provide a lower level of protection.

Encryption Algorithms

SQL Server 2008 supports a variety of encryption algorithms. These algorithms are used to secure the data, keys, and certificates.

The algorithms supported by SQL Server 2008 are

- Data Encryption Standard (DES)
- Triple DES
- Rivest Cipher (RC2)
- RC4
- 128-bit RC4
- DESX
- 128-bit Advanced Encryption Standard (AES)
- 192-bit AES
- 256-bit AES

Choosing an algorithm can be a complex undertaking because it requires balancing the strength of the algorithm, the resources required to use the algorithm, and the potential weaknesses of the algorithm.

Although these are all very valid considerations for choosing an algorithm, most organizations are, in reality, not encrypting data at all. Thus, using any of the preceding algorithms is a tremendous improvement in the level of security. Which particular algorithm is chosen matters less than just the fact of using any of them.

In the examples in this book, we used the tried-and-true Triple DES algorithm. It provides a good balance between performance and security.

Securing the Data Storage

Unencrypted data residing in SQL Server, it is vulnerable to being read by a hacker who can elevate his privileges or gain access to backup tapes. To secure the data that is stored in the database, you can encrypt the values to provide an additional layer of security.

Creating a Database for Testing

To facilitate running these examples, these exercises use data from the SQL samples found on Microsoft's sample website. The `customer.txt` file can be downloaded at http://www.codeplex.com/MSFTISProdSamples/ under the Package Samples "Execute SQL Statements in a Loop Sample SS2008." Before starting, you need to create the customer database and import the customer data that is located in the `customer.txt` file.

Note

If the Customer database already exists from previous exercises, delete the database prior to completing the exercises in this chapter.

To create the database, first download the `Customers.txt` file from http://www.codeplex.com/MSFTISProdSamples/ and follow these steps:

1. Open SQL Server Management Studio.
2. Connect to the Database Engine of the SQL Server.
3. Expand the Databases folder in the Object Explorer.
4. In the SQL Server Management Studio, create a new database named Customer.
5. Right-click the Customer database and select Tasks, Import Data.
6. Click Next.
7. Select Flat File Source as the data source.
8. Click the Browse button and select the `Customers.txt` file.
9. Click Open.

10. Check the Column names in the first data row check box.

11. Click Next.

12. Select the Customer database if not selected already and click Next.

13. Click Next to accept tables and views.

14. Click Next to execute immediately and not save the package.

15. Click Finish to run the import.

16. Click Close.

The basic database is now ready for the encryption exercises in this chapter.

Setting Up for Encryption

When the database is created, there is no database master key initially. You need to create this key for each database.

To create a Database Master Key, open a query window and execute the following query:

```
USE Customer;
GO
CREATE MASTER KEY ENCRYPTION BY
        PASSWORD = 'The secret password.';
GO
```

This query prepares the database for encrypting the data. Clearly, the secret password could use some additional complexity.

Note

As stated earlier, the Service Master Key is created when the SQL Server instance is installed, so you do not need to create it manually.

Creating the Encryption Certificate

Now you need to create a certificate to protect the keys that will actually be used to encrypt the data itself.

To create the certificate, execute the following query:

```
USE Customer;
GO
CREATE CERTIFICATE Customer01
        WITH SUBJECT = 'Customer';
GO
```

After creating the certificate, you can create and protect the symmetric key. This key will be used to encrypt the data. Using a symmetric key allows the data to be encrypted rapidly, whereas encrypting it with a certificate provides strong protection.

To create the symmetric key, execute the following query:

```
USE Customer;
GO
CREATE SYMMETRIC KEY YearlyIncome_Key_01
       WITH ALGORITHM = TRIPLE_DES
       ENCRYPTION BY CERTIFICATE Customer01;
GO
```

We chose the Triple DES algorithm because of its security and compatibility.

Encrypting the Data

With the database now prepared, the next step is to encrypt a column of data. In this case, the data to be protected is the YearlyIncome column.

To encrypt the YearlyIncome column, execute the following query:

```
USE [Customer];
GO

ALTER TABLE dbo.Customers
     ADD EncryptedYearlyIncome varbinary(128);
GO

OPEN SYMMETRIC KEY YearlyIncome_Key_01
     DECRYPTION BY CERTIFICATE Customer01;
UPDATE dbo.Customers
SET EncryptedYearlyIncome = EncryptByKey
(Key_GUID('YearlyIncome_Key_01'), YearlyIncome);
CLOSE SYMMETRIC KEY YearlyIncome_Key_01;
GO
```

Note that the query adds a new column named EncryptedYearlyIncome of type varbinary to hold the encrypted values.

> **Note**
>
> The Customers table still retains the original column named YearlyIncome with the unencrypted data. In a real-world situation, you would need to drop the column to protect the data. The query to do this is `ALTER TABLE Customer.dbo.Customers DROP COLUMN YearlyIncome;`.
>
> We did not drop this column in the examples, to allow comparisons and to allow the column to be re-encrypted.

Using Encrypted Data

The encrypted data is protected but can't be used directly. To select the data with no decryption, execute the following query:

```
SELECT EncryptedYearlyIncome
       FROM Customer.dbo.Customers;
GO
```

Rather than a nice set of Yearly Income numbers, the SELECT query returns a list of hexadecimal characters, as shown in Figure 11.3.

This result is good because it means that a hacker would not be able to discern the customer's yearly incomes. However, valid users need a way to see the actual values and cannot use the column of data directly. To actually use the data, you must decrypt it when selecting it.

To select the data with decryption, execute the following query:

```
OPEN SYMMETRIC KEY YearlyIncome_Key_01
     DECRYPTION BY CERTIFICATE Customer01;
GO
SELECT CONVERT(varchar, DecryptByKey(EncryptedYearlyIncome))
       AS 'Decrypted Yearly Income' FROM Customer.dbo.Customers;
CLOSE SYMMETRIC KEY YearlyIncome_Key_01;
GO
```

This query shows the actual values of the Yearly Income in unencrypted form, as shown in Figure 11.4.

The data is now secured while stored in the database and would be protected in backups.

Attacking the Encryption

Although the data is protected against being viewed, a hacker might be able to subvert the control of the data. One way to accomplish this is to replace the encrypted value with another encrypted value. This is referred to as an *inference attack*.

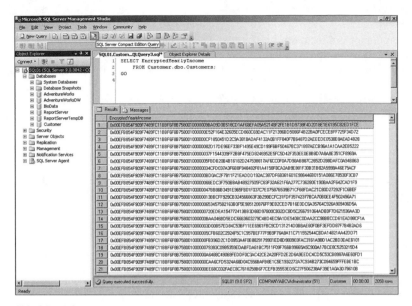

FIGURE 11.3
Encrypted data.

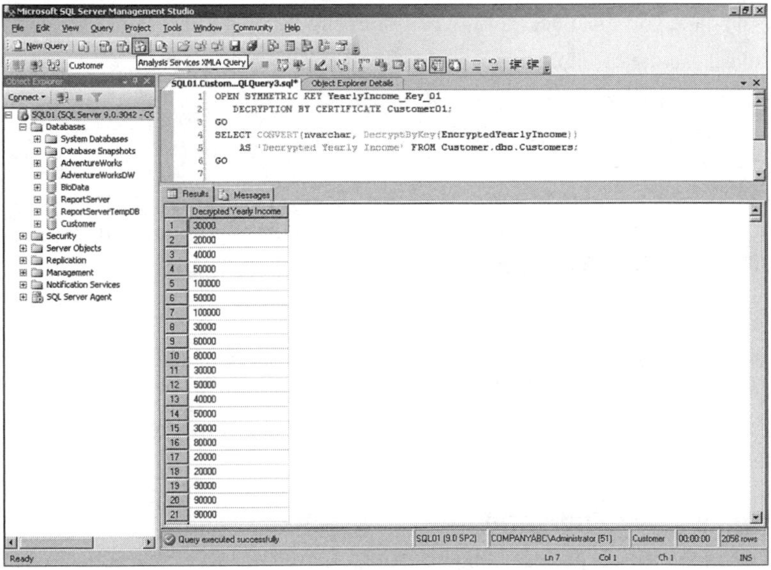

FIGURE 11.4
Decrypted data.

Consider the two rows in the Customer database shown in Table 14.1.

Table 14.1   **View of Two Customer Records**

Name	Occupation	Yearly Income
Craig Dominguez	Management	100,000
Meghan Gomez	Manual	10,000

The Yearly Income values are encrypted, so a hacker who subverts the access controls might be able to gather the information about the rows shown in Table 14.2.

Table 14.2   **Compromised View of Two Customer Records**

Name	Occupation	Yearly Income
Craig Dominguez	Management	Encrypted Value 1
Meghan Gomez	Manual	Encrypted Value 2

Although the hacker cannot determine the yearly income of either customer, he can make some assumptions based on their occupations. Without any prior knowledge, a hacker could safely assume that Mr. Dominguez earns more than Ms. Gomez. Using that basic assumption, the hacker can elevate the yearly income of Ms. Gomez simply by moving the encrypted value from Mr. Dominguez without ever needing to know what the value is. In effect, the hacker can elevate the yearly income to $100,000.

To demonstrate this hack, execute the following query to hack the database:

```
USE Customer;
GO


UPDATE Customer.dbo.Customers
SET EncryptedYearlyIncome =
        (SELECT EncryptedYearlyIncome FROM Customer.dbo.Customers
        WHERE EmailAddress = 'cdominguez@fabrikam.com')
        WHERE EmailAddress = 'mgomez@fabrikam.com';
GO
```

This query copies the Encrypted Value 1 in Table 14.2 over Encrypted Value 2 in the table, in effect replacing Ms. Gomez's income with Mr. Dominguez's income. To verify that the hack was successful, execute the following query:

```
USE Customer;
Go
OPEN SYMMETRIC KEY YearlyIncome_Key_01
```

```
        DECRYPTION BY CERTIFICATE Customer01;
GO
SELECT CONVERT(varchar, DecryptByKey(EncryptedYearlyIncome))
        AS 'Decrypted Yearly Income'
        FROM dbo.Customers where EmailAddress =
     'mgomez@fabrikam.com';
CLOSE SYMMETRIC KEY YearlyIncome_Key_01;
GO
```

The result returned is 100000, indicating that the yearly income for Ms. Gomez was elevated to management-level pay. Good for Ms. Gomez, but bad for the company!

You can foil these types of attacks by using an authenticator when encrypting and decrypting the data.

Using an Authenticator

An *authenticator*, also known as a "salt value" in cryptography, is another column value that is unique to the row that is used in conjunction with the key to secure the data being encrypted. This prevents a hacker from moving an encrypted value between rows.

It is worth mentioning that the Authenticator selected is one that is not likely to change and if it ever does you have lost your ability to decrypt the data.

To encrypt the YearlyIncome column with an authenticator (in this case, the EmailAddress), execute the following query:

```
USE Customer;
GO
OPEN SYMMETRIC KEY YearlyIncome_Key_01
        DECRYPTION BY CERTIFICATE Customer01;
UPDATE dbo.Customers
        SET EncryptedYearlyIncome = EncryptByKey(Key_GUID
                ('YearlyIncome_Key_01'),
                YearlyIncome, 1, convert (varbinary, EmailAddress));
CLOSE SYMMETRIC KEY YearlyIncome_Key_01;
GO
```

Note that the preceding query overwrites the data in the EncryptedYearlyIncome column with freshly encrypted data from the YearlyIncome column.

Verify that the EncryptedYearlyIncome column is still encrypted. To view the results, execute the following query:

```
USE Customer;
GO
SELECT EncryptedYearlyIncome AS 'Encrypted Yearly Income'
      FROM dbo.Customers;
GO
```

The values should be displayed as long hexadecimal numbers, similar to those shown in Figure 11.3. The next step is to see whether the hacker substitution will succeed. Execute the hack again using the following query:

```
USE Customer;
GO

UPDATE Customer.dbo.Customers
SET EncryptedYearlyIncome =
      (SELECT EncryptedYearlyIncome FROM Customer.dbo.Customers
      WHERE EmailAddress = 'cdominguez@fabrikam.com')
      WHERE EmailAddress = 'mgomez@fabrikam.com';
GO
```

The preceding query is the same query that was executed before and successfully hacked the database. Note that the value is still replaced. The question is whether the value will be accepted by the application or the hack will be foiled.

To verify that the hacker was foiled, execute the following query:

```
USE Customer;
GO
OPEN SYMMETRIC KEY YearlyIncome_Key_01
    DECRYPTION BY CERTIFICATE Customer01;
GO
SELECT CONVERT(nvarchar, DecryptByKey(EncryptedYearlyIncome))
      AS 'Decrypted Yearly Income'
      FROM dbo.Customers where EmailAddress =
'mgomez@fabrikam.com';
CLOSE SYMMETRIC KEY YearlyIncome_Key_01;
GO
```

Now the decrypted Yearly Income value displays NULL, indicating that the decryption failed and the hacker was not successful in replacing Ms. Gomez's yearly income.

To verify that an authorized user can still access the data correctly, execute the following query:

```
USE Customer;
GO
OPEN SYMMETRIC KEY YearlyIncome_Key_01
     DECRYPTION BY CERTIFICATE Customer01;
GO
SELECT CONVERT(varchar, DecryptByKey(EncryptedYearlyIncome, 1,
       convert (varbinary, EmailAddress)))
       AS 'Decrypted Yearly Income'
       FROM dbo.Customers;
CLOSE SYMMETRIC KEY YearlyIncome_Key_01;
GO
```

The Yearly Income values should be displayed for all, but Ms. Gomez.

Backing Up the Keys

The service master keys and database keys are critical values that need to be preserved. Losing these keys can result in the loss of any data that is encrypted. Backing up the service master and database master keys allows you to recover the data in case of problems.

To back up the Service Master Key, execute the following query:

```
BACKUP SERVICE MASTER KEY
TO FILE = 'c:\ServiceMasterKeyBackup.dat'
     ENCRYPTION BY PASSWORD = 'SecretPassword'; GO
```

To back up the Database Master Key, execute the following query for the Customer database:

```
USE Customer;
GO
BACKUP MASTER KEY
TO FILE = 'c:\CustomerDatabaseMasterKeyBackup.dat'
     ENCRYPTION BY PASSWORD = 'SecretPassword';GO
```

You repeat this query for each database master key that you need to back up.

You should store both key backup files offsite in case of server problems. In the event of a problem with the keys, the Service Master Key and Database Master Key can be restored from the files.

Extensible Key Management

SQL Server 2008 adds a new functionality called Extensible Key Management (EKM) that allows you to store your encryption keys outside of the Database Engine, using Hardware Security Modules (HSM). It allows you to store the encryption keys separately from the data being encrypted and provides additional level of security. This functionality is available only in the Enterprise and Developer editions of SQL Server 2008.

EKM works by allowing integration of SQL Server data encryption with third-party solutions for key generation, key storage, key management, and hardware acceleration of the encryption process. The main part of this solution is the cryptographic provider DLL that allows access from SQL Server to the Hardware Security Module. This DLL is provided by the vendor of your HSM and is written using a common interface allowing SQL Server to access the key stored on the HSM. This DLL must be signed by a trusted source in order to be accepted by SQL Server engine.

Enabling EKM

In order to use the EKM you need to follow this procedure.

First, you must enable the use of EKM providers on the database instance level by changing the configuration option 'EKM provider enabled':

```
sp_configure 'show advanced', 1
GO
RECONFIGURE
GO
sp_configure 'EKM provider enabled', 1
GO
RECONFIGURE
GO
```

This will allow you to create and use the cryptographic providers in SQL Server.

Creating the Cryptographic Provider

Next, you need to create the cryptographic provider using the DLL obtained from your HSM vendor. This DLL will provide SQL Server with access to the encryption keys stored on the HSM.

```
CREATE CRYPTOGRAPHIC PROVIDER MyHSM
FROM FILE='C:\MyHSM\HSMProvider.dll'
GO
```

Please note that this example is fictional and assumes that you have the provider DLL file stored in file C:\MyHSM\HSMProvider.dll.

Creating the Credential to Access the HSM

Most of the HSMs require additional authentication in order to access the keys stored on them. Depending on your HSM and cryptographic provider, it may or may not support basic authentication using username and password. If the basic authentication is supported, you should create the credential for the login that will be using the key stored in the HSM. Otherwise, the authentication to the HSM must be performed independently of SQL Server.

To create a credential that allows access to the keys stored on the HSM created in the previous step and assign it to SQL Server login Bob, you would use the following code:

```
CREATE CREDENTIAL CredentialForMyHSM
WITH IDENTITY='HSMUser',
SECRET='StrongP@ssw0rd'
FOR CRYPTOGRAPHIC PROVIDER MyHSM;
GO
ALTER LOGIN Bob
ADD CREDENTIAL CredentialForMyHSM;
GO
```

Creating the Encryption Key with EKM

After the preceding steps are completed, you can use your HSM to create and store the encryption keys that you want to use to encrypt the data in the database engine.

To create a symmetric key based on the existing encryption key stored on your HSM, you can use the following syntax:

```
CREATE SYMMETRIC KEY MyEKMKey
AUTHORIZATION Bob
FROM PROVIDER MyHSM
WITH PROVIDER_KEY_NAME='MyHSMKey',
CREATION_DISPOSITION=OPEN_EXISTING;
GO
```

This would allow you to use the key for data encryption within SQL Server. After the key is created and mapped to a key stored on the HSM, the usage of the encryption functions is analogous to the one described in the previous section of this chapter.

Advantages of EKM

Storing of encryption keys outside of the database engine and on the HSM provides several security benefits, namely:

- Encryption keys stored independently if the data encrypted with them
- Additional authorization checks for key retrieval
- Easier and more flexible key management for key generation, distribution, backup, recovery and disposal
- Higher performance in case of the HSM supporting hardware encryption and decryption

> **Note**
>
> Configuring EKM is vendor specific; therefore, each HSM will have different setup instructions to follow when configuring.

Transparent Data Encryption

Transparent Data Encryption (TDE) is a new feature, available in SQL Server 2008 Enterprise and Developer editions. It allows you to encrypt and protect the data in your database files, without having to change anything in your application and data access code (hence the name transparent). Using Transparent Data Encryption will allow you to meet regulatory requirements of having your data encrypted "at rest" with a minimal administrative effort. It can also protect your data in case the media containing your database files or database backup is lost or stolen.

> **Note**
>
> When TDE is implemented, the entire database is encrypted; however, TDE does not provide encryption across communication channels. In addition, the backups associated with the database are also encrypted.

Mode of Operation

Transparent Data Encryption works by encrypting data pages and log pages stored on disk. Encryption and decryption happens during I/O operations— data is encrypted as it is written to disk and decrypted as it is read from disk into memory. The performance overhead of TDE is relatively small as the data is only encrypted during I/O operations and remains decrypted while in memory. When you enable TDE, the entire database, including all data file and log files, is encrypted on disk. Such an encrypted database cannot be restored or attached to a different server without access to the server certificate from the original server.

> **Note**
>
> Data stored using FILESTREAM storage is not encrypted with TDE. If you use FILESTREAM data, you need to encrypt it separately, for instance using NTFS encryption.

Encryption Hierarchy

As with column encryption, there is an encryption hierarchy that protects the keys used by Transparent Data Encryption. The hierarchy is slightly different from the one used by the column encryption, but it serves the same purpose: to protect the key used for direct data encryption with some other, higher-level keys. In case of Transparent Data Encryption, the levels are

- **Windows level**—The highest level of the hierarchy is the Windows operating system. This level uses the Windows DP API to encrypt and protect the next level.

- **SQL Server level**—This level contains the Service Master Key (SMK), which is protected by the Windows level. The Service Master Key is used to protect the next level.

- **Master database level**—This level contains the Database Master Key (DMK) in the master database, which is protected by the Service Master Key. It also contains a server certificate, or asymmetric key stored in the master database and encrypted with DMK. The server certificate or asymmetric key is used to protect the Database Encryption Key on the next level.

- **Database level**—This level contains the Database Encryption Key (DEK) used by the server to encrypt that particular database with TDE.

Enabling Transparent Data Encryption

The following example illustrates the steps required to enable TDE on the sample database AdventureWorks2008. To be able to use TDE, you need to create all the necessary encryption keys on all the appropriate levels before you enable TDE for your database.

Creating a Database Master Key in the Master Database

The first key we need to create is Database Master Key in the master database. In some scenarios, you might have already created it (there can be only one DMK per database). Otherwise, you need to create it by running code similar to this:

```
USE master;
GO
CREATE MASTER KEY ENCRYPTION BY
    PASSWORD = 'MakeSureYouUseAStr0ngP@ssw0rd';
GO
```

Note

As indicated in this example, it is a best practice to select a strong password when creating the master key for encryption.

Creating Server Certificate in the Master Database

The next step is to create a server certificate or asymmetric key in the master database. From a TDE perspective, it does not matter if you choose to create a certificate or an asymmetric key—both are functionally equivalent and their respective private keys are encrypted by the Database Master Key.

You can create a server certificate using the following code:

```
USE master;
GO
CREATE CERTIFICATE ServerCert WITH
    SUBJECT = 'Certificate for use with TDE';
GO
```

Note

After you create the server certificate or asymmetric key, you should immediately take a backup of it, containing the private key. This backup copy of the key will be necessary in order to restore the encrypted databases in cases when you are restoring to another server or when the original key is no longer available for any reason. Make sure to protect the backup file containing the private key by using a strong password and storing it on an offline media.

Creating a Database Encryption Key

Next step is to create the Database Encryption Key (DEK) in the database you plan to use TDE on. This key is protected by the server certificate or asymmetric key and cannot be opened without it. Under normal operation, this ensures that the database can only be opened (and decrypted) by the server instance that "owns" the database.

You can create the Database Encryption Key using the following code:

```
USE AdventureWorks2008;
GO
CREATE DATABASE ENCRYPTION KEY
WITH ALGORITHM = AES_256
ENCRYPTION BY SERVER CERTIFICATE ServerCert;
GO
```

While creating your Database Encryption Key, you should consider the choice of the encryption algorithm used. For performance and security reasons, only certain symmetric algorithms are available for use with TDE:

- Triple DES
- 128-bit AES
- 192-bit AES
- 256-bit AES

From those, the best choice in terms of protection provided is Advanced Encryption Standard (AES) in its 256-bit form, but it is also the one that requires most processing power during encryption.

Enabling Transparent Database Encryption for the Database

After you have created the necessary encryption key hierarchy, you are ready to enable TDE on your database. To enable it, just run the following code:

```
USE master;
GO
ALTER DATABASE AdventureWorks2008
SET ENCRYPTION ON;
GO
```

Enabling TDE is a metadata operation and happens very quickly. The actual encryption process takes place in the background and, depending on the size of your database and the load on the server, can take several hours to finish. You can check the status of TDE on your database by querying the sys.dm_database_encryption_keys DMV:

```
SELECT *
FROM sys.dm_database_encryption_keys
```

```
WHERE database_id = DB_ID('AdventureWorks2008');
GO
```

The encryption_state column of that DMV shows you the status of TDE for that particular database. Possible values are:

- 0—No database encryption key present, no encryption
- 1—Unencrypted
- 2—Encryption in progress
- 3—Encrypted
- 4—Key change in progress
- 5—Decryption in progress

> **Note**
>
> After you enable TDE for any database on the SQL Server instance, the tempdb database is encrypted as well, in order to protect data stored in any temporary objects. This can have a performance impact on other databases and applications running on the same instance.

After the backup thread finishes encrypting your database, both data files and log files are fully encrypted. Any database, file, or log backups you take from this point forward will contain encrypted data, and such backups can only be restored if you have access to the server certificate protecting the Database Encryption Key.

Disabling Transparent Database Encryption for the Database

Should you ever decide that you no longer want your database to use TDE, disabling it is as simple as enabling:

```
USE master;
GO
ALTER DATABASE AdventureWorks2008
SET ENCRYPTION OFF;
GO
```

As with enabling, when you disable TDE, the actual decryption process takes place in the background and can take a considerable amount of time to finish. Again, you can check the status of this process by querying the sys.dm_database_encryption_keys DMV.

Securing Connections

When you use cell-level or TDE encryption, the data is encrypted while in the database. However, when the client selects the data, it is unencrypted. The data needs to be protected while being transmitted as well as while being stored. SQL Server 2008 can use SSL certificate-based encryption to encrypt all communications between the client and server.

Hacking the Transmission

To understand the problem, you can use Network Monitor tools for this example to view the contents of the network traffic between the SQL Server and client. This tool is available for Windows Server 2008 as an out-of-band download directly from Microsoft, http://www.microsoft.com/downloads/results.aspx?pocId=&freetext=network%20monitor%203&DisplayLang=en. The examples in this section assume that the SQL Server Workstation Components are installed on the client.

Start the Network Monitor on the server and then execute the following query from SQL Server Management Studio on the client:

```
USE Customer;
Go
OPEN SYMMETRIC KEY YearlyIncome_Key_01
     DECRYPTION BY CERTIFICATE Customer01;
GO
SELECT FirstName, LastName, BirthDate,
       CONVERT(nvarchar, DecryptByKey(EncryptedYearlyIncome, 1,
       convert (varbinary, EmailAddress)))
       AS 'Decrypted Yearly Income'
       FROM dbo.Customers where EmailAddress =
'cdominguez@fabrikam.com';
GO
```

The query returns the information shown in Table 14.3.

Table 14.3 **Query Results**

Decrypted FirstName	LastName	BirthDate	Yearly Income
Craig	Dominguez	7/20/1970	100000

This result is clearly confidential information that should be protected from the prying eyes of a hacker. It even includes the yearly income information that was encrypted in the Customer database to prevent unauthorized disclosure.

Figure 11.5 shows the results of the network capture of the preceding query. The highlighted frame in the figure contains the data sent from SQL Server (TOR-SQL01) to the client (172.16.2.1). The circled section of the figure shows the information that a hacker was able to capture simply by listening in on the network transmission. The information includes the name, birth date, and yearly income. Although the information is not formatted in a pretty manner, it is all there for the hacker to see.

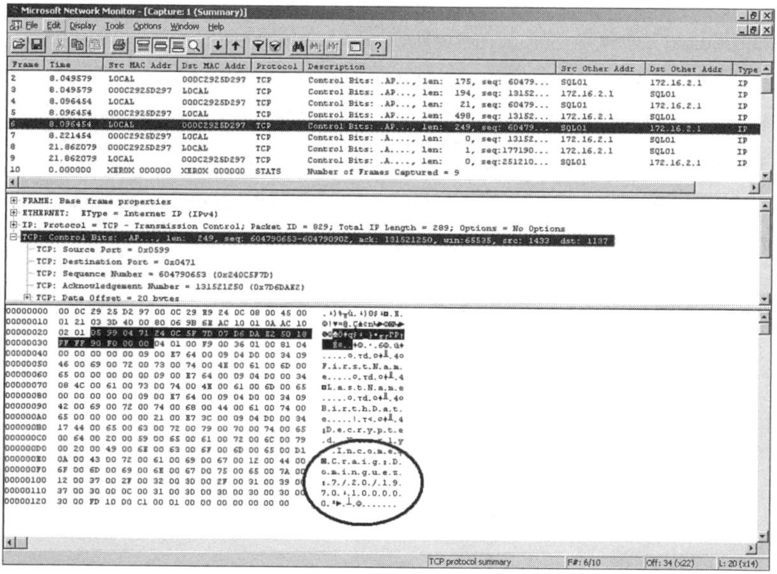

FIGURE 11.5
Hacked data transmission.

Most troubling is the fact that the information that was encrypted in the database is transmitted unencrypted over the wire. The reason is that the query decrypts the information at the server side prior to transmission. The bottom line is that encrypting the columns in the database does nothing to protect the data while it is being transmitted over the network.

To protect data transmissions, you need to encrypt the connections.

Configuring Server-Initiated Encryption

SQL Server 2008 can be configured to require SSL-based encryption. Configuring the ForceEncryption setting of SQL Server to Yes forces all client/server communications to be encrypted. By default, the ForceEncryption setting is set to No, so SQL Server client/server communications are not protected.

Note

The SQL Server 2008 login process is always encrypted, regardless of the ForceEncryption setting of the server. This ensures that login and password combinations are not compromised.

To configure the server to require encrypted connections, follow these steps:

1. Launch the SQL Server Configuration Manager.
2. Expand the SQL Server Network Configuration.
3. Right-click on Protocols for a SQL Server instance and select Properties.
4. On the Flags tab, change the ForceEncryption drop-down to Yes.
5. Click OK to save the setting.
6. Click OK on the dialog box indicating the service needs to be restarted.
7. Select the SQL Server Services folder.
8. Select the SQL Server (MSSQLSERVER) service.
9. Restart the SQL Server service.

The connections to your SQL Server 2008 server are now encrypted.

Hacking the Transmission: The Sequel

Now that the server has been configured to force encryption of the network transmissions, the hacker should not be able to see the contents of the network transmissions.

To verify that the transmissions are protected, start the Network Monitor on the server and then execute the following query from the SQL Server Management Studio on the client:

```
USE Customer;
Go
OPEN SYMMETRIC KEY YearlyIncome_Key_01
        DECRYPTION BY CERTIFICATE Customer01;
GO
SELECT FirstName, LastName, BirthDate,
        CONVERT(nvarchar, DecryptByKey(EncryptedYearlyIncome, 1,
        convert (varbinary, EmailAddress)))
        AS 'Decrypted Yearly Income'
        FROM dbo.Customers where EmailAddress =
'cdominguez@fabrikam.com';
GO
```

Figure 11.6 shows the results of the network capture of the preceding query. The highlighted frame in the figure is the frame that contains the data sent from SQL Server (SQL01) to the client (172.16.2.1). The circled section of the figure shows the information that a hacker was able to capture. The information is now a jumble of strange characters and protected from the hacker's prying eyes.

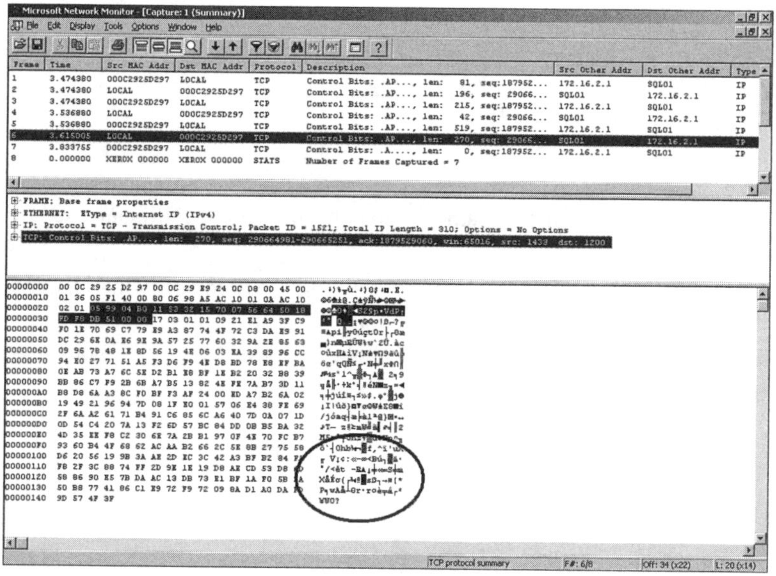

FIGURE 11.6
Encrypted data transmission.

Notice that the frames are a bit different. The encrypted frame length is 270 versus 249 for the unencrypted frame. Encryption carries some overhead both in the size of the frames and in the effort that the server and client have to make in processing the encryption.

Using Certificates

The encryption used until now in the chapter has been based on self-signed certificates. These certificates are generated when SQL Server does not have a certificate provisioned.

Self-signed certificates are vulnerable to certain attacks, most critically man-in-the-middle attacks. This means that without an independent verification of the identity of the SQL Server, there is no way to be sure that the communication is not really between a nefarious third party posing as the server to the client. Note that the communication is encrypted, as shown in Figure 11.7, but the encryption is between the hacker and the client and server.

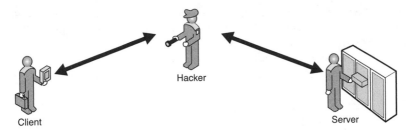

FIGURE 11.7
Man-in-the-middle attack.

Neither the client nor the server detects the ruse because there is no independent third-party certificate authority to confirm that the certificate used to encrypt the transmission is trusted.

This attack is thwarted by using a third-party certificate to verify the identity of the SQL Server. When the hacker attempts to insert himself between the client and server, as shown in Figure 11.8, the attack is detected by both the client and server.

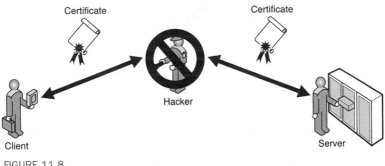

FIGURE 11.8
Third-party certificate protection.

The following sections detail how to configure a certificate server, and to provision and configure certificates for SQL Server 2008.

Setting Up the Certificate Server

The first step when implementing certificates is to request a certificate from a trusted certificate authority. The certificate authority can be a third-party vendor such as VeriSign, or it can be an internal Active Directory or standalone CA residing on the corporate Windows infrastructure. For this example, the first step will include setting up a certificate server on a Windows Server 2008 system, so that it can issue certificates for the SQL Server infrastructure.

The example uses Microsoft Certificate Services, but a third-party CA and certificates could be used as well. If you already have a certificate or a certificate server within your infrastructure, proceed to the next step, "Provisioning a Server Certificate."

The TOR-DC01.companyabc.com server was chosen for this example. The procedure assumes that the Windows 2008 operating system has been installed and that the TOR-DC01 server has joined the companyabc.com domain.

Install the Certificate Services role on the TOR-SQL01 server using the following steps:

1. Launch Server Manager.
2. In the Roles Summary pane, select Add Roles to start the wizard.
3. Click Next.
4. Select Active Directory Certificate Services, and click Next.
5. Click Next.
6. Check the Certification Authority Web Enrollment.
7. A window opens with an additional set of role services and features required to support web enrollment. Click Add Required Role Services to add these prerequisites.
8. Click Next.
9. Select Enterprise or Standalone option to create a stand-alone CA, and click Next.

Note

The Enterprise option should be used if the server is part of a domain and there is need to leverage the Directory Services for issuing and managing certificates. The Standalone option is used when Directory Services will not issue and manage certificates.

---

10. Leave the Root CA option selected, and click Next.
11. Leave the Create a New Private Key option selected, and click Next.
12. Click Next to accept the cryptography options for the CA.
13. Click Next to accept the CA name.
14. Click Next to accept the default validity period of five years.
15. Click Next to accept the default directories.
16. Click Next to accept the default web server role services.

17. Click Install to install the roles.

18. When the installation finishes, click Close to close the wizard.

Note

In order to complete certificate enrollments, the Website hosting the CA must be configured to use HTTPs authentication. This can be achieved on the default website in Internet Information Services by first adding HTTPs as a secure binding and then requiring SSL in the SSL settings.

This certificate server will be used on each of the components for the SQL Server infrastructure.

Provisioning a Server Certificate

The next step in protecting the data transmissions with a third-party certificate is to provision the certificate, which entails obtaining and installing a certificate form a third-party vendor or an internal Windows Certificate Authority that was created in the previous steps. The certificate requirements for SQL Server 2008 SSL encryption are as follows?

- The certificate must be in the local computer certificate store or the current user certificate store.

- The current system time must be in the certificate valid range of dates.

- The certificate must be meant for server authentication; that is, the Enhanced Key Usage property of the certificate specifies Server Authentication (1.3.6.1.5.5.7.3.1).

- The common name (CN) must be the same as the fully qualified domain name (FQDN) of the server computer.

To provision (install) a certificate on the server from a Windows certificate authority, follow these steps:

1. Launch Microsoft Internet Explorer on the SQL Server system, in this sample Tor-SQL01.

2. Enter the uniform resource locator (URL) for the Certification Authority Web Enrollment, which in this example is `https://tor-dc01.companyabc.com/certsrv`.

3. Click Request a Certificate to request a new certificate.

4. Click Advanced Certificate Request to request a certificate.

5. Click Create and Submit a Request to This CA.

> **Note**
>
> You might need to add the site to the trusted sites in Internet Explorer to allow ActiveX controls to run.

6. Enter the fully qualified domain name of the computer in the Name field, which, in this example, is `tor-sql01.companyabc.com`.

> **Note**
>
> The name must match the FQDN name of the computer exactly or the certificate will fail later on.

7. Enter email, company, department, city, state, and country.
8. Select Server for the type of certificate needed.
9. Check the Mark Keys as Exportable option.
10. Enter the FQDN for the friendly name, in this example `tor-sql01.companyabc.com`.
11. The request should look like the example shown in Figure 11.9. Click Submit to complete the request.

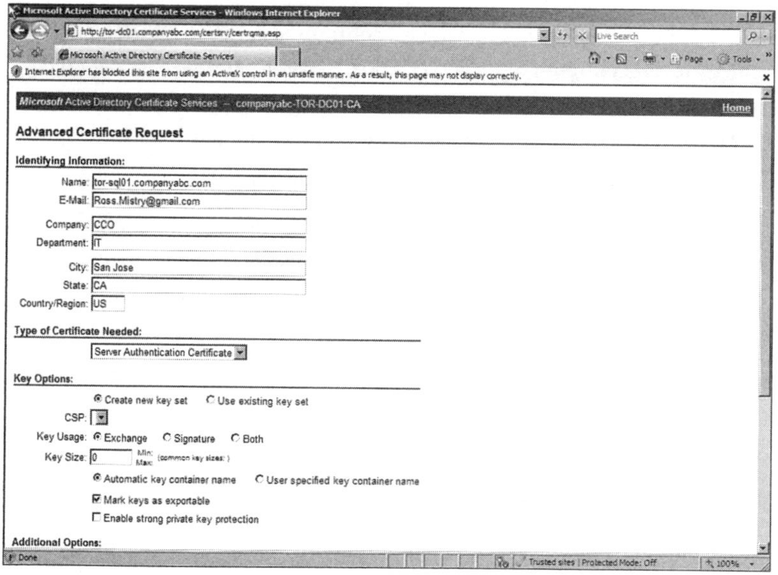

FIGURE 11.9
Certificate enrollment.

12. Click Yes to allow the website to request the certificate.

13. The website will show a Certificate Pending page. The page will have a Request ID number for the certificate request.

14. On the Certificate Authority server, launch the Certification Authority MMC from the Administrative Tools.

15. Expand the Certificate Authority name, and select the Pending Requests folder.

16. Locate the matching Request ID number in the Details pane.

17. Right-click on the request and select All Tasks, Issue.

18. Go back to the Internet Explorer window.

19. Enter the URL for the Certification Authority Web Enrollment, which in this example is `http://tor-sql01.companyabc.com/certsrv`.

20. Select View the Status of a Pending Certificate Request.

21. Click on the certificate request.

22. Click on Install This Certificate to add the certificate to the local computer store.

23. Click Yes to allow the certificate to be installed.

SQL Server Certificate Configuration

After a certificate has been obtained and configured on the SQL Server system, you can configure SQL Server 2008 to use it. You do this with the SQL Server Configuration Manager tool.

The steps to configure SQL Server to use the certificate are

1. Launch the SQL Server Configuration Manager.

2. Expand the SQL Server Network Configuration.

3. Right-click Protocols for the SQL Server instance, such as TOR-SQL01\Instance01 and select Properties.

4. Select the Certificate tab.

5. Select the certificate from the drop-down list for the Certificate box.

6. Click OK to save the settings.

7. Click OK to acknowledge that the service needs to be restarted.

8. Restart the SQL Server service to use the certificate.

The SQL Server is now protected against man-in-the-middle attacks with the CA certificate. However, the clients need to be configured to use the server certificate and trust the CA if an internal CA was used.

Client Certificate Configuration

The certificate is stored in the SQL Server certificate store and needs to be exported so that it can be shared. To export the server certificate, follow these steps:

1. Click Start, Run, and in the Open box, type MMC; and click OK.

2. In the MMC, on the File menu, click Add/Remove Snap-in.

3. In the Add/Remove Snap-in dialog box, click Add.

4. In the Add Standalone Snap-in dialog box, click Certificates and then click Add.

5. In the Certificates Snap-in dialog box, click Computer Account and then click Finish.

6. In the Add Standalone Snap-in dialog box, click Close.

7. In the Add/Remove Snap-in dialog box, click OK.

8. From the Certificates MMC snap-in, locate the certificate in the Certificates\Personal folder.

9. Right-click the Certificate, select All Tasks, and click Export.

10. Complete the Certificate Export Wizard, saving the certificate file in a convenient location.

The certificate, stored in the file, is now ready to be used by the client. To import the certificate into the client computer store, follow these steps:

1. Copy the exported certificate file to the client computer.

2. In the Certificates snap-in on the client, expand Certificates.

3. Expand the Personal folder.

4. Right-click on Personal, select All Tasks, and click Import.

5. Complete the Certificate Import Wizard.

The certificate is now ready to use. However, if you used a private CA to issue the certificate, you need to add the CA to the trusted CA list. For a Windows CA, use the following steps to do that:

1. On the client, launch Internet Explorer.

2. Enter the address http://TOR-SQL01.companyabc.com/certsrv to access the Certificate Service Web Request site. This assumes that the certificate services were installed on the dc1.companyabc.com server.

3. Click on the Download a CA Certificate link.

4. Click on the Install This CA Certificate Chain link to configure the SQL Server to trust the CA.

5. Click Yes to continue.

6. Click Yes to install the CA certificate.

The Windows Certificate Authority is now trusted by the client.

Client-Initiated Encryption

In some cases, there might not be the need or the option to configure the server to force encryption for all clients. Perhaps only a few connections need to be encrypted, or there is no administrative control over the configuration of SQL Server.

To configure the client to request encrypted connections using the ODBC, follow these steps:

1. Select Start, Control Panel.

2. Double-click on Administrative Tools to open the folder.

3. Double-click on the Data Sources (ODBC) applet.

4. Select the System DSN tab.

5. Click Add to add a new data source.

6. Select either SQL Server or SQL Native Client.

7. Click Finish to launch the configuration of the data source.

8. Enter a name for the data source, in this case `Customer Database`.

9. Enter the name of the SQL Server, in this case `TOR-SQL01\Instance01`.

10. Click Next.

11. Click Next to leave the default authentication.

12. Check the Change the Default Database box.

13. Select the Customer database from the drop-down list.

14. Click Next.

15. Check the Use Strong Encryption for Data box to encrypt the client/server traffic.

16. Click Finish.

17. Click Test Data Source to verify the settings.

18. Click OK three times to close out the settings.

The connection now forces itself to use strong encryption regardless of the SQL Server setting. This option does require that a certificate issued by a trusted third party be used.

SQL Server Management Studio

The SQL Server Management Studio is a potential source of exploits itself. Given the level of communications with data, code, and passwords, a hacker can discover a ton of information from the traffic generated by the SQL Server Management Studio tool. This is the case when the tool is loaded on a client computer rather than the server itself.

Fortunately, the communications from the SQL Server Management Studio on a client to SQL Server can easily be encrypted as well. The steps to do this are

1. On the Object Explorer toolbar, click Connect.
2. Select a service, in this case the Database Engine.
3. Select a server, in this case TOR-SQL01.
4. Click on the Options button.
5. Check the Encrypt Connection box.
6. Click Connect to connect.

Now all communications between the SQL Server Management Studio and SQL Server are protected with encryption.

SQL Server and BitLocker Drive Encryption

Microsoft added Windows BitLocker Drive Encryption to Windows 2008 mostly as a result of organizations demanding protection not only for their operating systems, but also for the vital data stored on the system volume and data storage volumes housing both the SQL Server Database and Transaction Logs. BitLocker Drive Encryption, commonly referred to as just BitLocker, is a hardware-enhanced, data-protection security feature included in all versions of the Windows 2008 family of operating systems. It is an optional component that you must install if you choose to use it.

BitLocker increases data protection for an operating system by merging two concepts together: encrypting a volume and guaranteeing the integrity of the operating system's boot components. The first component, drive encryption, safeguards data residing on the system volume and configured data volumes by preventing unauthorized users from compromising Windows system files encrypted with BitLocker. Encryption at the volume level is achieved by leveraging the new features available with BitLocker such as a Trusted Platform Module (TPM), which is discussed in the following section. The second component provides integrity verifications of the early boot components, which essentially refers to components used during the startup process, by validating that the hard disk has not been tampered with or removed from its original server. Equally important, when you use BitLocker, confidential data on a protected server cannot be viewed even if the hard disks are transferred to another operating system. If these two conditions are met, only then will data on a BitLocker volume be decrypted and the system allowed to boot.

If you have worked with previous versions of Windows Server, you will recognize immediately that BitLocker is a great addition to Windows 2008 as it protects all of the data residing on a server's hard disks because everything written to the disk including the operating system is encrypted. In previous versions of Windows Server, encryption based on integration with TPM hardware was not supported, which meant personal information could be compromised. In addition, with BitLocker now on the map, branch offices concerned over the physical security and theft of their domain controllers stand to benefit the most from leveraging BitLocker because this feature further bolsters security and ensures that confidential data is not disclosed without authorization.

> **NOTE**
>
> Many professionals are posing questions as they wonder about the differences between BitLocker and Encrypting File System (EFS). Both technologies offer tools for encryption; however, BitLocker is intended to protect all personal and system files on a system and after it is enabled, it is transparent as well as automatic. EFS, on the other hand, encrypts individual files based on an administrator's judgment call.

Examining BitLocker's Drive Encryption Components and Windows Server 2008 Enhancements

BitLocker was first introduced with the release of Windows Vista. Since entering the Windows 2008 family of operating systems, Microsoft has improved BitLocker by adding three new features: data volumes; three-factor authentication that includes TPM, USB, and PIN; and Unified Extensible Firmware Interface (UEFI). Furthermore, BitLocker Drive Encryption is designed to offer a seamless user experience.

> **NOTE**
>
> UEFI is only supported when running 64-bit processor architecture in the system.

You will recognize when first attempting to use BitLocker that there are different ways to deploy it. To ensure that your installation receives the highest level of security and protection, you need to remember that the server requires the Trusted Platform Module (TPM) microchip and BIOS based on version 1.2 or higher. Also required is the Static Root of Trust Measurement, which is defined by the Trusted Computing Group (TCG).

TPM is a component that provides enhanced protection of data and ensures boot integrity by validating the computer's boot manager integrity and boot files at startup. This hardware component confirms that the encrypted drive in a computer actually belongs to that computer.

TPM also runs a check of the hard disk to ensure it has not been subjected to unauthorized viewing while in an offline state by encrypting the entire Windows volume. This includes system and user files as well as swap files and hibernation files. In addition, BitLocker saves measurement details related to core operating system files in TPM, creating a sort of system fingerprint. The fingerprint remains the same unless someone tampers with the boot system.

BitLocker Drive Encryption provides seamless protection at system startup. Because this is transparent to the user, the user logon experience is unchanged. However, if the TPM is changed or missing, or if startup information has changed, BitLocker enters Recovery mode and the user must provide a recovery password to regain access to the data.

Two new major improvements to BitLocker on Windows Server 2008 include data volumes and a new authenticator. Both of these are discussed in the following sections.

Data Volumes

BitLocker extends the functionality included in Windows Vista by supporting encryption beyond the functionality of just the boot drive. All data volumes associated with a server can be encrypted by BitLocker, so SQL Server volumes associated with the database and transaction logs can be protected. A *data volume* is defined as any plug-and-play internal volume that does not contain the operating system files that are currently running. Typically, these could be volumes that store user data, such as Microsoft Office files, music, or other downloads. To enable data volumes on an operating system volume, you must have BitLocker enabled.

New Authenticator

Like many other security products in the industry that handle authentication, the IT security community requested Microsoft to include a multifactor form of authentication built into BitLocker. BitLocker on Windows 2008 supports three-factor authentication. For example, it is possible to configure BitLocker to use TPM, USB, and PIN to maximize security authentication.

Comprehending BitLocker's Drive Encryption Hardware Requirements

Configuring BitLocker Drive Encryption is not as simple as clicking through a few screens on a Windows 2008 wizard. A number of prerequisite steps must be fulfilled before BitLocker can be configured and implemented.

Before you implement BitLocker Drive Encryption, make certain the following hardware requirements and prerequisites are met and understood:

- The system should have a Trusted Platform Module (TPM) version 1.2 or higher.

- If the system does not have TPM, a removable USB memory device can be used to store the encryption key.

- There must be a minimum of at least two partitions on the system.

- One partition must be dedicated for the Windows operating system files.

- There must be an active system partition that is not encrypted. Therefore, the computer can be booted and/or started. The system volume must differ from the operating system volume and should be at least 1.5GB.

- All drives and partitions must be formatted with the NTFS file system.

- The system BIOS must support TPM and USB devices during startup.

Configuring BitLocker Drive Encryption on a SQL Server System

The following sections cover step-by-step procedures on how to implement BitLocker by first configuring the system partitions, installing the BitLocker feature, and then enabling BitLocker Drive Encryption. The enabling section includes steps for enabling BitLocker when using TPM hardware, when not using TPM hardware, and enabling BitLocker on additional volumes beyond the scope of the volume hosting the operating system. The final step-by-step procedures include how to utilize the BitLocker recovery password in the event of an issue and how to remove BitLocker after it has been installed and configured.

Configuring the System Partitions for BitLocker

As mentioned earlier, one of the prerequisite tasks when configuring an operating system for BitLocker is configuring a nonencrypted active partition also referred to as a system partition. Complete the following steps to configure this partition on a new server:

1. Insert the Windows Server 2008 media. The Install Windows screen should automatically launch; otherwise, click on `Setup.exe`.

2. Input the appropriate Language, Time, Currency, and Keyboard preferences, and then click Next.

3. Click Repair Your Computer on the Install Now page.

4. Select Command Prompt on the System Recovery Options page.

5. Click Next on the System Recovery Options page.

6. In the Command Prompt window, type **Diskpart** to create prerequisite partitions.

7. Type **select Disk 0** and press Enter. A message stating that Disk 0 is now the selected disk should appear.

8. Type **Clean** and then press Enter to erase the current partition table. A confirmation message stating that DiskPart succeeded in cleaning the disk message will be displayed.

9. Create the initial partition to boot the system by typing **create partition primary size=1500**.

NOTE

Allocate at least 1500MB for the system partition when creating the volume partitions.

---

10. Assign a drive letter to the partition by typing the following: **assign letter=z**. For this example, the letter Z was used to assign the drive letter to the partition. Another letter of your choice can be substituted.

11. Next, type **Active** to mark the newly created partition as an active partition for the system.

12. The next steps are used to create an additional partition for the Windows 2008 system files. This is accomplished by typing the words **create partition primary**.

13. Assign the new partition a drive letter such as C by typing the following: **assign letter=C**.

NOTE

It is possible to view the newly created volumes by typing the words *list volume* at the command prompt.

---

14. Now that the partitions have been created, type **Exit** to leave the DiskPart utility.

15. The final step requires both partitions to be formatted with NTFS. This can be done by typing **format X: /y /q /fs:NTFS**. Replace the letter *X* with the drive letters assigned in the previous steps. Repeat this step for both partitions created.

16. Type **Exit** to close the command prompt.

17. Close the System Recovery Options page by clicking the X icon in the upper-right corner or by pressing Alt+F4.

18. Now that the partitions have been created and formatted, click Install Now to proceed with the remainder of the Windows 2008 installation. Ensure that you install Windows on the larger partition, which was created in steps 12 and 13.

Installing BitLocker Drive Encryption

Now that the system partition has been configured, there are different ways to install BitLocker. Install it during the initial configuration through Server Manager or through a command prompt. The following sections illustrate how to execute both of these installations.

Installing BitLocker with Server Manager

To install the BitLocker server role using Server Manager, follow these steps:

1. Click Start, Administrative Tools, and Server Manager. The Server Manager tools appear.

2. Right-click on features in the left pane of Server Manager, and then select Add Features.

3. On the Select Features page, install BitLocker by selecting BitLocker Drive Encryption in the Features section, as shown in Figure 11.10, and then click Next.

4. On the Confirm Installation Selections page, review the roles, services, and features selected for installation, and then click Install to initiate the installation process.

5. Ensure the installation succeeded by reviewing the messages on the Installation Results page, and then click Close.

NOTE

Alternatively, the BitLocker Drive Encryption feature can also be installed by selecting Add Features in the Initial Configuration Tasks Wizard.

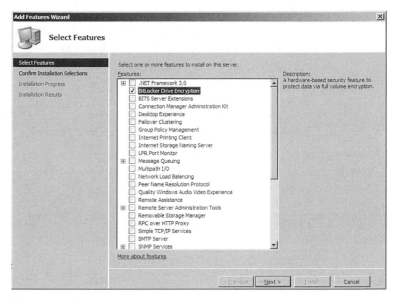

FIGURE 11.10
Selecting the BitLocker feature for installation.

Installing BitLocker via the Command Prompt

Another alternative to installing BitLocker is via the command prompt. This methodology should be reserved for branch office implementations using Windows 2008 Server Core installation because a graphical interface to manage the server does not exist. To install the BitLocker feature using the command prompt, follow these steps:

1. Click Start, Run, type **CMD**, and then click OK.

2. From the command prompt type **start /w pkgmgr /iu:BitLocker**.

3. After the installation is complete, click Yes on the Windows Package Manager to restart the system.

Enabling BitLocker Drive Encryption

By default, BitLocker is configured to use a Trusted Platform Module. To recap, however, BitLocker's full functionality will not be witnessed unless the system being used is compatible with the TPM microchip and BIOS.

Now that the system partition and BitLocker are installed, it is time to look at ways to enable BitLocker. The next section looks at how to enable BitLocker

Drive Encryption with TPM hardware. Microsoft recognizes that many laptops and computers do not have TPM chips (or are not "TPM enabled"). If you are in this situation, don't despair because you can use BitLocker without a compatible TPM chip and BIOS. As such, this section also covers information on how to enable BitLocker without TPM hardware.

Enabling BitLocker Drive Encryption with TPM Hardware

1. Click Start, Control Panel, and double-click BitLocker Drive Encryption.

2. Enable BitLocker Drive Encryption for the operating system volume by clicking Turn On BitLocker on the BitLocker Drive Encryption page. This will display the page shown in Figure 11.11.

FIGURE 11.11
Turning on BitLocker via Control Panel.

NOTE

The Initialize TPM Security Hardware screen will be displayed if the TPM is not initialized. Launch the wizard to initialize the hardware and then restart your computer. In addition, if the drive configuration is not suitable for BitLocker, repartition the hard disk based on the prerequisite tasks and then start over from step 1.

3. Review the message on the BitLocker Drive Encryption Platform Check page, and then click Continue with BitLocker Drive Encryption to start the BitLocker process.

4. Because TPM hardware is present on this system, select the option Use BitLocker Without Additional Keys, and then click Next. This option can be found on the Set BitLocker Startup Preferences page, as displayed in Figure 11.12. Additional keys such as a PIN or USB are not required as BitLocker stores both encryption and decryption keys within the TPM chip.

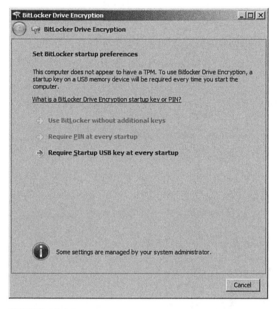

FIGURE 11.12
Specifying BitLocker startup preferences.

5. The Save the Recovery Password page is invoked. The administrator has the ability to save the BitLocker recovery password on a USB drive or to a folder on the system. In addition, the third option allows for printing of the password. Choose the desired storage alternative for saving the recovery password, and then click Next to continue.

6. On the Encrypt the Volume page, ensure that the Run BitLocker System Check option is enabled, and then click Continue. The system check guarantees that BitLocker can access and read the recovery and encryption keys before encrypting the volume.

7. The Encryption in Progress status bar is displayed. Restart the system when the encryption process is finalized.

Enabling BitLocker Drive Encryption When TPM Hardware Is Not Available

If TPM hardware is not available on the system, BitLocker must be configured to leverage a USB key at startup. The following example configures a local group policy for the group policy object titled "Enabling Advanced Startup Options: Control Panel Setup."

1. Click Start, Run, and then type **gpedit.msc**. Click OK and the Local Group Policy Object Editor is invoked.

2. In the Local Group Policy Object Editor, expand Local Computer Policy, Computer Configuration, Administrative Templates, Windows Components, and then select BitLocker Drive Encryption.

3. In the right pane, double-click Control Panel Setup: Enable Advanced Startup Options.

4. Enable the BitLocker group policy settings by selecting the Enabled option, and then click OK, as displayed in Figure 11.13.

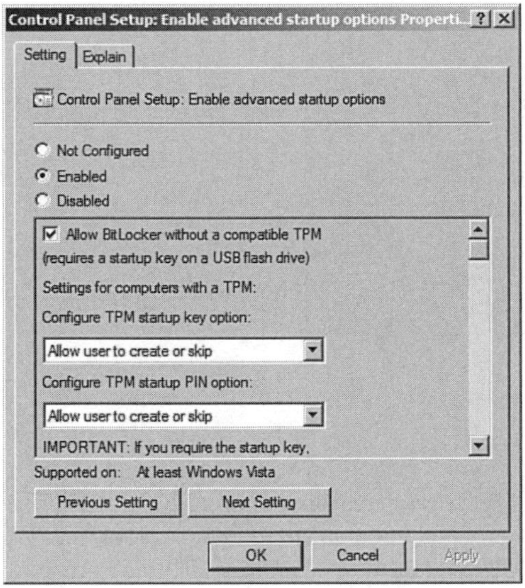

FIGURE 11.13
Enabling advanced startup options for BitLocker support.

5. Apply the new group policy settings by typing **gpupdate.exe /force** at the command prompt.

BitLocker Drive Encryption utilizing a USB device can now be configured by completing the following steps:

1. Click Start, Control Panel, and double-click BitLocker Drive Encryption.

2. Enable BitLocker Drive Encryption by clicking Turn On BitLocker on the BitLocker Drive Encryption page.

3. Review the message on the BitLocker Drive Encryption Platform Check page, and then click Continue with BitLocker Drive Encryption to start the BitLocker process.

4. Because a TPM does not exist in this example, select the option Require Startup USB Key at Every Startup, and then click Next. This option can be found on the Set BitLocker Startup Preferences page.

5. Ensure that a USB memory device has been inserted into the system. Then on the Save Your Startup Key page, specify the removable drive to which the startup key will be saved, and then click Save.

6. The Save the Recovery Password page is then invoked. The administrator has the ability to save the BitLocker recovery password on a USB drive or to a folder on the system. In addition, the third option allows for printing of the password. Choose the desired storage alternative for saving the recovery password, and then click Next to continue.

NOTE

It is a best practice to make additional copies of the recovery password and store them in a secure location like a vault. For maximum security, the recovery password should not be stored on the local system nor should the password be printed on paper. In addition, do not store the recovery password and the startup key on the same media.

---

7. On the Encrypt the Volume page, ensure that the Run BitLocker System Check option is enabled, and then click Continue. The system check guarantees BitLocker can access and read the recovery and encryption keys before encrypting the volume.

NOTE

Do not bypass the option to run a system check before encrypting the volume. Data loss can occur if there is an error reading the encryption or recovery key.

---

8. Insert the USB memory device containing the startup key into the system, and then click Restart Now. The Encryption in Progress status bar is displayed showing the completion status of the disk volume encryption.

NOTE

The USB device must be plugged into the system every time the system starts to boot and gain access to the encrypted volume. If the USB device containing the startup key is lost or damaged, you must use the Recovery mode and provide the recovery key to start the system.

Enabling BitLocker Drive Encryption on Additional Data Volumes

There might be situations when BitLocker Drive Encryption is warranted not only on the volume containing the operating system files, but also on the data volumes. This is especially common with domain controllers in branch offices where a lack of physical security and theft is a concern.

When encrypting data volumes with BitLocker, the keys generated for the operating system volume are independent of the drive volume. However, encryption of a data volume is similar to the encryption process of the operating system volume.

Follow these steps to enable BitLocker Drive Encryption for server data volumes:

1. Click Start, Run, and then type **Cmd**. Click OK to launch a command prompt.

2. From within the command prompt, type **manage-bde -on <volume>: -rp -rk <removable drive>:\\.**

NOTE

Replace the *<volume>* argument with the desired volume drive letter that you want to encrypt. In addition, replace the *<removable drive>* argument with the drive letter of a USB device. The USB device is utilized to store the recovery key.

The data volume must be unlocked each time the server is rebooted. This can be accomplished through a manual or automatic process. The syntax to manually unlock a data volume after every restart consists of the following two options:

```
manage-bde -unlock <volume>: -rp <recovery password>

manage-bde -unlock <volume>: -rk U:\<recovery-key-file name>
```

The first option uses the recovery password, whereas the second options takes advantage of passing the recovery key to decrypt the data volume. As mentioned in the previous paragraph, it is possible to enable automatic unlocking of a data volume by utilizing the following syntax at the command prompt:

```
manage-bde -autounlock -enable <volume>:
```

This command creates a recovery key and stores it on the operating system volume. The data volume is automatically unlocked after each system reboot.

> **NOTE**
>
> After the Windows Server 2008 operating system has been successfully installed, the next step is to install SQL Server 2008. For more information on installing SQL Server 2008, see Chapter 1, "Installing or Upgrading to the SQL Server 2008 Database Engine."

Utilizing the BitLocker Recovery Password

There might be situations when you need to leverage the recovery password to gain access to a volume that is encrypted with BitLocker. This situation might occur when there is an error related to the TPM hardware, one of the boot files becomes corrupt or modified, or TPM is unintentionally cleared or disabled. The following instructions outline the recovery steps:

1. Restart the system and the BitLocker Drive Encryption console will come into view.

2. Insert the USB device containing the recovery password, and then press Esc. If the USB device is not available, bypass step 2 and proceed to step 3.

3. Press Enter. You will be prompted to enter the recovery password manually.

4. Type the recovery password, press Enter, and then restart the system.

Removing BitLocker Drive Encryption

The course of action for turning off BitLocker Drive Encryption is the same for both TPM-based hardware configurations and USB devices. When you're turning off BitLocker, two options exist. You can either remove BitLocker entirely and decrypt a volume or you can temporarily disable BitLocker so that changes can still be made. The following steps depict the process for removing and disabling BitLocker:

1. Click Start, Control Panel, and double-click BitLocker Drive Encryption.

2. Turn off BitLocker Drive Encryption by clicking Turn Off BitLocker on the BitLocker Drive Encryption page.

3. The What Level of Decryption Do You Want dialog box will be invoked. Choose either Disable BitLocker Drive Encryption or Decrypt the Volume.

Summary

Confidential data is at risk if not protected by the appropriate measures. Access controls are not enough to secure confidential data, and an in-depth defense strategy is needed. A critical layer in this strategy is encryption.

Encryption is an effective method of protecting Microsoft SQL Server 2008 data, both while stored in the database and while on the wire. Encrypting data is an easy and straightforward process in SQL Server 2008, especially when you use Transparent Data Encryption.

The sections in this chapter illustrate how to encrypt data while in the database and how to encrypt data during transmission. Given the ease with which data can be compromised by a determined hacker, it is important to protect the data with encryption using the methods outlined in this chapter.

Best Practices

Some important best practices from the chapter include

- Encrypt client/server data transmissions.

- Use a third-party certificate to prevent man-in-the-middle attacks.

- Encrypt confidential data in the database to protect the data on disk and in backups.

- Encrypt entire databases by using Transparent Data Encryption for easy protection of data files and backups.

- Use an authenticator when encrypting data to protect against inference hacking.

- Force the clients to use strong encryption when SQL Server cannot be configured to always require encryption.

- Use self-signed certificates rather than nothing at all to secure data.

- Configure SQL Server Management Studio to use encryption when connecting to servers over the network.

- Leverage BitLocker in order to protect the operating system and data volumes associated with a SQL Server system.

PART III

SQL Server 2008 High Availability Alternatives

IN THIS PART

CHAPTER 12

Implementing and Managing Failover Clustering

Failover clustering is one of four SQL Server 2008 high-availability alternatives. Other SQL Server 2008 high-availability alternatives include database mirroring, log shipping, and peer-to-peer replication. These other high-availability technologies are discussed in other chapters in this book.

This chapter first focuses on an overview of SQL Server 2008 failover clustering based on Windows Server 2008, then on the new features associated with both SQL Server 2008 and Windows Server 2008 failover clustering, and finally, on hardware and software prerequisites.

The chapter also includes step-by-step procedures for installing a two-node single-instance and multiple-instance SQL Server 2008 failover cluster based on Windows Server 2008. The final portion of the chapter includes management tasks for managing a SQL Server failover cluster when running on Windows Server 2008.

SQL Server 2008 Failover Clustering Overview

Failover clustering with SQL Server 2008 running on Windows Server 2008 provides server-level redundancy by supporting the *shared-nothing cluster model*. In a shared-nothing cluster, two or more independent servers share resources; however, each computer, or *node*, owns and manages its local resources and provides nonsharing data services. In case of a node failure, the disks, resources, and services running on the failed node fail over to a surviving node in the cluster. With SQL Server failover clustering, specifically, only one node manages one particular SQL Server instance, set of disks, and associated services at any given time.

Note

SQL Server failover clustering provides high availability for mission-critical databases and server nodes. However, it does not replace the need for a comprehensive backup and recovery strategy for a SQL Server environment. Equally important, you should not rely on clustering as a replacement for disaster recovery and business continuity strategies.

What's New for SQL Server 2008 Failover Clustering When Running on Windows Server 2008?

Both Windows Server 2008 and SQL Server 2008 make significant enhancements to failover clustering. The majority of the noteworthy improvements are based on the radical redesign related to the underlying Windows Server 2008 Failover Clustering feature. The list of enhancements for both SQL Server 2008 and Windows Server 2008 failover clustering includes the following:

- The terminology for referencing clusters has changed, and they are now known as "failover clusters."

- Windows Server 2008 introduces a new Cluster Validation Tool that must be run before installing a cluster. The tool performs a test against all the components associated with the failover cluster to ensure that the components are suitable, meet the minimum requirements, and are configured correctly. There are over 100 tests with the central theme focusing on inventory, network, storage, and system configuration.

- The SQL Server 2008 failover cluster installation has been redesigned and is done on a per-node basis. Using the installation wizard, you first install the first node of the SQL Server failover cluster and then run the installation again, on all subsequent nodes. Using the new installation process, it is now possible to conduct rolling patches, upgrades, and service pack installations without causing downtime, something which was not achievable with SQL Server 2005.

- The SQL Server 2008 Installation Center includes a new tool for both advanced cluster preparation and advanced cluster completion. These tools allow a wizard to prepare a SQL Server 2008 failover cluster installation and another wizard to complete the installation.

- Windows Server 2008 introduces new installation wizards, which simplify the installation process so that a Windows Server 2008 failover cluster creation can be achieved in one step.

- The failover cluster installation process for both Windows Server 2008 and SQL Server 2008 is fully scriptable—making it effortless to automate the installation of more than one failover cluster.

- The cluster management interface in Windows Server 2008 has been completely revamped and optimized in order to enhance the administrator's day-to-day management experience.

- In previous releases of Windows, the quorum drive was a potential single point of failure as it maintained all the cluster configuration. With Windows Server 2008, a new quorum model eliminates the single point of failure associated with the quorum resource. It is possible to configure the quorum with the majority node cluster setting. Therefore, the cluster configuration is stored in multiple locations.

- From a network and security perspective, Windows Server 2008 failover clusters support the latest IP protocol, known as Internet Protocol version 6 (IPv6).

- Windows Server 2008 eliminates the need to have all nodes in a failover cluster reside in the same subnet, making it easier to establish a geographically dispersed failover cluster.

Note

An in-place upgrade from a previous SQL Server failover cluster to a SQL Server 2008 failover cluster running on Windows Server 2008 is not supported. It is necessary to build a new failover cluster with SQL Server 2008 and then conduct a data migration from the legacy cluster. This is based on the redesign of failover clustering with Windows Server 2008. Because of the enhanced security, backward compatibility with Windows Server 2003 failover clustering could not be achieved.

Determining When to Implement a SQL Server 2008 Failover Cluster

Typically, organizations implement a SQL Server 2008 failover cluster to address the following situations:

- To increase server availability for mission-critical applications and network services

- To provide high-availability support for an entire instance of SQL Server, not just a database

- To provide a seamless failover which minimizes the impact to client applications and end users

- To provide an automatic failover that does not require database administrator intervention

- To reduce downtime during routine maintenance or unplanned failures

- To perform Windows Server 2008 and SQL Server 2008 patches and service pack rolling upgrades

Failover Clustering Terminology

Before installing failover clustering, it is beneficial to understand the terminology associated with SQL Server 2008 and Windows Server 2008 failover clustering. Let's examine the terminology in the following list:

- **SQL Server virtual server**—A *SQL Server virtual server* is, in fact, a cluster-configured resource group that contains all resources necessary for SQL Server to operate on the cluster. This includes the NetBIOS name of the virtual server, a TCP/IP address for the virtual server and all disk drives, and vital SQL Server services required to operate in a clustered configuration. In a multiple instance, two or more node clusters and one SQL Server virtual server are created per node, whereas the NetBIOS name and TCP/IP address of the cluster form the virtual server. When failover occurs in this configuration, the entire SQL Server virtual server fails over to the surviving node in the cluster dynamically.

- **Heartbeat**—A single User Datagram Protocol (UDP) packet is sent every 500 milliseconds between nodes in the cluster across the internal private network. This packet relays health information about the cluster nodes as well as health information about the clustered application. If there is no response during a heartbeat to indicate that the node is alive, the cluster begins the failover process. In SQL Server 2008, this interval can be changed. This capability is useful when you are using a geographically dispersed cluster.

- **Failover**—*Failover* is the process of one node in the cluster changing states from offline to online, resulting in the node taking over responsibility of the SQL Server virtual server. The Cluster Service fails over a group in the event that node becomes unavailable or one of the resources in the group fails.

- **Failback**—*Failback* is the process of moving a SQL Server virtual server that failed over in the cluster back to the original online node.

- **Quorum resource**—The *quorum* resource, also referred to as the *witness* disk in Windows Server 2008, is the shared disk that holds the cluster server's configuration information. All servers must be able to contact the quorum resource to become part of a SQL Server 2008 cluster. In Windows Server 2003, the entire cluster's health and vitality depends on the quorum drive being available. With Windows Server 2008, a majority quorum model can be leveraged to eliminate this single point of failure.

- **Resource group**—A *resource group* is a collection of cluster resources such as the SQL Server NetBIOS name, TCP/IP address, and the services belonging to the SQL Server cluster. A resource group also defines the items that fail over to the surviving nodes during failover. These items also include cluster resource items such as a cluster disk. It is also worth noting that a resource group is owned by only one node in the cluster at a time.

- **Cluster resource**—*Cluster resources* contain vital information for the SQL Server virtual server and include its network TCP/IP addresses, NetBIOS name, disks, and SQL Server services, such as the System Attendant. These cluster resources are added to services or applications when the virtual server is created to form SQL Server virtual servers. With Windows Server 2008, a clustered resource is known as an application and a service.

- **Dependency**—A *dependency* is specified when creating cluster resources. Similar to a dependency on SQL Server services, a cluster resource identified as a dependency indicates that a mandatory relationship exists between resources. Before a cluster resource is brought online, the resource defined as a dependent must be brought online first. For instance, the virtual server NetBIOS name is dependent on the TCP/IP address; therefore, the TCP/IP address of the virtual server must be brought online before the NetBIOS name is brought online.

- **Majority Node cluster**—In this configuration, each node is responsible for contributing one local disk to the quorum disk set that is used as storage disks. This configuration limits the majority node resource to one owner at a time. Because the quorum does not require a shared disk, the solution is typically used for geographically dispersed clusters.

- **Failover Cluster Management**—Formerly known as Cluster Administrator, Failover Cluster Manager in Windows Server 2008 is a tool used by cluster and database administrators for accessing, creating, and administering Windows clusters. The Failover Cluster Administrator console is included in Windows Server 2008 and can be launched from any active node within the cluster. Additional administration and management tasks include viewing, creating, and deleting services or applications, cluster resources, and nodes.

- **Cluster witness disk or file share**—The *cluster witness* or the *witness file share* are used to store the cluster configuration information, and to help determine the state of the cluster when some if not all of the cluster nodes cannot be contacted.

- **LUNs**—LUN stands for *Logical Unit Number*. An LUN is used to identify a disk or a disk volume that is presented to a host server or multiple hosts by the shared storage device. Of course, there are shared storage controllers, firmware, drivers, and physical connections between the server and the shared storage, but the concept is that an LUN or set of LUNs is presented to the server for use as a local disk. LUNs provided by shared storage must meet many requirements before they can be used with failover clusters, but when they do, all active nodes in the cluster must have exclusive access to these LUNs. More information on LUNs and shared storage is provided later in this chapter.

SQL Server Failover Clustering Prerequisites

SQL Server failover clustering is based on the Windows shared-nothing model. Two or more nodes can control a single set of media that hold the application data. In the case of SQL Server 2008, this refers to a virtual instance where there is only a single copy of the database and logs residing on shared disks. Multiple nodes are available and can control these resources one at a time.

Before installing SQL Server clustering, ensure that the following prerequisites are met:

- A minimum of two identical servers running Windows Server 2008 Enterprise or Datacenter Edition are required.

- Two network interfaces are needed per server: one for the private heartbeat and the other for the public network. The public network should be the first network in the binding order.

- Shared disk storage is needed for the witness (quorum), database, and log files. This could be a storage area network (SAN), small computer system interface (SCSI), Serial Attached SCSI (SAS), or Internet SCSI (ISCSI) storage solution. All shared disks must be configured as basic because clustering does not support dynamic disks. In addition, all shared disks must be online, configured with NTFS, and be seen from all nodes.

- Distributed Transaction Coordinator (DTC) may need to be installed and configured prior to the installation of SQL Server. DTC is not required if only the Database Engine feature will be installed. However, it is required if the following components will be installed in conjunction with one another: Database Engine, Integration Services, and Shared components.

- Ensure that the shared disks have the same drive letter mappings on both nodes.

- If the Windows Server 2008 Firewall is enabled, then ensure that the SQL Server port, SQL Browser port, File and Printer Sharing (TCP 139/445 and UDP 137/138), and Remote Procedure Call (TCP port 135) have been allowed.

- The Failover Clustering feature of Windows Server 2008 must be configured prior to the installation of SQL Server. The clustering groups and resources should be available, operational, and online.

- Separate service accounts are needed for both the Microsoft Failover Cluster Server and SQL Server services.

- All nodes should be identical and have the same service pack hotfixes and identical software. This also includes the same processor version.

- NETBIOS must be disabled on all network adapters being used for the private heartbeat network.

- All hardware and software being used must be certified by Microsoft and be on its Windows Catalog and Hardware Compatibility List (HCL).

- Ensure that the network adapters are listed in the order in which they are accessed by network services. For example, the Public adapter should be listed first and then the Heartbeat adapter. This setting can be modified by going to Control Panel, Network Connections, Advanced, Advanced Settings.

- Create a spreadsheet with the network names, IP addresses, and cluster disks that will be used for the administrative cluster and the High Availability "Services and Applications" group or groups that will be deployed in the failover cluster. Each "Services and Applications" group will require a separate network name and IPv4 Address, but if IPv6 is used, the address can be added separately in addition to the IPv4 address or a custom or generic "Services and Applications" group will need to be created. The servers in the cluster must be using DNS for name resolution. All servers in the cluster must be in the same AD domain, and should have the same domain role (recommended member server).

Failover Clustering Alternatives

The following list describes the types of clustering options available with SQL Server 2008:

- **Single-instance failover**—In a SQL Server 2008 single-instance failover configuration, the cluster runs a single virtual instance of SQL Server on all nodes in the cluster. Only one node in the cluster can service end users at any one time; this is known as the *active node*. The passive node, on the other hand, is on standby. If a failure occurs, the clustered resources are shifted to the passive node, which then begins to service clients. In this configuration, one virtual SQL Server instance is configured and shared by one or both nodes.

- **Multiple-instance failover**—In a multiple-instance failover configuration, each active node runs its own virtual instance of SQL Server. Each instance of SQL Server includes a separate installation of the full service and can be managed, upgraded, and stopped independently. If you want to apply a multiple-instance failover configuration, at least two instances of SQL Server need to be installed on the cluster, and each instance should be configured to run on a certain node as its primary server.

- **N+1**—This is a deviation of the multiple-instance failover clustering topology just discussed. In this scenario, more than two nodes are configured within the failover cluster solution and share the same failover node in the event of a failure. For example, in a four-node cluster, there may be three active nodes and one passive node. The passive node acts as a hot standby for any or all of the three active nodes. This solution reduces hardware costs because there isn't a one-to-one mapping between active and passive nodes. However, the major disadvantage is that the passive node must have enough hardware resources to take on the load of all three active nodes if they crash at the same time. The chances of three nodes crashing is highly unlikely; however, in the computer industry, we all know there is a first time for everything.

- **N+M**—Sometimes there is more than one active node in the cluster, so having a single dedicated failover node such as in the N+1 scenario is not sufficient enough to provide redundancy. Therefore, more than one standby node (M) is included in the cluster and available for failover. The number of standby servers is a trade-off between cost and reliability requirements.

- **Geographically dispersed clusters**—SQL Server 2008 also offers geographically dispersed clusters. This scenario does not require a quorum drive to be configured on a shared disk, thus allowing active and passive nodes to be in separate physical locations. If you want to implement this solution, specific hardware is required from a vendor. This hardware must be certified from the vendor and Microsoft. This is a different list from the Microsoft Clustering HCL. Implementing geographically dispersed clusters is expensive. It is recommended to use database mirroring instead of building a geographical cluster because database mirroring is much cheaper and also provides high availability, seamless failover, and automatic client failover.

> **Note**
>
> Server load and performance degradation should be analyzed when working with multiple instances within a single SQL Server failover cluster. You must ensure that the surviving node can handle the load if running more than one SQL Server instance on a single server. This can be achieved by manually tuning processor and memory settings within SQL Server Management Studio.

SQL Server 2008 Failover Clustering Scalability Metrics

A discussion on cluster basics is always essential because it can help organizations define a suitable operating system for their business. SQL Server 2008 Enterprise Edition on Windows 2008 Enterprise or Windows 2008 Datacenter Edition can support up to 16 nodes within a single cluster. SQL Server 2008 Standard Edition can support up to 2 nodes. Failover clustering of SQL Server 2008 can be configured in two ways: a single-instance failover configuration or a multiple-instance failover configuration. When using multiple-instance failover clustering, SQL Server 2008 scales up to 50 instances on Enterprise Edition, whereas the Standard Edition supports up to 16.

> **Note**
>
> When implementing SQL Server multiple-instance failover clustering, you should be aware that each instance requires a separate virtual server and each virtual server requires a separate clustered group with dedicated resources such as disks, network name, and IP address.

SQL Server 2008 Cluster-Aware Features

The SQL Server 2008 Database Engine Services, Analysis Services, and Full-Text Search features are cluster aware. This means that these features can be installed on a failover cluster, they have failover capabilities, and they show up as cluster resources in the Windows Server 2008 Failover Cluster Management console. Unfortunately, Reporting Services and Integration Services are not cluster aware.

Combining Failover Clustering with Other SQL Server High-Availability Alternatives

Other SQL Server high-availability alternatives can be combined with failover clustering for maximum availability, business continuity, and disaster recovery. For example, CompanyABC may have a two-node failover cluster residing in its Toronto office. This cluster provides high availability for a production database at the server level in that physical location. Regulatory legislation such as the Sarbanes-Oxley Act may have a requirement that CompanyABC maintain a disaster recovery site, and all production databases must be available in another location in the event of a disaster in the Toronto location. Therefore, CompanyABC can implement database mirroring in conjunction with clustering and mirror the production databases from the Toronto location to its disaster recovery location in San Francisco. The production database would be available in San Francisco in the event of the total cluster failure (which is highly unlikely) or in the event that the Toronto site is unavailable.

On a side note, database mirroring is not the only other high-availability alternative that works with failover clustering: Log shipping and replication can also be used.

Additional Elements of Failover Clustering

Some additional elements DBAs should be aware of include enhancements associated with the Quorum models on Windows Server 2008 and the different types of shared storage available when configuring a failover cluster.

Windows Server 2008 Failover Cluster Quorum Models

As previously stated, Windows Server 2008 failover clusters support four different Cluster Quorum models. Each of these four models is best suited for specific configurations, but if all the nodes and shared storage are configured, specified, and available during the installation of the failover cluster, the best suited Quorum model will be automatically selected.

Node Majority Quorum

The Node Majority Quorum model has been designed for Failover Cluster deployments that contain an odd number of cluster nodes. When determining the quorum state of the cluster, only the number of available nodes is counted. A cluster using the Node Majority Quorum is called a *Node Majority cluster*. A Node Majority cluster will remain up and running if the number of available nodes exceeds the number of failed nodes. As an example, in a five-node cluster, three nodes must be available for the cluster to remain online. If three nodes fail in a five-node Node Majority cluster, the entire cluster will be shut down. Node Majority clusters have been designed and are well suited for geographically or network dispersed cluster nodes, but in order for this configuration to be supported by Microsoft it will take serious effort, quality hardware, a third-party mechanism to replicate any back-end data, and a very reliable network. Again, this model works well for clusters with an odd number of nodes.

Node and Disk Majority

The Node and Disk Majority Quorum model determines whether a cluster can continue to function by counting the number of available nodes and the availability of the cluster witness disk. Using this model the cluster quorum is stored on a cluster disk that is accessible and made available to all nodes in the cluster through a shared storage device using SAS, Fibre Channel (FC), or ISCSI connections. This model is the closest to the traditional single-quorum device cluster configuration model and is composed of two or more server nodes that are all connected to a shared storage device. In this model, only one copy of the quorum data is maintained on the witness disk. This model is well suited for failover clusters using shared storage, all connected on the same network with an even number of nodes. For example, on a two-, four-, six-, or eight-node cluster using this model, the cluster will continue to function as long as half of the total nodes are available and can contact the witness disk. In the case of a witness disk failure, a majority of the nodes will need to remain up and running. To calculate this, take half of the total nodes and add one; this will give you the lowest number of available nodes that are required to keep a cluster running. For example, on a six-node cluster using this model, if the witness disk fails, the cluster will remain up and running as long as four nodes are available.

Node and File Share Majority Quorum

The Node and File Share Majority Quorum model is very similar to the Node and Disk Majority Quorum model, but instead of a witness disk, the quorum is stored on file share. The advantage of this model is that it can be deployed similarly to the Node Majority Quorum model, but as long as the witness file share is available, this model can tolerate the failure of half of the total nodes. This model is well suited for clusters with an even number of nodes that do not utilize shared storage.

No Majority: Disk Only Quorum

The No Majority: Disk Only Quorum model is best suited for testing the process and behavior of deploying built-in or custom services and/or applications on a Windows Server 2008 failover cluster. In this model the cluster can sustain the failover of all nodes except one, as long as the disk containing the quorum remains available. The limitation of this model is that the disk containing the quorum becomes a single point of failure and that is why this model is not well suited for production deployments of failover clusters.

As a best practice, before deploying a failover cluster, determine whether shared storage will be used and verify that each node can communicate with each LUN presented by the shared storage device. When the cluster is created, add all nodes to the list. This will ensure that the correct recommended cluster quorum model is selected for the new failover cluster. When the recommended model utilizes shared storage and a witness disk, the smallest available LUN will be selected. This can be changed if necessary after the cluster is created.

Shared Storage for Failover Clusters

Shared disk storage is a requirement for SQL Server 2008 failover clusters when running on Windows Server 2008 when using the Node and Disk Majority quorum and the Disk Only Quorum models. Shared storage devices can be a part of any cluster configuration and when they are used, the disks, disk volumes, or LUNs presented to the Windows systems must be presented as basic Windows disks.

All storage drivers must be digitally signed and certified for use with Windows Server 2008. Many storage devices certified for Windows Server 2003 may not work with Windows Server 2008 and either simply cannot be used for failover cluster shared storage, or may require a firmware and driver upgrade to be supported. One main reason for this is that all failover shared storage must comply with SCSI-3 Architecture Model SAM-2. This includes any and all legacy and serial attached SCSI controllers, Fibre Channel host bus adapters, and ISCSI hardware- and software-based initiators and targets. If the cluster attempts to perform an action on an LUN or shared disk and the attempt causes an interruption in communication to the other nodes in the cluster or any other system connected to the shared storage device, data corruption can occur and the entire cluster and each SAN-connected system may lose connectivity to the storage.

When LUNS are presented to failover cluster nodes, each LUN must be presented to each node in the cluster. Also, when the shared storage is accessed by the cluster and other systems, the LUNs must be masked or presented only to the cluster nodes and the shared storage device controllers to ensure that no other systems can access or disrupt the cluster communication.

Shared Storage Requirements

There are strict requirements for shared storage support, especially with failover clusters. Storage Area Networks (SANs) or other types of shared storage must meet the following list of requirements:

- All Fibre Channel, SAS, and ISCSI host bus adapters (HBAs) and Ethernet cards used with ISCSI software initiators must have obtained the "Designed for Microsoft Windows" logo for Windows Server 2008 and have suitable signed device drivers.

- SAS, Fibre Channel, and ISCSI HBAs must use Storport device drivers to provide targeted LUN resets and other functions inherent to the Storport driver specification. SCSIport drivers were at one point supported for two-node clusters, but if a Storport driver is available it should be used, to ensure support from the hardware vendors and Microsoft.

- All shared storage HBAs and back-end storage devices including ISCSI targets, Fibre Channel, and SAS storage arrays must support SCSI-3 standards and must also support persistent bindings or reservations of LUNs.

- All shared storage HBAs must be deployed with matching firmware and driver versions. Failover clusters using shared storage require a very stable infrastructure, and applying the latest storage controller driver to an outdated HBA firmware can cause a very undesirable situation and may disrupt access to data.

- All nodes in the cluster should contain the same HBAs and use the same version of drivers and firmware. Each cluster node should be an exact duplicate of each other node when it comes to hardware selection, configuration, drivers, and firmware revisions. This allows for a more reliable configuration and simplifies management and standardization.

- When ISCSI software initiators are used to connect to ISCSI software- or hardware-based targets, the network adapter used for ISCSI communication must be connected to a dedicated switch, cannot be used for any cluster communication, and cannot be a teamed network adapter.

- For ISCSI shared storage, configure an additional, dedicated network adapter or hardware-based ISCSI HBA.

- Configure all necessary IPv4 and IPv6 addresses as static configurations. DHCP is supported but not recommended.

- Verify that any and all HBAs and other storage controllers are running the proper firmware and matched driver version suitable for Windows Server 2008 failover clusters.

- If shared storage will be used, plan to utilize at least two separate LUNs, one to serve as the witness disk and the other to support DTC.

- Ensure that proper LUN masking and zoning has been configured at the FC or Ethernet switch level for FC or ISCSI shared storage communication, suitable for failover clustering. Each node in the failover cluster, along with the HBAs of the shared storage device should have exclusive access to the LUNs presented to the failover cluster.

- If multiple HBAs will be used in each failover node or in the shared storage device, ensure that a suitable Multipath I/O driver has been installed. The Microsoft Windows Server 2008 Multipath I/O feature can be used to provide this function if approved by the HBA, the switch and storage device vendors, and Microsoft.

- Shut down all nodes except one and on that node, configure the shared storage LUNS as Windows basic disks, format as a single partition/volume for the entire span of the disk, and define an appropriate drive letter or mount point and volume label. Shut down the node used to set up the disks, bring each other node up one at a time, verify that each LUN is available, and if necessary configure the appropriate drive letter if it does not match what was configured on the first node.

- As required, test Multipath I/O for load balancing and/or failover using the appropriate diagnostic or monitoring tool to ensure proper operation on each node one at a time.

Types of Shared Storage

The final topic for storage that a DBA must fully understand is the different types of storage associated with Windows Server 2008. The storage items consist of:

- SAS (Serial Attached SCSI) Storage Arrays
- Fibre Channel Storage Arrays
- ISCSI Storage
- Multipath I/O

SAS Serial Attached SCSI Storage Arrays

SAS (Serial Attached SCSI) disks are one of the newest additions to the disk market. SAS storage arrays can provide organizations with affordable entry-level hardware-based Direct Attached Storage arrays suitable for Windows Server 2008 clusters. SAS storage arrays commonly are limited to four hosts, but some models support extenders to add additional hosts as required. One of the major issues not with SAS but with Direct Attached Storage is that replication of the data within the storage is usually not achievable without involving one of the host systems and software.

Fibre Channel Storage Arrays

Using Fibre Channel (FC) HBAs, Windows Server 2008 can access both shared and nonshared disks residing on a SAN connected to a common FC

Switch. This allows both the shared storage and operating system volumes to be located on the SAN, if desired, to provide diskless servers. In many cases, however, diskless storage may not be desired if the operating system performs many paging actions as the cache on the storage controllers can be used up very fast and can cause delay in disk read and write operations for dedicated cluster storage. If this is desired, however, the SAN must support this option and be configured to present the operating system dedicated LUNs to only a single host exclusively. The LUNs defined for shared cluster storage must be zones and presented to every node in the cluster, and no other systems. The LUN zoning or masking in many cases is configured on the Fibre Channel switch that connects the cluster nodes and the shared storage device. This is a distinct difference between Direct Access Storage and FC or ISCSI share storage. Both FC and ISCSI require a common Fibre Channel or Ethernet switch to establish and maintain connections between the hosts and the storage.

A properly configured FC zone for a cluster will include the World Wide Port Number (WWPN) of each cluster host's FC HBAs and the WWPN of the HBA Controller(s) from the shared storage device. If either the server or the storage device utilize multiple HBAs to connect to a single or multiple FC switches to provide failover or load-balancing functionality, this is known as Multipath I/O and a qualified driver for MPIO management and communication must be used. Also, the function of either MPIO failover and/or MPIO load balancing must be verified as approved for Windows Server 2008. Consult the shared storage vendor including the Fibre Channel switch vendor for documentation and supported configurations, and check the cluster HCL on the Microsoft website to find approved configurations.

ISCSI Storage

When organizations want to utilize ISCSI storage for Windows Server 2008 failover clusters, security and network isolation is highly recommended. ISCSI utilizes an initiator or the host that requires access to the LUNs or ISCSI targets. Targets are located or hosted on ISCSI target portals. Using the Target Portal interface, the target must be configured to be accessed by multiple initiators in a cluster configuration. Both the ISCSI initiators and target portals come in software- and hardware-based models, but both models utilize IP networks for communication between the initiators and the targets. The targets will need to be presented to Windows as a basic disk. When standard network cards will be used for ISCSI communication on Windows Server 2008 systems, the built-in Windows Server 2008 ISCSI Initiator can be used, provided that the ISCSI target can support the authentication and security options provided, if used.

Regardless of the choice of the Microsoft ISCSI initiator, software-based or hardware-based initiators or targets, ISCSI communication should be deployed on isolated network segments and preferably dedicated network switches. Furthermore, the LUNs presented to the failover cluster should be masked from any systems that are not nodes participating in the cluster by using authentication and IPSec communication as possible. Within the Windows Server 2008 operating system, the ISCSI HBA or designated network card should not be used for any failover cluster configuration and cannot be deployed using network teaming software, or it will not be supported by Microsoft.

Hopefully by now it is very clear that Microsoft only wants to support organizations that deploy failover clusters on tested and approved entire systems, but in many cases, failover clusters can still be deployed and can function as the Create a Cluster Wizard will allow a cluster to be deployed that is not in a supported configuration.

Note

When deploying a failover cluster, pay close attention to the results of the Validate a Cluster Wizard to ensure that the system has passed all storage tests to ensure that a supported configuration is deployed.

Multipath I/O

Windows Server 2008 supports Multipath I/O to external storage devices such as SANs and ISCSI targets when multiple HBAs are used in the local system or by the shared storage. Multipath I/O can be used to provide failover access to disk storage in case of a controller or HBA failure, but some drivers also support load balancing across HBAs in both stand-alone and failover cluster deployments. Windows Server 2008 provides a built in Multipath I/O driver that can be leveraged when the manufacturer conforms to the necessary specifications to allow for the use of this built in driver.

Volume Shadow Copy for Shared Storage Volume

The Volume Shadow Copy Service (VSS) is supported on shared storage volumes. Volume Shadow Copy can take a point-in-time snapshot of an entire volume, enabling administrators and users to recover data from a previous version. Furthermore, failover clusters and the entire Windows Backup architecture utilize VSS to store backup data. Many of today's services and applications that are certified to work on Windows Server 2008 failover clusters are VSS compliant, and careful choice and consideration should be made when choosing an alternative backup system, unless the system is provided by the shared storage manufacture and certified to work in conjunction with VSS, Windows Server 2008, and the service or application running on the failover cluster.

> **Note**
>
> Support for parallel SCSI as a shared bus type has been deprecated in Windows Server 2008 failover clusters. SAS is replacing parallel SCSI as a simple and low-cost cluster solution because Serial Attached SCSI (SAS) is the next evolution of parallel SCSI.

Implementing a Single-Instance SQL Server 2008 Failover Cluster

Based on the previous sections in this chapter, there are a tremendous number of prerequisites that must be configured from a hardware perspective before we can start the implementation of a single-instance SQL Server 2008 failover cluster. When the prerequisite tasks are completed, the Windows Server 2008 Failover Cluster feature can be installed. SQL Server 2008 failover clusters are deployed using a series of high-level steps:

- Configure the shared storage for the failover cluster.
- Install the Failover Cluster feature.
- Run the Validate Cluster Configuration Wizard.
- Create the Windows Server 2008 failover cluster.
- Implement DTC (depending on which features will be installed).
- Install the first SQL Server 2008 failover cluster node.
- Add additional SQL Server 2008 failover cluster nodes.

The following example illustrates the implementation of a two-node single-instance SQL Server 2008 failover cluster running on Windows Server 2008 Enterprise Edition for a fictitious organization called CompanyABC.

> **Note**
>
> Tables 12.1 and 12.2 and Figure 12.1 depict the layout of the failover cluster including settings that will be used for this example, "Implementing a Single-Instance SQL Server 2008 Failover Cluster" and the upcoming example, "Implementing a Multiple-Instance SQL Server 2008 Failover Cluster."
>
> The values in the table include the cluster node names, drives, IP addresses, network card, and NetBIOS information used for this example in this chapter.

Table 12.1   **CompanyABC's SQL Server Failover Clustering Settings**

Item	Description
Cluster Nodes	
NODE 1 NETBIOS Name	TOR-CL01
NODE 2 NETBIOS Name	TOR-CL02
NODE 1 Public IP Address	192.168.115.203
NODE 2 Public IP Address	192.168.115.204
NODE 1 Private(Heartbeat) IP Address	10.0.0.1
NODE 2 Private(Heartbeat) IP Address	10.0.0.2
Cluster Name	TOR-CLUS-SQL01
Cluster IP Address	192.168.115.205
SQL Server Virtual Instance01	
SQL Server Virtual Instance01 Name	TOR-CL01-SQL01\INSTANCE01
SQL Server Virtual IP Address	192.168.115.206
Instance01 Failover Components	Database Engine
SQL Server Virtual Instance02	
SQL Server Virtual Instance02 Name	TOR-CL01-SQL02\INSTANCE02
SQL Server Virtual IP Address	192.168.115.207
Instance02 Failover Components	Database Engine
Shared Storage Layout	
Quorum	Q Drive
Database Files - Instance01	D Drive
Database Logs - Instance01	L Drive
Database Files - Instance02	E Drive
Database Logs - Instance02	M Drive
DTC	R Drive
Distributed Transaction Coordinator	
DTC Resource Name	TOR-CLUS-SQL-DTC
DTC IP Address	192.168.115.208

Using the information in Table 12.1 and Figure 12.1, you can now turn your attention to preparing the operating system and configuring the Windows Server 2008 failover cluster.

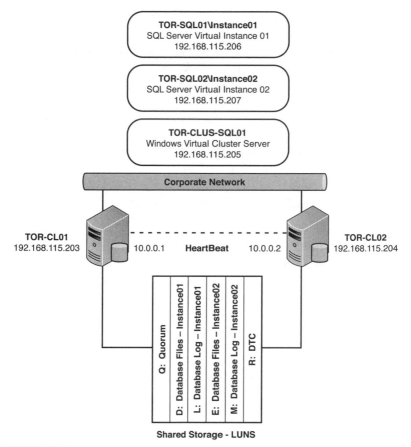

FIGURE 12.1
A multiple-instance failover cluster configuration including settings.

Preparing the Windows Server 2008 Operating System for Each Node

For this example, creating a SQL Server 2008 single-instance failover cluster starts out with a standard installation of Windows Server 2008, Enterprise or Datacenter Edition. Follow these steps to build the operating system based on the assumption that Windows Server 2008 Enterprise Edition will be leveraged:

1. For each node in the two-node cluster, install Windows Server 2008 Enterprise Edition. Use the typical settings when setting up Windows Server 2008.

2. Join the nodes to an Active Directory domain that will host the SQL Cluster such as CompanyABC.

3. Create a heartbeat network between the two nodes by addressing a network interface card (NIC) on a different IP space from the production network. Isolate these heartbeat NICs to an isolated VLAN or a separate network switch or use a crossover cable. This network will be used by the cluster nodes to communicate with each other. For this example, use the IP addresses based on the values in Table 12.1— 10.0.0.1 for node 1 and 10.0.0.2 for node 2. Disable NetBIOS on the heartbeat adapters. Ensure the public network card is the first in the network binding order.

4. Install the latest Windows service packs and hotfixes.

Configuring the Shared Storage for the Windows Server 2008 Failover Cluster

The next step in the process is configuring the shared storage for the failover cluster. In the case of a two-node single-instance failover cluster, you need to configure several shared drives to be accessible by both nodes. These drives include the quorum drive, the DTC drive, 2x database drives and 2x log drives, as shown in Table 12.2.

Table 12.2 **CompanyABC's Clustering Sample Storage Information**

Drive Description	Drive Letter
Quorum	Q Drive
Database Files - Instance01	D Drive
Database Logs - Instance01	L Drive
Database Files - Instance02	E Drive
Database Logs - Instance02	M Drive
DTC	R Drive

Tip

When running Windows Server 2008, it is possible to create a MS DTC resource for each cluster group within the failover cluster. This strategy prevents performance degradation and isolation for disparate applications within multiple cluster groups in the failover cluster. It is still recommended that the DTC resource should be placed on its own shared disk.

After the shared storage has been presented to the nodes in the failover cluster, it is necessary to initialize and format the disk using the Disk Management snap-in in Windows Server 2008.

1. Open the Disk Management snap-in by choosing Start, All Programs, Administrator Tools, and Server Manager.

2. In Server Manager, expand the Storage icon and then select Disk Management.

3. Most likely the shared disks will be offline and are required to be in an online state in order to initialize them. Therefore, right-click each shared disk and select Online.

4. When the shared disks are online, right-click each shared disk and initialize them.

5. In the Initialize Disk dialog box, select the disks to initialize and select the partition style to use, either master boot record (MBR) or GUID partition table (GPT), and then click OK.

Note

A GPT disk takes advantage of a GUID partition table disk partitioning system. GPT disks allow up to 128 partitions per disk, volume sizes of over 2 terabytes, and in general are more reliable and scalable. MBR, which is the traditional partition style, has a limitation of four primary partitions and a maximum size of 2 terabytes.

---

6. The disks that are initialized as basic disks, however, show up as unallocated. On each shared disk, create a new simple volume, specify a volume size, assign a drive letter, and format the drive with NTFS. Be sure to create them as primary partitions, and do not convert the disks to dynamic disks. For this example, the disk configuration is based on Table 12.2 and Figure 12.2.

Note

Disks made available to a cluster must be configured as basic disks. A Windows 2008 cluster can't access a dynamic disk.

Preparing the Windows Server 2008 Failover Cluster

Now that the nodes are prepared and the shared storage is created, initialized, and formatted, the Windows Server 2008 failover cluster can be formed. Be sure to have the following items ready for the cluster configuration: unique names for each node, unique name for the cluster identity, unique name for each SQL Server instance, and unique IP addresses for each of the names created previously. The following steps should be conducted in the order presented.

Installing the Windows Server 2008 Failover Cluster Feature on Each Node

With Windows Server 2008, the Failover Cluster feature is no longer installed by default. Before a failover cluster can be deployed, the necessary feature must be installed. To install the Failover Cluster feature, perform the following steps on a Windows Server 2008 node:

1. Log on to the Windows Server 2008 cluster node with an account with administrator privileges.

2. Click Start, All Programs, Administrative Tools, and then select Server Manager.

3. When Server Manager opens, in the Tree pane select the Features node.

4. In the Tasks pane, select the Add Features link.

5. In the Add Features window, select Failover Clustering and click Install.

6. When the installation completes, click the Close button to complete the installation and return to Server Manager.

7. Close Server Manager and install the Failover Cluster feature on each of the remaining cluster nodes.

Running the Windows Server 2008 Validate a Cluster Configuration Wizard

Failover Cluster Management is the new MMC Snap-in used to administer the Failover Cluster feature. After the feature is installed, the next step is to run the Validate a Configuration Wizard from the Tasks pane of the Failover Cluster Management console. All nodes should be up and running when the wizard is run. To run the Validate a Configuration wizard, perform the following steps:

1. Log on to one of the Windows Server 2008 cluster nodes with an account with administrator privileges over all nodes in the cluster.

2. Click Start, All Programs, Administrative Tools, and then select Failover Cluster Management.

3. When the Failover Cluster Management console opens, click the Validate a Configuration link in the Actions pane.

4. When the Validate a Configuration wizard opens, click Next on the Before You Begin page.

5. In the Select Servers or a Cluster page, enter the name of a cluster node and click the Add button. Repeat this process until all nodes are added to the list. For this example TOR-CL01 and TOR-CL02 were specified. Click Next to continue.

6. In the Testing Options page, read the details that explain the requirements for all tests to pass in order to be supported by Microsoft. Select the Run All Tests (Recommended) radio button and click Next to continue.

7. In the Confirmation page, review the list of servers that will be tested and the list of tests that will be performed, and click Next to begin testing the servers.

8. When the tests complete, the Summary window will display the results and whether the tests passed. Click Finish to complete the Validate a Configuration wizard. If the test failed, click the View Report button to review the details of the results and determine which test failed and why the test failed.

Note

Disks Even if the Validate a Configuration wizard does not pass every test, depending on the test, creating a cluster may still be possible. After the Validate a Configuration wizard is completed successfully, the cluster can be created.

Caution

You may stumble upon an error indicating that duplicate IP addresses were found on the Teredo Tunneling Pseudo-Interface network adapters among both nodes within the cluster. This error message is not accurate, but it will prevent you from going ahead and installing the failover cluster. The workaround is to disable the Teredo driver in Windows Server 2008 Device Manager on all nodes within the cluster.

Creating the Windows Server 2008 Failover Cluster

When the Windows Server 2008 Failover Cluster is first created, all nodes in the cluster should be up and running. The exception to that rule is when failover clusters utilize direct attached storage such as Serial Attached SCSI devices that require a process of creating the cluster on a single node and adding other nodes one at a time. For clusters that will not use shared storage or clusters that will connect to shared storage using ISCSI or Fibre Channel connections, all nodes should be powered on during cluster creation. To create the failover cluster, perform the following steps:

1. Log on to one of the Windows Server 2008 cluster nodes with an account with administrator privileges over all nodes in the cluster.

2. Click Start, All Programs, Administrative Tools, and then select Failover Cluster Management.

3. When the Failover Cluster Management console opens, click the Create a Cluster link in the Actions pane.

4. When the Create Cluster Wizard opens, click Next on the Before You Begin page.

5. In the Select Servers page, enter the name of each cluster node and click Add. When all the nodes are listed, click the Next button to continue.

6. In the Access Point for Administering the Cluster page, type the name of the cluster (**TOR-CLUS-SQL01**), specify the IPv4 address (**192.168.115.205**), and click Next, as shown in Figure 12.2.

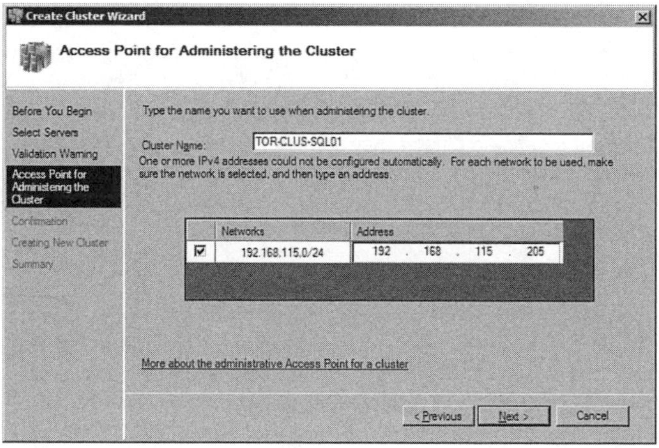

FIGURE 12.2
Defining the network name and IPv4 address for the failover cluster.

7. On the Confirmation page, review the settings and click Next to create the cluster.

8. On the Summary page, review the results of the cluster creation process and click Finish to return to the Failover Cluster Management console. If there are any errors, click the View Report button to reveal the detailed cluster creation report.

9. Back in the Failover Cluster Management console, select the cluster name in the Tree pane. In the Tasks pane review the configuration of the cluster.

10. In the Tree pane, select and expand the Nodes folder to list all of the cluster nodes.

11. Select Storage and review the cluster storage in the Tasks pane listed under Summary of Storage, as shown in Figure 12.3.

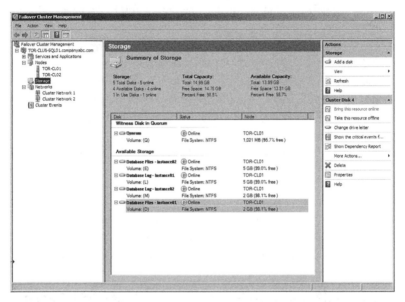

FIGURE 12.3
Displaying the dedicated cluster storage.

12. Expand Networks in the Tree pane to review the list of networks. Select each network and review the names of the adapters in each network.

13. When you have completed reviewing the cluster, close the Failover Cluster Management console and log off the cluster node.

After the cluster is created, additional tasks should be performed before any Services and Application groups are created using the High Availability Wizard. These tasks can include, but may not require, customizing the cluster networks, adding storage to the cluster, adding nodes to the cluster, changing the cluster Quorum model, and installing DTC.

Installing DTC as a SQL Server Failover Clustering Prerequisite

As discussed earlier in the chapter, DTC is required as a prerequisite for installing SQL clustering. To create the DTC resource, follow these steps:

1. In Failover Cluster Management, expand the failover cluster created in the previous steps and then expand the Services and Applications node.

2. In the Actions pane, double-click Configure a Service or Application.

3. Read the information presented on the Before You Begin page and then click Next.

4. On the Select Service or Application page, select Distributed Transaction Coordinator (DTC) and then click Next.

5. On the Client Access Point page, specify a name for the DTC service and then a dedicated IP Address. For this example, the DTC name is **TOR-CLUS-SQL-DTC** and the IP Address is **192.168.115.208**. Click Next to continue.

6. The next page is Select Storage. On this page, select the storage volume that you want to assign to the DTC clustered resource. For this example, use the DTC drive, which is the letter R. Click Next to continue.

7. Review the settings on the confirmation page, and then click Next.

8. Review the progress bar on the Configure High Availability page, then view the status on the installation on the Summary page and click Finish.

Installing the First Node in the Single-Instance SQL Server 2008 Failover Cluster

Follow the next set of steps to install failover clustering for the first virtual instance of SQL Server 2008. The features installed for this virtual instance are strictly for the Database Engine. These steps should be conducted on the first node of the Windows Cluster. The installation steps are based on the examples provided in Figure 12.1. Validate that the first node (TOR-CL01) is the owner for all cluster resources and then do the following:

1. Log into the first node with administrative privileges and insert the SQL Server 2008 media. Autorun should launch the SQL Server 2008 Installation Center landing page; otherwise, click Setup.exe.

> **Note**
>
> If SQL Server's setup software prerequisites have not been met, the installation wizard will prompt, and then install the prerequisites. After the prerequisites have been installed, the SQL Server installation process will resume. SQL Server 2008 software prerequisites may include .NET framework 3.5 and the latest Windows Installer, version 4.5. In addition, system restarts may be required after SQL Server's setup software prerequisites are installed. If so, rerun setup after the reboot to continue with the SQL Server installation.

2. To install a single-node SQL Server failover cluster, on the SQL Server Installation Center screen, first click the Installation link, and then New SQL Server Failover Cluster Installation, as illustrated in Figure 12.4.

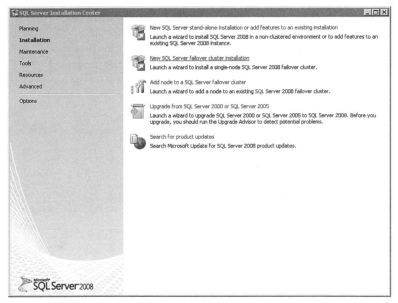

FIGURE 12.4
Selecting the option to install a new SQL Server failover cluster installation.

3. On the Setup Support Rules page, review the outcome of the System Configuration Checker. Ensure that all tests associated with the operation passed without any failures, warnings, or skipped elements. Alternatively, you can review a standard or comprehensive report by selecting the Show Details button or View Detailed Report. To continue with the installation, click OK.

4. On the Product Key page, enter the SQL Server Product Key and click Next.

5. On the License Agreement page, Accept the Licensing Terms, and then click Next.

6. On the Setup Support Files screen, the wizard will prompt if additional setup support files are required for the failover cluster installation. If additional files are required, review the status of the files required and click Install.

7. The Setup Support Rules page will be displayed again and will identify any outstanding items that may hinder the installation process associated with the SQL Server failover cluster. Review and correct failures and warnings before commencing the installation. If failures are not displayed, then click Next to start the installation.

8. On the Feature Selection page, select the desired clustered components and features to install. Then specify the installation path for the Shared Feature Directory and Shared Feature Directory (x86) folders. Click Next to continue as displayed in Figure 12.5. For this example, the Database Engine Services component, SQL Server Replication, and Full-Text Search features were selected.

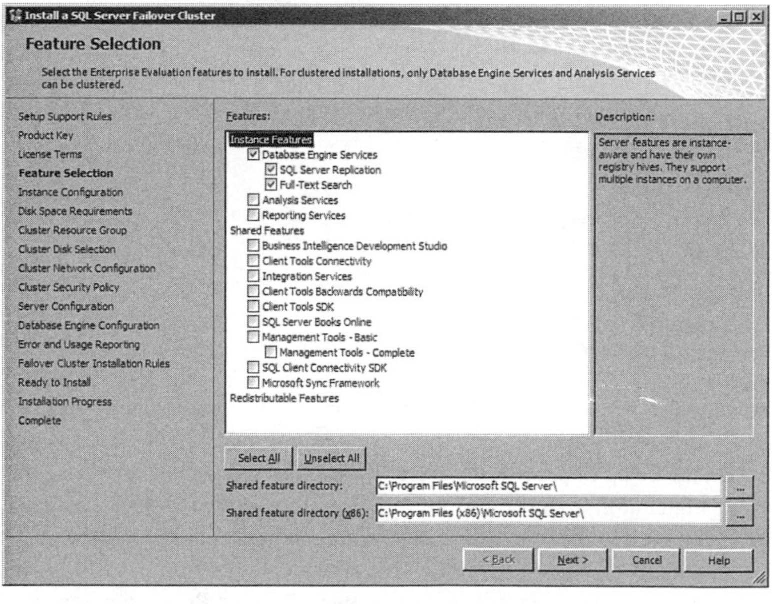

FIGURE 12.5
The Feature Selection page.

> **Note**
>
> Only the Database Engine Services and Analysis Services features are failover-cluster aware. In addition, if you want to install SSMS, select Management Tools in the Shared Features options.

9. On the Instance Configuration page, specify the SQL Server Failover Cluster Network Name, Instance Name, and Instance ID for the SQL Server failover cluster instance. In addition, provide the path for the Instance Root Directory, and then click Next. For this example, the items specified in the Instance Configuration page are based on Table 12.3.

Table 12.3   **CompanyABC's Instance Parameters**

Element Description	Element Value
SQL Server Failover Cluster Network Name	TOR-CL01-SQL01
Instance Name	Instance01
Instance ID	Instance01
Instance Root Directory	C:\Program Files\Microsoft SQL Server\

10. The next page is the Disk Space Requirements. Review the disk space summary for the SQL Server components and features selected and then click Next.

11. On the Cluster Resource Group page, specify a name for the new SQL Server resource group, and then click Next. The resource group is where the SQL Server virtual resources will be placed. This page also displays existing cluster resource groups installed within the failover cluster.

12. Now you must specify the shared cluster disks that will be used with the new SQL Server failover cluster installation. For this example, the DatabaseFiles-Instance-01 and DatabaseLogs-Instance01 shared disks will be used. Click Next to continue as displayed in Figure 12.6.

> **NOTE**
>
> By default, the first available disk located in the Available Shared Disks section will be selected for the installation. However, you can change this by specifying an alternative shared disk. Also, any disks already associated to another service or application, such as the quorum, will be unavailable.

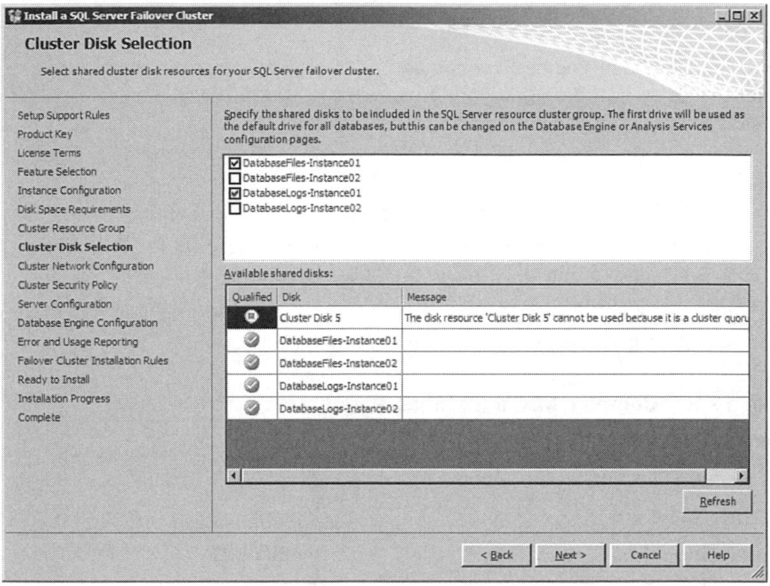

FIGURE 12.6
Specifying the cluster disk to be used for the failover cluster installation.

13. A SQL Server 2008 failover cluster on Windows Server 2008 supports both IPv4 and IPv6. On the Cluster Network Configuration page, first indicate which IP Type will be utilized; IPv4 and/or IPv6 and then enter a virtual IP address and subsequent Subnet Mask, and then Click Next. For this example, the IP address of 192.168.115.206 with a subnet mask of 255.255.255.0 was used.

> **Tip**
>
> When you're entering network configuration settings on a SQL Server 2008 cluster running Window Server 2008, it is possible to obtain a dynamic IP address via DHCP for the virtual instance. Using DHCP addresses for mission-critical services is not an industry best practice, hence not recommended.

14. On the Cluster Security Policy page, select the option to use either Service SIDs or Domain Groups; Service SIDs is recommended when using Windows Server 2008. If the Domain Groups option is selected, an already created domain group must be entered for each SQL Server service presented on this screen. Click Next to continue.

Note

During a SQL Server installation, SQL Server Setup creates a service group for each feature of SQL Server being installed. When running Windows Server 2008, it is possible to leverage service SIDs instead of creating predefined Service Account groups in Active Directory, which was a requirement of Windows Server 2003. When using service SIDs with Windows Server 2008, a higher level of service isolation is achieved as the service SID is added to the local security group instead of the SQL Server service account.

15. On the Collation tab, enter the desired collation option for the Database Engine. It is possible to change default collation settings used by the Database Engine and Analysis Services for language and sorting by selecting Customize. Click Next to continue.

16. The Database Engine Configuration page consists of three tabs: Account Provisioning, Data Directories, and FILESTREAM.

   a. On the first tab, in the Account Provisioning section, specify the Authentication Mode, which consists of either Windows Authentication Mode or Mixed Mode (SQL Server authentication and Windows authentication). If Mixed Mode is selected, enter and confirm the password for the Built-in SQL Server administrator account. The next step is to provision a SQL Server Administrator by either selecting the option Add Current User or clicking Add and specifying a SQL Server administrator account.

Note

From a hardening perspective, Microsoft recommends entering a separate service account for each SQL Server component and feature being installed. In addition, the account specified should follow the principle of least privilege. For more information on selecting the desired service account, and hardening a SQL Server implementation, reference Chapter 8, "Hardening a SQL Server Implementation."

   b. The second tab, Data Directories, located on the Database Engine Configuration page, is used for specifying the location of the default directories associated with the installation of this SQL Server instance. The directories include: Data Root Directory, System Database Directory, User Database Directory, User Database Log Directory, TempDB Directory, Temp DB Log Directory, and Backup Directory. Either maintain the default directories or specify a new directory residing on the shared disks.

Tip

Because I/O to log files is sequential and I/O to database files is random, it is a best practice for increased performance to place log files on separate disks from database files. In addition, placing the tempdb on its own disk also bolsters performance. Because this is a failover cluster configuration, all disks need to be shared disks—accessible by both nodes in the cluster.

    c. The final tab on the Database Engine Configuration page is FILESTREAM. Here, decide whether or not you want to enable FILESTREAM. If FILESTREAM is enabled, additional parameters must be entered such as Enable FILESTREAM for File I/O Streaming Access, Windows Share Name, and whether or not to allow remote clients to have streaming access to FILESTREAM data. Click Next to proceed. When working with clustering, FILESTREAM filegroups must be placed on shared disks with a cluster. In addition, FILESTREAM must be enabled on each node in the cluster.

17. On the Error and Usage Reporting page, help Microsoft improve SQL Server features and services by sending error reports and feature usage to Microsoft. Specify the level of participation, and then click Next.

18. The final check will take place to ensure that the failover cluster installation will not be blocked. On the Upgrade Installation Rules, review for any outstanding errors or warnings and then click Next to continue.

19. Before commencing the SQL Server 2008 failover installation, review the features to be upgraded on the Ready to Install page, and then click Install.

Note

If you need to review the installation and configuration logs after the installation is complete, please note the location of this file and path.

20. When the installation process starts, you can monitor its progress accordingly. When the installation setup completes, review the success status based upon each SQL Server Failover Cluster feature and then click Next.

21. On the Complete page, review the location of the SQL Server summary upgrade log file and additional items that can be found in the supplemental information section. Click Close to finalize the installation.

These steps conclude the installation of the first node associated with the single-instance failover cluster. As mentioned earlier, the SQL Server failover cluster installation is no longer a single-step process as the installation process is now on a per-node basis. Therefore, in order to finalize the SQL Server failover cluster, the steps in the following section must be completed and repeated for every additional nodes within the cluster.

Installing Additional Nodes in the Single-Instance SQL Server 2008 Failover Cluster

Based on conducting the steps in the previous section, we have successfully established the first node associated with the SQL Server 2008 failover cluster for TOR-CL01-SQL01\Instance01. As mentioned earlier, the failover clustering installation process in SQL Server 2008 has changed significantly. Each node within the cluster is a peer and completely independent of each other. Therefore, we now have to conduct the following steps to add additional nodes to the existing failover cluster configuration.

Note

The steps are very similar to adding the first node in the SQL Server 2008 failover cluster; however, the major difference is that you select the option Add Node to a SQL Server Failover Cluster instead of New SQL Server Failover Cluster Installation on SQL Server Installation Center.

---

1. Log in to the second node with administrative privileges and insert the SQL Server 2008 media. Autorun should launch the SQL Server 2008 Installation Center landing page; otherwise, click Setup.exe.

2. To install the additional node into the SQL Server failover cluster, on the SQL Server Installation Center page, first click the Installation link, and then Add Node to a SQL Server Failover Cluster.

3. On the Setup Support Rules page, review the outcome of the System Configuration Checker. Ensure that all tests associated with the operation passed without any failures, warnings, or skipped elements. Alternatively, you can review a standard or comprehensive report by selecting the Show Details button or View Detailed Report. To continue with the installation, click OK.

4. On the Product Key page, enter the SQL Server Product Key, and click Next.

5. On the License Agreement page, accept the Licensing Terms, and then click Next.

6. On the Setup Support Files page, the wizard will prompt if additional setup support files are required for the installation. If additional files are required, review the status of the files required and click Install.

7. The next page, Setup Support Rules, will identify any outstanding items that may hinder the installation process associated with the SQL Server cluster. Review and correct failures and click Next.

8. The Cluster Node Configuration page is now invoked. Use the drop-down box and select the name of the SQL Server instance name to join. The Name field of this node text box is prepopulated with the name of the associated node from which the installation is being conducted. For this example, use **TOR-CL01-SQL01\Instance01**. Click Next, as displayed in Figure 12.7.

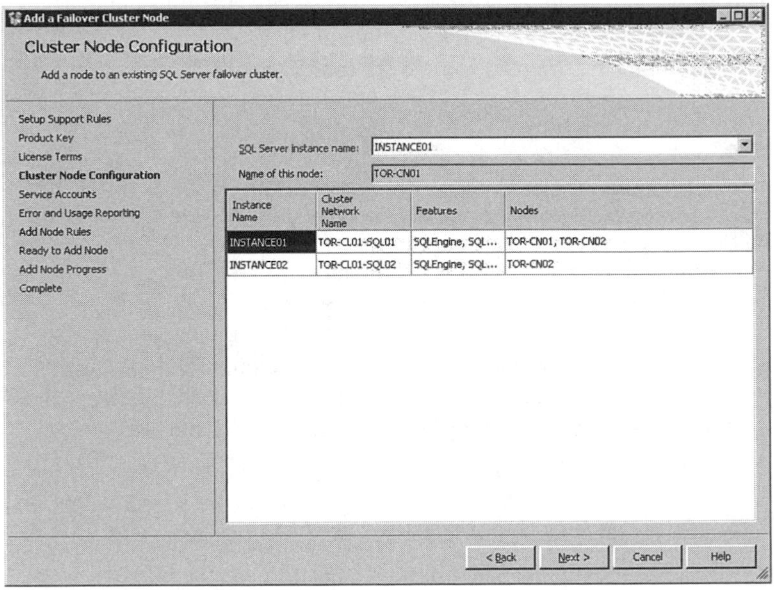

FIGURE 12.7
Specifying the name of the SQL Server instance to join.

9. On the Service Accounts page, specify the password for the accounts associated with each service, and then click Next.

10. On the Error and Usage Reporting page, help Microsoft improve SQL Server features and services by sending error reports and feature usage to Microsoft. Specify the level of participation, and then click Next.

11. Setup will run a final set of rules to ensure that the Add Node process will not be blocked. To continue, Click Next on the Add Node Rules page.

12. Before adding the node to the existing failover cluster, in the Read to Add Node page, review the components and features that will be installed and click Next.

13. Review the progress of the installation on the Add Node Progress page, and then click Next to finalize the installation.

14. On the final page, Complete, information about the setup operation, the location of the summary log file, and the next steps is presented. Review this information, and then click Close to exit the SQL Server Installation Wizard.

15. Repeat steps 1 to 13 if additional nodes exist within the SQL Server failover Configuration.

Implement a Multiple-Instance SQL Server 2008 Failover Cluster

One of the challenges that many DBAs face is understanding the concept of how to employ a multiple-instance SQL Server 2008 failover cluster. Implementing a multiple-instance failover cluster is as simple as creating a single-instance failover cluster; however, the new instance requires a dedicated SQL server name, instance name, instance ID, IP address, and shared cluster disks.

When working with multiple-instance configurations, it is also beneficial to configure the preferred node settings in Failover Cluster Management for maximum performance. For example, Instance01 would be operating on Node1 and Instance02 would be operating on Node2.

Note

Before installing additional instances onto a failover cluster, ensure that the first instance has been successfully established by following the steps in the previous sections. The steps include "Installing the First Node in the Single-Instance SQL Server 2008 Failover Cluster" and "Installing Additional Nodes in the Single-Instance SQL Server 2008 Failover Cluster."

The following example illustrates the implementation of a multiple-instance SQL Server 2008 failover cluster implementation using Windows Server 2008 Enterprise Edition for CompanyABC. This example is based upon implementing the second instance, TOR-SQL02\Instance02, for the fictitious organization ABC. The example is also depicted in Figure 12.1 and uses the data found in Table 12.1, specifically items associated with the SQL Server Virtual Instance02.

In order to start, a single-instance failover cluster that has already been established by following the preceding steps must exist. In addition, ensure that the additional shared cluster drives E and M are present within Failover Cluster Management before starting.

Using the information in Figure 12.1 and Table 12.1, you can now turn your attention to the following steps to install the first node in the multiple-instance SQL Server 2008 failover cluster.

Installing the First Node in the Multiple-Instance SQL Server 2008 Failover Cluster

To employ a multiple-instance failover configuration, follow the 21 steps in the section "Installing the First Node in the Single-Instance SQL Server 2008 Failover Cluster;" to be steps 9, 11, 12, and 13 with the following alternatives.

1. On the Instance Configuration page, which was step 9, specify the SQL Server Failover Cluster Network Name, Instance Name, and Instance ID for the new SQL Server failover cluster instance based on the values in Table 12.4. In addition, provide the path for the Instance Root Directory, and then click Next.

Table 12.4   **Values for New Failover Cluster**

Element Description	Element Value
SQL Server Failover Cluster Network Name	TOR-CL01-SQL02
Instance Name	Instance02
Instance ID	Instance02
Instance Root Directory	C:\Program Files\Microsoft SQL Server\

2. On the Cluster Resource Group page, which was step 11, specify a unique name for the new SQL Server resource group (TOR-CL01-SQL02\ Instance02), and then click Next. The cluster resource group is where the new SQL Server virtual resources associated with Instance02 will be placed. This page also displays existing cluster resource groups installed within the failover cluster. Click Next as illustrated in Figure 12.8.

3. On the Cluster Disk Selection page, which was formerly step 12, specify the shared cluster disks to be included in the SQL Server resource cluster group associated with the new multiple-instance SQL Server failover cluster installation. For this example, the DatabaseFiles-Instance-02 and DatabaseLogs-Instance02 shared disks will be used. Click Next to continue as displayed in Figure 12.9.

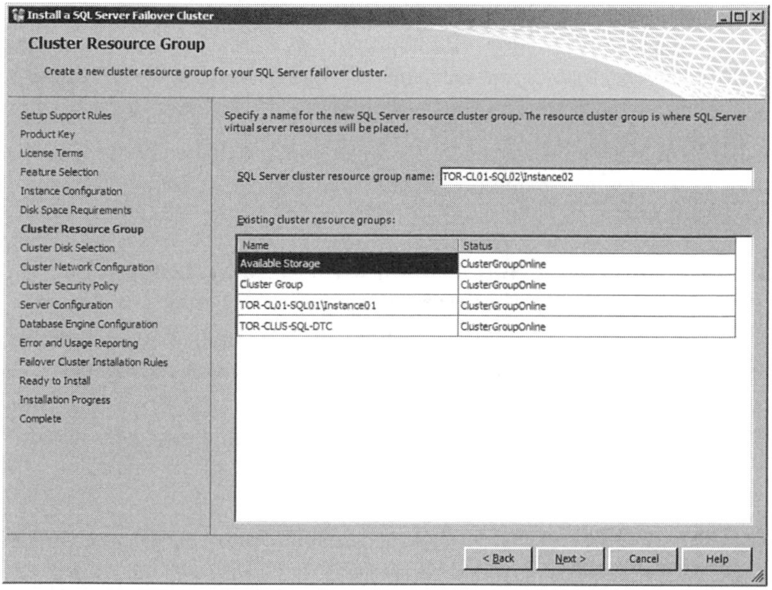

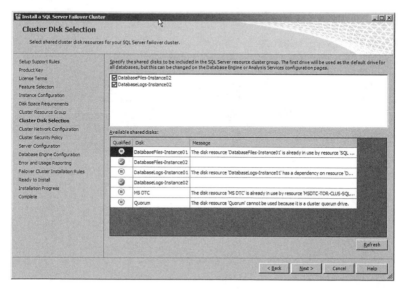

FIGURE 12.8
Specifying the name for the new SQL Server cluster resource group.

FIGURE 12.9
Specifying the shared disks for the new SQL Server instance.

4. On the Cluster Network Configuration page, which was step 13, first indi-
    cate which IP Type will be utilized; IPv4 and/or IPv6 and then enter a virtual
    IP address and subsequent subnet mask. For this example, the IP address of
    192.168.115.207 with a subnet mask of 255.255.255.0 was used. Click Next.

Finalize the remainder of the steps to complete the installation of the first node
associated with the new multiple-instance failover cluster called TOR-CL01-
SQL02\INSTANCE02.

Installing Additional Nodes in the Multiple-Instance SQL Server 2008 Failover Cluster

Conduct the following steps in order to finalize the additional nodes associated
with the multiple-instance SQL Server 2008 failover cluster TOR-CL01-
SQL02\Instance02.

1. Follow the 14 steps in the section "Installing Additional Nodes in the
    Single-Instance SQL Server 2008 Failover Cluster," but replace step 8 as
    follows.

2. The Cluster Node Configuration page, which was step 8, is now invoked.
    Use the drop-down box and select the name of the SQL Server instance
    name to join (TOR-CL01-SQL02\Instance02). The Name field of this
    node text box is prepopulated with the name of the associated node from
    which the installation is being conducted. Click Next to continue, as
    displayed in Figure 12.10.

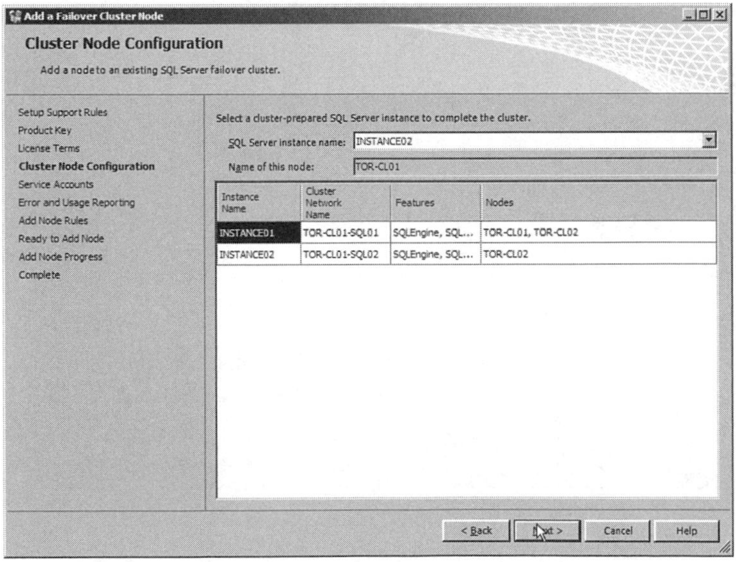

FIGURE 12.10
Adding a node to an existing SQL Server failover cluster.

3. Repeat steps 1 to 13 for any additional nodes that exist within the SQL Server failover configuration.

Managing Failover Clusters from a SQL Server 2008 Perspective

The following sections focus on management tasks after a SQL Server 2008 failover cluster has been implemented. These tasks are in no particular order and focus on the SQL Server aspect of failover clustering. The subsequent section of the chapter, "Managing Failover Clusters from a Windows Server 2008 Perspective," will focus on failover cluster management tasks from a Windows Server 2008 point of view.

Verifying the Status of Clustered Service and Applications, Nodes, Storage, and Networks

As database administrator, you frequently need to know which node is the owner of each clustered group, service, and application, whether or not a node is operational, status on storage, and whether any health issues are occurring. The first level of defense when reviewing status is to check cluster events. Cluster events can be found by expanding a cluster name in Failover Cluster Management, and then in the Tree pane selecting Cluster Events. Alternatively, status of a failover cluster element can be determined by following these steps.

1. In Failover Cluster Management, select and expand the cluster name.

2. In the Tree pane, select either Services and Applications, Nodes, Storage or Networks.

3. After the element has been selected, its status is displayed in the central pane.

Initiating Manual Service or Application Failovers

To manage service or application failovers, follow these steps:

1. In Failover Cluster Management, expand the desired failover cluster name.

2. Expand Services and Applications and then select a SQL Server Failover Service or Application, also formerly known as a cluster group.

3. From the Actions pane, select Move This Service or Application to Another Node and then specify the node to move to.

4. In the Please Confirm Action dialog box, read the warning message and select the option Move.

Managing SQL Server Failover Service Accounts

Sometimes a service account or a service account password needs to be changed for the failover cluster instance. Similar to a stand-alone SQL Server installation, all SQL Service account changes should be conducted with the SQL Server 2008 Configuration Manager tool. In addition, when you're working with clusters, all nodes must be online when a service account changes. As a reminder, when allocating service accounts, follow the practice of least privilege and isolation; as a result, the SQL Cluster Service Account should be a different account from the service account running the Windows cluster.

Managing Preferred Owners of a Cluster Node and Group

For each service or application, you can assign a preferred owner. In the example, there are two instances of SQL Server installed within the cluster. From a performance perspective, it is possible to configure node 1 to be the preferred owner of TOR-SQL/Instance01 and node 2 to be the preferred owner of TOR-SQL02/Instance02. Therefore, when the servers are brought online, the preferred owners maintain service operations of the desired Service or Application and SQL Server virtual instance. It is worth mentioning that preferred owners are necessary when you are running more than two nodes within a cluster. The preferred owners list dictates the failover behavior to the next available node based on the nodes in the list. For example, in an eight-node cluster, you may have dedicated passive standbys by having node 1 first fail over to node 3, then node 4, and then node 5.

Tip

When the cluster nodes are turned on, the cluster administrator tries to assign the SQL Server virtual server to the first node in the preferred owners list. If this node is not available, the server is assigned to the next server name in the list. This behavior is similar to the failover process. If a failover occurs, the SQL Server cluster fails over to the available passive nodes based on the preferred owners list.

Follow the next set of steps to configure preferred owners for a SQL Server failover cluster. For example, based on our example, TOR-CL01-SQL01\INSTANCE01 should be homed in on node 1 (TOR-CL01), and TOR-CL01-SQL02\INSTANCE02 should be homed in on node 2 (TOR-CL02). Follow these steps to make preferred node changes on a failover cluster:

1. In Failover Cluster Management, expand the desired failover cluster name.

2. Expand Services and Applications and then select a SQL Server failover service or application.

3. Right-click a SQL Server failover service or application and select Properties.

4. In the Service or Application Properties dialog box, specify the preferred owners of the service or application.

5. If more than one node is selected, use the Up and Down buttons to move the desired node owner to the top of the list.

6. In order to have the Service or Application automatically move to the particular node when the node becomes available, ensure that the Allow Failback option is selected on the Failover tab.

7. Click OK to finalize.

Managing Failover Clustering Failover Policies

There are a few ways to control how many failures will be allowed in a given period of time until the resource is left in a failed state. First, a global setting controls the threshold and period of a failover. This setting affects the whole service or application and dictates how many times a failover can occur during a period of time. Second, advanced parameters can be configured on each individual resource. Advanced parameters dictate whether the individual resource failure will affect the whole service or application and interval settings such as Looks Alive and Is Alive.

Follow these steps to configure failover settings for a Service or Application such as `TOR-CL01-SQL01\INSTANCE01`:

1. In Failover Cluster Management, expand the desired failover cluster name.

2. Expand Services and Applications and then select a SQL Server Failover Service or Application you plan on modifying.

3. Right-click the SQL Server failover service or application and select Properties.

4. In the Service or Application Properties box, select the Failover tab and specify the number of times the Cluster service will attempt to restart in a specified period.

5. Finally, in the Failback section, specify whether or not Failback is allowed.

6. Click OK to finalize.

Managing Failover Clustering Failback Policies

When a primary node fails, you can control the behavior of the failback after the primary node becomes active again. The failback can be set to immediately, between a specific time of the day, or can be prevented. For mission-critical production clusters, it is a best practice to either prevent automatic failback or set the failback during hours of nonpeak usage. By using these settings, you can fail back the node manually or during nonpeak usage. As a result, the end-user community and application are not affected, resulting in downtime when the node fails back.

Follow these steps to configure failback settings for a service or application such as `TOR-CL01-SQL01\INSTANCE01`:

1. In Failover Cluster Management, expand the desired failover cluster name.

2. Expand Services and Applications and then select a SQL Server failover service or application.

3. Right-click a SQL Server failover service or application and select Properties.

4. In the Service or Application Properties box, select the Failover tab and specify whether or not failback is allowed.

5. If the Allow Failback option is selected, specify the option to fail back immediately or between a desired interval.

6. Click OK to finalize.

Removing SQL Server 2008 Nodes from an Existing SQL Server Failover Cluster

Because the SQL Server 2008 Enterprise Edition supports up to 16 nodes in a cluster, sometimes you may need to remove a node from an existing SQL Server 2008 clustered instance. Unfortunately, to achieve this goal, you must rerun Setup and from the SQL Server Installation Center, select the Maintenance link and then double-click Remove Node from a SQL Server Failover Cluster. The good news is that the wizard for removing nodes is intuitive and the removal process does not negatively affect surviving nodes in the cluster because each node is an independent peer. Run the following steps on the node or nodes you plan on evicting from the SQL Server failover cluster:

1. On the SQL Server Installation Center screen, click the Maintenance link and then click Remove Node from a SQL Server Failover Cluster.

2. On the Setup Support Rules screen, review the outcome of the System Configuration Checker. Ensure that all tests associated with the operation passed without any failures, warnings, or skipped elements. Alternatively, you can review a standard or comprehensive report by selecting the Show Details button or View Detailed Report. Click OK to continue with the installation.

3. The Cluster Node Configuration page is now invoked. Use the drop-down box and specify an existing SQL Server failover cluster to modify. The Name field of this node text box is prepopulated with the name of the associated node from which the installation is being conducted. Therefore, as a reminder you must conduct these steps from the node you plan on removing. Click Next.

4. On the Ready to Remove Node page, verify the SQL Server 2008 features to be removed as part of the removed node operation and click Remove.

5. Review the remove node process on the Remove Node Progress page, and then click Next to finalize the removal process.

6. On the final page, Complete, information about the removal operation, the location of the summary log file, and the next steps is presented. Review this information, and then click Close to exit the SQL Server Installation Wizard.

Removing SQL Server Failover Clustering

There are multiple steps involved when removing SQL Server Failover Clustering completely from a Windows Server 2008 environment. First use the Remove Node functionality found in the SQL Server Installation Center, as depicted in the preceding section. Repeat this process on all SQL Server nodes within the cluster. Then, using Windows Server 2008 Program and Features, remove each SQL Server element. Repeat steps for each node within the cluster. Windows Server 2008 Programs and Features can be invoked by selecting Start, Control Panel, and then Programs and Features.

Managing Failover Clusters from a Windows Server 2008 Perspective

The upcoming section include step-by-step tasks for managing failover cluster from a Windows Server 2008 perspective.

Administering Patch Management on a SQL Server 2008 Failover Cluster

Similar to a traditional non-clustered SQL Server, the operating system and SQL Server application require ongoing patch management to keep the servers up to date. Patch management includes installing service packs and critical hotfixes for both the operating system and SQL Server. When you're working in a clustered environment, each node within the cluster should have the exact same service pack and hotfixes to ensure consistency.

One of the main benefits of using failover clusters is your ability to install software, service packs, and critical updates on a node without interrupting service of the cluster. This process is known as a *rolling upgrade*. For example, when you install service packs and critical fixes for Windows Server 2008, all the services or applications can be failed over to the second node, and the installation can then be conducted on the first node without affecting client operations. The node can be rolled back to node 1, and Windows Server 2008 service packs and critical fixes can be applied to the second node. The rolling upgrade strategy has been reintroduced in SQL Server 2008.

Pausing and Resuming a SQL Server Cluster Node

When you're conducting maintenance or rolling upgrades, it is common to pause a node. When a node is paused, the existing services or applications and resources stay online; however, additional groups and resources cannot be brought online. Follow these steps to pause and resume a SQL Server cluster node:

1. In Failover Cluster Management, expand the desired failover cluster name.
2. Expand the Node tree.
3. Right-click the node you plan on modifying and select Pause.
4. Repeat the steps, and choose Resume to recommence the node.

Adding Additional Windows Nodes to the Cluster

If additional Windows nodes need to be added to the cluster after the initial cluster creation process, perform the following steps:

1. In Failover Cluster Management, select and expand the cluster name.
2. Select and expand Nodes in the Tree pane.
3. Right-click Nodes and select Add Node.
4. When the Add Node Wizard opens, click Next on the Before You Begin page.

5. In the Select Server page, type the name of the cluster node and click the Add button. After the node has been added to the list, click Next to continue.

6. In the Confirmation page, review the names of the node or nodes that will be added and click Next to continue.

7. When the process completes, review the results in the Summary page and click Finish to close the wizard.

Adding Storage to the Cluster

When shared storage is used with failover clusters, all of the LUNs or targets presented to the cluster hosts may not have been added to the cluster during the initial configuration. When this is the case, and additional storage needs to be added to the cluster, perform the following steps:

1. In Failover Cluster Management, select and expand the cluster name.

2. In the Tree pane, select Storage, right-click and select Add a Disk.

3. If suitable storage is ready to be added to the cluster, it will be listed in the Add Disks to a Cluster window. If a disk is listed, check the box next to the desired disk or disks and click OK to add the disk(s) to the cluster.

4. When the process completes, if necessary, change the drive letter of the new disk.

5. Close the Failover Cluster Management console.

6. Click the Start button and select Computer.

7. Review the list of disks on the cluster node and note that disks managed by the cluster are listed as clustered disks instead of local disks. This is a distinct change from server clusters in previous versions of Windows Server.

8. Close the Explorer windows and log off the server.

Managing Cluster Drive Dependencies

Unless otherwise specified, a SQL Server virtual instance uses only one shared hard drive during the installation of SQL Server failover clustering. Therefore, even though additional share drives are available in the cluster, such as the log and backup drives, a SQL Server instance cannot leverage those shared drives unless each additional shared drive is added as a resource dependency for the SQL Server Name clustered resource in Failover Cluster Management. These tasks should be configured prior to installing a SQL Server failover cluster. However, if they haven't then these steps are a great way for adding additional shared disks to an existing cluster.

> **Note**
>
> In the past you had to take the service or application offline when adding additional shared disk resources; however, when running failover clustering with Windows Server 2008, this is no longer the case.

To add cluster drive dependencies, conduct the following steps in Failover Cluster Management.

1. In Failover Cluster Management, expand the desired failover cluster name.

2. Expand Services and Applications and then select SQL Server Name resource, which is located in the central pane.

3. From the Actions pane, select Properties and then the Dependencies tab.

4. On the Dependencies tab, click Insert and select the desired shared disk, such as DatabaseLogs-Instance01.

5. Click Apply and then Close to finalize this task.

6. Run the Show Dependency Report from the Action pane to verify that the newly added resource dependency drives are available to SQL Server.

Cluster Quorum Configuration

If all of the cluster nodes and shared storage was available during the creation of the cluster, the best suited Quorum model was automatically selected during the cluster creation process. When the existing cluster quorum needs to be validated or changed, perform the following steps:

1. In Failover Cluster Management, select and expand the cluster name.

2. In the Tree pane, select the Cluster name and in the Tasks pane the current Quorum model will be listed.

3. Review the current Quorum model and if it is correct, close the Failover Cluster Management console.

4. If the current Quorum model is not the desired model, right-click the cluster name in the Tree pane, click More Actions, and select Configure Cluster Quorum Settings.

5. In the Select Quorum Configuration page, select the radio button of the desired Quorum model or select the radio button of the recommended model and click Next to continue, as shown in Figure 12.11.

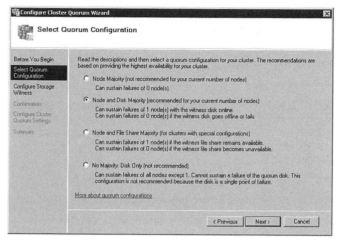

FIGURE 12.11
Configuring the Cluster Quorum model for a failover cluster.

6. If a Quorum model contains a witness disk or file share, select the designated disk or specify the path to the file share and click Next.

7. In the confirmation page, review the settings and click Next to update the Cluster Quorum model for the Failover Cluster.

8. Review the results in the Summary page and click Finish to return to the Failover Cluster Management console.

Summary

Failover clustering is a great high-availability alternative for maintaining maximum uptime for mission-critical databases and the whole SQL Server instance. Failover is seamless and transparent to end users and clients. The correct clustering topology must be selected based on Service Level Agreements, availability requirements, and budget.

Best Practices

- Before installing SQL Server failover clustering, understand the prerequisites and verify that the clustering hardware is supported and certified by both the hardware vendor and Microsoft.

- Leverage the Cluster Validation Tool included with Windows Server 2008 to ensure that all nodes within the cluster meet the prerequisites for deploying failover clustering.

- Use identical hardware for all nodes in the cluster. This includes processor, memory, and firmware.

- Configure Failover Clustering Feature from a Windows Server 2008 perspective prior to SQL Server 2008 Failover Clustering.

- Ensure disk drive letters are identical on all nodes within the cluster.

- Avoid having the quorum resource and other cluster resources from sharing the same disk.

- Ensure that the public network adapter is the first adapter in the network binding list.

- Disable NETBIOS on the private/heartbeat network adapters.

- Disable write-back caching on host controllers.

- Do *not* configure dynamic disks because clustering supports only basic disk configurations.

- Determine whether a single-instance or multiple-instance configuration will be implemented. Plan the disk layout accordingly while taking future growth into account.

- Identify which SQL Server features will be installed.

- Do *not* use the same service account for Windows and SQL Server failover clustering.

- Configure dependencies for shared disks so that they can be recognized and leveraged by SQL Server 2008.

- Before using multiple instances, understand the impact of multiple-instance configurations and performance degradation on the surviving node if a failover occurs.

- Change the service accounts only via SQL Server Configuration Manager.

- Do not configure DTC resources within the same service or application as the SQL Server virtual instances.

- Use the SQL Server Installation Center to modify a SQL Server failover cluster installation.

- Ensure that each virtual server name is unique on the Active Directory domain.

- Understand the benefit and impact associated with the different quorum models included in Windows Server 2008.

- For advanced SQL Server 2008 failover clustering installations, use the planning and deployment tools included with the SQL Server Installation Center.

CHAPTER 13

Administering and Managing Database Mirroring

This chapter takes a systematic look at database mirroring, one of the four high-availability alternatives offered with SQL Server 2008. Database mirroring was probably one of the most anticipated features of SQL Server 2005. Unfortunately, it wasn't ready for prime time and was actually pulled and not officially supported when Microsoft shipped SQL Server 2005, creating slight disappointment. It wasn't until the release of SQL Server 2005 Service Pack 1 that database mirroring was officially supported in production environments.

Database mirroring offers increased database availability and database protection by providing and maintaining a hot standby database on another instance of SQL Server 2008. A key point to note is that the mirror database is an exact copy of the principal database. With database mirroring, continuous support is given to organizations, bolstering operations by decreasing downtime and reducing data loss.

To ensure that organizations can reap the full benefits of database mirroring, the topics in this chapter are geared toward giving you the knowledge necessary to understand the full potential of database mirroring and how it meets different business scenarios, as well as how to implement and maintain it successfully. Specifically, the chapter focuses on an overview of database mirroring, terminology, and ways to use database mirroring. The middle sections of the chapter focus on database mirroring configuration and administration. The final sections of the chapter discuss how to manage and monitor database mirroring.

What's New for Database Mirroring with SQL Server 2008?

Microsoft realized that the introduction of database mirroring in SQL Server 2005 was widely accepted by many customers. It enabled organizations to implement high availability in a datacenter without the requirement of shared storage. Moreover, because shared storage was not required, the principal and mirrored servers could be placed in separate geographical locations for both high availability and disaster recovery. Unfortunately, in SQL Server 2005 there were some limitations.

With SQL Server 2005, the amount of network bandwidth required was a limitation when trying to mirror large amounts of data over the WAN. It was common for database mirroring to fail as the WAN would get saturated and transactions would either no longer make it or trickle across the wire. In addition, during these times of WAN saturation, performance degradation on the principal database would occur, especially if you were using the High Safety with Automatic Failover mode.

SQL Server 2008 addresses these issues by introducing a new feature called Database Mirroring Log Stream Compression. Application performance and throughput is enhanced over limited WAN connections as transaction log data in transit from the principal server to the mirrored server is extremely compressed. By compressing transaction log data by default, more data can be sent from the principal server to the mirrored server, thus increasing performance, and more log records can be shipped in a given time. Log Stream Compression rates of at least 13 percent or more have been achieved in specific lower-bandwidth networks.

Caution

The only caveat when using Database Mirroring Log Stream Compression is that there is increased overhead on the processor, as the processor must compress and decompress the logs, which translates to higher CPU usage. Depending on the workload, CPU usage could double compare to not using log compression. If WAN utilization and saturation is not an issue, then Log Stream Compression can be disabled with Trace Flag 1463. The behavior returns to the same functionality as in SQL Server 2005.

Automatic page repair and recovery from corrupted pages is another new feature for database mirroring when using SQL Server 2008. From a high level, the SQL Server hosting the mirrored database will try to resolve specific types of errors and corruption that prevent a data page from being read. If an error is detected, the server will attempt to obtain a fresh copy of the data and replace the corrupted data page, thus increasing data consistency among the principal and mirror databases and minimizing a database outage. It is typical to see an 823 or 824 error in the SQL Server logs indicating that an error took place causing an automatic page repair attempt. These errors are subsequently followed by an event indicating that SQL Server 2008 successfully repaired the physical page by obtaining a copy from the partner. Error 823 represents a cyclic redundancy check due to failed data and error 824 indicates logical errors.

Note

Automatic recovery from corrupted pages can only try to successfully resolve a failed data page when one or more of the following errors occur: page has been marked as restore pending, logical errors, or a cyclic redundancy check (CRC). These errors are also referred to by number: 823, 824, and 829.

Additional enhancements associated with database mirroring consist of the following:

- The mirror server writes received log records to disk asynchronously.

- Twenty-one new performance counters have been added in order to better troubleshoot and understand database mirroring workloads.

- If the principal database is configured for enhanced auditing, then the database mirrored server will also automatically include the SQL Server Audit Specification.

- Faster recovery on failover can now be achieved with SQL Server 2008.

- A new Dynamic Management View (DMV) has been implemented, sys.dm_db_mirroring_auto_page_repair, which allows tracking of 100 corrupt pages previously found in all mirroring sessions.

SQL Server 2008 Database Mirroring Overview

As mentioned earlier, database mirroring offers increased database availability and database protection by providing and maintaining a hot standby database on another instance of SQL Server 2008. Its usefulness is best witnessed when a failure takes place on a primary database. In this situation, the standby database becomes active and clients are redirected without the organization experiencing data loss or downtime.

Database mirroring is also commonly used to meet disaster recovery requirements and, therefore, should not be recognized only as an availability mechanism for a local site. When database mirroring becomes an integral part of an organization's disaster recovery plan, a hot or warm standby database is typically placed in a physical location other than the primary active database.

> **Note**
>
> The primary database is commonly referred to as the *principal* database, and the hot or warm standby is referred to as the *mirror* database.

The principal database handles client activity, whereas the mirror database receives continuous transaction log changes through a dedicated and secure TCP endpoint. This process keeps the mirror database up to date and ready to take on client operations in the event of a failure. Depending on the configuration/operating mode, database mirroring can be configured for either synchronous or asynchronous operations.

Figure 13.1 depicts the internals of a database mirroring session.

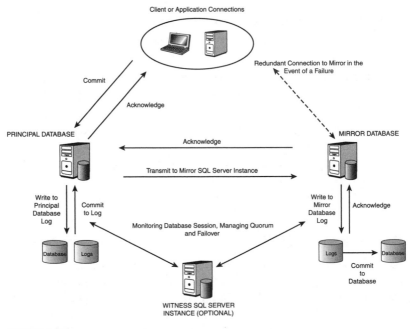

FIGURE 13.1
Overview of database mirroring.

Many database administrators find similarities between database mirroring and log shipping. They often refer to database mirroring as real-time log shipping or log shipping on steroids. However, in database mirroring, unlike log shipping, the primary server does not ship the logs to the standby server based on a time increment. Database mirroring transactions are continuously sent and committed between the principal and mirror; therefore, the databases are kept up to date.

> **Note**
>
> It is not possible to configure a database mirroring session on the SQL Server system databases, that is, the master, msdb, tempdb, or model databases. Failover clustering would be the alternative to provide high availability on the system databases.

Database Mirroring Terminology

Although you may be eager to install SQL Server 2008 database mirroring, you should take the time to fully understand all the new terminology and components that make up this new high-availability solution. By doing this, you and your organization can avoid running into roadblocks and will have an easier time with the installation. To prepare yourself for the installation, review the following terms regarding database mirroring:

- **Principal database**—The *principal database* is the primary server in a database mirroring solution. This server maintains a live copy of the database that is accessed by clients and applications.

> **Note**
>
> The principal database must reside on a separate instance of SQL Server than the mirror database.

- **Mirror database**—The *mirror database* is the target database, which reflects all the changes of the principal database through a secure dedicated channel. The mirror database is a hot or warm standby and is continuously updated by transferring transaction logs from the principal database in chunks.

> **Note**
>
> The Mirror SQL Server instance does not require a SQL Server license if the server is strictly used as a standby.

- **Witness server**—The *witness server* is an optional component in a database mirroring session. Typically, this component resides on a dedicated SQL Server instance independent of both the principal database and the mirroring database servers. The witness facilitates the quorum role and monitors the database mirroring session. It initiates a failover from the principal to the mirror database in the event of a disaster. You may view the witness server as a requirement to support automatic failovers between the principal and mirror database instances. The Express edition of SQL Server 2008 can host the Witness Server role.

- **Quorum**—The *quorum* monitors the state of a mirroring session. It controls the failover process based on communication among the principal, mirror, and witness databases. The principal server maintains the primary role of owning the database by maintaining quorum with either the mirror or witness. At least two servers are required to form a quorum; if the principal loses quorum with the mirror and/or the witness, a failover is initiated.

- **Synchronous/asynchronous**—A database mirroring session can transfer data between the principal database and mirror database by either a synchronous or an asynchronous operation. When you use the *synchronous* transfer mechanism, a transaction is successfully completed when it is committed on the principal and the principal receives an acknowledgment from the mirror that the same transaction has been written and committed. This process guarantees transactional consistency between the principal and mirror; however, transaction commits and client performance may be hindered based on the network speed, mirror location, and available bandwidth between the principal and mirror server instances.

  The *asynchronous* transfer mechanism commits transactions to the principal database much faster because it does not require an acknowledgment from the mirror. This process does not guarantee transactional consistency between the principal and mirror.

- **Automatic and manual failover**—Database mirroring supports both an automatic and manual failover process between the principal and mirrored databases. The type of failover is dictated by the type of database mirroring configuration mode selected, whether a witness server is present, and the type of client used.

- **Transparent client redirect**—In the event of a failure, clients and applications automatically redirect from the principal database to the mirror database, resulting in minimal downtime. Be aware that automatic failover requires the latest SQL client based on the .NET and SQL Server Native Client (SNAC) providers/libraries.

- **Database mirroring endpoint**—SQL Server 2008 uses endpoints to achieve secure server-to-server communication and authentication over the network. When you're configuring database mirroring, a dedicated endpoint is required exclusively for mirroring communications between both the principal and mirror database servers.

Database Mirroring Configuration/Operating Modes

Following are the database mirroring configuration and operating modes:

- **High Availability**—This database mirroring operating mode is also known as *High Safety with Automatic Failover* (synchronous with a witness). It provides maximum availability for a database mirroring session by using a synchronous form of mirroring. This operating mode requires a witness and supports automatic detection and automatic failover in the event the principal database is unavailable. Client performance is affected by the network speed and distance between the principal and mirror servers.

- **High Protection**—High protection is also referred to as *High Safety Without Automatic Failover* (synchronous without a witness). Like the high-availability operating mode, high protection uses a synchronous form of mirroring but does not require a witness. It does not require a witness SQL Server instance because failover is manual. With this mode, just as in the high-availability operating mode, principal performance is affected between the principal and mirror server based on network speed and distance.

- **High Performance**—High performance is the final operating mode and is also referred to as *High Performance Asynchronous*. High performance uses an asynchronous form of mirroring. In this situation, the principal server does not wait for confirmation that the transactions have been successfully committed to the mirror database instance. This increases performance because the network speed and distance are not factors. This solution does not require a witness. Therefore, there is no automatic detection or automatic failover as in high-availability mode.

Summary of Database Mirroring Configuration Modes

Table 19.1 provides an easy-to-read summary of the database mirroring configuration modes, detection levels, and failover process; it also indicates whether a witness server is required.

Table 19.1   **Database Mirroring Configuration Modes**

Database Mirroring Type	**Automatic Detection**	**Automatic or Manual Failover**	**Synchronous or Asynchronous Modes**	**Requires Witness**	**Transaction Safety**
High Availability	Yes	Automatic	Synchronous	Yes	Off
High Protection	No	Manual	Synchronous	No	Full
High Performance	No	Manual	Asynchronous	No	Full

Note

Asynchronous Database Mirroring (High-Performance Mode) is supported only by SQL Server 2008 Enterprise Edition.

When you use high-availability and high-protection modes, principal performance is affected by network speed, distance, and available bandwidth. Performance is not adversely affected when you use high performance. The mode you select ultimately determines how your organization wants to handle synchronization and failover processing.

SQL Server Database Mirroring Prerequisites

Configuring database mirroring is not as simple as clicking through a few pages of a SQL Server installation wizard. A number of prerequisite steps must be fulfilled before a database mirroring session can be configured and implemented. Following are the prerequisites:

- Register the principal, mirror, and witness SQL Server 2008 instances to ensure connectivity is present. The principal and mirror servers should be running the same edition of SQL Server 2008. Based on the features required, the Standard or Enterprise Edition can be used.
- The recovery model on the principal database must be set to Full.
- A full backup of the principal database is required.
- The mirror database needs to be initialized prior to implementing database mirroring by conducting a restore using the NORECOVERY option. All transaction logs taken after the full backup must also be restored.
- The database names for both the principal and mirror database must be identical.
- The server hosting the mirrored database requires adequate disk space.

When SQL Server 2008 Database Mirroring Is Desirable

Some of the key driving factors for implementing database mirroring with SQL Server 2008 are as follows:

■ There is a need to provide high-availability support for a specific database but not for an entire instance of SQL Server.

■ A seamless failover that does not affect client applications and end users is required.

■ An automatic failover that does not require intervention from a database administrator is favorable.

■ High availability for a database in another physical location other than the principal is required. Note that there is no distance limitation with mirroring.

■ There is a need for high availability, and the organization does not have identical servers and shared storage, which is an expensive requirement for failover clustering.

■ There is a need to fulfill the business continuity and disaster recovery requirements by placing and maintaining a redundant, up-to-date database in a different physical location than the principal.

■ There is a need to remove the single point of failure intrinsic in failover clusters. The single point of failure is typically the shared storage as it only maintains one copy of the production data.

■ Database mirroring can be used if there is a need to conduct a rolling upgrade of a SQL Server participating in a mirroring session without impacting database operations.

There are many other reasons organizations may turn to database mirroring. The first step your organization should take is to identify the gaps between the current and desired states of your business and then determine whether data mirroring fulfills your high-availability business goals.

Witness Server Placement

When an organization decides on using a witness server for high availability and automatic failure, it is often challenged with where to place the server. If the database mirroring session is configured over a wide area network (WAN), the witness can be placed either in the site with the principal or the site with the mirror. It is recommended to place the witness server in the same site as the mirror server. The reason is that if a site failure occurs where the principal resides, the witness server will still be operational and can initiate the failover with ease. On the other hand, some organizations place the witness server in the same site as the principal server because the network may not be reliable between the two sites. For these organizations, placing the principal and witness together minimizes unnecessary failovers due to network glitches.

Finally, if your organization is using database mirroring as a high-availability alternative, the witness server should be configured on a dedicated server that is not the principal or mirror. Placement on a dedicated server in this situation protects against hardware failure. It is important to mention that even if the witness is placed on a separate SQL Server instance, but the instance resides on the same server as the principal or mirror, you run into problems. If the physical hardware crashes, both instances fail and the witness cannot conduct an automatic failover, resulting in a longer downtime. Finally, the witness server can be placed on the SQL Server 2008 Express edition to reduce licensing and management costs.

It is worth noting that a witness server can run on any reliable system that supports SQL Server 2008. However, it is recommend that the instance used to host the witness corresponds to the minimum configuration that is required for SQL Server 2008 Standard Edition.

Combining Database Mirroring with Other SQL Server 2008 Technologies

Other SQL Server high-availability alternatives and technologies can be combined with database mirroring for maximum availability, reporting, business continuity, and disaster recovery. The following sections explain how database mirroring interacts with other SQL Server 2008 technologies.

Database Mirroring and Other High-Availability Alternatives

Database mirroring has its advantages and disadvantages, and it does not solve every high-availability requirement. This is why database mirroring can be combined with other SQL Server high-availability alternatives such as failover clustering, log shipping, and replication.

Database Mirroring and Failover Clustering

In many cases, database mirroring can be configured as a disaster recovery solution to a local SQL Server failover cluster instance by placing the principal database on the cluster and the hot standby mirror database in another physical location. If this combination is used, it is a best practice to use the high-protection or high-performance configuration mode because a cluster failover takes longer than the mirroring failover threshold. Therefore, if the high-availability configuration mode is being used, an automatic mirror failover takes place every time a cluster failover takes place between the two cluster nodes, making the cluster instance a mirrored database.

It is worth noting that the default threshold setting for controlling automatic failover with database mirroring is set to ten seconds. When combined with failover clustering, a mirroring failover might take place when a node failover occurs within the cluster. Most likely this behavior is unwanted and occurs because a failover within a cluster takes more than ten seconds. In order to address this concern, it is best practice to increase the partner time-out value. The following example illustrates changing the mirroring failover threshold to two minutes:

```
ALTER DATABASE AdventureWorks20082008
SET PARTNER TIMEOUT 120
```

Database Mirroring and Log Shipping

One of the limitations of database mirroring compared to log shipping is that database mirroring can have only one mirrored server associated with each principal, whereas log shipping can have multiple standby servers. The two technologies can be combined if there is a need to ship the principal database logs to a remote location other than the place where the mirror resides. In addition, log shipping databases can be used for reporting, whereas mirror databases cannot unless a snapshot is used.

Note

Log shipping needs to be reinitialized on the mirror SQL Server instance in the event of a failure or role change.

Database Mirroring and Replication

Finally, database mirroring can be used in conjunction with replication. The main focus is to provide availability for the publication database because the distribution and subscription databases are not supported with database mirroring. Because of the requirements and considerations, it is not a recommended practice to combine these two technologies; however, Microsoft includes a list of prerequisite tasks in SQL Server 2008 Books Online.

Database Mirroring and SQL Server 2008 Database Snapshots

Many organizations need to run reports against a production database for business purposes. To mitigate performance degradation and unnecessary locking due to sequential read and writes, it is a best practice to have a dedicated reporting server and not have reports run from the production database. Database mirroring offers this capability by allowing the mirror database to be used for reporting purposes. Unfortunately, the mirror database is in a constant recovering state, so it cannot be accessed directly. You can create a point-in-time database snapshot from the mirror database, which can be used for reporting.

Reporting against a mirrored database could be a great technology if offered by Microsoft because organizations would be able to create real-time reports from the mirror database without the need to constantly create snapshots. Perhaps this could be a new feature if enough DBAs requested Microsoft to create it.

> **Note**
>
> For more information on creating database snapshots, see Chapter 7, "Backing Up and Restoring the SQL Server 2008 Database Engine."

Administering a Database Mirroring Session

To administer a database mirroring session, first follow the steps to configure database mirroring. The following example simulates a database mirroring implementation that uses the high-availability configuration mode, including a witness for CompanyABC's AdventureWorks2008 production database located in San Francisco. The mirroring and witness partner is located in Toronto. The server names are shown in Table 19.2.

Table 19.2   **Roles and Server Names for Database Mirroring Example**

Role	SQL Server Instance	Location
Principal Server	SFC-SQL01\Instance01	San Francisco
Mirror Server	TOR-SQL01\Instance01	Toronto
Witness Server	TOR-SQL01\Instance02	Toronto

Configuring Database Mirroring Prerequisites

You must conduct the following tasks to configure database mirroring on the AdventureWorks2008 database from San Francisco to Toronto:

1. From the principal server (SFC-SQL01\Instance01), conduct a full backup of the AdventureWorks2008 database by using Transact-SQL (TSQL) code or SQL Server Management Studio (SSMS).

> **Caution**
>
> Use independent files when creating the database and transaction log backups. Do *not* append both of these backups to the same file; otherwise, an erroneous error such as Error 1418 may occur when setting up the database mirroring session. Error 1418 typically represents network connectivity or issues when resolving server names in a mirroring session.

2. Conduct a transaction log backup of the AdventureWorks2008 database by using TSQL code or SSMS.

3. Copy the backup files from the principal server (SFC-SQL01\ Instance01) to the mirror server (TOR-SQL01\Instance01).

Tip

You need to create the AdventureWorks2008 database on the mirror server if it does not already exist. To simplify the backup and restore process, it is a best practice to maintain the same file path for the database and transaction log files that the principal database is using. Otherwise, the MOVE command is required when you're conducting the restore.

---

4. From the Mirror Server SQL Server instance (TOR-SQL01\ Instance01), conduct a restore of the AdventureWorks2008 database file and then the transaction log. Use the recovery state option RESTORE WITH NORECOVERY for both restores. Therefore, the database is not in an operational state - for end users and applications - and ready to accept database mirroring transactions.

Note

For more information on backing up and restoring SQL Server with either SSMS or TSQL, see Chapter 7.

---

5. In SSMS, on the principal server, register the principal, mirror, and witness SQL Server instances to ensure successful connectivity and authentication.

Configuring Database Mirroring with High Safety and Automatic Failover

Now that you've configured the prerequisites, follow these steps to configure database mirroring with high safety and automatic failover:

1. From the principal server (SFC-SQL01\Instance01), choose Start, All Programs, Microsoft SQL Server 2008, SQL Server Management Studio.

2. In Object Explorer, first connect to the Database Engine, expand the desired server (SFC-SQL01\Instance01), and then expand the Database folder.

3. Right-click the AdventureWorks2008 database, select Tasks, and then choose Mirror.

4. On the Database Properties page, select the Configure Security button located on the Mirroring page.

Note

Because database mirroring requires the transaction logs for synchronization, you receive a warning message if the database recovery level is not set to Full. If this occurs, switch the recovery model to Full and restart the Database Mirroring Wizard.

---

5. On the Configure Database Mirroring Security Wizard Starting page, select Next.

6. Specify whether to include a witness server in the configuration by selecting the option Yes on the Include Witness Server page. For this example, you use a witness server instance (TOR-SQL01\Instance02) to operate database mirroring in synchronous mode with automatic failure.

7. In the Choose Servers to Configure page, select the principal, mirror, and witness server instances, as illustrated in Figure 13.2. Click Next.

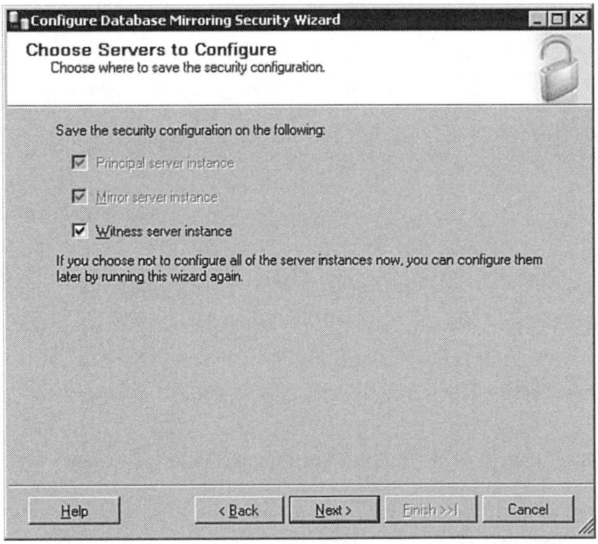

FIGURE 13.2
Configuring the database mirroring servers for security.

8. On the Principal Server Instance page, specify the endpoint properties for the principal server instance, as shown in Figure 13.3. Ensure that the option Encrypt Data Sent Through This Endpoint is selected, and then click Next to continue.

Note

Typically, the default listener port for each endpoint is 5022. However, if the principal, mirror, or witness is configured on the same SQL Server instance, its endpoints must use different ports.

---

9. On the Mirror Server Instance page, specify the mirror server instance and the endpoint properties for the mirrored server instance, as shown in Figure 13.4. Click Next to continue.

Note

Before specifying options for this page, you may have to click the Connect button in order to first pass credentials for the desired mirror server instance.

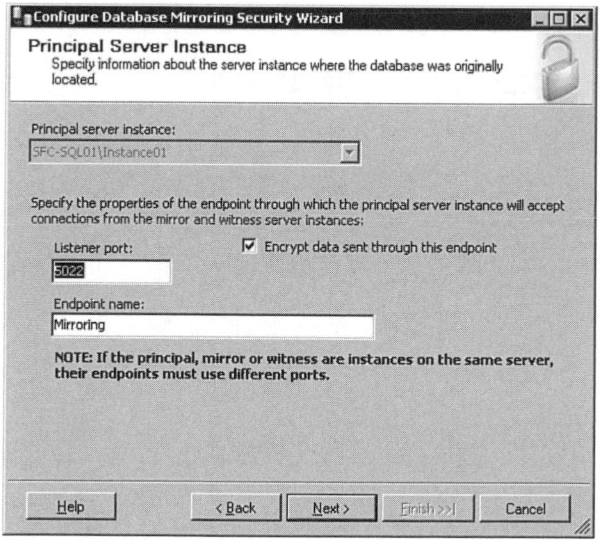

FIGURE 13.3
Entering the principal server instance information and settings.

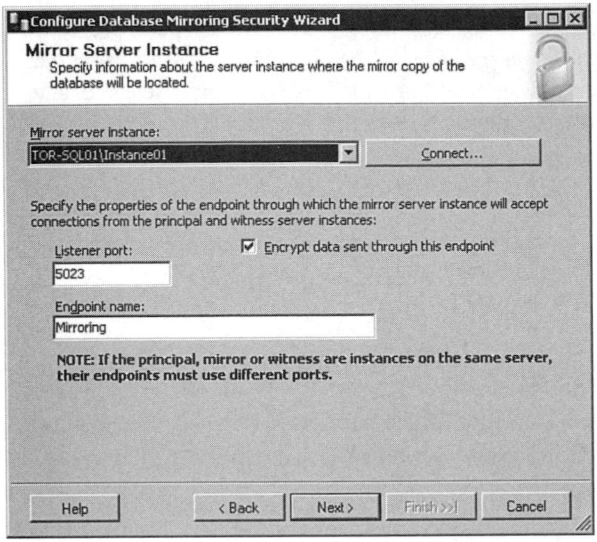

FIGURE 13.4
Entering the mirror server instance information and settings.

10. On the Witness Server Instance page, specify the witness server instance and the endpoint properties for the witness server instance, as shown in Figure 13.5. Click Next to continue.

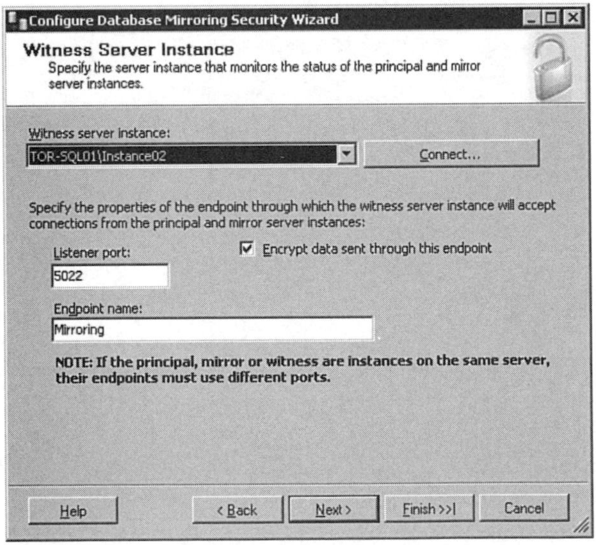

FIGURE 13.5
Entering the witness server instance information and settings.

11. On the Service Accounts page, enter the service account information for each instance partaking in the database mirroring session. If the service accounts are the same for each instance, as in this example, leave the text boxes blank, as illustrated in Figure 13.6, and click Next to continue.

Note

If the service accounts entered are different and the accounts do not already exist in the specific SQL Server instance, the wizard automatically creates the accounts, grants appropriate permissions, and associates the account credentials to the endpoints.

---

12. On the Complete the Wizard page, verify the configuration settings for each database mirroring instance, as shown in Figure 13.7, and then click Finish.

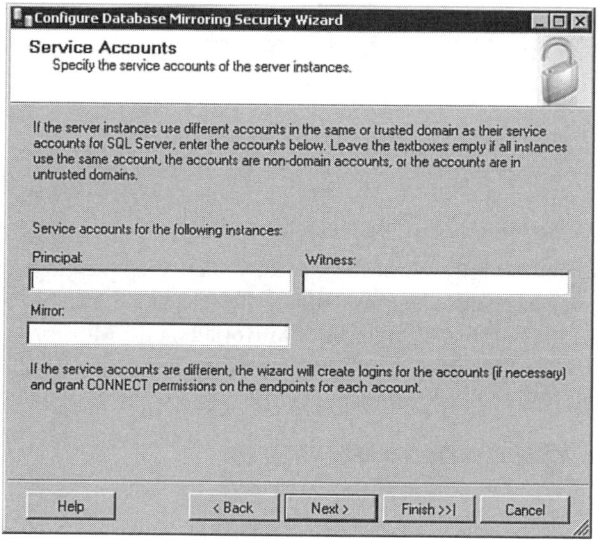

FIGURE 13.6
Specifying the database mirroring service accounts.

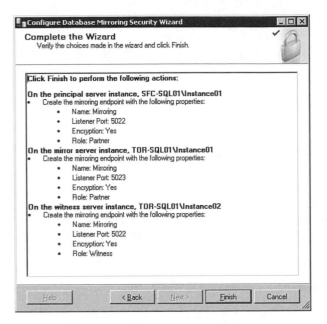

FIGURE 13.7
Verifying the database mirroring security settings.

13. On the Configuring Endpoints page, verify the status of each endpoint to ensure it was successfully created and click Close.

14. When this Endpoint Security Wizard is closed, you are prompted to either start the database mirroring session now by selecting Start Mirroring or start it later by selecting Start Mirroring on the Mirroring page of the Database Properties dialog box, as shown in Figure 13.8. For this example, click Start Mirroring.

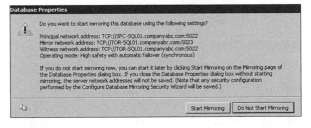

FIGURE 13.8
Starting the database mirroring.

Note

The mirrored database must be present on the mirrored server; otherwise, an error occurs, stating that the mirrored database does not exist and must be created via a backup and restore prior to initializing the database mirroring session.

---

15. Verify that the initial synchronization was successful by viewing the Status section located in the Database Properties page, as shown in Figure 13.9, and then click OK.

When databases are configured in a database mirroring session, a status message appears next to the database and includes the server role. For example, on the SFC-SQL01\Instance01 server, the principal AdventureWorks20082008 database status message indicates (Principal, Synchronized), and TOR-SQL01\ Instance01 database status message indicates (Mirror, Synchronized/ Restoring...).

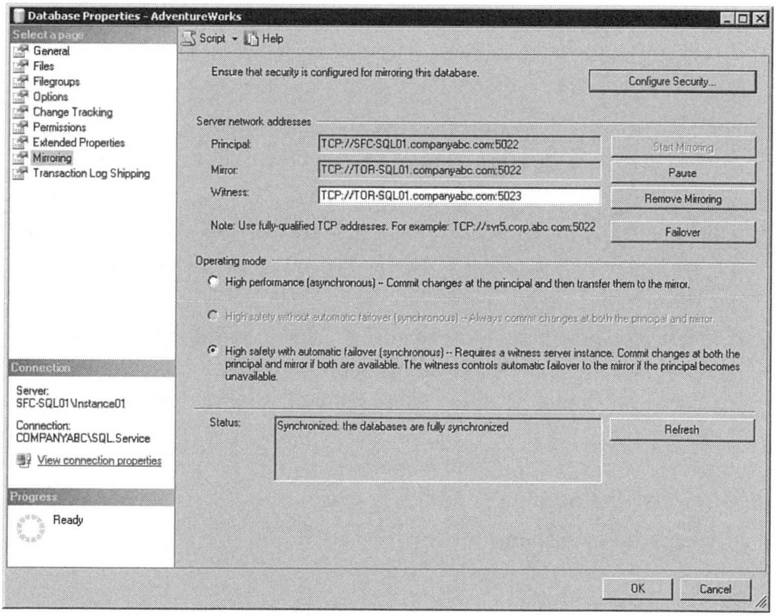

FIGURE 13.9
Viewing the database mirroring status in the Database Properties page.

Managing a Database Mirroring Session

The Mirroring page accessible from the Database Properties page allows you to manage a database mirroring session. With this tool, you can pause, remove, or fail over a database mirroring session. In addition, it is possible to change the database mirroring operation mode—for example, from high performance (asynchronous) to high safety (synchronous). Finally, you can use this page to initiate manual failovers and status verification. Alternatively, any database mirroring tasks that can be conducted from the management console can also be scripted with Transact-SQL (TSQL).

Pausing and Resuming a Database Mirroring Session

Occasionally, you need to either pause or resume a database mirroring session for administrative purposes. You can pause and resume a mirroring session by using SSMS or TSQL.

Follow these steps to either pause or resume a database mirroring session with SSMS:

1. From the principal server (SFC-SQL01), choose Start, All Programs, Microsoft SQL Server 2008, SQL Server Management Studio.

2. In Object Explorer, first connect to the Database Engine, expand the desired server (SFC-SQL01\Instance01), and then expand the Database folder.

3. Right-click the AdventureWorks2008 database, select Tasks, and then choose Mirror.

4. Click the Pause button located in the Server Network Address section on the Mirroring tab of the Database Properties page (refer to the previous Figure 13.9).

5. Click the Resume button to restart the database mirroring session. The Resume button is not displayed in Figure 13.9 because it only appears on the Mirroring tab after the Pause button has been clicked.

Alternatively, you can use the following sample TSQL syntax to pause and resume a database mirroring session:

Pausing database mirroring:

```
Use Master
ALTER DATABASE <database_name> SET PARTNER SUSPEND
GO
```

Resuming database mirroring:

```
Use Master
ALTER DATABASE <database_name> SET PARTNER RESUME
Go
```

Manually Failing Over a Database Mirroring Session

Follow these steps to swap the principal and mirror roles by manually failing over the database session from the principal server to the mirrored server:

1. From the principal server (SFC-SQL01), choose Start, All Programs, Microsoft SQL Server 2008, SQL Server Management Studio.

2. In Object Explorer, first connect to the Database Engine, expand the desired server (SFC-SQL01\Instance01), and then expand the Database folder.

3. Right-click the AdventureWorks2008 database, select Tasks, and then choose Mirror.

4. Click the Failover button located in the Server Network Addresses section on the Mirroring tab of the Database Properties page.

5. Read the warning message and click Yes to finalize the role swap.

In SSMS, notice how the status messages have changed based on the role swap. On the SFC-SQL01\Instance01 server, the AdventureWorks2008 database status message indicates (`Mirror, Synchronized/In Recovery`), whereas the TOR-SQL01\Instance01 database instance status message indicates (`Principal, Synchronized`).

The following sample TSQL syntax should be used to fail over a database mirroring session:

```
Use Master
ALTER DATABASE database_name SET PARTNER FAILOVER
Go
```

Changing the Database Mirroring Configuration/Operating Mode

In some situations, either you or your organization decides to change the operating mode. Reasons for changing the operating mode may include performance issues, the absence of a witness server, or even a need to manually control a failover as opposed to having SQL automatically conduct the role swap.

Follow these steps to change the database mirroring operating mode with SSMS:

1. From the principal server (SFC-SQL01), choose Start, All Programs, Microsoft SQL Server 2008, SQL Server Management Studio.

2. In Object Explorer, first connect to the Database Engine, expand the desired server (SFC-SQL01\Instance01), and then expand the Database folder.

3. Right-click the AdventureWorks2008 database, select Tasks, and then choose Mirror.

4. In the Operating Mode section, change the Operating Mode option to either High Performance, High Safety, or High Safety with Automatic Failover and click OK.

You can use the following basic TSQL syntax to change the database mirroring operating mode:

Enable Transaction Safety:

```
Use Master
ALTER DATABASE <database> SET PARTNER SAFETY FULL
GO
```

Disable Transaction Safety:

```
Use Master
ALTER DATABASE <database> SET PARTNER SAFETY OFF
GO
```

Removing a Database Mirroring Session

Similar to the management steps you used previously, you can remove database mirroring sessions with either TSQL or SSMS.

Follow these steps to swap roles by manually failing over the database session from the principal server to the mirrored server:

1. From the principal server (SFC-SQL01), choose Start, All Programs, Microsoft SQL Server 2008, SQL Server Management Studio.

2. In Object Explorer, first connect to the Database Engine, expand the desired server (SFC-SQL01\Instance01), and then expand the Database folder.

3. Right-click the AdventureWorks2008 database, select Tasks, and then choose Mirror.

4. Click the Remove Mirroring button located in the Server Network Addresses section on the Mirroring tab of the Database Properties page.

5. Read the warning message and click Yes to remove mirroring from the AdventureWorks2008 database.

6. In the Database Properties page, click OK to finalize the procedures.

The following TSQL syntax can also be used to remove a database mirroring session:

```
Use Master
ALTER DATABASE <database_name> SET PARTNER OFF
Go
```

Managing Database Mirroring Client Connections and Redirect

In the event of a principal database failure, the principal database fails over to the mirror either manually or automatically. Therefore, all client connections need to be redirected from the principal server instance to the new mirror database instance. The latest ADO.NET or SQL Server clients have built-in redirect technologies that allow an application to automatically redirect its connection in the event of a database failure. Either you, as database administrator, or an application developer must specify the principal and failover SQL Server instance in the connection string to make this happen.

Follow these steps to configure automatic client redirect by using the native SQL Server client:

1. Choose Start, All Programs, Administrative Tools, Data Sources (ODBC).

2. On the ODBC Data Source Administrator page, select System DSN.

3. Click Add to create a new System DSN connection to the principal and mirror SQL Server instance.

4. In the Create New Data Source page, select SQL Native Client 10.0 and then click Finish.

5. In the Create a New Data Source to SQL Server page, enter the name, description, and the principal database server instance, as illustrated in Figure 13.10. For this example, use the principal SQL Server instance SFC-SQL01\Instance01. Click Next.

6. Select the SQL Server authentication mode for the SQL Server connection and click Next.

7. Select the default database to connect to and enter the name of the mirror server, as shown in Figure 13.11. For this example, select AdventureWorks2008 database and TOR-SQL01\Instance01 for the mirror server instance. Click Next.

FIGURE 13.10
Creating a new SQL Server native client data source.

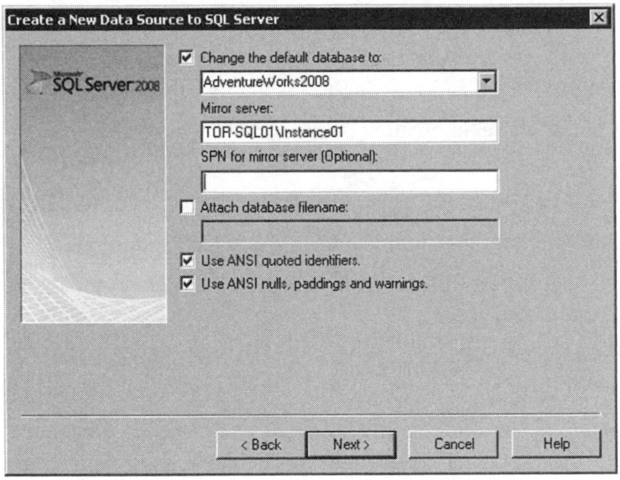

FIGURE 13.11
Specifying the mirror database settings.

8. Click Finish and then click Test Data Source to finalize the connection settings.

The new connection can be leveraged with a front-end SQL Server client such as Access, Visual Studio .NET, or Reporting Services. Use the newly created connection and display data from the AdventureWorks2008 database such as the Employee table. When a connection is established and the data is presented, fail over the database mirroring session. The application should still be able to display the Employee table because it automatically redirects to the AdventureWorks2008 database residing on the mirror instance of SQL Server.

Monitoring and Troubleshooting a Database Mirroring Session

After you have configured database mirroring, you should turn your attention to understanding the following tools available for monitoring and managing the mirroring session:

- Database Mirroring Monitoring tool
- System Performance
- System Catalogs
- Operations Manager 2007

Using the Database Mirroring Monitoring Tool to Manage Database Mirroring

The Database Mirroring Monitoring tool is included with SSMS and should be used to monitor databases configured in a mirroring session. The tool can be launched by right-clicking the database partaking in a database mirroring session and then selecting Tasks, Launch Database Mirroring Monitor. You can use the tool to identify the status of the database mirroring session, identify the role of each partner, determine whether the mirroring session is behind schedule, and estimate the time it will take to catch up.

Use the following procedure to monitor the state of the database mirroring session configured in the earlier examples:

1. From the principal server (SFC-SQL01), choose Start, All Programs, Microsoft SQL Server 2008, SQL Server Management Studio.

2. In Object Explorer, first connect to the Database Engine, expand the desired server (SFC-SQL01\Instance01), and then expand the Database folder.

3. Right-click the AdventureWorks2008 database, select Tasks, and then choose Launch Database Mirroring Monitor.

4. To register a mirrored database, either click the Register Mirrored Database hyperlink in the right pane or select Action, Register Mirrored Database from the Tools menu.

5. In the Register Mirrored Database page, select the server instance by clicking the Connect button.

6. In the Connect to Server dialog box, select the Mirrored Database SQL Server Instance (TOR-SQL01\Instance01) and click OK.

7. In the Register Mirrored Database page, click the Register check box next to the database to register the mirrored database instance and then click OK.

8. The Database Mirroring Monitoring tool automatically connects to both the principal and mirror instances partaking in the database mirroring session. In the Manage Server Instance Connections, edit the credentials if necessary or click OK.

The Database Mirroring Monitoring Tool Status Tab

The Status tab includes a plethora of database mirroring status information for both the principal and mirror databases. The status information located on the Status tab is broken into four sections: Status, Principal Log, Mirror Log, and General Information.

The Status section indicates the server instance, current role, and mirrored state, and it validates that the witness is operational. The final command in the status window provides a history log file, as shown in Figure 13.13.

The Principal Log section includes metrics on the following:

- Unsent Log Information in KB
- Oldest Unsent Transaction
- Time to Send Log (Estimated)
- Current Send Rate in KB per Second
- Current Rate of New Transactions

The General section located at the bottom of the Status tab page includes additional status for troubleshooting and diagnostics:

- Mirror Commit Overhead in Milliseconds
- Time Estimates to Send and Restore All Current Logs
- Witness Address
- Operation Mode

The Database Mirroring Monitoring Tool Warnings Tab

The Warnings tab allows you to set database mirroring warning thresholds for the principal and mirror SQL Server instances. The four warnings included with this tool are

- Warn If the Unsent Log Exceeds the Threshold
- Warn If the Un-Restored Log Exceeds the Threshold

- Warn If the Age of the Oldest Unsent Transaction Exceeds the Threshold
- Warn If the Mirror Commit Overhead Exceeds the Threshold

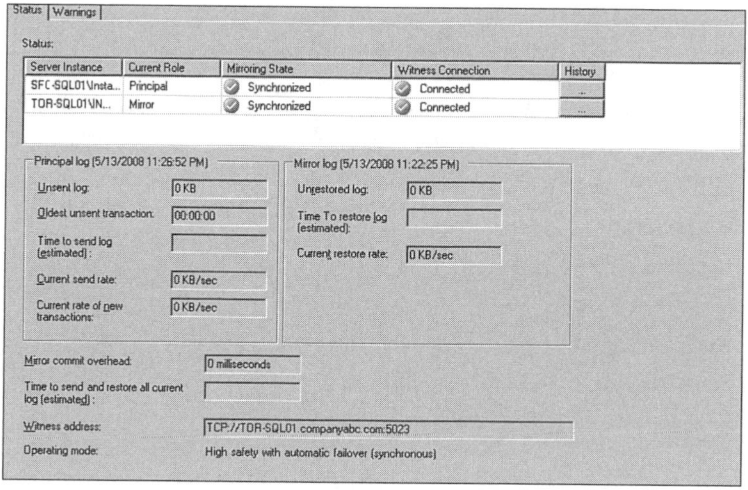

FIGURE 13.12
Displaying database mirroring history.

The Set Warning Thresholds page should be used to enable/disable warning per instance and set thresholds.

Monitoring Database Mirroring Performance

The Database Mirroring Monitoring tool is a great starting point for managing and analyzing a database mirroring session. When additional metrics are needed for analysis, or when troubleshooting or creating a performance baseline, you can use the Reliability and Performance Monitor tool included with Windows Server 2008. To launch the tool, choose Start, All Programs, Administrative Tools, and Reliability Performance Monitor.

Following are the specific counters included with the SQL Server Database Mirroring Performance Object:

- Bytes Received/sec
- Bytes Sent/sec
- Log Bytes Received/sec
- Log Bytes Redone from Cache/sec
- Log Bytes Sent from Cache/sec
- Log Bytes Sent/sec

- Log Compressed Bytes Rcvd/sec
- Log Compressed Bytes Sent/sec
- Log Harden Time (ms)
- Log Remaining for Undo KB
- Log Scanned for Undo KB
- Log Send Flow Control Time (ms)
- Mirrored Write Transactions/sec
- Log Send Queue KB
- Pages Sent/sec
- Receives/sec
- Redo Bytes/sec
- Redo Queue KB
- Send/Receive Ack Time
- Sends/sec
- Transaction Delay

Collecting and analyzing the preceding metrics assists organizations with planning their database mirroring solution. Before database mirroring is implemented in production, it is a best practice to simulate mirroring in a prototype test lab and analyze the metrics collected. If possible, a bandwidth simulator tool should also be used to mimic the production network speed, especially if Log Stream Compression will be used. This allows an organization to fully understand the database mirroring and bandwidth requirements when setting up database mirroring in production over a private network. When analyzing bandwidth requirements, your organization should also assess the current bandwidth utilization. Therefore, if the link is already fully saturated, more bandwidth may be necessary to support the mirroring solution. Alternatively, many organizations purchase dedicated network lines tailored specifically for database mirroring replication.

Using the System Catalogs to Monitor Database Mirroring

The catalog view included with SQL Server is another great source of information when monitoring status and performance.

The following catalog views should be used:

- Sys.database_mirroring
- Sys.database_mirroring_witness
- Sys.database_mirroring_endpoints
- Sys.tcp_endpoints
- Sys.Server_principals

- Sys.Server_recovery_status
- Sys.dm_db_mirroring_auto_page_repair

The catalog view provides database mirroring metadata for a session, including witness, endpoint, principal, and recovery status.

Monitoring Database Mirroring with Operations Manager 2007

Another great tool to proactively monitor database mirroring, including the health of the principal, mirror, and witness SQL Server instances, is Microsoft Operations Manager 2007. Operations Manager 2007 includes a dedicated Microsoft Management Pack tailored toward SQL Server. It includes a subcomponent that focuses on database mirroring.

> **Note**
>
> For more information on proactively monitoring a database mirroring session with Operations Manager 2007, refer to Chapter 18, " Proactively Monitoring SQL Server 2008 with System Center Operations Manager 2007".

Summary

Database mirroring is a SQL Server 2008 high-availability alternative that can be used for maintaining a redundant copy of the principal database on a standby server for increased availability and disaster recovery purposes. The new features and functionality introduced in SQL Server 2008 allow organizations to more easily implement database mirroring across physical sites with limited bandwidth, and automatic page repair protects the mirrored copy from corruption.

How well database mirroring performs is closely associated with the type of application, transaction safety level, and network performance between the principal and mirror servers. Understanding the application behavior in terms of the log generation rate, number of concurrent connections, and size of transactions is important in achieving the best performance.

In addition, the network plays a very important role in a database mirroring environment. When used with a high-bandwidth and low-latency network, database mirroring can provide a reliable high-availability solution against planned and unplanned downtime. With data centers in different geographical locations, database mirroring can provide the foundation for a solid, inexpensive disaster recovery solution.

Best Practices

The following are the best practices for this chapter:

- Database mirroring using the high-availability configuration mode is a practical alternative when the principal and mirror server reside in the same physical location. The reason is that most organizations' production environments are running fast networks without network latency.

- Database mirroring using the high-performance configuration mode is a practical alternative when the principal and mirror server reside in different physical locations. The reason is that production performance is typically of higher importance than automatic failover and availability in these situations.

- Leverage database mirroring to reduce planned downtime, increase availability for mission-critical databases, and satisfy disaster recovery requirements.

- To increase performance, implement and leverage a dedicated high-bandwidth network for synchronization communications between the principal and mirror database servers when possible.

- Leverage Database Mirroring Log Compression in environments where there isn't enough available bandwidth between the principal database instance and the mirrored database instance.

- In the event of a failure, the mirror server needs to maintain the same workload as the principal. Both servers should be of similar class and have the same number of processors and the same amount of memory and storage. Unlike in failover clustering, the hardware does not have to be an exact match, but the mirror needs to support the same load as the principal.

- Use failover clustering over database mirroring if there is a need to provide high availability on the whole SQL Server instance. This includes the master, model, msdb, and tempdb databases because these system databases cannot partake in a database mirroring session.

- To reduce the number of unforeseen issues with database mirroring, use the same edition of Windows and SQL Server for both the principal and mirror server. In addition, the service packs, hotfixes, drive letter layout, collation settings, and SQL Server configuration settings should be identical. Although this is not a requirement, it is a best practice.

- To reduce complications and troubleshooting, use a single mirror SQL Server instance if a principal instance is composed of multiple databases belonging to one application that needs to be mirrored.

- When using database mirroring, create items such as logins, scheduled jobs, and extended stored procedures that are identical on the mirrored database and instance.

- When configuring database mirroring, do *not* forget to initialize the mirror database by restoring the full backup and the last transaction log with the NORECOVERY option.

- If you configured the database mirroring session to use high-availability or high-protection mode and delays are experienced with client applications, switch to high-performance mode.

CHAPTER 14

Implementing and Managing Log Shipping

Log shipping is one of four SQL Server 2008 high-availability alternatives. Other SQL Server 2008 high-availability alternatives include database mirroring, failover clustering, and peer-to-peer replication, which are covered in the other high-availability chapters of this book: Chapter 12, "Implementing and Managing Failover Clustering"; Chapter 13, "Implementing and Managing Database Mirroring"; and Chapter 15, "Implementing and Administering SQL Server Replication."

What's New for Log Shipping in SQL Server 2008?

Not much has changed for log shipping with SQL Server 2008. However, when leveraging the Enterprise Edition of SQL Server 2008, it is now possible to compress the backups associated with the logs. Keep in mind that when you enable backup compression, CPU usage increases. At times additional CPU consumption can starve other tasks; therefore, if the increased CPU usage is a concern, leverage Resource Governor to limit CPU usage by backup compression. Finally, when using backup compression with log shipping, the compression options include: Use the Default Server settings, Enable Compression, and Do Not Compress Backup. For more information on backup compression, refer to Chapter 7, "Backing Up and Restoring the SQL Server 2008 Database Engine."

SQL Server 2008 Log Shipping Overview

Log shipping offers increased database availability and database protection by maintaining a warm standby database on another instance of SQL Server 2008. Unlike database mirroring, a log shipping failover is not done automatically because you must perform several manual steps to successfully complete a failover. Failover steps include manually redirecting clients from the primary database to the secondary database after manually bringing the secondary database online.

Caution

It is important to understand that some data loss might occur when a failover is performed and the original database is no longer available. Because transaction log backups are shipped and restored to the secondary servers on a schedule, any changes made between the time of the last "shipped" transaction log and the failure are lost because these changes have not been applied to the secondary server.

If data loss is unacceptable, other SQL Server high-availability options should be considered.

In previous versions of SQL Server, log shipping was commonly used for geographical fault tolerance because geographical failover clustering was often expensive and impractical. Now, with mirroring and the introduction of the new SQL Server 2008 geographically disbursed failover clustering, the use of log shipping for this role has been reduced.

In SQL Server 2008, log shipping is now more commonly used in conjunction with other SQL Server high-availability options such as clustering and mirroring. Log shipping is also useful when a delay in the restoration is desirable. In this scenario, the time between the backup and restore process is purposely delayed to provide recovery from catastrophic database operations.

With log shipping, the primary database handles client activity, whereas the secondary database copies and restores transaction log backups. SQL Server log shipping is simply composed of several SQL Server Agent jobs that back up the transaction log from a database on the primary server; each transaction log backup is then copied and restored in the correct order to a database on a secondary server. The restore process on the secondary server is kept "open" in recovery, allowing additional transaction log backups to be applied.

Figure 14.1 depicts the process used by log shipping.

Many database administrators find similarities between database mirroring and log shipping. However, key elements make these technologies different. For example, unlike with database mirroring, the log shipping primary server does not continuously send and commit data to the secondary servers; instead, data is sent on a defined schedule. This increases the chance of data loss when a log shipping failover occurs, while mirroring can be configured for synchronous and asynchronous operation. In addition, log shipping does not provide an automatic failover or failback mechanism, whereas database mirroring can be configured to automatically fail over and fail back the database. Log shipping does provide the ability to configure multiple secondary servers, whereas database mirroring can have only a single secondary database.

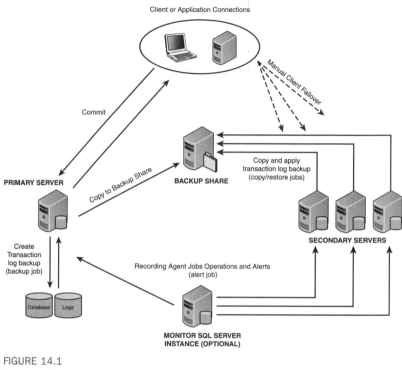

FIGURE 14.1
Overview of log shipping.

Understanding Log Shipping Terminology

To effectively administer and manage log shipping, you need to understand the terminology and components that make up this solution. To prepare you for administrative and management tasks, this section details some of the log shipping terms used throughout this chapter:

- **Primary server**—The primary server contains the source database used in the log shipping configuration.

- **Secondary server**—The secondary server contains the replica database. This database is a warm standby copy of the source database on the primary server.

- **Monitor server**—This optional server records various details about the log shipping activity between the primary and secondary servers. This information includes backup operations, restore operations, and any alerts that have been generated.

- **Backup job**—The backup job resides on the primary server; this job is used to back up the transaction logs and store them in the backup share. The backup share can be a network location, the secondary server, or a local drive on the primary server.

- **Copy job**—The copy job resides on each secondary server; this job is used to copy the transaction log backups from the backup location to the staging area. The staging area is usually a local drive on the secondary server.

- **Restore job**—The restore job resides on each secondary server; this job is used to restore the transaction log backups that were copied to the local staging area.

Considering Environmental Factors

The following environmental characteristics should be identified when configuring and managing log shipping, along with potential issues that may arise:

- **Network speed**—The available network bandwidth between each server affects the speed with which the transaction log backup can be copied from the primary server to the backup share and from the backup share to the secondary server. The time to copy the backup files cannot exceed the backup interval. If the copy time exceeds the backup interval, log shipping will become backlogged and eventually fail.

- **Server performance**—The performance of the server needs to be considered. Both the time to back up the transaction log on the primary server and the time to restore the transaction log backups on the secondary servers cannot exceed the defined backup interval. If the server cannot restore backups fast enough, log shipping will become backlogged and eventually fail.

- **Drive capacity**—Enough storage capacity is required to store the transaction log backup made by the backup job and the transaction log copy made by the copy job. The retention period for these files can be adjusted but should provide enough history to recover from an interruption. For example, creating a backup every 15 minutes generates 96 backups each day.

- **Monitor server placement**—The placement of the optional monitor server is important because this server is responsible for recording backups, restores, and alerts in a central location.

> **Note**
>
> SQL Server 2008 Enterprise Edition can compress the log shipped backups. If your principal database is Enterprise Edition and the transaction log backups are compressed, any version of SQL Server 2008 can restore the log to the secondary server. Remember that if your secondary database server is not Enterprise Edition, if it becomes the primary in a failover scenario, the transaction log files will not be compressed and will take up more space on the shared location.

When you're considering these factors, it is important to evaluate the total end-to-end transition time. For example, if the transaction log backup is executed every 15 minutes and takes 10 minutes to complete, and it takes 15 minutes to copy and restore the backup to the secondary server, the next backup job will start before the first iteration of the log shipping process can complete. In this scenario, a backlog of transaction log backups will accumulate in the backup share.

When a backlog occurs, the synchronization gap between the primary and secondary database will continue to grow. The transaction log backups are removed based on a predefined schedule. When the synchronization gap between the primary and secondary servers grows beyond the transaction log retention period, the backups are removed before the secondary database has a chance to copy and restore them, ultimately causing the log shipping process to fail.

Deciding When to Use Log Shipping

Some of the key driving factors for implementing log shipping with SQL Server 2008 include

- A controlled delay between the primary database and secondary databases is desirable.
- Automatic client failover is not necessary.
- An additional replication of an existing database mirror is necessary.
- Data must be replicated to multiple secondary servers.
- A need exists to host a replica database for reporting purposes.
- A secondary copy of the data is required for reporting purposes.

The first thing organizations should do when considering a high-availability solution is to identify the gaps between the current and desired states of their business and then determine whether log shipping fulfills their high-availability business goals or another high-availability solution is more appropriate.

Considering Design Factors

The following describes common design considerations that should be explored before configuring log shipping:

- **Security**—When you want to configure log shipping, the sysadmin role is required on each SQL Server that will take part in the implementation. This includes the primary server, each secondary server, and the monitor server. The agent account used to run the backup job on the primary server must be able to read and write to the backup location. The agent account on the secondary server used to copy the backups to the staging area must have read access to the backup share and read/write access to the staging area.

- **SQL Server version**—SQL Server 2008 Standard, Workgroup, and Enterprise Editions and above can be used for log shipping. All servers must be configured with the same case-sensitivity settings.

- **Recovery mode**—The recovery mode of the source database on the primary server must be configured as full or bulk-logged. The Simple recovery model commits data to the database and then removes transaction log files; the Full and Bulk-Logged recovery models truncate the transaction log until after a successful transaction log backup. Because the transaction log is a key part of log shipping, the Simple recovery model cannot be used.

- **Backup storage location**—The backup storage location is used to store the transaction log backups created by the backup job. In a large-scale environment, it is highly recommended to host the transaction log backups on a fault-tolerant server independent of the log shipping primary or secondary servers. However, in a small environment or test environment, it may be acceptable to store the data on local storage attached to the primary server. The account used to execute the backup job must have read/write access to this location.

- **Staging storage location**—The staging storage location is used to store the transaction log backups copied from the backup location. It is common to store these backups on local storage on the secondary server if enough drives are available. If adequate drives are unavailable, the staging area can be hosted on a different server. The account used to execute the copy job on each secondary server must have read/write access to this location and read access to the backup storage location.

- **Monitor server**—The monitor server is optional and is normally hosted on a SQL Server that is not part of the log shipping implementation. This server is important because it provides a central location for the log shipping status and alert messages. In the event of a failure, the monitor server can be used to determine when the last backup occurred. If a monitor server is not specified, each server in the log shipping implementation monitors itself.

Combining Log Shipping with Other SQL Technologies

In most cases, other SQL Server high-availability alternatives and technologies can be combined with log shipping. Log shipping often complements failover clustering or database mirroring because these technologies provide fast and automatic failover.

Log shipping complements these technologies by providing an additional layer of availability. For example, an organization may implement database mirroring between two offices to support hot failover of critical business data. Log shipping is often implemented in this scenario to make an additional replica of this data to a remote disaster recovery site.

The following sections describe how log shipping interacts with other SQL Server 2008 technologies.

Log Shipping and Failover Clustering

Log shipping can be combined with failover clustering to achieve maximum availability, business continuity, and disaster recovery. For example, CompanyABC may have a failover cluster supporting business data in the primary locations. In this case, database mirroring may be used to create a hot standby of the database in another office, and log shipping is used to create a third copy in a remote disaster recovery site.

Log Shipping and Database Mirroring

One of the limitations of database mirroring compared to log shipping is that database mirroring can have only one mirrored server associated with each principal, whereas log shipping can have multiple standby servers. The two technologies can be combined if there is a need to ship the principal database logs to a remote location other than where the mirror resides. In addition, log shipping databases can be used for reporting, whereas mirror databases cannot unless a snapshot is used.

Note

Log shipping needs to be reinitialized on the mirror SQL Server instance in the event of a failure and role change.

To ensure that log shipping is continuous after a mirror has failed over and is now the principal, simply create the primary/secondary relationship twice— once on the primary database and once on the mirror database. Because only one database is active at a time, the log shipping jobs never overlap.

Log Shipping and Replication

Log shipping can also be combined with database replication if necessary. However, replication must be manually reconfigured after a log shipping failover. Alternatively, if the failover is permanent, the secondary server can be renamed to allow replication to continue.

> **Note**
>
> Due to the requirements and manual work, database mirroring is often a better choice when high availability for replicated databases is necessary.

Administering Log Shipping

The following sections provide step-by-step tasks used to administer log shipping. These tasks include several prerequisites that you should understand because they affect the success of the log shipping solution. The examples provided throughout these sections simulate a log shipping implementation between two servers while using a third server to act as the monitor.

The AdventureWorks2008 database on INSTANCE01 on the primary server TOR-SQL01 will be shipped to INSTANCE01 on the secondary server NYC-SQL01. The SQL Agent service on each server is running under the SQL. Service domain credentials. Table 14.1 shows the log shipping configuration.

Table 14.1 **Server Names and Role**

Role	SQL Server Instance	Location
Primary Server	TOR-SQL01\Instance01	Toronto
Secondary Server	NYC-SQL01\Instance01	New York
Monitor Server	NYC-SQL01\Instance02	New York

Configuring the Log Shipping Storage Locations

Follow these steps to configure the backup storage location. In this example, the transaction log backups will be stored on a local drive on the primary server. This example uses the X drive. The SQL Agent service account or proxy account on the primary server must be granted access to the folders created in this procedure.

1. On the primary server (TOR-SQL01), navigate to the X:\ drive.
2. Create a folder called **LSBackup**.
3. Create a folder called **AdventureWorks2008** in LSBackup.

4. Right-click the `AdventureWorks2008` folder, and then select Share.

5. In the File Sharing dialog box, type the name of the SQL Service Account (SQL.Service), or click the arrow to select it.

6. Click the arrow by the Permission Level and select Owner or Contributor.

7. Click the Share button.

8. Click the Done button to close the dialog box.

Follow these steps to configure the staging storage location. In this example, the backups will be stored on a local drive on the secondary server. The SQL Agent service account or proxy account on the secondary server must be granted access to the folders created in this procedure.

1. On the secondary server (NYC-SQL01), navigate to the X:\ drive.

2. Create a folder called **LSCopy**.

3. Create a folder called **AdventureWorks2008** in LSCopy.

4. Right-click the `AdventureWorks2008` folder and select Share.

5. In the File Sharing dialog box, type the name of the SQL Service Account (SQL.Service), or click the arrow to select it.

6. Click the arrow by the Permission Level and select Owner or Contributor.

7. Click the Share button.

8. Click the Done button to close the dialog box.

Configuring the Database Recovery Model

SQL Server databases can support different types of recovery models. To support log shipping, the database recovery model must be set to full or bulk-logged. The Full and Bulk-Logged recovery models do not automatically truncate the transaction log; the transaction log is truncated only after a successful transaction log backup is performed.

Follow these steps to configure the AdventureWorks2008 database to use the Full recovery model:

1. Choose Start, All Programs, Microsoft SQL Server 2008, SQL Server Management Studio.

2. Connect to the Database Engine in Object Explorer.

3. Expand the SQL Server instance (TOR-SQL01\Instance01), and then the Database Folder.

4. Right-click the AdventureWorks2008 database and select Properties. The Database Properties window opens.

5. Select the Options page, specify Full from the Recovery model drop-down list, and then click OK.

The AdventureWorks2008 database now uses the Full recovery model. Alternatively, the following TSQL code can also be used to change the recovery model of the AdventureWorks2008 database:

```
ALTER DATABASE AdventureWorks2008 SET RECOVERY FULL
```

> **Note**
>
> On a heavily used database, the transaction log can grow very quickly and can consume a large amount of space. It is important to allocate enough space to store the transaction log, transaction log backup, and transaction log backup copies.

For additional information on database recovery models, see Chapter 7, "Backing Up & Restoring the SQL Server 2008 Database Engine. "

Implementing Log Shipping

After the prerequisites have been configured and the recovery model has been selected, the log shipping configuration can begin. Follow these steps to start the configuration of log shipping on the AdventureWorks2008 database:

1. From the primary server (TOR-SQL01), choose Start, All Programs, Microsoft SQL Server 2008, SQL Server Management Studio.

2. Select Database Engine from the Server Type drop-down list; then enter the server and instance name (**TOR-SQL01\Instance01**).

3. Select Windows Authentication from the Authentication drop-down list and then click the Connect button.

4. A connection to the database engine is made. If the Object Explorer pane is not visible, press the F8 key.

5. From within the Object Explorer pane, expand Databases; the AdventureWorks2008 database should be listed.

6. Right-click the AdventureWorks2008 database and select Properties. The Database Properties window opens.

7. Select the Transaction Log Shipping page. Select the Enable This as a Primary Database in a Log Shipping Configuration option.

Configuring the Transaction Log Backup Settings

The next step in the process is to configure the transaction log backup settings. The following options are available for the log shipping backup:

- **Network Path to Backup Folder**—This option is required and defines a network path to store the transaction log backups.

- **Local Path to Backup Folder**—This option defines the local path to store the transaction log backups and needs to be configured only if the transaction log backups will be stored locally.

- **Backup Retention**—The Delete Files Older Than option defines how long the transaction log backups are kept before being deleted. It is important to store enough backups to recover from small interruptions in the log shipping process. For additional information on recovering, see the section "Recovering from Log Shipping Interruptions" later in this chapter.

- **Alert Threshold**—The Alert If No Backup Occurs Within option defines the threshold that must be reached before an alert is generated when a successful backup does not occur.

- **Backup Job Schedule**—The backup schedule defines the reoccurring pattern for the transaction log backup.

- **Compression**—SQL Server 2008 allows backups to be compressed. The options associated with setting backup compression include: Use the Default Server Setting, Backup Compression, Compress Backup, and Do Not Compress Backup.

Note

It is important to ensure the transaction log for the database is not backed up by any other maintenance plans.

Normally, when the transaction log is successfully backed up, it is truncated. If a different maintenance plan truncates the transaction log before being shipped to the secondary server, the log shipping process will fail.

Follow these steps to continue the configuration of log shipping by establishing the log shipping backup options:

1. In the Transaction Log Shipping page of the database properties, select the Backup Settings button.

2. The Backup Setting window opens, allowing configuration of the log shipping backup.

3. Enter \\TOR-SQL01\AdventureWorks2008 in the Network Path to Backup Folder field.

4. Enter X:\LSBackup\AdventureWorks2008 in the Local Path field.

5. Keep the default 72 hours for the Delete Files Older Than option.

6. Keep the default 1 hour for the Alert If No Backup Occurs Within option.

7. Set the applied desired compression setting.

Figure 14.2 shows how the settings in the Transaction Log Backup Settings window should look after being configured using the preceding steps.

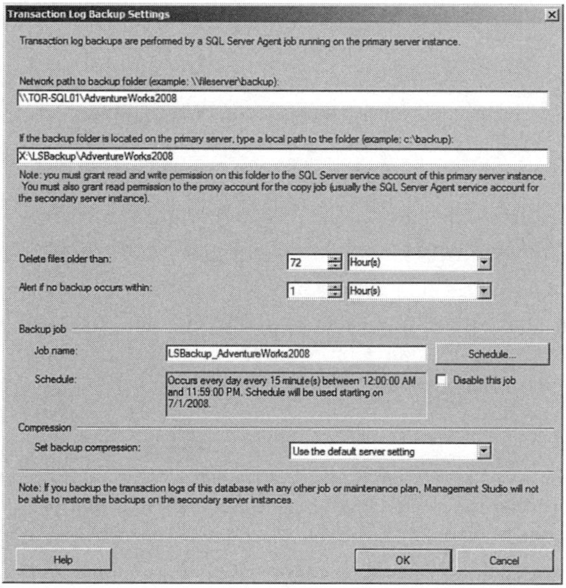

FIGURE 14.2
Transaction Log Backup Settings window.

At this point, you can configure the schedule for the log shipping backup by clicking the Schedule button. See the section "Managing Log Shipping Jobs" later in this chapter for additional details on configuring the transaction log backup schedule.

For the purposes of this exercise, accept the default schedule. The default schedule will run the backup job at 15-minute intervals throughout the day. Click OK to return to the Transaction Log Shipping page.

Adding a Secondary Database

The sysadmin role is required on the server being added as the log shipping secondary. Follow these steps to add NYC-SQL01\Instance01 as the secondary server:

1. In the Transaction Log Shipping page of the database properties, click the Add button.

2. When the Secondary Database Setting window opens, click the Connect button.

3. Enter the server and instance name (**NYC-SQL01\Instance01**).

4. Select Windows Authentication from the Authentication drop-down list and then click the Connect button.

5. The secondary database field is prepopulated to match the name of the source database. This name is acceptable in most instances but can be changed if necessary.

Before the backups can be shipped to the secondary server, the secondary server must be initialized. The initialization process simply restores a full copy of the source database to the target server. This restoration process leaves the database in a loading state ready to restore additional transaction log backups.

Initializing the Secondary Database

On the Initialization tab, the following options used to prepare the database on the secondary server are available:

■ **Generate Full Backup and Restore**—The option titled Yes, Generate a Full Backup of the Primary Database and Restore It into the Secondary Database kicks off the backup immediately following the completion of the configuration page and restores it to the secondary server.

■ **Restore Existing Backup**—The option titled Yes, Restore an Existing Backup of the Primary Database into the Secondary Database can be used to avoid the latency of copying the initial backup over the network if a recent backup of the database is close to the secondary server.

■ **Do Not Initialize**—The option titled No, the Secondary Database Is Initialized should be used only if a recent copy of the source database has already been created and is in a state ready for additional restores. This option is commonly used when recovering from a log shipping interruption and during a failover/failback scenario.

Follow these steps to configure the database initialization options and continue the log shipping implementation:

1. Select the option Yes, Generate a Full Backup of the Primary Database and Restore It into the Secondary Database.

2. Click the Restore Options button. The path to the database and transaction log on the secondary server can be specified.

3. Enter the path to the data files. For this example the path is: `D:\Program Files\Microsoft SQL Server\MSSQL.10.Instance01\MSSQL\Data`.

4. Enter the path to the log files. For this example the path is: `L:\Program Files\Microsoft SQL Server\MSSQL.10.Instance01\MSSQL\Data`. Click OK.

Note

The paths are based on where the database and log folders are placed. Make sure the path to each folder exists; otherwise, the log shipping configuration will fail.

The paths for the database and transaction log were configured to match the path for the AdventureWorks2008 database on the primary server. It is a best practice to standardize the path of the database and logs on each server.

Creating the Copy Files Job

The next step in the process is to configure the Copy Files job settings. This job is created on the secondary server and is used to copy the transaction log backups from the backup share to the staging folder. The Copy Files tab contains options used to configure the copy job.

Note

The target folder is normally in local storage on the secondary SQL Server. If the log backups are being shipped to a failover cluster, a shared storage location is highly recommended as the transaction log staging area.

The following options are available on the Copy Files tab:

- **Destination Folder**—This is the storage location for the copied transaction log backups. This folder is usually kept in local storage on the secondary server and in large-scale environments should be placed on a different set of disks than the database and transaction log.

■ **Backup Retention**—This option defines how long the transaction log backups are kept in the staging folder. The backup copies are kept for 72 hours by default. This option should be adjusted as necessary to keep the destination location from running out of space while providing enough backups to recover from minor interruptions.

■ **Schedule**—The schedule controls how often the copy job copies new backup files in the source folder to the staging area. The schedule of the copy file job is set to run all day at 15-minute intervals, as a default. The schedule of this job does not need to match the backup job and is commonly configured at a higher interval than the backup job. See the section "Managing Log Shipping Jobs" later in this chapter for additional details on managing transaction log schedules.

Follow these steps to configure the settings on the Copy Files tab:

1. Select the Copy Files tab in the Secondary Database Settings dialog box.

2. Enter `X:\LSCopy\AdventureWorks2008` in the Destination Folder field.

3. Accept the default 72-hour retention period and default schedule.

Figure 14.3 shows how the Copy Files tab should look after being configured using the preceding steps.

Note

The transaction log backups can be used for a point-in-time recovery of the database.

The default schedule executes the copy job every 15 minutes. With this schedule, a total of (72*60/15)=288 transaction log backups will be stored in the staging folder.

Defining the Restoration Options

The next step in the process is to configure the Restore Transaction Log job settings. This job is also created on the secondary server and is used to restore the transaction log backups located in the staging folder. The following options are available for the restoration process:

■ **No Recovery Mode**—This option restores the transaction log backups with the NORECOVERY option. The NORECOVERY option keeps the restore process open, allowing additional transaction log backups to be applied.

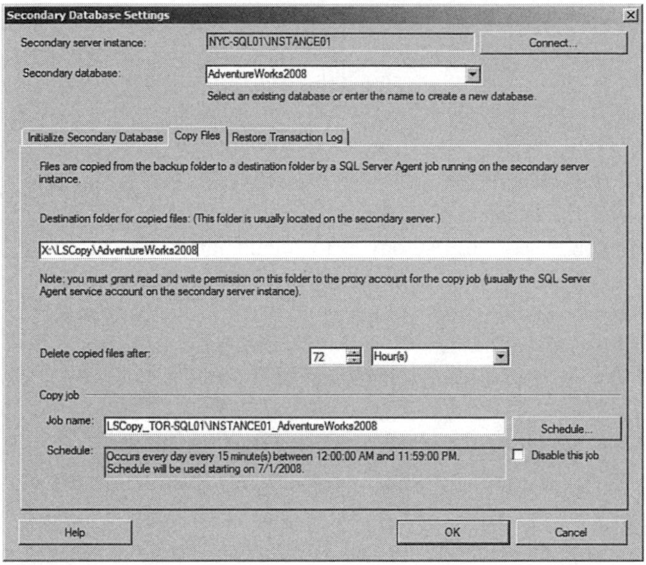

FIGURE 14.3
Copy Files tab settings.

- **Standby Mode**—This option is similar to the NORECOVERY option except that it allows the data on the secondary database to be queried for reporting purposes.

- **Delay Restoring Backup**—An optional delay can be configured. This option can be used to control when the transaction log backups are restored. A delay may be desirable in some situations when the warm standby server is used to recover from a point in time before a catastrophic operation occurred.

- **Alert Threshold**—An alert threshold can be configured to generate a SQL alert when a backup hasn't been performed within a specific time frame.

Select the Restore Transaction Log tab on the Secondary Database Settings dialog box. Accept the default option and then click OK to complete the configuration.

The default options on this tab specify the No Recovery mode, a delay option of 0, and an alert setting of 45 minutes. This configuration offers an adequate starting point, but these options can be fine-tuned to achieve maximum effectiveness for the environment.

> **Note**
>
> When using a log shipping server for reporting purposes, ensure that the restore job and reporting jobs don't overlap, because this can cause the reports to fail or show inaccurate data. Consider using replication as a great alternative for maintaining a real-time copy of the database for reporting.

Adding a Monitor Server

The final step in the configuration process is to define the monitor server. The monitor server is used to track the status of the backup and restoration process. If either the backup or restore exceeds the specified threshold, an alert can be generated.

> **Note**
>
> The monitor server must be defined during the initial configuration of log shipping. To add a monitor server after log shipping has been established, remove and re-create the log shipping configuration.

Use the following procedure to add the server NYC-SQL01\Instance02 as the monitor server:

1. In the Transaction Log Shipping page of the database properties, enable the Use a Monitor Server Instance option.

2. Click the Settings button. When the Log Shipping Monitor Setting window opens, click the Connect button.

3. Enter the server and instance name (`NYC-SQL01\Instance02`).

4. Select Windows Authentication from the Authentication drop-down list and then click the Connect button.

> **Note**
>
> The monitor role should be hosted on a server other than the primary or secondary server.

These log shipping configuration options are available:

- **Monitor Connections**—The agent that executes each of the log shipping jobs must be able to connect to the SQL Server. You can set the Monitor Connections option to impersonate the SQL Server agent proxy account or use a specific account.

- **History Retention**—This is the amount of time old log shipping transactions are kept in the monitor server database.
- **Alert Job**—The alert job name can be changed; however, the job
  schedule is hard-coded and doesn't normally need to be modified.

Click OK to accept the default settings and return to the Transaction Log
Shipping page. Figure 14.4 shows how the Log Shipping Monitor settings
page should look after being configured using the preceding steps.

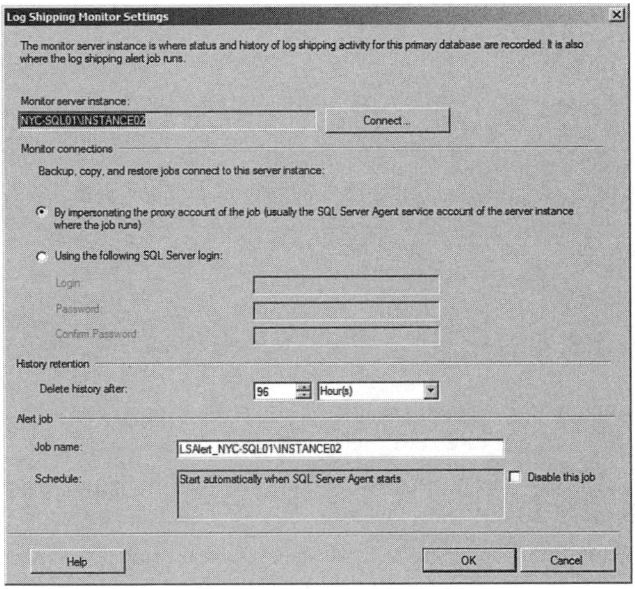

FIGURE 14.4
Transaction Log Shipping properties.

Now that the log shipping configuration is complete, click OK on the properties
page to apply the configuration to the primary, secondary, and monitor servers.

After you click OK, the database is backed up and restored on the secondary
server. Then the SQL Server jobs used to create backups are scheduled on the
source server, the copy job and restore jobs are created on the destination
server, and the alert job is created on the monitor server.

> **Note**
>
> Before clicking OK to implement log shipping, it is possible to script the entire log shipping configuration by clicking the Script Configuration button in the Transaction Log Shipping page.

Managing Log Shipping

The following sections describe common log shipping management tasks. These tasks include recovery steps that should be taken when the primary and secondary databases become unsynchronized, along with steps on how to fail over the database to a secondary server and then fail back to the original database after the primary server has been repaired.

Recovering from Log Shipping Interruptions

Log shipping interruptions can result in the log shipping process stopping until the problem is corrected. When the log shipping process is stopped, the database on the secondary server is no longer synchronized with the source data. It is important to correct these interruptions quickly to prevent transaction log backups in the backup share from being removed before they can be shipped to the secondary server. If the transaction log backups in the backup share are removed before being shipped to the secondary server, the log shipping configuration must be re-created and the secondary database must be reinitialized.

> **Note**
>
> Different factors should be considered when configuring the transaction log retention period. For example, the 72-hour default retention period allows easy recovery from a failure that may occur on Friday evening, without your needing to reinitialize the database on the secondary server when returning to work the following week.

Common problems are usually the result of inadequate disk space. If the transaction log backup job runs every 15 minutes and 72 hours of transaction log backups are retained, 288 transaction log backups are generated. These backups are stored in both the backup share and staging folders.

Additional problems usually occur if one of the jobs used in the log shipping process stops working, but all the transaction log backups are available. In this scenario, the problem can be corrected, and the log shipping process will catch up during the next execution cycle. For example, if a security setting was changed on the backup share and the agent on the secondary no longer has the appropriate permissions needed to access the share, the log shipping process stops. When the permissions are corrected, the next log shipping job cycle will copy and restore all transaction log backups from where it left off before the problem occurred.

In a worst-case scenario, a transaction log backup is lost or otherwise unable to be restored to the secondary server. In this scenario, the log shipping configuration must be rebuilt, and the database must be reinitialized. Follow these steps to remove log shipping from the database:

1. From the primary server (TOR-SQL01), choose Start, All Programs, Microsoft SQL Server 2008, SQL Server Management Studio.

2. Select Database Engine from the Server Type drop-down list; then enter the server and instance name (**TOR-SQL01\Instance01**).

3. Select Windows Authentication from the Authentication drop-down list and then click the Connect button.

4. A connection to the database engine is made. If the Object Explorer pane is not visible, press the F8 key.

5. From within the Object Explorer pane, expand Databases; the AdventureWorks2008 database should be listed.

6. Right-click the AdventureWorks2008 database and select Properties. The Database Properties window opens.

7. Select the Transaction Log Shipping page. Uncheck the Enable This as a Primary Database in a Log Shipping Configuration option.

After log shipping has been removed, the log files in the backup share and the staging area can also be removed because they cannot be applied to the database out of order and are most likely unusable. The database on the secondary server is not removed automatically and should be manually removed before re-creating log shipping.

Managing Log Shipping Jobs

The following options are available when configuring the schedule properties for the backup, copy, and restore log shipping jobs:

- **Name and Schedule Type**—The name of the backup job should be unique and allow easy identification of the job function. The schedule type for the log shipping backup job should be set to Reoccurring because the job must back up the transaction log backups repeatedly.

- **Frequency**—The frequency of the log shipping job is normally set to Daily. This option is adequate for most implementations of log shipping because the occurrence pattern option essentially keeps the job running at predefined intervals throughout the day.

- **Occurrence Pattern**—The occurrence pattern executes each transaction log shipping job at predefined intervals throughout the day. The default reoccurrence pattern is set to run the job every 15 minutes from 12:00:00 a.m. to 11:59:00 p.m. The reoccurrence pattern should be configured according to the organization's Service Level Agreements (SLAs).

- **Duration**—The duration of the log shipping agent jobs is commonly set to No End Date because keeping the target servers updated is key.

> **Note**
>
> The size of the transaction log backups, speed of the network, and length of time the restoration takes all play a significant role in the planning and scheduling process to prevent a backlog from occurring.
>
> Increasing the frequency of transaction log backups reduces the amount of data lost during a failure while directly increasing the network and system resources consumed.

The log shipping job schedules can be changed during the log shipping configuration or after log shipping has been implemented. The backup job is located on the primary server, and the copy and restore jobs are located on the secondary servers.

To change the log shipping jobs, navigate to SQL Server Agent, Jobs from within SQL Server Management Studio. Double-click one of the log shipping jobs and select the Schedule options page to change the schedule for the job.

Failing Over to a Secondary Server

There are two basic scenarios for initiating a log shipping failover from the primary to the secondary server. The first type of failover occurs when both the primary and secondary servers are up and running and the database on both systems is in a usable state. This scenario is referred to as a *controlled* failover and is usually performed to test the log shipping failover process.

The other scenario occurs when the primary server or database has failed and is unavailable, and the secondary database must be brought online. In this scenario, because the primary database is not available, the work performed between the last transaction log backup and the time of the failure is lost and must be manually re-created.

The process for the two scenarios is almost the same. However, the controlled failover scenario has some additional steps to ensure that no data is lost during the transition.

Preparing for a Controlled Failover

You can use the following procedure to initiate a controlled failover to the secondary database. This procedure is used to eliminate the possibility of data loss but is available only when the primary server is still online and the database is available.

Note

Before starting a controlled failover, ensure that no users or applications are using the database.

To start the process, disable the existing log shipping jobs on the primary and secondary servers. You can do this by navigating to SQL Server Agent, Jobs from within SQL Server Management Studio. Right-click each log shipping job and select Disable. Based on the steps found in the section "Implementing Log Shipping," the backup job on the primary server is called LSBackup_ AdventureWorks2008, whereas the copy and restore jobs on the secondary server are called LSCopy_TOR-SQL01_AdventureWorks2008 and LSCopy_ TOR-SQL01_AdventureWorks2008.

Place the database in single-user mode. You can do this by right-clicking the database from within SQL Server Management Studio and selecting Properties. When the Properties window opens, select the Options page. Change the Restrict Access option located at the bottom of the list to SINGLE_USER and then click OK.

The next step is to back up the primary database with the NORECOVERY option. This places the database in a state ready for the controlled "failback" process. This also backs up any changes that occurred between the current time and the time of the last transaction log backup. Use the following code to back up the database with the NORECOVERY option:

```
USE MASTER
BACKUP LOG [AdventureWorks2008]
TO  DISK = N'X:\LSBackup\AdventureWorks2008
➥ \AdventureWorks2008_Final.trn'
WITH  NORECOVERY
GO
```

The final changes are backed up and stored in a file called AdventureWorks 2008_Final in the LSBackup\AdventureWorks2008 folder.

The next step is to synchronize the primary and secondary databases, essentially making sure they are exactly the same by restoring the final transaction log backup.

The first part of this step simply involves manually running the copy and restore jobs on the secondary server. This restores any transaction log backups in the backup share that have not been applied to the database on the secondary server. To manually run the copy and restore jobs, from within SSMS on the secondary server (NYC-SQL01), right-click the LSCopy job and select Start Job at Step. After the LSCopy job has completed successfully, right-click the LSRestore job and select Start Job at Step.

The second part of this step involves manually copying and applying the AdventureWorks2008_Final.trn backup file to the database on the secondary server. You can use the following code to commit the last transaction log to the database on the secondary server:

```
USE MASTER
RESTORE LOG [AdventureWorks2008]
FROM DISK = N'X:\LSCopy\AdventureWorks2008\
➥ AdventureWorks2008_Final.trn'
WITH NORECOVERY
GO
```

This code assumes the AdventureWorks2008_Final.trn file has been copied to the LSCopy\AdventureWorks2008 folder on the secondary server.

The next step is to bring the secondary database online.

Bringing the Secondary Database Online

This section details the actual process used to bring the database on the secondary server online. These steps are a continuation of the controlled failover process. If the controlled failover process is not available, this is the starting point for a catastrophic failure that has caused the primary database and/or server to become unavailable.

To bring the database on the secondary server online, run the following command from the secondary server:

```
USE MASTER
RESTORE DATABASE AdventureWorks2008 WITH RECOVERY
```

The database is now online and ready to be used by clients. The next step in the process is to redirect any application or clients that use the database to the new server. This step can be different for each front-end application being used.

Failing Back to the Primary Server

Failing back to the original primary server is actually easy. When a failover was originally initiated, the secondary server that was brought online is now the primary server. To fail back to the original server, simply establish log shipping from the active database on the "new" primary server back to the "original" server. The "original" primary server then acts as the secondary server.

After log shipping is established, a controlled failover can be initiated, and the original server will once again be the primary server hosting the active database.

The only configuration option that changes is in the Secondary Database Settings dialog box: Select the option No, the Secondary Database Is Initialized.

Managing Log Shipping from the Command Line

SQL Server 2008 includes the SQLLogShip.exe application first introduced in SQL Server 2005 SP2. The application performs backup, copy, restore and clean up tasks from a log shipping perspective. Table 14.2 shows each option available with this program.

Table 14.2   SQLLogShip.exe **Options**

Option	Description
-server <*instance*>	Specifies the instance of SQL Server where the operation will run.
-backup <*p_id*>	Performs a backup operation for the primary database whose primary ID is specified by <*p_id*>.
-copy <*s_id*>	Performs a copy operation to copy backups from the specified secondary server for the secondary database, or databases, whose secondary ID is specified by <*s_id*>.
-restore <*s_id*>	Performs a restore operation on the specified secondary server for the secondary database, or databases, whose secondary ID is specified by <*s_id*>.
-verboselevel <*level*>	Specifies the level of messages added to the log shipping history. The level can be set from 0 to 4, with 0 = logging no output and 4 = logging all messages.
-logintimeout <*value*>	Specifies the amount of time in seconds allotted for attempting to log in to the server instance. The default is 15 seconds.
-querytimeout <*value*>	Specifies the amount of time in seconds allotted for starting the specified operation.

> **Note**
>
> For more information on SQLLogShip.exe refer to SQL Server 2008 Books online.

The backup, copy, and restore options cannot be combined and must be executed on the appropriate server. For example, the backup option must be run on the primary server, and the copy/restore option must be run on the secondary server.

The primary ID for the backup command can be obtained by querying the log_shipping_primary_database's system table. The secondary ID for the copy and restore commands can be obtained by querying the log_shipping_secondary system table.

Monitoring and Troubleshooting Log Shipping

The following sections describe the different administration and maintenance tables, stored procedures, and reports that can be used to troubleshoot and monitor log shipping.

It is important to become familiar with how to use each of these items because they help keep the high-availability solution running efficiently without issue.

Viewing Log Shipping Reports

Log shipping reports can be viewed from the primary, secondary, and monitor servers. However, viewing the reports from the monitor server is most effective because the monitor server contains records from both the primary and secondary servers. Viewing the log shipping report from the primary and secondary servers shows only half the data.

Follow these steps to view log shipping reports:

1. From the primary server (TOR-SQL01), choose Start, All Programs, Microsoft SQL Server 2008, SQL Server Management Studio.

2. Select Database Engine from the Server Type drop-down; then enter the server and instance name (**TOR-SQL01\Instance01**).

3. Select Windows Authentication from the Authentication drop-down list and then click the Connect button.

4. A connection to the database engine is made. If the Object Explorer pane is not visible, press the F8 key.

5. From within the Object Explorer pane, right-click the server name (TOR-SQL01\Instance01) at the top of the tree.

6. Select Reports, Standard Reports, and Transaction Log Shipping Status from the context menu.

7. The transaction log shipping report is displayed.

Figure 14.5 shows a sample log shipping report run from the monitor server.

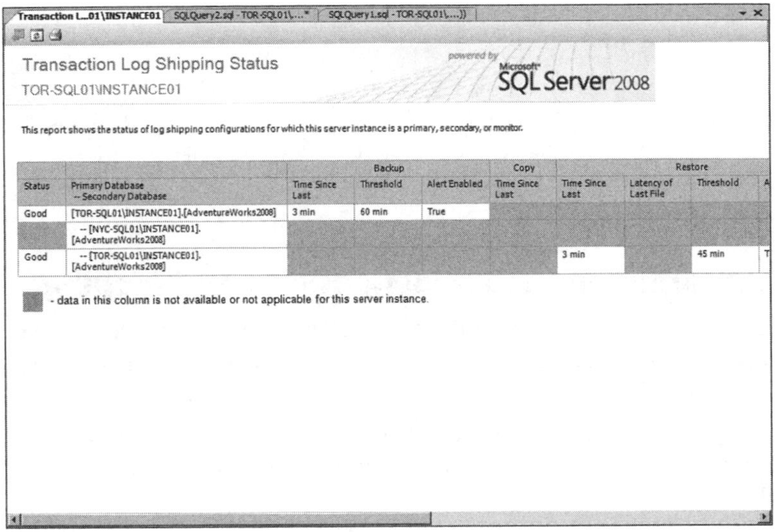

FIGURE 14.5
Transaction log shipping status report.

The report shows the backup and restore configuration and the current status of each log shipping server, along with the times the last backup and copy operation took place.

Querying Log Shipping Tables for Status

The tables listed in Table 14.3 store information about log shipping and can be used to monitor status and troubleshoot issues.

Table 14.3   **Log Shipping Tables**

Table Name	Description
log_shipping_monitor_alert	Stores alert job ID.
log_shipping_monitor_error_detail	Stores error details for log shipping jobs.

Table Name	Description
log_shipping_monitor_history_detail	Contains history details for log shipping agents.
log_shipping_monitor_primary	Stores one monitor record for the primary database in each log shipping configuration, including information about the last backup file and last restored file that is useful for monitoring.
log_shipping_monitor_secondary	Stores one monitor record for each secondary database, including information about the last backup file and last restored file that is useful for monitoring.

To use these tables, for example, you could execute a standard SQL query. Use the following code to locate all log shipping errors, sorted by the most recent:

```
USE msdb
SELECT * FROM log_shipping_monitor_error_detail
ORDER BY log_time Desc
```

Using Log Shipping Stored Procedures

The following stored procedures can be used to assist in troubleshooting and monitoring log shipping activity:

- **sp_help_log_shipping_monitor_primary**—Returns monitor records for the specified primary database from the log_shipping_monitor_primary table. This stored procedure can be run on monitor servers or primary servers.

- **sp_help_log_shipping_monitor_secondary**—Returns monitor records for the specified secondary database from the log_shipping_monitor_secondary table. This stored procedure can be run on the monitor server or secondary servers.

- **sp_help_log_shipping_alert_job**—Returns the job ID of the alert job. This stored procedure can be run on the monitor server or primary and secondary servers if no monitor is defined.

- **sp_help_log_shipping_primary_database**—Retrieves primary database settings and displays the values from the log_shipping_primary_databases and log_shipping_monitor_primary tables. This stored procedure can be run on the primary server.

- **sp_help_log_shipping_primary_secondary**—Retrieves secondary database names for a primary database. This stored procedure can be run on the primary server.

- **sp_help_log_shipping_secondary_database**—Retrieves secondary database settings from the log_shipping_secondary, log_shipping_secondary_databases, and log_shipping_monitor_secondary tables. This stored procedure can be run on secondary servers.

- **sp_help_log_shipping_secondary_primary**—This stored procedure retrieves the settings for a given primary database on the secondary server. This stored procedure can be run on secondary servers.

Summary

SQL Server 2008 log shipping is almost identical to log shipping in previous versions of SQL Server. However, the role of log shipping has been reduced because new technologies such as database mirroring provide substantial enhancements. Because these new technologies have limits, log shipping is commonly used to complement other high-availability technologies in scenarios such as replicating business-critical data to a disaster recovery site. However, log shipping is still prevalent when there is a need to maintain multiple copies of data and a secondary for reporting.

Best Practices

The following best practices can be taken from this chapter:

- Store enough backups to recover from interruptions in the log shipping process. This ensures that transaction log backups are not removed before the problem can be corrected.

- Use the transaction log backups for a point-in-time recovery of the database in the event of data corruption.

- On a heavily used database, transactions can be generated very quickly, and the log can consume a large amount of space. Be sure to allocate enough space to store the transaction log.

- Configure the backup and restore reoccurrence pattern according to acceptable loss and environmental limits. A more aggressive reoccurrence pattern lowers the amount of data lost during a catastrophic failure.

- The size of the transaction log backups, speed of the network, and length of time the restoration takes all play a significant role in planning and scheduling the log shipping solution.

- Make sure a backlog in the log shipping process does not occur.

- Ensure that the transaction log for the database is not backed up by any other maintenance plans, because other maintenance plans can truncate the transaction log before the changes are shipped to the secondary servers.

- Log shipping is most practical when multiple secondary servers are necessary. If only a single secondary server is being used, use database mirroring over log shipping.

- Apply transaction log backups in sequential order to the secondary database.

- Define the monitor server during the initial configuration of log shipping. To add a monitor server after log shipping has been established, remove and re-create the log shipping configuration.

- Standardize the path of the database on each server.

- When using a log shipping server for reporting purposes, ensure the restore job and reporting jobs don't overlap because this can cause the reports to fail or show inaccurate data. Consider using replication as a great alternative for maintaining a real-time copy of the database for reporting.

CHAPTER 15

Implementing and Administering SQL Server Replication

Replication is a native SQL Server feature that allows a DBA to copy tables, views, indexed views, functions, stored procedures, and so on from one database to another, and allows a DBA to control how synchronized the two copies are. In other words, you can replicate changes to both data and schema objects (that is, table, view, or stored procedure changes, and so on). Some replication types allow for bidirectional replication, where changes made on the destination database can be replicated back to the source database.

Replication is best used for the following purposes:

- **To move data closer to clients**—For example, branch offices might need to access data in a central office, and the network hop involved makes the applications run very slowly. Having a local copy of the data will make their data access much faster.

- **To offload reporting to another server**—Instead of having reporting clients accessing data from the production server, causing I/O and database user contention between the reporting users and the application users, data can be replicated to a reporting server and the reporting clients can access their data there. The end result is greater scalability for both sets of users.

- **To scale out performance**—Instead of having 1,000 users accessing a single server, 100 users can each access one of 10 servers with the end result being improved performance for all users.

- **To fulfill application requirements**—This includes consolidating data from branch offices to a central location, replicating to tables with different schemas, replicating to different RDBMSs, replicating to handheld devices, and so on.

Replication is also frequently used as a disaster recovery solution, but it is a poor choice for this for these reasons:

- There is no automatic failover of clients from the production server to the failover server.

- Latencies aren't predictable, and consequently exposure to data loss can be much greater than with other disaster recovery technologies.

- Not every object is replicated (for example, logins), and new objects require special handling.

- Replication requires licenses for both the production server and the failover server; the other Microsoft disaster recovery solutions for SQL Server do not.

The focus of this chapter is how to design, implement, and monitor replication topologies.

What's New in SQL Server 2008 Replication?

Although the changes in replication between SQL Server 2000 and 2005 were radically different, the changes between SQL Server 2005 and 2008 are much smaller. The following features are new in SQL Server 2008:

- Radical improvements in snapshot delivery

- A new interface for creating and modifying peer-to-peer topologies

- Peer-to-peer replication, which now supports conflict detection and replicates schema changes without having to go offline

- Deeper replication integration with database mirroring

- A class that developers can use for database synchronization that requires no DBA administration (Sync Services)

> **Note**
>
> The focus of the replication team for SQL Server 2008 was working on the features for change tracking, change data capture, and Sync Services, and as a consequence the base features for SQL Server 2008 replication have not changed significantly since SQL Server 2005 replication.

SQL Server 2008 Replication Essentials

To be able to administer SQL Server replication, you will need to understand the concepts behind it. Replication also has many components. This section introduces the main concepts and components of replication.

SQL Server 2008 Replication Roles

Replication uses metaphors from the world of publishing. The main components are as follows:

- **Publisher**—The source of the data and/or objects you are replicating. This could be a SQL Server or an Oracle Server; SQL Server Express is not supported as a Publisher.

- **Subscriber**—The destination server; again this could be a database on the same server, another SQL Server (2000, 2005 or 2008) or an Oracle or DB2 RDBMS. SQL Server Express and CE are also supported subscribers.

- **Distributor**—Transactional and snapshot replication (these replication types are covered in the next section) use a store-and-forward metaphor. The Distributor is a server that stores the replication commands before they are executed on the Subscriber. In merge replication, the Distributor only holds historical data. In most topologies the Distributor will be on the same server as the Publisher; however, if you expect large workloads on your Publisher, you might want to use a remote distributor.

  If you do not already have a Distributor, connect to your SQL Server in SQL Server Management Studio, and expand the Replication folder. If you do not see a folder labeled Local Publications, you are running SQL Server Express, which does not support the installation of a Distributor. If you see a menu item Distributor Properties, your SQL Server is already configured with a Distributor. If you do not have a Distributor, right-click and select Configure Distribution. Click Next and accept the default to create a local distributor. We will cover how to create a remote distributor in the section "Creating the Distributor."

- **Publications**—Publications contain the objects you want to replicate. Group the objects you want to replicate into publications according to replication type, logical grouping (such as business unit), publications that have common properties, or common objects that need to go to a group of subscribers.

- **Articles**—Articles are objects you can replicate. They include schema-only objects (functions, views, and stored procedures) and schema and data objects (tables and indexed views). Tables and indexed views can be vertically or horizontally partitioned; in other words, a subset of the columns or rows or a subset of both can be replicated.

- **Bidirectional replication**—This metaphor is not from the world of publishing. In bidirectional replication, data modifications (DML) originating on the Publisher are applied on the Subscriber and DML originating on the Subscriber are applied on the Publisher. The most common type of bidirectional replication used is merge replication. Please refer to the section "Configuring Merge Replication."

- **Push subscribers**—The Publisher pushes the schema and data to the Subscriber. This is normally used with a small number of subscribers on a Local Area Network (LAN).

- **Pull subscribers**—The Subscriber pulls the schema and data from the Publisher. This is normally used with large numbers of subscribers and most often over the Internet.

- **Publication Access List (PAL)**—A database group of subscriber SQL or Windows accounts that have rights to access the publication.

- **Conflict**—This metaphor is not from the world of publishing. In conflicts, a data modification occurs on one side of a replication topology that disagrees with a modification on another side of the replication topology. There are five basic types of conflicts:

  - **Primary key collision**—An insert originating on the Publisher has the same primary key values as an insert on the Subscriber, and the primary key constraint is violated when replication attempts to synchronize the two.

  - **Updating a deleted row**—This conflict occurs when a row is updated on one side of the replication topology (the Publisher for instance) and deleted on the Subscriber. The conflict occurs when replication attempts to synchronize the two.

  - **Lack of consistency**—One row is modified on the Publisher, but when replication attempts to modify the same row on the Subscriber, it does not exist or there is more than one row with the same key values.

  - **Column-level tracking**—A tuple or cell is updated on one side of a replication topology and updated with a different value on the other side of the replication topology.

  - **Row-level tracking**—A row is updated on one side of a replication topology and the same row is updated on the other side of the replication topology. Unlike column-level tracking, row-level tracking does not track to see if the change occurred in the same column.

Types of Replication Alternatives Available

There are three types of replication: snapshot, transactional, and merge, with some variants on the snapshot and transactional replication types.

Snapshot Replication

- **Snapshot replication**—This replication type generates an image of the data at a point in time (a *snapshot*) and distributes it to one or more subscribers. After the snapshot is deployed, no changes are replicated to the Subscriber(s) until the next time the snapshot is generated and distributed. This replication type is best used when your data changes infrequently and the bulk of it changes at one time, for example, catalog updates. There are no schema modifications using this replication type.

- **Snapshot replication with queued updating**—This replication type is a variation of snapshot replication; however, changes that occur on the Subscriber are replicated back to the Publisher on a continuous or scheduled basis. This replication type is best used in the following situations:
    - When the majority of the changes occur on the Publisher.
    - When there are fewer than 10 subscribers.
    - This replication type is resilient to network interruptions; if a failure occurs, replication will pick up where it left off and replicate changes back to the Publisher.
    - This replication type adds a GUID column and triggers to all tables that are replicated.
    - Adjustments must be made for constraints, triggers, and the identity property with this replication type.
    - Conflicts will be detected, but there are no facilities to roll them back (more on conflict detection later). This variant is deprecated in SQL Server 2008. Microsoft recommends that you use peer-to-peer replication, although it is only supported in the Enterprise Edition of SQL Server.

- **Snapshot replication with immediate updating**—This replication type is another variation of snapshot replication; however, changes that occur on the Subscriber are applied as a two-phase commit via Microsoft Distributed Transaction Coordinator (MS DTC) to the Subscriber. Essentially all transactions originating at the Subscriber are applied in a transactional context on the Publisher and then on the Subscriber. In addition to the same caveats with queued updating there are several important additional caveats to this replication type:
    - Latency of transactions originating on the Subscriber is increased. Now transactions have to make a network hop and be written on both sides. This latency can reduce scalability.

- If the link between the Subscriber and the Publisher goes down, transactions originating on the Subscriber will hang until the transaction is rolled back. The transactions typically hang between 15 and 20 seconds before being rolled back.

- **Snapshot replication with immediate updating and queued failover**—This variant of snapshot replication uses immediate updating by default; however, if your Publisher goes offline, you have the option to manually switch to queued updating. The same caveats as queued updating apply here as well.

  - The majority of the transactions originate at the Publisher.

  - There should be fewer than 10 subscribers.

  - Conflict detection but not conflict handling.

  - A GUID column will be added to your tables being replicated.

  - Conflicts will be detected but there are no facilities to roll them back (more on conflict detection later). This variant is deprecated in SQL Server 2008. Microsoft recommends that you use peer-to-peer replication, although it is only supported in the Enterprise Edition of SQL Server.

Transactional Replication

- **Transactional Replication**—This is the most common replication type. It is chosen because it tracks changes and replicates them to the Subscriber. The latency with this replication type can be very low (typically slightly less than 3 seconds) even for large workloads that involve *singletons* (one-row inserts, updates, and deletes). However, latencies can be large for batch updates, inserts, and deletes. In transactional replication, transactions that occur on the Publisher are read from the transaction log and stored in the distribution database on the Distributor. They are then applied on the Subscriber via stored procedures or SQL statements, within a transactional context. This replication type requires a primary key on every table you are replicating and is resilient to network interruptions. Transaction replication does not make any modifications to the tables it replicates.

- **Transactional Replication with Queued Updating**—This replication type is very similar to Snapshot replication with queued updating. Changes that originate on the Publisher are replicated via a Distribution Agent (more on this later in the next section). Changes that occur on the Subscriber are replicated back to the Publisher via a queue reader (more later). The same caveats with snapshot replication with queued updating also apply here. This variant is deprecated in SQL Server 2008. Microsoft recommends that you use peer-to-peer replication, although it is only supported in the Enterprise Edition of SQL Server.

■ **Transactional Replication with Immediate Updating**—This replication type is very similar to snapshot replication with immediate updating. Changes that originate on the Publisher are replicated via a Distribution Agent (more on this later in the next section). Changes that occur on the Subscriber are replicated back to the Publisher using a two-phase commit via MS DTC. The same caveats with snapshot replication with immediate updating also apply here. This variant is deprecated in SQL Server 2008. Microsoft recommends that you use peer-to-peer replication, although it is only supported in the Enterprise Edition of SQL Server.

■ **Transactional Replication with Immediate Updating and Queued Failover**—This is a variant of snapshot replication with immediate updating and queued failover. As the Subscriber will roll back all transactions that originate on the Subscriber when the Publisher is offline, the topology is designed to be failed over to queued updating until the Subscriber comes back online. The same caveats as in snapshot replication with immediate updating and queued failover hold here as well. This variant is deprecated in SQL Server 2008. Microsoft recommends that you use peer-to-peer replication, although it is only supported in the Enterprise Edition of SQL Server.

■ **Oracle Publishing**—In this type of replication, an Oracle RDBMs server replicates to SQL Server 2005 or 2008. This is supported on the Enterprise Edition of SQL Server. This is a variant of transactional replication. Support is deprecated for Oracle 8, with SQL Server 2008 you to run Oracle 9i and above as the Oracle Publisher.

■ **Bidirectional Transactional Replication**—This replication type is not available using the wizards and must be configured manually. Use transactional replication to replicate to the Subscriber, and then the Subscriber is configured as a Publisher to replicate back to the original Publisher. Set the @loopback_detection parameter to True in sp_addsubscription when configuring your subscribers. You must set the Not For Replication property on all constraints, triggers, and identity columns. You will also need to set the identity property to have different seeds on either side so that you don't get any primary key conflicts—configuring your primary keys or identity seeds to minimize primary key conflicts is called *partitioning*. This replication type does not require any schema modifications.

Although Microsoft recommends using peer-to-peer replication, which is an Enterprise Edition–only feature, bidirectional transactional replication is supported on the Standard Edition and above and is faster than peer-to-peer replication, but not scalable beyond a small number of nodes (two to three).

■ **Peer to Peer Transactional Replication**—Peer-to-peer transactional replication is bidirectional replication extended to many more Publisher/Subscriber pairs called *nodes*. The limit is 10 nodes; however, this depends on available network bandwidth and workload. Peer-to-peer replication is popular because a node can drop off (for maintenance, or if the link goes down) and the other nodes can continue to synchronize with each other. When the disconnected node comes back on, it will synchronize with the other partners. If the node is disconnected, due to a failed Wide-Area Network (WAN) link for example, local users could access this node and do work, and when the WAN link comes back, the changes the users made when the node was disconnected from the WAN will be replicated to all other nodes. Peer-to-peer replication, like bidirectional transactional replication, does not require any schema changes. Peer-to-peer replication is only available in the Enterprise Editions of SQL Server 2005 and 2008.

■ **Merge Replication**—Whereas all other bidirectional replication solutions are limited by the number of subscribers, merge replication is highly scalable. It has rich conflict detection and resolution features. Merge replication does tend to be slower than the other bidirectional replication options, but it is designed for low-bandwidth links. For example, it is an excellent fit where you have to replicate over phone lines. Merge replication is the only replication type that can be used with PDAs or handhelds running SQL Compact Edition.

So which replication type should you use? If the bulk of your data changes infrequently but at regular intervals, and you need one-way replication, use snapshot replication. If your data changes continuously, use transactional replication. If you need near-real-time bidirectional replication and have 2 to 3 subscribers and have partitioned your data to minimize conflicts, use bidirectional transactional replication. If you need near-real-time bidirectional replication and have between 2 and 10 subscribers, are running Enterprise Edition, and have partitioned your data to minimize conflicts, use peer-to-peer replication. If you need bidirectional replication, have a large number of subscribers, and need rich conflict detection and resolution, use merge replication. Use Oracle Publishing if you are publishing from an Oracle RDBMs and your SQL Server is the Enterprise Edition.

Additional Replication Components

Replication uses agents to detect changes and migrate them to the Subscriber and Publishers. These agents are executables that you can find in C:\Program Files\Microsoft SQL Server\100\Com, and they function as described in the following list:

- **Log Reader Agent**—This agent is used by transactional replication. Changes that occur to published articles are written to the transaction log. The Log Reader Agent reads these changes, constructs replication commands, and writes these commands to the distribution database, and also writes a marker in the distribution database indicating the last part of the log it read. The transaction log can be truncated to the last-read command. The distribution database is a repository on the Distributor that stores replication commands (for transactional replication only) and history and metadata for all replication types. The Log Reader Agent then writes a marker in the transaction log stating that it has read these changes out of the transaction log. This way, if the Log Reader Agent fails, it will retrieve the record from the distribution database indicating the last command read from the log and then start reading from this point on.

- **Snapshot Agent**—The Snapshot Agent is used by all replication types to create a base image of the published articles and all replication data necessary for the replication processes, for example, replication stored procedures, tracking and conflict tables, and tracking triggers.

- **Queue Reader Agent**—This agent is used in queued replication. *Queued replication* uses tracking triggers to capture changes that originate by user activity on the Subscriber database and writes them to a queue. The queue reader reads this queue and writes the changes in the publication database.

- **Distribution Agent**—The Distribution Agent reads the changes that the Log Reader has written to the distribution database and writes them to the Subscriber. It places a marker in the Subscriber database indicating the last transaction applied there, and also on the distribution database. This way, if the distribution agent fails, the next time it runs it will determine what the last command applied on the Subscriber was and pick up where it left off.

- **Merge Agent**—The Merge Agent connects to Subscriber and Publisher and determines the last time both synchronized. It then will determine what changes occurred on both sides since the last time it synchronized. It then processes all deletes at one time, and then processes all inserts and updates. While processing these changes, it determines whether any of the changes have occurred on the same row, or if you are using column-level tracking, it determines whether any of the changes have occurred on the same row and column. If so, the Merge Agent invokes the conflict detection mechanism specified for the article to which the row belongs. The Merge Agent also will write tracking metadata so that if the agent is interrupted, it will be able to pick up where it left off the next time the Publisher and Subscriber synchronize.

- **Replication Monitor**—The central point for monitoring publishers and subscribers. You can administer most agents in Replication Monitor; however you cannot modify the publishers, publications, subscribers, or subscriptions here. To access Replication Monitor, connect to your Publisher in SQL Server Management Studio and right click on the Replication Folder and select Launch Replication Monitor.

- **Conflict Viewer**—The Conflict Viewer allows you to see conflicts that have occurred in merge replication of one of the updatable subscriber variants of snapshot and transactional replication. The Conflict Viewer also lets you roll back and forth between conflicts if you are using merge replication. To use the Conflict Viewer, connect to your Publisher in SQL Server Management Studio, expand the Replication folder, expand the Local Publishers folder, right-click on your publication, and select View Conflicts.

- **Profiles**—*Profiles* are groups of settings that you can configure for your agents to use. For example, if your link between your Publisher and Subscriber is unstable, you can select the Slow Link Profiler for your Merge Agent. To select a profile, you need to launch Replication Monitor by right-clicking on the Replication folder, and selecting Launch Replication Monitor. Add your Publisher if it is not already added, by selecting Add Publisher. Expand the Publisher and in the right-hand pane, click on the Subscriber. Then right-click on the Subscriber and select Agent Profile. By default the Default Agent Profile will be selected. At this point choose another Profile, or click the New button to create your own.

SQL Server 2008 Replication Topologies

There are basically five types of replication topologies:

1. **Publisher-Distributor-Subscriber**—This is the most common replication topology and can be used by all replication types. This replication topology is illustrated in Figure 15.1. The publication originates at the

Publisher, and the schema, its data, and related metadata are replicated to the Subscriber(s). Depending on your replication topology, data moves from the Publisher to the Subscriber (transactional and snapshot), and for all other replication types it moves both ways.

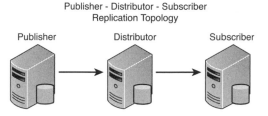

FIGURE 15.1
Publisher-Distributor-Subscriber topology.

2. **Republishing**—Here a Publisher replicates to the Subscriber, which in turn publishes its schema, data, and related metadata to the downstream subscriber. The schema, data, and related metadata originate on the upstream Publisher. Data moves from the main Publisher downstream to the Subscriber for transactional and snapshot replication. For all other replication types it can move both ways. This replication topology is illustrated in Figure 15.2.

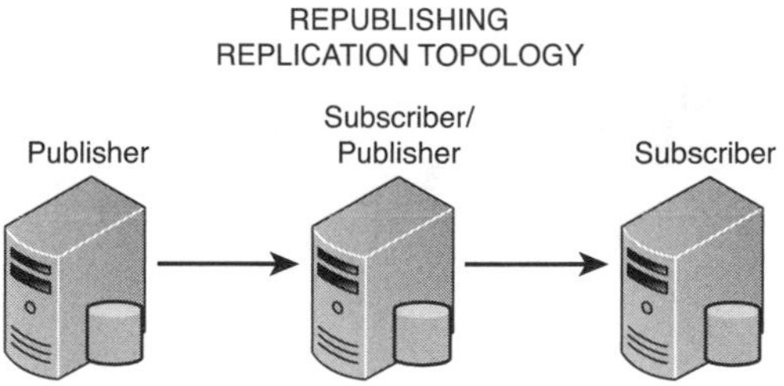

REPUBLISHING
REPLICATION TOPOLOGY

FIGURE 15.2
Republishing topology.

3. **Central Publisher**—In this replication topology, a central Publisher publishes to multiple subscribers. In some cases the subscribers may only get a subset of the data. This replication topology is illustrated in Figure 15.3.

4. **Central Subscriber**—In this topology, multiple publishers replicate to the same Subscriber. This replication topology is illustrated in Figure 15.4.

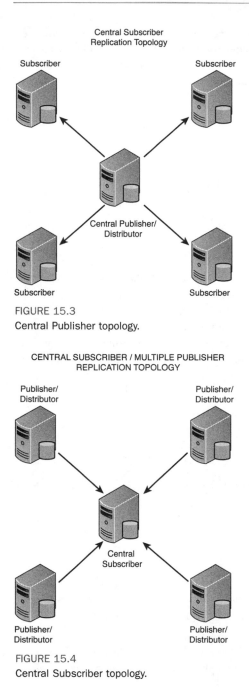

FIGURE 15.3
Central Publisher topology.

FIGURE 15.4
Central Subscriber topology.

5. **Mesh**—This topology is used in peer-to-peer replication. The path taken by data from one Subscriber to another is unpredictable, and one node can drop off the replication topology and return with no interruption to the other nodes in the mesh. This replication topology is illustrated in Figure 15.5.

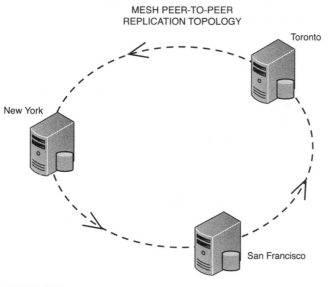

FIGURE 15.5
Mesh topology.

SQL Server 2008 Replication Prerequisites

Configuring replication is not as simple as clicking through a few screens of a SQL Server installation wizard. A number of prerequisite steps must be fulfilled before replication can be configured and implemented.

Before you install SQL Server replication, ensure that the following prerequisites are met or understood:

1. All merge replication types require the installation of a local or remote distributor.

2. A snapshot folder must be accessible by all the agents and be large enough to store all the snapshot files for the publications.

3. Transactional replication requires primary keys on every table you replicate.

4. You cannot have a table published in an immediate-updating publication and merge replication.

5. You need to have a network connection between the Publisher and the Subscriber. This link does not need to be always connected for most replication types.

6. You need to have at minimum an account that is in the dbo role on the Subscriber for push replication, and an account that is in the dbo role on the Distributor and in the PAL in the publication.

7. If you are using web synchronization, you will need a certificate issued by a certificate authority (CA) from a trusted 3rd party like VeriSign or an internal certificate server, and have your IIS Server configured to use this certificate for SSL.

To initialize a subscription from a backup in SQL Server 2008, a user must be a member of the dbcreator server role. In SQL Server 2005, membership in the db_owner database role was sufficient.

SQL Server 2008 Edition Limitations

There are several SQL Server edition–specific limitations to replication. SQL Server Express 2008 can only be used as a Subscriber. SQL Server 2008 Workgroup Edition can only have 5 Subscribers. SQL Server 2008 Standard Edition can have 25 Subscribers.

Knowing When to Implement SQL Server 2008 Replication

An organization can have many reasons for its implementation of SQL Server replication. Following are some of the situations organizations try to address by using SQL Server 2008 replication:

- **Distributing data**—This involves distributing data from one database to another database or one server to another server. For example, an organization must make data such as pricing or sales data residing at corporate headquarters readily available to all field offices.

- **Consolidating data**—An organization may be interested in consolidating data from many servers to one server for centralized reporting, analysis, or business intelligence. Examples include consolidating data from field offices, manufacturing facilities, or data residing in PDAs or mobile devices to a centralized SQL Server.

- **Ensuring high availability**—Replication is one of four SQL Server 2008 high-availability alternatives. It can be used to maintain redundant copies of a database on multiple servers residing in different locations.

Peer-to-peer transaction replication was introduced in SQL Server 2005 and is discussed later in this chapter. When replication is used for high availability, it does not provide automatic failover or automatic client redirect as failover clustering or database mirroring does.

- **Reporting**—If you want to minimize performance degradation on production databases/servers, it is advantageous to offload reporting from production database servers to dedicated reporting servers. Although there are a number of ways of achieving this goal, transactional replication provides a means of replicating data to one or more reporting servers with minimal overhead on the production database. Unlike with database mirroring, the reporting database can be accessed for reporting purposes in real time without the need for creating database snapshots.

- **Distributing or consolidating database subsets**—Unlike other high-availability alternatives or data distribution methods such as log shipping or database mirroring, replication offers a means to copy or replicate only a subset of the database if needed. For example, you can choose to replicate only a table, rows based on a filter, specific columns, or stored procedures.

- **Ensuring scalability**—The goal is to scale the workload across multiple databases with replication. This provides increased performance and availability.

Replication is essentially copying or distributing data from one location to another. However, there are other technologies you can also use to accomplish this.

- **SSIS**—SQL Server Integration Services (SSIS) does rich ETL (Extract Transform and Load); however, it does not easily track changes. SSIS is best for moving copying data from heterogeneous data sources. Transactional replication can be used to transform data but it is an involved task. Look up "Custom Sync Objects" in Books Online for more information on how to do this.

- **BCP**—Bulk Copy Program (BCP) is used to copy data out of the file system and into another SQL Server. It does not track changes easily, but you can use it for high-performance data loads, which can perform much better than the other data load methods.

- **Triggers**—Triggers can be used to replicate or transform data; however, they add latency to each transaction, do not scale well over a network, and there is an administrative burden with this method.

- **Two-phase commit**—This technology involves writing to the source table and then writing to the destination table within a transaction. There is considerable latency associated with this; however, for some applications that have very high consistency requirements, two-phase commits are necessary.

- **Backup and Restore**—Backup and restore can be used to replicate data; however, the source database is offline during the restore operation, and for large databases this can be unwieldy.

- **Log shipping**—Log shipping is continuous backup and restore. The destination database is offline while the log is being applied. Microsoft does not require you to maintain a SQL Server license for the standby server as it is only fulfilling a standby role.

- **Database mirroring**—This can be considered to be contiguous log shipping. The destination database (called a mirror) is offline when participating in database mirroring. Database mirroring has two modes: high performance and high safety. With high performance some data loss is possible, but performance is better than with high safety. With high safety there will be no data loss. Microsoft does not require you to maintain a SQL Server license for the mirror server as it is only fulfilling a mirroring role. Database mirroring is the only technology that does client redirects on failover. So if clients are connected to your source server (called a *principal*), they will be automatically failed over to the mirror server when the principal goes down. Mirroring is most practical in high-performance mode, which is only available in Enterprise Edition. Note that Database Mirroring does not support FILESTREAM, whereas replication does.

For high-availability and disaster-recovery scenarios, database mirroring, log shipping, and in some cases backup and restore are a much better fit than replication, mainly due to the unpredictable latencies that replication offers and the lack of automatic and client failover. SSIS and BCP work best if there is some form of change tracking. Triggers are seldom a good solution. Two-phase commit fits best when your source and destination must be identical at all times. In all other scenarios, replication is a much better fit for copying data.

Combining Replication with Other SQL Server High-Availability Alternatives

Frequently, high-availability and disaster-recovery plans require a combination of technologies. For example, you may require implementing database mirroring in conjunction with replication. Such a topology would keep the Publisher operational and redirect the clients to the mirror. Although clustering can achieve the same result, clustering has distance limitations, which mirroring can overcome. This section examines caveats associated with both technologies.

Combining Replication with Database Mirroring

You can mirror a published database or a subscriber database. The complications occur at failover.

If your publication database is mirrored and you are using a remote distributor, you can configure your log reader, distribution, queue reader, and merge agents to fail over to the mirror and pick up where they left off by configuring the `PublisherFailoverParameter` parameter with the mirror name in the agents. This ensures that if the principal is failed over to the mirror, the Log Reader, Snapshot, or Merge Agent will continue to work. You will need to enable trace flag 1448, and you may need to issue a `sp_replrestart` in your publication database to get the log reader to work again.

If your Subscriber is mirrored and you need to fail over to the mirror, you will need to configure the Distribution Agent for the new Subscriber (the former mirrored database). You will then need to configure the Subscriber. To do this you will need to clean up the old subscription in the principal database (use `sp_subscription_cleanup`), and then obtain the last Log Sequence Number (LSN) from the distribution database on the Distributor. You will need to query the transaction_timestamp value from MSReplication_Subscriptions. Then add your subscription using the `sp_addsubscription` stored procedure and the `subscriptionlsn` parameter. The value you supply for the `subscriptionlsn` will be the value obtained in the transaction_timestamp column. After you have done this, your distribution database and new principal will be in sync, and you can start mirroring to the old principal.

Replication is a good fit with database mirroring as database mirroring is the only high-availability (HA) option that provides real-time synchronization with no data loss (in the high-safety mode). When replication is used with mirroring, the Publisher's availability will be maximized.

Combining Replication with Log Shipping

If you have a remote distributor, you can configure the `PublisherFailoverPartner` parameter on the Log Reader Agent on your primary (the source database in your log shipping topology) with the name of your secondary (the destination database in your log-shipping topology). The

`PublisherFailoverPartner` should be the secondary server name. On failover the Publisher will start to replicate to the remote distributor. Please refer to the section in Books Online titled "Strategies for Backing Up and Restoring Snapshot and Transactional Replication."

Combining Replication with Failover Clustering

Clustering is replication aware. You can create any type of publication on a clustered server. The only complication is that your snapshot folder must be on a clustered shared disk resource. If your snapshot folder is not shared, the active node may not be able to access the snapshot folder. This will only be a problem during snapshot generation and deployment.

Administering SQL Server Replication

There are four parts involved in administering SQL Server Replication:

- Creating the Distributor
- Creating publications
- Creating subscriptions
- Administering and monitoring the publications and subscriptions

This section will cover each part in turn.

Creating the Distributor

For large workloads in a transactional replication topology, you should use a remote distributor on a clustered server. For merge replication, placement of the distribution database is not critical. Smaller transactional replication workloads can tolerate a local distributor without too much locking. If considerable locking occurs between Log Reader Agents and Distribution Agents, consider moving to a remote distributor. *Locking* occurs when two processes try to access the same resource (a table, index, page of a table, or index) simultaneously. A *remote distributor* is a SQL Server that hosts the distribution database, and is neither the Publisher or a Subscriber.

The topic of how to create a local distributor has already been briefly discussed in the "SQL Server 2008 Replication Roles" section. A *remote distributor* is essentially a server that is configured with a distributor database (in other words, is a Distributor), and then has remote publishers publishing to it.

There are three steps for configuring a remote distributor.

   1. Configuring a Distributor.

2. Enabling the Distributor for remote publishers. This step must be performed on your distributor.

3. Enabling your publishers to use the remote distributor. This step must be performed on your Publisher.

Configuring a Distributor

To create a remote distributor, you would follow the guidelines on how to create a local distributor in the "SQL Server 2008 Replication Roles" section.

Configuring a Distributor for Remote Publishers

After you have configured the Distributor, you need to configure which publishers you want to publish to.

1. In SQL Server Management Studio, right-click on the Replication folder on the remote distributor, select Distributor Properties, and click on the Publishers page.

2. Click Add, select Add SQL Server Publisher, connect to the Publisher in SQL Server Management Studio, click Remote Publisher Warning, and click OK.

3. Right-click on the Replication folder and select Configure Distribution. Click Next at the splash screen and select the Publishers tab.

4. Click the Add button and select Add SQL Server, enter the name of the server you want to add as a Publisher to use the remote distributor, and select an authentication mechanism. Click Connect.

You will get a message telling you "Remote Publishers must use a password when automatically connecting to the Distributor to perform replication administrator operations. You must specify the administrative link password for this Distributor."

The message is telling you that when you configure the Publisher to use this remote distributor, you must supply a password. You can configure the administrative link password in the Administrative Link Password text boxes displayed in Figure 15.6. Click OK to complete the operation.

Notice that in Figure 15.6, the Publisher NYC-SQL01\Instance01 uses the distribution database called Distribution. It is recommended that you use different distribution databases for each remote distributor to minimize contention.

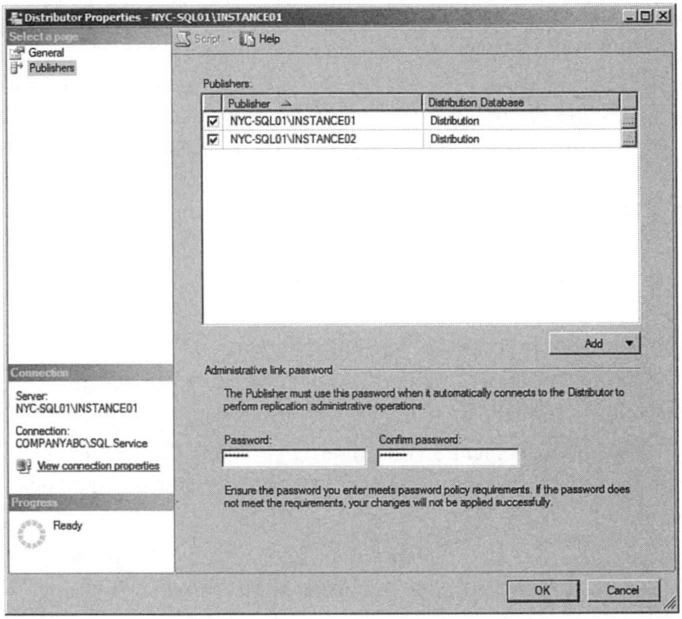

FIGURE 15.6
The Distributor Properties dialog box showing two distribution databases, one for each Publisher.

To create a new distributor:

1. In SQL Server Management Studio, connect to the SQL Server.

2. Right-click on the Replication folder, and click on Configure Distribution.

3. Click Next at the splash screen.

4. Select [Your Server Name] Will Act as Its Own Distributor. SQL Server will create a new distribution database and log. Click Next.

5. Accept the default for the snapshot folder, or locate it on a drive with ample room for your snapshots. During snapshot generation, there will be significant I/O activity; otherwise, there will be little. Click Next.

6. Accept the default for the distribution database name and folders. Click Next.

7. In the Publishers dialog, ensure that your server is enabled, and that your distribution database is selected. Click Next.

8. In the Wizard Actions dialog, ensure that Configure Distribution is selected.

9. Click Finish to create your distribution database and to configure this server as a Distributor, and click Close.

This will configure the Distributor for your Publisher.

Enabling the Publishers to Use the Remote Distributor

You must now connect to the Publisher in SQL Server Management Studio, right-click on the Replication folder, select Configure Distribution, click Next, and then select the Use the Following Server as the Distributor option. Then click Add and in the connection dialog, enter the server name of your Distributor (for this example, NYC-SQL01\Instance01) and select the correct authentication mechanism. You will then be prompted for the Administrative Link Password as illustrated in Figure 15.7.

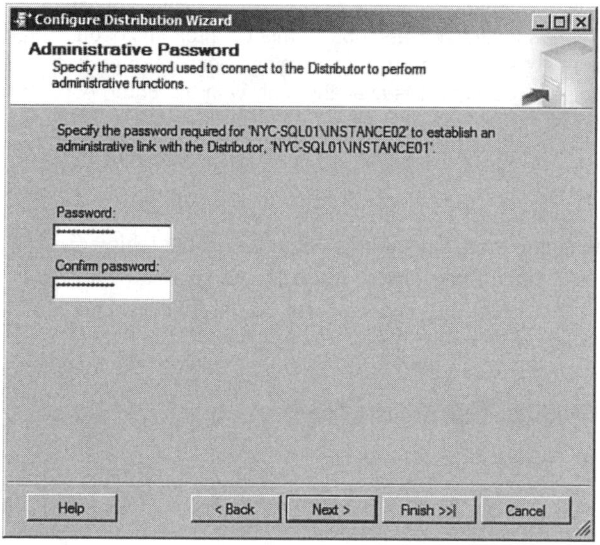

FIGURE 15.7
The Administrative Link Password dialog.

After you have entered the password, click Next, Next, Finish, and Close. Your Publisher is now configured to use your remote distributor.

Configuring Snapshot and Transactional Replication

The steps to create all replication types are very similar. We will create a Transactional Publication first as its setup is highly similar to that of a Snapshot publication. Along the way we will note the differences.

Configuring Publications for the AdventureWorks Database

1. To create a publication, connect to your Publisher in SQL Server Management Studio (NYC-SQL01\Instance02), expand the Replication folder, right-click on Local Publications, and select New Publication.

2. Click Next at the splash screen. If you get a dialog titled Distributor, follow the steps in the "SQL Server 2008 Replication Roles" section. In the Publication Database dialog box, select the AdventureWorks 2008 database.

3. In the Publication Types dialog, select Transactional Replication.

Note

Snapshot replication with Immediate Updating, Queued Updating, or Immediate Updating with Queued Failover is only available using replication stored procedures, which is beyond the scope of this chapter. Microsoft has deprecated updateable subscriptions in favor of using peer-to-peer replication. However Peer-to-peer replication is available only with the Enterprise Editions of SQL 2005 and SQL 2008.

---

4. After you have selected the replication type, click Next. You will then see the Articles dialog box. This allows you to select the tables, stored procedures, user-defined functions, views, and indexed views you will be able to replicate. Select the objects you want to replicate. This option is illustrated in Figure 15.8.

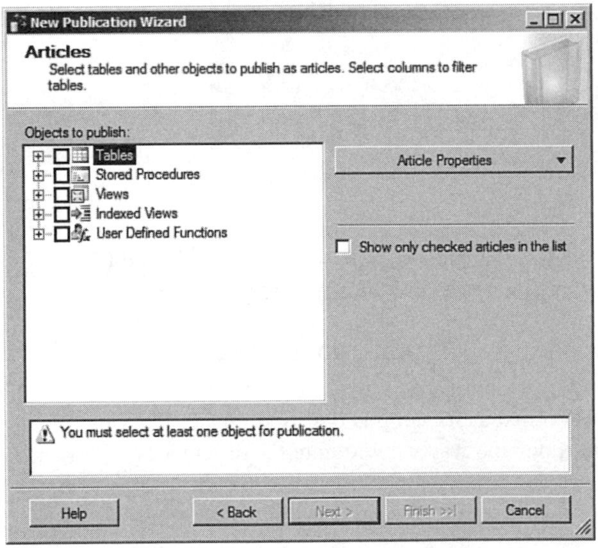

FIGURE 15.8
The Articles dialog.

In general, you will want to replicate all objects to support the requirements of the applications using the subscriber database. This can be all tables or a subset of them.

You can expand each object type, for example the tables object, to select individual tables, or check the check box to the left of the table icon to replicate all tables. In the Article Properties dialog box, you can select properties of the articles you want to replicate, for example, the choice to replicate nonclustered indexes, or to replicate a table to a table with a different name or schema owner.

There are some differences in some of the Article Properties dialog settings between snapshot and transactional replication. For example, in transactional replication there is the Statement Delivery option, which allows you to determine how incremental changes will be applied on the Subscriber. This section does not appear in the snapshot publication creation dialogs. Statement Delivery refers to whether replication will use stored procedures or SQL statements to keep the two databases synchronized.

You also have the option to select which columns you want to replicate. Expand the Tables node, and then expand the individual table you want to vertically partition (only replicate some of the columns). Figure 15.9 illustrates vertically partitioning the Address table to not replicate the City column. (We are choosing not to replicate the City column purely for illustrative puposes.)

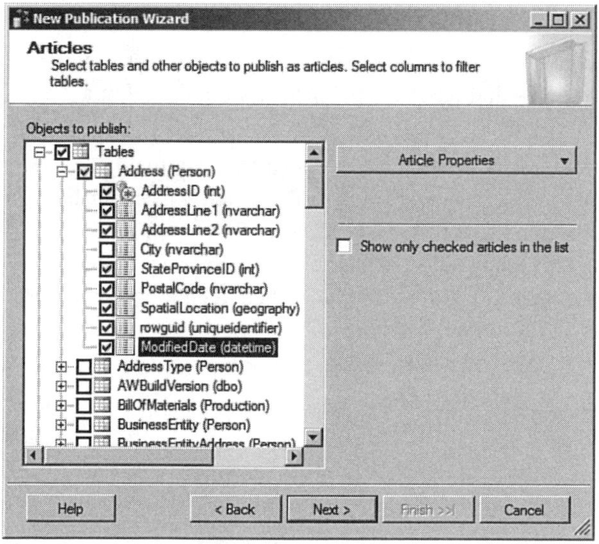

FIGURE 15.9
Vertically partitioning the Address table.

5. Click Next to launch the Filter Rows dialog illustrated in Figure 15.10. In Figure 15.10 we are now horizontally partitioning the Address table by only sending the rows with a StateProvinceID of 30 (Massachusetts) to the subscribers.

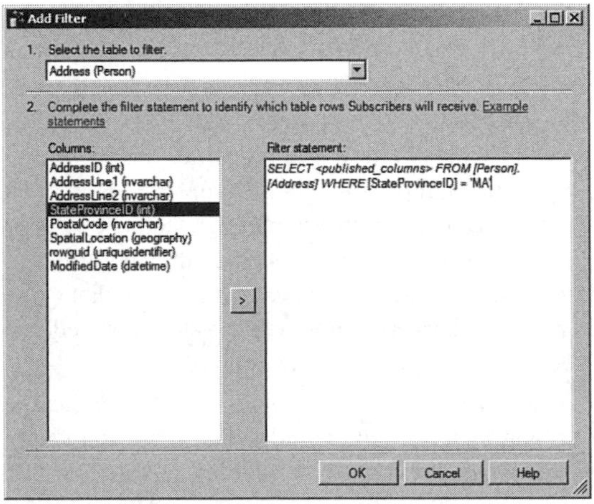

FIGURE 15.10
Horizontally partitioning the Address table.

6. Click OK to complete the Filter Rows dialog.

7. Click Next to continue. In the Snapshot Agent dialog, select Create the Snapshot Immediately and Keep the Snapshot Available to Initialize Subscriptions.

8. Click Next to continue advancing to the Agent Security dialog box. This allows you to select the account or authentication mechanism to use by the publication. Leave the User Security Settings from the Snapshot Agent check box selected, and click the Security Settings button beside the Snapshot Agent. The Snapshot Agent Security dialog box will appear as illustrated in Figure 15.11.

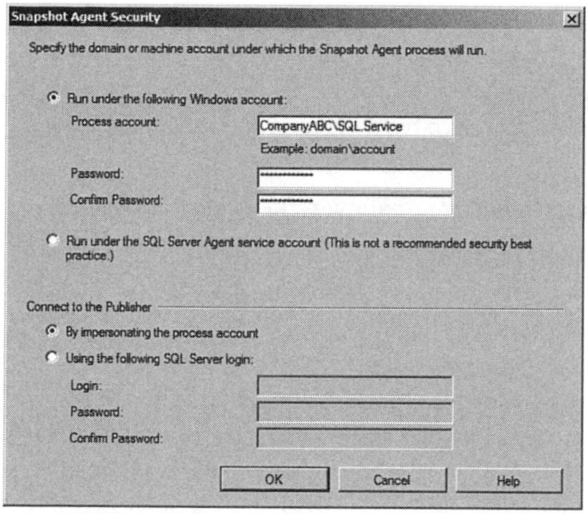

FIGURE 15.11
Snapshot Agent Security dialog box.

Note that for snapshot publications, this option will not appear as there is no Log Reader Agent.

You have two choices here for the security context that the Snapshot Agent will run under: The SQL Server Agent account's security context, or the context of a low-privilege Windows account. Microsoft has the following recommendations for the security context under which your agent will run:

- Run each replication agent under a different Windows account, and use Windows Authentication for all replication agent connections.

- Grant only the required permissions to each agent.

- Ensure that all Merge Agent and Distribution Agent accounts are in the publication access list (PAL).

- Follow the principle of least privilege by allowing accounts in the PAL only the permissions they need to perform replication tasks. Do not add the logins to any fixed server roles that are not required for replication.

- Configure the snapshot share to allow read access by all Merge Agents and Distribution Agents. In the case of snapshots for publications with parameterized filters, ensure that each folder is configured to allow access only to the appropriate Merge Agent accounts.

- Configure the snapshot share to allow write access by the Snapshot Agent.

- If you use pull subscriptions, use a network share rather than a local path for the snapshot folder.

If you do not select the SQL Server Agent accounts security context, ensure that the Windows account you chose has rights to read and list files and folders on the snapshot folder, or snapshot share. Microsoft recommends you do not use the SQL Server Agent account as it tends to run under an Administrator account, and if an exploit hijacks it, the exploit will have Administrator rights on your machine and possibly your domain. The Connect to Publisher dialog allows you to select how you want the Snapshot Agent executable to connect to the Publisher. You can use the account you specify the Snapshot Agent to run under, or a SQL login.

9. When you have finished configuring the Snapshot Agent Security, click OK, Next, and then Next (to create the publication).

10. In the Complete the Publication dialog, give your publication a meaningful name. In this case we will call it AdventureWorks. Click Finish. The wizard will then create your publication. Click Close to close the dialog. You are now ready to create your subscriptions.

Configuring Subscriptions for the AdventureWorks Database

Follow these steps to create your subscription:

1. In SQL Server Management Studio, connect to the Publisher, and expand the Replication folder.

2. Expand the Local Publications folder, locate your publication, right-click on it, and select New Subscriptions.

3. Click Next at the New Subscription Wizard splash screen. Select your publication (it should be highlighted—if not, you may need to expand the publication database to find it).

4. Click Next; this will launch the Distribution Agent Location. There are two choices:

- Run all of the Agents at the Distributor (push subscriptions). Use this option when you have a small number of subscribers or are replicating to a non–SQL Server RDBMs.
- Run each agent at the Subscriber (pull subscriptions). Use this option when you have a large number of subscribers.

Choose the option to run the agent at the Distributor.

5. Click Next to launch the Subscribers dialog. Click on the Subscriber if it appears in this dialog. If not, click the Add Subscriber button at the bottom (for push subscriptions) or the Add SQL Server Subscriber button (for pull subscriptions). You will need to connect to the Subscriber using Windows Authentication or a SQL Server login.

6. Click Connect and the Subscription database drop-down list will be populated. Select the subscription database here if it already exists—note that there is an option to create a new database on the Subscriber.

7. Click Next. You will then get the Distribution Agent Security dialog box. Click on the ellipsis button to set the accounts you want to use to connect to the Distributor and Subscriber. For the process login, enter a low-privilege Windows account that is in the dbo role on the Distributor. Note that if the Distributor is in an untrusted domain, you can use *pass-through authentication*, where the account has the same name and password and is a local machine or domain account on both the Distributor and the Subscriber. For the Connect to Subscriber dialog, either select to impersonate the process account (the SQL Server Agent account on the Distributor for push, or the SQL Server Agent account on the Subscriber for pull). You can select a SQL login here as well. This will use the security context of the SQL Server Agent account on the Subscriber to read the snapshot share.

8. After you have configured all of the accounts, click OK and then Next to launch the Synchronization Schedule. This will allow you to set a schedule for the Distribution Agent, have it run on demand, or have it run continuously.

9. Click Next to launch the Initialize Subscriptions dialog box. Notice the Initialize check box, which by default will be selected. This will create and distribute the snapshot to the Subscriber. This will be the metadata, replication objects, schema, and data that the Subscriber needs to be synchronized with the Publisher.

It is possible for you to configure the Subscriber for replication yourself by using a backup or by putting the schema and data in the Subscriber yourself.

You will likely need to put the replication stored procedures in place: Use the stored procedure sp_scriptpublicationcustomprocs 'PublicationName' in your publication database to generate these stored procedures, and then copy and paste them into a query window on your Subscriber and execute them. You also have the option of selecting whether the snapshot should be generated immediately, or at first synchronization. If you select the Immediately option, the Snapshot Agent will be run after your publication is created. If you select At First Synchronization, it will be generated when the Distribution Agent first connects with the Subscriber. Click Next for the option to create the subscription now or to script it out, or both. Click Next and then Finish to complete the creation of your subscription.

Testing Your Publication

To verify that your publication is replicating successfully, do the following:

1. In SQL Server Management Studio, connect to your Publisher.

2. Right-click the Replication folder, and select Launch Replication Monitor.

3. After Replication Monitor has launched, click on the Add Publisher hyperlink on the right-hand pane to monitor your Publisher.

4. When your Publisher has been added, expand it in the left-hand pane, so that your publication shows up. If there are any errors, your Publisher and publication will have a red circle with a white x on them.

5. After you have clicked on your publication, all subscriptions to that publication will be displayed in the right-hand pane. Click on the Publications and Agents tabs to see if there are any red circles with white x's on them and observe any status messages that might be displayed.

Typical errors you will see are connection errors; for example, the Distribution Agent is unable to connect to the subscriber. To fix these errors, right-click on the agent with the error icon on it and select View Details. Read and evaluate the error message. Most errors can be solved by right-clicking on the publication and changing the publication's properties, or in the case of a pull subscription, by right-clicking on the subscription and selecting Properties.

Validations

You can also run a validation to verify that your publication and subscription are consistent (that is, have the same data).

1. In SQL Server Management Studio, connect to your Publisher.

2. Right-click on your publication in SQL Server Management Studio and select Validate Subscriptions.

3. You will be offered a choice to validate all subscriptions or individual subscriptions. Make the appropriate choice and click the Validation Options button. The options are a fast row count based on cached information, an actual row count, or a fast row count and if differences are noted, an actual row count is done. You also have the option to perform a checksum and stop the Distribution Agent if a Subscriber fails validation. Click OK.

You can view the results on the validation in Replication Monitor in the Publications tab.

1. Launch Replication by right-clicking on your publication in the Replication folder for your SQL Server.

2. Drill down on the Publisher, and expand your publication.

3. Right-click on your subscription and select View Details.

4. Note the values in the Actions in the selected session—this appears as the lower half of the dialog.

Tracer Tokens

If you are concerned with latency issues or want to verify that replication is working, click on the Tracer Tokens tab in Replication Monitor (you need to drill down on the Publisher, Publication, and Subscription and look in the right-hand pane of Replication Monitor to see this). Click on Insert Tracer and watch the tracer token being injected into the publication. Replication Monitor will track how long it takes for the tracer token to make its way from the Publisher to the Distributor and then from the Distributor to the Subscriber.

You'll see the breakdown of the time it took the token to go from the Publisher to the Distributor, time from Distributor to Subscriber, and total latency. If latency is unacceptable, you may need to check network bandwidth, or attempt to optimize your replication topology performance. Optimizing your network link. is outside the scope of this book. Good values should be below a minute on a LAN (but can be as low as 2–4 seconds). WAN performance is highly variable and dependent on bandwidth and workloads. The tracer token can also be used to help determine the best QueryTimeout value. This can also be done by using TSQL.

Replication Monitor can also be used to view undistributed commands. If you view the details of a subscription, you can see how many commands are waiting to be distributed and an estimate of how long the distribution will take.

Configuring Peer-to-Peer Transactional Replication

To configure peer-to-peer replication, you must first create a transactional publication. Follow the steps that you used previously in creating your transactional replication publication AdventureWorks for the AdventureWorks2008 database. Do not create a subscription. If you already have the subscription created, drop it by right-clicking on the AdventureWorks publication (you can find it in the Local Publications folder), selecting Delete, and selecting Yes at the confirmation prompt.

After the publication is created, follow these steps:

1. Right-click on the AdventureWorks publication in the Local Publications folder, and select Properties.

2. In the Subscription Options tab, change Allow Peer to Peer Subscriptions from False to True.

3. Click OK to close the dialog.

4. Right-click on your publication (the AdventureWorks one) again and select Configure Peer to Peer Topology.

5. Click Next at the splash screen, drill down on your publication database (AdventureWorks2008), select your AdventureWorks publication (it should already be highlighted), and click Next.

6. The Configure Topology dialog will display, as illustrated in Figure 15.12.

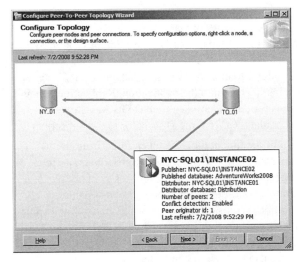

FIGURE 15.12
The Configure Topology dialog box.

7. Right-click anywhere on the screen (except the database icon in the center) and select Add a New Peer node.

8. Enter the server name of a server that you want to participate in peer-to-peer replication, select the appropriate authentication mechanism, and click Next. In this case, pick NYC-SQL01.

9. You will then be prompted for a database and Peer Originator ID as illustrated in Figure 15.13.

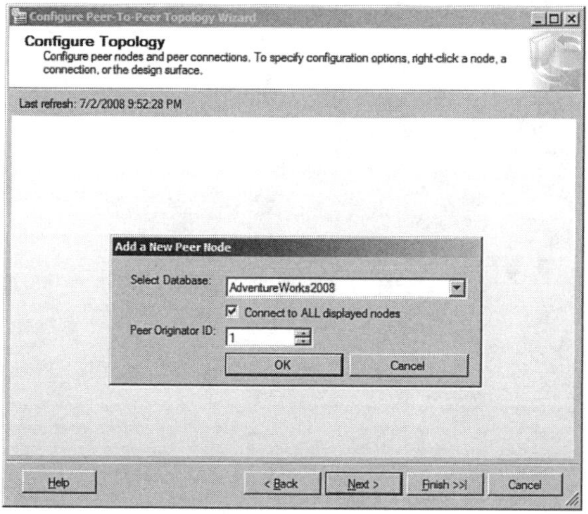

FIGURE 15.13
The Add a New Peer Node dialog box.

Let SQL Server auto-assign Peer Originator IDs. Click OK.

10. Right-click on the database icon in the center of the Configure Topology dialog box, and select Connect to All Displayed Nodes. Click Next.

11. The Log Agent Security dialog box, which is very similar to the Snapshot Agent Security dialog box, will display. Select an account that the Log Reader Agent should run under, and click Next.

12. You will then see a Distributor Security dialog box, which is very similar to the Snapshot Agent Security dialog box and the Log Reader Agent Security Dialog box. Select an account that the Distribution Agent should run under and how the Distribution Agent should connect

to the Subscriber. You will need to do this for each node in the topology. Note that in this example we have only selected one node in our topology. We could have added multiple nodes at one time in the Configure Topology dialog and then selected Connect to All Displayed Nodes and Configure Security.

13. Click Next when you are done configuring security. This will launch the New Peer Initialization dialog as illustrated in Figure 15.14.

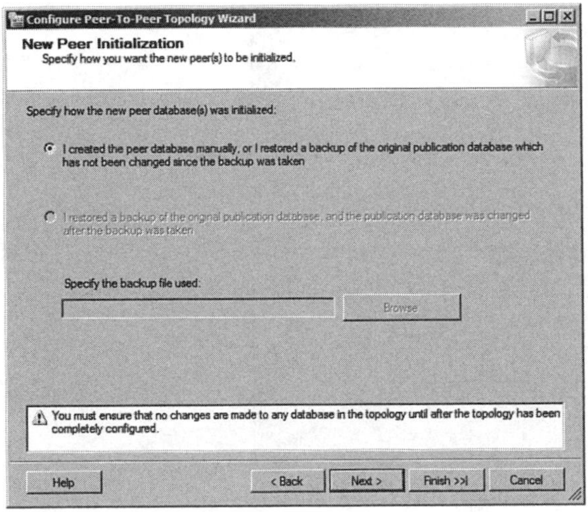

FIGURE 15.14
The New Peer Initialization dialog.

Either pre-create your subscriber databases by creating the tables and data, or restore them via a database backup. It is highly recommended that you restore the database from a backup as peer-to-peer replication can do conflict detection. Conflict detection is an optional feature, which is enabled by default.

14. Click Next and Finish to complete the Peer to Peer topology configuration.

If at any time you need to add a new node to your topology, right-click on one of the publications involved in peer to peer replication and select Configure Peer to Peer Topology. Then in the Configure Topology dialog box, right-click anywhere on the grey background and select Add a New Peer Node. Follow the dialogs as outlined in the preceding step sequences.

Configuring Merge Replication

Creating merge publications is very similar to creating snapshot or transactional publications. Here are the steps to create a merge replication topology:

1. In SQL Server Management Studio, connect to the SQL Server that will be your Publisher.

2. Expand the Replication folder, right-click on Local Publications, and click Next through the splash screen titled New Publication Wizard.

3. Select the database that contains the tables and data you want to merge replicate in the Publication Databases dialog. In this case, select the AdventureWorks2008 database.

4. On the Publication Types splash screen, select Merge Publication and click Next to move to the Subscriber Types dialog.

5. Choose the appropriate Subscriber type. Be very careful with the selection you make here. If you choose SQL 2000 Subscribers, for example, all future merge publications you create in this database after this choice will be limited to that subscription type. It is possible to select multiple subscriber types, keeping in mind that the lowest subscriber type will limit all future subscriber types and some of the new merge replication features will be unavailable to you.

6. Click Next to Advance to the Articles dialog box. Here you can select which type of objects you want to replicate as well as individual articles. You also have the option of horizontally partitioning your tables by deselecting individual columns. The Article Properties button allows you to find grained control of article properties, for example, that you can select to replicate user triggers to your subscribers. Click Next. The wizard will then warn you that a unique identifier (GUID) column will be added to all tables you are indexing.

Note

This may cause unqualified inserts to fail. For example, the following command will fail if there is not also a unique identifier column on the table you are inserting into:

```
Insert into tableName
Select * from OtherTableName
```

To get around this problem you will have to list all the columns in the SELECT and INSERT statements.

7. Click Next to advance to the Filter Rows dialog box. Merge replication is designed with a low-bandwidth footprint. In other words, it is tuned to replicate over low-bandwidth lines like telephone lines. One of the features that minimizes network traffic is join filters. Basically a join filter is a filter you place on a table, and this filter can be extended to all other tables that join to the original table. Consider the SalesTerritory table in the AdventureWorks2008 database. It is joined to the SalesOrderHeader table by TerritoryID and the SalesOrderHeaderTable is joined to the SalesOrderDetail table by the SalesOrderID column.

FIGURE 15.15
Schema illustrating the relationship between Territories and Sales.

Figure 15.15 illustrates this relationship. Consider what would happen if we were filtering on the Territory Name. Such a filter would ensure that only specific TerritoryIDs would go to specific Subscribers. The Territory names are Northwest, Northeast, Central, Southeast, Southwest, Canada, and so on. If you filter on Northwest, only sales that have a territory name of Northwest would go to the Northwest subscribers. The value of this is that the entire database would not have to go over the wire to the Northwest subscriber; only Northwest data would go there. Join filters ensure that all data related to the filter would also go to the Northwest subscriber—that is, all the orders (in the OrderHeader table) and order details from salespeople with a TerritoryName of Northwest.

And if, for example, there was consolidation of the Northwest into the Northeast and the Northwest Territory was now renamed Northeast, all of the sales orders that belonged to the Northwest would move to the Northeast subscriber. This is termed *partition realignment* and is normally a good thing. Join filters are what makes this happen; join filters will walk the relationships and ensure that all data that belongs to a filter will move with that filter. Without join filters, only the old Northeast row would move in the example, and none of the orders owned by the Northeast would move.

To use join filters, click the Add button in the Filter Table Rows dialog box and select Automatically Generate Filters (where SQL Server will walk the relationships in the tables you are publishing and automatically generate join filters), or click the Add Filter button and select the tables and rows you want to filter on. You then have the option of clicking the Add Button again and selecting Add Join to Extend the Selected Filter. You can also filter on Host_Name() and SUSER_NAME(), both of which can be overridden by the Merge Agent (HostName and PublisherLogin respectively).

   8. Click Next to launch the Snapshot Agent dialog box; in most cases you will want to accept the default. Click Next to launch the Snapshot Security Agent dialog box and set the appropriate accounts for your Snapshot Agent.

   9. Click Next to either generate your publication or script it out.

   10. Click Next to name your publication and then click Finish. When your publication has been created, click Close.

Configuring Merge Replication Subscriptions

Creating merge replication subscriptions is almost identical to creating subscriptions to transactional and snapshot publications. There are two differences. The first is that there is a Subscription type dialog box. This is illustrated in Figure 15.16.

The Subscription Type dialog controls how conflicts "stick." In this example we are using the Server-based subscription type with a priority of 75 percent. This means that a conflict caused by a Subscriber will have a priority of 75 percent. If the Publisher and this Subscriber conflict, the Publisher will win unless you use a different conflict resolver (you can set conflict resolvers in the Articles Properties dialog). If the Subscriber does win, its conflict has a priority of 75 percent. If other subscribers sync with a lower priority, the old value will win. If subscribers sync with a higher priority (90 percent, for example), the new value will win.

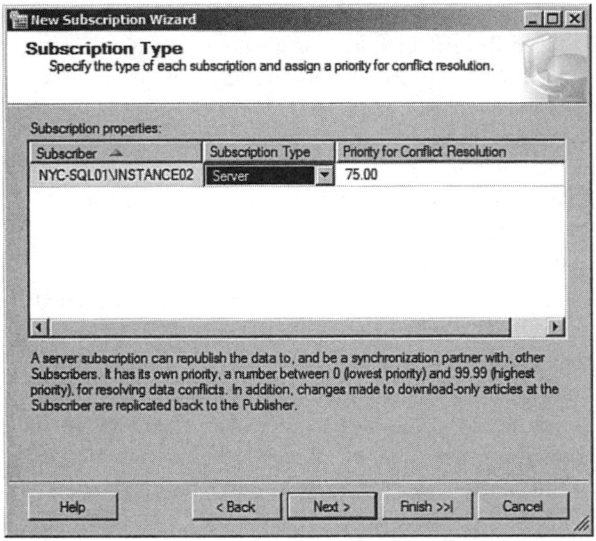

FIGURE 15.16
The Subscription Type dialog.

The other subscription type is Client, which means that the first value to the Publisher will stick and win any conflicts.

The other change is the Host_Name values, as illustrated in Figure 15.17.

If you are doing row filtering based on Host_name or PublisherLogin (SUser_Name), you can enter the value here to filter your subscription. This will ensure that your Subscriber only gets data that matches its filter, or data that is part of the extended join condition.

Managing the Distributor's Properties

There are several options for the Distributor. Right-click on the Replication folder on your Distributor and select Distributor Properties. In the General tab click on the ellipsis button to the right of the distribution databases. There are several text boxes of interest here:

- **Transaction Retention**—Transaction Retention has two options:

  - **Store Transactions: At Least**—This setting determines how long transactional replication commands remain in the distribution database after they are applied to all subscribers. In general, set this to 0, which means they are cleaned up the next time the distribution cleanup task runs. In some cases you will want to set this to higher values, normally when replication is involved in some disaster recovery scenario. Limit this setting as low as possible as it can cause performance degradation if set to high.

- **Store Transactions: But Not More Than**—This setting determines how long transactional replication commands can pool in the distribution database before the Subscriber expires. Again limit this setting as low as possible to cover any reasonable time periods your Subscriber could be offline so that it does not cause performance problems.

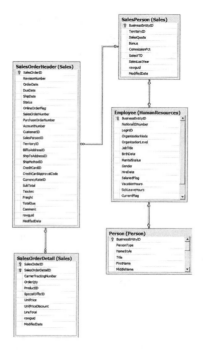

FIGURE 15.17
The Host_Name Values dialog box.

- **History Retention**—Store replication performance history at least; history retention is frequently needed for debugging purposes. The more history you collect, the slower your agents will run. Accepting the defaults is the best choice here.

There is also an option to set default profiles on the General tab of the Distributor Properties dialog box. You can set a default profile here for each agent. For example, you could set the Continue on Data Consistency Error Profile if you continually have problems with data collisions.

The Publishers tab of the Distributor properties dialog allows you to add Publishers and set an administrative link password.

Disabling Publishing and Distribution

If you need to disable replication on a server, connect to the server in SQL Server Management Studio, right-click on the Replication folder, and select Disable Publishing and Distribution. Click Next at the splash screen. A dialog will ask if you want to disable publishing on the server, or continue using replication on this server. Make your selection and click Next. You will then be prompted to delete existing publications and subscriptions. Click Next, and you will then be prompted to disable publishing and distribution and/or create a script to do so. Make the appropriate choice and click Next, then Finish and Close.

Choose Disable Publishing if you no longer want to use this server as a Publisher or Distributor. If you still have active publications on this server or want to use it as a distributor, select No, Continue Using this Server as a Publisher.

Deleting Local Subscriptions

If you need to delete a subscription, connect to the Publisher in SQL Server Management Studio and expand the Local Publications folder, expand your publication, right-click on your Subscription, and select Delete. Select Yes at the confirmation prompt. You can also delete the subscription by connecting to the Subscriber and expanding the Replication folder, expanding Local Subscriptions, right-clicking on the subscription, and selecting Delete. Click Yes at the confirmation prompt.

Deleting Local Publications

To delete a publication, connect to the Publisher in SQL Server Management Studio, expand the Replication Folder, expand the Local Publications folder, right-click on the publication you want to delete, select Delete, and click Yes.

Managing Replication Passwords

To modify the Administrative Link Password to connect to a Remote Distributor, right-click on the Replication folder and Select Update Replication Passwords. Enter the passwords and click OK.

Generating Replication Scripts

If you ever need to create a replication script, you can right-click on the publication or subscription and select Generate Script. In SQL Server 2008 you can generate a script to a file (the default), to the clipboard, or to a new query window. The dialog allows you to generate scripts to create the publication or subscription or to delete it.

You can also right-click on the Replication folder and generate scripts for selected databases or your entire server.

Monitoring and Troubleshooting SQL Server Replication

The central point to monitor and troubleshoot replication is through Replication Monitor. To launch Replication Monitor, right-click on the Replication folder. When Replication Monitor comes up, add your Publisher by clicking on the Add Publisher link. Then drill down on your Publisher in the left-hand pane and expand it to display all publications. As you click on each publication, all subscriptions to it will be displayed in the right-hand pane. Three to four tabs will be displayed depending on your replication type—these tabs are for monitoring and managing subscriptions.

- **All Subscriptions**—This tab is similar to the Publications tab; however, this tab displays information on subscriptions, of course, and not publications. The information displayed based on the columns available includes the status of each subscription, the subscription name, performance, and latency. In addition, it is possible to filter subscriptions based on All Subscriptions, 25 Worst Performing Subscriptions, 50 Worst Performing Subscriptions, Errors and Warnings Only, Errors Only, Warning Only, Subscriptions Running, and Subscriptions Not Running.

- **Tracer Tokens**—The second tab is a great utility to test the replication topology, including performance, by placing an artificial synthetic transaction into the replication stream. By clicking the Insert Tracer command button, you can review and calculate performance metrics between the Publisher to Distributor, Distributor to Subscriber, and finally the total latency for the artificial transaction.

- **Agents**—This tab provides job information and status on all publications on the Publisher. For each common job, the following information is displayed: Status, Job Name, Last Start Time, and Duration.

- **Warnings and Alerts** —When you're monitoring subscriptions, the final tab allows you to configure warnings, alerts, and notifications on subscriptions. The two warnings are Warn If a Subscription Will Expire Within Threshold and Warn If Latency Exceeds the Threshold. Click on the Alerts button to display the alerts. Each of these predefined replication alerts can be configured and customized based on a SQL Server event, SQL Server performance condition alert, WMI event alert, error numbers, or severity. In addition, a response can be created for each alert. These responses can execute a specific job or notify an operator on each replication alert that has been customized. The predefined alerts include the following:

  - **Peer-to-peer conflict detection alert**
  - **Replication Warning**—Long merge over dialup connection (Threshold:Mergelowrunduration)
  - **Replication Warning**—Long merge over LAN connection (Threshold: mergefastrunduration)
  - **Replication Warning**—Slow merge over dialup connection (Threshold: mereslowrunspeed)
  - **Replication Warning**—Slow merge over LAN connection (Threshold: mergefastrunspeed)
  - **Replication Warning**—Subscription expiration (Threshold: expiration)
  - **Replication Warning**—Transactional replication latency (Threshold: latency)
  - **Replication**—Agent custom shutdown
  - **Replication**—Agent failure
  - **Replication**—Agent retry
  - **Replication**—Agent success
  - **Replication**—Expired subscription dropped
  - **Replication**—Subscriber has failed data validation
  - **Replication**—Subscriber has passed data validation
  - **Replication**—Subscription reinitialized after validation failure

Summary

Replication in SQL Server 2008 is a mature technology and a great utility to distribute data among SQL Server instances. For the most part, replication is predominantly used for distributing data between physical sites within an organization. However, it is also commonly used for creating redundant read-only copies of a database for reporting purposes and for consolidating data from many locations.

Although replication can be used as a form of high availability or for disaster recovery, failover clustering, log shipping, and database mirroring are preferred alternatives because they guarantee transaction safety in the event of a disaster.

Best Practices

Some of the best practices that apply to replication include the following:

- Create a backup and restore strategy after the replication topology has been implemented. Don't forget to include the distribution, MSDB, and master databases on the Publisher, Distributor, and all subscribers.

- Script all replication components from a disaster recovery perspective. Scripts are also useful for conducting repetitive tasks. Finally, regenerate and/or update scripts whenever a replication component changes.

- Use Replication Monitor to create baseline metrics for tuning replication and validate that the hardware and network infrastructure live up to the replication requirements and expectations.

- Familiarize yourself with modifying database schema and publications after replication has been configured. Some replication items can be changed on the fly, whereas others require you to create a new snapshot.

- Place the Distribution system database on either a RAID 1 or RAID 1+0 volume other than the operating system. Finally, set the recovery model to Full to safeguard against database failures, and set the size of the database to accommodate the replication data.

- When configuring replication security, apply the principle of least privilege to ensure that replication is hardened and unwanted authorization is prevented.

- To address performance degradation on the Publisher, configure a Distributor on its own server.

- The Service Master Key needs to be available in order to recover from some HA scenarios.

PART IV

Monitoring and Troubleshooting SQL Server 2008

IN THIS PART

CHAPTER 16

Managing Workloads and Consumption with Resource Governor

Resource Governor is a new feature and one of the most antici-pated management features in SQL Server 2008. It bolsters SQL Server performance by allowing DBAs to establish resource limits and priorities on processor and memory-related workloads and resource pools. By defining resource limits on resource consump-tion, it is possible to prioritize multiple workloads in order to ensure consistent performance and maximize the experience of the end users and the efficiency of the applications without degrada-tion. It is important to realize from the start that Resource Governor will only throttle processes if SQL Server is experienc-ing CPU or memory pressure, and it will only throttle incoming requests. For example, a process that consumes high CPU will not be throttled, but the next process may be throttled.

Resource Governor is unable to throttle high I/O consumers (processes that read and write excessively from disk) in the SQL Server 2008 release, but this is planned for a future release.

Resource Governor is exciting for DBAs as it will allow them to control

- **Runaway processes**—Processes that could otherwise degrade overall SQL Server performance; for example, a badly written cursor would no longer be able to consume all CPU, or a query that does not have appropriate indexes could not cause a CPU spike, or a long-running query that returns a large rowset could not consume large amounts of memory in the process.

- **Login priorities**—The DBA can selectively give high prior-ities to groups of logins, and lower priorities to other logins; for example, reporting users could have a lower priority than logins associated with order entry applications.

- **Unpredictable responses**—By throttling high-resource consumers, SQL Server will be able to deliver predictable response times, as the high-resource consumers will not degrade SQL Server performance the way they would in an ungoverned SQL Server infrastructure.

> **Note**
>
> Resource Governor only applies to the SQL Server Database Engine; it does not apply to Reporting Services, Analysis Services, or Integration Servers. Also, it is not instance aware; in other words, another instance running on the same SQL Server can still degrade performance on all instances.

Resource Governor Concepts

Before we start using Resource Governor, it is essential to have a good grasp of its concepts. Resource Governor has three components. In this section we will look at these components which will help us to understand them and implement Resource Governor in your enterprise.

- **Workload**—A *workload* is a process that can be identified by Resource Governor and throttled by it. It can consist of one or more processes. Resource Governor cannot throttle active processes; it can only throttle processes when they log in.

- **Classifier function**—A *classifier function* is a TSQL function that is invoked at login and will determine which workload group the process will execute in. Resource Governor can only use a single classifier function at one time, but you can dynamically change the classifier function or change the classifier function that Resource Governor uses. Workloads will be classified by the classifier function after the login is authenticated and logon triggers are executed.

- **Resource pool**—Resource Governor parcels out CPU and RAM into groups called *pools*. Think of a resource pool as a SQL Server instance. A SQL Server shares resources among other instances running on a single physical machine. Similarly, Resource Governor shares resources among resource pools.

  By default two resource pools are created for Resource Governor, a default and an internal resource pool. All internal database engine processes will run in the internal resource pool. You cannot modify the properties of the internal resource pool, nor can you create workload groups to run inside it. The default resource pool is the pool that all workloads will run in, unless you define another resource pool, and the classifier function classifies workloads to run in workload groups that exist in other resource pools. You can create your own user resource pools and modify their properties on the fly. Changes to user resource pools will apply to newly logged-on workloads and not to current workloads.

A resource pool will have a minimum set of resources assigned to it; these resources are nonoverlapping. Other pools will not be able to use these resources, and the minimum settings for all pools combined cannot exceed 100 percent. A resource pool will also have a maximum set of resources, which are shared with other pools. Although a maximum resource setting for a particular pool can be 100 percent, the effective maximum will likely be less.

Consider the range of pool values in Table 16.1.

Table 16.1   **Minimum and Maximum Pool Values**

Name	Minimum	Maximum	Effective Max	Shared Max
Internal	0	100	100	100
Default	0	100	100-30-20=50	0
Resource Pool A	20	50	50-30-0=20	20 (50-20)
Resource Pool B	30	70	70-20-0=50	20 (70-50)

Resource Pool A will have a minimum value of 20 for CPU for example, and an effective max of 20 (the maximum for Pool A subtract the minimum for Pool B). We subtract the minimum of Pool B as it and the minimum for the default pool as these are dedicated to these pools and are not overlapping with the other pools. This means that it will share 20 percent of its resources with the other pools if it is not using them. Workload groups are placed in resource pools, and can be dynamically moved from one resource pool to another.

Note that if there is an error in your classifier function, or if the classifier function is unable to classify a workload, it will run in the default resource pool.

- **Workload Group**—A *workload group* is a container in which one or more workloads will run. A workload group has properties associated with it, like Max CPU, degree of parallelism, and so on, and you can monitor the resource consumption of workload groups inside a resource pool. This is valuable as it will allow you to move a workload from one workload group to another, or a newly created workload group. As with resource pools, by default there are two workload groups, the internal workload group, and the default workload group.

You cannot modify the internal workload group, but you can monitor it. The default group will handle all unclassified workloads.

Resource Governor Scenarios

As Resource Governor is a new feature in SQL Server 2008, most DBAs will want to understand where it will apply within their SQL Server infrastructure. Resource Governor will allow for predictable performance by allowing DBAs to "bucket" their workloads into resource pools, which will have preset limits on the amount of CPU and RAM they can consume. Consider a case where the DBA is using backup compression, which is a high-CPU consumer. While the backups are occurring, they will consume CPU that would otherwise be available to other workloads using the SQL Server. The net result is that all workloads using SQL Server will have degraded performance while the backup process is running. If the DBA were to implement a resource pool with a max CPU usage of 25 percent, the backup process would be throttled and the CPU hit while the backup is running would be considerably less than if you weren't using Resource Governor. The end result is that the backup process would take longer, but the other workloads running while the backup is in operation would continue to offer the same performance levels as before the backup started.

Also consider a case where a cursor or WHILE loop is missing a FETCH NEXT, or increment step. In this case the cursor or WHILE loop would execute the same portion of code and never exit the cursor or WHILE loop. Such a process, called a *runaway process*, would pre-empt other processes and consume all the CPU. Resource Governor would limit the impact of such runaway processes by limiting their priority and the resources these runaway processes could take.

Resource Governor can also be used to classify workloads and place them in workload groups, thereby isolating these workloads from other processes. For example, by placing a reporting workload in its own workload group, you can set limits on its workload group and minimize the impact of other workloads in other work load groups from adversely affecting the reporting workload. By doing this you can ensure predictable performance for the reporting workload. Another example, a high CPU process could manage so that other workloads would be able to get the CPU resource they require.

By isolating workloads into their own groups it is possible to monitor them and tune the resources that they consume. Resource Governor will allow you to closely monitor CPU and memory consumption of workloads in workload groups so you can correctly allocate resource to this workload to improve the overall performance of all workloads on your SQL Server.

While monitoring workloads with Resource Governor, you can selectively prioritize workloads as Low, Medium, or High, and then create workload groups for prioritized workloads. This will ensure that high priority processes complete faster than lower priority processes. Prior to Resource Governor it was impossible to monitor or perform such prioritizing of your workloads.

As you will see later in this chapter, the best way to deploy Resource Governor is to place all workloads in the default resource pool, observe their resource requirements, and then create resource pools that are appropriate for their resource demands, and resource pools that will limit the impact of these workloads on the entire SQL Server. After these resource pools have been created, these workloads can be moved into these resource pools and SQL Server will dynamically throttle new workloads as they exceed their resource limits.

Enabling Resource Governor

To control Resource Governor, you must be in the sys_admin role. Resource Governor is disabled by default. To enable Resource Governor, take the following steps:

1. In SQL Server 2008 Management Studio, connect to a SQL Server instance.
2. Expand the Management folder.
3. Right-click on Resource Governor and select Enable.

To enable Resource Governor using TSQL, issue the following command:

```
ALTER RESOURCE GOVERNOR RECONFIGURE
GO
```

Similarly, you can disable Resource Governor by using the following steps in Management Studio:

1. In SQL Server 2008 Management Studio, connect to a SQL Server instance.
2. Expand the Management folder.
3. Right-click on Resource Governor and select Disable.

Disabling Resource Governor will not drop classifier functions, workload groups, or resource pools. Essentially, disabling Resource Governor will place all workloads in the default resource pool and workload group. The next time you enable Resource Governor, it will govern newly logged-on workloads.

Use the following TSQL command to disable Resource Governor:

```
ALTER RESOURCE GOVERNOR DISABLE
RECONFIGURE
GO
```

Issuing repeat calls to disable or enable Resource Governor will not raise an error message.

If you disable Resource Governor, existing workloads will continue to be throttled based on their current resource pool/workload group settings. Only workloads that are connecting on will be assigned to the default resource pool and workload group.

> **Note**
>
> You cannot place the ALTER RESOURCE GOVERNOR statements within a transaction.

Creating a Classifier function

A *classifier function* is a TSQL function, created in the master database, which evaluates the properties of a workload at login and places the workload in a workload group. The classifier function works by detecting properties of the login and then returning the name of the workload group into which the workload is to be placed to Resource Governor.

The available properties that the classifier function can use are

- HOST_NAME()
- APP_NAME()
- SUSER_NAME()
- SUSER_SNAME()
- IS_SRVROLEMEMBER()
- IS_MEMBER()
- LOGINPROPERTY(suser_name(),'DefaultDatabase')
- LOGINPROPERTY('MyAccount,' DefaultLanguage')

However, you are free to use any function, or even a lookup table, to classify your workloads.

Be careful when writing your classification function, as a poorly written classification function will be applied to all login sessions and can cause performance problems. The Dedicated Admin Connection (DAC) will not be classified and can be used to troubleshoot problems with the classification function.

Here is an example of a classifier function:

```
CREATE FUNCTION [dbo].[MyClassifier] ()
    RETURNS sysname WITH SCHEMABINDING
AS
BEGIN
DECLARE @grp_name AS sysname
IF (SUSER_NAME() = 'Backup')
BEGIN
SET @grp_name = 'BackupGroup'
END
ELSE
BEGIN
IF (APP_NAME() LIKE '%MANAGEMENT STUDIO%')

OR (APP_NAME() LIKE '%QUERY ANALYZER%')
BEGIN
SET @grp_name = 'DevGroup'
END
ELSE
IF (APP_NAME() LIKE '%REPORT SERVER%')
BEGIN
SET @grp_name = 'ReportingGroup'
END
ELSE
SET @grp_name = 'WorkLoadGroup1'
END
RETURN @grp_name
END
GO
```

This function starts by determining whether the login is the Backup login. If it is, it returns the name BackupGroup, and Resource Governor places this login in the BackupGroup workload group.

It then checks to see if the application name is Management Studio, or Query Analyzer. If so, the classifier function returns the name DevGroup, and Resource Governor will place this login in the DevGroup workload group.

Finally, the classifier function checks to see if the application name is Report Server. If so, it returns the name ReportingGroup to Resource Governor and the workload will be placed in the ReportingGroup workload group. All other workloads will be placed in the workload group WorkLoadGroup1.

After you have written your classification function, you need to configure Resource Governor to use it. Here is an example of how to do this:

```
ALTER RESOURCE GOVERNOR WITH
(CLASSIFIER_FUNCTION = dbo.MyClassifier);
GO
```

> **Note**
>
> You will need Control Server permission to make any changes to Resource Governor configuration, including changing the classifier function, which Resource Governor uses.

There are some considerations when writing the classifier function. The classifier function must return the workgroup name using the data type sysname or nvarchar(128). Group names returned are case-sensitive comparisons. For example, Default (referring to the default workload group) might not resolve to the default workload group. The default resource pool and workload group are lowercased.

Troubleshooting Your Classifier Function

If your classifier function causes performance problems on your SQL Server, you have two options for logging on to your server and bypassing the classifier function to troubleshoot it:

1. Start SQL Server with the -m switch from the console. Here is an example of how to do this:

   At a command prompt, navigate to the location of your SQL Server binaries. They are likely to be at C:\Program Files\Microsoft SQL Server\MSSQL10.MSSQLSERVER\MSSQL\Binn. Then issue the following command:

   ```
   sqlservr -con –m
   This will put SQL Server into single-user mode. Using the
   DAC (explained below) is preferrable.
   ```

2. Alternatively, use the DAC (Dedicated Admin Connection). Log on to SQL Server using the DAC. The DAC will not be subject to the

classifier function. The DAC is disabled by default on SQL Server, and to enable the DAC, you will need to issue the following command in a Database Engine query window:

```
sp_configure 'show advanced options',1
reconfigure with override
go
sp_configure 'remote admin connections',1
reconfigure with override
GO
```

After you have done this you can use the DAC. There are two ways to log on using the DAC:

1. In SQLCMD, log on using the **-A** parameter. Here is an example:

   ```
   sqlcmd -S TOR-SQL01\Instance01 -U sa -P sapassword –A
   ```

   Where TOR-SQL01\Instance01 is the name of your SQL Server, sa is the sa account, and sapassword is the sa password.

2. To log on to SQL Server using the DAC in SQL Server Management Studio, take the following steps:

   a. In SQL Server 2008 Management Studio, connect to a SQL Server instance with no other DACs open, and on the toolbar, click Database Engine Query.

   b. In the Connect to Database Engine dialog box, in the Server name box, type **ADMIN:** followed by the name of the server instance. For example, to connect to a server instance named TOR-SQL01\Instance01, type **ADMIN: TOR-SQL01\Instance01**.

   c. Complete the Authentication section, providing credentials for a member of the sysadmin group, and then click Connect.

Creating a Resource Pool

To create a resource pool, take the following steps:

1. In SQL Server 2008 Management Studio, connect to a SQL Server Instance.

2. Expand the Management folder.

3. Right-click on the Resource Governor icon, and select New Resource Pool.

4. Enter the name of your resource pool (ResourcePoolName), the Minimum and Maximum CPU%, and the Minimum and Maximum Memory % as illustrated in Figure 16.1. Enter **20** for the minimum and **50** for the maximum CPU, and for memory enter the same values.

5. Click the OK button.

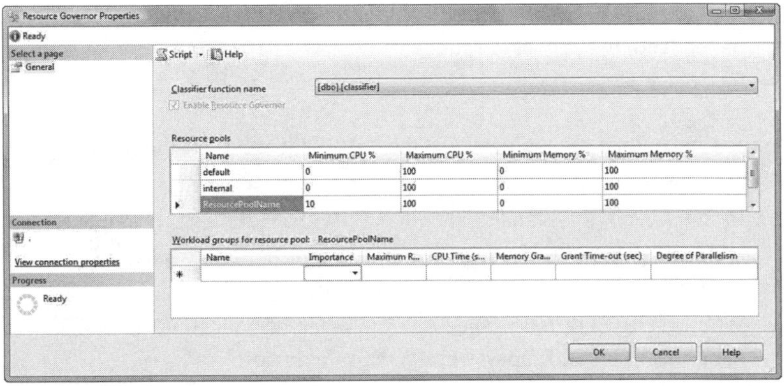

FIGURE 16.1
Dialog for creating a resource pool.

Your resource pool is now created. You will need to create some workload groups in it to make it useful.

To create a resource pool using TSQL commands, use the following syntax:

```
CREATE RESOURCE POOL ResourcePoolName
 WITH
(
MIN_CPU_PERCENT = 20,
MAX_CPU_PERCENT = 50,
MIN_MEMORY_PERCENT = 20,
MAX_MEMORY_PERCENT = 50
)
GO
ALTER RESOURCE GOVERNOR RECONFIGURE
GO
```

The value for MIN_CPU_PERCENT is the minimum CPU you want to dedicate to workloads in this resource pool. This value will not be shared among other resource pools. The value will be between 0 and 100 and must be less than the MAX_CPU_PERCENT. If you attempt to set the minimum larger than the maximum, you will get the following error message:

```
Msg 10908, Level 15, State 4, Line 5
Attribute 'max_cpu_percent' with value of 50 is less than
attribute 'min_cpu_percent' with value of 60.
```

The value for MAX_CPU_PERCENT is the maximum value of CPU you want to share among work loads using this resource pool. Note that this will not be the effective maximum CPU percent; the effective maximum will be the MAX_CPU_PERCENT less the minimum CPU percent values for all other resource pools.

When deriving values for max and min CPU, you will need to measure the CPU taken by these workloads using Profiler for a single execution and then multiply this value by the expected number of executions per second.

MIN_MEMORY_PERCENT is the minimum memory dedicated to this resource pool. The range is between 0 and 100 and must be less than the value assigned for the MAX_MEMORY_PERCENT. Estimating representative values for minimum and maximum memory is difficult. The best way to do this is to create workload groups that run in the default resource pool and measure the total and average memory taken by individual workloads over several days and then use these results for your minimum and maximum memory percentages. Use the performance monitor counter SQL Server:Resource Pool Stats:Default to get these values.

MAX_MEMORY_PERCENT is the maximum memory to dedicate to your resource pool. As with MAX_CPU_PERCENT, the effective maximum memory is the MAX_MEMORY_PERCENT less the MIN_MEMORY_PERCENT settings of all the other resource pools.

After you have configured your resource pool settings, you will need to apply them to Resource Governor by running the following command:

```
ALTER RESOURCE GOVERNOR RECONFIGURE
GO
```

Creating a Workload Group

To create a workload group, follow these steps:

1. In SQL Server 2008 Management Studio, connect to a SQL Server Instance.

2. Expand the Management folder, expand the Resource Governor node, and expand the Resource Pools folder.

3. Expand the resource pool in which you want to create your workload group, right-click on the Workload Groups folder, and select New Workload Group, as illustrated in Figure 16.2.

4. In the Resource Pools section, highlight your resource pool (in this case the resource pool named ResourcePoolName), and then in the bottom part of the dialog titled Workload Groups for resource pool: ResourcePoolName, enter the name of your workload group. Enter **BackupGroup**. For the rest of the settings in this area, enter the following values, as shown in Figure 16.2:

- For Importance, select Low.
- For Maximum Requests, select 0.
- For CPU Time, select 0.
- For Memory Grant %, select 25.
- For Grant Timeout, select 0.
- For Degree of Parallelism, select 0.

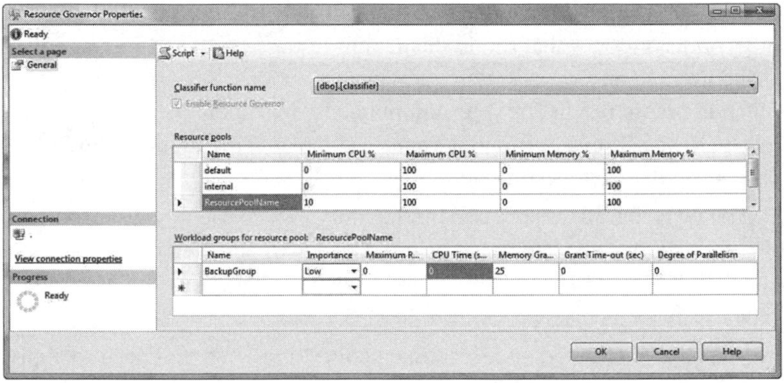

FIGURE 16.2
Creating a new workload group.

The following list gives additional details about the meaning of these settings:

- **Importance**—The Importance setting is the relative importance of a request in the workload group. Available settings are Low, Medium, and High. Importance *does not* imply a priority as we normally understand it in the context for threading and the process priority you see in Task Manager when you right-click on a process in the Processes tab, and select Set Priority.

  For Resource Governor, Importance is a simple weighting schema among active workers for the pool. SQL Server will at any one time be simultaneously executing several tasks. Tasks that are ready to run will be in a runable task queue. When a worker is added to the runable queue, the Importance is used as a factor for position in the list against other workers in the same pool on the same scheduler. The Importance does not carry across multiple schedulers nor does it carry across multiple pools on the same scheduler. It only applies to active workers of groups assigned to the same pool.

- **Maximum Requests**—Specifies the maximum number of simultaneous requests that are allowed to execute in the workload group. A setting of 0 indicates unlimited requests.

- **CPU Time (sec)**—Determines how much CPU time a request can use. 0 indicates unlimited time. The values are in seconds.

- **Memory Grant %**—The maximum amount of memory a single request can take from the resource pool.

- **Grant Time-out (sec)**—Refers to the maximum time a query will wait for resources to become available before timing out. Values are in seconds and can range from 0 and above.

- **Degree of Parallelism**—This setting controls the degree of parallelism, 0 meaning all processors may be used to return or manipulated large results sets. You can select a value between 0 and the maximum number of processors you have on your server. The maximum value is 64, which corresponds to the number of processors on the Wintel platform. Although parallelism can results in faster generations of results sets, it typically means high CPU consumption, which may degrade overall performance. Select a value that is best for your system.

To create a workload group using TSQL, use a command similar to the following:

```
CREATE WORKLOAD GROUP BackupGroup1
WITH(group_max_requests=0,
        importance=Medium,
        request_max_cpu_time_sec=0,
        request_max_memory_grant_percent=25,
        request_memory_grant_timeout_sec=0,
        max_dop=0)
USING [ResourcePoolName]
GO
ALTER RESOURCE GOVERNOR RECONFIGURE
GO
```

In the preceding example, we are creating a workload group called BackupGroup, and placing it in the resource pool ResourcePoolName.

Managing Resource Governor

While using Resource Governor, you will find it necessary to modify your classifier function to move workloads in and out of workload groups as your workload changes to consume more or fewer resources. Initially you will need to place some workloads in the default workload group until you understand that workload's memory consumption, and then move it to another more appropriate workload group, sometimes in a different resource pool.

To make these changes you can use SQL Server Management Studio, or use TSQL commands.

Here is an example of how to do this using SQL Server 2008 Management Studio.

1. Using SQL Server 2008 Management Studio, connect to a SQL Server instance.

2. Expand the Management folder, expand Resource Governor, expand the Resource Pools folder, right-click on your resource pool (called ResourcePoolName), and select Properties.

3. A dialog similar to the one you saw in Figure 16.1 will appear. You can make changes to the ResourcePoolName resource pool. For example, increase the minimum CPU to 25 percent.

4. Then click OK to reconfigure your resource pool to use this new minimum for CPU.

In TSQL you would issue the following command:

```
ALTER RESOURCE POOL [ResourcePoolName] WITH (min_cpu_percent=25)
GO
ALTER RESOURCE GOVERNOR RECONFIGURE
GO
```

To make changes to your classifier function, you can use the ALTER FUNC-TION command, and then issue a call to ALTER RESOURCE GOVERNOR RECON-FIGURE. This must be done in the query pane; you can't make any modifications through the Resource Governor menu items that show up in SQL Server 2008 Management Studio.

You will want to modify your classifier function when you need to change the workload group in which workloads will run.

To make changes to your workload groups, follow these steps:

1. Using SQL Server 2008 Management Studio, connect to a SQL Server instance.

2. Expand the Management folder, expand Resource Governor, expand the Resource Pools folder, expand your resource pool ResourcePoolName, expand the Workload Groups folder, and then right-click on your workload group (BackupGroup) and select Properties.

3. A dialog similar to the one you saw in Figure 16.2 will appear. You can make changes to the test workload group. For example, decrease the Importance to Low.

4. Then click OK to reconfigure your workload group to use this new Importance setting.

To make this change using TSQL, you would use the following commands:

```
ALTER WORKLOAD GROUP [BackupGroup] WITH (group_max_requests=0,
      importance=Low,
      request_max_cpu_time_sec=0,
      request_max_memory_grant_percent=25,
      request_memory_grant_timeout_sec=0,
      max_dop=0)
GO
```

In addition, it is possible to script configuration settings associated with Resource Governor. This can be achieved by right-clicking the Resource Governor folder in SQL Server Management Studio and selecting the appropriate statement.

Monitoring Resource Governor

Resource Governor needs to be closely monitored to get maximum benefit from it.

The three tools you can use to do this are

- Reliability and Performance Monitor
- Profiler
- Dynamic Management Views (DMVs)

Performance Monitor

In Performance Monitor, use the counters SQLServer:WorkloadGroup Stats and SQLServer:Resource Pool Stats to monitor the active workloads in a workload group or resource pool. If one workload group consumes a significant portion of the resources in the default resource pool, you will need to migrate it to its own resource pool to minimize the impact on the other works loads in this Workoad Group or resource pool.

Of the counters in the `SQLServer:WorkloadGroup Stats` object, the following will be most useful to you:

- **Active Parallel Threads**—Number of threads used by parallel queries in the workload group.
- **Active Requests**—Number of currently running requests in the workload group.
- **Blocked Tasks**—Number of blocked tasks in the workload group.
- **CPU Usage**—System CPU usage by all requests in this workload group.
- **Max Request CPU Time (ms)**—Maximum CPU time in milliseconds used by a request in the workload group.
- **Max Memory Grant (KB)**—Maximum value of memory grant in kilobytes used by a query in the workload group.
- **Queued Requests**—Number of requests waiting in the queue due to resource governor limits in the workload group.
- **Reduced Memory Grants/sec**—Number of queries per second getting a less than ideal amount of memory in the workload group.
- **Requests completed/sec**—Number of completed requests per second in the workload group.

Of the counters in the `SQLServer:Resource Pool Stats` object, the following will be most useful to you:

- **Active memory grant amount (KB)**—Total amount of granted memory in kilobytes in the resource pool.
- **Active memory grant count**—Number of query memory grants in the resource pool.
- **CPU Usage %**—System CPU usage by all requests in the specified instance of the performance object.
- **CPU Usage Target %**—Target value of "CPU usage %" for the resource pool based on the configuration settings and the system load.
- **Max Memory**—Maximum amount of memory in kilobytes that the resource pool can have based on the settings and server state.
- **Memory grant timeouts/sec**—Number of query memory grant timeouts per second occurring in the resource pool.
- **Memory grant/sec**—Number of query memory grants per second occurring in the resource pool.

- **Pending Memory grants count**—Number of queries waiting for memory grants in the resource pool.

- **Query exec memory target**—Current memory target for query execution memory grant in kilobytes.

- **Target Memory**—Target amount of memory in kilobytes that the resource pool is trying to attain based on the settings and server state.

- **Used Memory**—Amount of memory used in the resource pool in kilobytes.

Figure 16.3 illustrates the CPU Usage % counter for the SQLServer:Resource Pool Stats objects. In this figure there are three resource pools. The first pool uses maximum CPU, until a workload in the second pool requires CPU resources and Resource Governor throttles the first workload to give the second resource pool its maximum. Then the third resource pool requires resources and both other resource pools are throttled.

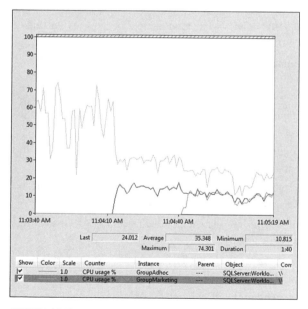

FIGURE 16.3
Each resource pool throttles workloads to the maximums for each pool.

Profiler

In Profiler, use the events `CPU Threshold Exceeded`, `PreConnect:Starting`, and `PreConnect:Completed`. `CPU Threshold Exceeded` will tell you when the `Request_Max_CPU_TIME_SEC` thresholds are exceeded for workloads. The `PreConnect` counters will tell you when the classifier function is operating.

DMVs

The following DMVs will give you a window into Resource Governor, the resource pools and the workload groups.

- **`Sys.dm_resource_governor_workload_groups`**—Returns workload group statistics and the current in-memory configuration of the workload group. The most significant columns that are returned by this DMV are the following:

  - **`Name`**—The name of the workload group.

  - **`pool_id`**—The ID of the pool in which the workload group is located.

  - **`total_request_count`**—The total number of requests for this workload group.

  - **`total_queued_request_count`**—The total number of requests queued in this workload group. This is an indication that some workloads in this workload group are being throttled.

  - **`active_request_count`**—The number of active requests in this workload group.

  - **`queued_request_count`**—The number of queued requests in this workload group.

  - **`total_cpu_limit_violation_count`**—The number of requests exceeds the maximum CPU limit.

  - **`total_cpu_usage_ms`**—The total CPU usage by workloads in this workload group.

  - **`max_request_cpu_time_ms`**—The maximum CPU usage for a single request in milliseconds.

  - **`blocked_task_count`**—The number of blocked tasks.

  - **`total_lock_wait_count`**—Cumulative number of lock waits.

  - **`total_lock_wait_time_ms`**—Total time spent waiting for locks.

  - **`total_reduced_memgrant_count`**—Cumulative count of memory grants that reached the maximum query size limit.

- **max_request_grant_memory_kb**—Maximum memory grant size, in kilobytes, of a single request since the statistics were reset.

- **active_parallel_thread_count**—Current count of parallel thread usage.

- **importance**—Current configuration value for the relative importance of a request in this workload group

- **request_max_memory_grant_percent**—Current setting for the maximum memory grant, as a percentage, for a single request.

- **request_max_cpu_time_sec**—Current setting for maximum CPU use limit, in seconds, for a single request.

- **request_memory_grant_timeout_sec**—Current setting for memory grant time-out, in seconds, for a single request.

- **group_max_requests**—Current setting for the maximum number of concurrent requests.

- **max_dop**—maximum degree of parallelism

This DMV will return a wealth of information about requests in each group. The following query will return a list of requests in each workload group:

```
SELECT r.group_id, g.name, r.status, r.session_id,
r.request_id, r.start_time, r.command, t.text
FROM sys.dm_exec_requests r
INNER JOIN sys.dm_resource_governor_workload_groups g
ON g.group_id = r.group_id
CROSS APPLY sys.dm_exec_sql_text(r.sql_handle) AS t
ORDER BY g.name
GO
```

- **Sys.dm_resource_governor_resource_pools**—Returns information about the current resource pool state, the current configuration of the resource pools, and the resource pool statistics.

- **Sys.dm_resource_governor_configuration**—Returns a row that contains the current in-memory configuration state of Resource Governor.

   This DMV will return two columns, classifier_function_id, and is_reconfiguration_pending. The classifier_function_id matches with the object_id column in sys.objects. A value of 0 for is_reconfiguration_pending confirms that there is no pending reconfiguration of the

Resource Governor due to changes in configuration, and the Resource Governor configuration metadata matches its in-memory configuration.

Here is an example query illustrating usage of sys.dm_resource_governor_configuration, returning the name of the classifier function:

```
select object_schema_name(classifier_function_id) +'.'+
OBJECT_NAME(classifier_function_id) AS
ClassifierFunction, is_reconfiguration_pending
```

You can use the following query to find out the name of the workload group and the resource pool, in Resource Governor, that the classifier function assigned to each session of a Microsoft SQL Server instance:

```
SELECT session_id as 'Session ID',
[host_name] as 'Host Name',
[program_name] as 'Program Name',
nt_user_name as 'User Name',
SS.[Name] as 'Group Assigned',
SES.[name] as 'Pool Assigned'
FROM sys.dm_exec_sessions SES
INNER JOIN
sys.dm_resource_governor_workload_groups SS
ON SDES.group_id = SDRGWG.group_id
INNER JOIN sys.dm_resource_governor_resource_pools DRGRP
ON SDRGWG.pool_id = DRGRP.pool_id
WHERE Session_ID>50
```

The following query will tell you how the classifier function is classifying workloads.

```
select Sessions.session_id, Sessions.group_id,
CONVERT(NCHAR(20), Groups.name)
as group_name from sys.dm_exec_sessions as Sessions
join sys.dm_resource_governor_workload_groups as Groups
on Sessions.group_id = Groups.group_id where session_id > 50
```

This query will display which CPU/Scheduler each workload/session is running on.

```
select Requests.session_id,
CONVERT(NCHAR(20), WorkLoadGroup.name) as group_name,
Tasks.scheduler_id,
```

```
Requests.status
from sys.dm_exec_requests Requests
join sys.dm_os_tasks Tasks on Requests.task_address =
Tasks.task_address
join sys.dm_resource_governor_workload_groups WorkLoadGroup on
Requests.group_id = WorkLoadGroup.group_id
where
Requests.session_id > 50
GO
```

Summary

Resource Governor is a new feature in SQL Server 2008 that allows DBAs to selectively throttle workloads so that resource-hungry workloads will not affect the performance of other processes on the box. Take care creating resource pools and workload groups so that you can get optimal performance out of your Resource Governor solution.

Best Practices

- Try to estimate the CPU and memory resources that workloads will consume and place them in a workload group that approximates this load. Monitor the resource consumption in using the DMVs and adjust the workload group settings if appropriate. Create a new resource pool if necessary.

- For workloads whose characteristics are unknown, place them in the default workload group for the default resource pool and monitor its resource consumption there. Create a new resource pool or Workload group if necessary and move it there if required.

- Ensure that your classifier function performs well, and if you need to use a large lookup table, ensure that there are covering indexes in place on it.

- Ensure that any application using Resource Governor has retry/recovery logic built into it, so that if a grant request should fail there will be no data loss.

CHAPTER 17

Monitoring SQL Server 2008 with Native Tools

The detection and resolution of anomalies within SQL Server will always be part of a DBA's duty. As such, DBAs should be aware that the effectiveness of the detection technique, and the first step to a resolution, lies in the department's commitment to monitoring. A strong commitment to monitoring is key for ensuring that a SQL Server 2008 system stays operational with as few unplanned interruptions as possible. When anomalies do occur, monitoring ensures that the issues are quickly identified and corrected. Without a strong commitment to monitoring, issues left unattended can quickly grow into major issues if not dealt with, eventually leading to a production outage.

For monitoring enthusiasts, there are many monitoring tools, new and old, to pique your interest in this chapter. For starters, the tools and utilities identified in this chapter are similar to those found in previous versions of SQL Server. As with most features associated with Microsoft, however, the features and functionality of the tools have been vastly improved and expanded upon in the latest edition. In addition, SQL Server 2008 also introduces new tools for monitoring. Some of the new features receiving close attention in SQL Server 2008 include Extended Events, SQL Server Audit, and Performance Studio.

This chapter first covers the tools and utilities that allow a DBA to gain quick insight into a SQL Server system running on Windows Server 2008. It then discusses and illustrates how to monitor changes on a SQL Server system and/or database with SQL Server Audit. The latter part of the chapter covers data collection gathering with Performance Studio and explains how to conduct performance monitoring with the Windows Server 2008 Reliability and Performance Monitor tools. The chapter ends with coverage of configuring SQL Server alerts, operators, and emails.

What's New for Monitoring in SQL Server 2008?

- The introduction of the SQL Server Audit object and SQL Server Audit Specification object improves compliance and security by enabling organizations to audit every SQL Server Event within an instance.

- DBAs can gain quick insight rather effortlessly with the new revamped Activity Monitor tool. With one click of a button, Activity Monitor provides graphical real-time performance data on a SQL Server system's processes, resource waits, and data file I/O, and it also illustrates expensive queries.

- On systems that run Windows Server 2008, DBAs can leverage the new Task Manager, Resource Monitor, and Reliability and Performance Monitoring tools to monitor, diagnose, and troubleshoot a SQL Server system.

- Performance insights can be achieved by implementing Performance Studio. Performance Studio is a new data collection utility that captures performance data from one or more SQL Server 2008 instances and stores it in a centralized management data warehouse.

- SQL Server 2008 also provides new Dynamic Management Views (DMVs) for mentoring and troubleshooting SQL Server instances.

Gaining Quick Insight into a SQL Server System

The preceding section is a testament to all the new monitoring tools introduced with SQL Server 2008. It is worth noting that even with these new tools, some DBAs will encounter situations when they need to gain insight into a SQL Server system quickly and effortlessly, but don't have the cycles to implement features such as SQL Server Audit, Performance Studio, or Profiler. The following sections will illustrate SQL Server 2008 and Windows Server 2008 tools and utilities that will ensure that a DBA's efforts are not impeded.

Leveraging Activity Monitor's New Performance Dashboard

The SQL Server Activity Monitor, as displayed in Figure 17.1, is one of the first tools a DBA should leverage when a quick overview of a SQL Server system's performance is needed. Activity Monitor has been completely rewritten in SQL Server 2008, and compared to its predecessors, it is no longer limited to displaying processes, locks by object, and locks by process. Activity Monitor introduced a newly redesigned performance dashboard with intuitive graphs and performance indicators with drill-down and filtering capabilities. The new tool's look and feel is very similar to the Resource Monitoring tool found in Windows Server 2008; however, the information captured and presented is broken down into five major sections dedicated to SQL Server performance monitoring. The sections, as illustrated in Figure 17.1, are Overview, Processes, Resource Waits, Data File I/O, and Recent Expensive Queries. The tool can be invoked by right-clicking a SQL Server instance within Object Explorer and specifying Activity Monitor.

- **Overview**—The first section is called Overview. It provides a dashboard of intuitive graphs and charts that illustrate the SQL Server system's Process Time, Waiting Tasks, Database I/O and Batch Requests/sec in real time.

- **Processes**—The next section in the dashboard is Processes. When this section is expanded, a DBA can quickly monitor and assess the status of a given SQL Server process currently running on the system. Activity Monitor displays a list of current processes on the server such as the session ID, the status of each process, who initiated it (by login ID), the database that the process is using, and the SQL command that the process is running. SQL Server assigns a unique number to each process; this unique number is called a server process ID ("SPID"). Moreover, metrics associated with each process ID are also presented. A tremendous amount of data is presented in this section, but it is possible to filter data by rows within a specific column. By right-clicking a process, a DBA can obtain more details, kill a process, or trace the process directly in SQL Server Profiler.

- **Resource Waits**— This section displays resource waits vertically that are based on the following wait categories: CPU, SQLCLR, Network I/O, Latch, Lock, Logging, Memory, Buffer I/O, Buffer Latch, and Compilation. From a horizontal perspective, the Wait Time, Recent Wait Time, Average Waiter Counter, and Cumulative Wait Time metrics are published for each Wait Category. As in the Processes section, data can be filtered based on items within a column.

- **Data File I/O**— The Data File I/O section displays I/O activity for relational database files within the Database Engine. It includes both the system and user databases. Information is broken down by database and database file name. In addition, MB/sec Read, MB/sec Written, and Response Time (ms) are presented.

- **Recent Expensive Queries**—The final section in Activity Monitor is Recent Expensive Queries, which provides DBAs the opportunity to capture the queries that are performing the worst and negatively impacting a SQL Server instance. Approximately 10 to 15 of the worst and most expensive queries are displayed in the performance dashboard. The actual query is displayed with augmenting metrics such as

Execution in Minutes, CPU ms/sec, Physical Reads/sec, Logical
Write/sec, Logical Reads/sec, Average Duration in ms, and Plan Count.
It is also possible to right-click the most expensive query and edit the
query text or show the execution plan.

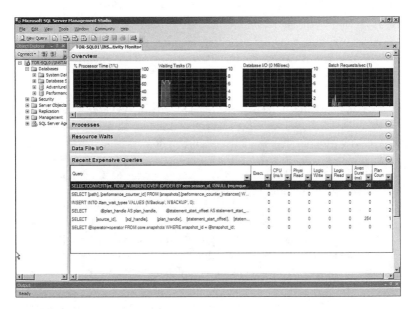

FIGURE 17.1
Viewing the Activity Monitor performance dashboard.

Leveraging Windows Server 2008 Task Manager

The Task Manager is a familiar monitoring tool found in Windows Server
2008. Ultimately, the tool is very similar to the Task Manager included with
previous versions of Windows such as Windows Server 2003. It still provides
an instant view of system resources such as processor activity, process activity, memory usage, networking activity, user information, and resource
consumption. However, there are some noticeable changes DBAs should be
aware of, including the addition of a Services tab and the ability to launch the
Resource Monitor directly from within the Performance tab.

The Windows Server 2008 Task Manager is very useful for an immediate view
of key system operations. It comes in handy when a user notes slow response
time, system problems, or other nondescript problems with the network. With
just a quick glance at the Task Manager, you can see whether a SQL Server
system is using all available disk, processor, memory, or networking resources.

There are three methods to launch the Task Manager:

- Right-click the taskbar and select Task Manager.
- Press Ctrl+Shift+Esc.
- Press Ctrl+Alt+Del, and select Start Task Manager.

When the Task Manager loads, you will notice six tabs, as shown in Figure 17.2: Applications, Processes, Services, Performance, Networking, and Users.

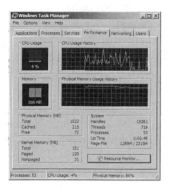

FIGURE 17.2
The Performance tab in Windows Task Manager.

The following sections provide a closer look at how helpful the Task Manager components can be.

Monitoring Applications

The first tab on the Task Manager is the Applications tab. The Applications view provides a list of tasks in the left column and the status of these applications in the right column. The status information enables you to determine whether an application like SQL Server Management Studio or SQL Server Configuration Manager is running and allows you to terminate an application that is not responding, in trouble, or causing problems for your server. To stop such an application, highlight the particular application and click End

Task at the bottom of the Task Manager. You can also switch to another application if you have several applications running. To do so, highlight the program and click Switch To at the bottom of the Task Manager. Finally, you can create a dump file that can be used when a point-in-time snapshot of every process running is needed for advanced troubleshooting. To create a dump file, right-click on an application and select Create Dump File.

Monitoring Processes

The second Task Manager tab is the Processes tab. It provides a list of running processes on the server. It also measures the performance in simple data format. This information includes CPU percent used, memory allocated to each process, and username used in initiating a process, which includes system, local, and network services.

If the initial analysis of the process on your server, such as SQL Server Integration Package or SQL Server instance, takes up too much CPU percentage or uses too many memory resources, thereby hindering server performance, you can sort the processes by clicking the CPU or Memory (Private Working Set) column header. The processes are then sorted in order of usage. This way, you can tell which one is slowing down performance on your server. You can terminate a process by selecting the process and clicking the End Process button.

Many other performance or process measures can be removed or added to the Processes view. They include, but are not limited to, process identifier (PID), CPU time, session ID, and page faults. To add these measures, select View, Select Columns to open the Select Column property page. Here, you can add process counters to the process list or remove them from the list.

Monitoring Services

The newest addition to the family of Task Manager tabs is the Services tab. When this tab is selected, you can quickly assess and troubleshoot a specific Windows or SQL Server service by viewing whether it has stopped or is still running. The Services tab also offers additional key details including the service name, service description, and service group. In addition, it is also possible to launch the Services snap-in if you need to make changes to a specific service. For example, if you know a given service should be running and you don't see it running in the Process tab (common services include SQL Server Browser, SQL Server, or SQL Server Agent), you can just go to the Services tab and attempt to start the service from there. It's very rudimentary, but in keeping with what Task Manager is typically used for, it does offer a quick overview of system status and preliminary problem resolution.

Monitoring Performance

The Performance tab allows you to view the CPU and pagefile usage in graphical form. This information is especially useful when you need a quick view of a performance bottleneck. The Performance tab makes it possible to graph a percentage of processor time in Kernel mode. To show this, select View, Show Kernel Times. The kernel time is represented by the red line in the graph. The kernel time is the measure of time that applications are using operating system services. The other processor time is known as User mode. User mode processor time is spent in threads that are spawned by applications on the system. If your server has multiple CPU processors installed, you can view multiple CPU graphs at a time by selecting View, CPU History. Also on the Performance tab you will find a button labeled Resource Monitor. You can invoke Resource Monitor for additional analysis of the system. Resource Monitor is covered in the section "Using the Windows Server 2008 Performance and Reliability Monitoring Tools."

Monitoring Network Performance

The Networking tab provides a measurement of the network traffic for the connections on the local server in graphical form. This utility is a great way to monitor database mirroring traffic between two SQL Server systems. For multiple network connections—whether they are dial-up, LAN connections, a WAN connection, a VPN connection, or the like—the Networking tab displays a graphical comparison of the traffic for each connection. It provides a quick overview of the adapter, network utilization, link speed, and state of your connection.

To show a visible line on the graph for network traffic on any interface, the view automatically scales to magnify the view of traffic versus available bandwidth. The graph scales from 0% to 100% if the Auto Scale option is not enabled. The greater the percentage shown on the graph, the less is the magnified view of the current traffic. To auto-scale and capture network traffic, select Options, Auto Scale.

It is possible to break down traffic on the graph into Bytes Sent, Received, and Total Bytes by selecting View, Network Adapter History and checking the selections you'd like graphed. This can be useful if you determine the overall throughput is high and you need to quickly determine if inbound or outbound traffic is an issue. In this situation, the default setting is displayed in Total Bytes.

You can also add more column headings by selecting View, Select Columns. Various network measures can be added or removed; they include Bytes Throughput, Bytes Sent/Interval, Unicast Sent and Received, and so on.

Tip

If you suspect a possible network server problem, launch the Task Manager and quickly glance at the information on CPU utilization, memory available, process utilization, and network utilization. When the utilization of any or all of these items exceeds 80 to 90 percent, there may be a bottleneck or overutilization of the resource. However, if all the utilization information shows demand being less than 5 percent, the problem is probably not related to server operations.

Monitoring User Activity

The final tab on the Task Manager is the Users tab, which displays a list of the users who can access the server, session status, and names. The following five columns are available on the Users tab:

- **User**—Shows the users logged on the server. As long as the user is not connected by means of a console session, it is possible to control the session remotely or send a message. Remote Control can be initiated by right-clicking the user and selecting Remote Control. The level of control is dictated by the security settings associated with Remote Desktop.

- **ID**—Displays the numeric ID that identifies the session on the server.

- **Client Name**—Specifies the name of the client computer using the session, if applicable.

- **Status**—Displays the current status of a session. Sessions can be either Active or Disconnected.

- **Session**—Displays the ID numbers of active sessions on the server.

Obtaining Monitoring Metrics with Dynamic Management Views

Here is yet another feature that gives DBAs the potential to gain quick insight into a system. Dynamic Management Views (DMVs) were first introduced in SQL Server 2005 to monitor performance and obtain state information on servers and databases without placing a heavy burden on the system from a performance perspective. Because DMVs are lightweight and less intrusive than other monitoring mechanisms, such as SQL Server Profiler and Performance Studio, they can be used to monitor, diagnose, and identify performance issues quickly. There is an extensive number of existing and new DMVs within SQL Server 2008. Some of them are tailored toward monitoring; however, others even provide server state information. From the perspective of SQL Server 2008 internals, Dynamic Management Views and their associated functions are organized into the following categories.

- Change Data Capture—related DMVs
- Query Notifications—related DMVs
- Common Language Runtime—related DMVs
- Replication-related DMVs
- Database Mirroring—related DMVs
- Resource Governor related DMVs
- Database-related DMVs
- Service Broker—related DMVs
- Execution-related DMVs and Functions
- SQL Server Extended Event related DMVs
- Full-Text Search—related DMVs
- SQL Server Operating System—related DMVs
- Index-related DMVs and Functions
- Transaction-related DMVs and Functions
- I/O-related DMVs and Functions
- Security-related DMVs
- Object-related DMVs and Functions

To view a DMV, in Object Explorer, expand the Views folder in a given database and then expand the Systems View folder. All DMVs reside in this folder and start with the prefix `sys.dm_`. The functions associated with a DMV can be found by expanding the master database, Programmability, Functions folder, System Functions, and Table Valued Functions. Unless you are a genius (and we aren't saying that you are not), it is challenging trying to remember all of the DMVs included in SQL Server 2008. Therefore the following script can be executed to provide a listing of over 100 DMVs that are available.

```
SELECT * FROM sys.all_objects
   WHERE [name] LIKE '%dm_%'
                AND [type] IN ('V', 'TF', 'IF')
                AND [schema_id] = 4
ORDER BY [name]
```

Useful DMVs for Monitoring SQL Server 2008
As mentioned earlier, not only can DMVs assist you with performance turning and monitoring, but they can also provided detailed information when you need to monitor a SQL Server system. For example, the `sys.dm_os_sys_info`

view can be used to determine the number of logical CPUs in a system, hyper-thread ratio between the logical and physical processors, and the amount of physical memory available in the system. Here is the Transact-SQL code that illustrates this example, including the results.

```
Select cpu_count,
hyperthread_ratio,
physical_memory_in_bytes
From sys.dm_os_sys_info
/*
Results
cpu_count¦hyperthread_ratio ¦physical_memory_in_bytes
1 ¦ 1 ¦ 072447488
```

Another useful DMV that is applicable at the database scope level is sys.dm_tran_locks. It allows a DBA to obtain information on currently active Lock Manager resources. Locks that have been granted or waiting are displayed.

Here are examples of index-related DMVs that gather information pertaining to index usage information within a database. The sys.dm_db_index_usage_stats view is a great DMV to validate which indexes are not being heavily utilized and which indexes are causing maintenance overhead. The sys.dm_db_missing_index_details DMV returns information about missing indexes. Additional parameters identify the database and the table where the missing index resides.

Using Predefined SQL Server 2008 Standard Reports for Monitoring

Reports were introduced in Chapter 2, "Administering the SQL Server 2008 Database Engine." The predefined standard reports included in SQL Server 2008 are a great way for a DBA to monitor a SQL Server system. These reports provide performance monitoring statistics, resource usage, and consumption at both the server-scope level and the database-scope level.

The predefined standard reports can be displayed by right-clicking a SQL Server instance in Management Studio and selecting Reports and then Standard Reports. The standard reports include

- Server Dashboard
- Configuration Changes History
- Schema Changes History
- Scheduler Health
- Memory Consumption

- Activity—All Blocking Transactions
- Activity—All Cursors
- Activity—Top Cursors
- Activity—All Sessions
- Activity—Top Sessions
- Activity—Dormant Sessions
- Activity—Top Connections
- Top Transactions by Age
- Top Transactions by Blocked Transactions Count
- Top Transactions by Locks Count
- Performance—Batch Execution Statistics
- Performance—Object Execution Statistics
- Performance—Top Queries by Average CPU Time
- Performance—Top Queries by Average IO
- Performance—Top Queries by Total CPU Time
- Performance—Top Queries by Total I/O
- Server Broker Statistics
- Transaction Log Shipping Status

The standard report, titled Server Dashboard, is a great overall report that provides an overview of a SQL Server instance, including activity and configuration settings. Actually, all the reports provide strategic value for a DBA when monitoring a SQL Server system, specifically the ones associated with performance. From a monitoring perspective, give them a try and familiarize yourself with the content and output.

In addition, it is also possible to create reports associated to specific databases. This can be achieved by right-clicking a database, selecting Reports, Standard Reports and then the specific report that you want displayed.

Monitoring Job Activity

The Job Activity Monitor allows the monitoring of all agent jobs for a specific SQL Server instance through the SQL Server Management Studio (SSMS). To view all jobs with the Job Activity Monitor:

1. In Object Explorer, expand SQL Server Agent and then select Job Activity Monitor.

2. Right-click the Job Activity Monitor.

3. Select View Job Activity.

Within the Job Activity Monitor, each job hosted by the SQL Server instance is listed. The columns above the display fields can be used to sort the different jobs. Both the Filter link located in the status pane and the Filter button located at the top of the window can be used to filter the list of agent jobs. If the SQL Server Agent is configured as a Master based on the Multi Server Administration, you will be able to see job activity for other SQL Server instances that are using this SQL Server Agent as a target.

Filter settings can be applied to each of the agent job columns. This capability is helpful when many jobs are listed. To apply a filter to the list of jobs, follow these steps:

1. From within the Job Activity Monitor, click the Filter button or the View Filter Settings link.

2. To configure the filter to show only failed jobs, select Failed from the Last Run Outcome drop-down.

3. When the filter is configured, enable the Apply Filter option near the bottom of the window.

4. Click OK to accept the settings.

Note

The filter icon changes from blue to green when a filter is applied to the list. To remove the filter, simply disable the Apply Filter option from within the Filter Settings dialog box.

The Details pane does not update automatically; however, you can configure it by selecting View Refresh Settings from the Status pane. Note that the refresh interval and the filter settings are not persistent. When the Job Activity Monitor is closed, the settings revert to the defaults.

The jobs shown in the Details pane can also be managed. The context menu allows you to start, stop, enable, disable, delete, and view the job history. You also can access the properties of the job by right-clicking the job and selecting Properties.

Monitoring SQL Logs

SQL Server 2008 keeps several different logs detailing the various processes that take place on the server. All the log files can be viewed through the Log File Viewer.

The SQL Server error logs are the primary logs kept for instances. By default, six archive logs and one active log are kept. A new log file is created each time an instance is started.

Follow these steps to access the SQL Server logs in SQL Server Management Studio:

1. In SQL Server Management Studio's Object Explorer, expand a SQL Server instance.

2. From within the Object Explorer pane, expand Management, and then expand the SQL Server Logs folder.

3. Double-click a log in order to view it.

You can change the number of SQL error logs kept by right-clicking the SQL Server Logs container in the Object Explorer and selecting Configure. In the Configure SQL Server Error Logs window, enable the option to limit the number of error log files and specify the number of error log files.

The SQL Server 2008 Agent error logs keep track of agent processes that take place on the SQL Server. If a problem with a SQL Server Agent process occurs, these logs should be checked to help determine the cause of the issue.

Nine Agent archive logs and one current log are kept. To access the Agent error logs from within the SSMS, expand the SQL Server Agent container and then expand the Error Logs container. You can configure the Agent error-logging levels by right-clicking on the Error Logs container and selecting Configure. By default, only error and warning messages are enabled. To enable informational logging messages, simply select the check box and click OK. Enabling informational logging may significantly increase the size of the log files.

Note

By right-clicking either an Agent or SQL Server error log and selecting View Log, you can open the Log File Viewer. The Log File Viewer allows you to view each log file individually. A powerful feature of the Log File Viewer is to combine the log files, including the Windows event log, into a single view. You can accomplish this by enabling and disabling the logs from the menu pane on the left side of the window. Figure 17.3 shows the current SQL Server logs combined with the current Windows logs.

This concludes the description of the tools and utilities that should be used to gain insight into a SQL Server system. The next portion of the chapter will focus on monitoring changes with SQL Server Audit and Performance Studio.

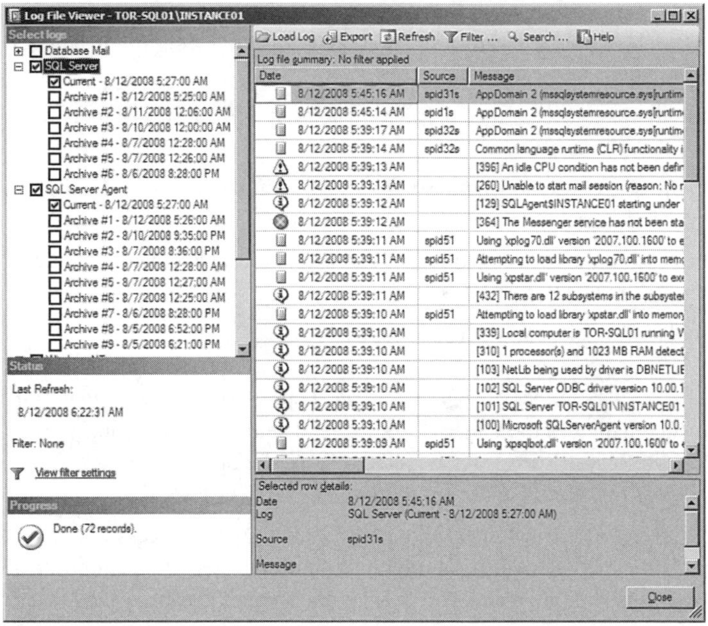

FIGURE 17.3
Viewing consolidated logs within the Log File Viewer screen.

Monitoring Events with SQL Server Audit

Auditing has long been a part of corporate America, not to mention the rest of the world. But lately, with investor confidence falling and the economy's health deteriorating, discussions about auditing have taken center stage. One only has to think about the recent wave of corporate deception involving Fortune companies like Enron and WorldCom to understand why there was so much talk about the future of auditing. The actions of these corrupt corporate entities got the government to take notice and ultimately take back the integrity of the profession of auditing through the introduction of government requirements such as Sarbanes-Oxley (SOX), PCI Compliance, and FDA oversight of data.

With government regulations in place, organizations are now held more accountable for securing and auditing sensitive data. This has resulted in a strong marriage between databases and auditing in SQL Server 2008 as auditing logs are no longer an exception, but a norm today for most companies. Accordingly, SQL Server 2008 incorporates a new auditing solution referred to as SQL Server Audit.

> **Note**
>
> Even if your organization is not governed by some form of regulatory compliance, it is still a best practice to leverage the new Audit object to increase awareness concerning log changes and access to sensitive company data.

By introducing the Audit object and the Audit Specification object, SQL Server 2008 significantly enhances the auditing capabilities compared to previous versions of SQL. It is now possible for organizations to audit all database and server events associated with the Database Engine. This is possible as the new SQL Server Audit object leverages the new Extended Events framework coupled with DDL commands.

In addition, by leveraging the logging improvements in Windows Server 2008 and/or the Audit Collection Services component with System Center Operations Management 2007, organizations can easily centralize and consolidate server and database auditing events across the enterprise, which simplifies compliance, reduces total cost of ownership, and provides rich analysis based on auditing trends. This was inconceivable with the past versions of SQL Server.

SQL Server 2008 Audit Components

With any new SQL Server 2008 feature, it is beneficial to first understand the terminology associated with the components before implementing it. The upcoming sections will further examine the SQL Server Audit components and their associated terminology.

SQL Server Audit and Audit Destinations

To set up auditing, a DBA first creates a SQL Server Audit object and then specifies the location to which the audited events will be written. Audits can be saved to the Windows Security Log, the Windows Application Log, or to a file on the network infrastructure. The audit destination is also referred to as a *target*. Creating a SQL Server Audit object can be performed by using SSMS or Transact-SQL. Within a SQL Server instance, it is possible to generate more than one SQL Server Audit object; however, each Server Audit object would have its own audit destination.

In mission-critical environments where security and auditing are a major concern or requirement, it is a best practice to write auditing data to the Windows Security Log. The Windows Application Log is inferior compared to the Windows Security Log as it requests lower permissions and any authenticated user can read or write to and from the log. In addition, files on the network are vulnerable to anyone who has access to the file system. Therefore, the Windows Security Log is the best choice as it offers the highest level of security, making audit data less subject to tampering.

Server Audit Specification

A Server Audit Specification object is associated with a SQL Server Audit object. It defines the server event that will be audited based on a predefined set of SQL Server Audit action types. Examples of Server Audit Action Groups include: Server Permission Change Group, Database Ownership Change Group, and Failed Login Group. There is a plethora of Server Audit action types that a DBA can choose from for auditing a SQL Server instance. Review the topic "Server-Level Audit Action Groups" in SQL Server 2008 Books Online for a full listing of Server-Level Audit Action Groups.

There is a one-to-one mapping between server audit specifications and server audits. Multiple server audit specifications can be created; however, they cannot be bound to the same server audit. Each specification requires its own server audit.

Database Audit Specification

A Database Audit Specification object is also associated with a server audit. It is similar to the Server Audit Specification object. In this case, however, the Database Audit Specification object defines the database event that will be audited based on a predefined set of Database-Level Audit Action Groups. Examples of Database-Level Audit Action Groups include DATABASE_ROLE_MEMBER_CHANGE_GROUP, DATABASE_OPERATION_GROUP, and SCHEMA_OBJECT_CHANGE_GROUP. As with server audit specifications, there are many predefined Database-Level Audit Action Groups that are applicable to a database. In addition, database-level audits can be linked to a specific database action; for example, an event can be raised whenever a SELECT, UPDATE, INSERT, DELETE, EXECUTE, or RECEIVE statement is issued. Review the topic "Database-Level Audit Action Groups and Database-Level Audit Actions" in SQL Server 2008 Books Online for a full listing of Database-Level Audit Action Groups and respective actions.

It should be noted that there is a one-to-one mapping between database audit specifications and server audits. Multiple database audit specifications can be created; however, they cannot be bound to the same server audit. Each specification requires its own server audit.

Note

When creating and implementing server or database audit specifications, a server audit must already exist as it is a prerequisite task because a specification must be bound to the audit.

SQL Server Audit Failed Logon Attempt Example

The implementation of SQL Server Audit is relatively straightforward and involves four steps: The first step involves generating an audit and choosing a target. In the second step, the decision to create either a server audit specification or a database audit specification is required. The final two steps include enabling the audit and then reviewing the captured audit events on a periodic basis. The upcoming section will further examine the SQL Server Audit components and the terminology associated with this four-step installation process.

Before we dive into the step-by-step creation of an Audit object and audit specification with SQL Server Management Studio, let's first examine an example that captures failed logon attempts on a server via Transact-SQL. The example demonstrates the creation of a SQL Server audit with the target being a file on the file system with Transact-SQL.

Phase 1: Create the SQL Server Audit Object with Transact-SQL

The first step in this four-phase process is to create the Audit object. This example creates an audit called TOR-SQL01-Audit, which stores the audit logs to a file residing in a SQLServerAudit folder located on the L: drive. In addition, a queue delay of 1000 is used and maximum and minimum rollover settings are set to unlimited.

```
/* Create the SQL Server Audit. */
USE [master]
GO
CREATE SERVER AUDIT [TOR-SQL01-Audit]
TO FILE
(    FILEPATH = N'L:\SQLServerAudit'
    ,MAXSIZE = 0 MB
    ,MAX_ROLLOVER_FILES = 2147483647
    ,RESERVE_DISK_SPACE = OFF
)
WITH
(    QUEUE_DELAY = 1000
    ,ON_FAILURE = SHUTDOWN
)
GO
```

Phase 2: Enable the Newly Created Audit Object with Transact-SQL

Now that the audit has been created, the next step is to enable the audit. This can be done by executing the following Transact-SQL syntax.

```
/* Enable the SQL Server Audit. */
USE [master]
GO
ALTER SERVER AUDIT [TOR-SQL01-Audit]
WITH (STATE = ON) ;
GO
```

Phase 3: Create the SQL Server Audit Specification Object with Transact-SQL

The following Transact-SQL syntax illustrates how to create a server audit specification to capture failed logins based on our example.

```
/* Create the Audit Specification Object. */
USE [master]
GO
CREATE SERVER AUDIT SPECIFICATION
[ServerAuditSpecification-Failed-Login]
FOR SERVER AUDIT [TOR-SQL01-Audit]
ADD (FAILED_LOGIN_GROUP)
GO
```

Phase 4: Viewing the Newly Created Audit Log

The final phase in the process is to view the audit log for any irregularities or suspicious activity. Ironically, this is one of the most critical steps, which is too often overlooked. Before viewing the log, let's first generate some failed logon attempts on the server. This can be done by selecting File, Connect Object Explorer in SQL Server Management Studio. In the Connect to Server dialog box, ensure that the Server Type is set to the Database Engine, and enter the name of the SQL Server instance that is hosting the audits. Change the authentication to SQL Server Authentication. Enter the SA as the Login, type the incorrect password, and then click Connect. You should receive an Error 18456 message indicating that you cannot connect to the SQL Server because the login failed for user SA. Repeat the login attempt two more times so that a few more audit events are generated.

Follow the steps to review the audit log we generated in Phase 1.

1. In Object Explorer, expand a SQL Server instance, the Security folder, and then the Audits folder.

2. Right-click the audit, TOR-SQL01-Audit, and specify View Audit Logs.

3. The SQL Server Log File Viewer will be invoked as shown in Figure
    17.4. Take note of the failed login attempts that were captured based on
    our audit specification. If you click on an event where the Action ID
    states LOGIN FAILED, you will be able to review addition details
    such as time, audit collection name, user account, and so on.

4. Click Close when you have finished reviewing the log.

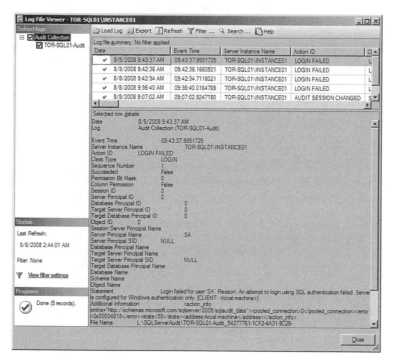

FIGURE 17.4
Viewing the Failed Login Group audit log.

Creating SQL Server Audits with SQL Server Management Studio

As mentioned earlier, the first step to monitoring changes on a SQL Server
instance or database is to create the SQL Server Audit object. Follow these
steps to create a SQL Server Audit object with SQL Server Management
Studio:

1. In Object Explorer, expand a SQL Server instance, expand the Security
    folder, and then select the Audit folder.

2. Right-click the Audit folder and select New Audit, which will invoke the Create Audit dialog box, as illustrated in Figure 17.5.

3. On the General tab in the Create Audit dialog box, first specify a name for the audit in the Audit Name field.

4. Either maintain the Queue Delay default setting or enter a value in milliseconds between 0 and 2,147,483,647. The queue delay indicates the quantity of time that can elapse before audits are forced to be committed. The value of 0 indicates synchronous delivery.

5. Next, enable or disable the Shut Down Server on Audit Log Failure option. When enabled, this setting forces the server to shut down if a SQL Server instance cannot successfully write audit events to a specified target. This setting is typically enabled for organizations dealing with strict auditing requirements.

Tip

Let's take a moment to understand the ramifications of enabling the Shut Down Server on Audit Log Failure option. When an event captured by the audit cannot be successfully written, the server will shut down. If this SQL Server instance is a mission-critical production server, a major outage will result and will continue to negatively impact the organization and users until the auditing functionality is fixed. So tread carefully when making the decision to use this option, as your decision will impact either security or functionality.

---

6. The next step includes selecting a destination for the audit from the predefined options in the Audit Destination drop-down box. The options include File, Security Log, and Application Log. Choose the appropriate destination.

7. If a file destination is selected, specify the additional options for the file based on the settings in the following list. If either the Security Log or Application Log was selected, the additional File options are grayed out, so click OK to finalize the creation of the new audit. The additional File settings in the Create Audit dialog box consist of the following:

   - **File Path**—Indicates the location of the file to which audit data will be written.

   - **Maximum Rollover**—Controls how many audit files should be maintained within the file system. The default option is set to Unlimited. This means that files will not be overwritten. A file restriction can be imposed by entering a number that represents the maximum number of files that can be maintained. The maximum number is 2,147,483,647.

- **Maximum File Size**—The maximum size of an audit file can be 2,147,483,647 terabytes, which is the default setting. Alternatively, you can specify a size between 1024KB and 2,147,483,647TB.

- **Reserve Disk Space**—The final option, Reserve Disk Space, guarantees that the maximum size allocated to the file in the previous setting is preallocated to the file system.

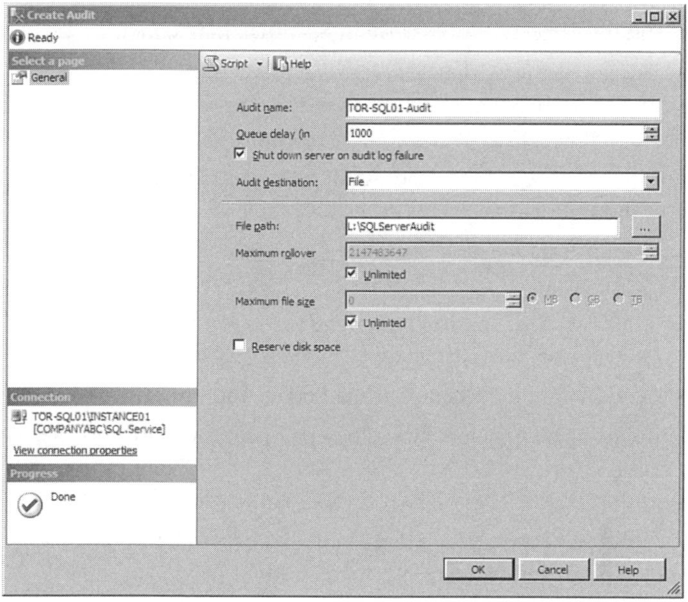

FIGURE 17.5
Creating an audit with SQL Server Management Studio.

Enabling a SQL Server Audit with SQL Server Management Studio

The next step in the process is to enable the newly created audit. This can be done by expanding the Audits folder in Object Explorer, right-clicking the new audit, and then selecting Enable Audit. A red down arrow on the audit represents Disabled.

Create Server Audit Specification with SQL Server Management Studio

As mentioned earlier in the four-step example, after the SQL Server audit has been created and enabled, the next phase is to create the actual server audit specification. The following steps illustrate the creation of the server audit specification, which will monitor failed logins using SQL Server Management Studio.

1. In SQL Server Management Studio, connect to the Database Engine.

2. In Object Explorer, expand a SQL Server instance, expand the Security folder, and then select the Server Audit Specifications folder.

3. Right-click the Server Audit Specifications folder and select New Server Audit Specification to invoke the Create Server Audit Specification dialog box, as illustrated in Figure 17.6.

4. On the General page in the Create Audit dialog box, first specify a name for the audit in the Name text box.

5. Select an audit from the drop-down list. An audit must already exist prior to this step.

6. In the Actions section, specify the desired server-level Audit Action Type from the drop-down list, such as FAILED_LOGIN_GROUP.

7. Click OK to finalize the creation of the Server Audit Specification.

8. Similar to the Audit Specification, the Server Audit Specification needs to be enabled by right-clicking the new Server Audit Specification and then selecting Enable Server Audit Specification.

9. When the logon attempt fails, close the dialog box and proceed to the steps in the following section, "Viewing an Audit Log."

Viewing an Audit Log

After the audit and audit specification have been established, take the following steps to review an audit log within SQL Server Management Studio. This is the fourth and final step in the process:

1. In Object Explorer, expand a SQL Server instance, the Security folder, and then the Audits folder.

2. Right-click the audit for which you plan on reviewing the associated logs, and select View Audit Logs.

3. The SQL Server Log File Viewer will be invoked. Take note of the audit events of interest, then click Close.

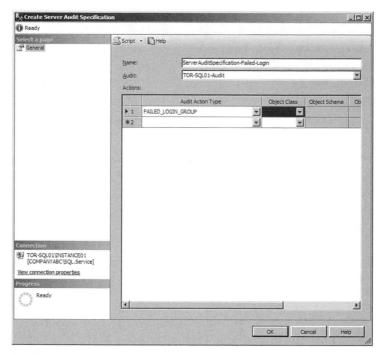

FIGURE 17.6
Creating a Server Audit Specification with SQL Server Management Studio.

Create a Database Audit Specification with Transact-SQL

Instead of creating a server database audit specification, a DBA may choose to create an audit specification that is applicable to a user or system database. If a database audit specification is created, the Database Action Group will collect data on all databases within the SQL Server instance. On the other hand, if you want to audit only one database, that is possible by generating a database audit specification and applying it to one specific database.

When working with database audit specifications, a DBA must still create the Server Audit object and enable it as a prerequisite task. The following steps demonstrate the creation of the database audit specification using TSQL, which will monitor SELECT and INSERT statements on the AdventureWorks database.

```
— STEP 1, Create the SQL Server audit
USE [master]
GO
CREATE SERVER AUDIT [AdventureWorks-Person-Password-Audit]
```

```
TO FILE
(    FILEPATH = N'L:\SQLServerAudit'
    ,MAXSIZE = 0 MB
    ,MAX_ROLLOVER_FILES = 2147483647
    ,RESERVE_DISK_SPACE = OFF
)
WITH
(    QUEUE_DELAY = 1000
    ,ON_FAILURE = SHUTDOWN
)
GO
- STEP 2, Enable the SQL Server audit
ALTER SERVER AUDIT [AdventureWorks-Person-Password-Audit]
WITH (STATE = ON) ;
GO
- STEP3 Create the Database Audit
    Specification on the AdventureWorks2008
USE AdventureWorks2008
GO
CREATE DATABASE AUDIT SPECIFICATION [Audit-Person-Password-Table]
FOR SERVER AUDIT [AdventureWorks-Person-Password-Audit]
ADD (SELECT , INSERT
    ON Person.Password BY dbo )
WITH (STATE = ON)
GO
```

Let's generate a few audit events by running the following SELECT statements against the Person.Password table.

```
Use AdventureWorks2008
Select *
From Person.Password
Go
```

Now open the AdventureWorks-Person-Password-Audit log file by right-clicking the Audit folder in Object Explorer and choosing View Audit Logs. Notice how the SELECT statements against the Person.Password table have been captured in the log based on the ActiveID SELECT. The details of the log entry show the Session Server Principal Name and the Server Principal Name including the user SID who accessed the table based on the SELECT statement.

Managing Audits and Audit Specifications

The next few sections include tasks associated with managing audits and audit specifications.

Using the Windows Server 2008 Security Log as an Audit Target

Compared to other locations, the Windows Server 2008 Security log is the best place to record audit object access, as it is the least likely to be tampered with. When using the Windows Server 2008 Security log as a Audit target, two tasks must be initiated as prerequisites. First the Audit Object Access setting must be configured on the Windows Server 2008 system in order to allow audit events to be recorded. Second, the account used to generate audit events to the Security log, which is the SQL Server Agent, must be granted the Generate Security Audits permissions.

The following example illustrates how to conduct the first step by enabling Audit Object Access on a SQL Server 2008 system running Windows Server 2008.

1. Log on to a Windows Server 2008 system with administrative permissions.

2. Launch a command prompt with administrative privileges. This is achieved by choosing Start, All Programs, Accessories, right-clicking the Command Prompt, and then selecting Run as Administrator.

3. Execute the following code from the command prompt.

   ```
   auditpol /set /subcategory:"application generated"
   /success:enable /failure:enable
   ```

4. Close down the command prompt. Note that the setting takes place immediately.

The next step is to open up the local security policy on the Windows Server 2008 system that will be hosting the SQL Server Audit object and grant the account associated with the SQL Server Agent permission to record data to the Security Log. This can be accomplished by conducting the following steps:

1. Log on to a Windows Server 2008 system with administrative permissions.

2. Click Start, Run, type **secpol.msc**, and then click OK to invoke the Windows Server 2008 Local Security Policy.

3. In the Local Security Policy screen, first expand the Local Policies folder and then the User Rights Assignment.

4. In the right-hand pane, double-click on Generate Security Audits.

5. In the Generate Security Audits Properties dialog box, click Add User or Group.

6. In the Select Users, Computers or Groups dialog box, enter the name of the security account of the SQL Server Agent, and then click OK.

7. Click Apply and then close the Local Security Policy tool.

8. Restart the SQL Server and SQL Server Agent Service.

Note

When more than one Windows Server 2008 Security Log is being used to capture audits, a Windows Server 2008 Active Directory Group Policy can be used to automatically grant and enforce the SQL Server Agent Account the appropriate permissions on the Security.. It is a best practice to first create an Organizational Unit in Active Directory, place the desired SQL Server computers within the Organizational Unit, create the Group Policy, and then link the Group Policy to the Organizational Unit where the SQL Server computers reside.

Viewing Security Events from an Audit File via Transact-SQL

A new function can be leveraged to view security events associated with an audit file residing on a SQL Server system. Here is the default syntax:

```
fn_get_audit_file ( file_pattern,
{default ¦ initial_file_name ¦ NULL },
{default ¦ audit_file_offset ¦ NULL } )
```

The DBA will need to specify the directory and path to the actual filename that needs to be viewed. Here is an example based on the audit file Payrole_Security_Audit, which was created in the steps earlier in the chapter.

```
Select * From fn_get_audit_file
('L:\SQLServerAudit\*',null,null)
```

Dropping Audits and Audit Specifications

Using SQL Server Management Studio, right-click on an audit, click Server Audit Specification and/or Database Audit Specification, and select Delete. It would be best to first delete the audit specification and then the audit associated with the audit specification. The drop can also be achieved with Transact-SQL. Here are the three basic syntaxes.

```
— Drop Server Audit Specification
DROP SERVER AUDIT SPECIFICATION audit_specification_name
[ ; ]
—Drop Database Audit Specification
DROP DATABASE AUDIT SPECIFICATION audit_specification_name
```

```
    [ ; ]
  —Drop Server Audit
  DROP SERVER AUDIT audit_name
    [ ; ]
```

Data Collection with Performance Studio

Performance Studio is a new integrated framework introduced in SQL Server 2008 for performance monitoring and troubleshooting. Performance Studio is involved in the collection of performance and diagnostic data from one or more SQL Server systems. The captured data is stored in a centralized management data warehouse (MDW). With the information yielded, DBAs are able to proactively analyze, troubleshoot, and monitor SQL Server as a result of the trends and historical knowledge they gain from just firing intuitive reports against a SQL Server system in question.

The outlook on Performance Studio is very promising, and the tool would be faultless if it weren't for one issue; Performance Studio only captures performance and diagnostic data for SQL Server 2008 systems, specifically the Database Engine. Not to worry, though, as future releases will focus on the other SQL Server components and features such as Reporting Services and Analysis Services.

Note

So as not to get confused when reviewing other books or online materials, readers should remember that Performance Studio is synonymous with Data Collector. They are the same tool.

Performance Studio Components and Architecture

The Performance Studio infrastructure is based on a simple framework involving a few new components:

- **Data provider**—Sources of performance or diagnostic information.

- **Collector type**—A logical wrapper that recognizes how to leverage, obtain, and expose data from a specific data provider. Examples include Generic T-SQL Query Collector Type, Query Activity Collector Type, and Performance Counters Collector Types.

- **Collection item**—A *collection item* is an example of a collector type that defines the items to be collected in a collection set. When defining collection items, a name, collector type, and collection frequency must be established as a collection item cannot exist on its own.

- **Collection set**—A logical unit of data collection items associated with a SQL Server instance.
- **Collection mode**—Indicates how data will be collected, stored, and uploaded to the management data warehouse. The options include Non-Cached and Cached modes.
- **Management data warehouse**—A relational database that acts as a repository for maintaining all historical data captured via Performance Studio.

A data collector is installed by default on each SQL Server instance. After a collection set is established on a target, performance data and diagnostic information will upload on demand or based on a specified time interval to the management data warehouse as a result of a series of jobs executed by the SQL Server Agent. Also, depending on the collection set, some data may be cached on the SQL Server instance before it's uploaded. After the data is captured and consolidated within the management data warehouse, reports can be generated based on a specific collection set.

> **Note**
>
> Based on the schema design of the management data warehouse, the MDW must be hosted on a SQL Server 2008 instance.

Configuring the Management Data Warehouse

The first step in conducting a Performance Studio implementation is creating and establishing the management data warehouse. Even though performance monitoring and diagnostic data is captured with minimal overhead, it is a best practice to implement the management data warehouse on a dedicated SQL Server system especially if more than one SQL Server instance target is anticipated. In return, Performance Studio will not skew the performance numbers as a result of additional performance overhead from the data collector when data is being captured and analyzed from a SQL Server system.

By default, data from a target is uploaded to the MDW every 15 minutes. This event screams a potential performance bottleneck if there are hundreds of instances uploading data to the same MDW. To avoid this situation, it is a best practice to stagnate the start time of the upload process when working with multiple instances; therefore, an MDW bottleneck will be alleviated because data is being uploaded at a distributed rate.

The space requirement for a system collection set is approximately 200 to 500 megabytes per day. Consider these numbers seriously when creating and allocating space for the MDW. It also makes sense to ensure that the recovery model is set to Simple to minimize excessive log growth. However, maintain the Full recovery model if there is a need to restore the database to the point of failure.

Tip

When creating customized collection sets, it is a best practice to test the amount of data captured in a dedicated prototype lab before going live in production. By simulating a production workload in the lab, the DBA will be able to accurately size the MDW and interpret the stress on the system. Performance may degrade and storage costs may increase when implementing a number of collection sets with a large number of services and performance counters being captured.

Follow these steps to implement the management data warehouse with SQL Server Management Studio:

1. Launch SQL Server Management Studio and then connect to a SQL Server Database Engine instance that you plan on using as the management data warehouse.

2. In Object Explorer, expand a SQL Server instance, expand the Management Folder, and then select the Data Collection node.

3. Right-click the Data Collection node and then select Configure Management Data Warehouse.

4. Click Next in the Welcome to the Configure Management Data Warehouse Wizard.

5. On the Select Configuration Task page, select the option Create or Upgrade a Management Data Warehouse, and then click Next.

6. On the next page, select a server and database to host the management data warehouse. If the database does not already exist, click New to manually generate a new management data warehouse database. Click Next to continue.

7. The next page, Map Logins and Users, is used for mapping logins and users to the predefined management data warehouse roles. If the desired login is not displayed, click New Login and add the account. The management data warehouse roles that need to be mapped to a login include mdw_admin, mdw_reader, and mdw_writer. After all logins are added and mapped to the management data warehouse roles, click Next, as displayed in Figure 17.7.

- mdw_admin—Ultimately this role is the superuser role associated with management data warehouse as members of this role have read, write, and delete access to the MDW. Members can also modify the schema and run maintenance jobs.

- mdw_reader—Similar to write permissions with a database, members of this role can upload and write data to the MDW; however, they cannot read the data.

- mdw_writer—This group can strictly read data in the MDW and that's it.

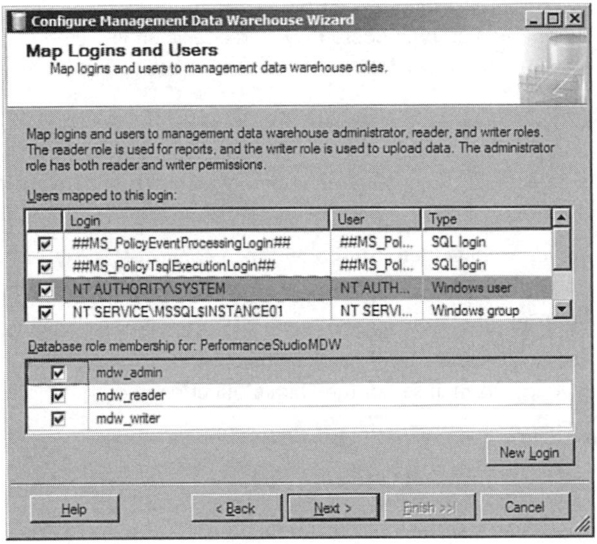

FIGURE 17.7
Mapping logins and users to the MDW roles.

8. Review the management data warehouse configuration settings in the Complete the Wizard page, and then click Finish.

9. The final page will indicate the status of the installation. Verify that all actions were successful and then click Close.

10. When the wizard is complete, connect to the same SQL Server instance and ensure that the new management data warehouse database exists in Object Explorer. In addition, ensure that the database recovery model is set to Simple.

A simple review of the MDW database will show that the database objects are grouped together based on three schemas. The Core schema represents objects associated with collected data. The Snapshot schema is used for storing system collected data sets, which are included with SQL Server 2008 and the Custom Snapshot schema is used when adding new data types for out-of-the-box data collector types or for third-party collector types for user-defined collector sets.

Set Up a Data Collection

Now that the management data warehouse is created and initialized, the next step is to set up a data collection on one or more SQL Server instances.

1. Launch SQL Server Management Studio and then connect to a SQL Server Database Engine instance that you plan on collecting data from.

2. In Object Explorer, expand a SQL Server instance, expand the Management Folder, and then select the Data Collection node.

3. Right-click the Data Collection node and then select Configure Management Data Warehouse.

4. Click Next in the Welcome to the Configure Management Data Warehouse Wizard.

5. On the Select Configuration Task page, select the option Set Up Data Collection to configure this SQL Server instance, which will start collecting data for an existing management data warehouse. Click Next to continue.

6. Ensure that the names of the SQL Server instance and management data warehouse hosting the management data warehouse are accurate. Then specify the cache directory that will store collected data before it is updated to the management data warehouse. The TEMP directory of the collector process will be used automatically if these settings are left blank. Click Next as displayed in Figure 17.8.

7. Review the management data warehouse configuration settings on the Complete the Wizard page, and then click Finish.

8. The final page should communicate the following: the appropriate management data warehouse is selected, the collection sets are started, and the data collection is enabled. Click Close when all actions are completed successfully.

9. Expand the System Data Collection Sets folder under the Data Collection node in Object Explorer to see the newly created system data collection sets.

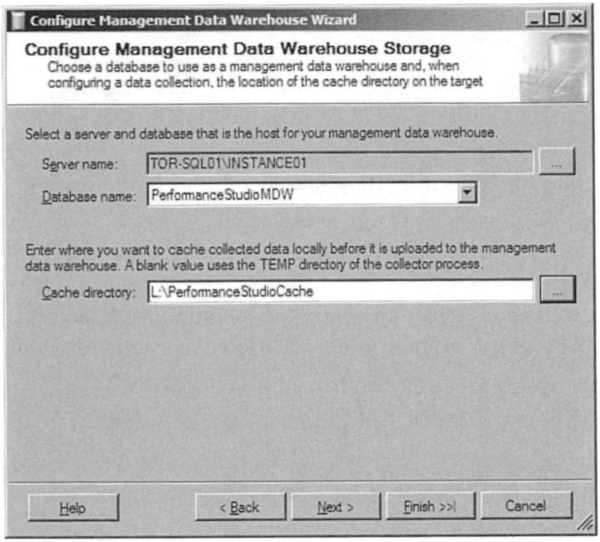

FIGURE 17.8
Configuring a data collection.

Examining the System Data Collection Sets Included with Performance Studio

Based on the SQL Server 2008 RTM release in August of 2008, Microsoft included three built-in system data collection sets, which are installed when a data collection is set up on a SQL Server instance. Each of these built-in collection sets also includes Collection Set Reports.

Microsoft plans on releasing many more predefined collection sets; however, this will most likely occur only with future releases or new service packs. The new data collection sets will also focus on gathering performance metrics on other components such as Analysis Services and Reporting Services.

Each data collection set included with SQL Server 2008 is explained in the following sections:

- **Disk Usage System Data collection set**—The Disk Usage System Data collection set, as illustrated in Figure 17.9, captures data files and log files of disk usage performance data associated with SQL Server 2008 relational databases via the Generic T-SQL Query Collection collector type. Also, the disk usage data uploads to the MDW every six hours where it is then retained for 90 days. After the data is collected it is stored in MDW tables under the snapshot schemas Snapshots.disk_usage and Snapshots.log_usage. Performance counters for free drive space are also captured. Additional performance data associated with a database can be obtained if you double-click on a database. This is presented in Figure 17.10.

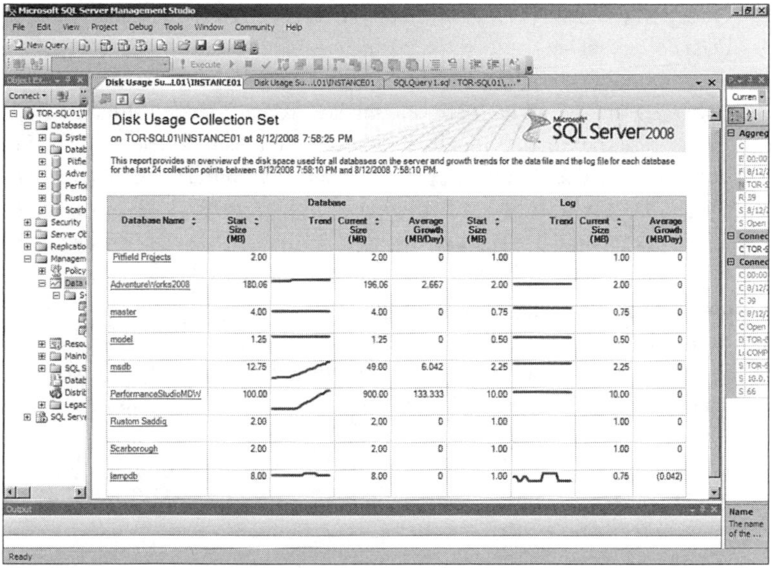

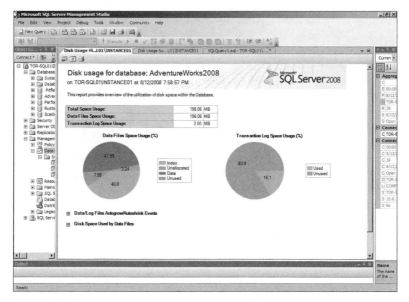

FIGURE 17.9

Viewing the Disk Usage Summary Data Collection report.

FIGURE 17.10

Viewing the Disk Usage Data Collection report for a specific database.

■ **Query Statistics System Data collection set**—The Query Statistics
Data collection set captures performance data that allows DBAs to
analyze and identify "interesting" queries along with query plans that
have been altered without conducting a full server-side profiler trace.
Server-side traces are typically costly transactions that degrade system
performance. The Properties page associated with the Query Statistics
System Data collection set is illustrated in Figure 17.11. By leveraging
the dm_exec_query_stats DMV, troublesome queries can be identified because snapshot plan caches are being captured on a periodic
basis. By comparing query stats against previous snapshots, the top
most interesting queries can be identified. When data is captured it is
stored in the snapshots.query_stats, snapshots.notable_query_text, and
snapshots.notable_query_plan tables.

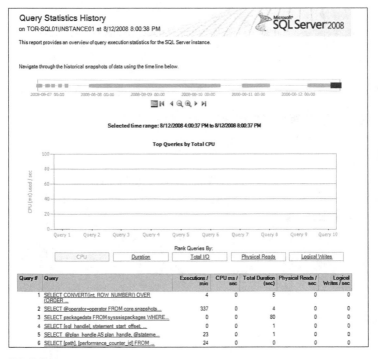

FIGURE 17.11
Viewing the Query Statistics History Data Collection report.

■ **Server Activity Data collection set**—This is another data collection set
included out of the box that collects performance data on active sessions

and requests, memory, performance counters, schedules, and wait statistics. The data associated with this collection is captured every 10 to 60 seconds, cached on the local system, and uploaded every 15 minutes. The Server History Data Collection report can be seen in Figure 17.12.

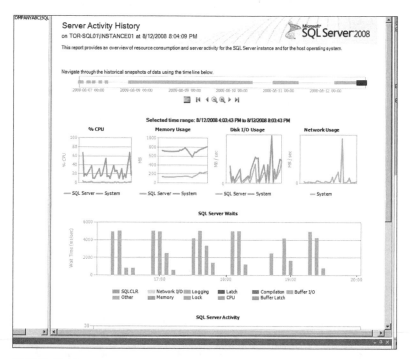

FIGURE 17.12
Viewing the Query Statistics History Data Collection report.

Managing Data Collection Set Properties

It is possible to manage the properties associated with a data collection set by right-clicking a data collection set in Object Explorer and then selecting Properties. Examples of built-in system data collection sets in SQL Server 2008 include: Disk Usage Collection Set, Query Activity Collection Set, and Server Activity Collection Set. Each of these collection sets can be managed.

The Data Collection Set Properties dialog box has a total of three pages. The settings in many sections on these pages are customizable. Become familiar with these pages by reading the next section.

The Data Collection Set General Page

The General page is broken down into the following sections as depicted in Figure 17.13.

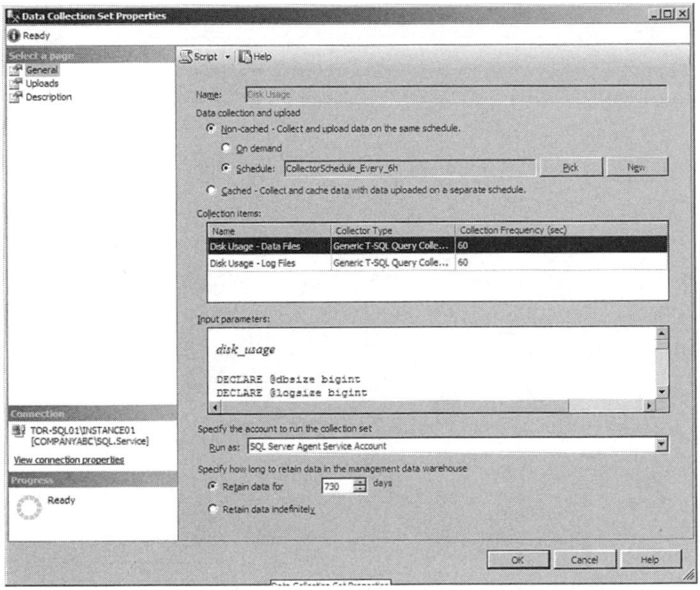

FIGURE 17.13
Viewing the General page associated with the properties of a data collection set.

- **Name**—This text box is self-explanatory; it displays the name of the data collection set.

- **Data Collection and Upload**—The two options available in this section include Non-Cached and Cached mode. These options dictate how data is collected and uploaded to the management data warehouse. The Non-Cached mode is the default option involved in collecting performance data based on a scheduled interval. Alternatively, non-cached data is collected and uploaded on demand. The second option, known as Cached mode, collects performance data at collection frequencies and then uploads the data based on a separate schedule.

- **Collection Items**—The next section located on the general page is Collection Items. A DBA can review the collected items including names, category type, and collection frequency in seconds. For example, performance data associated with Disk Files or Log Files disk usage can be collected based on the Generic T-SQL Collector type every 60 seconds.

> **Note**
>
> The Collection frequency time interval can be modified only if the Data Collection and Upload setting is configured as Cached.

- **Input Parameters**—This section presents the input parameters used for the collection set based on Transact-SQL.
- **Specify the Account to Run the Collection Set**—This setting indicates the account used to run the collection set. The SQL Server Agent account is the default account; however, if proxy accounts are configured and available, there is the option to select an account from the drop-down list.
- **Specify How Long to Retain Data in the Management Warehouse**—The final setting indicates how long performance data that is based on a collection should be retained in the management data warehouse. Of course, DBAs can change the frequency by specifying a new value or selecting the option to retain data indefinitely.

The Data Collection Set Uploads Page

The Data Collection Set Uploads page is used for viewing or setting upload schedules for collected data. Settings are only displayed and cannot be changed unless the Cached option is configured on the General tab for Data Collection and Uploaded. The settings and information include the Server hosting the management data warehouse, the MDW name being written to, the time associated with the last upload, and the upload schedule.

The Data Collection Set Description Page

The final page in the Data Collection Set Properties dialog box is the Description Page. Here you can view detailed description for the data collection set. For example, the detailed description for the Server Activity Data Collection Set gathers top-level performance indicators for the computer and the Database Engine. DBAs can benefit from this page by conducting an analysis on resource use, resource bottlenecks, and Database Engine activity.

Viewing Collection Set Logs

When viewing collection set logs, a DBA has two choices: either review logs associated with all the collection sets, or drill down on a specific collection set and view just one log file. Follow these steps to review the logs associated with all of the collection sets.

1. Launch SQL Server Management Studio, and then connect to a SQL Server Database Engine instance for which you plan to view the collection set's logs.

2. In Object Explorer, expand a SQL Server instance, expand the Management folder, and then select the Data Collection node.

3. Right-click the Data Collection node and then select View Logs.

Capturing Performance Counters from Multiple SQL Server 2008 Instances

If there is a need to capture performance data from one or more SQL Server instances, the best practice is to use one MDW within the SQL Server infrastructure. Again, ensure that the MDW can support the workload based on the number of instances recording performance data to the MDW.

Follow these steps to implement a data collection on a SQL Server instance that is not hosting the MDW. For this example, our MDW is residing on TOR-SQL01\ Instance01 and a data collection will be configured on TOR-SQL01\Instance02 to record performance data to the MDW residing on TOR-SQL01\Instance01.

1. Launch SQL Server Management Studio, and then connect to a SQL Server Database Engine instance for which you plan on setting up a data collection (TOR-SQL01\Instance02).

2. In Object Explorer, expand a SQL Server instance (TOR-SQL01\Instance02), expand the Management folder, and then select the Data Collection node. This SQL Server instance should not be hosting the MDW database.

3. Right-click the Data Collection node and then select Configure Management Data Warehouse.

4. Click Next in the Welcome to the Configure Management Data Warehouse Wizard.

5. On the Select Configuration Task page, select the option Set Up Data Collection, and then click Next.

6. On the subsequent page, specify a SQL Server instance that is already hosting the MDW, such as TOR-SQL01\Instance01. Next, specify the database name of the MDW and the Cache directory and then click Next, as shown in Figure 17.14.

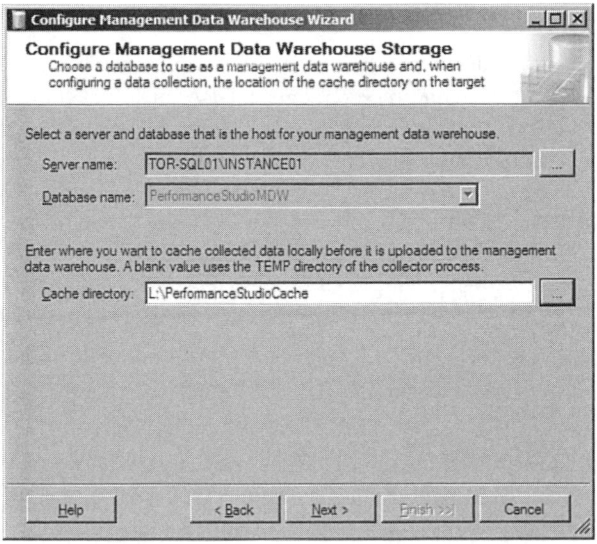

FIGURE 17.14
Configure a data collection to use a MDW on another SQL Server instance.

7. Verify the configuration on the Complete the Wizard page, and then click Finish.

8. The final page will indicate the status of the installation. Verify that all actions were successful, and then click Close.

9. Repeat steps 1 through 8 on all SQL Server instances for which you want to capture performance monitoring data.

Running Data Collection Reports

Each built-in data collection set includes intuitive reports that should be leveraged for analyzing trends and diagnostics. To generate a report, conduct the following steps:

1. In Object Explorer, expand a SQL Server instance, expand the Management folder, and then select the Data Collection node.

2. Right-click the Data Collection node, select Reports, Management Data Warehouse, and then select a report to preview like Disk Usage Summary, which was displayed in Figure 17.9.

Creating Operators and Sending Email Alerts

Being proactive by obtaining alerts via email is another form of monitoring within SQL Server 2008. To send and receive alerts, a DBA must first configure the Database Mail feature, define an operator, and then create an alert and bind it to an operator. The upcoming sections will depict this process.

Configuring Database Mail

The mail delivery architecture in SQL Server 2008 is very similar to Database Mail in SQL Server 2005; However, it is significantly different compared to SQL Server 2000 and previous versions. Although the legacy SQL Mail functionality is still available for backward compatibility, its use is not encouraged. In addition, it is not supported on 64-bit editions of SQL Server 2008.

Database Mail in SQL Server 2008 continues to offer mail functionality without the installation of a MAPI client such as Outlook on the server just to send email. Email continues to be sent using standard Simple Mail Transfer Protocol (SMTP). This also means that one or more available SMTP servers in the organization can be used to relay mail, which could include an existing Exchange Server 2007 running either the Hub Transport or Edge role.

To use the new Database Mail feature, the user must be part of the DatabaseMailUserRole role in the MSDB database. This role allows the execution of the `sp_send_dbmail` stored procedure.

Implementing Database Mail

After installing and configuring the SMTP server, follow these steps to configure Database Mail for a SQL Server instance:

1. In Object Explorer, expand a SQL Server instance and then the Management folder. Database Mail should be listed.

2. Right-click Database Mail and select Configure Database Mail.

3. On the Welcome page, click Next.

4. Select the Set Up Database Mail option and click Next.

5. If prompted, click Yes to enable Database Mail.

6. Type **Email Notification** in the Profile Name field.

Note

If the Database Mail feature is not available, a message will be displayed. Click Yes to enable the Database Mail feature.

The next step is to establish a Database Mail account, which is simply a list of SMTP servers used to send the email.

Multiple Database Mail accounts can be used. When email is sent, each mail account is tried in order until one of them is successful. When the email is successfully sent through an account, that account is used for subsequent email delivery until it becomes unavailable.

Each account can be configured with a different authentication, depending on the requirements of the environment. Follow these steps to add the Database Mail account:

1. Still on the New Profile page, click the Add button to open the New Database Mail Account page.

2. Type `Local SMTP` in the Account Name field.

3. Type an email address such as **dbSupport@companyabc.com** for the Email Address field.

4. Type a display name such as `Email Notification` in the Display Name field.

5. The Server Name field must be populated with the name of your SMTP server. For this example, type **TOR-HB01.companyabc.com** in the Server Name field.

6. Select the type of SMTP authentication to use, such as Windows Authentication using Database Engine Service Credentials, Basic Authentication, or Anonymous Authentication. The setting selected will be based on the relay security associated with the SMTP server.

7. Click OK and then click Next.

Figure 17.15 shows how the New Database Mail Account page should look. You can add additional accounts using the same procedure.

On the Manage Profile Security page, you can configure the profile as public or private. Public profiles can be used by any user in the DatabaseMailUserRole role, whereas private profiles can be used only by specific database users. The profile can also be configured as the default profile.

To continue using the wizard, enable the Email Notification Profile by checking the Public check box and then click Next.

On the Configure System Parameters page, you can configure the setting that controls how Database Mail operates. For example, to configure the system to retry delivery if an error is experienced, set the Account Retry Attempts and Account Retry Delay (Seconds) options.

To continue the wizard, accept the default values and click Next. Click Finish to complete the wizard and execute the defined configuration.

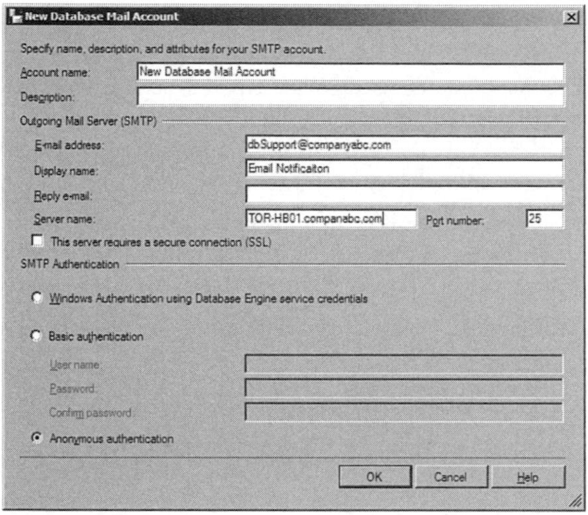

FIGURE 17.15
New Database Mail account.

Tip

From a security perspective, it is a best practice to use a dedicated SMTP server within the infrastructure and not the SQL Server system. Adding the IIS and SMTP roles on a SQL Server system increases the surface area of attack. On systems that are running Exchange Server 2007, relaying can be achieved on an Exchange Server system running the Hub Transport or Edge Transport role.

Validating the Database Mail Configuration

To test the email delivery and validate that email is working correctly, follow these steps from within SSMS:

1. Right-click Database Mail.
2. Select Send Test E-Mail.
3. Select Email Notification as the profile.
4. Enter an email address in the To field.
5. Click Send Test E-mail and then click OK.

The Database Mail log can be used to validate that the email was sent from the SQL Server to the SMTP server. To view the log, right-click the Database Mail container and select View Database Mail Log from the menu.

The following stored procedures can be used to configure Database Mail using the data definition language (DDL):

- sysmail_add_account_sp
- sysmail_add_profile_sp
- sysmail_add_profileaccount_sp
- sysmail_add_principalprofile_sp
- sp_send_dbmail

For example, you can now use the following code to send an email notification:

```
EXEC msdb.dbo.sp_send_dbmail @recipients='user@companyabc.com',
    @profile_name = 'Email Notification',
    @subject = 'Test Email Notification',
    @body = 'Email message from TOR-SQL01\INSTANCE01',
    @body_format = 'HTML';
```

Adding Operators

An *operator* is a user or a group that receives notifications. Notifications can include email, pagers, and net send. The schedule of the operator can also be configured; for example, an operator can be defined to receive notification during business hours, and a different operator can be defined to use notifications during nonbusiness hours or on the weekend.

From within SSMS, you can define new operators. To add a new operator to the SQL Server instance, follow these steps:

1. From within SQL Server Management Studio, expand SQL Server Agent.
2. Right-click Operators and select New Operator.
3. Enter the name of the operator in the field provided.
4. Enter the email address in the Email Name field.
5. Enable a suitable schedule for the operator, for example, from 8 a.m. to 9 p.m. Monday through Friday.
6. Click OK.

You can use the Notification section of the New Operator page to enable notifications for existing alerts on the server.

Defining Alerts

Alerts can be defined for a wide range of SQL Server events. You can receive alerts on the following types of events:

- SQL Server events
- SQL Server performance conditions
- WMI events

Follow these steps to generate an alert when the used log file space falls below 100MB in the AdventureWorks2008 database:

1. Expand the SQL Server Agent in Object Explorer.
2. Right-click Alerts and select New Alert.
3. In the Name field, type `AW Log Files Used Size`.
4. Select SQL Server Performance Condition Alert from the Type drop-down.
5. Select MSSQL$INSTANCE01:Databases for the object. The first part of the object corresponds to the instance name; if the SQL Server was installed as the default instance, the object name is SQLServer:Databases.
6. Select Log File(s) Used Size (KB) for the counter.
7. Select AdventureWorks for the instance.
8. Select Falls Below for the alert condition.
9. Enter `102400` for the value.

You can also define a response to an alert. Responses can include executing a job or notifying an operator. The following steps demonstrate how to add an operator to the previously created alert:

1. In the New Alert window, select the Response option page.
2. Enable the Notify Operators option.
3. Enable the Email column for the operator created earlier.
4. Click OK to finish creating the alert.

You can use the Options page of the new alert to specify whether the error text is included in the different types of alerts.

Using the Windows Server 2008 Performance and Reliability Monitoring Tools

Performance is a basis for measuring how fast application and system tasks are completed on a computer, and *reliability* is a basis for measuring system operation. How reliable a system is will be based on whether or not it regularly operates at the level at which it was designed to perform. Based on these descriptions, it should be easy to recognize that performance and reliability monitoring are crucial aspects in the overall availability and health of a SQL Server system running on Windows Server 2008. To ensure maximum uptime, a well-thought-through process needs to be put in place to monitor, identify, diagnose, and analyze system performance. This process should invariably provide a means for quickly comparing system performances at varying instances in time and detecting and potentially preventing a catastrophic incident before it causes system downtime.

The Reliability and Performance Monitor, which is a Microsoft Management Console (MMC) snap-in on Windows Server 2008, provides a myriad of new tools for DBAs so they can conduct real-time SQL Server system monitoring, examine system resources, collect performance data, and create performance reports from a single console. This tool is literally a combination of three legacy Windows server monitoring tools: System Monitor, Performance Monitor, and Server Performance Advisor. However, new features and functionalities have been introduced to shake things up including data collector sets, Resource Overview, Reliability and Performance Monitor, scheduling, diagnosis reporting, and wizards and templates for creating logs. To launch the Reliability and Performance Monitor MMC snap-in tool, select Start, All Programs, Administrator Tools, Reliability and Performance Monitor, or type **perfmon.msc** at a command prompt.

The Reliability and Performance Monitor MMC snap-in is made up of the following elements:

- Resource Monitor
- Performance Monitor
- Reliability Monitor
- Data Collector Sets
- Report Generation

The upcoming sections further explore these major elements found in the Performance and Reliability Monitoring tool.

Resource Monitor

The first area of interest in the Reliability and Performance Monitor snap-in is the Resource Overview screen, also known as the Resource Monitor. It is displayed in the home page central details pane after the Performance and Reliability Monitoring tool is invoked and looks similar to the new Activity Monitor in SQL Server 2008. Alternatively, you can review the Resource

Overview screen by selecting Reliability and Performance in the navigation tree. Resource Monitor can also be launched from within the Performance tab in the Windows Task Manager.

The Resource Monitor Overview screen presents a holistic real-time graphical illustration of a SQL Server system's CPU usage, disk usage, network usage, and memory usage, as displayed in Figure 17.16.

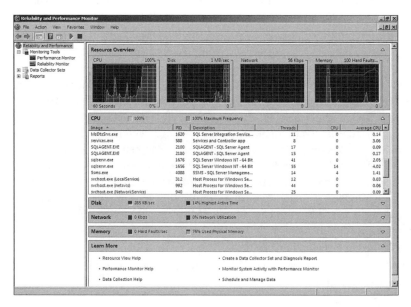

FIGURE 17.16
Viewing the Resource Overview home page in Reliability and Performance Monitor.

You can view additional process-level detail to better understand your system's current resource usage by expanding subsections beneath the graphs. For example, when expanded, the CPU subsection includes CPU consumption by application such as SQL Server, and the Disk subsection displays disk activity based on read and write operations. For example, you can view disk activity associated with SQLServer.exe. In addition, the Network subsection exhibits bytes being sent and received based on an application. This comes in handy when measuring Network Utilization monitoring SQL Server database mirroring between two systems. Finally, the Memory subsection reveals information about the memory use of SQL Server.

The Resource Monitor Overview screen is the first level of defense when there is a need to get a quick overview of a SQL Server system's resources.

If quick diagnosis of an issue cannot be achieved, an administrator should leverage the additional tools within the Reliability and Performance Monitor. These are covered in the upcoming sections.

Performance Monitor

Windows Server 2008 comes with two tools for performance monitoring. The first tool is called Performance Monitor and the second tool is known as Reliability Monitor. These tools together provide performance analysis and information that can be used for bottleneck, performance, and troubleshooting analysis of a SQL Server system.

First, defining some terms used in performance monitoring will help clarify the function of Performance Monitor and how it ties in to software and system functionality. The three components noted in the Performance Monitor, Data Collector Sets, and Reports are as follows:

- **Object**—Components contained in a system are grouped into objects. Objects are grouped according to system functionality or by association within the system. *Objects* can represent logical entities such as memory or a physical mechanism such as a hard disk drive. The number of objects available in a system depends on the configuration. For example, if Microsoft SQL server is installed on a server, some objects pertaining to Microsoft SQL would be available.

- **Counter**—*Counters* are subsets of objects. Counters typically provide more detailed information for an object such as queue length or throughput for an object. The System Monitor can collect data through the counters and display it in either a graphical format or a text log format.

- **Instances**—If a server has more than one similar object, each one is considered an *instance*. For example, a server with multiple processors has individual counters for each instance of the processor. Counters with multiple instances also have an instance for the combined data collected for the instances.

The Performance Monitor provides an interface that allows for the analysis of system data, research performance, and bottlenecks. The System Monitor displays performance counter output in line graphs, histogram (bar chart), and report format.

The histogram and line graphs can be used to view multiple counters at the same time. However, each data point displays only a single value that is independent of its object. The report view is better for displaying multiple values.

Launching the Performance Monitor is accomplished by selecting Performance Monitor from the Monitoring Tools folder in the Reliability and Performance MMC snap-in. You can also open it from a command line by typing `perfmon.msc`. When a new Performance console is started, it loads a blank system monitor graph into the console with % Processor Time as the only counter defined.

Adding Counters with Performance Monitor

Before counters can be displayed, they have to be added. The counters can be added simply by using the menu bar. The Counter button on the button bar includes Add, Delete, and Highlight. You can use the Add Counter button to display new counters. On the other hand, use the Delete Counter button to remove unwanted counters from the display. The Highlight button is helpful for highlighting a particular counter of interest; a counter can be highlighted with either a white or black color around the counter.

The following step-by-step procedures depict how to add counters to the Performance Monitor:

1. In the navigation tree of Event Viewer, first expand Reliability and Performance, Monitoring Tools, and then Performance Monitoring.

2. Either click the Add icon in the menu bar or right-click anywhere on the graph and select Add Counters.

Note

Typical baseline counters consist of Memory - Pages / Sec, Physical Disk - Avg. Disk Queue Length and Processor - % Processor time.

---

3. The Add Counters dialog box is invoked as shown in Figure 17.17. In the Available Counters section, select the desired counters and click Add.

4. Review the selected counters in the Added Counters section and then click OK.

Note

This chapter focuses on monitoring. Chapter 19, "Performance Tuning and Troubleshooting SQL Server 2008," illustrates the useful SQL Server counters that should be utilized when performance tuning and troubleshooting SQL Server 2008.

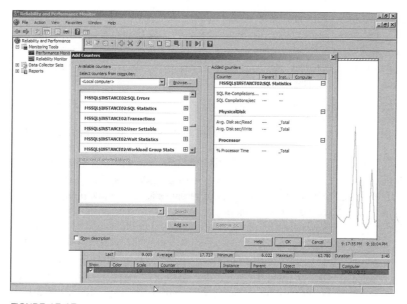

FIGURE 17.17
Adding counters to Performance Monitor.

Managing Performance Monitor Settings

In the Performance Monitor display, update displays by clicking the Clear Display button. Clicking the Freeze Display button or pressing Ctrl+F freezes displays, which suspends data collection. Data collection can be resumed by pressing Ctrl+F or clicking the Freeze Display button again. Click the Update Data button to display an updated data analysis.

It is also possible to export and import a display by using the Cut and Paste buttons. For example, a display can be saved to the Clipboard and then imported into another instance of the Performance Monitor. This is commonly used to view or analyze system information on a different system such as information from a production server.

The Properties page of Performance Monitor has five additional tabs of configuration: General, Source, Data, Graph, and Appearance. Generally, the Properties page provides access to settings that control the graph grid, color, style of display data, and so on. Data can be saved from the monitor in different ways. The easiest way to retain the display features is to save the control as an HTML file.

The Performance Monitor enables you to also save log files in comma-separated (CSV) or tab-separated (TSV) format, which you can then analyze by using third-party tools such as Seagate Crystal Reports. Alternatively, a comma-separated or tab-separated file can be imported into a spreadsheet or database application such as Microsoft Excel or Access.

Reliability Monitor

The Reliability Monitor is a brand new tool first introduced with the release of Windows Vista and now reintroduced with Windows Server 2008. This enhanced system management tool is the second monitoring tool available with Microsoft's Reliability and Performance Monitor MMC snap-in. Use this tool when you need help troubleshooting the root cause associated with reduced reliability of a SQL Server system running on Windows Server 2008. Reliability Monitor provides event details through system stability charts and reports that help diagnose items that may be negatively impacting the reliability of a system.

The tool uses a System Stability Index to rate the stability of a system each day over its lifetime by means of an index scorecard that identifies any reduction in reliability. An index rating of 1 represents a system in its least stable stage, whereas an index rating of 10 indicates a system in its most stable stage. Each day's index rating is displayed in a System Stability Chart graph, as illustrated in Figure 17.18. This graph typically helps administrators to identify dates when stability issues with the Windows Server 2008 system occurred. Additional itemized system stability information can be found in an accompanying System Stability Report section of the Reliability Monitor screen. The additional stability information further assists by identifying the root cause of the reliability issues. This information is grouped into the following categories: Software Installs and Uninstalls, Application Failures, Hardware Failures, Windows Failures, and Miscellaneous Failures.

Reliability Monitor is an essential tool for identifying problems with Windows Server 2008. With Reliability Monitoring, an administrator can quickly identify changes in a system that caused a negative trend with system reliability. As such, this tool can also help administrators anticipate other problems, which all ultimately leads to solving issues efficiently and effectively.

Data Collector Sets

The Data Collector Set is a vital new feature available as a subfolder within the Performance and Reliability snap-in. The purpose of a data collector set is to review or log system performance data. This is achievable through a single component that encompasses organized multiple data collection points. This information can then be analyzed to diagnose problems, correct system performance issues, or create baselines.

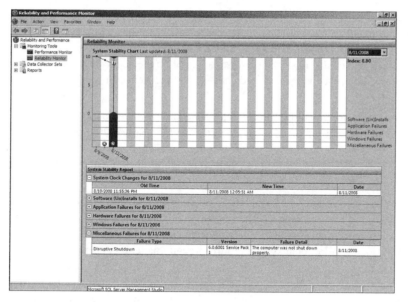

FIGURE 17.18
The Reliability Monitor.

Performance counters, event trace data, and system configuration information are all data collector elements that can be captured and contained in a data collector set. Data collector sets can be based on a predefined template, created from a data collector set that already exists, created manually or with a wizard, or can be user defined. Data collector sets can be exported and used for multiple systems easing the administrative load involving the configuration of new systems producing more effective monitoring. Wizards facilitate the creation of data collector sets and enable an administrator to quickly create collections based on server roles or the type of information that is required.

Note

When capturing and consolidating SQL Server performance Metrics, DBAs should leverage Performance Studio as a data-collecting mechanism over the Data Collector Sets feature in Windows Server 2008.

Reports

The final folder in the Reliability and Performance console is Reports. The Reports folder provides diagnostic reports to support administrators in troubleshooting and diagnosing system performance problems including reliability. Reports are viewed in the central details pane of the Reliability and Performance Monitor snap-in.

The reports are based on data collector sets that were previously defined by users or preconfigured and included with Windows Server 2008 Reliability and Performance Monitoring. The report console's features and functionality are very similar to those seen using the reports introduced with Server Performance Advisor in Windows Server 2003.

The Reporting folder is broken into two main subfolders: User Defined Reports and System Reports. The default System Reports subfolder typically includes reports relating to LAN diagnostics, system diagnostics, and system performance. Additional system reports are automatically generated depending on the server role installed on the Windows Server 2008 system. For example, an Active Directory diagnostics system report is automatically included in the console when the Active Directory Domain Services server role is installed on the Windows Server 2008 system.

Additional Tools to Monitor SQL Server 2008

SQL Server 2008 provides several additional built-in tools that assist in your ongoing monitoring efforts. Database administrators commonly use these tools to verify that the different SQL Server components are running correctly and to troubleshoot problems as they are encountered. These tools will be introduced here; however, they are covered in greater detail in the other chapters of the book.

Using the SQL Server Profiler

The SQL Server Profiler tool captures SQL Server 2008 events as they are generated on a SQL Server. The captured information, referred to as a *workload*, can be reviewed in the UI or saved to a trace file. The workload can be used to analyze performance or can be replayed to conduct N+1 testing. The SQL Server Profiler tool is invaluable for getting detailed insight into the internal workings of applications and databases from a real-world and real-time perspective.

For additional information on using the SQL Server Profiler, see Chapter 19.

Using the Database Engine Tuning Advisor

The Database Engine Tuning Advisor automates the process of selecting an optimized set of indexes, indexed views, statistics, and partitions and even provides the code to implement the recommendations it makes. The Database Engine Tuning Advisor can work with a specific query or can use a real-world workload as gathered by the SQL Server Profiler tool. The advantage of the latter approach is that the workload is generated based on actual usage, and the tuning recommendations reflect that.

The Database Engine Tuning Advisor is customizable and allows you to select the level of recommendation that the tool recommends. This feature allows you to maintain the existing database design and make appropriate fine-tuning recommendations for just indexes. Or you can make the existing design flexible and then have the tool recommend far-reaching changes to the structure such as partitioning.

For additional information on using the Database Engine Tuning Advisor, see Chapter 19.

Summary

The built-in monitoring tools in SQL Server 2008 provide a tremendous amount of proactive monitoring by allowing you to audit events, create alerts, collect performance data, send email notification, and review monitoring metrics via the newly established performance dashboards. In addition, when monitoring a SQL Server system, do not forget the new tools in Windows Server 2008 such as the new Task Manager. Performance Monitor and Reliability Monitor also bolsters a DBA's monitoring experience.

Best Practices

- Leverage Activity Monitor as the first line of defense when there is a need to gain quick and effortless insight into a SQL Server system.
- Use the predefined standard reports included with SQL Server for monitoring performance and state information.
- Leverage the existing and new DMVs when gathering performance, state, and monitoring metrics.
- Monitor server and database events by creating audits, database audit specifications, and server audit specifications.
- Don't forget to view audit logs on a regular basis for trends, irregularities, and issues.

- Leverage Performance Studio to capture performance data from one or more SQL Server instances.

- When using Performance Studio, take advantage of the Windows Server Log as a target as it is the least likely log to be tampered with.

- Review the reports associated with the built-in collections for monitoring state and historical information.

- Use the SQL Server Profiler to generate workloads and test performance of databases.

- Use the Database Engine Tuning Advisor to assist in the creation of indexes, indexed views, statistics, and partitions for the database and to test the results of the changes.

- Examine the use of System Center Operations Manager 2007 for monitoring SQL Servers.

CHAPTER 18

Proactively Monitoring SQL Server 2008 with System Center Operations Manager 2007

System Center Operations Manager (OpsMgr) 2007, also known as SCOM, provides the best-of-breed approach to proactively monitoring and managing a SQL Server 2008 infrastructure. Through the use of monitoring and alerting components, OpsMgr helps to identify specific environmental conditions before they evolve into problems.

OpsMgr provides a timely view of important conditions in SQL Server 2008, as displayed in Figure 18.1, and intelligently links problems to knowledge provided in the monitoring rules. Critical events and known issues are identified and matched to technical reference articles in the Microsoft Knowledge Base for troubleshooting and quick problem resolution.

The monitoring is accomplished using standard operating system components such as Windows Management Instrumentation (WMI), Windows event logs, and Windows performance counters, along with OpsMgr-specific components designed to perform synthetic transactions and track the health and availability of network services such as SQL Server 2008. In addition, OpsMgr provides a reporting feature that allows administrators to track problems and trends occurring on the network. Reports can be generated automatically, providing database administrators, network administrators, managers, and decision makers with a current and long-term historical view of environmental trends in SQL Server.

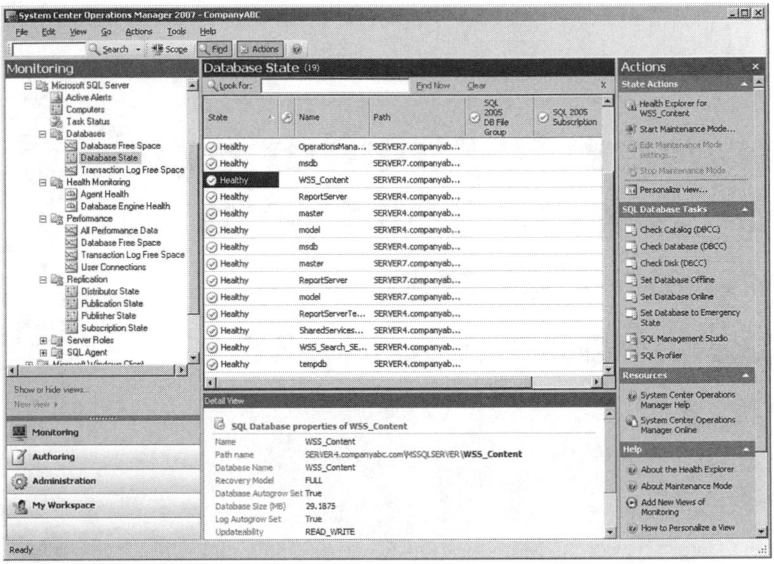

FIGURE 18.1
Monitoring SQL Server systems with OpsMgr 2007 Console.

Note

System Center Operations Manager was originally developed by NetIQ and then purchased and released as Microsoft Operations Manager (MOM) 2000. OpsMgr was subsequently updated and released as MOM 2005. Recently, the product has been completely redesigned and was released as System Center Operations Manager 2007. OpsMgr 2007 contains powerful management capabilities and presents a fundamental change in the way systems are monitored. In addition to individual server monitoring, groups of systems can now be monitored together as a service with multiple interdependent and distributed components.

Overview of System Center Operations Manager

OpsMgr is a sophisticated monitoring system that effectively allows for large-scale management of mission-critical servers. Organizations with a medium to large investment in Microsoft technologies will find that OpsMgr has an unprecedented ability to keep on top of the tens of thousands of event log messages that occur on a daily basis. In its simplest form, OpsMgr performs two functions: processing monitored data and issuing alerts and automatic responses based on that data.

The model-based architecture of OpsMgr presents a fundamental shift in the way a network is monitored. The entire environment can be monitored as groups of hierarchical services with interdependent components. Microsoft, in addition to third-party vendors and a large development community, can leverage the functionality of OpsMgr components through customizable monitoring rules.

OpsMgr provides for several major pieces of functionality as follows:

- **Management packs**—Application-specific monitoring rules are provided within individual files called *management packs*. For example, Microsoft provides management packs for Windows server systems, SQL Server, Exchange, SharePoint, DNS, and DHCP, along with many other Microsoft technologies. Management packs are loaded with the intelligence and information necessary to properly troubleshoot and identify problems. The rules are dynamically applied to agents based on a custom discovery process provided within the management pack. Only applicable rules are applied to each managed server.

- **Event monitoring rules**—Management pack rules can monitor for specific event log data. This is one of the key methods of responding to conditions within the environment.

- **Performance monitoring rules**—Management pack rules can monitor for specific performance counters. This data is used for alerting based on thresholds or archived for trending and capacity planning.

- **State-based monitors**—Management packs contain *monitors*, which allow for advanced state-based monitoring and aggregated health rollup of services. Monitors also provide self-tuning performance threshold monitoring based on a two- or three-state configuration.

- **Alerting**—OpsMgr provides advanced alerting functionality by enabling email alerts, paging, short message service (SMS), instant messaging (IM), and functional alerting roles to be defined. Alerts are highly customizable, with the ability to define alert rules for all monitored components.

- **Reporting**—Monitoring rules can be configured to send monitored data to both the operations database for alerting and the reporting database for archiving.

- **End-to-end service monitoring**—OpsMgr provides service-oriented monitoring based on System Definition Model (SDM) technologies. This includes advanced object discovery and hierarchical monitoring of systems.

Processing Operational Data

OpsMgr proactively manages and monitors Windows networks including a SQL Server infrastructure through monitoring rules used for object discovery, Windows event log monitoring, performance data gathering, and application-specific synthetic transactions. Monitoring rules define how OpsMgr collects, handles, and responds to the information gathered. OpsMgr monitoring rules handle incoming event data and allow OpsMgr to react automatically, either to respond to a predetermined problem scenario, such as a failed hard drive, with predefined corrective and diagnostic actions (for example, trigger an alert, execute a command or script) to provide the operator with additional details based on what was happening at the time the condition occurred.

Generating Alerts and Responses

OpsMgr monitoring rules can generate alerts based on critical events, synthetic transactions, or performance thresholds and variances found through self-tuning performance trending. An alert can be generated by a single event or by a combination of events or performance thresholds. Alerts can also be configured to trigger responses such as email, pages, Simple Network Management Protocol (SNMP) traps, and scripts to notify you of potential problems. In brief, OpsMgr is completely customizable in this respect and can be modified to fit most alert requirements.

Outlining OpsMgr Architecture

OpsMgr is primarily composed of five basic components: the operations database, reporting database, Root Management Server, management agents, and Operations Console. These components make up a basic deployment scenario. Several optional components are also described in the following bulleted list; these components provide functionality for advanced deployment scenarios.

OpsMgr was specifically designed to be scalable and can be configured to meet the needs of any size company. This flexibility stems from the fact that all OpsMgr components can either reside on one server or can be distributed across multiple servers.

Each of these various components provides specific OpsMgr functionality. OpsMgr design scenarios often involve the separation of parts of these components onto multiple servers. For example, the database components can be delegated to a dedicated server, and the management server can reside on a second server.

The following list describes the different OpsMgr components:

- **Operations database**—The operations database stores the monitoring rules and the active data collected from monitored systems. This database has a 7-day default retention period.

- **Reporting database**—The reporting database stores archived data for reporting purposes. This database has a 400-day default retention period.

- **Root Management Server**—This is the first management server in the management group. This server runs the software development kit (SDK) and Configuration service and is responsible for handling console communication, calculating the health of the environment, and determining what rules should be applied to each agent.

- **Management server**—Optionally, an additional management server can be added for redundancy and scalability. Agents communicate with the management server to deliver operational data and pull down new monitoring rules.

- **Management agents**—Agents are installed on each managed system to provide efficient monitoring of local components. Almost all communication is initiated from the agent with the exception of the actual agent installation and specific tasks run from the Operations Console. Agentless monitoring is also available with a reduction of functionality and environmental scalability.

- **Operations Console**—The Operations Console is used to monitor systems, run tasks, configure environmental settings, set author rules, subscribe to alerts, and generate and subscribe to reports.

- **Web console**—The Web console is an optional component used to monitor systems, run tasks, and manage maintenance mode from a web browser.

- **Audit Collection Services**—This is an optional component used to collect security events from managed systems; this component is composed of a *forwarder* on the agent that sends all security events, a *collector* on the management server that receives events from managed systems, and a special database used to store the collected security data for auditing, reporting, and forensic analysis.

- **Gateway server**—This optional component provides mutual authentication through certificates for nontrusted systems in remote domains or workgroups.

- **Command shell**—This optional component is built on PowerShell and provides full command-line management of the OpsMgr environment.

- **Agentless Exception Monitoring**—This component can be used to monitor Windows and application crash data throughout the environment and provides insight into the health of the productivity applications across workstations and servers.
- **Connector Framework**—This optional component provides a bidirectional web service for communicating, extending, and integrating the environment with third-party or custom systems.

Understanding How OpsMgr Stores Captured Data

OpsMgr itself utilizes two Microsoft SQL Server databases for all collected data. Both databases are automatically maintained through OpsMgr-specific scheduled maintenance tasks.

The operations database stores all the monitoring rules and is imported by management packs and operational data collected from each monitored system. Data in this database is retained for 7 days by default. Data retention for the operations database is lower than the reporting database to improve efficiency of the environment. This database must be installed as a separate component from OpsMgr but can physically reside on the same server, if needed. The reporting database stores data for long-term trend analysis and is designed to grow much larger than the operations database. Data in the reporting database is stored in three states: raw data, hourly summary, and daily summary. The raw data is only stored for 14 days, whereas both daily and hourly data are stored for 400 days. This automatic summarization of data allows for reports that span days or months to be generated very quickly.

Determining the Role of Agents in System Monitoring

The *agents* are the monitoring components installed on each managed computer. They monitor the system based on the rules and business logic defined in each of the management packs. Management packs are dynamically applied to agents based on the various discovery rules included with each management pack.

Defining Management Groups

OpsMgr utilizes the concept of *management groups* to logically separate geographical and organizational boundaries. Management groups allow you to scale the size of OpsMgr architecture or politically organize the administration of OpsMgr.

At a minimum, each management group consists of the following components:

- An operations database
- An optional reporting database

- A Root Management Server
- Management agents

OpsMgr can be scaled to meet the needs of different sized organizations. For small organizations, all the OpsMgr components can be installed on one server with a single management group. In large organizations, on the other hand, the distribution of OpsMgr components to separate servers allows the organizations to customize and scale their OpsMgr architecture. Multiple management groups provide load balancing and fault tolerance within the OpsMgr infrastructure. Organizations can set up multiple management servers at strategic locations, to distribute the workload among them.

> **Note**
>
> The general rule of thumb with management groups is to start with a single management group and add more management groups only if they are absolutely necessary. Administrative overhead is reduced, and there is less need to re-create rules and perform other redundant tasks with fewer management groups.

Understanding How to Use OpsMgr

Using OpsMgr is relatively straightforward. The OpsMgr monitoring environment can be accessed through three sets of consoles: an *Operations Console*, a *Web console*, and a *command shell*. The Operations Console provides full monitoring of agent systems and administration of the OpsMgr environment, whereas the Web console provides access only to the monitoring functionality. The command shell provides command-line access to administer the OpsMgr environment.

Managing and Monitoring with OpsMgr

As mentioned in the preceding section, two methods are provided to configure and view OpsMgr settings. The first approach is through the *Operations Console* and the second is through the *command shell*.

In the Administration section of the Operations Console, you can easily configure the security roles, notifications, and configuration settings. In the Monitoring section of the Operations Console, you can easily monitor a quick "up/down" status, active and closed alerts, and overall environment health.

In addition, a web-based monitoring console can be run on any system that supports Microsoft Internet Explorer 6.0 or higher. This console can be used to view the health of systems, view and respond to alerts, view events, view performance graphs, run tasks, and manage maintenance mode of monitored objects.

Reporting from OpsMgr

OpsMgr management packs commonly include a variety of preconfigured reports to show information about the operating system or the specific application, such as SQL Server, they were designed to work with. The reports provide an effective view of systems and services on the network over a custom period, such as weekly, monthly, or quarterly. They can also help you monitor your networks based on performance data, which can include critical pattern analysis, trend analysis, capacity planning, and security auditing. Reports also provide availability statistics for distributed applications, servers, and specific components within a server.

The reports can be run on demand or at scheduled times. OpsMgr can also generate HTML-based reports that can be published to a web server and viewed from any web browser. Vendors can also create additional reports as part of their management packs.

Using Performance Monitoring

Another key feature of OpsMgr is the capability to monitor and track server performance. OpsMgr can be configured to monitor key performance thresholds through rules that are set to collect predefined performance data, such as memory and CPU usage over time. Rules can be configured to trigger alerts and actions when specified performance thresholds have been met or exceeded, allowing network administrators to act on potential performance issues. Performance data can be viewed from the OpsMgr Operations Console.

In addition, performance *monitors* can establish baselines for the environment and then alert the administrator when the counter subsequently falls outside the defined baseline envelope. Performance Monitoring with Operations Manager works in conjunction with SQL Server 2008's Performance Studio. In essence, SQL Server Performance Studio can write performance data to the local Windows Server 2008 application and security logs. Operations Manager can then comb these logs and centralize data into a central warehouse for further analysis and reporting.

Using Active Directory Integration

Active Directory integration provides a way to install management agents on systems without environment-specific settings. When the agent starts, the correct environmental settings, such as the primary and failover management servers, are stored in Active Directory. The configuration of Active Directory integration provides advanced search and filter capabilities to fine-tune the dynamic assignment of systems.

Integrating OpsMgr with Non-Windows Devices

Network management is not a new concept. Simple management of various network nodes has been handled for quite some time through the use of the SNMP. Quite often, simple or even complex systems that utilize SNMP to provide for system monitoring are in place in an organization to provide for varying degrees of system management on a network.

OpsMgr can be configured to integrate with non-Windows systems through monitoring of syslog information, log file data, and SNMP traps. OpsMgr can also monitor TCP port communication and website transaction sequencing for information-specific data management.

Special connectors can be created to provide bidirectional information flows to other management products. OpsMgr can monitor SNMP traps from SNMP-supported devices as well as generate SNMP traps to be delivered to third-party network management infrastructures.

Integrating OpsMgr with Legacy Management Software

Network management is not a new concept. Simple management of various network nodes has been handled for quite some time through the use of SNMP. Quite often, simple or even complex systems that utilize SNMP to provide for system monitoring are in place in an organization to provide for varying degrees of system management on a network.

OpsMgr can be configured to integrate with these network systems and management infrastructures. Special connectors can be created to provide bidirectional information flows to other management products. OpsMgr can monitor SNMP traps from SNMP-supported devices as well as generate SNMP traps to be delivered to third-party network management infrastructures. In addition, OpsMgr can also monitor live events on Unix systems using the syslog protocol.

Recently the OpsMgr team has released new extensions for Cross Platform monitoring and management. Systems that can be monitored include; including HP-UX, Sun Solaris, Red Hat Enterprise Linux, and Novell SUSE Linux Enterprise. Currently this technology is still in Beta.

Exploring Third-Party Management Packs

Software and hardware developers can subsequently create their own management packs to extend OpsMgr's management capabilities. These management packs extend OpsMgr's management capabilities beyond Microsoft-specific applications. Each management pack is designed to contain a set of rules and product knowledge required to support its respective products. Currently, management packs have been developed for APC, Cisco, Citrix, Dell, F5, HP, IBM, Linux, Oracle, Solaris, UNIX, and VMware, to name a few. A complete list of management packs can be found at the following Microsoft site:

> http://www.microsoft.com/technet/prodtechnol/mom/catalog/catalog.aspx

Understanding OpsMgr Component Requirements

Each OpsMgr component has specific design requirements, and a good knowledge of these factors is required before beginning the design of OpsMgr. Hardware and software requirements must be taken into account, as well as factors involving specific OpsMgr components, such as the Root Management Server, gateway servers, service accounts, mutual authentication, and backup requirements.

Exploring Hardware Requirements

Having the proper hardware for OpsMgr to operate on is a critical component of OpsMgr functionality, reliability, and overall performance. Nothing is worse than overloading a brand-new server only a few short months after its implementation. The industry standard generally holds that any production servers deployed should remain relevant for three to four years following deployment. Stretching beyond this time frame might be possible, but the ugly truth is that hardware investments are typically short term and need to be replaced often to ensure relevance. Buying a less expensive server might save money in the short term but could potentially increase costs associated with downtime, troubleshooting, and administration. That said, the following are the Microsoft-recommended minimum requirements for any server running an OpsMgr 2007 server component:

- 1.8Ghz+ Pentium or compatible processor
- 20GB of free disk space
- 2GB of random access memory (RAM)

These recommendations apply only to the smallest OpsMgr deployments and should be seen as minimum levels for OpsMgr hardware. Future expansion and relevance of hardware should be taken into account when sizing servers for OpsMgr deployment.

Determining Software Requirements

OpsMgr components can be installed on either 32-bit or 64-bit versions of Windows Server 2008, Windows Server 2003 R2, or Windows Server 2003 SP1. The database for OpsMgr must be run on a Microsoft SQL Server 2005 (Standard or Enterprise SP1 or above) server. The database can be installed on the same server as OpsMgr or on a separate server, a concept that is discussed in more detail in following sections.

OpsMgr itself must be installed on a member server in a Windows Active Directory domain. It is commonly recommended to keep the installation of OpsMgr on a separate server or set of dedicated member servers that do not run any other applications that could interfere in the monitoring and alerting process.

A few other factors critical to the success of an OpsMgr implementation are as follows:

- DNS must be installed to utilize required mutual authentication between domain members and management servers.
- Microsoft .NET Framework 2.0 and 3.0 must be installed on the management server and the reporting server.
- Client certificates must be installed in environments to facilitate mutual authentication between nondomain members and management servers.
- SQL Reporting Services must be installed for an organization to be able to view and produce custom reports using OpsMgr's reporting feature.

OpsMgr Backup Considerations

The most critical piece of OpsMgr, the SQL databases, should be backed up regularly using a standard backup software that can effectively perform online backups of SQL databases. If integrating these specialized backup utilities into an OpsMgr deployment is not possible, it becomes necessary to leverage built-in backup functionality found in SQL Server, such as the SQL Server backup utility included in SQL Server Management Studio.

Deploying OpsMgr Agents

OpsMgr agents are deployed to all managed servers through the OpsMgr existing deployment functionality, or by using software distribution mechanisms such as Active Directory GPOs or System Center Configuration Manager 2007. Installation through the Operations Console uses the fully qualified domain name (FQDN) of the computer. When searching for systems through the Operations Console, you can use wildcards to locate a broad range of computers for agent installation. Certain situations, such as monitoring across firewalls, can require the manual installation of these components.

Understanding Advanced OpsMgr Concepts

OpsMgr's simple installation and relative ease of use often betray the potential complexity of its underlying components. This complexity can be managed with the right amount of knowledge of some of the advanced concepts of OpsMgr design and implementation.

Understanding OpsMgr Deployment Scenarios

As previously mentioned, OpsMgr components can be divided across multiple servers to distribute load and ensure balanced functionality. This separation allows OpsMgr servers to come in four potential "flavors," depending on the OpsMgr components held by those servers. The four OpsMgr server types are as follows:

- **Operations database server**—An operations database server is simply a member server with SQL Server 2005 and above installed for the OpsMgr operations database. No other OpsMgr components are installed on this server. The SQL Server component can be installed with default options and with the system account used for authentication. Data in this database is kept for 4 days by default.

- **Reporting database server**—A reporting database server is simply a member server with SQL Server 2005 and above and SQL Server Reporting Services installed. This database stores data collected through the monitoring rules for a much longer period than the operations database and is used for reporting and trend analysis. This database requires significantly more drive space than the operations database server. Data in this database is kept for 13 months by default.

- **Management server**—A management server is the communication point for both management consoles and agents. Effectively, a management server does not have a database and is often used in large OpsMgr implementations that have a dedicated database server. Often, in these configurations, multiple management servers are used in a single management group to provide for scalability and to address multiple managed nodes.

- **All-in-one server**—An all-in-one server is effectively an OpsMgr server that holds all OpsMgr roles, including that of the databases. Subsequently, single-server OpsMgr configurations use one server for all OpsMgr operations.

Multiple Configuration Groups

As previously defined, an OpsMgr management group is a logical grouping of monitored servers that are managed by a single OpsMgr SQL database, one or more management servers, and a unique management group name. Each management group established operates completely separately from other management groups, although they can be configured in a hierarchical structure with a top-level management group able to see "connected" lower-level management groups.

The concept of connected management groups allows OpsMgr to scale beyond artificial boundaries and also gives a great deal of flexibility when combining OpsMgr environments. However, certain caveats must be taken into account. Because each management group is an island in itself, each must subsequently be manually configured with individual settings. In environments with a large number of customized rules, for example, such manual configuration would create a great deal of redundant work in the creation, administration, and troubleshooting of multiple management groups.

Deploying Geographic-Based Configuration Groups

Based on the factors outlined in the preceding section, it is preferable to deploy OpsMgr in a single management group. However, in some situations an organization needs to divide its OpsMgr environment into multiple management groups. The most common reason for division of OpsMgr management groups is division along geographic lines. In situations in which wide area network (WAN) links are saturated or unreliable, it might be wise to separate large "islands" of WAN connectivity into separate management groups.

Simply being separated across slow WAN links is not enough reason to warrant a separate management group, however. For example, small sites with few servers would not warrant the creation of a separate OpsMgr management group, with the associated hardware, software, and administrative costs. However, if many servers exist in a distributed, generally well-connected geographical area, that might be a case for the creation of a management group. For example, an organization could be divided into several sites across the United States but decide to divide the OpsMgr environment into separate management groups for East Coast and West Coast, to roughly approximate their WAN infrastructure.

Smaller sites that are not well connected but are not large enough to warrant their own management group should have their event monitoring throttled to avoid being sent across the WAN during peak usage times. The downside to this approach, however, is that the reaction time to critical event response is increased.

Deploying Political or Security-Based Configuration Groups

The less common method of dividing OpsMgr management groups is by political or security lines. For example, it might become necessary to separate financial servers into a separate management group to maintain the security of the finance environment and allow for a separate set of administrators.

Politically, if administration is not centralized within an organization, management groups can be established to separate OpsMgr management into separate spheres of control. This would keep each OpsMgr management zone under separate security models.

As previously mentioned, a single management group is the most efficient OpsMgr environment and provides for the least amount of redundant setup, administration, and troubleshooting work. Consequently, artificial OpsMgr division along political or security lines should be avoided, if possible.

Sizing the OpsMgr Database

Depending on several factors, such as the type of data collected, the length of time that collected data will be kept, or the amount of database grooming that is scheduled, the size of the OpsMgr database will grow or shrink accordingly.

It is important to monitor the size of the database to ensure that it does not increase well beyond the bounds of acceptable size. OpsMgr can be configured to monitor itself, supplying advance notice of database problems and capacity thresholds. This type of strategy is highly recommended because OpsMgr could easily collect event information faster than it could get rid of it.

The size of the operations database can be estimated through the following formula:

```
Number of agents x 5MB x retention days +
➥1024 overhead = estimated database size
```

For example, an OpsMgr environment monitoring 1,000 servers with the default 7-day retention period will have an estimated 35GB operations database.

```
(1000 * 5 * 7) + 1024 = 36024 MB
```

The size of the reporting database can be estimated through the following formula:

```
Number of agents x 3MB x retention days +
➥1024 overhead = estimated database size
```

The same environment monitoring 1,000 servers with the default 400-day retention period will have an estimated 1.1TB reporting database.

```
(1000 * 3 * 400) + 1024 = 1201024 MB
```

Defining Capacity Limits

As with any system, OpsMgr includes some hard limits that should be taken into account before deployment begins. Surpassing these limits could be cause for the creation of new management groups and should subsequently be included in a design plan. These limits are as follows:

- **Operations database**—OpsMgr operates through a principle of centralized, rather than distributed, collection of data. All event logs, performance counters, and alerts are sent to a single centralized database, and subsequently there can only be a single operations database per management group. The use of a backup and high-availability strategy for the OpsMgr database is, therefore, highly recommended, to protect it from outage. It is recommended to keep this database with a 50GB limit to improve efficiency and reduce alert latency.

- **Management servers**—OpsMgr does not have a hard-coded limit of management servers per management group. However, it is recommended to keep the environment between three to five management servers. Each management server can support approximately 2,000 managed agents.

- **Gateway servers**—OpsMgr does not have a hard-coded limit of gateway servers per management group. However, it is recommended to deploy a gateway server for every 200 nontrusted domain members.

- **Agents**—Each management server can theoretically support up to 2,000 monitored agents. In most configurations, however, it is wise to limit the number of agents per management server, although the levels can be scaled upward with more robust hardware, if necessary.

- **Administrative consoles**—OpsMgr does not limit the number of instances of the Web and Operations Consoles; however, going beyond the suggested limit might introduce performance and scalability problems.

Defining System Redundancy

In addition to the scalability built in to OpsMgr, redundancy is built in to the components of the environment. Proper knowledge of how to deploy OpsMgr redundancy and place OpsMgr components correctly is important to the understanding of OpsMgr redundancy.

Having multiple management servers deployed across a management group allows an environment to achieve a certain level of redundancy. If a single management server experiences downtime, another management server within the management group will take over the responsibilities for the monitored servers in the environment. For this reason, it might be wise to include multiple management servers in an environment to achieve a certain level of redundancy if high uptime is a priority.

The first management server in the management group is called the *Root Management Server*. Only one Root Management Server can exist in a management group, and it hosts the software development kit (SDK) and Configuration service. All OpsMgr consoles communicate with the management server, so its availability is critical. In large-scale environments, the Root Management Server should leverage Microsoft Clustering technology to provide high availability for this component.

Because there can be only a single OpsMgr database per management group, the database is subsequently a single point of failure and should be protected from downtime. Utilizing Windows Server 2008 clustering or third-party fault-tolerance solutions for SQL databases helps to mitigate the risk involved with the OpsMgr database.

Securing OpsMgr

Security has evolved into a primary concern that can no longer be taken for granted. The inherent security in Windows 2008 is only as good as the services that have access to it; therefore, it is wise to perform a security audit of all systems that access information from servers. This concept holds true for management systems as well because they collect sensitive information from every server in an enterprise. This includes potentially sensitive event logs that could be used to compromise a system. Consequently, securing the OpsMgr infrastructure should not be taken lightly.

Securing OpsMgr Agents

Each server that contains an OpsMgr agent and forwards events to management servers has specific security requirements. Server-level security should be established and should include provisions for OpsMgr data collection. All traffic between OpsMgr components, such as the agents, management servers, and database, is encrypted automatically for security, so the traffic is inherently secured.

In addition, environments with high security requirements should investigate the use of encryption technologies such as IPSec to scramble the event IDs that are sent between agents and OpsMgr servers, to protect against eavesdropping of OpsMgr packets.

OpsMgr uses mutual authentication between agents and management servers. This means that the agent must reside in the same forest as the management server. If the agent is located in a different forest or workgroup, client certificates can be used to establish mutual authentication. If an entire nontrusted domain must be monitored, the gateway server can be installed in the nontrusted domain, agents can establish mutual authentication to the gateway server, and certificates on the gateway and management server are used to establish mutual authentication. In this scenario, you can avoid needing to place a certificate on each nontrusted domain member.

Understanding Firewall Requirements

OpsMgr servers that are deployed across a firewall have special considerations that must be taken into account. Port 5723, the default port for OpsMgr communications, must specifically be opened on a firewall to allow OpsMgr to communicate across it. The following describes communication for other OpsMgr components:

- Operations Console to RMS—TCP 5724
- Operations Console to Reporting Server—TCP 80
- Web console to Web console server—TCP 51908, 445
- Agent to Root Management Server—TCP 5723
- ACS forwarder to ACS collector—TCP 51909
- Agentless management—Remote Procedure Call (RPC)
- Management server to databases—OLEDB TCP 1433

Outlining Service Account Security

In addition to the aforementioned security measures, security of an OpsMgr environment can be strengthened by the addition of multiple service accounts to handle the different OpsMgr components. For example, the Management Server Action account and the SDK/Configuration service account should be configured to use separate credentials, to provide an extra layer of protection in the event that one account is compromised.

- **Management Server Action account**—The account responsible for collecting data and running responses from management servers.
- **SDK and Configuration service account**—The account that writes data to the operations database; this service is also used for all console communication.
- **Local Administrator account**—The account used during the agent push installation process. To install the agent, local administrative rights are required.
- **Agent Action account**—The credentials the agent will run as. This account can run under a built-in system account, such as Local System, or a limited domain user account for high-security environments.

- **Data Warehouse Write Action account**—The account used by the management server to write data to the reporting data warehouse.

- **Data Warehouse Reader account**—The account used to read data from the data warehouse when reports are executed.

- **Run As accounts**—The specific accounts used by management packs to facilitate monitoring. These accounts must be manually created and delegated specific rights as defined in the management pack documentation. These accounts are then assigned as run-as accounts used by the management pack to achieve a high-degree of security and flexibility when monitoring the environment.

Exploring the SQL Server Management Pack

When imported, the SQL Server management pack automatically discovers the following objects on managed SQL Server systems in the management group:

- SQL Server 2008 Database Engine
- SQL Server 2008 Analysis Services
- SQL Server 2008 Reporting Services
- SQL Server 2008 Integration Services
- SQL Server 2008 Distributor
- SQL Server 2008 Publisher
- SQL Server 2008 Subscriber
- SQL Server 2008 DB
- SQL Server 2008 Agent
- SQL Server 2008 Agent Jobs
- SQL Server 2008 DB File Group
- SQL Server 2008 DB File
- SQL Server 2008 Transaction Log File

As you can see, OpsMgr finds many of the components associated with a SQL Server and not just the server itself. Availability statistics of each component can be calculated independently or together as a group. For example, an availability report can be scheduled for a single database on a server or the entire server. This type of discovery also allows each component to be placed into maintenance mode independently of other components on the server. For example, a single database can be placed into maintenance mode to prevent alerts from being generated when the database is worked on or repaired while other databases on the server are still being monitored.

In addition to basic monitoring of SQL Server—related events and performance data, the SQL Server management pack provides advanced monitoring through custom scripts associated with rules in the management pack. The following rules are specific to SQL Server monitoring. Each rule can be customized for the environment or even a specific server being monitored.

- **Block Analysis**—When an SPID is blocked for more than one minute, an alert is generated. This detection can be configured through the Blocking SPIDs monitor associated with the SQL 2008 DB Engine object. Alert details include; blocked SPID, blocked by SPID, program name, block duration, login name, database name and resources.

- **Database Configuration**—SQL Server—specific configurable options such as Auto Close, Auto Create Statistics, Auto Shrink, Auto Update, DB Chaining, and Torn Page Detection. This detection can be configured through the corresponding configuration monitors associated with the SQL 2008 DB object.

- **Database Health**—Tracks the availability and current state of databases on SQL Servers in the environment. This detection can be configured through the Database Status monitor associated with the SQL Server 2008 DB object.

- **Database and Disk Space**—The free space within database and transaction logs is monitored. An *alert* is an event generated when predefined thresholds are exceeded or a significant change in size is detected. This detection can be configured through the corresponding performance monitors associated with the SQL Server 2008 DB object.

- **Replication Monitoring**—The whole SQL Server replication topology is monitored indicating overall health and alerts based on replication failures.

- **Backups** —Monitoring of all backup items such as failed and successful backups are captured and presented.

- **Jobs**—Agent jobs that run for more than 60 minutes will generate an alert by default. This detection can be configured through the Long Running Jobs performance monitor associated with the SQL 2008 Agent object. Other jobs and associated items such as failed SQL Server Agent jobs, job corruption and SQL Server Mail are also monitored and alerted upon.

- **Security Monitoring**—Tracks security and audit events such as; license compliance, shutdowns, configuration issues, collection of audit data, denied administration functions, and both successful and failed logons.

- **Service Pack Compliance**—The current service pack level can be monitored by configuring the Service Pack Compliance configuration monitor associated with the SQL Server 2008 DB Engine object. An alert is generated when a server is not at the required service pack level.

Within the Monitoring area of the Operators console, the following views are available to assist with monitoring the environment:

- Alerts view
- Computers View
- Database Free Space Performance
- Transaction Log Free Space Performance
- Database State
- Agent Health State
- Database Engine Health State
- Analysis Services State
- Database Engines State
- Integration Services State
- Reporting Services State
- Database Mirroring State
- Server Resource Utilization
- SQL Agent Job State
- SQL Agent State

The SQL Server management pack also includes several default reports to help with trend-specific SQL:

- SQL Broker Performance
- SQL Server Database Counters
- SQL Server Configuration
- SQL Server Lock Analysis
- SQL Server Service Pack
- SQL User Activity
- Top Five Deadlocked Databases
- User Connections by Day
- User Connections by Peak Hours
- SQL Database Space Report

The latest version of management packs should always be used because it includes many improvements and updates from the release code.

Downloading and Extracting the SQL Server 2008 Management Pack

As previously mentioned, management packs contain intelligence about specific applications and services and include troubleshooting information specific to those services. The SQL Server 2008 Management Pack is required for effectively proactively monitoring a SQL Server 2008 infrastructure.

To install the SQL 2008 Management Pack on an OpsMgr management server, first download it from the Microsoft downloads page at www.microsoft.com/technet/prodtechnol/mom/catalog/catalog.aspx?vs=2007.

To install the SQL Server 2008 Management Pack on the OpsMgr management server, follow these steps:

1. Double-click on the downloaded executable.

2. Select I Agree on the license agreement page and click Next to continue.

3. Select a location to which to extract the management pack and then click Next.

4. Click Next again to start the installation.

5. Click Close when the file extraction is complete.

Importing the SQL Server 2008 Management Pack File into OpsMgr 2007

After extracting the management pack, follow these steps to upload the management pack files directly into the OpsMgr administrator console:

1. From the OpsMgr Console, navigate to the Administration node.

2. Click the Import Management Packs link.

3. From the Select Management Packs to Import dialog box, browse to the location where the files were extracted and select all of them. Click Open.

4. From the Import Management Packs dialog box, shown in Figure 18.2, click Import.

5. Click Close when finished.

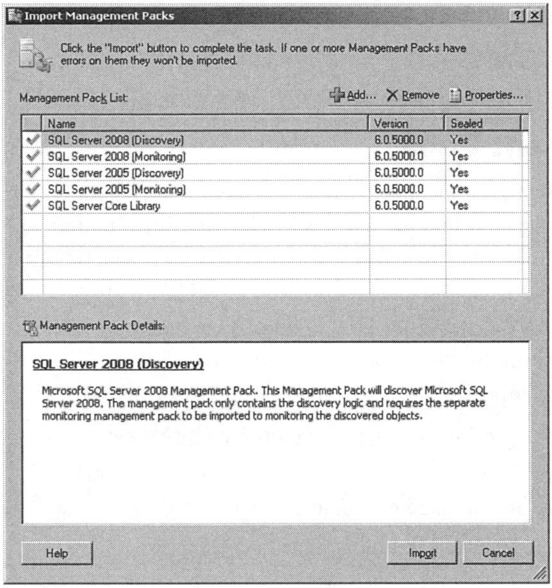

FIGURE 18.2
Beginning the SQL Management Pack import process.

> **Note**
>
> When managing a Windows infrastructure, it is a best practice not to down-load only the SQL Server Management Pack. Other management packs that should be downloaded and installed include: Windows Server 2003/2008 Base Operating System Management Pack and the Windows Server 2003/2008 Active Directory Management Pack.

Installing the OpsMgr Agent on the SQL Server

Installation of OpsMgr agents on SQL Server can be automated from the OpsMgr console. To initiate the process of installing agents, follow these steps:

1. From the OpsMgr 2007 Console, click the Monitoring node.

2. Click the Required: Configure Computers and Devices to Manage link.

3. From the Computer and Device Management Wizard, shown in Figure 18.3, select Next to start the process of deploying agents.

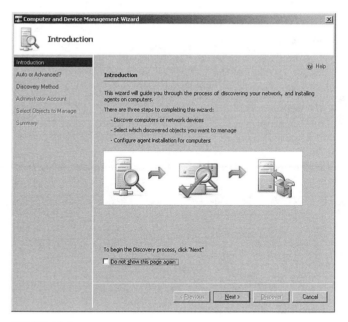

FIGURE 18.3
Deploying agents to SQL Servers.

4. In the Auto or Advanced dialog box, select Automatic Computer Discovery or experiment by doing a selective search. Note that Automatic Computer Discovery can take a while and have a network impact. Click Next to continue.

5. Enter a service account to perform the search; it must have local admin rights on the boxes where the agents will be installed. You can also select to use the Action account. Click Discover to continue.

6. After discovery, a list of discovered servers is displayed, as shown in Figure 18.4. Check the boxes next to the servers where the agents will be installed and click Next.

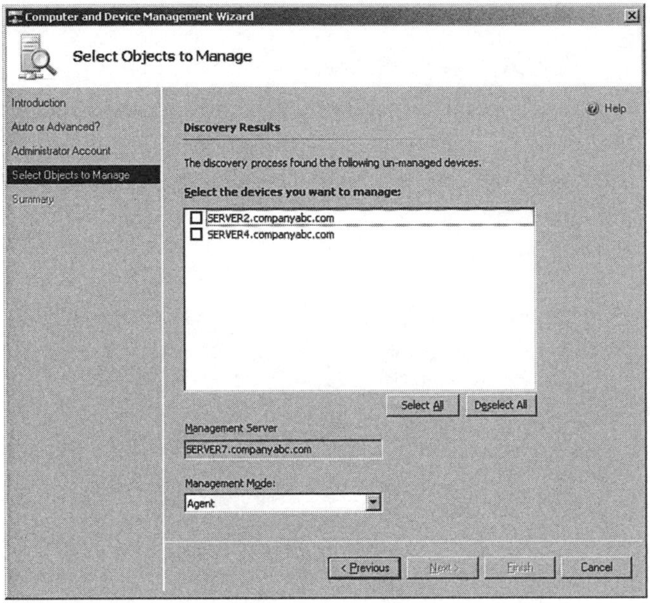

FIGURE 18.4
Selecting servers to deploy the agents to.

7. On the summary page, leave the defaults and click Finish.

8. Click Close when complete.

After completing the installation, you might need to wait a few minutes before the information from the agents is sent to the console.

Monitoring SQL Functionality and Performance with OpsMgr

After the management pack is installed for SQL Server and the agent has been installed and is communicating, OpsMgr consolidates and reacts to every event and performance counter sent to it from the SQL Server. This information is reflected in the OpsMgr operations console, as shown in Figure 18.5.

For more information on OpsMgr 2007, see the Microsoft website at www.microsoft.com/opsmgr.

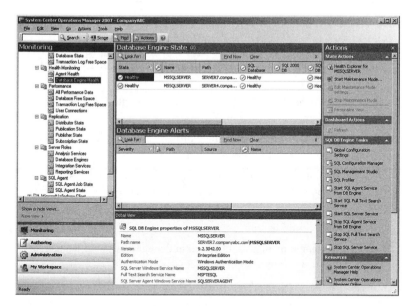

FIGURE 18.5
Monitoring SQL functionality in the OpsMgr 2007 console.

Summary

The built-in monitoring tools provide a limited amount of proactive monitoring by allowing you to configure events as necessary to alert operators. Built-in monitoring tools also provide a historical analysis through logs, greatly assisting the troubleshooting process.

System Center Operations Manager 2007 is an ideal monitoring and management platform for a SQL Server farm and has proven its value in proactively identifying potential server issues before they degrade into server downtime. OpsMgr for SQL Server provides the built-in reliability of the OS and allows for greater control over a large, distributed server environment. In addition, proper understanding of OpsMgr components, their logical design and configuration, and other OpsMgr placement issues can help an organization to fully realize the advantages that OpsMgr can bring to a SQL Server 2008 environment.

Best Practices

The following are best practices from this chapter:

- Examine the use of System Center Operations Manager 2007 for monitoring SQL Servers.

- Install the updated SQL 2008 Management Pack into the OpsMgr management group.

- Take future expansion and relevance of hardware into account when sizing servers for OpsMgr deployment.

- Keep the installation of OpsMgr on a separate server or set of separate dedicated member servers that do not run any other separate applications.

- Use SQL Server Reporting Services to produce custom reports using OpsMgr's reporting feature.

- Start with a single management group and add additional management groups only if they are absolutely necessary.

- Use a dedicated service account for OpsMgr.

- Monitor the size of the OpsMgr database to ensure that it does not increase beyond the bounds of acceptable size.

- Archive collected data.

- Modify the grooming interval to aggressively address space limitations and keep the database consistent.

- Configure OpsMgr to monitor itself.

- Satisfy regulatory compliance by leveraging OpsMgr's Audit Collection Services (ACS) for centralizing and auditing SQL Server events.

CHAPTER 19

Performance Tuning and Troubleshooting SQL Server 2008

Speak with any DBA and the conversation will eventually turn to performance issues and troubleshooting. This is because a large part of a DBA's time is spent on performance tuning and resolving issues that can ultimately affect a SQL Server system, database, or application. It is also worth mentioning that performance tuning and troubleshooting are such popular subjects simply because they are entwined with so many other tools and processes—making it one very large topic. Specifically, performance tuning and troubleshooting performance issues are iterative processes that include monitoring, troubleshooting, and adjusting. When troubleshooting SQL Server performance issues, it is helpful to have a baseline or a goal in mind, such as having a specific query execute in fewer than X milliseconds.

Performance tuning and troubleshooting can be viewed as a layered model. The layers consist of the hardware, operating system, SQL Server, database, and application. Each layer is dependent on the layers below for its performance, as illustrated in Figure 19.1. For example, if the hardware layer is not performing due to a lack of resources, this affects the performance of the database layer. It makes little or no sense to optimize the upper layers if the lower layers have not been optimized. It some cases, the application and database may be on the same level.

This chapter augments other performance-tuning and troubleshooting techniques covered in previous chapters including such topics as Performance Studio, Operations Manager 2007, Resource Governor, and Dynamic Management Views in SQL Server 2008, and Reliability and Performance Monitor in Windows Server 2008.

This chapter builds on the information already presented in the book with new concepts in performance tuning and troubleshooting, such as which key performance counters should be utilized when using Performance Monitor, how to analyze workloads with SQL Server Profiler, how to leverage SQL Server Database Engine Tuning Advisor to make index recommendations, and how to use Dynamic Management Views (DMV) and Extended Events.

Note

Throughout the chapter, there are references to collecting performance counters and various logs such as the SQL Server logs and Windows event logs. Although they are not covered in this chapter, Performance Studio and Operations Manager 2007 are great tools for collecting and keeping a long-term history of all the counters covered in this chapter. It is strongly recommended that you deploy and use either Performance Studio or Operations Manager 2007 to monitor the SQL Server 2008 infrastructure. Performance Studio is covered in Chapter 17, "Monitoring SQL Server 2008 with Native Tools." See Chapter 18, "Proactively Monitoring SQL Server 2008 with System Center Operations Manager 2007," to learn how to use Operations Manager 2007.

Appropriately, this chapter starts with troubleshooting performance at the lowest level, the platform.

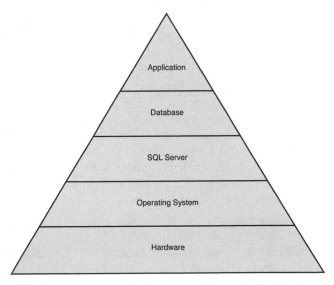

FIGURE 19.1
Optimization layers.

Platform Troubleshooting and Optimization

At the root of almost all optimization efforts are the hardware and operating system that a SQL Server instance resides on, which is collectively referred to as the *platform*. These areas are likely to be the first place to consider optimization as the SQL Server 2008 infrastructure rests on a solid platform. The initial efforts should focus on investigating disk activity, processor utilization, and memory usage. Typically, one of these three elements will be the likely cause for performance degradation.

This is where key objects and counters become a necessary part of the optimization and troubleshooting process. This section of the chapter discusses these objects and counters and how to leverage them when performance tuning and troubleshooting a SQL Server system. In addition, this section focuses on how to interpret the key counters against baseline thresholds.

This section should not be confused with Chapter 17, which also discusses the new Performance and Reliability Monitoring tool included with the Windows Server 2008 operating system. Chapter 17, specifically the section titled "Adding Counters with Performance Monitor," focuses on how to use the Performance Monitoring tool to monitor a SQL Server system, whereas this chapter emphasizes the key counters to utilize when performance tuning and troubleshooting.

Note

Both SQL Server 2008 and Windows Server 2008 include a remarkable number of objects and counters to choose from when conducting performance tuning and troubleshooting of a SQL Server system. Providing detailed information about what each counter does in this chapter would be great, but with so much other information to cover it is unrealistic. Readers who are interested in finding out more about a counter, however, can get detailed information about counters by enabling the Show Description option in the Add Counters dialog box and highlighting a specific counter to obtain a detailed explanation of it.

Platform Performance Measures

If the hardware is not sufficient for the load placed on it by SQL Server, performance issues and failures will result. In cases like these, it is best to first turn your attention to performance objects and counters included with SQL Server. With the use of the Performance tool and a set of key performance objects and counters, DBAs can learn whether the platform is experiencing performance problems. DBAs should capture the following counters at a minimum to understand how the hardware and operating system are performing. The common counters are broken down by memory, network, processor, and disk.

Memory Objects and Counters

- **Memory: Pages/sec**—The Pages/sec counter indicates the rate at which pages are read or written to disk during hard page faults. When memory pages are transferred to and from a relatively slow disk, the system will experience slow performance. The counter should be 20 or less on average, but preferably close to 0 would be best, although the number may spike. Add memory to the server if this number is continually high. If nothing is done, it is more than likely that SQL Server will experience memory pressure.

- **Memory: Available Bytes**—The Available Bytes counter illustrates the amount of physical memory available for allocation. There should be at least 100MB of free RAM. If there is less than 100MB, then consider adding more RAM to the server.

When these two counters indicate memory pressure, DBAs should look more deeply into the situation by reviewing the following counters associated with SQL Server memory:

- Process: Working Set
- SQL Server: Buffer Manager: Buffer Cache Hit Ratio
- SQL Server: Buffer Manager: Total Pages
- SQL Server: Memory Manager: Total Server Memory (KB)
- SQL Server: Buffer Manager: Buffer Cache Hit Ration
- SQL Server: Plan Cache: Cache Hit Ration

Network Objects and Counters

- **Network Interface: Bytes Total/sec**—The Network Interface: Bytes Total/sec counter identifies the rate in seconds at which data is passing though the network interface card (NIC). It is beneficial to track both input and output on all network cards installed on the SQL Server. For a 100Mbps network adapter the value should be below 6 to 7Mbps, and for a 1000Mbps network adapter should be below 60 to 70Mbps.

- **Network Interface: Packets Outbound Errors**—Indicates the number of packages that should not be transmitted because of errors. The expected value should be 0 at all times.

Page File Objects and Counters

- **Paging File: %Usage**—This counter indicates the amount of page file being used as a percentage. The value should be less than 70 percent.

- **Paging File: %Usage Peak**—The Paging File: %Usage Peak counter indicates the peak usage of the Page File instance based on a percentage. This amount should be either less than 70 percent or greater than the %usage value.

Physical Disk Objects and Counters

- **Physical Disk: % Disk Time**—The % Disk Time counter illustrates the amount of time the disk is busy as a percent. This should be less than 55 percent over any sustained period of time, although that number may spike occasionally. If this number is too high, consider adding drives to the array to increase the spindles and spread the load, adding additional channels, or changing the RAID version to a higher performance version (for example, RAID 5 to RAID 0+1).

- **Physical Disk: Avg. Disk Queue Length**—The Avg. Disk Queue Length counter exposes the number of disk requests that are waiting in the queue. According to queuing theory, this should be less than two over any sustained period of time or the queue could become backlogged. If this number is too high, then consider using faster drives such as 15K RPM and/or adding drives to the array to increase the spindles and spread the load, adding additional channels, or changing the RAID version to a higher performance version (for example, RAID 5 to RAID 0+1).

- **Physical:Disk Reads/sec**—indicates the rate of read operations on the disk. Poor performance is indicated by a value greater than 20 milliseconds. Average performance is acceptable when the value is between 12 and 20 milliseconds, and an optimal setting is less than 8 milliseconds.

- **Physical:Disk Writes/sec**—indicates the rate of write operations on the disk. If writes are high , it is possible that read latencies are also affected as of direct correlations with high write times. The average value should be below 100ms at all times.

If an organization is using a SAN as the storage device, then a DBA should leverage the performance monitoring tools included with the SAN for accurately troubleshooting disk issues. In addition, in order to isolate SQL Server I/O activity from all the other I/O activity on a system, use these SQL Server counters—SQL Server:Buffer Manager:Page reads/sec and SQL Server:Buffer Manager:Page writes/sec.

Note

When monitoring physical counters, it is recommended to not only include the total disk counters, however, each individual disk counter should also be included based on the drives in the system. This will ensure that the results are not skewed and it is possible to assess the exact disk which is causing the performance issue.

Processor Objects and Counters

- **Processor: % Processor Time**—The % Processor Time counter exposes the time the processor is doing actual work. This value is arrived at in a backward fashion by measuring the percentage of time the processor is idle and subtracting that from 100 to get the time the processor is busy doing work. This should be less than 75 percent over any sustained period of time, although it will spike occasionally. If this number is too high, consider adding or upgrading the processors on the server.

- **System: Processor Queue Length**—The Processor Queue Length counter displays the number of threads in the processor queue. There is a single queue for processor time even on computers with multiple processors. If this exceeds two per processor (that is, four on a two-processor server or eight on a four-processor server), consider adding or upgrading the processors on the server. It is common for queries without the proper indexes or with memory pressure occurring on a system to cause this spike.

- **System: Processor % Privileged Time**—This counter displays the percentage of time a process was running in privileged mode. The value should be less than 30 percent of the Total % Processor Time.

The example in Figure 19.2 shows a log for the recommended common performance counters. The nice part of this log is that the tool summarizes the average, minimum, and maximum for each counter.

Database Engine and Integration Services Performance Measures

Over time, DBAs learn that they need to approach each issue methodically if they are to resolve them successfully and in a timely fashion. For instance, if bottlenecks were not found while troubleshooting the platform based on the common performance objects and counters recommended, the next step is dissecting the issue at a deeper level like troubleshooting specific features of the SQL Server 2008, such as the Database Engine and Integration Services. It should be noted that each SQL Server 2008 Database Engine feature requires a slightly different approach and tools to troubleshoot performance issues.

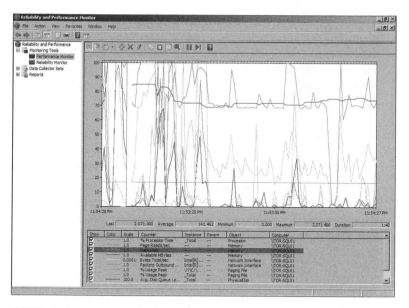

FIGURE 19.2
Performance log counters.

The Database Engine

There are a number of counter objects and counters that SQL Server 2008 uses to monitor the SQL Server Database Engine. Below, you will find the primary counters for performance troubleshooting of the Database Engine.

- **SQLServer:Access Methods Page Splits/sec**—This counter indicates the number of page splits per second that occur as the result of an overflow of index pages. The ideal threshold should be less than 20 per 100 Batch Requests/Sec. If the value is very high, I/O overhead might be occurring due to random inserts. In a case like this, evaluate the Fill factors or consider reindexing.

- **SQLServer:Access Methods Index Searches/sec and Full Scans/sec**—Index searches are used to start range scans, perform single-index record fetches, and reposition within an index. Full Scans/sec represents the number of unrestricted full scans, which can be either a base table or full index scan. The value of Index Searches/sec and Full Scans /sec should be greater than 1000. Obviously, these values will not be presented, if SQL Server is idle.

- **SQL Server:Buffer Manager Buffer Cache Hit Ratio**—Percentage of pages that were found in the buffer pool without having to incur a read from disk. The actual ratio is based on the total number of cache hits divided by the total number of cache lookups over the last few thousand page accesses. The counters start getting captured after a SQL Server system is restarted. If the Buffer Cache Hit Ratio is too low, you need to install additional memory in the SQL Server system. The value should be at least 90 percent and ideally at 99 percent. However, with large databases with extensive access, this number might be difficult to achieve. This ratio should be high, typically above 90 percent as you want SQL Server to read from cache instead of reading from disk. Potential problems could be based on memory pressure.

- **SQL Server:Buffer Manager Page Life Expectancy**—Represents the number of seconds a page will stay in the SQL Server cache. If low page life occurs, it could be due to memory issues, missing indexes, or high page faults. The threshold should be greater than 300. If it is less than 300, SQL Server is experiencing memory pressure.

- **SQL Server:General Statistics: User Connections**—Counts the number of users currently connected to SQL Server. Although there is no specific guideline on the number of users shown by the User Connections counter, the utilization of SQL Server is proportional to the number of users. The more users the server is supporting, the higher the load on the server.

- **SQLServer:General Statistics Logins/sec**—Total number of logins occurring per second that are not already pooled. The preferred threshold should be < 2.

- **SQLServer:General Statistics Logouts/sec**—Total number of logout operations started per second. The preferred threshold should be < 2.

- **SQL Server:Latches Latch Waits/sec**—Indicates the number of latch requests that could not be granted immediately. The preferred threshold should be calculated with this formula: (Total Latch Wait Time) / (Latch Waits/Sec) < 10. If the value is high, it is likely there is an I/O or memory bottleneck, which can be relieved by adding more RAM and I/O capacity.

- **SQL Server:Latches Total Latch Wait Time (ms)**—The Total Latch Wait Time identifies the latch requests that had to wait in the last second and presents them in milliseconds. The formula, which is (Total Latch Wait Time) / (Latch Waits/Sec) < 10, is similar to the formula for Latch Waits/sec and suggests that there are I/O or memory issues if the value is greater than 10.

- **SQL Server:Locks Lock Waits/sec**—This counter shows the number of lock requests that could not be satisfied immediately and required the caller to wait before being granted the lock. Ideally, the counter's value should be very low; the closer to zero, the better. Essentially, the lower the number, the shorter the transaction, which means the transaction is not causing a lock.

- **SQLServer:SQL Statistics: SQL Compilations/sec**—The number of SQL compilations per second is referenced by this counter, which indicates the number of times the compile code path is entered. Includes compiles caused by statement-level recompilations in SQL Server. After SQL Server user activity is stable, this value reaches a steady state. < 10 percent of the number of Batch Requests/Sec. Batch Requests/sec represents then number of TSQL command batches received per second.

- **SQLServer:SQL Statistics:SQL Re-Compilations/sec**—This counter identifies the number of times statements recompiled per second. A low recompilation rate is ideal, such as < 10 percent of the number of SQL Compilations/sec. In later versions of SQL Server, recompilations are statement-scoped instead of batch-scoped as they are in Microsoft SQL Server 2000. Therefore, direct comparison of the counter values between SQL Server 2008 and earlier versions is not possible.

Integration Services

Integration Services fundamentally depends on the performance of the queries; hence, optimizing queries and database access is critical to the performance of Integration Services.

Review the Progress tab information to see where the longest-running components are and then optimize them. This information can also be captured in the package and data flow logs.

Integration Services also includes a number of performance counters in the SQL Server:SSIS Pipeline object that can be used to troubleshoot performance problems. These counters are listed in Table 19.1.

Table 19.1   **Integration Services Performance Counters**

Counter	Description
BLOB Bytes Read	The number of bytes of binary large object (BLOB) data that the data flow engine has read from all sources.
BLOB Bytes Written	The number of bytes of BLOB data that the data flow engine has written to all destinations.
BLOB Files in Use	The number of BLOB files that the data flow engine currently is using for spooling.

Table 19.1   continued

Counter	Description
Buffer Memory	The amount of memory in use. This may include both physical and virtual memory. When this number is larger than the amount of physical memory, the Buffers Spooled count rises as an indication that memory swapping is increasing. Increased memory swapping slows performance of the data flow engine.
Buffers in Use	The number of buffer objects of all types that all data flow components and the data flow engine are currently using.
Buffers Spooled	The number of buffers currently written to the disk. If the data flow engine runs low on physical memory, buffers not currently used are written to disk and then reloaded when needed.
Flat Buffer Memory	The total amount of memory, in bytes, that all flat buffers use. Flat buffers are blocks of memory that a component uses to store data. A flat buffer is a large block of bytes that is accessed byte by byte.
Flat Buffers in Use	The number of flat buffers that the data flow engine uses. All flat buffers are private buffers.
Private Buffer Memory	The total amount of memory in use by all private buffers. A buffer is not private if the data flow engine creates it to support data flow. A private buffer is a buffer that a transformation uses for temporary work only. For example, the Aggregation transformation uses private buffers to do its work.
Private Buffers in Use	The number of buffers that transformations use.
Rows Read	The number of rows that a source produces. The number does not include rows read from reference tables by the Lookup transformation.
Rows Written	The number of rows offered to a destination. The number does not reflect rows written to the destination data store.

When you're troubleshooting a package executing within Integration Services, use event handlers to troubleshoot package execution problems.

One of the most resource-intensive and performance-impacting operations is sorting within a package flow. This consumes large quantities of memory and processing resources. This is true if the package contains either the Sort transformation or a query within the data flow that includes the ORDER BY clause. The IsSorted hint property can be used to indicate to down-level components that the data is already sorted and bypass the sorting overhead.

SQL Server Logs

There are other important areas to monitor when troubleshooting the SQL Server 2008 Database Engine, including the Windows application log and SQL Server error logs. The Windows application log contains application-level logs, including those from the SQL Server 2008 application. In addition, SQL Server and SQL Server Agent both log events to the SQL Server log. Because of all the information accessible through these logs, DBAs should make it a practice to review them when troubleshooting SQL Server 2008.

When more detailed information is warranted, DBAs should also inspect the SQL Server error log. In many ways this log is also more important to the SQL Server application. The SQL Log File Viewer allows you to view various logs at the same time, interleaving the log entries for easy correlation as shown in Figure 19.3. The figure shows the aggregation of the SQL Agent log, SQL Server log, Windows application log, and Windows security log. This presentation of data reduces the level of effort needed to troubleshoot problems because causative and related events can be analyzed in the same window.

You can access the SQL Server logs from the SQL Server Management Studio by selecting Management, and then SQL Server Logs.

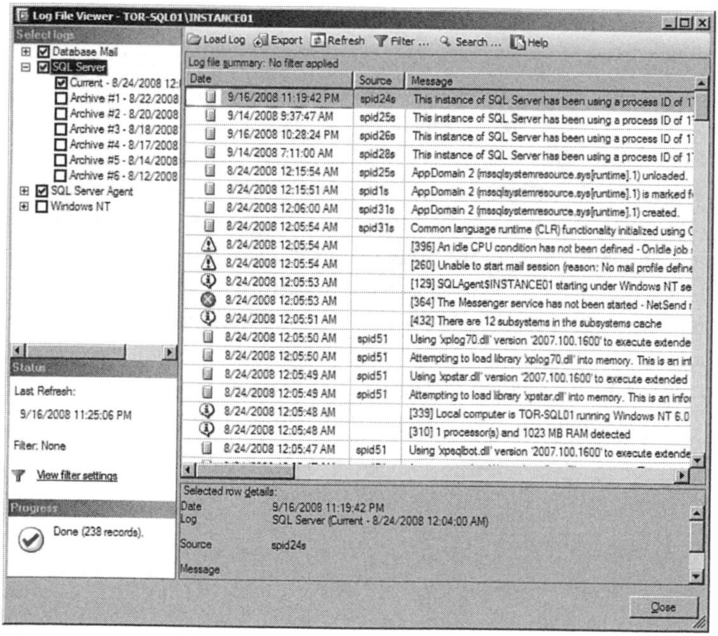

FIGURE 19.3
SQL Log File Viewer correlation.

Database Troubleshooting and Optimization

When thinking about database tuning, DBAs should have the mindset that database tuning will always be a work in process. Let me explain more by starting from the beginning. Database tuning can result in a tremendous boost in performance and address the root cause of many troubleshooting issues. When you're setting up a database, it can be difficult to know exactly what indexes to create because it may not be completely clear how applications will use the database or which stored procedures will be created. Database administrators rarely have insight into the types of queries and data access patterns an application will present to the database, especially if they have inherited a third-party database and application. On the other end, application developers rarely have any understanding about the inner workings of a database and may not even know precisely what their application is doing from a data perspective. Given the complexity of the situation, developing a fully tuned database for any given application straight out of development is extremely difficult.

Fortunately, it is possible to cut the Gordian knot by capturing the application behavior during actual use and then using that captured data to make tuning recommendations. There are two specialized tools to do this: SQL Server Profiler and the Database Engine Tuning Advisor.

The following sections conduct a basic optimization walkthrough to show how you can use the tools to optimize a database.

SQL Server Profiler

The SQL Server Profiler tool captures SQL Server 2008 events as they are generated on a SQL Server instance. The captured information, referred to as a *workload*, can be reviewed in the graphical user interface or saved to a trace file. The workload can be used to analyze performance or can be replayed to conduct N+1 testing. In N+1 testing, the workload would be replayed and the results analyzed. Adjustments would be made to the system, and then the workload would be replayed and the results analyzed again. This is repeated N times until finally all issues are resolved in the final N+1 time.

You can use the tool to

- Step through queries to troubleshoot problems
- Identify and optimize slow queries
- Capture traces for replay or analysis
- Conduct security audits of database activity
- Provide input to the Database Engine Tuning Advisor for database optimization

- Identify the worst performance queries
- Identify the cause of a deadlock
- Correlate a trace with data collected from Windows Server 2008 Performance Monitor

The SQL Server Profiler is invaluable for getting detailed insight into the internal workings of applications and databases from a real-world and real-time perspective.

Profiler Trace Templates

The Profiler tool can capture a wide variety of different event classes and data columns in the trace. They are easily specified in the trace templates.

The different default trace templates are shown in Table 19.2. Additional templates can be created for specific needs.

Table 19.2   **Default Trace Templates in the Profiler Tool**

Template	Template Purpose	Event Classes
Tuning	This template captures information about stored procedures as well as Transact-SQL batch execution. Use this to produce trace output for the Database Engine Tuning Advisor to use as a workload to tune databases.	RPC:Completed SP:StmtCompleted SQL:BatchCompleted
Standard	This is a generic starting point for creating a trace. Will capture all stored procedures and TSQL batches that are run. Use to monitor general database server activity.	Audit Login Audit Logout ExistingConnection RPC:Completed SQL:BatchCompleted SQL:BatchStarting
SP_Counts	Captures stored procedure execution behavior over time.	SP:Starting
TSQL	Captures all TSQL statements submitted to SQL Server by clients and the time issued. Use TSQL to debug client applications.	Audit Login Audit Logout ExistingConnection RPC:Starting SQL:BatchStarting
TSQL_Duration	Captures all TSQL statements submitted to SQL Server by clients, their execution time (in milliseconds), and groups them by duration. Use to identify slow queries.	RPC:Completed SQL:BatchCompleted

Table 19.2 **continued**

Template	Template Purpose	Event Classes
TSQL_Grouped	Captures all TSQL statements submitted to SQL Server and the time they were issued. Groups information by user or client that submitted the statement. Use to investigate queries from a particular client or user.	Audit Login Audit Logout ExistingConnection RPC:Starting SQL:BatchStarting
TSQL_Replay	Captures detailed information about TSQL statements required in case trace will be replayed. Use to perform iterative tuning.	CursorClose CursorExecute CursorOpen CursorPrepare CursorUnprepare Audit Login Audit Logout Existing Connection RPC Output Parameter RPC:Completed RPC:Starting Exec Prepared SQL Prepare SQL SQL:BatchCompleted SQL:BatchStarting
TSQL_Locks	Captures all of the Transact-SQL that are submitted to SQL Server by clients along with exceptional lock events. Use this troubleshoot deadlocks, lock timeout, and lock escalation events.	Blocked Process Report SP:StmtCompleted SP:StmtStarting SQL:StmtCompleted SQL:StmtStarting Deadlock Graph (Use against SQL Server 2005 or SQL Server 2008 instance.) Lock:Cancel Lock:Deadlock Lock:Deadlock Chain Lock:Escalation Lock:Timeout (Use against SQL Server 2000 instance.) Lock:Timeout (timeout>0) (Use against SQL Server 2005 or SQL Server 2008 instances.)

Template	Template Purpose	Event Classes
TSQL_SPs	Captures detailed information about all executing stored procedures. Use this to analyze the component steps of stored procedures.	Audit Login Audit Logout ExistingConnection RPC:Starting SP:Completed SP:Starting SP:StmtStarting SQL:BatchStarting

Although you do not need to use a template when creating a trace, when performance tuning, most often the Tuning template will be leveraged. It captures the events and columns that are used by the Database Engine Tuning Advisor. With SQL Server 2008, there are various ways to launch SQL Server Profiler. Any of these scenarios will do the trick and achieve the same result:

- Choose Start, All Programs, Microsoft SQL Server 2008, Performance Tools, and then SQL Server Profiler.

- Select SQL Server Profiler from the Database Engine Tuning Advisor Tools menu.

- From within SQL Server Management Studio, select SQL Server Profiler from the Tools menu.

Let's first examine the Database Engine Tuning Advisor before creating a trace or analyzing a workload with SQL Server Profiler. The two tools go hand in hand when conducting performance tuning and troubleshooting.

Database Engine Tuning Advisor

The Database Engine Tuning Advisor automates the process of selecting an optimized set of indexes, indexed views, statistics, and partitions and even provides the code to implement the recommendations it makes. It also provides recommendations on dropping existing indexes which do not make sense. To make your life even easier, you can use the tool to implement recommendations right from within the SQL Server Management Studio console.

The Database Engine Tuning Advisor can work with a specific query or can use a real-world workload as gathered by the SQL Server Profiler. The advantage of the latter approach is that the workload is generated based on actual usage, and the tuning recommendation reflects that.

The Database Engine Tuning Advisor is customizable and allows you to select the level of recommendation that the tool will recommend. This way, you can maintain the existing database design and make appropriate fine-tuning recommendations for just indexes. Or you can make the existing design flexible and then have the tool recommend far-reaching changes to the structure, such as partitioning.

Some of the new features associated with the Database Engine Tuning Advisor in SQL Server 2008 consist of improved workload parsing, enhanced scalability by using workload compression, integrated tuning, simultaneously tuning multiple databases at the same time, reducing production overhead by offloading tuning to a test server, command-prompt integration, XML support, and "what if" support.

The following sections walk you through running the Database Engine Tuning Advisor, starting with capturing a workload.

Capturing a Workload

The first part of the process to run the SQL Server Profiler is to capture a workload. So far we have been utilizing the AdventureWorks2008 database for all of our examples in this book. However, since the AdventureWorks2008 database is already optimized, let's first create a new Customer database and import customer-related data to create a workload against.

Creating a Database in Order to Capture a Workload

The Customers.txt file can be downloaded from the Microsoft's sample Integration Services website at http://www.codeplex.com/MSFTISProdSamples. The package sample name is "Execute SQL Statements in a Loop Sample Package"

To create the database and import the customer data, follow these steps:

1. In SQL Server Management Studio, in the Object Explorer, expand a SQL Server instance.

2. Right-click the Database folder and select New Database.

3. Create a new database called Customer.

4. To import data, right-click the Customer database and select Tasks, Import Data.

5. Click Next on the Welcome Screen.

6. Select Flat File Source as the data source.

7. Click the Browse button and provide the path to the Customers.txt file.

8. Check the Column names in the first data row check box, and then click Next.

9. In the Choose a Destination dialog box, select the Customer database if not already selected, and click Next.

10. Click Next to accept tables and views.

11. Click Next to execute immediately and not save the package.

12. Click Finish to run the import.

13. Click Close.

Capturing a Workload with Database Engine Tuning Advisor
To capture a workload with SQL Server Profiler, follow these steps:

1. Choose Start, All Programs, Microsoft SQL Server 2008, Performance Tools, and then SQL Server Profiler.

2. In SQL Server Profiler, select File, and then New Trace.

3. Connect to the Database Engine, which will capture the workload, in this case TOR-SQL01.

4. On the General tab of the Trace Properties window, enter **Customer Database Trace** for the Trace name.

5. Select the Tuning template from the Use the Template drop-down.

6. Check the Save to File box and select a location for the trace file.

7. Change the maximum file size to 100MB, although this example will not need this much space.

8. Select the Events Selection tab.

9. Review the events and columns that are preselected by the template you chose, in this case the Tuning template. Other templates select other events and columns.

10. Click Run to start the trace.

The trace window shows the server activity. By selecting any line in the trace window, you can review the event class, the duration of the statement (in milliseconds), the name of the database, the login name of the executing process, and even the detailed statement itself in the details window.

Now that the SQL Server Profiler is tracing the events on the server, a workload needs to be generated. Usually, you would do this during normal operations, and the trace would gather a production workload seamlessly. However, in this example, there are no normal operations. A series of query statements need to be executed to simulate a workload.

Launch SQL Server Management Studio, and then execute the following series of queries.

The first statement selects all columns from the database:

```
USE Customer;
GO
SELECT *
FROM dbo.Customers;
GO
```

The first statement returns too many columns, so the following query narrows the data to just the columns needed:

```
USE Customer;
GO
SELECT FirstName, LastName, EmailAddress, Occupation, State
FROM dbo.Customers;
GO
```

This statement still returns too many rows, so the following query returns just the rows of management:

```
USE Customer;
GO
SELECT FirstName, LastName, EmailAddress, Occupation, State
FROM dbo.Customers
WHERE Occupation = 'Management'
GO
```

However, the rows needed are just for California rather than all states, so the following query returns exactly what is required:

```
USE Customer;
GO
SELECT FirstName, LastName, EmailAddress, Occupation,
State FROM dbo.Customers
WHERE Occupation = 'Management' and State = 'CA';
GO
```

This final query should return 192 rows. This is a simple workload, but effective for a demonstration of the process.

The workload has been generated, so the next step is to stop the Profiler tool and save the workload for analysis. Follow these steps:

1. Switch to the SQL Server Profiler tool.

2. Select File, Stop Trace to stop the trace.

3. Scroll through the events and locate each of the query statements that you just executed. Note the duration, database, login name for each statement, and query for each event.

4. Close the SQL Server Profiler.

Now the workload has been saved and is ready for analysis.

Analyzing the Workload

Run the Tuning Advisor to analyze the workload as follows:

1. Choose Start, All Programs, Microsoft SQL Server 2008, Performance Tools, Database Engine Tuning Advisor.

2. Connect to the Database Engine, in this case TOR-SQL01.

3. In the Workload section on the General tab, select the file that the trace was saved to, in this case `Customer Database Trace.trc`.

4. Select the Customer database from the Database for Workload Analysis drop-down.

5. In the Select Databases and Tables to Tune section, check the Customer database. The configuration should look similar to that in Figure 19.4.

6. Select the Tuning Options tab. There are a number of tuning options for the advisor to use. By default, the advisor recommends index and statistical changes but can recommend changes to the physical design structures as well. Leave these at the default, which is to recommend index changes only.

7. Select Actions, Start Analysis to begin the analysis. In a real-world situation, the workload would be much longer, and an analysis would take a significant amount of time. In the case of this simple simulation, the analysis will take less than a minute.

> **Note**
>
> The Database Engine Tuning Advisor can make recommendations on clustered and nonclustered indexes, as well as indexed views and filtered indexes.

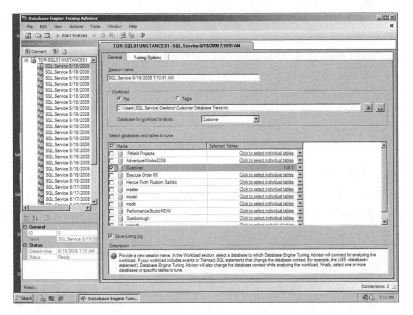

FIGURE 19.4
Database Engine Tuning Advisor settings.

Reviewing the Results

After the analysis, the Database Engine Tuning Advisor shows the Recommendations tab of the tool, which offers a set of recommendations for the Customers database based on the workload. This view is shown in Figure 19.5.

> **Note**
>
> The results, values and recommendations included in the upcoming examples may slightly deviate from your results due to system variables.

The top line of the recommendations window shows an Estimated Improvement percentage. In the case of the Customer database analysis, the estimated improvement is 58 percent. Clearly, a gain of approximately 58 percent is a big gain in improvement, so the tool is doing something useful.

Based on the database and workload, the tool recommends that a clustered index be created for the State and Occupation columns and a nonclustered index for Occupation, FirstName, LastName, and EmailAddress. It also recommends that statistics be created for State and Occupation as well as for FirstName.

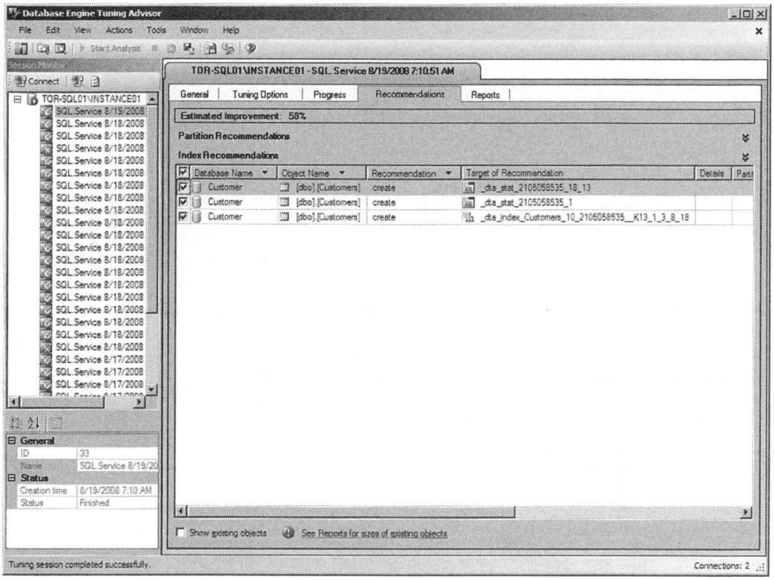

FIGURE 19.5
Database Engine Tuning Advisor recommendations.

For the recommended indexes, the tool shows the estimated size of the new indexes. This helps you plan for the additional space needed by the recommended indexes.

You can view the existing structures in the database along with the recommended objects by selecting the Show Existing Objects check box. This shows the existing nonclustered indexes that already exist in the Customers database.

The last column in each recommendation, Definition, shows the definition for the object. These recommendation definitions are hyperlinks that show you the query needed to create the object. This information assists in the implementation of the recommendations.

Selecting the Reports tab shows the tuning summary and gives access to a collection of reports to interpret the recommendations. Table 19.3 shows the summary of the analysis.

Table 19.3   **Database Engine Tuning Advisor Tuning Summary**

Description	Value
Date	9/05/2008
Time	10:51:48 AM
Server	TOR-SQL01\Instance01
Database(s) to tune	[Customer]
Workload file	C:\data\Customer Database Trace.trc
Maximum tuning time	47 Minutes
Time taken for tuning	1 Minute
Expected percentage improvement	58.56
Maximum space for recommendation (MB)	3
Space used currently (MB)	2
Space used by recommendation (MB)	2
Number of events in workload	103
Number of events tuned	103
Number of statements tuned	4
Percent SELECT statements in the tuned set	100
Number of indexes recommended to be created	0
Number of statistics recommended to be created	2

In the Tuning Reports section, select the Statement Cost Report from the drop-down list. The report shows the four query statements in the simulated workload. More importantly, it shows the percent improvement that the recommendations will have on each statement. For the more complex statement, the recommendations will generate an impressive 89.38 percent improvement in the performance.

Select the Workload Analysis Report from the drop-down list. The report shows the number of query statements in the workload and the net impact of the tuning recommendation on the statements. In the case of this example, three statements would have a net decrease in cost and one would have no change in cost. Cost is measured in the time needed to execute the query. Depending on the recommendation, the cost might actually increase for some queries, as shown in the report.

Other reports show various aspects of the workload usage, such as which tables are used in the database and which columns in each table. These are useful for understanding how the data is being used by the workload.

After reviewing the recommendations, you can apply the recommendations to the database.

Applying the Recommendations

The Database Engine Tuning Advisor tool provides several options for applying the recommendations:

- Cut/paste individual recommendations.
- Apply the recommendation from the tool.
- Save the recommendations to a file.

On the Recommendations tab, the Definition column of each recommendation is a hyperlink that pops up a window with the TSQL query needed to implement that specific recommendation. The window shows the specific code and has a Copy to Clipboard button to copy the code. This code can be pasted directly into the SQL Server Management Studio query window or any other TSQL query tool.

The easiest method of applying the recommendations is to select Actions, Apply Recommendations. This generates and runs the TSQL statements on the database to implement the recommended changes. They can be executed immediately or scheduled for a later date. Figure 19.6 shows the successful application of the recommendations to the Customer database.

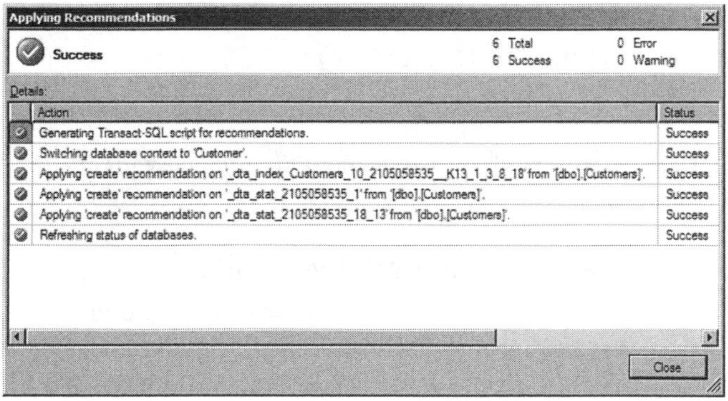

FIGURE 19.6
Applying the recommendations.

The tool also allows the recommendations to be exported to a SQL file for execution at a later time or for editing of the query statements. Select Actions, Save Recommendations to save the query statements to a file.

The saved recommendations for the Customer Database Tuning session are as follows:

```
use [Customer]
go
CREATE NONCLUSTERED INDEX [_dta_index_
➥Customers_10_2105058535__K13_1_3_8_18] ON [dbo].[Customers]
(
    [Occupation] ASC
)
INCLUDE ( [FirstName],
[LastName],
[EmailAddress],
[State]) WITH (SORT_IN_TEMPDB = OFF,
IGNORE_DUP_KEY = OFF, DROP_EXISTING = OFF,
ONLINE = OFF) ON [PRIMARY]
Go
use [Customer]
go
CREATE STATISTICS [_dta_stat_2105058535_1]
ON [dbo].[Customers]([FirstName])
go
use [Customer]
go
CREATE STATISTICS [_dta_stat_2105058535_18_13]
ON [dbo].[Customers]([State], [Occupation])
go
```

These statements can be preserved for documentation or to apply to other databases in a replicated environment.

Monitoring Processes with the Activity Monitor

The Activity Monitor was introduced and discussed, from a monitoring perspective, in Chapter 17. It is another tool that should be utilized not only for monitoring a SQL Server system, but also for troubleshooting and performance tuning. The Activity Monitor in SQL Server Management Studio graphically displays information about these measures:

- Running processes
- Resource Waits
- Data File I/O
- Recent Expensive Queries

Using this information, you can review activity, tune performance, and troubleshoot a SQL Server instance in real time. When troubleshooting and tuning, DBAs will probably find the most value if they dive into the Processes, Resource Waits, and Recent Expensive Queries sections. You can launch the Activity Monitor by right-clicking a SQL Server instance that you want to monitor within Management Studio and then selecting Activity Monitor. Alternatively, Activity Monitor can be invoked by clicking the Activity Monitor icon on the SQL Server Management Studio toolbar.

For example, the Activity Monitor shows a list of the worst-performing queries based on the Recent Expensive Queries section. Therefore, as a DBA, if you are experiencing performance issues based on a resource-intensive query, this is one of the first places you should check to verify if a bottleneck occurs. Execution in minutes, CPU consumption, physical reads per second, logical writes per second, average duration n milliseconds, and the plan count are displayed for each recent expensive query residing in the SQL Server cache. Additional detail can be found in order to assist with the investigation by right-clicking any query and selecting either Edit Query Text or Show Execution Plan. By doing this, you can view the entire query or display the graphical execution plan of the query from within one utility.

The Running Processes section should be utilized when there is a need to troubleshoot or terminate processes and user connections within a SQL Server instance. By right-clicking a Session ID, a DBA can either obtain additional details, kill the process, or trace the process in SQL Server Profiler.

Application Optimization and Troubleshooting

Application optimization and troubleshooting are typically beyond the scope of the database administrator. Application developers typically are responsible for the troubleshooting and optimization of applications, as they are fully aware of the database schema, stored procedures and/or queries developed in the database.

However, you may find that certain query statements are consuming resources or taking a long time. This is typically discovered in database troubleshooting and optimization. Therefore, you can take key information and assist developers in their tasks.

Query Analysis with Execution Plan

The Query Editor in the SQL Server Management Studio allows you to analyze the execution plans of queries to determine their specific breakdown and costs for each step. Use the tool to ensure that your queries are executing at an optimal level or if remediation work is necessary.

For example, consider the following query that runs against the Customer database, which was configured in the previous examples:

```
USE Customer;
GO
SELECT FirstName, LastName, EmailAddress,
Occupation, YearlyIncome, City, State
FROM dbo.Customers
WHERE Gender = 'F' and MaritalStatus = 'S' and
        YearlyIncome = (SELECT MAX(YearlyIncome)
FROM dbo.Customers) ORDER BY City;
GO
```

This query essentially selects the data for the highest-income single females in California and displays it sorted by city. To analyze this query, follow these steps:

1. Launch SQL Server Management Studio and open the Query Editor by selecting New Query.

2. Enter the preceding Transact-SQL query into the editor.

3. Select Query, Display Estimated Execution Plan.

Figure 19.7 shows the resulting graphical view of the query. The index scans are clearly the highest-cost items at 45 percent each. The sort is the next highest at 7 percent. Optimizing this query could significantly reduce the cost.

The following are some specific areas to look out for in the execution plan of a query:

- **Index or Table Scans**—They indicate that additional indexes are needed on the columns.

- **Sorts**—Sorting might be better done at the client or not at all.

- **Filters**—Filtering might require additional indexes, indicating that views are being used in TSQL or that there are functions in the statement.

Adjusting the query to smooth out the high-cost areas that the execution plan exposes can improve the performance of the application immensely.

If the database needs tuning, such as additional indexes, you can use the Database Engine Tuning Advisor to assist in that process.

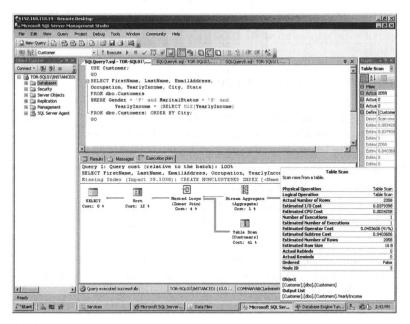

FIGURE 19.7
Estimated execution plan.

Query Analysis with the Tuning Advisor

Another method of troubleshooting a query is to use the Database Engine
Tuning Advisor to analyze the query. To do this, follow the steps based on
the query that was used in the previous set of steps:

1. In SQL Server Management Studio, select Query, Analyze Query in
   the Database Engine Tuning Advisor.

2. The query information is prepopulated by the SQL Server Management
   Studio, so select Actions, Start Analysis to generate recommendations.

3. Review the recommendations, which are to create a clustered index
   and to collect statistics.

4. Select Actions, Apply Recommendations to implement the recommendations.

5. Click Close to acknowledge the changes.

6. Close the Database Engine Tuning Advisor tool.

This procedure optimizes the database to run the query.

Back in the SQL Server Management Studio Query Editor, select Query, Display Estimated Execution Plan to see the difference in the query execution costs.

Cursors and the Lazy Developer

Another area to bring to the attention of application developers is the use of cursors. A SELECT statement normally returns a set of rows called a *resultset*, and the application has to work with the entire resultset. A *cursor* is a database object that lets applications work with single rows within the resultset. The cursor allows

- Positioning within the resultset
- Retrieving a single row at the current position in the resultset
- Modifying the row at the cursor position in the resultset

Although this feature makes the developer's job easy, cursors are resource intensive. The use of cursors is normally associated with lazy development practices. Extensive use of cursors can affect the performance of the database, and their use is generally frowned on.

This information can all be passed on to the application developers for recommendations on how to optimize the application.

Locking and Deadlock Detection

Locking allows users and processes to synchronize access to data and objects. This allows users in a multiaccess environment to prevent data from being corrupted. For example, when process A begins a transaction to modify a chunk of data X, the SQL Server Database Engine locks that data. If process B attempts to modify data X before the first transaction finishes, process B is paused (that is, sleeping). After process A finishes, process B is awakened and gets its lock on data X.

This process is all well and good, except when deadlocks occur. A deadlock condition occurs when two processes are mutually waiting for each other to free up locks on data. For example, consider what happens if process A locks data Y and then requests a lock on data Z. At the same time, process B locks data Z and requests a lock on data Y. Both processes are paused and waiting for the other to free up the lock—which, in theory, will never happen, and the processes will sleep forever; that is, the processes are deadlocked.

Resources that can deadlock include

- Locks
- Worker threads

- Memory
- Parallel queries
- Multiple active resultsets

Deadlocks can completely kill application performance and are unavoidable in a multiuser application such as SQL Server 2008.

Luckily, SQL Server 2008 has a mechanism for dealing with this condition. The SQL Server Database Engine runs deadlock detection to find and resolve these deadlock conditions. The deadlock detection is somewhat atavistic, basically selecting a deadlock victim and then resolving the situation by

- Terminating the ill-fated process's current batch command
- Rolling back the transaction, which frees all the locks it held
- Notifying the application with a 1205 error

The other, considerably luckier, process is then free to complete its transaction with the deadlock resolved. The deadlock victim is chosen on the basis of the least expensive transaction to roll back. This can be changed by setting the DEADLOCK_PRIORITY, which allows you or the application developer to force the selection.

The Database Engine executes deadlock detection on a periodic basis to locate deadlocks. The default interval is 5 seconds, but if a deadlock is encountered, the process triggers more often until it stops detecting deadlocks. Then it reverts to the 5-second interval.

Even though deadlocks are resolved, the delays that they cause affect performance. It is important to monitor SQL Server for errors and review the application code or logic if errors occur frequently.

Alternatively, the Dynamic Management View sys.dom_tran_locks returns information about active locks within a database. Each row represented in the result set displays an active request to the lock manager for a lock that has been granted or is waiting to be established. The following example illustrates the active locks associated with the AdventureWorks2008 database:

```
Use AdventureWorks2008
Go
Select * from sys.dm_tran_locks
```

Note

If a deadlock is found, you can kill the process by right-clicking the process within Activity Monitor and then selecting Kill.

Introducing Extended Events to Troubleshoot SQL Server

Extended Events, also referred to as XEVENTS, is a new high-performing diagnostic mechanism introduced with SQL Server 2008 that, as its name suggests, handles events. By leveraging the new event-based infrastructure, DBAs can define the events they want to monitor and apply them to targets. The numerous event concepts available allow this diagnostic mechanism to be highly customizable for pinpointing a problem. For instance, DBAs can look forward to quickly diagnosing runtime issues by analyzing, filtering, and responding on events generated by the SQL Server system. In addition, Extended Events is tightly integrated with the Windows Server 2008 operating system. This means visibility is available at a deeper level for diagnosing, troubleshooting, and obtaining event-based information beyond SQL Server.

Processing of events can be based on real-time (synchronous) or can be queued and processed later (asynchronous). Another characteristic of extended events is that a DBA can take action on events when they are executed. This provides flexibility if a deeper dive is required when diagnosing an issue. Finally, from a cost perspective, a single extended event is relatively cheap and does not consume a lot of system processes/resources, hence impact performance.

There was speculation that the SQL Server production team originally intended to leverage Extended Events strictly as a tool for internal purposes when diagnosing customers' problems. We are elated that they changed their minds and made Extended Events available to everyone.

DBAs should remember to exploit Extended Events when there is a need to troubleshoot the following situations: excessive CPU usage is experienced, SQL Server is not responding quickly to memory pressure, investigation of deadlocks is warranted, transient performance issues are taking place that occur for a short period of time, and correlating request activity with Windows ETW logs is necessary.

Event-Related Components and Terminology

- **Events**—An *event* is a program that monitors a specific point of interest within a code. Events are defined against modules and deliver a specific payload. The `sys.dm_xe_objects` dynamic management view provides a list of all available events within SQL Server system.

  ```
  This query depicts that SELECT * FROM sys.dm_xe_objects
  WHERE type = 'event'
  ```

  There are over 200 event objects to choose from in SQL Server 2008. Some examples of events include: Database Started, Checkpoint Has Begun, and SQL Statement Completed.

- **Actions**—*Actions* are programmatic responses that are bound to an event. Actions can capture and inspect data, store state information, aggregate event data, and write to event data. It is worth mentioning that the occurrence of an action takes place even before the event is available and can be consumed by a target. To become familiar with all the actions included with a SQL Server instance, query the sys.dm_xe_objects DMV. Some examples include: Collect Database ID, Collect Transaction ID, Collect Current CPU ID, and Run Time Statistics Calculation, Collect the Current Task Execution Time. SQL Server 2008 has 35 actions preinstalled and ready to use.

- **Predicates**—*Predicates* are essentially used as filters allowing a DBA to selectively capture event data based on specific criteria. Also, event costs are lowered with the use of predicates, whose filtering action takes place before events have an opportunity to get to their targets or prompt an action. Predicates can operate using local data or data from a global perspective. Predicates also leverage full Boolean expressions; therefore, they conform to True and False statements to filter events. Finally, predicates can also store state data in local context. As such, it is possible to set a counter to publish the number of times an event fires every nth time. In this way, sample data is collected systematically for analysis, which beats recording data for every single event.

- **Targets**—Most of the time targets are referred to as *event consumers*; they are synonymous. *Targets* are responsible for processing events and can be set up to do quite a lot, including kicking off a task and targeting event data to a file. In addition, targets can be set up to process a single event or a buffer, which is full of events. Data can be processed either synchronously or asynchronously and event data can be targeted to a file or can trigger a specific task, which is applicable to the event. Query the sys.dm_xe_objects DMV to obtain a list of all the targets available to a SQL Server system. For example:

```
Select *
From sys.dm_xe_objects
Where object_type = 'event'
```

SQL Server is shipped with 13 targets installed.

- **Types and Maps**—Types are found in packages and they define how events, targets, actions, and predicates will be interpreted. A map table maps an internal value to a string.

- **Packages**—A *package* is a logical container that maintains extended event information from a holistic perspective. A package consists of events, targets, actions, types, predicates, and maps. It can contain any or all the objects. For identification purposes, each package must have a unique name and GUID. For a list of installed packages on a SQL Server instance, query the sys.dm_xe_packages DMV.

Creating an Extended Event with DDL Statements

The new DDL Create Event Session allows you to add triggers, events, predicates, actions, and event session-level options all in one statement.

Based on SQL Server Books Online, the following syntax depicts how to create an Extended Event session.

```
CREATE EVENT SESSION event_session_name
ON SERVER
{
    <event_definition> [ ,...n]
    [ <event_target_definition> [ ,...n] ]
    [ WITH ( <event_session_options> [ ,...n] ) ]
}
;


<event_definition>::=
{
    ADD EVENT [event_module_guid].event_package_name.event_name
        [ ( {
                [ SET { event_customizable_
            ➥attribute = <value> [ ,...n] } ]
                [ ACTION ( { [event_module_guid].event_
            ➥package_name.action_name [ ,...n] } ) ]
                [ WHERE <predicate_expression> ]
        } ) ]
}


<predicate_expression> ::=
{
    [ NOT ] <predicate_factor> ¦ {( <predicate_expression> ) }
    [ { AND ¦ OR } [ NOT ] { <predicate_factor> ¦
        ➥ ( <predicate_expression> ) } ]
    [ ,...n ]
}
```

```
<predicate_factor>::=
{
    <predicate_leaf> | ( <predicate_expression> )
}
<predicate_leaf>::=
{
      <predicate_source_declaration>
    ⮕{ = | < > | ! = | > | > = | < | < = } <value>
    | [event_module_guid].event_package_name.
    ⮕predicate_compare_name
    ⮕( <predicate_source_declaration>, <value> )
}
<predicate_source_declaration>::=
{
        event_field_name | (
[event_module_guid].event_package_name.
    ⮕predicate_source_name )
}


<value>::=
{
        number | 'string'
}
<event_target_definition>::=
{
    ADD TARGET [event_module_guid].event_package_name.target_name
        [ ( SET { target_parameter_name = <value> [ ,...n] } ) ]
}
<event_session_options>::=
{
    [    MAX_MEMORY = size [ KB | MB ] ]
    [ [,] EVENT_RETENTION_MODE =
⮕{ ALLOW_SINGLE_EVENT_LOSS | ALLOW_MULTIPLE_EVENT_LOSS |
⮕ NO_EVENT_LOSS } ]
    [ [,] MAX_DISPATCH_LATENCY = { seconds SECONDS | INFINITE } ]
    [ [,] MAX_EVENT_SIZE = size [ KB | MB ] ]
    [ [,] MEMORY_PARTITION_MODE = { NONE | PER_NODE | PER_CPU } ]
    [ [,] TRACK_CAUSALITY = { ON | OFF } ]
    [ [,] STARTUP_STATE = { ON | OFF } ]
}
```

This Transact-SQL example illustrates how to create an Extended Event session based on capturing two events:

```
CREATE EVENT SESSION Create_Extended_Event_Example
ON SERVER
    ADD EVENT sqlos.async_io_requested,
    ADD EVENT sqlserver.lock_acquired
    ADD TARGET package0.etw_classic_sync_target
        (SET default_etw_session_logfile_path =
    ➥ N'C:\Create_Extended_Event.etl' )
    WITH (MAX_MEMORY=4MB, MAX_EVENT_SIZE=4MB);
GO
```

Leveraging the Extended Events Catalog Views

The following Extended Events catalog views should be exploited in order to ascertain the metadata that is generated with a event session.

- **sys.server_event_sessions**—When this catalog view is executed, it displays all of the event session definitions associated with a SQL Server instance.

- **sys.server_event_session_actions**—The sys.server_event_session_actions catalog view displays a row for each action on each event of an event session.

- **sys.server_event_session_events**—Returns information pertaining to each event in an event session.

- **sys.server_event_session_fields**—Displays information pertaining to each customizable column that was explicitly set on events and targets.

- **sys.server_event_session_targets**—Returns a row for each event target for an event session.

Leveraging the Extended Events Dynamic Management Views

The following Dynamic Management Views return Extended Event information for a SQL Server instance.

- **sys.dm_xe_map_values**—Returns a mapping of internal numeric keys to human-readable text.

- **sys.dm_os_dispatcher_pools**—Returns information about session dispatcher pools.

- **sys.dm_xe_objects**—Returns a row for each object that is exposed by an event package.

- **sys.dm_xe_object_columns**—Returns the schema information for all the objects and relative columns.

- **sys.dm_xe_packages**—Displays all the packages registered with the extended events engine.

- **sys.dm_xe_sessions**—Returns information about an active extended events session.

- **sys.dm_xe_session_targets**—Returns information about session targets in real time.

- **sys.dm_xe_session_events**—Returns information about session events.

- **sys.dm_xe_session_event_actions**—Returns information about event session actions.

- **sys.dm_xe_map_values**—Provides a mapping of internal numeric keys to human-readable text.

- **sys.dm_xe_session_object_columnsv**—Shows the configuration values for objects that are bound to a session.

Summary

Performance tuning and troubleshooting a SQL Server system, database, and related objects can be a daunting task. Fortunately, SQL Server 2008 and Windows Server 2008 contains the tools and instrumentation to allow you to easily conduct performance troubleshooting. These tools include Activity Monitor, Windows Server 2008 Reliability and Performance Monitor, SQL Server Profiler, Database Engine Tuning Advisor, Dynamic Management Views, and Extended Events.

Best Practices

Here are some important best practices from the chapter:

- Use the new Windows Server 2008 Reliability and Performance Monitoring tool to troubleshoot SQL Server objects and to capture performance baselines.

- Performance baselines should be captured on a regular basis so that when performance issues transpire, they can be correlated to the baseline to ensure that a SQL Server is running at a desired state.

- Use the SQL Server Profiler to gather workloads when troubleshooting SQL Server.

- Use the Database Engine Tuning Advisor to recommend indexes, statistics, and partitions based on the specific workloads.

- Use SQL Server Performance Studio and Operations Manager 2007 to automate the collection of performance metrics and to maintain a historical record of the data.

- Review the logs when troubleshooting SQL Server.

- Augment performance tuning and troubleshooting capabilities by using Dynamic Management Views to return server state information.

- Use SQL Server Performance Studio and Operations Manager 2007 to automate the collection of performance metrics and to maintain a historical record of the data.

- Leverage Activity Monitor to troubleshoot processes, resource waits, data file I/O and recent expensive queries.

- Utilize built in reports to quickly determine what areas should be looked at to improve performance.

- Extended Events should be exploited to correlate data from both SQL Server and the underlying operating system.

PART V

SQL Server 2008 Bonus Content

IN THIS PART

CHAPTER 20

Administering SQL Server 2008 with PowerShell

Windows PowerShell is Microsoft's next-generation scripting language. More and more server-based products are starting to come out with various levels of support for this new scripting language.

This chapter starts by providing an overview of what Windows PowerShell is. Then it describes some of the basic features of Windows PowerShell that SQL Server 2008 users should find useful. Practical examples later in the chapter demonstrate the use of these features with SQL Server 2008.

The chapter then reviews the features that have been added in SQL Server 2008 to support this new scripting language. Step-by-step examples of using Windows PowerShell for various OS and database tasks will be discussed.

The chapter closes by providing sources for more information and some best practices to follow when using Windows PowerShell.

Overview of PowerShell

Windows PowerShell is Microsoft's next-generation automation and scripting language. It is built on the Microsoft .NET 2.0 Framework.

Windows PowerShell was first released to the public in November 2006 as version 1.0. It was released as a separate install for Windows XP and Windows 2003, and shortly after, an install for Windows Vista was made available. Since its release, Windows PowerShell has been downloaded over 2 million times.

> **Note**
>
> From this point on, Windows PowerShell will be referred to as simply PowerShell.

When Windows Server 2008 was released, PowerShell was provided with the operating system. To have access to PowerShell, you simply had to add the Windows PowerShell feature through the new Server Manager.

> **Note**
>
> Currently, PowerShell is not available on Windows Server 2008 Core, because of the .NET Framework requirement. Server 2008 Core officially doesn't support the .NET Framework.

In 2008, Microsoft announced that PowerShell is now part of their Common Engineering Criteria for 2009 and beyond. That basically means that all of Microsoft's server products should have some level of PowerShell support. Microsoft Exchange 2007 was the earliest server-class product to come out with full PowerShell support. In fact, all of Exchange's administrative tasks are all based on PowerShell. The PowerShell functionality in Exchange is actually named Exchange Management Shell.

A preview (CTP, or Community Technology Preview) of the next version, PowerShell version 2, was released in November 2007, along with a newer build in May 2008. V2 introduces some things that didn't make it when v1 was set to release. It is possible that v2 will be officially released some time in 2009.

> **Note**
>
> PowerShell must be installed on a system before attempting to install SQL Server 2008. When installing Server 2008 on Windows Server 2008, a prompt will appear to install PowerShell if the feature isn't currently installed.

> **Note**
>
> For general information on PowerShell, be sure to check out the main PowerShell address: http://www.microsoft.com/powershell and also the PowerShell team blog: http://blogs.msdn.com/powershell.

Start Using PowerShell Now

The process of installing PowerShell will be reviewed later. PowerShell supports all the regular DOS commands and can run scripts written in any other language (the script engine specific to that scripting language still needs to be used). If any kind of scripting is currently being done, there is no reason why users can't start using PowerShell now, even if they are not using its vast functionality.

Common Terminology

Here are some of the common terms that are used when working with PowerShell:

- **Cmdlet**—This is the name given to the built-in commands in PowerShell. Cmdlets are the most basic component within PowerShell and are used when doing anything in PowerShell. Cmdlets are always of the form "verb-noun." Cmdlets also have arguments called *parameters*, and values can be passed to these.

- **Script**—With automation comes the requirement for scripts. This is as simple as putting a single cmdlet in a file, and then executing the file. In PowerShell, scripts will have the extension .ps1, and can be executed or invoked by simply calling it as ./my_script.ps1.

- **Pipeline**—PowerShell functionality in which a series of cmdlets can be combined together using the pipe character (¦). The output from one cmdlet is then piped to the following cmdlet for further processing.

- **Provider**—PowerShell functionality where a data store is presented to the user in a format similar to a file system. Some of the "core" cmdlets are typically used to do various tasks like creating items like files and/or folders, and so on.

- **Snap-in**—PowerShell functionality can be extended with the use of snap-ins. These are basically DLL files written in a .NET programming language such as C# or VB.NET. DBAs can load these snap-ins in their PowerShell session to add additional functionality such as additional cmdlets and/or providers.

- **Tab completion**—PowerShell functionality that allows the user to press the Tab key to autocomplete supported commands and parameters.

- **Aliases**—Shorter names that can be used for cmdlets. For example, some typical UNIX and DOS commands have had aliases for them created in PowerShell. These aliases map to the actual PowerShell cmdlet.

Object Based

As mentioned earlier, PowerShell is built on the .NET Framework. This implies that everything within PowerShell is object based. This is a familiar concept for anyone who is already familiar with the .NET Framework or .NET programming languages like C# or VB.NET.

It is an important concept to remember if you want to dive deeper into PowerShell. PowerShell provides many features, and it can also use additional features provided by other .NET assemblies.

Going into any more details is beyond the scope of this chapter.

SQL Server Management Objects (SMO)

SQL Server Management Objects (SMO) are a very useful tool to advanced users and developers when dealing with the automation of SQL Server 2005 and 2008. A lot of the features within SQL Server (core engine, agent, mail, and so on) are packaged up into easy-to-access .NET libraries that can be accessed from PowerShell.

Most of the functionality provided by the new PowerShell support in SQL 2008 is based on SMO.

As for SQL Server 2005, PowerShell can still be used to administer this version via SMO. The only difference is that the relevant assemblies must be loaded manually.

WMI

Windows Management Instrumentation (WMI) is a Windows service that provides remote control and management. PowerShell provides some built-in support for retrieving information via WMI.

Although the main goal of WMI may be to provide remote access, it can also be used locally, and can provide a wealth of information about a system. For example, WMI can be used to easily query disk space and installed patches. Examples of using WMI will be shown later in this chapter.

Installing PowerShell

As of Windows Server 2008, adding the PowerShell feature is easy using the new Server Manager application. With previous versions of Windows, PowerShell was a separate install, which required downloading and installing an external package.

To install PowerShell on Server 2008, start Server Manager, go to the Features node, then click Add Features, and simply check the box for Windows PowerShell, as shown in Figure 20.1.

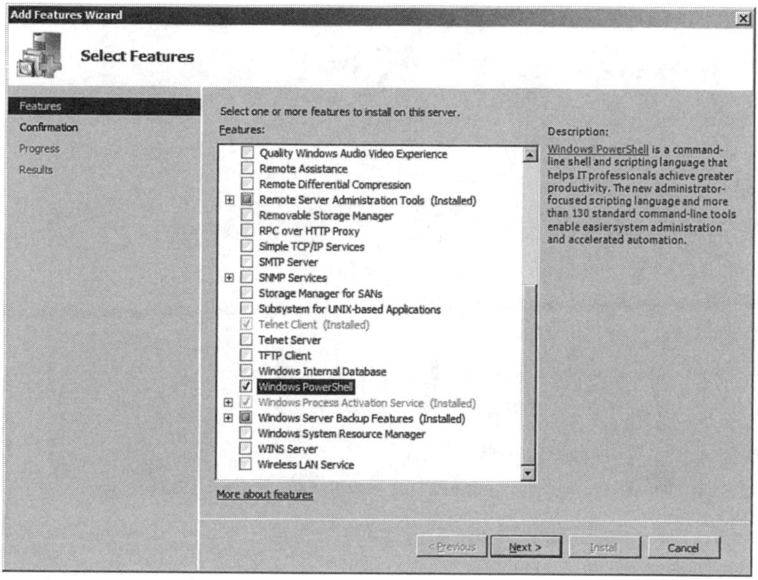

FIGURE 20.1
Selecting the Windows PowerShell feature.

PowerShell Console

You can accessing PowerShell directly from the Start menu, by opening
All Programs, and choosing Windows PowerShell 1.0, then finally Windows
PowerShell. The Windows PowerShell console will open as shown in
Figure 20.2.

> **Note**
>
> The prompt displayed in examples of the PowerShell console in this chapter
> has been changed from the default.

Scriptable and Interactive

PowerShell can be used as a scripting language, by creating reusable scripts
that can automate various tasks, and it can also be used interactively, by
opening up a console window and entering commands line by line.

In interactive mode, PowerShell is intelligent enough to know when a
command is not complete and will actually display >> on a new line when it
believes a complete command has not been entered.

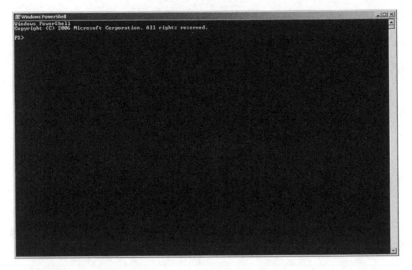

FIGURE 20.2
Opening the PowerShell console.

Default Security

After PowerShell has been installed, it is very secure out of the box. Here are two of the default security features:

- PowerShell cannot run any scripts. If you attempt to double-click on any .ps1 script, it will simply open the contents in Notepad.
- PowerShell cannot be accessed remotely.

Execution Policy

By default, PowerShell can only be used interactively from the console. This is part of the default security. To be able to actually run scripts, you must set the execution policy. The easiest way to set this is using the Set-ExecutionPolicy cmdlet.

```
PS>Set-ExecutionPolicy RemoteSigned
```

Basically, by using the value of RemoteSigned, PowerShell has been set to be able to run scripts that have been created locally, but if a script is downloaded from the Internet, for example, it must be signed.

> **Note**
>
> The details of the different execution policy settings that are available or the advantages/disadvantages of different possibilities will not be discussed here. Using `RemoteSigned` is one of the better trade-offs between function-ality and security for most users.

Profiles

As users become more and more familiar with PowerShell, they will typi-cally have customizations that they may want to save for the next time PowerShell is opened. PowerShell has several profiles that can be used to configure user and system-wide settings. All the possibilities won't be discussed here because this is beyond the scope of this chapter, but the system-wide profile is easy to access:

```
PS>notepad $profile
```

> **Note**
>
> On a new install, this file typically won't exist, so don't be surprised if there is a window that pops up asking to create the file. Adding commands to the profile is usually as easy as adding the exact same commands directly into it.

Built-in Help Features

As mentioned earlier, cmdlets are the most basic component of PowerShell. Three of these cmdlets are essential in attempting to learn PowerShell. Even advanced users may still use these cmdlets on a daily basis:

- `Get-Command`—This cmdlet is essential in discovering what commands can be used and what might be available on the system to help with a certain task.

- `Get-Help`—When looking for additional details, specifically on other cmdlets, this is the main cmdlet to use.

- `Get-Member`—Absolute beginners won't typically start using this cmdlet when first initiated into PowerShell, but for advanced users, and easier discovery, this cmdlet is very useful.

Let's look at each of these cmdlets in a bit more detail.

Get-Command

The Get-Command cmdlet can be used to get a listing of an entire list of cmdlets on the system, but it can also be used to get cmdlets that can be used for a specific task or purpose. For example, Get-Command alone in the console prints the entire list of available cmdlets available in the current console.

```
PS>Get-Command
```

For example, if this is the first time you have ever opened a PowerShell console, how do you write to the console? How about displaying something as simple as "Welcome to SQL 2008"? Something basic can be passed to Get-Command, such as the string "*write*":

```
PS>Get-Command *write*
```

What results is a listing of all the cmdlets that have the string "write" in any part of their name.

In addition, the last command will also display any applications and aliases (aliases will be discussed a bit later) that are found in the current user's path.

Now, PowerShell can be pretty smart. The sample that we just saw is actually a shortcut for something longer like this:

```
PS>Get-Command –Name *write*
```

Based on how the cmdlet is programmed, cmdlets can automatically assign a particular value to a parameter even when the parameter isn't explicitly typed out.

Originally we were looking for a cmdlet to display something on the console and found the cmdlet Write-Host. Let's try it:

```
PS>Write-Host "Welcome to SQL 2008"
```

Get-Help

The learning curve with PowerShell can be relatively steep. Sometimes you can find a particular command for a particular task, such as the Write-Host cmdlet in the previous section, but you might not always be sure how to actually use it. Write-Host was simple, but what if Write-Host had other useful features, or help was required for some other cmdlet?

Get-Help is a very useful cmdlet. Just doing Get-Help alone provides some default help information.

```
PS>Get-Help
```

Now, to get help on a particular cmdlet, use `Get-Help` and pass the other cmdlet as an argument.

```
PS>Get-Help Write-Host
```

That might not provide a lot of useful information; perhaps the `-Full` and `-Examples` parameters are more useful:

```
PS>Get-Help Write-Host -Full
```

Passing the `-Full` parameter gives a detailed description of the cmdlet and all its parameters (including what types of values they accept). For the more experienced user, the `-Examples` parameter is very useful, because it just gives some examples of using the cmdlet, which is an easy way to remember the syntax of a particular command.

```
PS>Get-Help Write-Host -Examples
```

> **Note**
>
> `Get-Help` works on other cmdlets, but it can also be used when looking for additional details on other concepts in PowerShell. To get a listing of the built-in help for various concepts in PowerShell, run the command `Get-Help about_*`.

Get-Member

Because everything in PowerShell is object based, some of the features that can be accessed are always visible. To find out more about a particular object, the `Get-Member` cmdlet can be used to look at all of its members (the more interesting members of a .NET object are usually its properties and methods).

Using something simple like "AdventureWorks2008" you can easily look at PowerShell's members (possibly without having to consult any .NET developer-focused documentation). "AdventureWorks2008" is a string, in other words, a combination of alphanumeric characters (that can include spaces). The following example is another way to display a string in the PowerShell console.

```
PS>"AdventureWorks2008"
```

PowerShell automatically recognizes this is a simple string and displays it.

A string can be easily displayed to the console, but what else can you do with a string object? In the .NET Framework, a string is really a `System.String` object. The .NET Framework provides a lot of functionality that can be used to deal with strings.

```
PS>" AdventureWorks2008"¦Get-Member
```

From the preceding command, more information is displayed now including `TypeName:System.String`, which confirms that this is a `System.String` object. One particular feature that `Get-Member` indicates is that there is a `ToLower` method that is supported by this particular object.

```
PS>"AdventureWorks2008".ToLower()
```

In this example, the `ToLower` method of the `System.String` object has been used to change the string into all lowercase letters.

PowerShell Scripting Basics

In the following sections, some of the basics of scripting with PowerShell will be covered. Hopefully this information will help you understand how PowerShell can be used in various situations to automate various tasks.

A Few Basic Cmdlets

The following is a list of a few basic cmdlets and how they can be used, with a brief example:

- `Get-ChildItem` (aka `dir`, `gci`)—Cmdlet used to list out child items in a provider. Mostly used to list out things like files and directories in a file system. Example: `Get-ChildItem *.ps1`

- `Select-Object`—Cmdlet used to retrieve only the specific properties. See `Get-Help Select-Object –Examples` for examples.

- `Group-Object`—Cmdlet used to group objects based on their properties. See `Get-Help Group-Object –Examples` for examples.

- `Sort-Object`—Cmdlet used to sort objects based on their properties. See `Get-Help Sort-Object –Examples` for examples.

- `Read-Host`—Cmdlet used to read input from the screen, usually from a user, before continuing. Example: `Read-Host "Enter a database name"`

- `Measure-Command`—Cmdlet used to measure how much time a particular scriptblock took to run. Example: `Measure-Command {Get-Command}`

- `Write-Host`—Cmdlet used to basically display output to the console. This cmdlet was covered earlier.

- `New-Object`—Cmdlet used to create an instance of a .NET (or COM) object. Examples will be provided later.

- `Get-Alias`—Cmdlet used to get a listing of the aliases on the system. `Get-Alias`, with no arguments, will list all the aliases configured on the local system.

- `Get-Content`—Cmdlet used to read the contents of a file. Typically, only text-based files are supported. Example: `Get-Content my_script.ps1`

- `Add-Content`—Cmdlet used to add or append content to a file. Example: `Add-Content my_file.txt "testing"`

- `Set-Content`—Cmdlet used to set the contents of a file (this will overwrite any existing content). Example: `Set-Content my_file.txt "testing 123"`

- `Start-Transcript`—Cmdlet used also with `Stop-Transcript` to record everything in the console to a specific text file. Example: `Start-Transcript`

Creating a PowerShell Script

Creating a PowerShell script is very easy. It is as simple as placing a few commands into a .ps1 script, and then invoking that script. Here's a simple example of putting the `Write-Host` cmdlet into a script and then running it.

```
PS>Write-Host `"testing`""¦Add-Content test.ps1
PS>./test.ps1
testing
PS>
```

In the preceding example, a `Write-Host` cmdlet was placed in a file named test.ps1, and then the file was invoked. The output resulted in the string "testing" being output to the script. Notepad or any other simple text editor could also be used to create more complicated scripts.

Note

Notice that the location where the script was created is not within the SQL Server provider, which will be discussed in more detail later. To move to the local file system, the cmdlet `Set-Location` or even the alias cd can be used to change to a particular location in the current provider or to change to a new one.

An example of a PowerShell script that directly applies to SQL Server administration will be provided later in this chapter.

Adding Comments

Adding comments to a PowerShell script is as simple as adding a simple # character at the beginning of the line. To comment out entire blocks of code, a # must be used on each line.

> **Note**
>
> There is another way to comment out blocks of code using something called a *here string*. This technique will not be covered in this book.

Variables

Strings and objects were already discussed earlier in this chapter. A very useful feature of PowerShell, and thus of SQL-PowerShell, is the ability to place objects into a variable. This allows you to run any kind of command and place any objects produced into a variable for later use.

Examples of using variables are presented later in this chapter. For now, a string can be easily saved as a variable.

```
PS>$var="AdventureWorks2008"
PS>$var
AdventureWorks2008
```

In the preceding example, the string was saved as the variable $var and then output to the script when the variable was simply invoked.

```
PS>$database=read-host "Enter a database name"
Enter a database name:AdventureWorks2008
PS>$database
AdventureWorks2008
```

The Read-Host cmdlet was introduced briefly already. In this example, the Read-Host cmdlet was used to read input from the console, and the information input was passed to the $database variable.

> **Note**
>
> When doing certain things in a script, a function, and even from the command line, the scope assigned to the variable or function determines how this variable will be seen by other scripts, functions, and so on. The details of scoping will not be discussed any further, but it is still an important concept to remember as one uses PowerShell more and more.

> **Note**
>
> See Get-Help about_shell_variable and Get-Help about_scope for more information and examples.

An example will be provided later in this chapter demonstrating that objects much more complicated than simple strings can be saved to a variable for later use.

Escaping Characters

Often a special character may be used, for example, in DOS commands, but PowerShell will try to interpret it differently. Take the example of the dollar sign character ($). PowerShell will normally try to interpret this as a variable:

```
PS C:\> $var="$5 dollars"
PS C:\> $var
 dollars
PS C:\> $var="`$5 dollars"
PS C:\> $var
$5 dollars
PS C:\>
```

The preceding example shows how the escape character, which is the backtick (`), is used to escape the dollar sign, so that PowerShell doesn't try to interpret the character literally as the beginning of a variable.

> **Note**
>
> See Get-Help about_escape_character for more information and examples.

Special Variable $_

In PowerShell, $_ is a special variable that represents the current object in the pipeline. When several cmdlets are piped together, this special variable will be used often. Several examples of using this special variable will be shown later in this chapter.

> **Note**
>
> There is also a special variable named $input, which also represents objects passed along the pipeline, but this will not be looked at in any further detail in this chapter.

> **Note**
>
> See Get-Help about_automatic_variables for more information and examples.

Joining Variables and Strings

The concept of objects was already introduced briefly. When dealing with simple strings, these can be easily added together to create a new one.

```
PS>$last_name="Doe"
PS>$first_name="John"
PS>$full_name=$last_name+", "+$first_name
PS>$full_name
Doe, John
PS>
```

In this example, two variables containing simple strings were defined, and they were simply added together to create a third variable, which was then displayed to the console.

> **Note**
>
> This kind of addition works when both variables are strings. An error may be returned.

An example will be provided later with the AdventureWorks2008 database where string variables from two different columns in the same table will be joined together using this feature.

Passing Arguments

There is a special reserved variable in PowerShell named $args. This can be used with scripts and functions, and represents any arguments passed to the script or function when it is invoked.

```
PS>Get-Content parameter.ps1
$args.count
$args[0]
PS>./parameter.ps1 1 2 3
3
1
PS>
```

In the preceding example, a two-line script is created, and then it is invoked while passing some arguments to it. $args.count gives the number of elements passed to the script, whereas $args[0] gives the first element only.

Later, an example of a PowerShell script that can do a database backup is provided. The example will be extended to show how a script could be used to accept an argument that would be the name of the database that the script will back up.

Using Param

A special construct, param, can be used to force how arguments are passed to a script or function.

```
PS>function test_param {
>> param([string]$arg1)
>> write-host "Argument 1 is $arg1"
>> }
>>
PS>test_param "testing"
Argument 1 is testing
PS>test_param -arg1 "testing"
Argument 1 is testing
PS>
```

In this example, param is used to specify that a parameter passed to this script will be a string object, and will be contained in the variable $arg1 for later use in the script.

> **Note**
>
> The biggest difference between using `param` or `$args` with arguments is when the number of arguments is known versus unknown. The `param` keyword should not be used when the number of arguments passed is not known.

> **Note**
>
> `[string]` is a shortcut in PowerShell where we are specifying that the argument, as in the preceding example, will be a string, and not something else like a number or integer. There are a dozen or so of these shortcuts in PowerShell, and they are typically known as *type accelerators*.

Arrays

To PowerShell, *arrays* are simply a listing of data. They can be used for various tasks, and can be created easily.

```
PS>$var="foo","bar"
PS>$var
foo
bar
PS>
```

In this example, an array is created with two values, and then it is simply invoked, which simply results in outputting each element of the array, one per line.

When an array is created, a reference can be made to a particular element of the array using a special "[]" syntax.

```
PS>$var[0]
foo
PS>
```

> **Note**
>
> The first element of an array is the element zero, therefore the first record in an array is retrieved by referencing the element id `[0]`.

The count property is also very useful as a property of array objects (remember: everything in PowerShell is .NET objects).

```
PS>$var.count
2
PS>
```

The count property is used to iterate through each element of an array.

> **Note**
>
> Arrays can also be defined in at least two other ways: with a type accelerator; [array]$var is an example (there are several type accelerators in PowerShell, but they will not be discussed further here), or using a notation like this: $var=@("foo","bar").

> **Note**
>
> See Get-Help about_array for more information and examples.

An example will be provided later where this feature of retrieving a particular element of an array will be used with the AdventureWorks2008 database.

Operators

Something that is commonly done both from the console and also in scripts is to compare two strings against each other. The most common operators are

- **Arithmetic**—When comparing numbers or integers, for example:

  ```
  5 -gt 4
  ```

- **Comparison**—When comparing strings, for example:

  ```
  "user" -eq "user"
  ```

In both of these cases, a Boolean value is returned (True or False).

> **Note**
>
> See Get-Help about_operator for more information and examples.

Conditional Statements

Often in scripting, some kind of decision must be made by comparing values before a script or set of commands continues.

Operators can provide a simple example of how conditional statements work.

```
PS>if("userA" -eq "userA")
>> {
>>    Write-Host "Equal"
>> }
```

```
>> else
>> {
>>    Write-Host "Not equal"
>> }
>>
Equal
PS>$user="userB"
PS>if("userA" -eq "$user")
>> {
>>    Write-Host "Equal"
>> }
>> else
>> {
>>    Write-Host "Not equal"
>> }
>>
Not equal
PS>
```

The preceding code provides a simple example and shows how interactive the PowerShell console can be. The >> character is simply PowerShell informing the user that the commands entered are basically not complete, and more input is required.

An example will be provided later using the AdventureWorks2008 database that will use a conditional statement to make a particular decision based on the results from evaluating a particular expression.

Functions

Quite often, as the usage of SQL-PowerShell increases, some efficiencies are gained by using functions. Functions are especially useful when creating things either directly in the console or in a script that are done on a regular basis.

For example, a long script may have been developed that contains several checks for the existence of a file, such as a long database filename.

```
PS>Function test {
>> param($user1,$user2)
>> if("$user1" -eq "$user2")
>> {
>>    Write-Host "Equals"
>> }
>> else
```

```
>> {
>>    Write-Host "Not equal"
>> }
>> }
>>
PS>test "userA" "userB"
Not equal
PS>test "userA" "userA"
Equals
PS>
```

Using the earlier example of comparing two strings, a function named test
was written, so if future comparisons are required, the typing requirements
will be greatly reduced.

Note

See Get-Help about_function for more information and examples.

An example is provided later where a function is used to create a quick reference for sending out an email via PowerShell.

Looping Statements

Often a script needs to loop through items and act on each. PowerShell
supports several looping constructs. Examples of the for and foreach
constructs will be demonstrated here. Others like while do exist but are not
covered.

```
PS>for($i=0;$i -lt 5;$i+=2){
>> $i
>> }
>>
0
2
4
PS>
```

The preceding example shows a for loop. The method to jump or how to use
a step is shown. A jump or step is indicated by the last part of the for loop
above, where $i+=2 is used. If $i++ was usedinstead, the output would be
each number from 0 to 5. Here's an example of using foreach:

```
PS>dir
    Directory: Microsoft.PowerShell.Core\FileSystem::C:\book
Mode                LastWriteTime     Length Name
----                -------------     ------ ----
d----         8/4/2008   11:29 PM            directory
-a---         8/5/2008   12:01 AM         53 database.csv
-a---         8/4/2008   11:27 PM          0 file.ps1
-a---         8/4/2008   11:27 PM          0 file.txt
-a---         8/4/2008   11:47 PM       1813 list.csv
PS>$contents=dir
PS>$contents
    Directory: Microsoft.PowerShell.Core\FileSystem::C:\book
Mode                LastWriteTime     Length Name
----                -------------     ------ ----
d----         8/4/2008   11:29 PM            directory
-a---         8/5/2008   12:01 AM         53 database.csv
-a---         8/4/2008   11:27 PM          0 file.ps1
-a---         8/4/2008   11:27 PM          0 file.txt
-a---         8/4/2008   11:47 PM       1813 list.csv
PS>foreach($each in $contents){
>> $each.name
>> }
>>
directory
database.csv
file.ps1
file.txt
list.csv
PS>
```

In this example, within the foreach scriptblock, any number of commands
could have been added, and these would have acted on each object.

Note

See Get-Help about_for, Get-Help about_foreach, and Get-Help
about_while for more information and examples.

> **Note**
>
> Another feature that can also be useful in scripting is *keywords*, such as break, continue, and return. These can be used in various circumstances to basically end the execution of conditional statements and also looping statements. See Get-Help about_break and Get-Help about_continue for more information and examples.

Filtering Cmdlets

PowerShell also has a few filtering cmdlets that are very useful:

- Where-Object (alias where and ?)—Participates in a pipeline by helping to narrow down the objects that are passed along the pipeline based on some specific criteria.

- ForEach-Object (alias foreach and %)—Participates in a pipeline by applying a scriptblock to every object that has been passed along the pipeline.

By looking at a few files and a directory contained within a test directly, the use of both cmdlets is easy to demonstrate.

```
PS C:\book> dir

    Directory: Microsoft.PowerShell.Core\FileSystem::C:\book

Mode              LastWriteTime     Length Name
----              -------------     ------ ----
d----        8/4/2008   11:29 PM           directory
-a---        8/4/2008   11:27 PM         0 file.ps1
-a---        8/4/2008   11:27 PM         0 file.txt

PS C:\book> dir|ForEach-Object{$_.Name.ToUpper()}
DIRECTORY
FILE.PS1
FILE.TXT
PS C:\book> dir|Where-Object{$_.PsIsContainer}

    Directory: Microsoft.PowerShell.Core\FileSystem::C:\book

Mode              LastWriteTime     Length Name
----              -------------     ------ ----
d----        8/4/2008   11:29 PM           directory

PS C:\book>
```

In this example, first the ForEach-Object cmdlet is demonstrated, where each object passed along from the dir command is acted on, and the name of the object (filename or directory name) is changed to uppercase.

After, the Where-Object cmdlet is demonstrated, where each object passed along is evaluated this time to determine whether it is a file or directory. If it is a directory (the scriptblock {$_.PsIsContainer} returns as True), the object continues along the pipeline, but in this case, the pipeline has ended.

> **Note**
>
> There is a ForEach-Object cmdlet and a foreach keyword, and these are not the same. Something useful to remember is that ForEach-Object would be used as part of a pipeline.

Formatting Cmdlets

There are several formatting cmdlets that are very useful:

- Format-Table (alias ft)—Cmdlet that prints out properties in a table-based format.

- Format-List (alias fl)—Cmdlet that prints out properties in a list-style format.

Some simple examples of Format-Table can be easily demonstrated.

```
PS C:\book\test> Get-Process powershell
Handles  NPM(K)     PM(K)      WS(K) VM(M)   CPU(s)
Id ProcessName
-------  ------     -----      ----- -----   ------
-- -----------
    548      13     54316      13192   164    25.55
2600 powershell


PS C:\book\test> Get-Process powershell¦ `
>> Format-Table -autosize handles,id
>>
Handles    Id
-------    --
    561  2600


PS C:\book\test>
```

In this example, the Get-Process cmdlet is used to list the properties of the powershell.exe process. By default, the PowerShell formatting subsystem determines what properties to display. Using Format-Table, the properties displayed can be modified. The –autosize parameter is used to left-align all the columns neatly.

> **Note**
>
> There are also Format-Custom and Format-Wide cmdlets. See the built-in help for each cmdlet for more information and examples.

Dealing with CSV Files

PowerShell provides two cmdlets that help greatly when dealing with files in the comma-separated value (CSV) format:

- Import-Csv—This cmdlet will read in a CSV file, and create objects from its contents.
- Export-Csv—This cmdlet will take an object (or objects) as input, and create a CSV file.

```
PS>dir ¦ Export-Csv file.csv
```

This is a simple example of outputting the contents of the current directory to a CSV-formatted file. Looking at the contents of this file will display information about the objects, though, instead of just plain strings like filenames, and so on.

```
PS C:\book> Get-Content database.csv
server,database
server1,database1
server2,database2
PS C:\book> Import-Csv database.csv¦Format-Table -AutoSize
server database
------ --------
server1 database1
server2 database2

PS C:\book> Import-Csv database.csv¦Select-Object database
database
--------
database1
database2

PS C:\book>
```

In this example, a simple CSV-formatted file was created, and then read in using the `Import-Csv` cmdlet. The `Select-Object` cmdlet is used to display only the database column.

> **Note**
>
> The `Format-Table` cmdlet is used above simply to format the data in a more appropriate format for this book.

Dealing with Dates and Times

Being able to do date/time calculations is very useful. Fortunately PowerShell provides all kinds of quick date/time calculations. Some of the more common tricks are shown in the following example:

```
PS>[DateTime]::Now
Tuesday, August 05, 2008 2:01:22 PM


PS>([DateTime]::Now).AddDays(-1)
Monday, August 04, 2008 2:01:44 PM


PS>
```

Here a .NET method is being used to get a new value from the original object. This is done in a "single step," in contrast to saving the object to a variable and then using the method on the variable. The use of a minus sign indicates that a value is being requested from the past.

Other common date/time methods include

- **AddHours**—Add/subtract based on a number of hours.
- **AddMilliseconds**—Add/subtract based on a number of milliseconds.
- **AddMinutes**—Add/subtract based on a number of minutes.
- **AddMonths**—Add/subtract based on a number of months.
- **AddSeconds**—Add/subtract based on a number of seconds.
- **AddYears**—Add/subtract based on a number of years.

-WhatIf/-Confirm **Parameters**

Several of the core PowerShell cmdlets support –whatif and/or –confirm parameters. The cmdlets that support these parameters could actually make system changes that cannot be reserved, such as deleting a file.

```
PS>New-Item -Type File -Path file.tmp

    Directory: Microsoft.PowerShell.Core\FileSystem::C:\book

Mode                LastWriteTime     Length Name
----                -------------     ------ ----
-a---          8/4/2008  10:33 PM          0 file.tmp

PS>Remove-Item -Path file.tmp -WhatIf
What if: Performing operation "Remove File" on Target
"C:\book\file.tmp".
PS>
```

Two new cmdlets are demonstrated in this preceding example: New-Item, used to create things such as files, and Remove-Item, used to delete or remove things such as files.

PowerShell in SQL Server 2008

This section covers what has been specifically added to SQL Server 2008 to provide support for PowerShell.

Adding PowerShell Support

> **Note**
>
> This discussion is based on SQL Server 2008 Enterprise Edition. SQL Server 2008 Express doesn't provide all the same features. For example, the Express version doesn't provide the SQL Server Agent functionality briefly discussed later.

Details were provided earlier on installing the default PowerShell application, and now the process required to install the SQL Server 2008–specific PowerShell features will be covered.

Either during the initial installation of SQL 2008 or afterward while changing the installed features, adding the SQL Server–specific PowerShell features is done by using setup. The feature Management Tools-Basic must be added as shown in Figure 20.3.

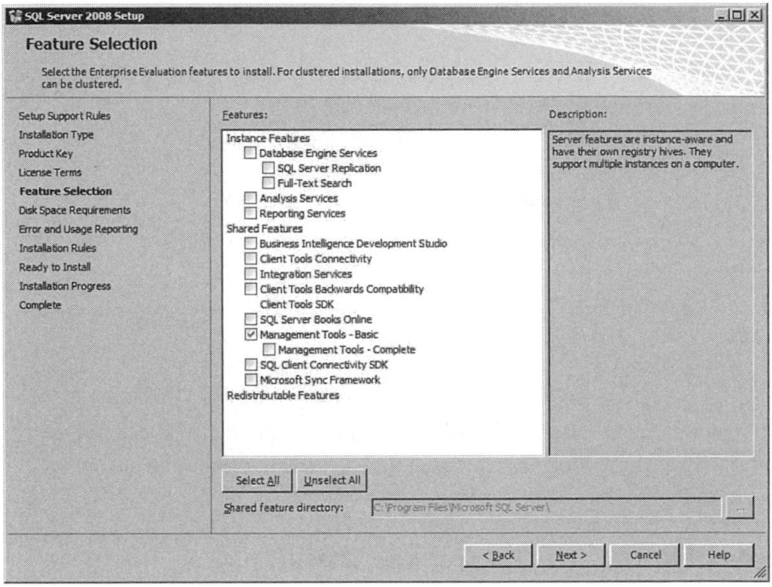

FIGURE 20.3
Installing the PowerShell features.

The Management Studio add-on is also required to get the PowerShell specific features installed. This specific feature adds:

- **Management Studio**—Graphical user interface for managing SQL 2008.
- **SQLCMD**—The utility that SQL scripters should already be familiar with.
- **SQL Server PowerShell provider**— The PowerShell-specific extra functionality.

Note

An added bonus is that you can install Management Studio by itself on either the server or another remote system, and be able to administer your SQL Server database remotely. Consideration should be given to whether the SQL Server is set up for remote connections, and the appropriate firewall changes have been made to the network and on the database server, if applicable.

Accessing PowerShell

Now that the SQL Server–specific PowerShell features have been added, there are two ways to access a SQL Server PowerShell session.

> **Note**
>
> From this point on, the distinction between PowerShell and SQL ServerPowerShell will be made. The details will be discussed shortly, but for now "PowerShell" is the basic or default PowerShell console, and "SQL ServerPowerShell" is a more restricted version of PowerShell that has all the SQL Server–specific PowerShell features basically packaged-in.

> **Note**
>
> Actually, there are three ways. When opening the default PowerShell console as discussed earlier in the chapter, you may notice that it doesn't include any of the SQL Server–specific PowerShell features that we are about to discuss. Going into the details here is beyond the scope of this chapter.

SQL Server PowerShell can be accessed in either of two ways:

- Opening SQL Server PowerShell via the SQL Server Management Studio by right-clicking on a particular object in the Object Explorer and selecting Start PowerShell, as shown in Figure 20.4. This way is handy because it provides a prompt in the SQL provider (which will be discussed shortly) in the location of the object that was right-clicked.

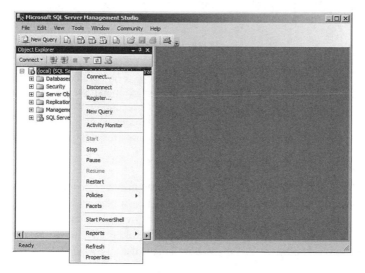

FIGURE 20.4
Accessing PowerShell via SSMS.

- SQL Server PowerShell can also be opened either from regular DOS directly or a regular PowerShell console by simply navigating to the appropriate location, as shown in Figure 20.5.

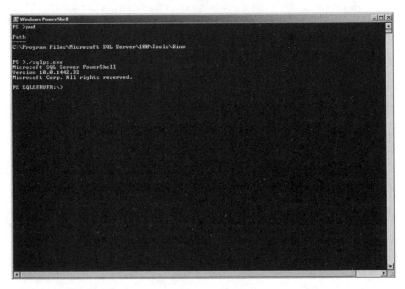

FIGURE 20.5
Accessing PowerShell using *SQLPS.exe*.

> **Note**
>
> When the shell is first opened, some errors may appear on the screen, which simply indicates that PowerShell execution policy should be set. This was covered near the beginning of the chapter. The execution policy for SQL Server PowerShell should also be RemoteSigned, at least.

SQL Server PowerShell

When you first get into SQL Server PowerShell, you might notice that this is a restricted version of the default PowerShell console. In other words, several of the core cmdlets are not available in SQL Server PowerShell, and others may not work exactly the same way. For example, invoking the Get-Command cmdlet alone with no other arguments will no longer list all the available commands.

Going into the details of why SQL Server PowerShell is restricted is beyond the scope of this chapter.

> **Note**
>
> Profiles were discussed earlier in this chapter. The SQL Server PowerShell minishell also has its own profile, and it can also be managed by simply typing `notepad $profile` in SQL Server PowerShell. A prompt may come up that the file cannot be found and asking if it should be created.

SQL Provider

Earlier in this chapter, the term *provider* was briefly introduced. The SQL team decided to implement a SQL Server provider. What this provides is a layout of the SQL object structure, which resembles that of a regular file system.

The SQL provider is used when accessing SQL Server PowerShell via SQL Server Management Studio: depending on what object is right-clicked to access SQL Server PowerShell, a prompt is opened up in the context of that particular object. Basically, the way certain commands work will also be affected by the current location within the SQL Server provider. Here are two different examples of being placed in different locations within the SQL Server provider. In the first example, the database AdventureWorks2008 was right-clicked within SSMS, as shown in Figure 20.6. In the second example, a specific table within the AdventureWorks2008 database was right-clicked, as shown in Figure 20.7.

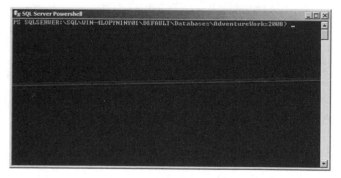

FIGURE 20.6
SQL Server provider at the database level.

Also, when the SQL Server PowerShell minishell is started by simply invoking `sqlps.exe` as seen earlier, a prompt is opened at the root of the SQL Server provider.

FIGURE 20.7
SQL Server provider at the table level.

Note

Some of the core cmdlets like Get-Item, Remove-Item, and New-Item are typically used within providers to retrieve, remote, and create items respectively. Within the SQL Server provider, creating items using the New-Item cmdlet is currently not supported. Other methods are required to actually create items.

Note

There are actually four SQL-based providers. Only the provider that provides functionality for the database engine itself will be looked at in any detail in this chapter. Please refer to the SQL documentation for more information on the other three providers.

SQL Cmdlets

A number of cmdlets are available in SQL Server PowerShell that are part of the basic PowerShell functionality. However, within SQL Server PowerShell, there are five additional cmdlets that are only available once the minishell is started (or if the snap-in is loaded manually, which will not be covered in any detail here):

- Invoke-PolicyEvaluation—A cmdlet that evaluates a SQL Server Policy Based Management policy (or policies) against a target server.

- Invoke-SqlCmd—A cmdlet that runs any regular TSQL command and any languages and commands supported by the sqlcmd utility, which may be more familiar to most users.

- Encode-SqlName—A cmdlet that helps to encode SQL Server identifiers into a format that PowerShell can use.

- Decode-SqlName—A cmdlet that helps to return the original SQL Server identifiers from a value previously given by the Encode-SqlName cmdlet.

- Convert-UrnToPath—A cmdlet that converts the SMO Uniform Resource Name to a SQL Server provider path.

Later, examples will be provided of using the core cmdlets, as well as the first two cmdlets just introduced in the preceding list.

> **Note**
>
> For more details on the three other cmdlets that will not be discussed, see the built-in help for more information and examples.

> **Note**
>
> The intent is to ship more cmdlets as part of SQL-PowerShell in the future after more database users become more familiar with SQLServer PowerShell.

SQL Server Agent support

PowerShell has also been integrated into the SQL Agent subsystem. In other words, jobs can be created that call PowerShell-specific commands to run.

Please consult the provided documentation for more details.

Step-By-Step Examples

This section provides examples of using PowerShell both for general tasks and for SQL Server 2008–specific tasks. Some of the basic concepts introduced earlier will be expanded upon with SQL Server 2008–specific examples.

General Tasks

Often there may be a requirement to send out emails containing particular reports and/or output from commands run.

To do so, features from the .NET Framework can be used via PowerShell to send out emails.

```
Function Send-Mail {
param([string]$To,[string]$From,[string]$Subject, `
  [string]$Body,[string]$File,[string]$SmtpServer)
  If($SmtpServer -eq ""){
    $SmtpServer = "FQDN of your SMTP server here"
```

```
}
$Smtp = New-Object System.Net.Mail.SMTPclient($SmtpServer)
$Message = New-Object
System.Net.Mail.MailMessage($From,$To,$Subject,$Body)
If ($File -ne "") {
  $Attach = New-Object System.Net.Mail.Attachment $File
  $Message.Attachments.Add($Attach)
}
$smtp.Send($message)
}
```

The preceding code could be entered into a script or directly to the console. If you type the code in the console, you must press the Enter key twice (once to close the function, and another on a empty line) before the PowerShell prompt returns.

In the preceding code listing, functionality from the .NET Framework has been used to get SMTP functionality. A function was used so that this code could be easily copied as required into new scripts, and so on. Calling the function is then very easy, and passing the command-line arguments is shown here (the PowerShell prompt can vary depending on whether the default PowerShell is being used or the new SQL minishell):

```
PS>Send?Mail  -To "end_user@user.com " -From "user@user.com" -Sub-
ject "Automated Email" -Body "Testing" -File
"C:\reports\report.txt"
```

> **Note**
>
> Some antivirus programs might need to be configured to allow the `PowerShell.exe` process (or `sqlps.exe`) to "talk" over the SMTP protocol port (TCP 25).

Scheduling Scripts

From time to time, it may be useful to have a method to schedule PowerShell scripts to run automatically based on a particular schedule (when the SQL Server Agent isn't available locally, for example).

The method to call PowerShell scripts can be viewed easily by simply typing `powershell.exe /?` from a PowerShell session.

```
PS>powershell.exe /?
...
PowerShell -Command "& {Get-EventLog -LogName security}"
...
```

Only a very small section of the text displayed is shown in this example. This command string can be used for scheduling regular PowerShell scripts. Using `sqlps.exe` works very similarly and its help can also be accessed by passing a slash (/) to the command.

Note

How do you know whether `powershell.exe` or `sqlps.exe` should be used when scheduling jobs? If anything relating to SMO and/or the SQL cmdlets are being used in the script, `sqlps.exe` would seem to be easier to use as all the prerequisites to using SMO and the SQL cmdlets are already loaded, which can save several lines in a script. As a reminder, the SQL minishell is limited in its functionality, so `powershell.exe` may be required in particular if you need to load some PowerShell functionality from another application, like Exchange, for example.

As discussed briefly earlier, SQL Server Agent can also be used to run scheduled PowerShell commands.

Common OS-Related Tasks

Let's start by looking at some more OS-related tasks, while keeping our focus on SQL Server–related tasks.

Let's check the status of the SQL Server service using the `Get-Service` cmdlet in the regular PowerShell console.

```
PS>Get-Service "mssqlserver"
Status     Name                  DisplayName
------     ----                  -----------
Stopped    MSSQLSERVER     SQL Server (MSSQLSERVER)
PS>
```

Note

When multiple instances are in use, the service name will be something like `MSSQL$INSTANCE01`. To start such an instance from PowerShell or even the SQL minishell, the following syntax would have to be used for the service name: `MSSQL`$INSTANCE01`. The dollar sign ($) character is being escaped so that PowerShell doesn't try to interpret this as the beginning of a variable when the string is parsed.

The service is stopped. Using the pipeline feature of PowerShell, the service will be started.

```
PS>Get-Service "mssqlserver"¦Start-Service
WARNING: Waiting for service 'SQL Server (SQLSERVER)
  (MSSQLSERVER)' to finish starting...
WARNING: Waiting for service 'SQL Server (SQLSERVER)
  (MSSQLSERVER)' to finish starting...
PS>
```

This demonstrates using the pipeline to chain commands together. Alternatively, Start-Service could have been used directly.

```
PS>Start-Service "mssqlserver"
```

The difference between the two methods demonstrates some of the power in PowerShell. When Get-Service is used, a service object is being retrieved. Using the pipeline, this object is being passed to Start-Service. Start-Service is built to basically accept input from the pipeline, and autofills its parameters based on what was input, and thus it knows to start the SQL Server service.

> **Note**
>
> SQL Server PowerShell could have been used, but since SQL Server wasn't started, Management Studio would not have been able to connect, and SQL Server PowerShell could not have been opened by right-clicking. PowerShell could have been used to start sqlps.exe, though, and then the Get-Service and Start-Service cmdlets could be used to start SQL Server. If SQL Server PowerShell was used by calling sqlps.exe directly from within a default PowerShell console, the SQL Server could still be started, but a connection wouldn't be automatically made to the default instance of the database.

Most administrators have probably already used the Windows Task Manager to look at the SQL Server processes. Perhaps it was to determine whether SQL seemed to be using too much memory, or some other issue. PowerShell provides the Get-Process cmdlet to look at running processes.

```
PS>Get-Process sqlservr
Handles  NPM(K)    PM(K)      WS(K) VM(M)   CPU(s)
  Id ProcessName
-------  ------    -----      ----- -----   ------
  -- -----------
    318      45    64156      44288 1554      2.03
  572 sqlservr
PS>
```

Another common OS-related task is to look for events in the Windows application event log:

```
PS>Get-EventLog Application -New 10
PS>Get-EventLog Application -New 10| `
  Where {$_.EntryType -eq "Error"}
PS>Get-EventLog Application -New 10| `
  Where {$_.EntryType -eq "Error"}|Select-Object TimeWritten
```

The preceding example demonstrates another useful feature of the PowerShell pipeline where we can join several commands together to get specific results. First, only the ten newest entries are retrieved; then a pipe is used to get only the entries that are classified as an error, and finally, only the TimeWritten property is displayed.

WMI was mentioned earlier in this chapter as a method for remote control and administration of servers. WMI is packed full of features that are useful for system administration. A few examples of using PowerShell's built-in WMI features are shown here.

- Getting a listing of all the fixed local logical drives:

  ```
  PS>Get-WmiObject -query "select * from Win32_LogicalDisk `
    where DriveType='3'"
  ```

- Getting a listing of all the fixed remote logical drives:

  ```
  PS>Get-WmiObject –computerName server -query `
    "select * from Win32_LogicalDisk where DriveType='3'"
  ```

- Getting a listing of all the local patches/hotfixes installed (the –computerName parameter could be used with a value to retrieve this information from a remote system):

  ```
  PS>Get-WmiObject Win32_QuickFixEngineering
  ```

Note

Remote WMI connections may require that appropriate firewall rules be open in the network and as well with a client firewall on the remote system. In addition, remote WMI queries must also be authenticated. By default, WMI queries will use the current user's authentication credentials. There are some scenarios where WMI authentication can be more complicated. Covering these scenarios is beyond the scope of this chapter.

That is only the beginning of all the things WMI can provide quick access to. Another common task is trying to find files or folders. The Get-ChildItem cmdlet can be used to recursively search through a directory structure. The following line is an example of searching for the location of the powershell.exe executable.

```
PS>Get-ChildItem c:\ -recurse powershell.exe
```

SQL Server–Specific Tasks

Before jumping into more hardcore SQL Server PowerShell features, let's briefly look at the SQL Server event log. Fortunately, these are simply text-based files, which PowerShell can read. The Get-Content cmdlet could be used to view the entire log, but instead, the Select-String cmdlet will be used to look for a specific string or pattern in the error log file. First, the current location will be changed to the SQL Server log directory.

```
PS>Set-Location 'C:\Program Files\Microsoft SQL Server"
PS>Set-Location (join-path $pwd "MSSQL10.MSSQLSERVER\MSSQL\Log')
PS>Select-String "error" ERRORLOG
```

The PowerShell prompt in the preceding example is simply a generic one, as the preceding commands would work both in the default PowerShell console and in the SQL Server PowerShell minishell.

An example of taking this further would be to retrieve all the errors that are in the ERRORLOG file. Using Get-Member and Format-List to look at the object outputted by Select-String, the date is hidden inside a string in the Line property.

```
PS >
PS>Select-String "error" ERRORLOG¦ ` foreach{$_.line}¦where{$_ -
match "^20*"}¦ `
foreach{
  $date,$time=$_.split()[0],$_.split()[1]
  [datetime]$($date+" "+$time)
```

The preceding example demonstrates looking for the string "error" in the current SQL Server ERRORLOG file. For all the lines that match, the Line property is passed along the pipeline. Next, based on some testing, it appears that we only wanted to search lines that started with "2008-". From that object, two values are retrieved: $_.split()[0] and $_.split[1]. These values are placed in the $date and $time variables respectively. From there, these are recombined, and a type accelerator is used to indicate that this is a date/time object, so any calculations against this value will be simplified. What is finally output is the timestamp showing when the error occurred.

Using the Provider

Using the SQL Server provider can be very handy in navigating the system. Starting PowerShell from SSMS, DBAs can easily find their way through different objects as if working with file and directories.

When the SSMS is used to start PowerShell at the server level, the databases are up one level, and from there things like tables and users, for example, can also be easily accessed.

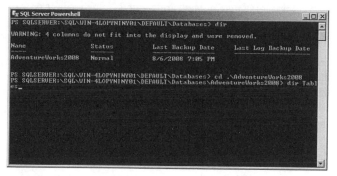

FIGURE 20.8
Navigating the SQL Server provider.

In the session shown in Figure 20.8, the user navigates to a particular database, and enters a dir Table command. The output from the last command would scroll beyond the current screen, so the only the command is displayed.

Creating a Database Table

Creating a database and a table are common tasks that a DBA may undertake. TSQL can be used with the Invoke-SqlCmd cmdlet to do this, but a demonstration on how to do this with the SQL Server PowerShell minishell using SMO is presented here to help better understand the new functionality that is available.

```
$my_db=New-Object Microsoft.SqlServer.Management.Smo.Database
$my_db.Name="my_database"
$my_db.Parent=(Get-Item ..)
$my_db.Create()
cd my_table
cd tables
```

```
$my_tbl=New-Object Microsoft.SqlServer.Management.Smo.Table
$my_tbl.Name="my_table"
$my_tbl.Parent=(Get-Item ..)
$my_col=New-Object Microsoft.SqlServer.Management.Smo.Column
$my_col.Name="my_column"
$my_col.Parent=$my_tbl
$my_col.DataType= `
  ([Microsoft.SqlServer.Management.Smo.DataType]::Int)
$my_tbl.Columns.Add($column)
$my_tbl.Create()
```

In the preceding example, some new objects are created, some of their properties are set, and some methods are called. You can search for the particular SMO classes used in this example to gain further information.

In the future, there may be something like New-Database and New-Table cmdlets that help to create a database and table, which would likely reduce the preceding code to less than five lines.

Doing a Database Backup

Another example that may be useful is how to do a database backup using SMO. Using the AdventureWorks2008 database, this can be done in a few lines.

```
$server=New-Object Microsoft.SqlServer.Management.Smo.Server
$backup=new-object Microsoft.SqlServer.Management.Smo.Backup
$file=new-object `
  Microsoft.SqlServer.Management.Smo.BackupDeviceItem
$file.Name="C:\backup\AW_DB.bak"
$backup.Devices.Add($file)
$backup.Database="AdventureWorks2008"
$backup.SqlBackup($server)
```

The preceding code could be copied into a .ps1 file, and it could be changed to accept two arguments. The preceding code could be modified to the following code snippet so that it will accept parameters from the command line.

```
param([string]$device=$(throw Write-Host "Device required"), `
[string]$database=$(throw Write-Host "Database required"))
Write-Host "backup of $database to $device starting..."
$server=New-Object Microsoft.SqlServer.Management.Smo.Server
$backup=new-object Microsoft.SqlServer.Management.Smo.Backup
$file=new-object `
  Microsoft.SqlServer.Management.Smo.BackupDeviceItem
```

```
$file.Name=$device
$backup.Devices.Add($file)
$backup.Database=$database
$backup.SqlBackup($server)
Write-Host "backup complete"
Get-Item $device
```

The changes in the preceding example introduce a new keyword, throw. Without it, error messages would be thrown to the console, but this might not help the end user to understand why it failed. For the purpose of printing feedback to the console, the Write-Host and Get-Item cmdlets were also added to provide a limited amount of feedback and to finally provide the details of the final backup file.

Then to invoke the script, two parameters would simply need to be passed to the script: the names of the file to back up to and the database to actually back up.

```
PS>$backup_to="C:\backup\AdventureWorks2008.bak"
PS>$db="AdventureWorks2008"
PS>./backup.ps1 $backup_to $db
```

As an example of using a conditional statement in the preceding script, perhaps a check could be done to see if a backup has already been completed within the last seven days. To accomplish this, this particular section of code would be added just before the first call to Write-Host.

```
param([string]$device=$(throw Write-Host "Device required"), `
[string]$database=$(throw Write-Host "Database required"))
If((Test-Path $device) –and (Get-Item $device).LastWriteTime `
  -gt (Get-Date).AddDays(-7)){
  "Done in last 7 days"
  Break
}
Write-Host "backup of $database to $device starting..."
(..remainder of script is not changed…)
```

In the preceding code, a conditional statement is added to accomplish the check. The AddDays() method was already briefly covered in this chapter.

Note

When using the param keyword, this section of code must be on the first noncommented line in all scripts. Otherwise, the PowerShell parser will return an error.

Again, using SMO isn't necessarily for beginners, but the good thing is that scripts can easily be created and passed around. The preceding example is the bare minimum required to do a database backup; several other options are available, and the preceding code would actually overwrite the backup each time it is run. There also isn't any error checking of any sort, which isn't the best way to develop scripts. Error handling is beyond the scope of this chapter.

Along with the New-Database and New-Table cmdlets that may come in the future, maybe a Start-DbBackup will be another good cmdlet to have available.

Checking Server Settings

From the SSMS, by right-clicking on the SQL Server node and then starting a SQL Server PowerShell session, you can open a console directly in the root of the default SQL Server in the example.

From here, information on the SQL Server is easily obtained. First, the location is set to the instance that is to be queried, and then an object representing the SQL Server is saved to a variable (this demonstrates the advanced features mentioned earlier where objects can be saved to variables). The properties of that variable can then be accessed easily.

```
PS>Set-Location SQLSERVER:\SQL\<servername>\<instance_name>
PS>$sql_server=get-item .
PS>$sql_server.Information.VersionString
```

Using the Get-Member cmdlet discussed earlier, other members of the object contained in $sql_server can be easily discovered, but this will be left as an exercise for the reader.

Note

This example demonstrates an important feature of the SQL Server provider: context sensitivity. In the preceding example, the current location was in the root of the SQL Server provider or database, and the command Get-Item . was used, where the dot basically indicates that we want an object that represents the current location in the provider. If moved to a different location, this would no longer work the same way.

Checking the Database Usage

Using the object that was retrieved in the $sql_server variable, a quick report of database usage can be created using the databases property of that object.

```
PS SQLSERVER:\SQL\<servername>\<instancename>> $sql_
➥server.databases¦ `
  Format-Table -autosize Name,@{ `
    Label=
"% Used"

Expression={[math]::round((($_.spaceavailable/1kb)/$_.size),2)}
  }
Name                % Used
----                ------
AdventureWorks2008  0.08
master              0.27
model               0.08
msdb                0.05
tempdb              0.8
```

Using the Format-Table cmdlet, all kinds of reports can be easily and quickly created. Some capabilities that haven't been discussed yet were used to create this report:

- **Calculated properties**—The values displayed by Format-Table can be calculated using scriptblocks. That allows the logic to be highly customized. These are laid out as follows:

```
@{Label="some text value"
  Expression={the scriptblock to evaluate here}
  }
```

- **Direct access to the .NET Framework**—The following line is directly from the .NET Framework:

```
"[math]::round(value,decimal)"
```

.NET functionality is being used to round out the numbers to the second decimal point.

PowerShell has special meaning for 1kb, 1mb, 1gb and 1tb, which all present the value of the counterpart in number of bytes, for example, 1kb=1024. The values can also be uppercase.

Getting Table Properties

Another common task is to get a row count of the tables in a particular database.

```
PS SQLSERVER:\SQL\<servername>\<instancename>\Databases\
➥AdventureWorks2008\Tables>Get-ChildItem .¦ `
  Sort-Object –descending¦Select-Object –First 10¦ `
  Format-Table –autosize Name,RowCount
```

> **Note**
>
> An easy-to-remember alias for Get-ChildItem is basically dir.

In the preceding example, using the AdventureWorks2008 database, the top ten tables with the highest row count value are returned.

> **Note**
>
> The preceding example shows how many features are packaged within PowerShell, which not only applies to SQL tables, but all .NET objects. Simply doing a Get-Item on a particular table only returns the default properties of Schema, Name, and Created. Piping something like Get-Item [table_name] to either Format-Table * or Get-Member will expose all the properties available for a particular object.

Cmdlet Example: Invoke-SqlCmd

The Invoke-SqlCmd cmdlet was already briefly mentioned. It is likely going to be the most commonly used cmdlet currently provided. Here is a simple example of using the cmdlet.

```
Invoke-sqlcmd –query "exec sp_help"
```

Using Invoke-SqlCmd, you can simply pass any TSQL-based query as a value to the cmdlet. The preceding basic example is provided by running a basic built-in stored procedure: sp_help.

This demonstrates several important things, especially how powerful the provider can be. Based on the location in the SQL provider, some of our values passed to the cmdlet were automatically provided to the cmdlet by the provider itself: The server and database to query weren't required in the command line.

Let's take this example a bit further and do a few extra things with it.

First, this cmdlet can accept input from the pipeline.

```
"exec sp_help"¦ForEach-Object{Invoke-SqlCmd $_}
```

The above demonstrates a few more things that have already been discussed: the ForEach-Object cmdlet, the special variable $_, and also how parameters can automatically match values to parameters even when the parameter name isn't explicitly added to the command entered.

The sp_help stored procedure provides a lot of information. What if only the extended stored procedures were required?

Using Get-Member, the members from this particular query were inspected, and it was determined that the Object_type property was the value that indicated what kind of stored procedure was being dealt with.

Note

A little trick when using Get-Member to understand what an object looks like is to prepend our pipeline with a simple comma.

For example, something as simple as:

```
"exec sp_help"|ForEach-Object{Invoke-SqlCmd $_}|Get-Member
```

versus:

```
"exec sp_help"|ForEach-Object{Invoke-SqlCmd $_}|Get-Member
```

The latter will provide us with the members of the object that we are dealing with, but it's much, much faster when dealing with a large collection of objects.

The query to get only extended SPs is now the following:

```
"exec sp_help"|ForEach-Object{Invoke-SqlCmd $_}| `
  Where{$_.Object_type –eq "extended stored proc"}|Select Name
```

Finally, the output consists only of extended stored procedures.

Cmdlet Example: Invoke-PolicyEvaluation

Another one of the provided cmdlets is Invoke-PolicyEvaluation. This cmdlet is used to specify a SQL Server Policy-Based Management policy (or policies) that will be evaluated against the target server. You can easily cycle through all of the available policies and evaluate each one, or simply provide a list of policies to evaluate separated by a comma.

```
PS C:\Program Files\Microsoft SQL Server\100\tools\Policies
➥\DatabaseEngine\1033>
  Invoke-PolicyEvaluation -policy `
   ".\Database Status.xml" -targetserver "nb517949\sqlexpress"
```

The preceding command will return the output to the console of the result of the policy evaluation. By default, the particular policy passed to the cmdlet is only checked. In other words, by default, properties won't actually be changed so that they are now compliant with the policy.

Joining Columns

Quite often, databases will provide a table for users. Frequently, these users will have their last name and first name in separate columns. Because these are typically simple strings, a feature, already discussed, allows two strings to be easily joined together.

The following code snippet shows how two columns from the AdventureWorks 2008 database are easily joined together from within the SQL minishell.

```
PS SQLSERVER:\SQL\WIN-4LOPYNINY01\DEFAULT\Databases\
➥AdventureWorks2008\Tables> I
nvoke-SqlCmd "Select * from Person.Person"¦ `
   Select-Object -First 10¦ForEach-
Object{$_.LastName + ", " + $_.FirstName}
```

Here, the first ten records are being selected, and then the LastName and FirstName values are being combined together.

Retrieving an Entry

On occasion, getting a particular entry from a table may be required. When the following code snippet is run, an array will be automatically returned.

```
PS SQLSERVER:\SQL\WIN-4LOPYNINY01\DEFAULT\Databases\
➥AdventureWorks2008\Tables> I
nvoke-SqlCmd "Select * from Person.Person"
```

PowerShell provides a simple way to look at particular elements within an array. In the following examples, entry 100 is being returned and then entries 95 to 105.

```
PS SQLSERVER:\SQL\WIN-4LOPYNINY01\DEFAULT\Databases\
➥AdventureWorks2008\Tables> (I
nvoke-SqlCmd "Select * from Person.Person")[100]
PS SQLSERVER:\SQL\WIN-4LOPYNINY01\DEFAULT\Databases\
➥AdventureWorks2008\Tables> (I
nvoke-SqlCmd "Select * from Person.Person")[95..105]
```

> **Note**
>
> The first element of an array is the element zero, therefore the first record in an array is retrieved by referencing the element id [0].

Summary

This chapter provided an overview of PowerShell and how it has been specifically implemented in SQL Server 2008.

Microsoft is putting a lot of effort into integrating PowerShell into all of its server-based products.

PowerShell support in SQL Server 2008 still has a way to go before PowerShell could ever be considered as the main scripting language.

It is definitely good to start learning more about PowerShell, and what you learn will definitely help when dealing with other PowerShell-enabled server products.

Best Practices

The following are best practices from this chapter:

- Start using PowerShell now. It will work with all kinds of other scripting languages.

- Do set the execution policy to RemotedSigned at least (AllSigned could be considered even more secure).

- Use functions when possible, to help keep scripts more compact.

- Remember that functions can also be added to the profile so that they are available the next time PowerShell is started.

- When scripting, add comments and do not use aliases.

- Use the SQLSERVER:\SQL folder to start paths that can represent any object that is supported by the SMO object model.

- Use the SQLSERVER:\SQLPolicy folder to execute Policy Based Management objects such as policies, facets, and so on.

- By default, system objects will not be listed when using Get-ChildItem or dir. The –force parameter can be used to view them.

CHAPTER 21

Consolidating and Virtualizing SQL Server 2008 with Hyper-V

More and more organizations are making the move to SQL Server because of an increase in the number of both Microsoft applications and line-of-business applications that call for SQL Server as the back-end database platform. Currently, many DBAs install a SQL Server instance every time their organization requires a SQL Server database, resulting in a proliferation of SQL Server installations within the infrastructure.

Take, for example, a DBA who installs a dedicated SQL Server installation to support databases associated with SharePoint, Symantec Enterprise Vault, and an antivirus application. Most likely, three independent SQL Server installations are not required, especially if each application is being underutilized. This action gets the job done, but it also translates into high costs for organizations in many areas including, but not limited to, hardware, licensing, power, cooling, management, and maintenance.

In an effort to help organizations reduce cost and even simplify their infrastructure while managing even larger workloads on their systems, Microsoft invites organizations to consolidate and/or virtualize on fewer systems using Hyper-V, a product introduced with Microsoft Windows Server 2008. A proliferation of SQL Server within the infrastructure is known as SQL Server *"sprawl"*.

Hyper-V is a long-awaited virtualization technology that has been much anticipated by Microsoft and the public. It is rumored to be the technology that will also help Microsoft leap past rival virtual server technologies like EMC's VMware.

Although Microsoft has had a virtual server technology for a few years, its features and capabilities have always lagged behind those of its competitors. Windows Server 2008 was written to provide enhanced virtualization technologies through a rewrite of the Windows kernel itself to support virtual server capabilities equal to, if not better than, other options on the marketplace.

This chapter focuses on consolidating and virtualizing SQL Server 2008 with Windows Server 2008 Hyper-V.

Understanding Microsoft's Virtualization Strategy

Server virtualization uses a single system to host multiple guest operating-system sessions by effectively taking advantage of the processing capabilities of a very powerful server. With most servers in datacenters utilizing only 5 to 10 percent of their processor, there is a large amount of space on servers that is unused. By combining the capabilities of multiple servers through virtualization, organizations can better exploit the processing power available in their networking environment.

Take, for example, the metrics gathered by SQL Server virtualization studies; the typical SQL Server installation runs on two physical cores with 4GB of RAM. Based on this configuration, the average SQL Server workload consumes less than 10 percent of the CPU, only 60 percent of the memory installed is being utilized, and the average network traffic for each system is 400 kilobytes per second. As you can see, this type of SQL Server system is heavily underutilized, which makes this type of system a good candidate to virtualize with Hyper-V.

By virtualizing servers such as SQL Server 2008, organizations can completely isolate the operating system and gain numerous benefits:

- Reducing Total Cost of Ownership associated with procuring and managing physical hardware.

- Drastically reducing power consumption costs.

- Running both 64-bit and 32-bit versions of SQL Server on the same virtual host.

- Consolidating many databases within the infrastructure into one or more virtual SQL Server implementations.

- Consolidating many underutilized SQL Server servers and instances into one or more virtual guest operating systems.

- Scaling up by installing more than one instance on a virtual guest operating system.

- Reducing SQL Server license costs as a single SQL Server license is valid for unlimited instances of SQL Server in multiple virtual machines on the same physical computer.

- Isolating database workloads such as OLTP and OLAP.

- Isolating SQL Server features such as the Database Engine, Analysis Services, and so on.

Integration of Hypervisor Technology in Windows Server 2008

To leap beyond its competition in the area of server virtualization, Microsoft had to make some significant changes to the operating system that hosted its next-generation virtual server technology. With Windows 2008 in development, Microsoft took the opportunity to add a core technology to Windows 2008 that provided the basis of Microsoft's future dominance in server virtualization. The core technology is called *hypervisor*, which effectively is a layer within the host operating system that provides better support for guest operating systems. Microsoft calls their hypervisor-based technology *Hyper-V*.

Prior to the inclusion of Hyper-V in Windows 2008, the Virtual Server application sat on top of the host operating system and effectively required all guest operating systems to share system resources, such as network communications, video-processing capabilities, memory allocation, and system resources. In the event that the host operating system has a system failure of something like the host network adapter driver, all guest sessions failed to communicate on the network. This monolithic approach is similar to how most server virtualization technologies operate.

Technologies like VMware ESX as well as Hyper-V leverage a hypervisor-based technology that allows the guest operating systems to effectively bypass the host operating system and communicate directly with system resources. In some instances, the hypervisor will manage shared guest session resources, and in other cases will pass guest session requests directly to the hardware layer of the system. By providing better independence of systems communications, the hypervisor-supported environment provides organizations with better scalability, better performance, and, ultimately, better reliability of the core virtual host environment.

Hyper-V is available in Windows 2008 Standard, Enterprise, and Datacenter editions. Each of these SKUs are available with and without Hyper-V, so from product launch in February 2008, Windows 2008 was ready to be a virtual server host system.

> **Note**
>
> Hyper-V in Windows 2008 is only supported to run on x64-bit systems that have hardware-assisted virtualization support.

What's New in Hyper-V?

There are many long-awaited features and technologies built into Hyper-V that give Microsoft the ability to compete with other server virtualization products on the market. Some of the key additions to Hyper-V include the following:

- **Support for x64-bit guest sessions**— Microsoft supports 64-bit guest sessions with Hyper-V. On a Windows 2008 server running Hyper-V, the system can host 32-bit and 64-bit guest sessions.

- **Support for greater guest session memory**—Windows 2008 virtualization supports guest session memory allocation greater than 64GB of memory per session.

- **Support for up to four cores per guest session**—Windows 2008 virtualization provides the capability to have up to four core processors allocated to a single guest session, providing individualized guest session performance enhancements.

> **Note**
>
> Although Hyper-V provides the capability to host guest operating systems for Windows servers, client systems, and non-Windows systems, many of the tools enterprises use in virtual server environments require the addition of the System Center Virtual Machine Manager (VMM) tool.
>
> Virtual Machine Manager provides a more centralized view and administration of multiple virtual guest sessions; the tools to do physical-to-virtual image creation, virtual-to-virtual image copying, and load balancing of virtual images across VMM servers; and the capability to do quick migration of guest sessions for disaster recovery between virtual host systems. VMM adds the administrative tools that take the basic virtual server sessions, and enables administrators to better manage the guest sessions.

Microsoft Hyper-V Server as a Role in Windows Server 2008

Even though Windows 2008 x64-bit has the hypervisor built into the core operating system, Microsoft has chosen to release the virtual server capability as a separate download. As a download, the virtual server installation option will be enabled as a server role just as Windows 2008 Active Directory

Certificate Services, Active Directory Domain Services, File Services, or Print Services are added to the server as a separate server role.

The installation of the Microsoft Hyper-V Server role is covered later in this chapter in the section "Installation of the Microsoft Hyper-V Server Role."

Planning Your Implementation of Hyper-V

For the organization that chooses to leverage the capabilities of Windows 2008 virtualization, a few moments should be spent to determine the proper size, capacity, and capabilities of the host server that would be used as the virtual server host system for SQL Server. Many server system applications get installed with little assessment of the resource requirements of the application itself, because most servers in a datacenter are running at less than 10 percent server utilization, so there is plenty of excess server capacity to handle server workload capabilities.

However, with Hyper-V, because each guest session is a completely running operating system, the installation of as few as three or four high-performance SQL Server guest sessions could quickly bring a server to 50 or 60 percent of the server performance limits. So, the planning phase is an important step in a Hyper-V configuration.

Sizing Your Windows Server 2008 System to Support SQL Server 2008 Virtualization

The host Windows 2008 Server needs to run Windows Server 2008 x64-bit edition. In addition, because server virtualization is the focus of this server system, the minimum Windows Server 2008 server requirements are insufficient to run Windows Server 2008 virtualization, specifically when running SQL Server 2008 as SQL Server's minimum requirements are typically higher.

In addition, only in theory does Windows 2008 have maximum processor and memory capabilities that reach into a dozen or more core processors and hundreds of gigabytes of RAM. In reality, the scaling of Windows virtualization comes down to the raw capabilities of network I/O that can be driven from a single host server. In many environments where a SQL Server virtualized guest system has a relatively low system utilization and network traffic demand, a single host system could easily support a dozen, two dozen, or more SQL Server guest sessions. In other environments where a virtualized SQL Server guest session has an extremely high system utilization, lots of disk I/O, and significant server communications traffic I/O, organizations might find that a single host server maximizes its capacity with as few as seven or eight guest sessions.

RAM for the Host Server

The rule of thumb for memory of a Windows 2008 server running Hyper-V is to have 2GB of RAM for the host server, plus enough memory for each guest session. Therefore, if a guest SQL Server session needs to have 2GB of RAM and there are three such guest sessions running on the host system, the host system should be configured with at least 8GB of RAM. If a guest session requires 8GB of memory and three of those systems are running on the system, the server should be configured with 24GB of memory to support the three guest sessions, plus at least 2GB of memory for the host system itself.

When establishing the amount of RAM required for the system hosting the virtual SQL Server sessions, it is a best practice to calculate and total the memory utilization of each physical SQL Server instance you plan on virtualizing. Don't forget to include the amount of RAM required to support each SQL Server instance and factor in a minimum of least 512 MB of RAM for each SQL Server instance being installed.

Processors for the Host Server

The host server itself in Windows 2008 virtualization has very low processor I/O requirements. In the virtualized environment, the processor demands of each guest session dictate how much processing capacity is needed for the server. If a guest session requires 2 cores to support the processing requirements of the SQL Server application, and seven guest sessions are running on the system, the server should have at least 15 cores available in the system. With quad-core processors, the system would need four processors. With dual-core processors, the system would need at least eight processors.

With Windows 2008 virtualization, each guest session can have up to 4 cores dedicated to the session, or processing capacity can be distributed either equally or as necessary to meet the performance demands of the organization. By sharing cores among several virtual machines that have low processing needs, an organization can make more use of their investment of hardware systems.

When deciding on the number of processors needed for the system hosting the virtual SQL Server sessions, it is a best practice to calculate and total the processor utilization of each physical SQL Server instance you plan on virtualizing. It is also a good idea to ensure that there are enough CPUs and cores to handle all the SQL Server workloads.

Disk Storage for the Host Server

A host server would typically have the base Windows 2008 operating system running on the host system itself with additional guest sessions either sharing the same disk as the host session, or the guest sessions being linked to a storage area network (SAN) or some form of external storage for the virtualized guest session images. From a SQL Server perspective, it is a best practice to leverage a SAN for maximum I/O performance.

Each guest session takes up at least 4GB of disk space. For guest sessions running databases or other storage-intensive configurations, the guest image can exceed 10GB, 20GB, or more. When planning disk storage for the virtual server system, plan to have enough disk space to support the host operating system files (typically about 10GB of actual files plus space for the pagefile when running Windows Server 2008) and then disk space available to support the SQL Server guest sessions.

Designing the back-end storage for a virtualized SQL Server implementation is very similar to designing a solution for a physical SQL Server. It is a best practice to isolate the I/O workload by dedicating spindles for database files, transaction logs and tempdb, and then isolating the workloads on each spindle. Additional spindles should be leveraged for isolation of additional databases, database filegroups, and SQL Server instances.

SQL Server Virtualization Considerations

When consolidating and virtualizing SQL Server, a DBA should first take an inventory of all the SQL Server instances within the infrastructure. The next step is to determine potential virtualized candidates by analyzing SQL Server workloads and performance metrics during peak hours for each database and instance. After a baseline is established for each potential candidate, a DBA can make a decision on whether or not to consolidate this SQL Server instance. In addition, understanding the performance baseline of each SQL Server instance will ensure that the host server selected has the correct amount of processor, memory, and disk space to support all virtualized candidates. The following are some considerations for virtualizing SQL Server 2008:

- A single guest SQL Server session should be selected if there is a need to completely isolate the operating system and/or SQL Server installation from others.

- Multiple virtual operating systems can be installed on one physical host. Each virtual operating system can handle the installation of one or more SQL Server instances.

- If a virtual host cannot handle any more SQL Server guest sessions due to resource constraints, another virtual host can be implemented within the infrastructure.

- Multiple databases can be hosted on a single instance of SQL Server running on a virtualized guest SQL Server session.

- If databases have different security, coalition, and management requirements, these databases can be placed on different SQL Server instances. Each SQL Server instance can reside on one or more SQL Server guest sessions.

Running Other Services on the Hyper-V System

On a system running Hyper-V, typically an organization would not run other roles or services on the host system, such as making the virtual server dedicated for the SQL Server guest operating system also a file and print server, or making the host server a Domain Controller, and so on. Typically, a server running virtualization is already going to be a system that will maximize the memory, processor, and disk storage capabilities of the system. So, rather than impacting the performance of all of the guest sessions by having a system-intensive application like SQL Server running on the host system, organizations choose to make servers running virtualization dedicated solely to the operation of virtualized guest sessions.

Planning for the Use of Snapshots on the Hyper-V System

A technology built into Hyper-V is the concept of a snapshot. A *snapshot* uses the Microsoft Volume Shadow Copy Service (VSS) to make a duplicate copy of a file; however, in the case of virtualization, the file is the entire virtual SQL Server server guest image. The first time a snapshot is taken, the snapshot contains a compressed copy of the contents of RAM on the system along with a bitmap of the virtual disk image of the guest session. If the original guest image is 8GB in size, the snapshot will be significantly smaller in size; however, the server storage system still needs to have additional disk space to support both the original disk image, plus the amount of disk space needed for the contents of the snapshot image.

Subsequent snapshots can be taken of the same guest session; however, the way VSS works, each additional snapshot just identifies the bits that are different from the original snapshot, thus limiting the required disk space for those additional snapshots to be just the same as needed for the incremental difference from the original snapshot to the current snapshot. This difference might be just megabytes in size.

The use of snapshots in a Windows virtualization environment is covered in more detail later in this chapter in the section titled "Using Snapshots of Guest Operating System Sessions."

Installation of the Microsoft Hyper-V Server Role

With the basic concepts of Windows virtualization covered so far in this chapter, and the background on sizing and planning for server capacity and storage, this section now focuses on the installation of the Microsoft Hyper-V Server role on a Windows Server 2008 system.

Installing Windows Server 2008 as the Host Operating System

The first step is to install an x64 version of Windows 2008 with Hyper-V as the host operating system. Step-by-step guidance for the installation of the Windows operating system is covered in the book *Windows Server 2008 Unleashed*, in Chapter 3, "Installing Windows Server 2008 and Server Core." Typically, the installation of a Windows 2008 server to run the Virtualization role is a new clean server installation, so the section in Chapter 3, "Installing a Clean Version of Windows Server 2008 Operating System," in the book *Windows Server 2008 Unleashed*, is the section to follow for getting the base Windows Server 2008 operating system up and running for virtualization.

Running Server Manager to Add the Hyper-V Role

After the base image of Windows 2008 has been installed, some basic initial tasks should be completed The basic tasks are as follows:

1. Change the server name to the name that you want the virtual server to be.

2. Configure the server to have a static IP address.

3. Join the server to an Active Directory domain (assuming the server will be part of a managed Active Directory environment with centralized administration).

4. Run Windows Update to confirm that all patches and updates have been installed and applied to the server.

After these basic tasks have been completed, the next step is to install the server virtualization software on the server and then add in the Hyper-V role to the server system. Because Windows virtualization did not ship with Windows Server 2008 at the time of the Windows Server 2008 product release, the Hyper-V role software must first be downloaded from Microsoft and then installed on the server system.

Note

It is not recommended to use the beta version of Hyper-V that is included with the RTM version of Windows Server 2008. If you do, use it only for testing purposes. It is a best practice to install the out-of-band version of Hyper-V, which must be downloaded from Microsoft's website. If you are leveraging the beta version, you can also update to the final version via Microsoft Update.

After the code of Hyper-V has been downloaded and installed on the system, do the following to add the server role to the system:

1. Make sure that you are logged on to the server with local Administrator or Domain Admin privileges.

2. Click Start and then click Run.

3. In the Run dialog box, type **ServerManager.msc**, and click OK. This will start the Server Manager console if it is not already running on the system.

4. Right-click on Roles in the left pane of the console, and select Add Roles, as shown in Figure 21.1.

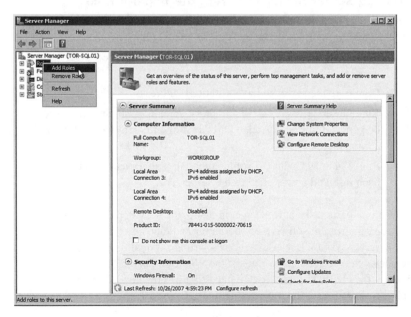

FIGURE 21.1
Adding the Hyper-V role to the Server Manager console.

5. After the Add Roles Wizard loads, click Next to continue past the Welcome screen.

6. On the Select Server Roles page, select the Microsoft Hyper-V Server role, and click Next.

Note

Hyper-V requires a supported version of hardware-assisted virtualization. Both Intel VT or AMD-V chipsets are supported by Hyper-V. In addition, virtualization must be enabled in the BIOS. Please check your server documentation for details on how to enable this setting.

---

7. On the Hyper-V page, read the notes and information about the role, and then click Next.

8. On the Create Virtual Networks page, select the LAN adapters you want to have shared with guest sessions. Click Next to continue.

9. On the Confirm Installation Selections page, review the selections made, and then click Install.

10. On the Installation Results page, review the results, and click Close.

11. When prompted to restart the server, click Yes.

12. After the server restarts, log on to the server with local Administrator or Domain Admin privileges.

13. After you've logged on, the installation and configuration will continue for a few more moments. When complete, the Installation Results page will be displayed. Review the results in the page and confirm that the Windows Hyper-V role has been installed successfully. Click Close.

Becoming Familiar with the Hyper-V Administrative Console

After Hyper-V has been installed, the next step is to install guest images, such as SQL Server 2008, that will run on the virtual server. However, before jumping into the installation of guest images, here is a quick guide on navigating through the Hyper-V Administrative console and the virtual server settings available to be configured that apply to all guest sessions on the server.

Launching the Hyper-V Administrative Console

To open the Hyper-V Administrative console, there are two ways to access the configuration options. One way is to use the Server Manager tool and administer the host server through Server Manager, or the other option is to launch the freestanding Microsoft Management Console (MMC) to perform administrative tasks for the host system.

Note

The functions and settings on the Server Manager console and the stand-alone MMC application are the same. Administrators who manage several server roles tend to use the Server Manager console because they have access to more than just the Virtualization role to manage; they can also manage DNS, Terminal Services, Network Policy Server, or other roles that might be applicable to their job. Those who do nothing but administer Windows virtualization systems might choose the freestanding MMC application for administering and managing just Windows virtual server systems.

Using the Server Manager Tool to Manage Hyper-V Systems

For administrators who want to manage their Hyper-V systems from a centralized console, the Server Manager tool provides a common administrative interface for all of the server roles installed on a particular system. To start the Server Manager tool to view and edit Hyper-V settings, do the following:

1. Click Start and then click Run.

2. In the Run dialog box, type **ServerManager.msc**, and click OK. This will start the Server Manager application if it is not already running on the system.

3. Expand the Roles section of the tree by clicking on the plus sign (+).

4. Expand the Hyper-V branch of the tree, and expand the Virtualization Services branch of the tree.

Using the Hyper-V MMC Tool to Manage Hyper-V Systems

For administrators who want to manage their Hyper-V systems from a dedicated console just for Hyper-V administration, the Hyper-V tool should be used. To start the Hyper-V administration tool, do the following:

1. Click Start, All Programs, Administrative Tools, and then choose Hyper-V Management for the tool to launch.

2. Click on Virtualization Services to see the virtual servers to which you are connected.

3. Click on the name of one of the virtual servers listed to see the virtual machines and actions available for the confirmation of the server system. By default, the Hyper-V MMC will have the local virtual server system listed, as shown in Figure 21.2.

FIGURE 21.2
Virtualization Management Console.

Connecting to a Different Virtual Server System

If you want to administer or manage a different virtual server system, you need to log on and connect to another server. To connect to a different virtual server, do the following:

1. From within the Hyper-V Management Console, click on the Virtualization Services option in the left pane.

2. Select Action, Connect to Server.

3. Select Another Computer and either enter the name of the server and click OK, or click on Browse to search Active Directory for the name of the server you want to remotely monitor and administer.

4. When the server appears in the Hyper-V Management Console, click to select the server to see the actions available for administering and managing that server.

Navigating and Configuring Host Server Settings

Regardless of whether you have chosen to use Server Manager or the MMC tool, the configuration options and settings are the same. When you click on the virtual server system you want to administer, action settings become available. These action settings allow you to configure the host server settings for the system you have chosen to administer.

Virtualization Settings

When you select the Virtualization Settings action item, you have access to configure default paths and remote control keyboard settings. Specifics on these settings are as follows:

- **Default Paths**—This option allows you to set the drive path for the location where virtual hard disks and snapshots are stored. This might be on the local C: drive of the server system or on an external SAN or storage system.

- **Remote Control**—The remote control settings include how to switch to Local, Remote, or Full Screen mode. There is also a remote control setting that allows you to choose which keystroke is used to release the mouse and keyboard control back to the host when you have been administering a guest session.

- **Keyboard Release Key**—By default, the key that releases the guest session so the administrator can gain keyboard control back to the host console is Ctrl+Alt+Left Arrow. The Remote Control/Release Key option allows for the selection of other key options.

Virtual Network Manager

By selecting the Virtual Network Manager action item, you have access to configure the virtual network switches, as shown in Figure 21.3 where you can configure the local area network (LAN) and WAN connections available for the guest sessions of the virtual server host.

Specific to these settings are as follows:

- **Add New Network Switch**—This configuration option allows for the addition of a new internal or external network segment available to the guest sessions. An *external network segment* would be a connection to a LAN adapter in the host server so that a guest session could gain access out of the virtual server. An *internal network segment* would be a connection that is solely within the virtual server system where you might want to set up a virtual LAN so that the virtual server guests within a system can talk to each other. By combining both internal and external network switch segments, virtual guest sessions can communicate with each other (internal) or outside of the virtual server (external) just as if the organization had physical switches and routers in a data center.

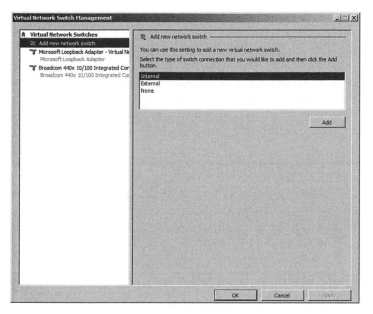

FIGURE 21.3
Virtual network switch management.

- **Existing virtual network switches**—If the system you are managing already has virtual network switches configured, they will be listed individually in the left pane of the Virtual Network Switch Management dialog box. By selecting an existing virtual network switch, you can change the name of the virtual switch, change the internal or external connection that the switch has access to, or remove the network switch altogether.

Edit Disk

The Edit Disk option in the Virtual Network Manager action item menu allows you to modify an existing virtual hard disk image. Specifically, the options are as follows:

- **Compact**—This option allows you to shrink a virtual hard disk to remove portions of the disk image file that is unused. This is commonly used when a disk image will be archived and stored, and having the smallest disk image file possible is preferred.

- **Convert**—This option allows you to convert a virtual hard disk file to another type other than the default Microsoft VHD disk format.

■ **Expand**—This option allows you to grow the size of a dynamic disk image. For example, you might have initially created the disk image to be only 8GB maximum in size and now that you've added a lot of applications to the guest image, you are running out of space in the image file. By expanding the image file, you effectively have the ability to add more applications and data to the guest session without having to re-create the guest session all over again.

Inspect Disk

The Inspect Disk option in the Virtual Network Manager action item menu allows you to view the settings of an existing virtual image file. For the example shown in Figure 21.4, the disk image is currently 8GB in size, can dynamically grow up to the maximum limit of 2040GB, and is located on the local hard drive in the directory C:\VPCs.

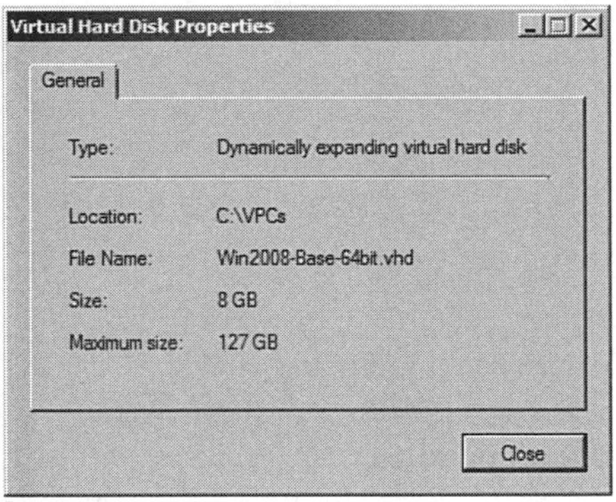

FIGURE 21.4
Virtual Hard Disk properties shown under the Inspect Disk option.

Stop Service

The Stop Service option in the Virtual Network Manager action item menu provides for the ability to stop the Windows virtualization service on the machine being managed. You might choose to stop the service if you needed to perform maintenance or begin the shutdown process of an administered system.

New Configuration Wizard

One of the wizards listed in the Virtual Network Manager action item menu allows for the creation of new virtual machines, hard disks, and floppy disks. Specifics of this configuration option are as follows:

- **New—Virtual Machine**—This option allows you to create a new virtual guest session. The whole purpose of running Windows virtualization is to run virtual guest sessions, and this option is the one that allows you to create new guest sessions.

- **New—Hard Disk**—This option allows you to create a new hard disk image. Typically, you would create an entire new virtual machine in the first option that includes creating a hard disk image; however, if you have already created a virtual machine with all of the RAM, network adapter, video, CD/DVD, and other settings and want to use that virtual machine setting and simply create a new hard disk image for that configuration, this wizard walks you through the configuration of a hard disk image.

- **New—Floppy Disk**—This option allows you to take an existing floppy disk and create a virtual floppy disk image from the physical disk. This might be used to create an image of a bootable floppy disk that would later be used in configuring or managing a guest image, or used to create a floppy disk image of a disk that has drivers or utilities on it that will be used in a virtual guest session.

Installing a SQL Server 2008 Guest Operating System Session

One of the key tasks noted in the previous section is to begin the installation of a new guest operating system session. The guest operating system installation is wizard driven and provides the administrator with the ability to configure settings for the guest session, and to begin the installation of the guest operating system software itself. When working with SQL Server 2008, a guest operating system should be Windows Server 2008, however, you can also use Windows Server 2003.

Gathering the Components Needed for a Guest Session

When creating a guest operating system, the DBA needs to make sure they have all of the components needed to begin the installation. The components needed are as follows:

- **Operating system media**—A copy of the operating system is required for the installation of the guest image. The media could be either a DVD or an ISO image of the media disc itself.

- **License key**—During the installation of the operating system software, if you are normally prompted to enter the license key for the operating system, you should have a copy of the license key available.

Here are some other things you should do before starting to install a guest operating system on the virtual server system:

- **Guest session configuration settings**—You will be prompted to answer several core guest session configuration setting options, such as how much RAM you want to allocate for the guest session, how much disk space you want to allocate for the guest image, and so on. Either jump ahead to the next section on "Beginning the Installation of the SQL Server 2008 Guest Session" so that you can gather up the information you'll need to answer the questions you'll be asked, or be prepared to answer the questions during the installation process.

- **Host server readiness**—If you are preplanning the answers to the questions that will be asked, ensure that the host system has everything it needs including, but not limited to, RAM and disk space to support the addition of a guest session on the virtual server system. If your requirements exceed the physical capacity of the server, stop and add more resources (memory, disk space, and so on) to the server before beginning the installation of the guest operating system.

- **SQL Server 2008 Installation Media**—A copy of the SQL Server 2008 media is required when the installation of the guest image is complete. The media could be either a DVD or an ISO image of the media disc itself.

Beginning the Installation of the SQL Server 2008 Guest Session

When you are ready to begin the installation of the guest operating system, launch the guest operating system installation wizard, as follows:

1. From the Actions pane, choose New, Virtual Machine.

2. Click Next to continue past the initial Welcome screen.

3. Give your virtual machine a name that will be descriptive of the virtual guest session you are creating, such as **SQLServer01**, **SQLOLTP01**, or **SQLVirtual01**, and so on.

4. If you had set the default virtual machine folder location where guest images are stored, the new image for this virtual machine will be placed in that default folder. However, if you need to select a different location where the image files should be stored, click Create a New Folder for the Virtual Machine Files, and select Browse to choose an existing disk directory or to create a new directory where the image file for this guest session should be stored. Click Next to continue.

5. Enter the amount of RAM you want allocated to this guest image (in megabytes), and then click Next.

6. Choose the network segment to which you want this guest image to be initially connected. This would be an internal or external segment created in the section "Virtual Network Manager" earlier in this chapter. Click Next.

Note

You can choose Not Connected during this virtual machine creation process and change the network segment option at a later date.

---

7. The next option allows you to create a new virtual hard disk or use an existing virtual hard disk for the guest image file. Creating a new virtual hard disk creates a VHD disk image in the directory you choose. By default, a dynamic virtual disk image size setting is set to 127GB. The actual file itself will only be the size needed to run the image (potentially 4GB or 8GB to start) and will dynamically grow up to the size noted in this setting. Alternately, you can choose an existing hard disk image you might have already created (including an older image you might have created in Microsoft Virtual Server 2005), or you can choose to select a hard disk image later. The options for this configuration are shown in Figure 21.5. Click Next to continue.

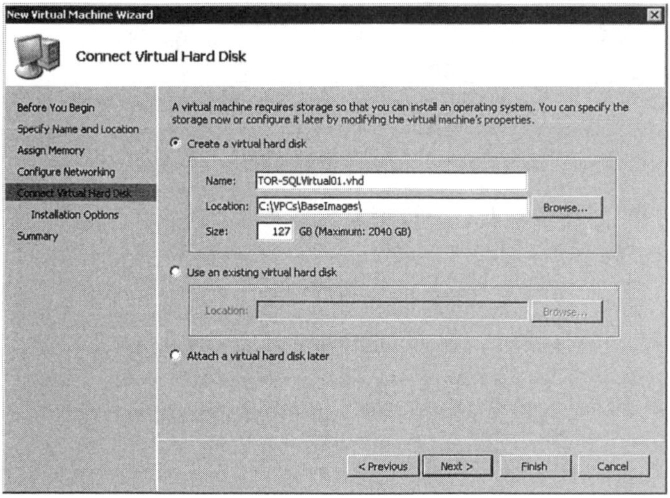

FIGURE 21.5
Virtual Hard Disk creation or selection option.

8. The next option, shown in Figure 21.6, allows for the installation of an operating system on the disk image you created in the previous step. You can choose to install an operating system at a later time, install an operating system from a bootable CD/DVD or ISO image file, install an operating system from a floppy disk image, or install an operating system from a network-based installation server (such as Remote Installation Service [RIS]). Typically, operating system source discs are on either a physical disc or ISO image file, and choosing a CD or DVD or an associated ISO image file will allow for the operating system to be installed on the guest image. Select your option, and then click Next to continue.

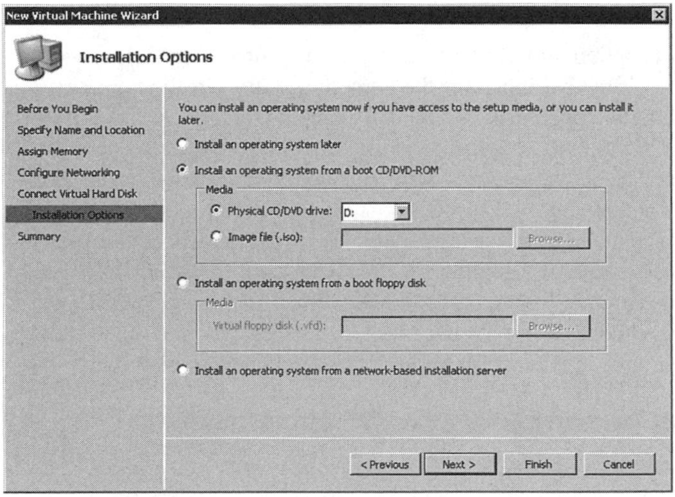

FIGURE 21.6
Choosing the installation mechanism for the guest session.

9. Review the summary of the options you have selected and either click Previous to go back and make changes, or click Finish if the settings you've chosen are fine. Choosing the Start the Virtual Machine Once This Wizard Is Finished check box will launch the guest session and begin the guest session installation process. If you need to make changes to the settings, you would not want to select this option yet—just click Finish so that you can make configuration setting changes and start the installation process after that.

Completing the Installation of the Guest Session

The guest operating system installation will proceed to install just like the process of installing the operating system on a physical system. Typically, at the end of an operating system installation, the guest session will restart and bring the session to a logon prompt. Log on to the guest operating system and configure the guest operating system as you would any other server system. This typically requires you to do things such as the following:

1. Change the system name to the name that you want for the virtual server. For many versions of operating systems, you will be prompted to enter the name of the system during the installation process.

2. Configure the guest session with an appropriate IP address. This might be issued by DHCP; however, if you are building a server system, a static IP address is typically recommended.

3. Provision the storage for the SQL Server system.

4. Join the system to an Active Directory domain (assuming the system will be part of a managed Active Directory Domain Services environment with centralized administration).

5. Download and apply the latest patches and updates on the guest session to confirm that all patches and updates have been installed and applied to the system.

The installation of the guest operating system typically requires yet another reboot, and the operating system will be installed and operational.

Installing SQL Server 2008 on the Guest Session

With the guest session's operating system successfully installed, the next step is to install SQL Server 2008. The steps for performing the SQL Server 2008 installation are the exact same steps for performing an installation on a physical server. Therefore, leverage the steps included in Chapter 1, "Installing or Upgrading to the SQL Server 2008 Database Engine," to perform the installation of SQL Server 2008 on the guest session.

Modifying SQL Server 2008 Guest Session Configuration Settings

After a guest session has been installed, the SQL Server 2008 host configuration settings for the guest session can be changed. Common changes to a SQL Server 2008 guest session include things such as the following:

- Adding or limiting the RAM of the guest session

- Changing network settings of the guest session
- Mounting a CD/DVD image or mounting a physical CD/DVD disc

Adding or Limiting the RAM of the Guest Session

One common configuration change made to a SQL Server guest session involves increasing or decreasing the amount of memory allocated to the guest session. The default memory allocated to the system typically is fine for a basic SQL Server system configuration; however, depending on the components being installed and the expected workload, there may be a need to increase the memory. As long as the host server system has enough memory to allocate additional memory to the guest session, adding memory to a guest session is a very simple task.

To add memory to the guest session, carry out the following steps:

1. From the Server Manager console or from the Virtualization MMC snap-in, click to select the guest session for which you want to change the allocated memory.
2. Right-click the guest session name, and choose Settings.
3. Click on Memory and enter the amount of RAM you want allocated for this guest session (in megabytes).
4. Click OK when you are finished.

Note

You cannot change the allocated RAM on a running virtual guest session. The guest session must be shut down first, memory reallocated to the image, and then the guest image booted for the new memory allocation to take effect. In addition, ensure that you revisit the Max Memory setting in SQL Server if you have hardcoded the memory based on a specific threshold.

Changing Network Settings for the Guest Session

Another common configuration change made to a guest session is to change the network setting for the guest session. An administrator of a virtual server might choose to have each guest session connected directly to the network backbone just as if the guest session had a network adapter connected to the backbone, or the network administrator might choose to set up an isolated network just for the guest sessions. The configuration of the internal and external network segments that the administrator can configure the guest sessions to connect to is covered earlier in this chapter in the section "Virtual Network Manager."

The common configuration methods of the virtual network configurations can be broken down into two groups, as follows:

- **Direct addressing**—The guest sessions can connect directly to the backbone of the network to which the virtual server host system is attached. In this instance, an administrator would configure an external connection in the Virtual Network Manager and have an IP address on that external segment.

- **Isolated network**—If the administrator wants to keep the guest sessions isolated from the network backbone, the administrator can set up an internal connection in the Virtual Network Manager and the guest sessions would have an IP address of a segment common to the other guest sessions on the host system. In this case, the virtual server acts as a network switch connecting the guest sessions together. This is a great option when implementing a SQL Server prototype or test lab that needs to be fully isolated from the production network.

> **Note**
>
> To connect the internal network segment with the external network segment, a guest session can be configured as a router or gateway between the internal network and external network.

Mounting a Physical CD/DVD Image or Mounting a CD/DVD Image File

When installing software on a guest session of a virtual server system, the administrator would either insert a CD or DVD into the drive of the physical server and access the disc from the guest session, or mount an ISO image file of the disc media.

To access a physical CD or DVD disc or to mount an image of a CD or DVD, such as the SQL Server media, do the following:

1. From the Server Manager console or from the Hyper-V MMC snap-in, click to select the guest session for which you want to change the allocated memory.

2. Right-click the guest session name, and choose Settings.

3. Click on DVD Drive and choose Physical CD/DVD Drive if you want to mount a disc in the physical drive of the host system, or click on Image File and browse for the ISO image file you want to mount as a disc image.

4. Click OK when you are finished.

Other Settings to Modify for a Guest Session Configuration

There are other settings that can be changed for a guest session. These options can be modified by going into the Settings option of the guest session and making changes. These other settings include the following:

- **BIOS**—This setting allows for the selection of boot order on the guest machine: the boot order can include floppy, CD, IDE (disk), or network boot.

- **Processor**—Hyper-V provides the ability to allocate core processors to the guest image, so a guest image can have up to four core processors allocated for each session. Additionally, resource control can be weighted between guest sessions by allocating system resource priority to key guest server sessions versus other guest sessions.

- **IDE Controller**—The guest session initially has a single virtual hard drive associated with it. Additional virtual hard drives can be added to a virtual guest session.

- **SCSI Controller**—A virtual SCSI controller can be associated with a virtual guest session as well as providing different drive configuration options for the different drive configurations.

- **COM Ports**—Virtual communication ports such as COM1 or COM2 can be associated with specific named pipes for input and output of information.

Launching a Hyper-V Guest Session

After a Hyper-V guest session has been created, and the settings have been properly modified to meet the expected needs of the organization, the virtual guest session can be launched and run. You need to make decisions about whether you want the guest session to launch automatically as soon as the server is booted, or whether you want to manually launch a guest session. Additionally, a decision needs to be made on the sequence in which guest sessions should be launched so that systems that are prerequisites to other sessions come up first. As an example, you'd want a global catalog server session and DHCP server session to come up before an application server such as SQL Server that logs on and authenticates to Active Directory comes online and needs to authenticate to Active Directory before the server service begins.

Automatically Launching a Guest Session

One option for launching and loading guest sessions is to have the guest session boot right after the physical server completes the boot cycle. This is typically the preferred option if a guest session is core to the network infrastructure of a network (such as a domain controller or host server system) so that in the event of a physical server reboot, the virtual guest sessions boot up automatically as well. It would not be convenient to have to manually boot each virtual server session every time the physical server is rebooted.

The option for setting the bootup option for a virtual session is in the configuration settings for each guest session.

To change the bootup action, perform the following steps:

1. From the Server Manager console or from the Hyper-V MMC snap-in, right-click the virtual machine for which you want to change the setup option, and select Settings.

2. In the Management section of the settings, click Automatic Start Action.

3. Three options are provided, as shown in Figure 21.7, of what to do with this virtual guest session upon bootup of the physical server. Either click Nothing (which would require a manual boot of the guest session), or click Automatically Start If It Was Running When the Service Stopped, or click Always Start This Virtual Machine Automatically. To set the virtual session to automatically start after the physical server comes up, choose the Always Start This Virtual Machine Automatically option.

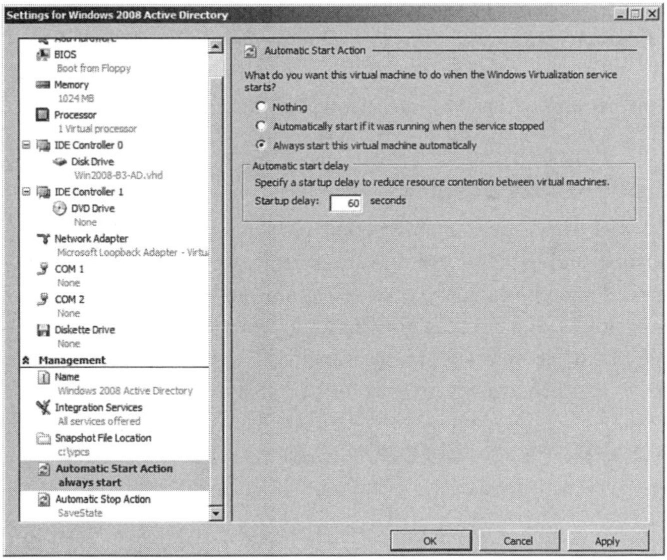

FIGURE 21.7
Automatic start actions.

4. Also on this settings page is the choice of an *automatic start delay*. This allows you to sequence the bootup of image files by having some images take longer to automatically start than others. Click OK to save these settings.

Manually Launching a Guest Session

Another option for guest session bootup is to not have a guest session auto-matically start after a physical server boots up. This is typically the preferred option if a guest session will be part of a demonstration or test server where the administrator of the system wants to control which guest sessions are automatically launched, and which sessions need to be manually launched. It would not be convenient to have a series of demo or test sessions automati-cally boot up every time the system is booted. The administrator of the system would typically want to choose to boot up guest sessions.

To set the bootup action to manually launch a guest session, do the following:

1. From the Server Manager console or from the Hyper-V MMC snap-in, right-click the virtual machine for which you want to change the setup option, and select Settings.

2. In the Management section of the settings, click Automatic Start Action.

3. In the three options of what to do with this virtual guest session upon bootup of the physical server, either click Nothing (which would require a manual boot of the guest session), or click Automatically Start If It Was Running When the Service Stopped, or click Always Start This Virtual Machine Automatically. If you choose the Nothing option, the session will need to be manually started.

Save State of a Guest Session

In Windows 2008 Hyper-V, there are two concepts for saving guest images, one being snapshots and the other being a saved state. At any time, an admin-istrator can select a guest session and choose Action, Save State. This Save State function is similar to a Hibernate mode on a desktop client system. It saves the image into a file with the option of bringing the saved state image file back to the state the image was in prior to being saved.

Using Snapshots of Guest Operating System Sessions

A highly versatile function in Windows 2008 Hyper-V is the option to create a snapshot of a guest session. A snapshot in Windows Hyper-V uses Microsoft Volume Shadow Copy Service (VSS) technology that captures an image of a file on a server—in this case, the file is the VHD image of the virtual server itself. At any point in time in the future, the snapshot can be used for recovery. With regards to SQL Server, many DBAs use snapshots to roll back changes after a test is complete and to maintain a pristine test envi-ronment for training end-users and other DBAs.

Snapshots for Image Rollback

One common use of a guest image snapshot is to roll back an image to a previous state. This is frequently done with guest images used for demonstration purposes, or test labs where a scenario is tested to see the results and compared with identical tests of other scenarios, or for the purpose of preparing for a software upgrade or migration.

For the case of a guest image used for demonstration purposes, a user might run through a demo of a software program where they add information, delete information, make software changes, or otherwise modify information in the software on the guest image. With a snapshot, rather than having to go back and delete the changes, or rebuilding the image from scratch to do the demo again, the user can simply roll the image back to the snapshot that was available before the changes were made to the image.

Image rollback has been successfully used for training purposes where an employee runs through a process, and then rolls back the image so they can run through the same process all over again, repeating the process on the same base image but without previous installations or configurations.

In network infrastructures, a snapshot is helpful when an organization applies a patch or update to a server, or a software upgrade is performed and problems occur; the administrator can simply roll the image back to the point prior to the start of the upgrade or migration.

Snapshots for Guest Session Server Fault Tolerance

Snapshots are commonly used in business environments for the purpose of fault tolerance or disaster recovery. A well-timed snapshot right before a system failure can help an organization roll the server back to the point right before the server failed or problem occurred. Rather than waiting hours to restore a server from tape, the activation of a snapshot image is nothing more than choosing the snapshot and selecting to start the guest image. When the guest image starts up, it is in the state that the image was in at the time the snapshot was created.

Creating a Snapshot of a Guest Image

Snapshots are very easy to create. To create a snapshot, do the following:

1. From the Server Manager console or from the Hyper-V MMC snap-in, click to select the guest session for which you want to create a snapshot.

2. Right-click the guest session name, and choose Snapshot. A snapshot of the image will immediately be taken of the guest image and the snapshot will show up in the Snapshots pane, as shown in Figure 21.8.

FIGURE 21.8
Viewing snapshots of a guest server.

Rolling Back a Guest Image to a Previous Snapshot Image

The term used in Windows 2008 Hyper-V to roll back an image is called
"applying" a snapshot to an existing image. When an image is rolled back,
the image that is currently running has the snapshot information applied to
the image, thus bringing the image back to an earlier configuration state. To
apply a snapshot, do the following:

1. From the Server Manager console or from the Hyper-V MMC snap-in,
   click the snapshot to which you want to revert the running guest image.

2. Right-click the snapshot image and choose Apply. The configuration
   state of the image will immediately be reverted to the state of the
   image when the snapshot was taken.

Note

By default, the name of the snapshot image takes on the date and time the
image was created. As an example, if the image was called "Windows 2008
IIS," an image taken on April 26, 2008 at 6:19 a.m. would show up as
"Windows 2008 IIS-20080426-061900."

Reverting a Snapshot Session

When working with snapshots, if you create a snapshot of a session and then apply an older session snapshot to the current session, to effectively undo the rollback, choose Action, Revert to bring the server back to the state it was in before the rollback occurred.

Summary

Microsoft Hyper-V has come a long way in just a few short years. As recently as 2003, one could not even find Microsoft in the virtualization game. Today, with the use of Windows 2008, virtualization provides organizations with an effective and efficient way of consolidating server applications such as SQL Server onto fewer virtual server systems. One of the key aspects of Windows 2008 Hyper-V is its ability to run 64-bit guest sessions and also allow for memory, disk, and processor support that meet the demands of enterprise-level physical servers into individualized guest operating sessions.

Hyper-V in Windows 2008 also gives organizations the chance to host SQL Server guest sessions with the ability to consolidate dozens of physical servers into a single virtual server system. By adding more virtual server systems to an enterprise, organizations can drastically reduce the number of physical servers they own, plus provide a method for implementing server redundancy, clustering, and disaster recovery without the need to double the number of physical servers the organization requires to provide better computing services.

Many DBAs and organizations feel that SQL Server is not a good candidate to virtualize as the workload is typically I/O intensive. However, with Windows Server 2008 and the hardware associated with today's servers, it is possible to virtualize even the heaviest SQL Server workload.

When consolidating and virtualizing SQL Server instances, it is possible to place all databases on one guest SQL Server session, or one guest session can host many SQL Server instances. Again, the number of sessions and instances supported is based on the hardware selected for the host system and workloads associated with each SQL Server database and instance to be virtualized.

Best Practices

The following are best practices from this chapter:

- Consolidate and virtualize SQL Server systems in order to centralize data management and to reduce hardware costs.
- Plan for the number of virtual SQL Server guest sessions you will have on a server to properly size the host system with respect to memory, processor, and disk space requirements.

- Do *not* virtualize just for the sake of virtualizing. For example, if you are planning to virtualize a SQL Server system that may consume all of the host system's resources and no other guest sessions can be created, this type of server is not an ideal candidate to virtualize.

- Save on SQL Server licensing by leveraging the SQL Server Enterprise Edition and virtualize as many SQL Server systems on one physical host as possible.

- Save on virtualization licensing by using the Windows Server 2008 Enterprise Edition.

- Leverage Resource Governor to manage SQL Server performance, resources, workloads, and priorities among virtualized SQL Server sessions.

- Virtualize SQL Server components that are not resource intensive such as Integration Services and Reporting Services.

- Leverage a SAN and spread SQL Server sessions and resources across multiple spindles for maximum I/O performance.

- For Microsoft Windows guest sessions, install the Windows add-in components to improve the use and operation of the guest session.

- Leverage the Hyper-V performance counters in order to monitor resource utilization.

- After installing the guest session and its associated applications, confirm whether the memory of the guest session is enough, and adjust the memory of the guest session accordingly to optimize the performance of the guest session.

- Allocate enough disk space to perform snapshots of images so that the disk subsystem can handle both the required guest image and the associated snapshots of the guest session.

- Leverage pass-through disks or fixed VHDs for best performance for storage.

- Consider using snapshots before applying major patches, updates, or upgrades to an image session to allow for a rollback to the original image.

- Have the installation media and license keys needed for the installation of the guest operating system handy when you are about to install the guest operating system session.

- Apply all patches and updates on guest sessions soon after installing the guest operating system just as you would for the installation of updates on physical systems.

Index